TECHNOLOGY

Library of Congress Classification

1999 EDITION

Prepared by the
Cataloging Policy
and Support Office,
Library Services

Library of Congress, Cataloging Distribution Service, Washington, D.C.

The additions and changes in Class T adopted while this work was in press will be cumulated and printed in List 277 of *LC Classification — Additions and Changes*

Library of Congress Cataloging-in-Publication Data

Library of Congress.
  Library of Congress classification. T. Technology / prepared by the Cataloging Policy and Support Office, Collections Services. — 1999 ed.
    p. cm.
    Includes index.
    1. Classification—Books—Technology. 2. Classification, Library of Congress. I. Title: Technology. II. Library of Congress. Cataloging Policy and Support Office. III. Title.
  Z696.U5 T 2000
  025.4'66—dc21   99-086968
                                                                          CIP

  ISBN 0-8444-1005-5

For sale by the Library of Congress, Cataloging Distribution Service, Washington, DC 20541-5017

PREFACE

The precursor to Class T, Technology, was a series of subclasses prepared between 1903 and 1907. The first edition of Class T as a whole was published in 1910, the second in 1922, the third in 1937, the fourth in 1948, and the fifth in 1971. An edition cumulating changes made during the period 1971-1995 was published in 1995. This 1999 edition cumulates additions and changes that have been made since 1995.

New or revised numbers and captions are added to the L.C. Classification schedules as a result of development proposals made by the cataloging staff of the Library of Congress and cooperating institutions. Upon approval of these proposals by the weekly editorial meeting of the Cataloging Policy and Support Office, new classification records are created or existing records are revised in the master classification database. The Classification Editorial Team, consisting of Lawrence Buzard, editor, and Barry Bellinger, Kent Griffith, Nancy Jones, and Dorothy Thomas, assistant editors, is responsible for creating new classification records, maintaining the master database, and creating index terms for the captions.

Thompson A. Yee, Acting Chief
Cataloging Policy and Support Office

December 1999

TECHNOLOGY (General)	**T**
ENGINEERING (General) CIVIL ENGINEERING (General)	**TA**
HYDRAULIC ENGINEERING	**TC**
ENVIRONMENTAL TECHNOLOGY • SANITARY ENGINEERING	**TD**
HIGHWAY ENGINEERING • ROADS AND PAVEMENTS	**TE**
RAILROAD ENGINEERING AND OPERATION	**TF**
BRIDGE ENGINEERING	**TG**
BUILDING CONSTRUCTION	**TH**
MECHANICAL ENGINEERING AND MACHINERY	**TJ**
ELECTRICAL ENGINEERING • ELECTRONICS • NUCLEAR ENGINEERING	**TK**
MOTOR VEHICLES • AERONAUTICS • ASTRONAUTICS	**TL**
MINING ENGINEERING • METALLURGY	**TN**
CHEMICAL TECHNOLOGY	**TP**
PHOTOGRAPHY	**TR**
MANUFACTURES	**TS**
HANDICRAFTS, ARTS AND CRAFTS	**TT**
HOME ECONOMICS	**TX**
	TABLES
	INDEX

OUTLINE

OUTLINE

T	1-995	Technology (General)
	10.5-11.9	Communication of technical information
	11.95-12.5	Industrial directories
	55-55.3	Industrial safety. Industrial accident prevention
	55.4-60.8	Industrial engineering. Management engineering
	57-57.97	Applied mathematics. Quantitative methods
	57.6-57.97	Operations research. Systems analysis
	58.4	Managerial control systems
	58.5-58.64	Information technology
	58.6-58.62	Management information systems
	58.7-58.8	Production capacity. Manufacturing capacity
	59-59.2	Standardization
	59.5	Automation
	59.7-59.77	Human engineering in industry. Man-machine systems
	60-60.8	Work measurement. Methods engineering
	61-173	Technical education. Technical schools
	173.2-174.5	Technological change
	175-178	Industrial research. Research and development
	201-342	Patents. Trademarks
	351-385	Mechanical drawing. Engineering graphics
	391-995	Exhibitions. Trade shows. World's fairs
TA	1-2040	Engineering (General). Civil engineering (General)
	164	Bioengineering
	165	Engineering instruments, meters, etc. Industrial instrumentation
	166-167	Human engineering
	168	Systems engineering
	170-171	Environmental engineering
	174	Engineering design
	177.4-185	Engineering economy
	190-194	Management of engineering works
	197-198	Engineering meteorology
	213-215	Engineering machinery, tools, and implements
	329-348	Engineering mathematics. Engineering analysis
	349-359	Mechanics of engineering. Applied mechanics
	365-367	Acoustics in engineering. Acoustical engineering
	401-492	Materials of engineering and construction. Mechanics of materials
	495	Disasters and engineering
	501-625	Surveying
	630-695	Structural engineering (General)
	703-712	Engineering geology. Rock mechanics. Soil mechanics. Underground construction

OUTLINE

TA		Engineering (General). Civil engineering (General) - Continued
	715-787	Earthwork. Foundations
	800-820	Tunneling. Tunnels
	1001-1280	Transportation engineering
	1501-1820	Applied optics. Photonics
	2001-2040	Plasma engineering
TC	1-978	Hydraulic engineering
	160-181	Technical hydraulics
	183-201	General preliminary operations. Dredging. Submarine building
	203-380	Harbors and coast protective works. Coastal engineering. Lighthouses
	401-506	River, lake, and water-supply engineering (General)
	530-537	River protective works. Regulation. Flood control
	540-558	Dams. Barrages
	601-791	Canals and inland navigation. Waterways
	801-978	Irrigation engineering. Reclamation of wasteland. Drainage
TC	1501-1800	Ocean engineering
TD	1-1066	Environmental technology. Sanitary engineering
	159-168	Municipal engineering
	169-171.8	Environmental protection
	172-193.5	Environmental pollution
	194-195	Environmental effects of industries and plants
	201-500	Water supply for domestic and industrial purposes
	419-428	Water pollution
	429.5-480.7	Water purification. Water treatment and conditioning. Saline water conversion
	481-493	Water distribution systems
	511-780	Sewage collection and disposal systems. Sewerage
	783-812.5	Municipal refuse. Solid wastes
	813-870	Street cleaning. Litter and its removal
	878-894	Special types of environment Including soil pollution, air pollution, noise pollution
	895-899	Industrial and factory sanitation
	896-899	Industrial and factory wastes
	920-934	Rural and farm sanitary engineering

OUTLINE

TD Continued		Environmental technology. Sanitary engineering -
	940-949	Low temperature sanitary engineering
	1020-1066	Hazardous substances and their disposal
TE	1-450	Highway engineering. Roads and pavements
	175-176.5	Highway design. Interchanges and intersections
	177-178.8	Roadside development. Landscaping
	200-205	Materials for roadmaking
	206-209.5	Location engineering
	210-228.3	Construction details
		Including foundations, maintenance, equipment
	250-278.8	Pavements and paved roads
	279	Streets
	279.5-298	Pedestrian facilities
	280-295	Sidewalks. Footpaths. Flagging
	298	Curbs. Curbstones
TF	1-1620	Railroad engineering and operation
	200-320	Railway construction
	340-499	Railway equipment and supplies
	501-668	Railway operation and management
	670-851	Local and light railways
	840-851	Elevated railways and subways
	855-1127	Electric railways
	1300-1620	High speed ground transporation
TG	1-470	Bridge engineering
TH	1-9745	Building construction
	845-895	Architectural engineering. Structural engineering of buildings
	900-915	Construction equipment in building
	1000-1725	Systems of building construction
		Including fireproof construction, concrete construction
	2025-3000	Details in building design and construction
		Including walls, roofs
	3301-3411	Maintenance and repair
	4021-4977	Buildings: Construction with reference to use
		Including public buildings, dwellings
	5011-5701	Construction by phase of the work (Building trades)
	6014-6081	Environmental engineering of buildings. Sanitary engineering of buildings
	6101-6887	Plumbing and pipefitting

OUTLINE

TH		Building construction - Continued
	7005-7699	Heating and ventilation. Air conditioning
	7700-7975	Illumination. Lighting
	8001-8581	Decoration and decorative furnishings
	9025-9745	Protection of buildings
		Including protection from dampness, fire, burglary

TJ		Mechanical engineering and machinery
	1-1570	Mechanical engineering and machinery
	163.13-163.25	Power resources
	163.26-163.5	Energy conservation
	170-179	Mechanics applied to machinery. Dynamics
	181-210	Mechanical movements
	210.2-211.47	Mechanical devices and figures. Automata. Ingenious mechanisms. Robots (General)
	212-225	Control engineering systems. Automatic machinery (General)
	227-240	Machine design and drawing
	241-254.7	Machine construction (General)
	255-265	Heat engines
	266-267.5	Turbines. Turbomachines (General)
	268-740	Steam engineering
	603-695	Locomotives
	751-805	Miscellaneous motors and engines
		Including gas, gasoline, diesel engines
	807-830	Renewable energy sources
	836-927	Hydraulic machinery
	940-940.5	Vacuum technology
	950-1030	Pneumatic machinery
	1040-1119	Machinery exclusive of prime movers
	1125-1345	Machine shops and machine shop practice
	1350-1418	Hoisting and conveying machinery
	1425-1475	Lifting and pressing machinery
	1480-1496	Agricultural machinery. Farm machinery
	1501-1519	Sewing machines

TK		Electrical engineering. Electronics. Nuclear engineering
	1-9971	Electrical engineering. Electronics. Nuclear engineering
	301-399	Electric meters
	452-454.4	Electric apparatus and materials. Electric circuits. Electric networks
	1001-1841	Production of electric energy or power. Powerplants. Central stations
	2000-2891	Dynamoelectric machinery and auxiliaries
		Including generators, motors, transformers
	2896-2985	Production of electricity by direct energy conversion

OUTLINE

TK		Electrical engineering. Electronics. Nuclear engineering - Continued
	3001-3521	Distribution or transmission of electric power
	4001-4102	Applications of electric power
	4125-4399	Electric lighting
	4601-4661	Electric heating
	5101-6720	Telecommunication
		Including telegraphy, telephone, radio, radar, television
	7800-8360	Electronics
	7885-7895	Computer engineering. Computer hardware
	8300-8360	Photoelectronic devices (General)
	9001-9401	Nuclear engineering. Atomic power
	9900-9971	Electricity for amateurs. Amateur constructors' manuals
TL	1-4050	Motor vehicles. Aeronautics. Astronautics
	1-484	Motor vehicles. Cycles
	500-777	Aeronautics. Aeronautical engineering
	780-785.8	Rocket propulsion. Rockets
	787-4050	Astronautics. Space travel
TN	1-997	Mining engineering. Metallurgy
	263-271	Mineral deposits. Metallic ore deposits. Prospecting
	275-325	Practical mining operations. Safety measures
	331-347	Mine transportation, haulage and hoisting. Mining machinery
	400-580	Ore deposits and mining of particular metals
	600-799	Metallurgy
	799.5-948	Nonmetallic minerals
	950-997	Building and ornamental stones
TP	1-1185	Chemical technology
	155-156	Chemical engineering
	200-248	Chemicals: Manufacture, use, etc.
	248.13-248.65	Biotechnology
	250-261	Industrial electrochemistry
	267.5-301	Explosives and pyrotechnics
	315-360	Fuel
	368-456	Food processing and manufacture
	480-498	Low temperature engineering. Cryogenic engineering. Refrigeration
	500-660	Fermentation industries. Beverages. Alcohol
	670-699	Oils, fats, and waxes
	690-692.5	Petroleum refining. Petroleum products

OUTLINE

TP		Chemical technology - Continued
	700-746	Illuminating industries (Nonelectric)
	751-762	Gas industry
	785-869	Clay industries. Ceramics. Glass
	875-888	Cement industries
	890-933	Textile bleaching, dyeing, printing, etc.
	934-945	Paints, pigments, varnishes, etc.
	1080-1185	Polymers and polymer manufacture
TR	1-1050	Photography
	250-265	Cameras
	287-500	Photographic processing. Darkroom technique
	504-508	Transparencies. Diapositives
	510-545	Color photography
	550-581	Studio and laboratory
	590-620	Lighting
	624-835	Applied photography
		Including artistic, commercial, medical photography, photocopying processes
	845-899	Cinematography. Motion pictures
	925-1050	Photomechanical processes
TS	1-2301	Manufactures
	155-194	Production management. Operations manageme
	195-198.8	Packaging
	200-770	Metal manufactures. Metalworking
	780-788	Stonework
	800-937	Wood technology. Lumber
	840-915	Wood products. Furniture
	920-937	Chemical processing of wood
	940-1047	Leather industries. Tanning
	1060-1070	Furs
	1080-1268	Paper manufacture and trade
	1300-1865	Textile industries
	1870-1935	Rubber industry
	1950-1982	Animal products
	2120-2159	Cereals and grain. Milling industry
	2220-2283	Tobacco industry
	2284-2288	Animal feeds and feed mills. Pet food industry
TT	1-999	Handicrafts. Arts and crafts
	161-170.7	Manual training. School shops
	174-176	Articles for children
	180-200	Woodworking. Furniture making. Upholstering
	201-203	Lathework. Turning
	205-267	Metalworking
	300-382.8	Painting. Wood finishing

OUTLINE

TT		Handicrafts. Arts and crafts - Continued
	387-410	Soft home furnishings
	490-695	Clothing manufacture. Dressmaking. Tailoring
	697-927	Home arts. Homecrafts
		Including sewing, embroidery, decorative crafts
	950-979	Hairdressing. Beauty culture. Barbers' work
	980-999	Laundry work
TX	1-1110	Home economics
	301-339	The house
		Including arrangement, care, servants
	341-641	Nutrition. Foods and food supply
	642-840	Cookery
	851-885	Dining-room service
	901-946.5	Hospitality industry. Hotels, clubs, restaurants, etc. Food service
	950-953	Taverns, barrooms, saloons
	955-985	Building operation and housekeeping
	1100-1105	Mobile home living
	1110	Recreational vehicle living

Technology (General)
    Periodicals and societies. By language of publication

1	English
2	French
3	German
4	Other languages (not A-Z)
5	Yearbooks
6	Congresses
	Industrial museums, etc , see T179 +
	International exhibitions, see T391 +
7	Collected works (nonserial)
8	Symbols and abbreviations
	Dictionaries and encyclopedias
9	General works
10	Bilingual and polyglot
	Communication of technical information
10.5	General works
	Information centers
10.6	General works
	Special countries
	United States
10.63.A1	General works
10.63.A2-Z	By region or state, A-Z
10.65.A-Z	Others, A-Z
10.68	Risk communication
10.7	Technical literature
10.8	Abstracting and indexing
	Language. Technical writing
	Cf. QA42, Mathematical language. Mathematical authorship
11	General works
11.3	Technical correspondence
11.4	Technical editing
11.5	Translating
11.8	Technical illustration
	Cf. Q222, Scientific illustration
	Cf. T351 +, Mechanical drawing
11.9	Technical archives
	Industrial directories
11.95	General works
	By region or country
	United States
12	General works
12.3.A-Z	By region or state, A-Z
	Under each state:
.x	*General works*
.x2A-Z	*Local, A-Z*
12.5.A-Z	Other regions or countries, A-Z
	Under each country:
.x	*General works*
.x2A-Z	*Local, A-Z*
13	General catalogs. Miscellaneous supplies

14   Philosophy. Theory. Classification. Methodology
                  Cf. CB478, Technology and civilization
14.5   Social aspects
                  Class here works which discuss the impact of
                      technology on modern society
                  For works on the role of technology in the history and
                      development of civilization, see CB478
              History
                  Including the history of inventions
14.7   Periodicals, societies, serials, etc.
15   General works
16   Ancient
17   Medieval
18   Modern
19   19th-20th centuries
20   20th century
                  Including "technological wonders of the modern
                      world"
              Special regions or countries
                  America. United States
21   General works
                  Special divisions (United States)
21.5.A-Z   By region, A-Z
                      e.g.
21.5.N4   New England
22.A-W   States, A-W
22.5.A-Z   Cities, A-Z
23   Canada (Table T4)
24   Latin America. West Indies (Table T4)
25   South America (Table T4)
26   Europe (Table T4)
27   Asia (Table T4)
27.3   Arab countries (Table T4)
28   Africa (Table T4)
29   Australia (Table T4)
29.5   New Zealand (Table T4)
30   Pacific Islands (Table T4)
31   Arctic regions (Table T4)
32   Primitive peoples
                  see GN429-GN434
33   Lost arts
35   Historical atlases of progress, invention, etc.
36   Women in technology
37   Industrial archaeology
                  For local areas, see T21+
              Biography
                  Including inventors
39   Collective
40.A-Z   Individual, A-Z
                  Class preferably with special subject in classes TA-
                      TT
              General works
44   Before 19th century

	General works -- Continued
45	19th century and later
47	Elementary and popular works. Home educators
48	Juvenile works
49	Pocketbooks. Receipts. Formulas
	Early to 1800, see T44
49.5	General special
	Including international cooperation
	Addresses, essays, lectures, see T185
50	Technical mensuration
	Cf. TA329+, Engineering mathematics
	Cf. TS172, Tolerances
50.5	Metric system in industry
	Class metric system in special industries with the industry
	Cf. QC90.8+, Metric system (General)
51	Tables
	Cf. TA151, Engineering (General)
	Cf. TA635, Structural engineering (General)
	Cf. TH151, Building (General)
	Cf. TH434+, Estimates, quantities and cost (Building)
(54)	Dangerous occupations. Industrial accidents see HD7262-HD7262.5
	Industrial safety. Industrial accident prevention
	Cf. TA169.7, System safety
	Cf. TS175, Safety of consumer products
55.A1	Periodicals, societies, congresses, etc.
55.A2-Z	General works
55.2	Study and teaching
55.25	Research
55.3.A-Z	Special topics, A-Z
	Including special measures and appliances
55.3.A87	Authorship of safety manuals
55.3.A93	Awards programs
55.3.B43	Behavior modification
55.3.B56	Biorhythms and industrial accidents
55.3.C6	Color as a safety measure
55.3.E96	Explosion prevention and protection
55.3.G3	Gas masks. Respirators
55.3.H3	Hazardous substances
	Cf. HE5623+, Transportation by country
	Cf. TD1020+, Waste disposal
55.3.L5	Lifting and carrying
55.3.M35	Manipulators
55.3.M37	Marking
55.3.P67	Posters
55.3.P75	Protective clothing
	Radiation environment procedures and equipment, see TK9151.4+
55.3.S23	Safety helmets
55.3.S72	Statistical methods

Industrial engineering
Including management engineering and management science
Class here works on the solving of management problems concerned with design, improvement, and installation of complex industrial systems of men, materials, and equipment; employing the methods of operations research and engineering analysis and design, with stress on optimum use of resources. For applications in special fields, see the field
For engineering economy, see TA177.4+
For industrial psychology, see HF5548.7+
For industrial safety, see T55+
For labor relations, see HD6958.5+
For personnel management, see HF5549+
For production management, see TS155+
For wage and salary administration, see HD4909+
For works on the organization and operation of industrial institutions and business enterprises, see HD28+

55.4	Periodicals. Societies. Collections
55.45	Congresses
55.5	Dictionaries and encyclopedias
55.52	Symbols and abbreviations
55.54	Directories
55.6	History
	Special countries
	United States
55.7	General works
55.72.A-W	States, A-W
55.74.A-Z	Other American countries, A-Z
55.75.A-Z	Europe. By country, A-Z
55.76.A-Z	Africa. By country, A-Z
55.77.A-Z	Asia. By country, A-Z
55.775	Australia
55.778	New Zealand
	Biography
55.8	Collective
55.85.A-Z	Individual, A-Z
	General works
55.9	Early to 1930
56	Treatises
56.23	Pocketbooks, tables, etc.
56.24	General special
56.25	Addresses, essays, lectures
56.3	Industrial engineering as a profession. Industrial engineers. Management consultants
	Study and teaching
56.4	General works
56.42	Research
56.8	Project management
	Applied mathematics. Quantitative methods
57	General works

Industrial engineering
Applied mathematics.
Quantitative methods -- Continued
57.2 Problems, exercises, etc.
Probability theory
57.3 General works
Stochastic processes
Cf. TS160 +, Inventory control
57.32 General works
57.33 Renewal theory
Statistical methods
Cf. HA154 +, Statistical data
Cf. TS156 +, Quality control
Cf. TS173, Reliability
Cf. TS178.5, Line balancing
57.35 General works
57.36 Sampling theory
57.37 Experimental design
57.4 Schematic and graphic analysis
57.5 Data processing
Cf. HF5548.125 +, Business data processing
Operations research. Systems analysis
Cf. QA402 +, Analytical methods connected with
physical problems
57.6.A1 Periodicals, societies, etc.
57.6.A2-Z General works
Simulation
Cf. QA76.9.C65, Computer science
Cf. TA343, Engineering mathematics
57.62 General works
57.64 Monte Carlo method
Programming
57.7 General works
Linear programming
57.74 General works
Simplex model
57.76 General works
57.77 Allocation method
57.78 Transportation method
57.79 Stochastic programming
Nonlinear programming
57.8 General works
57.815 Convex programming
57.817 Nonconvex programming
57.82 Quadratic programming
57.825 Geometric programming
57.83 Dynamic programming
57.84 Heuristic programming
57.85 Network systems theory
Including network analysis
Cf. TS157.5 +, Scheduling
57.9 Queuing theory. Waiting line problems

Industrial engineering
Applied mathematics. Quantitative methods
Operations research.
Systems analysis -- Continued
57.92   Game theory
                   Cf. HD30.26, Management games
57.95   Decision theory
                   Cf. HD30.23, Administrative decisions
57.97   Search theory
58.4   Managerial control systems
           Information technology. Information systems (General)
58.5   General works
                Management information systems
                   Cf. HD30.213, Industrial management
                   Cf. HF5549.5.C6+, Communication in personnel
                     management
                   Cf. TS158.6, Automatic data collection
                     systems (Production control)
58.6   General works
58.62   Decision support systems
                     Cf. HD30.213, Industrial management
58.64   Management of information systems
           Production capacity. Manufacturing capacity
                Cf. HD69.C3, Economics
                Cf. TS176+, Manufacturing engineering
58.7   General works
58.8   Productivity. Efficiency
           Standardization
                Cf. TA368, Standards (Collections, indexes,
                     etc.)
59.A1   Periodicals, societies, etc.
59.A2-Z   General works
59.2.A-Z   By region or country, A-Z
59.4   Mechanization
59.5   Automation
                Cf. HD45.2, Economics
                Cf. TA165, Engineering instruments
                Cf. TJ212+, Automatic control
                Cf. TJ1180+, Machine tools
                Cf. TS156.8, Process control
           Human engineering in industry. Man-machine systems
59.7   General works
59.72   Fatigue aspects of man-machine systems
59.77   Working environment
                Cf. TS187, Plant utilities
           Work measurement. Methods engineering
                Including time and motion study, work study, etc.
60.A2   Periodicals
60.A3-Z   General works
                Work measurement
60.2   General works
                  Production standards
60.3   General works

	Industrial engineering
	Work measurement. Methods engineering
	Work measurement
	Production standards -- Continued
60.35	Labor productivity
	Cf. HD57, Economics
	Time study
60.4	General works
60.42	Standard times
60.45	Allowances
60.47	Setup time
	Predetermined motion time systems
60.5	General works
60.52	Methods time measurement
60.55	Work sampling
	Methods engineering
60.6	General works
60.7	Motion study
60.74	Machine assignments
60.8	Work design. Job design
	Technical education. Technical schools
	Cf. LB1594 +, Industrial training in the
	elementary school
	Cf. LC1081 +, Industrial education (Theory)
	Cf. LC2780.5, Industrial education of Blacks and
	Afro-Americans
	Cf. T175 +, Industrial research
	Cf. TT161 +, Manual training
61	Periodicals, societies, etc.
62	Congresses
63	Dictionaries and encyclopedias
64	Directories
65	General works
65.3	General special
	Including international cooperation
65.5.A-Z	Special methods, A-Z
65.5.B5	Blackboard drawing
65.5.C3	Case method
65.5.C65	Computer-assisted instruction
65.5.M6	Motion pictures
65.5.P7	Programmed instruction
65.5.S9	Synthetic training devices
65.5.T4	Television
	History
66	General works
67	Ancient
68	Medieval
69	Modern
	Special countries
	For special schools, see T171 +
71	America
72	North America
	United States

	Technical education. Technical schools
	Special countries
	United States -- Continued
73	General works
73.1	New England. North Atlantic States
73.3	Southern States
73.5	Central States
73.7	Western States
74.A-Z	Special states, A-Z
75.A-Z	Special cities, A-Z
	Canada
76	General works
77.A-Z	Local, A-Z
	Mexico
78	General works
79.A-Z	Local, A-Z
	Central America
80	General works
81.A-Z	Special countries, A-Z
	West Indies
82	General works
83.A-Z	Special countries or islands, A-Z
	South America
84	General works
	Argentina
86	General works
87.A-Z	Local, A-Z
	Bolivia
88	General works
89.A-Z	Local, A-Z
	Brazil
91	General works
92.A-Z	Local, A-Z
	Chile
93	General works
94.A-Z	Local, A-Z
	Colombia
95	General works
96.A-Z	Local, A-Z
97	Ecuador
	Guiana
98	Guyana
99	Surinam
100	French
101	Paraguay
102	Peru
103	Uruguay
104	Venezuela
	Europe
105	General works
	Great Britain. England
107	General works
107.5	Colonies

	Technical education. Technical schools
	Special countries
	Europe
	Great Britain. England -- Continued
108.A-Z	English counties or cities, A-Z
	Ireland
109	General works
110.A-Z	Local, A-Z
	Scotland
111	General works
112.A-Z	Local, A-Z
	Wales
113	General works
114.A-Z	Local, A-Z
	Austria
115	General works
116.A-Z	Local, A-Z
(116.H8)	Hungary
	see T128.5
	Belgium
117	General works
118.A-Z	Local, A-Z
	Denmark
119	General works
120.A-Z	Local, A-Z
	France
121	General works
122.A-Z	Local, A-Z
	Germany
	Including West Germany
123	General works
124.A-Z	Local, A-Z
	East Germany
124.5	General works
(124.6.A-Z)	Local
	see T124.A-Z
	Greece
125	General works
126.A-Z	Local, A-Z
	Holland
127	General works
128.A-Z	Local, A-Z
128.5	Hungary
	Italy
129	General works
130.A-Z	Local, A-Z
	Norway
131	General works
132.A-Z	Local, A-Z
	Portugal
133	General works
134.A-Z	Local, A-Z
	Russia

	Technical education. Technical schools
	Special countries
	Europe
	Russia -- Continued
135	General works
136.A-Z	Local, A-Z
	Spain
137	General works
138.A-Z	Local, A-Z
	Sweden
139	General works
140.A-Z	Local, A-Z
	Switzerland
141	General works
142.A-Z	Local, A-Z
	Turkey
143	General works
144.A-Z	Local, A-Z
146.A-Z	Balkan States, A-Z
147.A-Z	Other countries, A-Z
	Asia
149	General works
	China
151	General works
152.A-Z	Local, A-Z
	India
153	General works
154.A-Z	Local, A-Z
	Japan
155	General works
156.A-Z	Local, A-Z
	Iran. Persia
157	General works
158.A-Z	Local, A-Z
(159-160)	Asia Minor
	see T143+
(161-162)	Siberia
	see T136
163.A-Z	Other Asian countries, A-Z
164	Arab countries
	Africa
165	General works
166.A-Z	Special countries, A-Z
	Indian Ocean islands
166.5	General works
166.6.A-Z	Special divisions, A-Z
	Australia
167	General works
168.A-Z	Local, A-Z
168.5	New Zealand
	Pacific islands
169	General works
170.A-Z	Special divisions, A-Z

Technical education. Technical schools -- Continued
  Special schools
      Including technical departments of universities
      Cf. TT167.A+, Manual training schools
    American schools

171.A-Z	General. By name, A-Z

        Under each school:
      .xA1-.xA4   *Official serials*
      .xA5-.xA7   *Official monographs*
      .xA8-.xZ   *Nonofficial publications. By author,*
                     A-Z

172.A-Z	Correspondence schools. By name, A-Z
173.A-Z	Other schools. By city where located, A-Z

      Expand Cutter number for city to provide
        alphabetical arrangement of schools, e.g.

173.L832	Borough Polytechnic (London, England)
173.L88	City of London Polytechnic

Technological change
  For economic aspects of technological innovations, see
    HD45
  For technological innovations in economic history, see
    HC79.T4

173.2	General works
	Special countries
173.4	United States
173.5.A-Z	Other countries, A-Z
	Inventions, see T212
173.8	Technological innovations
174	Technological forecasting
174.2	Technology indicators
174.3	Technology transfer
	Cf. HF1429, Foreign licensing agreements
174.5	Technology assessment
174.7	Nanotechnology
	Industrial research. Research and development
	Cf. T56.42, Industrial engineering
	Cf. TA160+, Engineering
	Cf. TS171+, Product design
175	General works
175.5	Management. Organization
175.7	Research parks
	Special countries
176	United States
177.A-Z	Others, A-Z
178.A-Z	Special research laboratories. By name, A-Z
	Museums. Exhibitions of local societies
179	General works
	Special museums
	United States
180.A1	General works
180.A2-Z	By city and museum, A-Z

	Museums. Exhibitions of local societies
	Special museums -- Continued
183.A-Z	Other regions or countries, A-Z
	Under each country:
	.x *General works*
	.x2A-Z *By city and museum, A-Z*
185	Addresses, essays, lectures
	Patents
	Cf. HD69.B7, Brand name products
	For patents pertaining to particular subjects, see the
	subject, e.g. TK7850, Patents in electronics
201	Periodicals, societies, congresses, etc.
	International patent conferences
203	General works. By date of conference
205	History and discussions of international agreements
	("conventions") resulting from the conferences
207	Collected works (nonserial)
	Addresses, essays, lectures, see T333
209	Dictionaries and encyclopedias
210	Patent literature
210.2	Translating. Translating services
210.5	Directories
211	Theory of patents
212	Inventors and inventions. How to invent
	Cf. T14.7+, History of inventions
	Cf. T173.8, Technology innovations
	History of patents
221-323.7	By region or country (Table T1 modified)
	Add country number in table to T200
	For patent law, see class K
	Under each region or country subarrange as
	follows:
	A2 *Periodicals*
	B2 *Specifications*
	C2 *Lists other than regular periodicals*
	D7 *Indexes to patents*
	F4 *Classification*
	H3 *Annual reports (Patent Office)*
	J4 *Special reports (Patent Office)*
	P2 *General works (Patent Office)*
	U3 *Designs and models*
	V1 *Periodicals (Trademarks)*
	V2 *General works (Trademarks)*
	V3 *Registers. Lists (Trademarks)*
	(Including lists of trademarks for
	special products and industries)
	Pacific islands
323.A1	General works
323.A5-Z	Special islands, A-Z
323.2	Arctic regions
323.3	Antarctica
323.7	Developing countries

	Patents -- Continued
324	Designs and models of patents (General)
	For special regions or countries, see T221+
325	Trademarks
	For special regions or countries, including
	trademarks for special products or industries
	of those regions or countries, see T221+
333	Addresses, essays, lectures
339	Inventors' manuals. Publications of patent solicitors
	Including works on how to protect, patent, and
	merchandise inventions
342	Industrial design coordination
	Mechanical drawing. Engineering graphics
	Cf. QA501+, Descriptive geometry
	Cf. T11.8, Technical illustration
	Cf. TA337+, Schematic and graphic methods in
	engineering
	Cf. TJ227+, Machine drawing
351	Periodicals, societies, etc.
351.3	Dictionaries and encyclopedias
351.5	Study and teaching
352	Drawing-room management and practice
	Cf. T375+, Drawing-room equipment and supplies
353	General works
353.5	Juvenile works
354	Problems, exercises, etc.
355	Structural drawing
	Cf. NA2685+, Architecture
357	General special
	Including tinting, standards
359	Freehand drawing for technical purposes
361	Technical blackboard drawing
	Projection
362	General works
363	Orthographic projection
	Including axonometric and isometric projection
365	Oblique projection
	Including cavalier and cabinet projection
369	Perspective projection
	Cf. NC748+, Drawing, design, illustration
	(Fine arts)
371	Lettering
	Cf. NK3600+, Alphabets, calligraphy and
	initials
	Cf. NK8705, Stonework
	Cf. TT360.A1+, Signs
	Drawing instruments and materials
375	General works
377	Catalogs
379	Working drawings and their use. Blueprint reading
	Cf. TA175, Engineering drawings
	Cf. TR915+, Reproduction of drawings
385	Computer graphics

	Exhibitions. Trade shows
	Including the great national and international
	exhibitions
391	Periodicals, societies, collections
393	Documents
	Cf. T395+, History
394	Directories
	History
395	General works
395.5.A-Z	By region or country, A-Z
	Organization, methods, classifications, etc.
	Including display techniques
396	General works
396.5	Display technique. Pavilions
397.A-Z	Special. By city, A-Z
	e.g.
397.C5	Chicago. World's Columbian Exposition, 1893
	Special exhibitions
	Arrange by place and subarrange by year
402	Aberdeen (Table T2)
402.2	Accra (Table T2)
403	Adelaide, 1897 (Table T2)
405	Agra, 1867 (Table T2)
	Agram, see T992
407	Alexandria (Table T2)
410	Algiers (Table T2)
412	Alma-Ata (Table T2)
	Amsterdam
414	1859 (Table T2)
415	1869 (Table T2)
416	1883 (Table T2)
417	Antananarivo, Madagascar (Table T2)
	Arrange by date
420	Antwerp, 1984 (Table T2)
424	Athens (Table T2)
	Atlanta
426	1881 (Table T2)
427	1895 (Table T2)
428.7	Bagdhad (Table T2)
429	Bahia, 1872 (Table T2)
430	Baltimore (Table T2)
433	Barcelona (Table T2)
436	Basel (Table T2)
439	Batavia (Table T2)
439.3	Belgrad (Table T2)
439.5	Bergen, 1898 (Table T2)
440	Berlin (Table T2)
450	Birmingham (Table T2)
452	Bogota (Table T2)
452.5	Bolzano (Table T2)
453	Bombay (Table T2)
456	Bordeaux (Table T2)
460	Boston, 1883 (Table T2)

	Exhibitions
	Special exhibitions -- Continued
	Brisbane
463	1875 (Table T2)
463.2	1988 (Table T2)
464	Brno (Table T2)
	Arrange by date
	Brussels
465	Before 1910 (Table T2)
	Arrange by date
467	1910 (Table T2)
468	1935 (Table T2)
469	1958 (Table T2)
475	Bucharest (Table T2)
	Budapest
478	1885 (Table T2)
479	1896 (Table T2)
479.2	1925 (Table T2)
479.3	Later (Table T2)
	Arrange by date
	Buenos Aires
481	1875 (Table T2)
482	1880 (Table T2)
483	1882 (Table T2)
484	1910 (Table T2)
484.5	Later (Table T2)
	Arrange by date
485	Buffalo, 1901 (Table T2)
486	Cadiz (Table T2)
487	Cairo (Table T2)
488	Calcutta (Table T2)
489	Calicut (Table T2)
491	Canton (Table T2)
494	Capetown (Table T2)
495	Caracas (Table T2)
496	Caserta, 1864 (Table T2)
	Charleroi
496.7	1911 (Table T2)
496.8	Later (Table T2)
	Arrange by date
497	Charleston, 1901-1902 (Table T2)
	Chicago
499	1873 (Table T2)
499.5	1883 (Table T2)
500	1893 (Table T2)
501	1933-1934 (Table T2)
502	1992 (Table T2)
	Christiania, see T797
	Cincinnati
515	1870-1872 (Table T2)
516	1888 (Table T2)
517	1935 (Table T2)
519	Ciudad Trujillo (Table T2)

	Exhibitions
	Special exhibitions -- Continued
	Cleveland
520	1909 (Table T2)
521	Later (Table T2)
	Arrange by date
523	Colombo, Ceylon (Table T2)
525	Constantinople (Table T2)
535	Copenhagen (Table T2)
536	Cordoba, 1871 (Table T2)
537	Cork, 1852 (Table T2)
540	Curitiba, 1875 (Table T2)
541	Dairen (Table T2)
	Arrange by date
543	Dallas, 1936-1937 (Table T2)
544	Delhi, India (Table T2)
545	Denver, 1882-1883 (Table T2)
	Detroit
550	1892 (Table T2)
551	Later (Table T2)
	Arrange by date
552	Djakarta (Table T2)
553	Dnepropetrovsk, 1910 (Table T2)
555	Dresden (Table T2)
	Dublin
560	1853 (Table T2)
561	1865 (Table T2)
563	Dusseldorf (Table T2)
	Dunedin
565	1865 (Table T2)
566	1925-1926 (Table T2)
570	Edinburgh (Table T2)
590	Florence (Table T2)
599	Fukuoka (Table T2)
606	Geneva (Table T2)
610	Genoa, 1892 (Table T2)
615	Ghent (Table T2)
	Arrange by date
	Glasgow
618	1888 (Table T2)
618.3	1938 (Table T2)
618.5	Gorki, 1896 (Table T2)
619	Graz (Table T2)
619.5	Guadalajara, 1880 (Table T2)
620	Guatemala, 1878 (Table T2)
620.5	Guimarães, 1884 (Table T2)
621	Haarlem, 1861 (Table T2)
624	Hague (Table T2)
627	Hakodate (Table T2)
631	Hamburg (Table T2)
632	Hangchow (Table T2)
	Arrange by date
632.5	Hannover, 2000 (Table T2)

	Exhibitions
	Special exhibitions -- Continued
	Hanoi
633	1902 (Table T2)
633.5	Since 1902 (Table T2)
	Arrange by date
635	Havana (Table T2)
640	Hong Kong (Table T2)
645	Indianapolis (Table T2)
647	Izmir (Table T2)
648	Jamestown, 1907 (Table T2)
650	Johannesburg (Table T2)
650.8	Kanazawa, Japan (Ishikawa Prefecture) (Table T2)
651	Karachi (Table T2)
	Arrange by date
652	Khartoum (Table T2)
	Arrange by date
653	Kiev (Table T2)
654	Kimberley, 1892 (Table T2)
655	Kingston, Jamaica, 1891 (Table T2)
658	Kishinev (Table T2)
670	Klagenfurt, 1838 (Table T2)
670.2	Knoxville, 1982 (Table T2)
670.4	Kobe-shi (Japan) (Table T2)
670.5	Kōchi, Japan (Table T2)
	Arrange by date
670.7	Kure, Japan (Table T2)
670.8	Kyoto, Japan (Table T2)
671.3	Lagos (Table T2)
671.5	La Paz, Bolivia (Table T2)
671.8	Lausanne (Table T2)
673	Leeds (Table T2)
678	Leipzig (Table T2)
	Liége
679	1905 (Table T2)
679.3	1930 (Table T2)
679.5	Later (Table T2)
	Arrange by date
680	Lima (Table T2)
681	Lisbon (Table T2)
684	Liverpool, 1886 (Table T2)
687	Loanda (Table T2)
	London
690	1851 (Table T2)
691	1862 (Table T2)
695	1871-1874 (Table T2)
695.5	1884 (Table T2)
695.6	1885 (Table T2)
696	1886 (Table T2)
	1887
697	General works (Table T2)
697.3	East London (Table T2)
698	1906 (Table T2)

	Exhibitions
	Special exhibitions
	London -- Continued
699	1908 (Table T2)
700	1910 (Table T2)
700.2	1912 (Table T2)
700.5	1917 (Table T2)
700.8	1928 (Table T2)
701	1929 (Table T2)
702	Later (Table T2)
	Arrange by date
703	Long Beach, Calif. (Table T2)
704	Los Angeles, Calif. (Table T2)
705	Louisville, 1886 (Table T2)
	Lyons
710	1894 (Table T2)
711	Later (Table T2)
	Arrange by date
712	Madras (Table T2)
	Arrange by date
	Madrid
714	Before 1891 (Table T2)
	Arrange by date
715	1891 (Table T2)
716	Later (Table T2)
	Arrange by date
718	Malmö, 1896 (Table T2)
719	Manchester, 1887 (Table T2)
723	Manila (Table T2)
725	Mar del Plata (Table T2)
727	Marseilles (Table T2)
729	Medellín, Colombia (Table T2)
	Melbourne
730	1861 (Table T2)
730.1	1866-1967 (Table T2)
730.6	1875 (Table T2)
731	1880-1881 (Table T2)
732	1888-1889 (Table T2)
739	Memphis (Table T2)
742	Mexico (City) (Table T2)
744	Milan (Table T2)
745	Milwaukee (Table T2)
748	Minneapolis (Table T2)
750	Minsk (Table T2)
750.4	Mogadishu, Somalia (Table T2)
	Arrange by date
751	Moji (Table T2)
752	Montreal (Table T2)
757	Moscow (Table T2)
760	Mukden (Table T2)
762	Munich (Table T2)
766	Nagasaki (Table T2)
766.5	Nagoya-shi (Japan) (Table T2)

Exhibitions
Special exhibitions -- Continued

768	Nancy (Table T2)
770	Nanking (Table T2)
773	Naples (Table T2)
774	Naruto-shi (Japan) (Table T2)
775	Nashville, 1897 (Table T2)
775.6	Neuchâtel, 2001 (Table T2)

New Orleans

776	1854 (Table T2)
777	1884-1885 (Table T2)
778	1885-1886 (Table T2)
779	Later (Table T2)
	Arrange by date

New York

783	1853-1854 (Table T2)
784	1855-1938 (Table T2)
	Arrange by date
785	1939-1940 (Table T2)
786	Later (Table T2)
	Arrange by date
787	Niagara Falls, 1926 (Table T2)
788	Nicosia (Cyprus) (Table T2)
	Arrange by date
789	Novgorod (Table T2)
793	Odessa (Table T2)
796	Omaha, 1898 (Table T2)
796.5	Oporto (Table T2)
796.7	Osaka (Table T2)
	Arrange by date
797	Oslo (Christiania) (Table T2)
797.5	Otaru, Japan (Table T2)
798	Panama (Table T2)
	Panama-Pacific exposition, see TC781+

Paris

799	Before 1855 (Table T2)
	Arrange by date
800	1855 (Table T2)
801	1867 (Table T2)
801.5	1875 (Table T2)
802	1878 (Table T2)
803	1889 (Table T2)
804	1900 (Table T2)
805	Later (Table T2)
	Arrange by date
820	Peking (Table T2)

Philadelphia

825	1876 (Table T2)
826	1877-1879 (Table T2)
826.3	1926 (Table T2)
828	Pisa, 1868 (Table T2)
830	Pittsburgh (Table T2)
830.5	Plovdiv (Table T2)

	Exhibitions
	Special exhibitions -- Continued
830.7	Poona (Table T2)
831	Port-au-Prince, 1949-1950 (Table T2)
832	Portland, Maine (Table T2)
	Portland, Oregon
834	1905 (Table T2)
834.2	Later (Table T2)
	Arrange by date
835	Porto, 1865 (Table T2)
836	Prague (Table T2)
836.8	Pushkin (Russia) (Table T2)
837	Quito (Table T2)
	Rio de Janeiro
839	Before 1875 (Table T2)
	Arrange by date
840	1875 (Table T2)
841	1876-1907 (Table T2)
	Arrange by date
843	1908 (Table T2)
844	Later (Table T2)
	Arrange by date
845	Rio Grande do Sul (Table T2)
850	Rome (Table T2)
860	St. Louis, 1904 (Table T2)
865	St. Paul (Table T2)
868	St. Petersburg (Table T2)
871	San Antonio, Texas (Table T2)
	San Diego
872	1915 (Table T2)
872.3	Later (Table T2)
	Arrange by date
	San Francisco
874	1894 (Table T2)
875	1895-1914 (Table T2)
	Arrange by date
	1915. Panama-Pacific exposition, see TC781 +
876	Later (Table T2)
	Arrange by date
877	San José, 1886 (Table T2)
878	San Juan, Puerto Rico (Table T2)
	Santiago de Chile
879	1872 (Table T2)
879.1	1873 (Table T2)
880	1875 (Table T2)
881	1942-1943 (Table T2)
882	1989
884	Sarajevo (Table T2)
888	Schwerin, 1861 (Table T2)
	Seattle
890	1909 (Table T2)
890.2	Later (Table T2)
	Arrange by date

	Exhibitions
	Special exhibitions -- Continued
	Seoul
891.5	1929 (Table T2)
892	1982 (Table T2)
	Seville
894	1929-1930 (Table T2)
894.1	1992 (Table T2)
895	Shan-t'ou chuan ch'u, China (Table T2)
896	Shanghai (Table T2)
896.5	Shizuoka (Japan) (Table T2)
	Arrange by date
897	Singapore (Table T2)
898	Sofia (Table T2)
902	Spokane (Table T2)
903	Springfield, Mass. (Table T2)
910	Stockholm, 1897 (Table T2)
915	Strassburg (Table T2)
920	Sydney, 1879-1880 (Table T2)
923	Taejŏn-si (Korea), 1993 (Table T2)
925	T'ai-pei (City) (Table T2)
926	Takayama-shi (Japan) (Table T2)
	Arrange by date
930	Tananarivo (Table T2)
933	Tbilisi, 1850 (Table T2)
934	Thessalonikē (Table T2)
	Tokyo
937	Before 1912 (Table T2)
	Arrange by date
938	1912- (Table T2)
	Arrange by date
939	Toluca, Mexico (Table T2)
940	Toronto (Table T2)
941	Toyama (Table T2)
944	Trieste (Table T2)
945	Tripoli (Table T2)
946	Tsukuba Kenkyū Gakuen Toshi (Japan) (Table T2)
	Turin
947	1884 (Table T2)
948	Later (Table T2)
	Arrange by date
948.5	Ulm (Table T2)
948.7	Utsunomiya-shi (Japan) (Table T2)
949	Valladolid, 1850 (Table T2)
951	Valparaiso (Table T2)
953	Vancouver, B.C. (Table T2)
	Arrange by date
955	Venice (Table T2)
	Vienna
960	1873 (Table T2)
960.2	1995 (Table T2)
967	Villanueva y Geltrú (Table T2)
975	Warsaw (Table T2)

Exhibitions
   Special exhibitions -- Continued
      Washington
983   1846 (Table T2)
984   Since 1846 (Table T2)
           Arrange by date
986   Wellington, N. Z., 1885 (Table T2)
988   Wembley, Eng., 1924-1925 (Table T2)
990   Yokohama (Table T2)
992   Zagreb (Agram) (Table T2)
995   Zurich (Table T2)

	Engineering (General). Civil engineering (General)
	Periodicals and societies
1	English
2	French
3	German
4	Other languages (not A-Z)
5	Congresses
	Exhibitions. Museums
6.A1	General works
6.A2-Z	By region or country, A-Z
	Under each country:
	.x *General works*
	.x2A-Z *Special. By city, A-Z*
7	Collected works (nonserial)
9	Dictionaries and encyclopedias
	Engineering literature, see T10.7
11	Symbols and abbreviations
12	Directories of engineering companies and engineers
	History
15	General works
16	Ancient
17	Medieval
	Modern
18	To 1800
19	1800-
21-127	Country divisions (Table T1)
	Class here general historical and descriptive literature, reports on public works, etc.
	Add country number in Table to TA0
	Cf. HD3881+, Economic aspects of public works
	Biography
139	Collective
140.A-Z	Individual, A-Z
	General works. Civil engineering, etc.
144	Early to 1850
145	1850-
147	Elementary textbooks
148	Popular works
149	Juvenile works
151	Handbooks, manuals, etc.
	Cf. TA332, Pocketbooks, tables, etc. (Engineering mathematics)
	Cf. TA685, Tables of structural shapes and sections of steel and iron
152	Laboratory manuals
153	General special
155	Addresses, essays, lectures
	Engineering as a profession. Engineers
	Including working conditions, ethics, etc.
157	General works
	Industrial technicians
	Cf. TS155.4+, Manufacturing personnel
158	General works

	Engineering as a profession. Engineers
	Industrial technicians -- Continued
158.3	Instrumentation technicians
	Communication in engineering
158.5	General works
158.7	Computer network resources
	Including the Internet
	Technical education. Technical schools, see T61 +
159	Examinations, questions, etc.
	Research
160	General works
	Special countries
160.4	United States
160.6.A-Z	Other regions or countries, A-Z
164	Bioengineering
	Cf. R856 +, Medical engineering
165	Engineering instruments, meters, etc. Industrial
	instrumentation
	Cf. TJ212 +, Control engineering
165.5	Coordinate measuring machines
	Human engineering
	Class particular applications with the field of
	application, e.g. TL240 +, Automobile design
	Cf. T59.7 +, Industrial engineering
166	General works
167	Man-machine systems
168	Systems engineering
	Cf. T57.6 +, Systems analysis (Industrial
	engineering)
168.5	Reverse engineering
	Systems reliability
	Cf. TS173, Reliability of industrial products
169	General works
169.3	Accelerated life testing
169.5	System failure
169.6	Fault location
169.7	System safety
	Cf. T55 +, Industrial safety
	Cf. TS175, Product safety
	Environmental engineering
	Cf. TD1 +, Environmental technology
	Cf. TH6014 +, Environmental engineering in
	buildings
170	General works
171	Environmental testing
174	Engineering design
175	Drawings and designs
	Cf. T351 +, Mechanical drawing
177	Engineering models
	Engineering economy
	Cf. TS165 +, Cost control. Value engineering
	Cf. TS181 +, Planning for machinery. Tool life
177.4	General works

	Engineering economy -- Continued
177.7	Cost effectiveness. Benefits-to-costs ratios
178	Valuation and depreciation
	Specifications
	Cf. HD2365+, Competitive letting of contracts in industry
	Cf. TH425, Construction of buildings
180	General works. Methods, etc.
181.A-Z	By region or country, A-Z
	Including the official manuals of public works
183	Estimates, quantities, and costs
	Cf. TH434+, Construction of buildings
185	Accounting for engineers
	Management of engineering works
190	General works
190.5	Office systems and records
191	Inspection of workmanship
	Cf. TH439, Building inspection
	Cf. TS156.2+, Inspection of manufactures
192	Safety measures
194	Planning of operations. Critical path analysis
	Engineering meteorology
197	General works
198	Industry and meteorology
	Class special industries and applications with the field e.g. TH7392.M6, Heating of factories
	Contractors' operations and equipment. Contracting
	Cf. TH11, Builders' and contractors' bulletins
201	Periodicals
210	General works
	Engineering machinery, tools, and implements
	Cf. TA735+, Excavating machinery
	Cf. TH900+, Construction equipment in building construction
	Cf. TS181+, Planning for machinery
213	General works
214	Directories
215	Trade and general catalogs, circulars, etc.
	Consulting engineering
	Cf. T56.3, Management consultants
	Directories, see TA12
216	General works
217.A-Z	Special companies. By name, A-Z
219	Forensic engineering
(221-327)	Engineering law see class K
	Engineering mathematics. Engineering analysis
	Cf. TA640+, Computational methods of structural engineering
329	Periodicals. Societies. Collections. Congresses
330	General works
331	General special
332	Pocketbooks, tables, etc.

	Engineering mathematics.
	Engineering analysis -- Continued
	Study and teaching
332.5	General works
333	Problems, exercises, examinations
335	Numerical methods. Approximations
	Schematic and graphic methods
337	General works
338.A-Z	Special topics, A-Z
338.B6	Bond graphs
338.F5	Flowgraphs
338.G7	Graph theory
338.N6	Nomograms
340	Probabilistic and statistical methods
	Mathematical models
	Cf. TA177, Engineering models
342	General works
343	Analogs. Simulation methods
	Cf. T57.62+, Industrial engineering
	Electronic data processing. Computer-aided
	engineering
345	General works
345.5.A-Z	Special systems, A-Z
345.5.A57	ANSYS
345.5.D47	DesignCAD
345.5.I2	ICES
345.5.M16	MESY
345.5.R73	RS/1
345.5.U53	UNISURF CAD
347.A-Z	Other specific mathematical aids in the solution of
	engineering problems, A-Z
347.B69	Boundary value problems
347.C3	Calculus of variations
347.C54	Closed circular ring problems
347.C6	Combinatorial analysis
347.C64	Complex analysis. Functions of complex variables
	Complex variables, Functions of, see TA347.C64
347.C68	Coupled problems
347.D4	Determinants and matrices
347.D45	Differential equations
347.D5	Dimensional analysis
347.D52	Dimensionless numbers
347.F5	Finite element method
347.F86	Functional analysis
	Functions of complex variables, see TA347.C64
347.I5	Integral equations
347.L5	Linear algebras
	Matrices, see TA347.D4
347.N46	Nets
347.N6	Normal numbers
347.T4	Tensor analysis
347.T7	Transfer functions
347.V4	Vector analysis

	Engineering mathematics.
	Engineering analysis -- Continued
348	Power spectra
	Mechanics of engineering. Applied mechanics
	Cf. TA405+, Mechanics of materials
	For mechanics applied to machinery, see TJ170+
	For structural engineering, see TA630+
349	Periodicals, societies, congresses, etc.
349.5	Dictionaries and encyclopedias
350	General works
350.2	Laboratory manuals
350.3	Addresses, essays, lectures
350.5	Study and teaching
350.7	Problems, exercises, examinations
351	Applied statics
	Applied dynamics
352	General works
353	Contact mechanics
354	Impact
354.5	Penetration mechanics
355	Vibration in engineering
	Cf. TA654+, Structural engineering
	Cf. TG265, Bridges
	Cf. TH153, Building (General)
	Cf. TJ208, Vibrators
356	Vibration of vehicles
	For vibration of specific vehicles, see the type
	of vehicle, e.g. TF, Railroad vehicles; TL,
	Motor vehicles
	Applied fluid mechanics
	Including fluid dynamics
	Cf. TC160+, Technical hydraulics
	Cf. TJ267, Theory of turbines
357	General works
357.3	Problems, exercises, etc.
357.5.A-Z	Special topics, A-Z
	Aerodynamics, see TA358
357.5.C38	Cavitation
357.5.C65	Convection
357.5.D37	Data processing
357.5.F55	Flow visualization
357.5.F58	Fluid-structure interaction
	Fluid transients, see TA357.5.U57
	Mathematics, see QA901+
357.5.M43	Measurements
357.5.M59	Mixing
357.5.M84	Multiphase flow. Two-phase flow
357.5.R44	Reduced gravity environments
357.5.S57	Sloshing
357.5.T87	Turbulence
	Two-phase flow, see TA357.5.M84
357.5.U57	Unsteady flow
357.5.V56	Viscous flow

	Mechanics of engineering. Applied mechanics
	Applied fluid mechanics -- Continued
358	Aerodynamics in engineering
	Cf. TL570+, Mechanics of flight
359	Aerodynamics of vehicles
	For aerodynamics of specific vehicles, see the vehicle, e.g. TF, Railroad vehicles; TL, Motor vehicles
	Acoustics in engineering. Acoustical engineering
	Class particular uses in the field of application, e.g. ML3805, Music; NA2800, Architectural acoustics; TK5981-TK5990, Electroacoustics
	Cf. TA418.84, Acoustical properties of materials
	Cf. TD891+, Noise control
	Cf. TH1725, Sound control in buildings
365	General works
365.5	Anechoic chambers
367	Ultrasonics in engineering
	Cf. TA417.4, Ultrasonic testing
367.5	Lasers in engineering
368	Standards (Collections, indexes, etc.)
	Class special collections of standards by subject in T-TX, e.g. TJ1330, Bolts and nuts
	Cf. T59+, Standardization
	Materials of engineering and construction
	Including building materials
	For constitution and properties of matter, see QC170+
401	Periodicals. Societies. Collections. Yearbooks
401.3	Congresses
	Exhibitions
401.6.A1	General works
401.6.A2-Z	By region or country, A-Z
	Apply table at TA6.A2-Z
402	Dictionaries and encyclopedias
402.3	Directories of materials scientists
402.5.A-Z	Special regions or countries, A-Z
402.7	Developing countries
403	Treatises
403.2	Popular works. Juvenile works
403.4	Pocketbooks, tables, etc.
403.6	General special
	Including transportation, quality control, etc.
403.8	Addresses, essays, lectures
403.9	Materials science as a profession
404	Study and teaching
404.2	Research
	Cf. TA416+, General engineering and testing laboratories
404.23	Data processing
	Including computer simulation
404.25	Communication in materials engineering
	Including materials databases
404.3	Problems, exercises, etc.

	Materials of engineering
	and construction -- Continued
404.5	Specifications and standards
	Specific characteristics of materials
	For chemical properties, see QD, TN, and TP
	For electric and magnetic properties, see QC501-QC764; TK
	Mechanical properties. Behavior of materials under applied forces
404.8	General works
	Strength of materials. Mechanics of materials
405	General works
407	General special
	Including stress analysis
407.2	Pocketbooks, tables, etc.
407.4	Problems, exercises, examinations
407.6	Study and teaching
409	Failure of materials. Fracture
	Cf. TA417.6, Deformation of materials
409.2	Service life of materials
409.3	Strengthening mechanisms
	Testing of materials (General and mechanical)
410	General works
412	Laboratory machines
	Testing machines
413	General works
413.5	Strain gages
	General engineering and testing laboratories
	Cf. TJ148, Mechanical engineering laboratories
416	General works
416.5.A-Z	By region or country, A-Z
417.A-Z	Special laboratories. By name, A-Z
	Nondestructive tests
417.2	General works
	Acoustic emission testing, see TA418.84
417.23	Microscopy
417.25	Radiographic examinations
417.3	Magnetic analysis
417.35	Electric analysis
417.4	Ultrasonic testing
417.45	Holographic testing
417.5	Infrared examinations
417.55	Penetrant inspection
417.6	Deformation of materials under stress
417.7.A-Z	Behavior of materials under specific stresses, A-Z
	For specific properties and tests, see the subject, e.g. TA418-TA418.12, Elastic properties and tests
	For specific properties and tests, see the subject, e.g. TA418.14-TA418.22, Plastic (inelastic) properties and tests

	Materials of engineering and construction
	Specific characteristics of materials
	Mechanical properties.
	Behavior of materials under applied forces
	Testing of materials (General and mechanical)
	Behavior of materials
	under specific
	stresses, A-Z -- Continued
	Bending, see TA417.7.F5
417.7.C6	Composite materials
417.7.C65	Compression
417.7.F5	Flexure
417.7.H53	High gravity
417.7.H55	High temperature
417.7.R43	Reduced gravity
417.7.S5	Shear
417.7.T4	Tension
417.7.T6	Torsion
	Specific properties and tests
	Elastic properties and tests
418	General works
418.12	Photoelasticity
	Plastic (inelastic) properties and tests
418.14	General works
418.15	Photoplasticity
	Ductile and brittle states
418.16	General works
418.17	Notch effect
418.18	Strain hardening
418.2	Viscous flow. Viscoelasticity
418.22	Creep behavior
	Temperature-dependent properties and tests
	Including effects of temperature on yield
	strength, viscous flow, etc.
	Cf. TA418.52 +, Thermal properties and
	tests
418.24	General works
418.26	Heat resistant materials. Refractory
	materials
	Cf. TN677 +, Metallurgical furnaces and
	refractory materials
418.28	Cold resistant materials
	Time-dependent properties and tests
418.3	General works
	Dynamic properties
418.32	General works
418.34	Impact strength
	Endurance properties and tests
418.36	General works
418.38	Fatigue behavior
418.4	Mechanical wear
	Cf. TA418.72, Friction properties
418.42	Hardness properties and tests

	Materials of engineering and construction
	Specific characteristics of materials
	Mechanical properties.
	Behavior of materials under applied forces
	Specific properties and tests -- Continued
418.45	Hard materials
	Physical properties
418.5	General works
	Thermal properties and tests
418.52	General works
418.54	Thermal conductivity
	Cf. TH1715+, Insulation and insulating
	materials
	Thermal expansion
418.56	General works
418.58	Thermal stresses
418.59	Space environmental effects and tests
418.6	Radiation effects and tests
418.62	Optical properties and tests
418.64	Moisture content
	Surface effects and tests
418.7	General works
418.72	Friction properties
	Cf. TJ1075+, Lubrication and friction
	Corrosion properties. Deterioration
	Cf. TA462, Corrosion of metals
418.74	General works
418.75	Corrosion-resistant materials
418.76	Protective coatings
	Materials as particles, with tests
418.78	General works
418.8	Particle size determination
418.82	Porosity and denseness, with tests
418.84	Acoustical properties and tests
	Cf. TH1725, Soundproof construction
	Cf. TH1727, Acoustical materials
418.9.A-Z	Materials of special composition or structure, A-Z
418.9.A58	Amorphous substances
418.9.C57	Coatings
	Cf. TA418.76, Protective coatings
	Cf. TA446, Cement coating
	Cf. TA491, Metal coating
	Cf. TP156.C57, Coating processes
	Cf. TP934+, Paints
	Cf. TP935.A2+, Protective coatings
	Cf. TP1175.S6, Plastic coating
	Cf. TS653+, Plastic coating
418.9.C6	Composite materials
	Including fibrous composites
	Cf. TA481+, Metallic composites
418.9.C7	Crystalline solids
418.9.F5	Fibers
	For fibrous composites, see TA418.9.C6

	Materials of engineering and construction
	Materials of special composition
	or structure, A-Z -- Continued
418.9.F6	Foamed materials
418.9.F85	Functionally gradient materials
418.9.I53	Inhomogeneous materials
418.9.L3	Laminated materials
418.9.L54	Liquid crystals
418.9.N35	Nanostructure materials
418.9.P6	Porous materials
418.9.R4	Reinforced materials
418.9.S62	Smart materials
418.9.S64	SPM materials
418.9.T45	Thin films
	Special materials
	For design and construction in special materials, see TA663+
	Nonmetallic materials
418.95	General works
	Wood
	Cf. TA666+, Wooden construction
	Cf. TS800+, Lumber and woodwork
	Cf. TS920+, Chemical processing of wood
419.A1	Periodicals, societies, congresses, etc.
419.A2-Z	General works
419.5	Standards
420	Strength and testing of wood
	Deterioration and preservation of wood
	Cf. TC200, Deterioration of structures exposed to sea water
422	General works
	Special destructive agents
	Including their control
423	General works
	Fungi. Decay
423.2	General works
423.3	Dry rot
423.4	Stain fungi
	Insects
423.6	General works
423.63	Beetles
423.7	Termites
	Preservation of wood
	Cf. TT300+, Painting
424	General works
424.2	Testing
424.4	Special preservation methods
	Including pressure-impregnation
424.6.A-Z	Special preservatives, A-Z
424.6.C7	Creosote
424.6.F8	Fungicides
424.6.O4	Oil-soluble preservatives
424.6.R8	Rubber

Materials of engineering and construction
Special materials
Nonmetallic materials
Wood
Deterioration and preservation of wood
Preservation of wood
Special preservatives, A-Z -- Continued
424.6.S3   Salt
424.6.W3   Water-soluble preservatives
Masonry materials
Cf. TA670+, Construction
425   General works
Stone
426   General works
427   Strength and testing of stone
428.A-Z   Special kinds of stone, A-Z
428.L5   Limestone
428.M3   Marble
430   Ceramic materials
Artificial materials
431   General works
Brick, tile, terra cotta
432   General works
433   Strength and testing of brick, etc.
Cement, lime, mortar, etc.
Cf. TP875+, Cement industries
434   General works
435   Strength and testing of cement, etc.
Mortar
436   General works
437   Strength and testing
438   Cement composites
Concrete
Including Portland cement concrete
Including mixing
439   General works
440   Strength and testing
Including concrete corrosion
441   Aggregates
Including use of slag, clinkers, etc
442   Concrete and timber
Special types of concrete
442.5   General works
443.A-Z   By cementing substance, A-Z
443.A7   Asphalt
443.C64   Colloidal concrete
443.P58   Polymers
443.R4   Resin
Reinforced concrete
444   General works
445   Strength and testing
445.5   Corrosion of reinforcing bars
Reinforcing bar practice, see TA683.42

Materials of engineering and construction
Special materials
Nonmetallic materials
Masonry materials
Artificial materials
Concrete -- Continued
446 Gunite, cement-guns, etc.
447 Pipes of cement, concrete, and clay
Including drain tiles, culverts, etc.
Cf. TP885.P5, Pipe manufacture
448 Plastic pipes
Cf. TH6330, Plastic pipes in plumbing
Cf. TP1185.P5, Manufacture of plastic pipes
450 Glass
Including fiber glass
455.A-Z Other nonmetallic materials, A-Z
455.A3 Abrasives
455.A34 Adhesives
455.A6 Asbestos
455.A62 Asbestos substitutes
455.A63 Ashes
Cf. TA455.F55, Fly ash
455.A7 Asphalt
455.B3 Bamboo
455.B5 Bituminous materials
455.B65 Borides
455.C3 Carbon
455.C43 Ceramic materials (General)
Cf. ML86, Music on ceramics
Cf. NK3700+, Art industries
Cf. R857.C4, Biomedical engineering
Cf. RK655, Ceramics in dentistry
Cf. TA430, Ceramic masonry materials
Cf. TA479.6, Ceramic metals
Cf. TK7871.15.C4, Electronics
Cf. TP785+, Chemical technology
Cf. TP825+, Ceramics, Architectural
Cf. TT919+, Pottery craft
For ceramic materials for heat-engines, see
TJ255.5
455.C45 Chromic materials
455.C55 Clay minerals
455.C6 Cork
455.C65 Corundum
455.E4 Elastomers
455.E5 Enamels
455.E6 Epoxy resins
455.F3 Faolite
455.F5 Fire clay
455.F55 Fly ash
Cf. TE210.5.F55, Soil stabilization
materials
455.G44 Geosynthetics

	Materials of engineering and construction
	Special materials
	Nonmetallic materials
	Other nonmetallic materials, A-Z -- Continued
455.G7	Graphite
455.G73	Gravel
455.G9	Gypsum
455.L3	Laterite
455.L6	Loess
455.M5	Mica
455.N5	Nitrides
455.P4	Peat
455.P45	Perlite
455.P49	Plant fibers
	Plastics
455.P5	General works
455.P55	Reinforced plastics
455.P58	Polymers
455.R4	Reed
	Refractory materials, see TN677 +
455.R8	Rubber
455.S3	Sand
455.S35	Semimetals
455.S4	Shale
455.S43	Shells (Sea shells)
455.S46	Silicates
455.S5	Slag
455.S6	Soil
455.S8	Straw
455.S84	Stucco
455.S93	Sulphur
455.T3	Talc
455.V4	Vermiculite
455.W3	Wallboard
	Metals
	Cf. TA684 +, Metal construction
	Cf. TN689 +, Metallography
459	General works
460	Strength and testing
461	Specifications
462	Corrosion and protection against corrosion
	Cf. TS653 +, Metal finishing
	Cf. TT300 +, Industrial and structural
	painting
463	Liquid metals
	Cf. QC173.4.L56, Physics
	Iron and steel
	Cf. TN701.482 +, Metallurgy
	Cf. UG408 +, Iron and steel for land
	defenses
464	General works
465	Strength and testing
466	Specifications

	Materials of engineering and construction
	Special materials
	Metals
	Iron and steel -- Continued
467	Corrosion and protection against corrosion
	For electrolytic corrosion, see TK3255
	For stray currents from electric traction, see TF912
	Wrought iron
	Including specifications
469	General works
470	Strength and testing
	Steel
	Including specifications
472	General works
473	Strength and testing
	Cast iron
	Including specifications
474	General works
475	Strength and testing
	Iron and steel alloys
478	General works
479.A-Z	Special, A-Z
479.A88	Austenitic steel
479.B6	Boron steel
479.C37	Carbon steel
479.C5	Chromium steel
479.C7	Copper steel
	Ferritic steel, see TA479.S7
479.H43	Heat resistant steel
	Cf. TA485, Heat resistant alloys
	Maraging steel, see TA479.N5
479.N5	Nickel steel
479.S5	Silicon alloys
479.S7	Stainless steel
479.V3	Vanadium steel
479.3	Nonferrous metals
479.6	Ceramic metals
480.A-Z	Special metals, including their alloys, A-Z
480.A6	Aluminum
	Including duralumin
480.B4	Beryllium
480.C5	Chromium
480.C6	Cobalt
480.C7	Copper
	Including brass and bronze
480.G4	Germanium
480.I53	Indium
480.L4	Lead
480.L5	Lithium
480.M3	Magnesium
480.M35	Manganese
480.M4	Mercury

Materials of engineering and construction
Special materials
Metals
Special metals, including
their alloys, A-Z -- Continued

480.M6	Molybdenum
480.N6	Nickel
480.N63	Nickel-titanium alloys
480.N65	Niobium
480.R3	Rare earth metals
480.R5	Rhenium
480.R8	Rubidium
480.S5	Silver
480.T34	Tantalum
480.T5	Tin

Including babbitt

480.T54	Titanium
480.T9	Tungsten
480.U7	Uranium
480.Y8	Yttrium
480.Z6	Zinc
480.Z65	Zirconium

Metallic composites

481	General works
481.5	Fiber-strengthened composites

Alloys

483	General works
484	Lightweight alloys

Cf. TA480.A6, Aluminum

485	Heat resistant alloys

Cf. TA479.H43, Heat resistant steel
Cf. TA479.6, Ceramic metals

486	Corrosion-resistant alloys
487	Shape memory alloys
491	Metal coatings

Cf. TP1175.M4, Metal coating of plastics
Cf. TS590+, Metal manufactures

492.A-Z	Special forms and shapes in metal, A-Z
492.A3	Adhesive joints
492.A6	Angles
492.B3	Balls
492.B63	Bolts and nuts
492.C6	Chains
492.C7	Columns
492.C9	Cylinders
492.F4	Fillets
492.F5	Flanges
492.G5	Girders
492.H6	Hooks
492.N2	Nails and spikes
492.P6	Pipes
492.P7	Plates

	Materials of engineering and construction
	Special materials
	Metals
	Special forms and
	shapes in metal, A-Z -- Continued
492.R6	Rivets
	Cf. TA891, Riveting
492.S25	Sandwich construction elements
492.S3	Screws
492.S5	Shafting
492.T4	Tee stiffeners
492.T8	Tubes
492.W4	Welded joints
492.W7	Wire
492.W77	Wire netting
492.W8	Wire rope
495	Disasters and engineering
	Cf. TC181, Earthquakes and hydraulic structures
	Cf. TC530+, Flood control
	Cf. TF539, Damage to railroads
	Cf. TH1095, Earthquakes and building
	Surveying
501	Periodicals, societies, etc
502	Congresses
504	Collected works (nonserial)
505	Dictionaries and encyclopedias
506	Directories
	History
514.7	Periodicals, societies, serials, etc.
515	General works
516	Ancient
517	Medieval
518	Modern
519	19th-20th centuries
520	20th century
521-531	Special regions or countries
	America. United States
521	General works
	Special divisions (United States)
521.5.A-Z	By region, A-Z
	e.g.
521.5.N4	New England
522.A-W	States, A-W
522.5.A-Z	Cities, A-Z
523.A1-Z	Canada (Table T4)
524.A1-Z	Latin America. West Indies (Table T4)
525.A1-Z	South America (Table T4)
526.A1-Z	Europe (Table T4)
527.A1-Z	Asia (Table T4)
528.A1-Z	Africa (Table T4)
529.A1-Z	Australia (Table T4)
529.5.A1-Z	New Zealand (Table T4)
530.A1-Z	Pacific islands (Table T4)

	Surveying
	History
	Special regions or countries -- Continued
531.A1-Z	Arctic regions (Table T4)
	Biography
532	Collective
533.A-Z	Individual, A-Z
534	Surveying as a profession
	Study and teaching
535	General works
537	Examinations, questions, etc.
538.A-Z	By region or country, A-Z
	General works
544	Early to 1800
545	1800-
549	General special
551	Pocketbooks, field manuals, etc.
552	Tables
555	Addresses, essays, lectures
556.A-Z	Special topics, A-Z
556.M38	Mathematics
	Instruments
562	General works
	Special instruments
563	Compass
565	Levels
571	Planetable
575	Theodolite and transit
579	Other instruments
581	Trade catalogs, circulars, etc.
583	Triangulation for engineering works
	Cf. QB311, Geodesy
	Cf. TA593.8+, Photographic triangulation
585	Traverses
588	Stadia surveying
590	Topographical surveying
	Photography in surveying, aerial surveying, etc.
	For special applications of photographic surveying, see the application
592	Periodicals. Societies. Serials
592.2	Congresses
592.3	Collected works (nonserial)
592.4	Dictionaries and encyclopedias
	History
592.5	General works
592.6.A-Z	By region or country, A-Z
	Under each country:
.x	*General works*
.x2A-Z	*Local, A-Z*
593	General works
593.2	General special
593.25	Handbooks, tables, etc.
593.3	Addresses, essays, lectures

	Surveying
	Photography in surveying,
	aerial surveying, etc. -- Continued
593.35	Instruments, cameras, etc.
593.4	Photographic reading, interpretation, etc.
593.5	Mathematical models. Data processing
593.6	Standards, specifications, etc.
593.7	Stereophotogrammetry
	Photographic triangulation
593.8	General works
593.83	Strip adjustment. Block adjustment
593.9.A-Z	Other topics, A-Z
593.9.E75	Errors
	Graphic plotting, see TA611
593.9.T54	Tilt
	Other methods. Compass surveying, etc.
595	General works
595.5	Satellite surveying
597	Applications of astronomy
	e.g. Azimuth observations
	Cf. QB201+, Geodesy
	Cf. VK563, Navigation
601	Measurement of distances
603	Measurement of angles
	Leveling
606	General works
607	Spirit leveling. Precise leveling
609	Trigonometric
	Barometric hypsometry, see QC895
610.A-Z	Lists of bench marks. By country, A-Z
611	Plotting
	Computation of areas
613	General works
614	Planimeter
	Class here works on application only
616	Topographic drawing
	Class here engineering works only
	Cf. GA125, Cartography
	Cf. UG470+, Military topography
	Surveying for special purposes
622	Public land
623	Hydraulic surveying for engineering purposes
	Hydrographic surveying, see VK588+
	City surveying, see TD167
	Geodetic surveying, see QB301+
	Geophysical surveying, see TN269+
	Military surveying, see UG470+
	Mine surveying, see TN273
	Railroad surveying, see TF210+
	Road surveying, see TE209+
625	Other special applications

Structural engineering (General)
     Cf. TA660.A+, Specific structural forms without
         regard to material used
     Cf. TA663+, Structures in special materials,
         including their structural parts
     For structural engineering of a specific kind of
         structure, see the structure, e.g. TC540, Dams;
         TG, Bridges; TH, Buildings; TJ, Machinery; TL,
         Vehicles; VM, Ships

630	Periodicals, societies, congresses, etc.
631	Dictionaries and encyclopedias
	General works
632	Early to 1850
633	1850-
634	Juvenile works
635	Pocketbooks, tables, etc.
636	General special
637	Addresses, essays, lectures
638	Study and teaching
638.2	Research
638.5	Examinations, questions, etc.

Structural engineering project management, see TA190+
Structural drawing, see T355
Computational methods

640	General works
640.2	General special
640.4	Problems, exercises, etc.
640.6	Graphic statics

         Cf. TG270, Graphic statics in bridge
            engineering
         Cf. TJ235, Graphic statics in mechanical
            engineering

640.8	Influence lines
641	Electronic computer methods
642	Matrix methods
643	Model analysis. Simulation methods
	Structural analysis. Theory of structures
645	General works
646	General special
647	Data processing
	Static loading conditions
648	General works
648.2	Dead loads
648.3	Stresses
648.4	Shear. Bending moments
648.5	Strains and deflections
	Statistically indeterminate structures

         Including the slope-deflection method,
            moment-distribution method, Cross method,
            Castigliano's theorem, three-moment theorem,
            etc.

650	General works
651	Continuous systems

Structural engineering (General)
Structural analysis.
Theory of structures -- Continued

652	Limit analysis. Plastic analysis. Yield stress analysis
653	Elastic analysis

Dynamic loading conditions. Structural dynamics. Vibrations

654	General works
654.15	Modal analysis
654.2	Impact loading
654.3	Live loads. Moving loads
654.4	Snow and ice loads
	Cf. TG304, Bridges
	Cf. TH895, Snow loads in building
654.5	Wind loads
	Cf. TG303, Wind pressure on bridges
	Cf. TH891, Wind pressure in building
654.55	Water wave loads
654.6	Earthquake forces
	Including general earthquake engineering
	Cf. QE539.2.S34, Earthquake safety measures and hazard analysis
	Cf. TA658.44, Earthquake resistant design
	Cf. TC181, Hydraulic structures
	Cf. TF539, Railroads
	Cf. TH1095, Earthquakes and building
654.7	Blast loads
	Cf. TA658.42, Blast resistant design
	Cf. TH1097, Bombproof construction
654.8	Thermal stresses
654.9	Dynamic control

Stability of structures. Structural failure

656	General works
656.2	Buckling
656.3	Fatigue
656.4	Brittle fracture
656.5	Probability of safety

Structural design
For design of structures of a specific material, see the specific material in TA663-TA695

658	General works
658.2	General special
658.3	Pocketbooks, tables, etc.
658.35	Problems, exercises, examinations

Structural design for dynamic loads

658.4	General works
658.42	Blast resistant design
658.44	Earthquake resistant design
	Cf. TA654.6, Earthquake forces and earthquake engineering
	Cf. TH1095, Earthquakes and building

	Structural engineering (General)
	Structural design
	Structural design for dynamic loads -- Continued
658.48	Wind resistant design
	Cf. TA654.5, Wind loads
	Cf. TH891, Wind pressure in building
658.6	Limit design. Plastic design
658.8	Structural optimization
660.A-Z	Specific structural forms, analysis, and design, A-Z
660.A53	Angles
660.A7	Arches
	Cf. TG327+, Arched bridges
	Cf. TH2150+, Arches in building detail
660.B3	Bars
660.B4	Beams
	Cf. TG350+, Beams and girders of bridges
660.B43	Beams, Continuous
660.B45	Bearings
	Cf. TJ1061+, Mechanical engineering
660.C3	Cables. Cable structures
660.C37	Castellated beams
660.C47	Channels
660.C6	Columns
660.C9	Cylinders
660.D52	Diaphragms
660.D6	Domes
	Cf. TH2170+, Domes in building detail
660.E9	Expansion joints
	Cf. TJ424, Pipe fittings
	Cf. TL784.E9, Rockets
660.F53	Flexible structures
660.F57	Flitch beams
660.F6	Floors (General)
	Cf. TH2521+, Floors in building design and construction
660.F7	Frames
660.F72	Frames, Continuous
660.F73	Frames, Multistory
	Girders, Plates, see TA660.P59
660.G7	Grillages
660.H66	Honeycomb structure
660.J64	Joints
660.P55	Pipelines
660.P59	Plate girders
660.P6	Plates
660.P63	Plates, Folded
660.P65	Plates, Twisted
660.P73	Polyhedra
	Pressure vessels, see TA660.T34
660.S3	Sandwich elements
660.S5	Shells
	Cf. TH2416+, Shell roofs of buildings
660.S6	Slabs

	Structural engineering (General)
	Specific structural forms,
	analysis, and design, A-Z -- Continued
660.S63	Space frame structures
660.S66	Steel beams
660.S67	Steel-wood I-beams
660.S7	Struts
660.T34	Tanks. Pressure vessels
	Cf. TF271, Track tanks
	Cf. TH4935, Silos
	Cf. TP692.5, Petroleum storage tanks
	Cf. TP756, Gasholders
	Cf. TP756.5, Underground storage
660.T48	Thick-walled elements
660.T5	Thin-walled elements
660.T6	Towers
660.T8	Trusses
	Cf. TG375 +, Trussed bridges
	Cf. TH2392, Roof trusses
660.W3	Walls (General)
	Cf. TH2201 +, Walls in building detail
	Design and construction in special materials
	For properties of special engineering materials
	without regard to their structural use, see
	TA418.95 +
663	Lightweight construction
	Cf. TH1100, Building construction
664	Composite design and construction
665	Prestressed construction
	Wooden construction
	Cf. TH1101, Building construction
666	General works
666.5.A-Z	Individual structural members, A-Z
666.5.B43	Beams
666.5.J64	Joints
666.5.P35	Panels. Paneling
668	Plastic construction
	Masonry construction
	Cf. TH1199 +, Building construction
	Cf. TH5311 +, Practical masonry
670	General works
672	Stereotomy
	Cf. TH5401 +, Stonecutting
676	Stone
	Cf. TH1201, Building construction
679	Brick
	Cf. TH1301, Building construction
	Cement and concrete
	Cf. TH1461 +, Building construction
680	Periodicals, societies, congresses
680.5	Directories
681	General works
	Analysis and design of structures

TA   ENGINEERING (GENERAL). CIVIL ENGINEERING
(GENERAL)
     TA

TA

	Structural engineering (General)
	Design and construction in special materials
	Masonry construction
	Cement and concrete
	Analysis and design
	of structures -- Continued
681.5	General works
682	Pocketbooks, tables, etc.
682.25	Specifications and standards
682.26	Estimates and costs
682.3	Joints. Hinges
	Practical construction methods
682.4	General works
682.42	Amateurs' manuals
682.43	Cold weather conditions
682.44	Formwork
682.445	Bearing pads
682.45	Pump placing
682.455	Roller compacting
682.46	Vibration processes
682.47	Vacuum processes
682.48	Hot weather conditions
682.485	Underwater construction
682.49	Finishing processes
682.5.A-Z	Individual structural members, A-Z
682.5.S5	Slabs
	Reinforced concrete construction
	Cf. TA444+, Construction materials
	Cf. TH1501, Building construction
	Periodicals, societies, congresses, see TA680
683	General works
	Analysis and design of structures
683.2	General works
683.22	Pocketbooks, tables, etc.
683.23	Examinations, questions, etc.
683.24	Specifications and standards
683.26	Estimates
683.28	Drawings. Detailing
683.3	Joints
	Practical construction methods
683.4	General works
683.42	Reinforcing bars
	Cf. TA445.5, Corrosion of reinforcing bars
683.44	Formwork
683.45	Inserts
683.46	Vibration methods
683.5.A-Z	Individual structural members, A-Z
683.5.B3	Beams
683.5.C7	Columns
683.5.F8	Frames
683.5.P35	Panels
683.5.P65	Poles

	Structural engineering (General)
	Design and construction in special materials
	Masonry construction
	Cement and concrete
	Reinforced concrete construction
	Individual structural
	members, A-Z -- Continued
683.5.S4	Shells
683.5.S6	Slabs
683.5.T7	Trusses
683.5.W34	Walls
683.7	Precast construction
	For individual members, see TA683.5.A+
	Prestressed concrete construction
	For individual members, see TA683.5.A+
683.9	General works
683.94	Post-tensioned prestressed concrete
	construction
	Metal construction
	Iron and steel
	Cf. TA890+, Cutting, bending, riveting of
	iron and steel
684	General works
685	Catalogs. Pocketbooks, tables, etc.
690	Aluminum and aluminum alloys
695.A-Z	Other metal construction, A-Z
	Engineering geology
	Cf. TC542, Dam geology
703	Periodicals. Societies. Serials
703.5	Congresses
704	Dictionaries and encyclopedias
705	General works
	By region or country
	United States
705.2	General works
705.3.A-Z	By region or state, A-Z
705.4.A-Z	Other regions or countries, A-Z
	Apply table at TA592.6.A-Z
	Rock mechanics
706	General works
706.3	Drill cores
706.5	Testing methods
709	Rockfills
709.5	Residual materials
	Soil mechanics
	Including properties of soils, water in soil, strength
	properties, consolidation, etc.
	Cf. TE208+, Soil surveys in highway engineering
	Cf. TL243+, Dynamics of motor vehicles
710.A1	Periodicals, societies, congresses, etc.
710.A15	Dictionaries and encyclopedias
710.A2-Z	General works
	By region or country

	Soil mechanics
	By region or country -- Continued
	United States
710.2	General works
710.3.A-Z	By region or state, A-Z
710.4.A-Z	Other regions or countries, A-Z
	Apply table at TA592.6.A-Z
710.5	Laboratory manuals. Testing of soils. Measurements
	Soil dynamics
711.A1	Periodicals, societies, congresses, etc.
711.A2-Z	General works
711.5	Soil-structure interaction
712	Underground construction
713	Frozen ground construction
	Cf. GB2400+, Physical geography
714	Snow mechanics. Avalanche control
	Cf. GB2400+, Physical geography
	Cf. QC929.A8, Avalanches (Meteorology)
	Cf. QC929.S7, Snow (Meteorology)
714.5	Ice mechanics
	Earthwork
715	General works
721	Tables, calculations, etc. Estimates
725	Earthmoving machinery
	Cf. TA735+, Excavating machinery
	Excavations
730	General works
732	Juvenile works
	Excavating machinery
	Cf. TC187+, Dredging
	Cf. TF225+, Railroads
735	General works
737	Trade catalogs
	Rock excavation
740	General works
743	Rock drilling
	Cf. TA800+, Tunneling
	Cf. TD412, Well boring
	Cf. TN275+, Mining operations
	Rock drills
745	General works
747	Trade catalogs
748	Blasting
749	Soil stabilization
	Including soil compaction
	Cf. S593.23, Agriculture
	Cf. TE210.4+, Highway engineering
750	Hydraulic filling
755	Grouting
	Embankments, retaining walls, dams, etc.
	Cf. TC540+, Dams
760	General works
765	Earth pressure

	Earthwork
	Embankments, retaining
	walls, dams, etc. -- Continued
770	Retaining walls
772	Anchorage (Structural engineering)
	Foundations
	Cf. TC197, Foundations under water
	Cf. TG320, Foundations of bridges
	Cf. TH2101, Foundations of buildings
775	General works
777	Guy anchors
	Piles and pile-driving
780	General works
783	Screw-piles
785	Sheet-piling
786	Steel piling
787	Concrete piling
	Tunneling. Tunnels
	Including vehicular tunnels
	Cf. TF230 +, Railroad tunnels and tunneling
	Cf. TN285, Mine tunneling
800	Periodicals, societies, congresses, etc.
	History
803	General works
804.A-Z	By region or country, A-Z
805	General works
807	Popular works. Juvenile works
810	Pocketbooks, tables, etc.
814	Ventilation and lighting
815	Special topics and methods
820.A-Z	Tunnels. By place, A-Z
	Scaffolding, see TH5281
	Practical masonry, stonecutting, bricklaying, etc , see
	TH5311 +
(881)	Centering of arches
	see TH5591
	Iron and steel work
	Including cutting, bending, etc.
	Cf. TA684 +, Construction
890	General works
891	Riveting
900	Protection of structures
	Cf. TH9025 +, Protection of buildings
901	Waterproof construction
	Cf. TH9031 +, Protection of buildings from
	dampness
	Transportation engineering
	Class individual types of transportation with the
	type, e.g. TF, Railroads; TL, Motor vehicles,
	airplanes, etc.
	For economics of transportation, see HE1 +
1001	Periodicals and societies
1004	Yearbooks

	Transportation engineering -- Continued
1005	Congresses
	Museums. Exhibitions
1006.A1	General works
1006.A2-Z	By region or country, A-Z
	Apply table at TA6.A2-Z
1007	Collected works (nonserial)
1009	Dictionaries and encyclopedias
1015	History
1021-1127	Country divisions (Table T1)
	Add country number in table to TA1000
1145	General works
1147	Popular works
1149	Juvenile works
1151	Handbooks, tables, etc.
1155	Addresses, essays, lectures
1160	Transportation engineering as a profession
1163	Study and teaching
	Route surveying, see TA551, TA625
1200	Coordination of forms of transportation
	Urban and metropolitan transportation systems
	For local, see TA1021 +
1205	General works
1207	Personal rapid transit
	Freight
1210	General works
1215	Containerization
1225	Terminals. Transport centers
1227	Food service
	Cf. TF668.A1 +, Dining car service
1230	Automation
1235	Electronics in transportation
	Signaling equipment
1245	General works
1250	Signal lights
1280	Heating, ventilation, and air conditioning equipment
	Applied optics. Photonics
	Class applications in a special field with the field
	Cf. QC370.5 +, Optical instruments and apparatus
	Cf. QH201 +, Microscopes and microscopy
	Cf. TK5103.59, Optical communications
	Cf. TK8300 +, Optoelectronic devices.
	Photoelectronic devices
	Cf. TR1 +, Photography
	Cf. TS510 +, Optical instrument manufacture
1501	Periodicals, societies, yearbooks, etc.
1505	Congresses
1509	Dictionaries and encyclopedias
1520	General works
1521	Juvenile works. Popular works
1522	General special

	Applied optics. Photonics -- Continued
	Applied holography
	Cf. HD9707.5.H34+, Holography industry
	Cf. QC244.5, Acoustic holography (Physics)
	Cf. QC449+, Holography (Physics)
	Cf. TA417.45, Holographic testing of
	engineering materials
1540	General works
1542	General special
1550	Acoustic holography
1552	Microwave holography
1555	Holographic interferometry
1570	Infrared technology
	Cf. QC457, Infrared rays
	Cf. TK4635, Infrared heating
	Cf. TP363, Heating, drying, cooling, etc.
	Cf. TR755, Photography
1600	Ultraviolet technology
	Cf. QC459+, Ultraviolet rays
	Optical data processing
	Cf. TA1540+, Applied holography
	Cf. TK7895.O6, Optical equipment (Computers)
	Cf. TK8315+, Imaging systems
1630	General works
1632	General special
1634	Computer vision
	Cf. TJ211.3, Robot vision
1635	Optical data storage
1637	Image processing
	Cf. T385, Mechanical drawing
	Cf. TK8315+, Imaging systems
	Cf. TR267, Digital photography
	Cf. TR897.7+, Computer animation
1640	Optical character recognition
1650	Optical pattern recognition
1660	Integrated optics
	Lasers and laser applications
	Cf. QC685+, Laser physics
	Cf. TK7871.4, Masers
	For application in special fields, see the field,
	e.g. RE992.P5, Laser coagulation; TA1540-
	TA1555, Applied holography; TJ1191, Laser beam
	cutting; TK5103.6, Laser communication
	systems; TK6592.O6, Optical radar
1671	Periodicals, societies, etc.
1673	Congresses
1674	Directories
1675	General works
1677	General special
1680	Popular works
1682	Juvenile works
1683	Handbooks, tables, etc.
1684	Addresses, essays, lectures

	Applied optics. Photonics
	Lasers and laser applications -- Continued
1688	Mode-locked lasers
1690	Chemical lasers. Dye lasers
1693	Free electron lasers
1694	Gamma ray lasers
1695	Gas lasers
1696	Infrared and far infrared lasers
1700	Semiconductor lasers
1705	Solid-state lasers (Ruby, etc.)
1706	Tunable lasers
1707	X-ray lasers
1715	Laser ablation
	Applied electrooptics. Electrooptical devices.
	Optoelectronics
	Cf. QC673 +, Electrooptics
	For specific optoelectronic devices, see TK8300 +
1750	General works
	Electroluminescent devices, see TK7871.68 +
	Photoelectronic devices, see TK8300 +
1770	Applied acoustooptics. Acoustooptical devices
1773	Applied neutron optics. Neutron optical devices
1775	Applied X-ray optics
	Applied fiber optics
	Cf. QC447.9 +, Fiber optics (Physics)
1800	General works
1815	Optical fiber detectors
1820	Stroboscopy
	Plasma engineering. Applied plasma dynamics
	Class applications in a special field with the field
2001	Periodicals, societies, yearbooks, etc.
2005	Congresses
2020	General works
2030	Plasma devices (General)
	Cf. TK2970, Magnetohydrodynamic generators
	Cf. TL783.6, Plasma rockets
2040	Magnetohydrodynamics. Magnetohydrodynamic devices
	Cf. TK2970, Magnetohydrodynamic generators

	Hydraulic engineering
	For hydraulic machinery, see TJ840.A2+
	For municipal water supply, see TD201+
1	Periodicals, societies, etc.
5	Congresses
	Exhibitions. Museums
6.A1	General works
6.A2-Z	By region or country, A-Z
	Under each country:
	.x *General works*
	.x2A-Z *Special. By city, A-Z*
7	Collected works (nonserial)
9	Dictionaries and encyclopedias
12	Directories
	History and description
15	General works
16	Ancient
17	Medieval
18	Modern
19	19th century
20	20th century
21-127	Country divisions (General hydraulic works)
	(Table T1)
	Add country number in table to TC0
	Biography
139	Collective
140.A-Z	Individual, A-Z
	e.g.
140.K5	Klír, Antonín
	General works
144	Early to 1800
145	1800-
146	Juvenile works
147	Waterpower engineering. Hydraulic powerplants
	Including use of tidal power
	Cf. TJ840.A2+, Hydraulic machinery
	Cf. TK1081+, Hydroelectric power production
	Cf. TK1421+, Hydroelectric powerplants
	For power utilization of specific rivers, see TC415+
151	Pocketbooks, tables, etc.
153	General special
155	Addresses, essays, lectures
	Study and teaching
157	General works
157.5	Problems, exercises, etc.
157.8	Electronic data processing
158	Hydraulic laboratories
159	Safety measures
	Technical hydraulics
160	General works
163	General special
163.5	Environmental hydraulics
	Hydraulic models

	Technical hydraulics
	Hydraulic models -- Continued
164	General works
164.6	Movable bed models
	Hydrostatics (Water at rest)
165	General works
167	Dams, reservoirs
169	Gates, sluices, etc.
	Hydrodynamics (Water in motion)
171	General works
171.5	Water tunnels
172	Water waves
173	Orifices. Nozzles. Jets
	Cf. TH9323, Fire streams
	Cf. TP156.S6, Spraying
	Cf. TP159.A85, Atomizers
174	Pipes and conduits
	Including water hammer
	Open channels, rivers, and canals. Sluices, flumes, weirs. Stream gaging
175	General works
175.2	Sediment transport
	For sediment transport of specific rivers, etc., see TC421 +
176	Underground flow
177	Hydraulic measurements. Hydraulic instruments, meters, registers, etc.
	Cf. TD499 +, Domestic meters
179	Tables, diagrams, etc.
180	Hydraulic structures
	Cf. TA654.55, Water wave loads
181	Earthquakes and hydraulic structures
	General preliminary operations
183	General works
	Diving, see VM975 +
	Dredging
187	General works
188	Dredges
	Submarine blasting
191	General works
192	Hell Gate
193	Submarine drilling
	Cf. TN871.3, Petroleum well drilling
	Submarine building
195	General works
197	Submarine foundations. Cribwork, etc.
	For bridge pier foundations, see TG320
198	Cofferdams
199	Caissons
200	Deterioration of structures exposed to sea water
	Including corrosion

General preliminary operations

Submarine building -- Continued

201   Control of organisms injurious to submerged structures

           Cf. QH91.8.M3, Marine biology

           Cf. TA422 +, Wood

Harbors and coast protective works. Coastal engineering

203   Periodicals. Societies. Yearbooks

203.5   Congresses

203.7   Dictionaries and encyclopedias

General works

204   Early to 1800

205   1800-

209   General special

215-327   History and country divisions (Table T1)

           Class here special harbors, inlets, channels, etc.

           Add country number in table to TC200

328   Marinas

Coast protective works

           For local, see TC215 +

330   General works

332   Beach nourishment

333   Breakwaters

335   Seawalls

337   Dikes, levees, embankments

           For canal embankments, see TC759 +

           For river levees, see TC533

339   Dunes (as defense works)

339.8   Sand bypassing

340   Tree planting

Reclamation and preservation of land from the sea. Polders

           Cf. TC970 +, Land drainage and reclamation of bogs, swamps, and lakes

343   General works

345.A-Z   By region or country, A-Z

Harbor engineering

           Cf. HE550 +, Economic aspects

           Cf. SH337.5, Fishing port facilities

352   Approach channels

353   Sea locks

355   Docks

357   Piers, quays, and wharves

361   Drydocks

363   Floating harbors

           Including floating docks, piers, etc.

365   Other special docks

370   Mechanical equipment of docks for cargo handling, etc.

           Including cranes

           For cargo handling, etc., see VK235

373   General special

           Including mooring berths, fenders

Lighthouses (Construction and equipment)

	Lighthouses (Construction
	and equipment) -- Continued
375	General works
377	Lights, lamps, etc.
379	Lenses
380	Buoys
	River, lake, and water-supply engineering (General)
	Class here development of the water resources of a watershed
	Cf. TD201+, Municipal water supply
401	Periodicals, societies, congresses, etc.
403	Dictionaries and encyclopedias
	General works
404	Early to 1800
405	1800-
406	Popular works
407	Pocketbooks, tables, etc.
409	General special
	Including estimation of value, simulation methods, watershed management
411	Addresses, essays, lectures
415-527	History and country divisions (Table T1 modified)
	Class here special rivers and lakes
	Add country number in table to TC400
	Cf. GB1200+, Physical geography of rivers
	Cf. HE380.8+, Economic aspects of waterways
	United States
423	General works
423.3	Great Lakes
	Including diversion of water from Lake Michigan
	Mississippi River
	The detailed arrangement for Mississippi River should not be used for other rivers
425.M6	General works
425.M61	Conventions
	Arrange by date
425.M62	Levees
425.M63A-W	Levees of special states, A-W
425.M65	Jetties
425.M66A-W	Special states, A-W
425.M67A-Z	Special cities, A-Z
	e.g.
425.M67M5	Memphis
	Rivers of Canada
426	General works
426.5.A-Z	Provinces, A-Z
427.A-Z	Special rivers and lakes, A-Z
	e.g.
427.S3	St. Lawrence River
	Rivers of Great Britain
457	General works
464.A-Z	Special rivers and lakes, A-Z
	e.g.

	River, lake, and water-supply engineering (General)
	History and country divisions
	Rivers of Great Britain
	Special rivers and lakes, A-Z -- Continued
464.T4	Thames
	Rivers of Austria
465	General works
466.A-Z	Special rivers and lakes, A-Z
	e.g.
466.D2	Danube
	Rivers of France
471	General works
472.A-Z	Special rivers and lakes, A-Z
	e.g.
472.S4	Seine
	Rivers of India
503	General works
503.5.A-Z	Provinces, etc., A-Z
504.A-Z	Special rivers and lakes, A-Z
	e.g.
504.I4	Indus River
	Rivers of Japan
505	General works
505.5.A-Z	Prefectures, etc., A-Z
506.A-Z	Special rivers and lakes, A-Z
529	Stream channelization. Channel improvement
	River protective works. Regulation. Flood control
	Cf. HD1675+, Economic aspects
	For local, see TC415+
530	General works
531	Flood control channels
533	Levees
535	Jetties
537	Tree planting. Streambank planting
	Dams. Barrages
540	General works
	Damsite selection
542	Dam geology
	For the geology of damsites of special areas, see TC556+
542.5	Earthquakes and dams
	Dam types
543	Earthen dams
545	Wooden dams
547	Masonry dams. Concrete dams
549	Other (not A-Z)
	Including steel, movable, beartrap, needle
550	Dam safety
	For local, see TC556+
550.2	Dam failures
	For local, see TC556+
553	Sluices and gates
554	Trashracks

TC

	Dams. Barrages -- Continued
555	Wasteways, spillways, weirs, etc.
	Special countries
	United States
556	General works
556.5.A-Z	By region, A-Z
557.A-W	By state, A-W
	e.g.
	Under each:
.x	*General works*
.x2A-Z	*Special dams, A-Z*
	California
557.C2	General works
557.C3A-Z	Special dams, A-Z
	e.g.
557.C3C2	Cachuma Dam
557.3.A-Z	By river, A-Z
	Class here only rivers located in two or more states
	e.g.
557.3.P6	Potomac River
557.5.A-Z	Other special dams, A-Z
	Class here only dams located in two states
	e.g.
557.5.H6	Hoover Dam
558.A-Z	Other regions or countries, A-Z
	e.g.
	Apply table at TC557.A-W
	Egypt
558.E4	General works
558.E5A-Z	Special dams, A-Z
	e.g.
558.E5A8	Aswan High Dam
	Canals and inland navigation. Waterways
	Cf. HE380.8+, Economic aspects
	Cf. TC930, Irrigation canals
601	Periodicals, societies, etc.
605	Congresses
607	Collected works (nonserial)
615-727	History and country divisions (Table T1 modified)
	Class here special canals and locks
	Add country number in table to TC600
	America
	United States
623	Canals (General)
623.1	Great Lakes to Atlantic
623.2	Great Lakes to Gulf of Mexico
623.3	Mississippi to Atlantic
	Intracoastal waterways
623.4	Atlantic
623.5	Gulf of Mexico
623.7	Miscellaneous general projects
624.A-W	Special states, A-W

	Canals and inland navigation. Waterways
	History and country divisions
	America
	United States -- Continued
625.A-Z	Special canals and locks, A-Z
	e.g.
	Under each:
	.xA1-.xA3 *Serial documents*
	.xA5 *Special documents, by date*
	.xA6-.xZ *General works*
625.E6	Erie Canal
625.M6	Middlesex Canal
	Isthmian canals, see TC773+
	Europe
655	General works
656.A-Z	Special projects, A-Z
	e.g.
656.R5	Rhine-Main-Danube Waterway
	Great Britain. England
664.A-Z	Cities (or other special), A-Z
	e.g.
664.M2	Manchester Ship Canal
	Balkan Peninsula
695.A2	General works
695.A3A-Z	Special projects, A-Z
	e.g.
695.A3D3	Danube-Aegean project
	Africa
	Egypt
718.A-Z	Local or special, A-Z
	Suez Canal, see TC791
	General works
744	Early to 1800
745	1800-
751	Pocketbooks, tables, etc.
753	General special
755	Addresses, essays, lectures
	Special aspects
759	Canal embankments
761	Canal locks
	For special locks, see TC615+
762	Canal gates
	Including operating devices
763	Lifts and inclines
764	Canal aqueducts
765	Canalboats
766	Resistance of water
	Motive power. Towing
767	General works
769	Mechanical and electrical
770	Ship canals (General)
	For economic studies, traffic statistics, etc., see HE380.8+

	Canals and inland navigation. Waterways
	Special aspects -- Continued
	Ship and boat railways
771	General works
772	Special (except Tehuantepec)
	Tehuantepec Ship Railway, see TC786
	Isthmian canal projects (General)
773	General works
	Panama Canal
774	General works
	For economic aspects, see HE537+
777	Operation of the canal
	Cf. HE538.A1+, Administration of the canal
777.5	Miscellaneous uncataloged matter
	Compagnie universelle du canal interocéanique de Panama
778	General works
778.B9	Bulletin du canal interocéanique
(778.1)	Annual report of directors
	see HE537.33
778.2	Annual report of chief engineer
778.3	Other serial reports
778.5	Special reports. By date
(778.7)	Charter, bylaws
	see HE537.37
778.8	Other printed matter
	Compagnie nouvelle du canal de Panama
779	General works
779.B9	Bulletin
(779.1)	Annual report of directors
	see HE537.43-45
779.2	Annual report of chief engineer
779.3	Other serial reports
779.5	Special reports. By date
(779.7)	Charter, bylaws
	see HE537.47
779.8	Other printed matter
780	The "Panama affair" and history of the companies
	Panama Exposition
	Preliminary
	United States
781.A1-A3	Documents
781.A4A-W	States, A-W
781.A5A-Z	Cities, A-Z
781.A6A-Z	Other regions or countries, A-Z
781.A7	Nonofficial. By author
	The Exposition
781.A8	Official guides
781.B1-N1	Other works (Table T2 modified)
	Other Isthmian canal projects
784	Nicaragua Canal
785	Tehuantepec Canal
786	Tehuantepec Ship Railway

	Canals and inland navigation. Waterways
	Isthmian canal projects (General)
	Other Isthmian canal projects -- Continued
788	Darien, Atrato and others
791	Suez Canal
	Irrigation engineering. Reclamation of wasteland
	Cf. HD1690+, Water rights
	Cf. HD1710.2+, Economic situation, history, etc.
	Cf. S604.8+, Agriculture
	Cf. SB112, Irrigation farming
	Cf. TC343+, Reclamation of land from the sea
801	Periodicals, societies, etc.
803	Congresses
804	Dictionaries and encyclopedias
805	General works
809	General special
812	Management of irrigation projects
815-927	History and country divisions (Table T1 modified)
	e.g.
	Add country number in table to TC800
	India
903	General works
904.4.A-Z	Special projects, A-Z
904.4.G2	Ganges Canal
(927)	Irrigation by pumping
	see TC929
	Biography
928	Collective
928.2.A-Z	Individual, A-Z
929	Irrigation pumps
930	Irrigation canals
933	Irrigation flumes and conduits
937	Gates and other incidental structures
	Flooding of deserts and wastelands
950	General works
	Special
953	United States
955	Sahara
957.A-Z	Other, A-Z
	Drainage
	Cf. HD1681+, Economics, public policy, etc.
	Cf. S621, Farmers' manuals
970	General works
973	Relief wells
974	Wellpoint system
974.2	Vertical drains
975	Reclamation of bogs, swamps, lakes, etc.
	Cf. TC343+, Reclamation of land from the sea
	Country divisions
	United States
976	General works
977.A-Z	Regions or states, A-Z

Drainage
Country divisions -- Continued
978.A-Z   Other regions or countries, A-Z
Under each country:
.x   *General works*
.x2A-Z   *Local, A-Z*

TC

Ocean engineering
    Cf. GC1000+, Marine resources
    Cf. TN291.5, Ocean mining
1501   Periodicals, societies, etc.
1505   Congresses
1550   Directories
1645   General works
1650   General special
1655   Study and teaching
1657   Electricity in ocean engineering
1660   Patents
1662   Remotely operated vehicles
        Offshore structures
1665   General works
1670   Corrosion
1680   Models
            Compliant platforms
1700   General works
1702   Semi-submersible offshore structures
1703   Tension leg platforms
1800   Underwater pipelines

	Environmental technology. Sanitary engineering
	Including the promotion and conservation of the public health, comfort, and convenience by the control of the environment
	Cf. GE170+, Environmental policy
	Cf. GF51, Human beings and the environment
	Cf. RA565+, Environmental health
	Cf. TH6014+, Environmental engineering in buildings
	Periodicals and societies. By language of publication
1	English
2	French
3	German
4	Other languages (not A-Z)
5	Congresses
	Exhibitions. Museums
6.A1	General works
6.A2-Z	By region or country, A-Z
	Under each country:
	.x General works
	.x2A-Z Special. By city, A-Z
7	Collected works (nonserial)
9	Dictionaries and encyclopedias
12	Directories
	History
15	General works
16	Ancient
17	Medieval
18	Modern to 1800
19	Nineteenth century
20	Twentieth century
21-127	Country and city subdivisions (Table T1 modified)
	Including municipal reports of public sanitary works
	Add country number in table to TD0
	Under each two number country, unless otherwise specified:
	1.A1 General works
	1.A6-Z States, provinces, etc., A-Z
	2.A-Z Local (Cities, etc.), A-Z
	Biography
139	Collective
140.A-Z	Individual, A-Z
	General works
144	Early to 1850
145	1850-
146	Elementary textbooks
148	Popular works
151	Pocketbooks, tables, etc.
153	General special
155	Addresses, essays, lectures
156	Environmental and sanitary engineering as a profession
	Study and teaching
157	General works
157.15	Problems, exercises, etc.

	Study and teaching -- Continued
	By region or country
	United States
157.2	General works
157.3.A-Z	By region or state, A-Z
	Under each state:
	.x *General works*
	.x2A-Z *Local, A-Z*
157.4.A-Z	Other regions or countries, A-Z
	Under each country:
	.x *General works*
	.x2A-Z *Local, A-Z*
157.5	Research
158	Remote sensing
	Municipal engineering
	Cf. GV421+, Playgrounds
	Cf. HD7285+, Housing
	Cf. SB481.A1+, Parks
	Cf. TE1+, Streets and roads
	Cf. TH350, Engineering of the subdivision
159.A1	Periodicals, societies, congresses, etc.
159.A5-Z	General works
159.3	General special
	By region or country, see TD21+
159.5	Department organization and management
	Planning and laying out cities
	Cf. HT165.5+, City planning (Urban sociology)
	Cf. HT170+, Urban renewal
	Cf. NA9000+, City planning (Architecture)
160	General works
163	General special
167	City surveying
168	Underground utility lines
	Environmental protection
	Cf. HC79.E5, Environmental policy
169	Periodicals, societies, congresses, etc.
169.3	Dictionaries and encyclopedias
169.5	Information services
169.6	Directories
170	General works
170.15	Juvenile works
170.2	General special
170.3	Addresses, essays, lectures
	Study and teaching
170.6	General works
	By region or country
170.7	United States
170.8.A-Z	Other regions or countries, A-Z
	Research
170.9	General works
	By region or country
170.93	United States
170.94.A-Z	Other regions or countries, A-Z

	Environmental protection -- Continued
	Special regions or countries
	United States
171	General works
171.3.A-Z	By region or state, A-Z
	Apply table at TD157.3.A-Z
171.5.A-Z	Other regions or countries, A-Z
	Apply table at TD157.4.A-Z
171.7	Citizen participation
171.8	Decision making
171.9	Environmental geotechnology
	Environmental pollution
	Including its control
	Class special types of pollution with the type, e.g.
	GC1080-GC1581, Marine pollution; TD196.R3,
	Radioactive pollution; TD419-TD428, Water pollution;
	TD881-TD890, Air pollution; TD891-TD894, Noise
	pollution, etc.
	Cf. SB744.5+, Crops and pollution
172	Periodicals, societies, etc.
172.5	Congresses
173	Dictionaries and encyclopedias
173.5	Directories
174	General works
175	Popular works
176	Juvenile works
176.4	Pocketbooks, tables, etc.
176.7	Addresses, essays, lectures
177	General special
177.8	Vocational guidance for pollution control personnel
	Study and teaching
178	General works
	Special countries
178.3	United States
178.4.A-Z	Other countries, A-Z
	Research
178.5	General works
	Special countries
178.6	United States
178.7.A-Z	Other countries, A-Z
	Environmental laboratories
178.8.A1	General works
178.8.A2-Z	By region or country, A-Z
	Under each country:
	.x *General works*
	.x2A-Z *By state, province, etc., A-Z*
	.x3A-Z *Special. By city, A-Z*
179	History
	Special countries
	North America
179.5	General works
	United States
180	General works

Environmental pollution
  Special countries
    North America
      United States -- Continued
181.A-Z   By region or state, A-Z
                 Apply table at TD157.3.A-Z
             Canada
182   General works
182.4.A-Z   By region or province, A-Z
                 Under each province:
               .x   *General works*
               .x2A-Z   *Local, A-Z*
             Mexico
182.6   General works
182.7.A-Z   By region or state, A-Z
                 Apply table at TD157.3.A-Z
           Central America
183   General works
183.5.A-Z   By country, A-Z
                 Under each:
               .x   *General works*
               .x2A-Z   *Local, A-Z*
           West Indies
184   General works
184.5.A-Z   By country, A-Z
                 Apply table at TD183.5.A-Z
           South America
185   General works
185.5.A-Z   By country, A-Z
                 Apply table at TD183.5.A-Z
           Europe
186   General works
186.5.A-Z   By country, A-Z
                 Apply table at TD183.5.A-Z
           Asia
187   General works
187.5.A-Z   By country, A-Z
                 Apply table at TD183.5.A-Z
           Africa
188   General works
188.5.A-Z   By country, A-Z
                 Apply table at TD183.5.A-Z
           Oceania
189   General works
189.5.A-Z   By country, A-Z
                 e.g.
                 Apply table at TD183.5.A-Z
189.5.A8   Australia
189.5.N4   New Zealand
           Polar regions
190   General works
190.5   Arctic regions
190.7   Antarctica

	Environmental pollution
	Special countries -- Continued
191	Developing countries
	Pollution control methods
191.5	General works
192	Equipment and supplies
	Special methods
	Chemical treatment
192.2	General works
192.3	Catalysis
192.4	Lime treatment
192.45	Oxidation
	Biological treatment. Bioremediation
192.5	General works
192.6	Fertilization
192.7	Seeding
192.75	Phytoremediation
192.8	In situ remediation
	Measurement of pollution. Sampling and analysis.
	Environmental chemistry
	For measurement or analysis of specific pollutants,
	see TD196.A +
193	General works
(193.2)	Environmental indicators
	see GE140-GE160
193.3	Cross-media pollution
193.4	Environmental forensics
193.5	Risk assessment
	Cf. GE145 +, Environmental risk assessment
	Environmental effects of industries and plants
	Cf. HD30.255, Environmental aspects of industrial
	management
	Cf. TD419 +, Water pollution
	Cf. TD881 +, Air pollution
	Cf. TD891 +, Noise pollution
	Cf. TD896 +, Industry and factory wastes
194	General works
194.4	General special
	Environmental impact statements
194.5	General works
	By region or country
	United States
194.55	General works
194.56.A-Z	By region or state, A-Z
	Apply table at TD157.3.A-Z
194.58.A-Z	Other regions or countries, A-Z
	Apply table at TD157.4.A-Z
	Environmental impact analysis
194.6	General works
	By region or country
	United States
194.65	General works

	Environmental effects of industries and plants
	Environmental impact analysis
	By region or country
	United States -- Continued
194.66.A-Z	By region or state, A-Z
	Apply table at TD157.3.A-Z
194.68.A-Z	Other regions or countries, A-Z
	Apply table at TD157.4.A-Z
194.7	Environmental auditing
195.A-Z	Special industries, facilities, activities, etc., A-Z
195.A27	Aeronautics
	Including air transportation
195.A33	Aggregate industry
195.A34	Agriculture
	Class here works on agricultural pollution, i.e. agriculture as a source of pollution
	Cf. S589.7, Agricultural ecology
	Cf. S589.75+, Agriculture and the environment
	Cf. TD930+, Agricultural wastes
195.A36	Airports
195.A37	Aluminum industry. Bauxite industry
195.A44	Ammonia industry
195.A75	Armed Forces
	Atomic power plants, see TD195.E4
195.B34	Ballistic missile defenses
	Bauxite industry, see TD195.A37
195.B56	Biomass energy
195.B58	Biotechnology
195.B63	Boats and boating
195.B74	Bridges
195.B84	Building materials industry
195.C42	Ceramic industries
195.C45	Chemical plants
195.C47	Church facilities
195.C54	Civil engineering
195.C58	Coal industry
195.C59	Cobalt mines and mining
195.C6	Cooling towers
195.D35	Dams
195.D5	Diamond mines and mining
195.D53	Diaper industry
195.D72	Dredging
195.D78	Drug factories
195.E25	Economic development
195.E37	Electric lines
195.E4	Electric power plants
	Cf. SH173, Effect on fish culture
195.E43	Electrochemistry, Industrial
195.E45	Electroplating
195.E49	Energy development
195.E5	Energy facilities
195.F46	Fertilizer industry
195.F52	Fishery processing industries

Environmental effects of industries and plants
Special industries, facilities,
activities, etc., A-Z -- Continued

195.F57	Food industry
	Forestry, see SD387.E58
195.F6	Foundries
195.G3	Gas industry
195.G46	Geothermal power plants
195.G57	Glass manufacture
195.G64	Gold industry
195.G66	Golf courses
195.H39	Hazardous waste management industry
195.H54	High technology industries
195.H67	Hotels
195.H93	Hydraulic engineering
195.I52	Incineration
195.I54	Industrial districts
195.I76	Ironworks
195.L4	Leather industry
195.L53	Lignite industry
195.L55	Limestone industry
195.M33	Magnesium industry and trade
195.M37	Marinas
195.M39	Marine terminals
195.M45	Military aeronautics
195.M48	Mine subsidences
195.M5	Mineral industries
195.M67	Motorsports
195.N47	New towns
195.N65	Nonferrous metal industries
195.N83	Nuclear facilities (General)
	Cf. TD195.E4, Electric power plants
	Nuclear power plants, see TD195.E4
195.N85	Nuclear weapons plants
195.O25	Ocean mining
195.O4	Oil-shale industry
195.P26	Package goods industry
195.P35	Paint industry
195.P37	Paper and pulp mills
195.P38	Peat mining
195.P39	Petrochemicals industry
195.P4	Petroleum industry
	Cf. TD427.P4, Water pollution
	Cf. TD888.P4, Air pollution
195.P46	Phosphate mines and mining
195.P47	Phosphatic fertilizer industry
195.P5	Pipelines
195.P52	Plastics industry
	Power resource development, see TD195.E49
195.P7	Printing industry
195.P76	Proving grounds
195.Q3	Quarries and quarrying
195.R33	Railroads

	Environmental effects of industries and plants
	Special industries, facilities,
	activities, etc., A-Z -- Continued
195.R34	Rainmaking
195.R4	Reactor fuel reprocessing plants
195.R45	Research natural areas
195.R47	Reservoirs
195.R49	Resource recovery facilities
195.R63	Roads
195.S26	Salt mines and mining
195.S3	Sand and gravel industry
195.S36	Scrap metal industry
195.S47	Sewage disposal plants
195.S52	Shopping centers
195.S54	Silicon industry
195.S64	Solar energy
195.S65	Spillways
195.S7	Steelworks
195.S75	Strip mining
	Cf. QH545.S84, Ecology
195.S9	Subways
195.S93	Sugar cane industry
195.S95	Synthetic fuels industry
195.T35	Tanneries
195.T48	Textile industry
195.T56	Tin mines and mining
195.T68	Tourist trade
195.T7	Transportation
	Cf. TD195.R63, Roads
	Cf. TD195.S9, Subways
195.U7	Uranium industry
195.W29	War
195.W295	Waste disposal sites
195.W3	Water-supply engineering
195.W54	Wind power industry
195.W6	Wood-using industries
	Special environmental pollutants
	Acid precipitation. Acid rain. Acid deposition
	Cf. QC926.5+, Meteorological aspects
195.4	Periodicals, societies, congresses, etc.
195.42	General works
195.44	Juvenile works
195.46	Handbooks, manuals, etc.
	By region or country
	United States
195.5	General works
195.52.A-Z	By region or state, A-Z
	Apply table at TD157.3.A-Z
195.54.A-Z	Other regions or countries, A-Z
	Apply table at TD157.4.A-Z
195.56.A-Z	Special topics, A-Z
	For local, see TD195.5+
195.56.E35	Economic aspects

	Special environmental pollutants -- Continued
196.A-Z	Other environmental pollutants, A-Z
196.A2	Acetates
196.A22	Acetic acid
196.A34	Agricultural chemicals
196.A75	Aromatic compounds
196.A77	Arsenic
196.A78	Asbestos
196.B38	Benzene
196.B4	Benzpyrene
196.B85	Building materials
196.C28	Cadmium
	Calcium oxide, see TD196.L55
196.C33	Carbolic acid
196.C45	Chemicals
196.C5	Chlorine organic compounds
196.C53	Chromium
196.C63	Coal
196.C93	Cyanides
196.C95	Cyclohexane
196.D48	Detergents
	Cf. RA1242.D4, Toxicology of detergents
	Cf. TD427.D4, Detergent pollution of water
196.E86	Ethylene oxide
196.F47	Fertilizers
196.F54	Fluorine compounds
196.F55	Fluorocarbons
	Cf. TD887.F67, Fluorocarbon pollution of air
196.F65	Formaldehyde
196.F67	Fossil fuels
	Cf. TD887.F69, Fossil fuel pollution of air
196.F85	Fumigants
196.H35	Halogen organic compounds
196.H4	Heat
	Cf. TD427.H4, Heat pollution of water
196.H43	Heavy elements
	Heavy metals, see TD196.M4
196.H47	Herbicides
196.H94	Hypochlorites
196.L4	Lead
196.L55	Lime
196.M38	Mercury
	Cf. TD427.M4, Mercury pollution of water
	Cf. TD887.M37, Mercury pollution of air
196.M4	Metals. Heavy metals
	Cf. TD427.M44, Heavy metal pollution of water
196.N48	Nickel
196.N55	Nitrogen and nitrogen compounds
196.O73	Organic compounds
196.O75	Organolead compounds
196.O76	Organometallic compounds
196.O95	Oxidizing agents
196.P36	Peroxyacetyl nitrate

Special environmental pollutants

Other environmental pollutants, A-Z -- Continued

196.P38	Pesticides
	Cf. QH545.P4, Effect on plants and animals
196.P4	Petroleum
	Cf. TD427.P4, Petroleum pollution of water
	Cf. TD879.P4, Petroleum pollution of soil
196.P45	Phosphates
196.P46	Phosphogypsum
196.P47	Phthalate esters
196.P5	Plastics
	Cf. TD798, Plastic waste
196.P65	Polychlorinated biphenyls
196.P67	Polythylene glycols
196.R3	Radioactive pollution
	Cf. TD427.R3, Radioactive pollution of water
	Cf. TD812+, Municipal radioactive wastes
	Cf. TD879.R34, Radioactive pollution of soils
	Cf. TD887.R3, Radioactive substances in air
	Cf. TD898, Radioactive substances in air
196.R33	Radon
196.S48	Silver
196.S52	Sodium hydroxide
196.S54	Solvents
196.S56	Soot
196.S95	Sulphur
196.T45	Thallium
196.T7	Trace elements
196.T74	Tritium
196.U73	Urea
196.V35	Vanadium
196.Z56	Zinc

Water supply for domestic and industrial purposes

Class here works on the supplying of usable water to consumers, including works on the water-supply systems and available resources of specific localities and works dealing with both water supply and sewerage

For general works on water-supply engineering (including the design and construction of works to procure water), as well as works on the development of the water resources of a watershed, see TC401+

For rural water supply, see TD927

For water supply and public health, see RA591+

For works describing the hydrology of a region without regard to development, see GB651+

For water supply in specific industries, see the industry, e.g. TS1116.2, Paper industry

Periodicals. Societies. Congresses. By language of publication

201	English
202	French

	Water supply for domestic and industrial purposes
	Periodicals. Societies.
	Congresses. By language
	of publication -- Continued
203	German
204	Other languages (not A-Z)
208	Dictionaries and encyclopedias
	Communication of water supply information
209	General works
211	Information services
	History
215	General works
216	Ancient
217	Medieval
218	Modern
219	Nineteenth century
220	Twentieth century
221-327	Country subdivisions (Table T1 modified)

TD

Including all local or departmental reports
Add country number in Table to TD200
Apply table at TD21-127

	General works
344	Early to 1800
345	1800-
346	Elementary textbooks
348	Popular works. Juvenile works
351	Pocketbooks, tables, etc.
353	General special
355	Addresses, essays, lectures
357	Study and teaching
360	Water rates
	Cf. TD499+, Meters
	For local, see TD221+
	Water quality management
	For local, see TD221+
365	General works
365.5	Biomanipulation
	Water quality monitoring
	For local, see TD221+
367	General works
368	Particle counting
	Qualities of water. Water quality
	For local, see TD221+
370	General works
372	Softness
374	Hardness and its correction
	Chemical purification, see TD451+
375	Sensory qualities
	Examination and analysis of water
	Including results
	Cf. GB855+, Natural water chemistry
	For specific pollutants of water, see TD427.A+
380	General works

Watter supply for domestic and industrial purposes
Examination and analysis of water -- Continued
Chemical, see QD142

384   Microscopial. Bacteriological
387.A-Z   Special bodies of water, A-Z
                 For water supplies of a special region or city,
                     see TD221+
             Water conservation
                 For local, see TD221+
                 For special methods of conservation, see the method,
                     e.g. SB439.8, Drought-tolerant plants;
                     SB475.83, Landscape architecture; TD397,
                     Evaporation control in reservoirs;
                     TC401-TC558, Water resources development;
                     TD495-TD497, Location of leaks in mains
388.A1   Periodicals, societies, congresses, etc.
388.A5-Z   General works
388.5   General special
             Sources of water supply
                 Cf. GB651+, Hydrology
390   General works
392   Rivers, lakes, ponds, etc.
             Reservoirs
                 Cf. QH96.8.R35, Reservoir drawdown
                     (Freshwater biology)
                 Cf. QH541.5.R4, Ecology
                 Cf. TD195.R47, Environmental effects
                 For dams and their construction, see TC540+
                 For special reservoirs, see TD221+
395   General works
396   Sedimentation
397   Evaporation control
398   Aqueducts, conduits, etc.
             Groundwater
                 Cf. GB1000+, Hydrology
                 Cf. TD426+, Pollution of groundwater
                 For local, see TD221+
403   General works
404   Artificial recharge
                 Cf. TD765, Disposal of sewage effluent
404.5   Aquifer storage recovery
404.7   Qanats
             Wells
                 Cf. TD426.8, Water pollution
                 For local, see TD221+
405   General works
407   General special
                 Including standards
410   Artesian wells
412   Well digging and boring
414   Boring machinery
                 Including catalogs
             Pumps, see TJ899+

Water supply for domestic and industrial purposes
Sources of water supply -- Continued
418   Rainwater (Collection and use)
Water pollution
Cf. GC1080+, Marine pollution
Cf. QH545.W3, Effect on plants and animals
Cf. RA591+, Public health
419   Periodicals. Societies. Serials
419.5   Congresses
420   General works
422   Juvenile works
423   General special
Study and teaching
424   General works
By region or country
United States
424.3   General works
424.35.A-Z   By region or state, A-Z
424.4.A-Z   Other regions or countries, A-Z
424.5   Research
424.8   Nonpoint source pollution
For local, see TD221+
425   Pollution of streams
For effect of oil pollution on marine organisms,
see QH91.8.O4
For pollution of special water supplies and bodies
of water, see TD221+
For sewage effluent disposal into streams, etc.,
see TD763+
For sewage sludge disposal into streams, etc., see
TD771.5
Pollution of groundwater
426   General works
426.8   Wells
427.A-Z   Specific pollutants and organisms, A-Z
Including presence of naturally occurring
substances
427.A27   Acid deposition
427.A28   Acid mine drainage
427.A35   Agricultural chemicals
427.A45   Aluminum
427.A68   Aquatic pests
Cf. SH174.5, Fish culture
427.A77   Arsenic
427.A84   Atmospheric deposition
427.A86   Atrazine
427.B37   Bacteria
427.B67   Boron
427.B75   Bromate
427.C37   Carbon dioxide
427.C48   Cesium
427.C54   Chemical weapons
427.C57   Chromium

	Water supply for domestic and industrial purposes
	Water pollution
	Specific pollutants, A-Z -- Continued
427.C66	Copper
427.C78	Cryptosporidium
427.C9	Cyanides
427.D34	DDT (Insecticide)
427.D4	Detergents
427.D47	Dibutyltin
427.D52	Dibromochloropropane
427.E83	Ethylene dibromide
427.F45	Fertilizers
427.F58	Fly ash
427.F68	Fouling organisms
427.G55	Glyphosate
	Halogenated hydrocarbons, see TD427.H93
427.H3	Hazardous substances
427.H4	Heat pollution
	Heavy metals, see TD427.M44
427.H46	Herbicides
427.H49	Hexazinone
427.H85	Humus
427.H93	Hydrocarbons
	Including halogenated hydrocarbons and polycyclic aromatic hydrocarbons
427.I55	Inorganic compounds
427.M35	Marine debris
427.M4	Mercury
427.M44	Metals
	Including heavy metals
427.M53	Microoganisms
427.N5	Nitrogen and nitrogen compounds
427.N87	Nutrients
427.O7	Organic compounds
427.P27	Particles
427.P35	Pesticides
427.P4	Petroleum
	Cf. SH177.O53, Effect on fish culture
427.P53	Phenols
427.P56	Phosphorus and phosphorus compounds
	Including phosphates
427.P62	Plastic scrap
427.P63	Plutonium
427.P65	Polychlorinated biphenyls
	Polycyclic aromatic hydrocarbons, see TD427.H93
427.P67	Polyelectrolytes
427.R3	Radioactive substances
427.S24	Salt
427.S33	Sediment
427.S38	Selenium
427.S94	Sulphur and sulphur compounds
	Including sulphides
	Cf. TD196.S95, Environmental pollutants

	Water supply for domestic and industrial purposes
	Water pollution
	Specific pollutants, A-Z -- Continued
427.T42	Technetium
	Thermal pollution, see TD427.H4
427.T7	Trace elements
427.T73	Tributyltin
427.T75	Trichloroethylene
427.T77	Trihalomethanes
427.V55	Viruses
427.V64	Volcanic ash, tuff, etc.
427.Z43	Zebra mussel
428.A-Z	Sources of pollution, A-Z
	Class here works which limit their discussions to wastes from specific industries, facilities, etc., as pollutants of water
	For nonpoint source pollution, see TD424.8
	For waste disposal and control in specific industries, see TD899.A +
428.A37	Agriculture
428.A48	Aluminum mines and mining. Bauxite mines and mining
428.A68	Aquaculture
428.A86	Atomic power plants
	Bauxite mines and mining, see TD428.A48
428.C58	Coal-fired power plants
428.C6	Coal mines and mining
428.C64	Construction industry
428.C66	Copper mines and mining
428.D78	Dry cleaning industry
428.F67	Forestry
428.G64	Gold mines and mining
428.I74	Iron mines and mining
428.L35	Land use
428.M47	Metallurgical plants
428.M49	Methane industry
428.M56	Mineral industries
428.M68	Motorboat racing
	Nuclear power plants, see TD428.A86
428.O33	Offshore oil industry
428.O35	Oil sands extraction plants
428.P35	Paper industry
428.P47	Petroleum refineries
428.P54	Pharmaceutical industry
428.P67	Power plants
428.R63	Road construction
428.R84	Runoff from roads
428.S47	Sewerage. Sewage disposal plants
428.S55	Ships
428.S64	Soil management
428.T78	Trucking
428.U73	Uranium mines and mining
428.W65	Woodpulp industry

	Water supply for domestic
	and industrial purposes -- Continued
429	Water reuse
	Water purification. Water treatment and conditioning
	Cf. RA591+, Public health
	Cf. TD485+, Waterworks, etc.
	Cf. TD745+, Purification of sewage
429.5	Periodicals, societies, congresses, etc.
430	General works
433	General special
434	Water treatment plants
	Special methods
	Mechanical treatment
437	General works
439	Screening. Settling. Sedimentation
	Including sedimentation tanks and basins
	Cf. TD455, Coagulation
	Filtration
441	General works
442	Direct filtration
442.5	Membrane filtration
443	Natural filtration
444	Roughing filtration
445	Sand filtration
446	Diatomaceous earth filtration
447	Filter basins and plants
449	Domestic filters
449.5	Adsorption
	Chemical treatment
451	General works
455	Chemical precipitation. Coagulation. Flocculation
457	Odor control
458	Aeration
	Disinfection
459	General works
460	Ultraviolet ray treatment
461	Ozone treatment
	Chlorination
462	General works
463	Hypochlorite treatment
464	Other methods, A-Z
465	Algae control by copper sulphate and other chemicals
466	Removal of dissolved minerals. Water softening
	Cf. TD478+, Saline water conversion
467	Fluoridation
468	Other methods
	Including color removal, stabilization, nitrification
471	Electrolytic treatment
473	Foam fractionation and flotation
475	Biological treatment

Water supply for domestic and industrial purposes
 Water purification. Water
  treatment and conditioning
   Special methods -- Continued

476	Irradiation
477	Other methods
	Water treatment plant residuals, see TD899.W3
	Saline water conversion
478	Periodicals, societies, congresses, etc.
	Special countries
	United States
478.3	General works
478.5.A-W	By state, A-W
478.6.A-Z	Other countries, A-Z
479	General works
479.15	Juvenile works
479.2	General special
479.25	Pocketbooks, tables, etc.
479.3	Estimates and costs
	Desalination plants
	For plants in specific locations, see TD478.3+
	For special conversion methods, see TD480+
479.4	General works
479.5	Combined purpose plants
479.6	Nuclear powered plants
479.7	Solar powered plants
479.8	Pretreatment of saline waters. Scale
	Special conversion methods
480	Distillation methods
480.2	Freezing methods
480.3	Hydrate process
	Membrane methods
480.4	General works
480.5	Electrodialysis
480.7	Ion exchange desalting
	Water distribution systems
	For local, see TD221+
	Aqueducts, see TD398
	Reservoirs, see TD395+
481	General works
482	General special
	Including smaller plants, fountains, pumps, etc.
	Waterworks, pumping stations, etc.
485	General works
487	General special
	Pumping machinery, see TJ899+
489	Water towers, standpipes, etc.
	Cf. TH9332+, Fire extinction
491	Mains, pipes, valves, etc.
	Cf. TK3255, Electrolytic corrosion
	Flow of water, see TC171+
493	Water withdrawals
	For local, see TD221+

	Water supply for domestic
	and industrial purposes -- Continued
	Water waste and its prevention
	Including location of breaks or leakage in mains
495	General works
497	General special
	Including unauthorized users of water
	Water meters and metering
	Cf. TC177, Hydraulics (Current meters)
499	General works
500	Special makes of meters
	Water supply for farms, country houses, etc , see TD927
	Sewage collection and disposal systems. Sewerage
	Cf. HD4475+, Economic aspects of sewage disposal
	Cf. RA567+, Public hygiene
	For industrial wastes, see TD896+
511	Periodicals, societies, congresses, etc.
	History
515	General works
516	Ancient
517	Medieval
518	Modern
519	19th century
520	20th century
521-627	Country subdivisions (Table T1 modified)
	Including all local departmental reports
	Add country number in table to TD500
	Under each country:
	1.A1 General works
	1.A6-Z States provinces, etc.
	2.A-Z Local (Cities, etc.), A-Z
	General works
644	Early to 1800
645	1800-
646	Elementary works
648	Popular works
651	Pocketbooks, tables, etc.
653	General special
	Including costs
655	Addresses, essays, lectures
	Urban runoff
	Cf. TD665, Storm sewer system
657	General works
657.5	Stormwater infiltration
658	Sewerage systems design
659	Layout of the system
	Sewerage systems
662	Combined system
664	Separate system
665	Storm sewer system
666	Liernur system
668	Shone system
670	Other systems

Sewage collection and
    disposal systems. Sewerage -- Continued
  Sewers
    For testing the strength of cement pipe, see TA447
    For testing the strength of metal pipe, see TA492.P6

673	General works
	Shape and size. Theory of flow
675	General works
676	Tables, formulas, diagrams
	Design and construction
678	General works
680	Brick
682	Cement and clay. Concrete
684	Clay pipe
686	Steel and iron pipe
688	Other material
690	Sewer gas, explosions, etc.
691	Sewer corrosion
692	Ventilation of sewers
	Sewer appurtenances
695	General works
696	Manholes
698	Flushing apparatus
701	Regulators
705	River crossings, etc.
711	Intercepting and outfall sewers
	Maintenance and repair
716	General works
719	Inspection and cleaning
722	Collecting reservoirs
725	Pumping stations
	Sewage
730	General works
733	General special
735	Analysis, sampling methods, etc.
736	Bacteriology
737	Biochemical oxygen demand
	Sewage disposal systems
	For local, see TD521 +
741	General works
743	General special
	Treatment, purification, etc.
745	General works
746	Sewage disposal plants
746.5	Oxidation ponds. Stabilization ponds. Lagoons
	Disinfection. Deodorization
747	General works
747.5	Ultraviolet ray treatment
747.7	Chlorination
747.9	Neutralization
748	Screening. Skimming
	Sedimentation. Settling tanks
	Cf. TD778, Septic tanks

TD

	Sewage collection and disposal systems. Sewerage
	Sewage disposal systems
	Treatment, purification, etc.
	Sedimentation. Settling tanks -- Continued
749	General works
750	Imhof tanks
751	Sedimentation with coagulation. Chemical precipitation. Flocculation
753	Filtration. Screening
753.5	Adsorption
754	Membrane methods
754.5	Form fractionation and flotation
	Biological purification. Bacterial purification
	Cf. TD746.5, Oxidation ponds
	Cf. TD764, Self-purification of streams, etc.
755	General works
756	Activated sludge method
756.5	Constructed wetlands
757	Electrolytic treatment
757.5	Ion exchange
758	Aeration. Oxidation
758.5.A-Z	Removal of specific chemical elements, compounds, etc., A-Z
758.5.C45	Chlorine
758.5.C65	Color removal
758.5.C93	Cyanides
758.5.H39	Hazardous wastes
758.5.H43	Heavy metals
758.5.N58	Nitrogen
758.5.O37	Oil
758.5.O75	Organic compounds
758.5.P53	Phenols
758.5.P56	Phosphorus
758.5.P64	Polychlorinated biphenyls
758.5.S44	Silver
	Disposal of sewage effluent
759	General works
760	Disposal on land. Irrigation. Sewage farming
761	Subsurface disposal. Deep-well injection
	Disposal by dilution. Discharge into streams, lakes, oceans
763	General works
764	Self-purification of streams, etc.
765	Other methods
	Including recharge of groundwaters
	Cf. TD429, Water reuse
	Sewage sludge treatment and disposal
767	General works
	Properties of sewage sludge. Tests
767.4	General works
767.7	Activated sludge
	Treatment

	Sewage collection and disposal systems. Sewerage
	Sewage disposal systems
	Sewage sludge treatment and disposal
	Treatment -- Continued
768	General works
	Sludge digestion. Digestion tanks
769	General works
769.4	Sludge gas production and utilization
769.7	Dewatering. Drying
769.8	Irradiation
	Special disposal methods
	Incineration
770	General works
770.3	Sewage sludge ash
771	Sanitary landfills. Burial
771.5	Discharge into streams, ocean
772	Manufacture into fertilizer, soil builder, etc.
	Disposal as fertilizer, soil builder, etc.
	Cf. SD408, Forest fertilization
774	General works
775	Cesspools, middens, privies, latrines
	Cf. TH4975, Design and construction of privies
776	Earth closets
778	Septic tanks
779	Aerated package treatment systems
780	Pail systems. Can privies
	Municipal refuse. Solid wastes
	Class here collection and disposal
785	Periodicals, societies, congresses, etc.
785.5	Dictionaries and encyclopedias
786	Directories
	Special countries
	United States
788	General works
788.4.A-Z	By region or state, A-Z
	Apply table at TD157.3.A-Z
789.A-Z	Other countries, A-Z
	Apply table at TD183.5.A-Z
790	Developing countries
791	General works
792	Juvenile works
793	General special
	Study and teaching
793.2	General works
	By region or country
	United States
793.25	General works
793.26.A-Z	By region or state, A-Z
793.27.A-Z	Other regions or countries, A-Z
793.3	Research
793.7	Estimates and costs
	Waste minimization

	Municipal refuse. Solid wastes
	Waste minimization -- Continued
793.9	General works
793.95	Source reduction
	Special industries, plants, processes, etc , see TD899.A +
794	Collection and haulage
794.2	Integrated solid waste management
	For local, see TD788 +
	Recycling
	Cf. SB454.3.R43, Gardening
	Cf. TS169, Waste control
794.5	General works
794.8	Source separation
	Special disposal methods
	Open dumps
795	General works
795.4	Junkyards and automobile graveyards
795.7	Sanitary landfills
	Incineration. Incinerators
796	General works
796.2	Waste heat utilization
796.5	Composting
796.7	Other methods
	Special wastes and their disposal
797	Ashes
	Automobile-related wastes
797.5	General works
797.7	Waste tires
	Packaging waste
797.9	General works
797.92	Cushioning materials
798	Plastic waste
799	Glass
799.5	Metal
799.7	Household appliances
799.8	Household batteries
799.85	Electronic apparatus and appliances
800	Petroleum waste
800.5	Waste paint
	Garbage
801	General works
803	Incinerators
	Organic wastes
804	General works
805	Paper waste
810	Wood waste
810.5	Yard waste
(811)	Animal waste
	see TD930.2
	Hazardous substances, see TD1020 +

	Municipal refuse. Solid wastes
	Special wastes and their disposal -- Continued
	Radioactive wastes and their disposal
	Cf. TD897.85+, Industrial wastes
	Cf. TD1020+, Hazardous wastes and their disposal
812	General works
	By region or country
	United States
812.2	General works
812.3.A-Z	By region or state, A-Z
812.4.A-Z	Other regions or countries, A-Z
812.5.A-Z	Special chemical elements, compounds, etc., A-Z
812.5.A48	Aluminum
812.5.C66	Copper
812.5.O73	Organohalogen compounds
	Street cleaning. Litter and its removal
	Cf. TE220.55, Roadside litter control
813	General works
	Special countries
	America
815	General works
	United States
817	General works
818.A-W	States, A-W
819.A-Z	Cities, A-Z
	Canada
820	General works
821.A-Y	Provinces, A-Y
822.A-Z	Cities, A-Z
823	Latin America
	Mexico
824	General works
825.A-Z	Cities, A-Z
	Central America
826	General works
827.A-Z	Special countries, A-Z
	West Indies
829	General works
830.A-Z	Special islands, A-Z
	South America
832	General works
833.A-Z	Special countries, A-Z
	Europe
835	General works
836.A-Z	Special countries, A-Z
	Asia
838	General works
839.A-Z	Special countries, A-Z
	Africa
841	General works
843.A-Z	Special countries, A-Z
	Australia

	Street cleaning. Litter and its removal
	Special countries
	Australia -- Continued
845	General works
846.A-Z	States, A-Z
847	New Zealand
	Pacific islands
848	General works
849.A-Z	Special islands, A-Z
860	Tools and appliances
	Street sprinkling
863	General works
865	Sprinkling carts
	Control of snow and ice on streets
	Cf. TE220.5, Control of snow and ice on roads
	and highways
868	General works
870	Use of chemicals
	Including salt, etc.
(877)	Street lighting
	see TK4188, (Electric); TP741, (Nonelectric)
	Special types of environment
	Soil pollution. Soil remediation
	Cf. RA571, Environmental health
	Cf. S622 +, Soil conservation
878	General works
	By region or country
	United States
878.2	General works
878.3.A-Z	By region or state, A-Z
878.4.A-Z	Other regions or countries, A-Z
	Special remediation methods
878.5	Soil vapor extraction
878.6	Soil bioventing
879.A-Z	Particular pollutants, A-Z
879.A35	Agricultural chemicals
	Class here works on the pollution of soils by
	agricultural chemicals
	For general works on agricultural chemicals and
	their behavior in soils, see S592.6.A34
879.C33	Cadmium
879.C63	Cobalt
879.C93	Cyanides
879.H38	Hazardous wastes. Hazardous substances
879.H4	Heavy metals
879.H47	Herbicides
879.I55	Inorganic compounds
879.L43	Lead
879.M47	Metals
879.O73	Organic compounds

	Special types of environment
	Soil pollution. Soil remediation
	Particular pollutants, A-Z -- Continued
879.P37	Pesticides
	Cf. S592.6.P43, Behavior and movement in soils
	Cf. SB951.145.S65, Soil pesticides
879.P4	Petroleum
879.P64	Polychlorinated biphenyls
879.P66	Polycyclic aromatic hydrocarbons
879.R34	Radioactive pollution
880.A-Z	Special industries, facilities, activities, etc., A-Z
880.L35	Land use
	Air pollution and its control
	Cf. HC79.A4, Economic aspects
	Cf. QC882+, Atmospheric pollutants
	Cf. QH545.A3, Influence on plants and animals
	Cf. QP82.2.A3, Physiological effect
	Cf. RA576+, Public health
881	Periodicals, societies, congresses, etc.
881.5	Dictionaries and encyclopedias
882	Directories
883	General works
883.1	General special
883.13	Juvenile works
883.14	Addresses, essays, lectures
	Study and teaching
883.143	General works
	By region or country
	United States
883.144	General works
883.145.A-Z	By region or state, A-Z
883.148.A-Z	Other regions or countries, A-Z
883.15	Research
883.17	Indoor air pollution
	Including indoor air quality
	Special regions or countries
	United States
883.2	General works
883.5.A-Z	By region or state, A-Z
	Apply table at TD157.3.A-Z
883.7.A-Z	Other regions or countries, A-Z
	Apply table at TD157.4.A-Z
	Particular air pollutants and their control
884	Smoke
	Cf. QC882.6, Meteorology
	Cf. TH1088.5, Smoke control systems
	Cf. TH2281+, Chimneys
884.3	Smog. Fog-pollutant mixtures
884.5	Dusts, fumes, and mists; particulate matter
	Cf. QC882.5, Meteorology
	Gases. Flue gases
885	General works

	Special types of environment
	Air pollution and its control
	Particular air pollutants and their control
	Gases. Flue gases -- Continued
885.5.A-Z	Individual gases and groups of gases, A-Z
885.5.C3	Carbon dioxide
885.5.C33	Carbon monoxide
885.5.C47	Chlorine
885.5.C5	Chlorofluoromethane
885.5.C66	Combustion gases
885.5.F57	Fluorine
885.5.F67	Formaldehyde
885.5.G73	Greenhouse gases
885.5.H9	Hydrogen sulphide
885.5.L35	Landfill gases
885.5.M48	Methane
885.5.N38	Natural gas
885.5.N5	Nitrogen oxides
885.5.O74	Organic compounds
885.5.O85	Ozone
885.5.R33	Radon
885.5.S8	Sulphur dioxide
885.5.S85	Sulphur oxides
886	Odors
886.5	Automobile exhaust
	Including emissions from motor vehicles in general
	Cf. TL214.P6, Pollution control devices for motor vehicles
886.7	Aircraft exhaust emissions
886.8	Diesel exhaust
887.A-Z	Other pollutants, A-Z
887.A37	Acrylonitrile
887.A66	Ammonia
887.A8	Asbestos
887.B43	Benzene
887.B45	Benzpyrene
887.B58	Bituminous materials
887.C34	Cadmium
887.C37	Carbon disulphide
887.C47	Chlorofluorocarbons
887.D56	Dioxins
887.E64	Epichlorohydrin
887.E83	Ethylene dichloride
887.F48	Fibers
887.F63	Fluorides
887.F67	Fluorocarbons
887.F69	Fossil fuels
887.H3	Halocarbons
887.H4	Heavy metals
887.H48	Hexylene glycol
887.H93	Hydrocarbons
887.L4	Lead

Special types of environment
  Air pollution and its control
    Particular air pollutants and their control
      Other pollutants, A-Z -- Continued

887.M34	Manganese
887.M37	Mercury
887.M4	Metals
887.O95	Ozone-depleting substances
887.P34	Peat
887.P45	Pesticides
887.P65	Pollen
887.R3	Radioactive metals
887.S78	Sulphates
887.S82	Sulphur
887.T75	Trichloroethylene
887.V55	Vinyl chloride
888.A-Z	Sources of pollution, A-Z

        Cf. TD899.A+, Waste control in special
          industries and plants

888.A53	Aerospace industries
888.A56	Aluminum plants
888.A86	Asphalt plants
888.C4	Cement plants
888.C5	Chemical plants
888.C58	Coaling stations
888.C6	Coffee processing plants
888.C63	Construction industry
888.C65	Cotton gins
888.E43	Electric power-plants
888.F3	Factories
888.F45	Fertilizer industry
888.F6	Foundries
888.G37	Gas manufacture and works
888.H43	Heating plants
888.H9	Hydrochloric acid plants
888.M26	Machinery industry
888.M4	Metallurgical plants
888.N8	Nuclear facilities
888.O35	Oil sands extraction plants
888.P38	Petroleum chemicals industry
888.P4	Petroleum refineries
888.P67	Power plants
888.P73	Printed circuits industry
888.P8	Pulp and paper mills
888.R4	Reactor fuel reprocessing plants
888.R48	Resource recovery facilities
888.R62	Road construction, maintenance, and repair
888.R66	Roofing industry
888.S38	Sewage disposal plants
888.S54	Ships
888.S6	Solvents industry
888.S7	Steam power plants
888.S72	Steelworks

	Special types of environment
	Air pollution and its control
	Sources of pollution, A-Z -- Continued
888.S77	Sugar factories
888.S8	Sulphuric acid plants
888.W6	Wood industry. Lumber industry
	Cf. TD888.P8, Pulp and paper mills
889	Air pollution control equipment
	Cf. TH7692 +, Dust removal (by pneumatic suction, etc.)
890	Measurement. Air sampling and analysis
	For measurement or analysis of specific pollutants, see TD884 +
	Noise and its control
891	Periodicals, societies, congresses, etc.
891.5	Directories
892	General works
892.5	Juvenile works
	Special countries
	United States
893	General works
893.3.A-Z	By region or state, A-Z
893.5.A-Z	Other regions or countries, A-Z
893.6.A-Z	Special industries, facilities, activities, etc., A-Z
893.6.A57	Airplanes
	Cf. TL671.65, Aeronautical engineering
893.6.B58	Blast furnaces
893.6.B68	Bottling plants
893.6.C45	Chemical plants
893.6.C6	Construction industry
893.6.C78	Crushed stone industry
893.6.E4	Electric lines
893.6.F58	Flour mills
893.6.F64	Food industry
893.6.F65	Forge shops
893.6.G37	Gasworks
893.6.G7	Grain elevators
893.6.M3	Machine shops
893.6.M35	Materials handling
893.6.M43	Meat industry
893.6.M45	Metalwork
893.6.M5	Mineral industries
893.6.O34	Offices
893.6.P35	Paper industry
893.6.P47	Petroleum refineries
893.6.P55	Pipe industry
893.6.P68	Power plants
893.6.P74	Precast concrete industry
893.6.P75	Printing plants
893.6.Q35	Quarries and quarrying
893.6.R3	Railroads
893.6.S48	Sewage disposal plants
893.6.T4	Textile industry

	Noise and its control
	Special industries, facilities,
	activities, etc., A-Z -- Continued
893.6.T7	Transportation
893.6.T86	Tunneling
893.6.W37	Water treatment plants
893.6.W65	Woodworking industries
894	Noise measurement
	Industrial and factory sanitation
	Cf. HD3656+, Factory inspection
	Cf. HD7260+, Industrial hygiene (Administrative
	aspects)
	Cf. T55+, Industrial safety
	Cf. TS193, Plant housekeeping
895	General works
	Industrial and factory wastes
	Cf. HD30.255, Environmental aspects of
	industrial management
896	Periodicals, societies, congresses, etc.
897	General works
897.5	General special
897.6	Industrial waste treatment facilities
	Including centralized facilities
	Special regions or countries
	United States
897.7	General works
897.75.A-Z	By region or state, A-Z
897.8.A-Z	Other regions or countries, A-Z
	Special topics
897.842	Biodegradation
897.843	Incineration
897.845	Recycling
897.847	Waste minimization
	Special wastes and their disposal
	Radioactive waste disposal
	Cf. TK9152.17, Transportation of
	radioactive substances
	For municipal and industrial hazardous wastes,
	see TD1020+
	For municipal radioactive waste, see TD812+
	For temporary storage at the facility, see
	TK9152.165
897.85	Periodicals, societies, congresses, etc.
898	General works
	By region or country
	United States
898.118	General works
898.12.A-Z	By region or state, A-Z
898.13.A-Z	Other regions or countries, A-Z
	Apply table at TD157.4.A-Z
898.14.A-Z	Special topics, A-Z
	For local, see TD898.118+
898.14.B55	Biodegradation

Industrial and factory sanitation
Industrial and factory wastes
Special wastes and their disposal
Radioactive waste disposal
Special topics, A-Z -- Continued

898.14.E36	Economic aspects
898.14.E58	Environmental aspects
898.14.E83	Evaluation
898.14.G46	Geochemistry
898.14.G47	Geology
898.14.G68	Government policy
898.14.I57	International cooperation
898.14.M35	Management
898.14.R57	Risk assessment
898.14.S34	Safety measures
898.14.S63	Social aspects

Radioactive waste sites
Cf. TK9152.2, Decontamination.
Decommissioning of facilities
For local, see TD898.118 +

898.15	General works
898.155.A-Z	Special topics, A-Z
898.155.D47	Design and construction
898.155.E83	Evaluation
898.16	Radioactive waste treatment facilities (General)

For local, see TD898.118 +
Special disposal methods
For temporary storage at the facility, see
TK9152.165

898.17	General works
898.173	Bituminization
898.175	Incineration
898.178	Transmutation
898.179	Vitrification
898.18	Stabilization. Solidification
898.2	Disposal in the ground

For local, see TD898.118 +

898.4	Disposal in the water

For local, see TD898.118 +

898.6	Disposal under the seabed

For local, see TD898.118 +

898.7.A-Z	Special substances, A-Z
898.7.A46	Alpha-bearing wastes
898.7.P48	Plutonium
898.8.A-Z	Other wastes, A-Z
898.8.A76	Arsenic wastes
898.8.C67	Corrosive wastes
898.8.M47	Metal wastes
898.8.P45	Pentachlorophenol
898.8.P64	Polychlorinated biphenyls
898.8.S65	Solvent wastes

	Industrial and factory sanitation
	Industrial and factory wastes -- Continued
899.A-Z	Waste control in special industries, plants, processes, etc., A-Z
	Cf. TD428.A+, Pollution of water by special industries, etc.
	Cf. TD888.A+, Air pollution by special industries, etc.
	Agriculture, see TD930+
899.A44	Aluminum industry
899.A76	Arsenals
899.A8	Atomic power plants
899.B48	Beverage container industry
899.C25	Cadmium industry
899.C27	Camp sites, facilities, etc.
899.C3	Canneries
899.C5	Chemical industry
899.C55	Citrus processing plants
899.C57	Clay industries
899.C58	Cleaning and dyeing industry
899.C585	Coal liquefaction
899.C588	Coal preparation plants
899.C5885	Construction industry
899.C59	Copper industry
899.C6	Cotton industry
899.D3	Dairy plants. Milk plants
899.D5	Distilleries
899.F4	Feedlots
899.F47	Fertilizer industry
899.F5	Fisheries
899.F57	Fishery processing industries
899.F585	Food industry
899.F6	Foundries
899.F7	Fruit processing plants
899.G3	Gas industry
899.G47	Glass fiber industry
899.G63	Gold industry
899.G85	Gums and resins industry
	Health facilities, see RA969.45
899.H65	Hotels
899.L32	Laboratories
899.L37	Laundries
899.M2	Machinery industry
899.M29	Manufactures
899.M4	Meat industry. Packinghouses. Slaughterhouses
899.M43	Metallurgical plants
899.M45	Metalworking and finishing industry
	Milk plants, see TD899.D3
899.M47	Mineral industries
899.M5	Mines
	Nuclear power plants, see TD899.A8
899.O54	Oil industries
	Packinghouses, see TD899.M4

Industrial and factory sanitation
Industrial and factory wastes
Waste control in special
industries, plants, processes,
etc., A-Z -- Continued

899.P25	Paint industry and trade
899.P3	Paper industry
899.P37	Pesticides industry
899.P4	Petroleum industry
899.P45	Phosphate industry
899.P46	Phosphoric acid industry
899.P48	Photographic industry
899.P55	Plastics industry
899.P6	Potato chip industry
899.P65	Poultry industry
899.P69	Printed circuits industry
899.P7	Printing industry
899.R26	Railroads
899.R3	Reactor fuel reprocessing plants
899.R34	Refractories industry
899.R8	Rubber industry
	Seafood processing, see TD899.F57
	Slaughterhouses, see TD899.M4
899.S46	Service stations
899.S68	Steam power plants
899.S7	Steelworks
899.S8	Sugar industry
899.T3	Tanneries
899.T4	Textile industry
899.T55	Tile industry
899.U73	Uranium industry
899.W3	Water treatment plants
899.W6	Wood industry
899.W65	Woodpulp industry
899.W73	Wrecking industry

Sanitary engineering as applied to buildings
see TH6014-TH6729

(905)	General works
(909)	General special
(913)	House drainage
	see TH6571-TH6675
(915)	Earth closets
	see TD776
(918)	Sanitary inspection
	see RA565-RA568

Rural and farm sanitary engineering
Including all small isolated plants for country and
farmhouses, etc.
For local, see TD21+

920	General works
923	General special
927	Water supply
	For local, see TD221+

	Rural and farm sanitary engineering -- Continued
	Sewage and refuse disposal and drainage
	For local, see TD521+
929	General works
	Agricultural wastes
930	General works
930.2	Animal waste
930.3	Crop residues
930.4	Dairy waste
	Pesticide waste, see TD1066.P47
931	Parks, recreation areas, campgrounds, etc.
	Cf. GV198.S3, Sanitation of organized camps
	Cf. RA604, Environmental health
(935)	Sanitary engineering of other isolated plants
	see TH6057-TH6059
	Low temperature sanitary engineering
940	General works
943	General special
947	Water supply
949	Sewage and refuse disposal and drainage
(1015)	Washhouses and public laundries
	see TH6057.L3
	Hazardous substances and their disposal
	Including both municipal and industrial hazardous
	wastes other than radioactive
	For industrial radioactive waste, see TD897.85+
	For municipal radioactive wastes, see TD812+
1020	Periodicals, societies, congresses, etc.
1024	Directories
1030	General works
1030.5	Juvenile works
1032	Handbooks, manuals, etc.
	By region or country
	United States
1040	General works
1042.A-Z	By region or state, A-Z
	Apply table at TD157.3.A-Z
1045.A-Z	Other regions or countries, A-Z
	Apply table at TD157.4.A-Z
1050.A-Z	Special topics, A-Z
	For local, see TD1040+
1050.C57	Citizen participation
1050.C67	Cost control
1050.E58	Environmental aspects
1050.P64	Political aspects
1050.R57	Risk assessment
1050.S24	Safety measures
1050.T43	Technological innovations
1050.T73	Tracking
1050.W36	Waste minimization
1052	Hazardous waste sites (General)
	For local, see TD1040+

	Hazardous substances and their disposal -- Continued
1054	Hazardous waste treatment facilities (General)
	Including surface impoundments
	For local, see TD1040+
	Special disposal methods
1060	General works
1061	Biodegradation
1062	Incineration
1063	Stabilization. Solidification
1064	Land disposal
1066.A-Z	Special substances, A-Z
1066.D45	Dense nonaqueous phase liquids
1066.G48	Glycols
1066.L57	Lithium
1066.M46	Metals
1066.O55	Oil
1066.O73	Organic compounds
1066.P47	Pesticides
1066.P64	Polychlorinated biphenyls

	Highway engineering. Roads and pavements
	Cf. HD9717.5.R6+, Road construction industry
	Cf. HE331+, Traffic engineering; economics of roads
	Cf. QH545.R62, Environmental effects
	Cf. TD888.R62, Air pollution
	Periodicals, societies, etc. By language of publication
1.A1	International or polyglot
1.A3-Z	English
2	French
3	German
4	Other languages (not A-Z)
5	Congresses
	Exhibitions. Museums
6.A1	General works
6.A2-Z	By region or country, A-Z
	Under each country:
	.x *General works*
	.x2A-Z *Special. By city, A-Z*
7	Collected works (nonserial)
9	Dictionaries and encyclopedias
12	Directories
	History
15	General works
16	Ancient
17	Medieval
18	Modern to 1800
19	1800-
21-127	Country divisions (Table T1 modified)
	Class special roads limited to a particular province,
	city, etc. with the province, city, etc.
	Add country number in table to TE0
	Under each country with two numbers, unless otherwise
	specified:
	1 *General works*
	Including government publications
	2.A-Z *Local (Provinces, cities, etc.) or special*
	roads, A-Z
	America
	North America
	United States
	For works on federal aid to highways, see HE355+
25.5.A-Z	Special roads not limited to one state or
	region. By name, A-Z
	Biography
139	Collective
140.A-Z	Individual, A-Z
	e.g.
140.M3	MacAdam
	General works
144	Early to 1800
145	1800-
147	Elementary textbooks
149	Juvenile works

TE

General works -- Continued
151 Pocketbooks, tables, etc.
153 General special
155 Addresses, essays, lectures
175 Highway design
Including drawings and designs
Interchanges and intersections
176 General works
176.3 Left-turn lanes
176.5 Traffic circles
176.8 Motor vehicle scales
Roadside development. Landscaping
177 General works
178 Vegetation
178.8 Rest areas
180 Specifications
183 Estimates, quantities, and costs
185 Records, timekeeping, etc.
For accounts and accounting, see HF5686.R6
191 Study and teaching
192 Highway research
195 Highway engineering management
Materials for roadmaking (stone, etc.)
200 General works
203 General special
Including road-marking materials
205 Testing and inspection. Laboratory manuals
Location engineering
206 General works
Soil surveys
Including physical tests, analysis of subgrade
soils, soil profiles, etc.
208 General works
208.5 Trafficability of soils
Road surveys
209 General works
209.5 Aerial surveys
Construction details
Foundations
210 General works
Soil stabilization
Including soil compaction
Cf. S593.23, Agriculture
Cf. TA749, Earthwork
210.4 General works
210.5.A-Z Special methods and materials, A-Z
210.5.B5 Bitumen
210.5.C3 Calcium chloride
210.5.F55 Fly ash
210.5.L5 Lime
210.5.S3 Salt
210.5.S6 Soil cement
210.8 Fills and embankments

	Construction details
	Foundations -- Continued
211	Subgrade structure
212	Base course
212.5	Shoulders
213	Culverts and small bridges
	Cf. TF282, Railroad engineering
215	Drainage
216	Bridge approaches
	Maintenance and repair
	Cf. TD813+, Street cleaning
220	General works
220.3	Overlays
220.5	Snow and ice control on roads and highways
	Cf. TD868+, Control of snow and ice on streets
220.55	Roadside litter control
	Cf. TD813+, Street litter and its removal
220.63	Dust control
221	Road binders, dust preventives, etc., for unpaved roads
	Including bituminous materials
	Machinery, road rollers, etc.
223	General works
227	Catalogs
228	Safety and traffic control devices
	Cf. HE370.A+, Traffic regulations
	Cf. TE203, Road-marking materials
228.3	Communication systems
	Including Intelligent Vehicle Highway Systems
228.5	Low-volume roads
228.7	Frontage roads
	Country roads
	Cf. TE280+, Paths
229	General works
229.2	Farm roads
229.5	Forest roads
	Cf. SD389, Forestry
229.8	Mountain roads
229.9	Scenic byways
	Special kinds of unpaved roads
230	Earth and sand
233	Gravel
	Broken stone
235	General works
237	Stonebreaking for roads
239	Stonecrushers for road material
241	Telford roads
243	Macadam roads
244	Tarred roads (Construction)
245	Other varieties
	Including plank roads
247	Ice roads. Ice crossings. Ice bridges
	Pavements and paved roads
250	General works

	Pavements and paved roads -- Continued
251	Design
251.5	Performance
252	Specifications
253	Wood
255	Brick
	Stone
257	General works
259	Cobblestone
	Stone blocks
261	General works
263	Belgian
265	Oblong
	Bituminous pavements
	Cf. TE221, Road-binders, dust preventives, etc.
	Cf. TE244, Tarred roads (Construction)
266	Congresses
270	General works
273	Asphalt mixing machinery and plants
275	Asphalt and asphalt mixtures
276	Asphalt block
	Concrete roads and pavements
	Including reinforced concrete
278	General works
278.2	Joints
278.6	Prestressed concrete
278.8	Precast concrete
279	Streets
279.3	Driveways
	Pedestrian facilities
	Cf. NA9074, Architecture
279.5	General works
	Sidewalks. Footpaths. Flagging
	Cf. TH4970, Garden walks
280	General works
283	Earth, gravel, cinder
285	Wood
287	Brick
289	Stone
291	Cement. Concrete
293	Asphalt
295.A-Z	Other, A-Z
298	Curbs. Curbstones
301	Bicycle paths and tracks
303	Equestrian roads
304	Trails
305	Racetracks for automobiles (Construction)
(315-427)	Laws and legislation
	see class K
450	Hauling tests. Traction tests

	Railroad engineering and operation
	Cf. HE1001+, Economic aspects of railroads
	Cf. TD893.6.R3, Noise control
	Periodicals and societies. By language of publication
1	English
2	French
3	German
4	Other languages (not A-Z)
5	Congresses
	Exhibitions. Museums
6.A1	General works
6.A2-Z	By region or country, A-Z
	Under each country:
	.x General works
	.x2A-Z Special. By city, A-Z
7	Collected works (nonserial)
9	Dictionaries and encyclopedias
12	Directories, etc.
	For directories of other railroads, see HE2801+
	For directories of purchasing agents, see TF359
	For directories of supply dealers, see TF355
	For directories of U.S. railroads, see HE2721
	History
15	General works
16	Antiquities
	Including early curiosities of railroad development and horse railroads
19	Nineteenth century
20	Twentieth century
21-127	Country divisions (Table T1)
	Class here only technical works, including works on the physical plants of individual railroads
	Add country number in table to TF0
	Biography
139	Collective
140.A-Z	Individual, A-Z
	General works
144	Early to 1850
145	1850-
146	Elementary textbooks
147	Popular works
148	Juvenile works
149	Pictorial works
151	Pocketbooks, tables, etc. (General)
153	General special
155	Addresses, essays, lectures
	Study and teaching. Research
	America
171	General works
173	United States
176	Canada
179	Latin America
180	Europe

	Study and teaching. Research -- Continued
181	Asia
182	Africa
183	Australia
190	Economics of location
	Class here only technical works
	Cf. HE1612 +, Location, right of way, etc.
	(Economic aspects)
	Cf. TF215 +, Railroad surveying (General)
193	Estimates, costs, etc.
195	Specifications
197	Model railways
	Safety measures, see TF610
	Railway construction
200	General works
	Including reconnaissance, surveying, and location
203	General special
205	Railroad engineering (Fieldbooks, tables, etc.)
208	Preliminary operations
	Railroad surveying
210	General works
212	Reconnaissance
213	Preliminary surveying
213.5	Aerial photography in railroad surveying
214	Plotting, profiles, etc.
	Location
215	General works
216	Curves and turnouts
217	Transition spiral, etc.
	Earthwork
	Including rock cuttings
220	General works
222	Tables, calculations, etc.
	Excavating machinery, steam shovels, etc.
225	General works
226	Catalogs
	Tunnels and tunneling
230	General works
232	General special
	Including special methods of tunnels, e.g.
	Pressure tunneling
	Maintenance and operating of tunnels
234	General works
235	Ventilation
236	Lighting
238.A-Z	Special tunnels, A-Z
	Permanent way. Superstructure. Roadway. Track
	Cf. TF530 +, Maintenance and repair
240	General works
241	General special
243	Grades
244	Gauges
245	Drainage

	Railway construction
	Permanent way. Superstructure.
	Roadway. Track -- Continued
248	Tracklaying machinery
	Details of the permanent way
250	Roadbed. Ballast
	Ties. Sleepers
252	General works
254	Wood
255	Iron and steel
256.A-Z	Other, A-Z
257	Tie plates
	Rails
258	General works
260	Section-books, tables, etc.
261	Rail fastenings (fishplates, bolts, etc.)
262	Continuous rails
263	Crossings
	Cf. HE1617+, Grade crossings
264	Turnouts and curves (Construction)
	For location of curves and field work, see TF216
	Switches, frogs, etc. Points (English)
266	General works
267	Frogs
268	Guardrails
	Railway structures and buildings
	Cf. NA6310+, Architecture
270	General works
	Accessories to the permanent way
271	Track tanks
272	Ashpits, etc.
274	Y tracks
275	Turntables
276	Transfer tables (Chariots transbordeurs)
277	Fences, cattle guards, snow guards
	Viaducts, bridges, etc , see TG445
282	Culverts, small bridges, cattle passes, etc.
(284)	Trestles
	see TG365-TG370
	Buildings, etc., other than structures enumerated above
288	General works
290	Water columns, cranes, and pipes
292	Sand plants and bins
294	Coalsheds and coaling plants
296	Enginehouses. Roundhouses
298	Shops
	Passenger depots, stations, and terminals
300	General works
302.A-Z	Special places, A-Z
	Freight yards and terminals
305	General works
308.A-Z	Special places, A-Z

TF

Railway construction
  Railway structures and buildings -- Continued
315   Railway docks
320   Railway ferries
  Railway equipment and supplies
    General works
340   Periodicals, societies, etc.
345   Treatises
347   General special
            Including standardization
350   Railway machinery and tools
355   Directories of dealers and manufacturers
357   Catalogs of dealers and manufacturers
            Including reports, histories, etc. of individual
              firms
            Cf. TJ625.A +, Locomotives
359   Directories of purchasing agents
361   Inspection. Testing
363   Specifications
365   Railway patents
368   Electrical equipment
    Rolling stock and car building
      For car service, see TF600 +
      For rolling stock of special places and roads, see
        TF21 +
371   Periodicals
373   Dictionaries and encyclopedias
375   General works
            Including atlases
376   Railway shops and shop practice. Repair shops
            Cf. TJ680 +, Locomotive shops
377   General special
    Details of car construction
      Car trucks
380   General works
383   Wheels
386   Axles
389   Bearings and lubrication
391   Springs
393   Shock absorbers
400   Car bodies
410   Couplers
413   Draft gear
      Brake gear
415   General works
        Airbrakes
420   General works
425   Westinghouse
430   New York
440   Car furnishings
      Car sanitation, heating, lighting, and ventilation
445   General works
        Lighting

Railway equipment and supplies
  Car sanitation, heating, lighting, and ventilation
    Lighting -- Continued

447	General works
449	Electric lighting
451	Drinking water
453	Air conditioning

  Varieties of cars
    Passenger cars

455	General works
457	Parlor cars
459	Sleeping cars
461	Dining cars
	Cf. TF668.A1+, Service
463	Baggage cars
467	Mail cars

    Freight cars

470.A1	Periodicals, societies, congresses, etc
470.A3-Z	General works
475	Stock cars
477	Refrigerator cars
479	Coal and ore cars
481	Tank cars
485	Cabooses, tool cars, etc.
490	Derrick cars and wrecking cars

    Motorcars

494	General works
495	Stream motorcars
497	Gasoline motorcars
498	Diesel motorcars
499	Gas-turbine motorcars

Railway operation and management
  For business administration, see HE1621+
  Periodicals and societies. By language of publication
    For engineering and construction periodicals, see
      TF1+

501	English
502	French
503	German
504	Other languages (not A-Z)
505	General works
506	Cold weather operation
507	General special

  Organization, etc., of staff and force

510	General works
512	General special
	For wage tables, see HD4966.R1+
515	Classification of correspondence, maps, records, etc.
518	Education and training of employees

  Service rules and regulations
    For regulations of particular branches of the
      service, see TF530+

520	General works

	Railway operation and management
	Service rules and regulations -- Continued
522	Special roads
	Maintenance and repair of permanent way
530	General works
	Roadmasters' and trackmasters' regulations
535	General works
536	Special roads
537	Inspection. Testing
538	Roadmasters' and trackmasters' manuals, etc.
538.5	Track maintenance equipment
539	Damage by natural disasters and its control
541	Protection against sand. Removal of sand
542	Protection against snow. Removal of snow and ice
544	Removal of wrecks
546	Removal of weeds. Weed-burners, etc.
548	Ditches
	Trains
	Including the movement of trains and cars
550	General works
552	Train resistance
	Cf. TF962, Car resistance
	Train speed
553	General works
554	Tables
555	Trainload. Ton-miles and coal computations
556	Train running
	Trainmen's manuals, etc.
557	General works
(558)	Wage tables
	see HD4966.R45 +
559	Train rules
561	Right-of-way
563	Train dispatching
565	Time schedules, etc., for making timetables
	For timetables themselves, see HE1805
	Special kinds of trains
	For named trains and trains of special roads, see TF21 +
	Passenger
570	General works
573	Fast express
	Freight
580	General works
582	Piggyback trains
583	Unit trains
	Circus trains, see GV1822
585	Other special kinds
	Terminal and yard management
590	General works
592	Switching of cars. Shunting
593	Making up trains
595	Roundhouse management

Railway operation and management
  Trains -- Continued
    Cars (Utilization and care)
        Cf. HE1821+, Railway economics
        Cf. TF371+, Car building
600   General works
        Car interchange systems. Car service associations
605   Periodicals, societies, etc.
606   General works
610   Safety measures, signals, etc.
        For airbrakes, etc.,, see TF420+
    Signaling
        Including telegraphic equipment
615   General works
617   General special
620   Tests of vision, color blindness, etc.
625   Hand signals, etc.
        Telegraph and telephone system. Radio and other
          electronic systems
            Cf. TK5569.T7, Train telegraph
627   General works
628   Special systems
                Including Bopp's
630   Block systems
635   Interlocking systems
638   Automatic train control
639   Other systems
            Including coded centralized traffic control
640   Catalogs of signaling appliances
    Railroad accidents, see HE1779+
    Traffic operations
650   General works
652   Station management
653   Passenger traffic
            Cf. HE2561+, Economic aspects
654   Passenger tickets
656   Baggage
659   Express
        Freight
662   General works
(663)   Classification
                see HE2123, HE2311, etc.
664   Rate tables, etc.
666   Prorating and adjustment tables, etc.
667   Refrigerator service
        Dining car service
668.A1   Periodicals, societies, etc.
668.A2-Z   General works
    Local and light railways
        For special places, see TF21+
670   General works
        General special
673   General works

	Local and light railways
	General special -- Continued
675	Narrow gauge railways
	For special places, see TF21+
677	Industrial railways
678	Logging railways
	For special places, see TF21+
	Mountain railways
680	General works
682	Cable
	Cf. TF835, Street railways
684	Rack
686	Gravity
688.A-Z	Special railways. By place, A-Z
692	Atmospheric railways
693	Suspended railways
	Cf. TJ1385+, Cableways, telpherage
694	Single-rail railways
695	Miscellaneous and curious railways
	Municipal and street railways. Interurban railways
701	Periodicals, societies, etc.
703	Directories
	Exhibitions. Museums
704.A1	General works
704.A2-Z	By region or country, A-Z
	Apply table at TF6.A2-Z
705	General works
707	General special
	Rapid transit question
	Cf. HE5351+, Interurban electric railways (Economic aspects)
710	General works
	Special places, see TF721+
	Rolling stock, track, and equipment of street car systems, see TF863+
721-827	Country subdivisions (Table T1)
	Add country number in table to TF700
	For special freight subways, see TF851.A+
	For special subways, see TF847.A+
830	Horse railways
835	Cable railways
	Cf. TF682, Mountain railways
838	Compressed air railways
	Elevated railways
840	General works
841.A-Z	Special places, A-Z
	Underground railways. Subways
845	General works
847.A-Z	Special places, A-Z
	Freight subways
850	General works
851.A-Z	Special places, A-Z

	Electric railways
	For special places, see TF1021+
	Periodicals and societies, see TF701
855	General works
856	Juvenile works
857	General special
	Electrification of steam railroads
858.A1	Periodicals. Societies. Serials
858.A2	Congresses
858.A4	General works
858.A5-Z	Special countries, A-Z
859.A-Z4	Special cities (Terminals, etc.), A-Z
859.Z5A-Z	Special railroads, A-Z
	Construction
863	Power production and distribution
	Cf. TK1191+, Electric powerplants
865	Roadbed
	Track
870	General works
872	Rails
873	Rail bonds, etc.
875	General special
	Power transmission systems
880	General works
885	Trolley (overhead wiring)
890	Third-rail
895	Underground conduits
900	Other systems
912	Losses in transmission. Stray currents
	Cars. Street cars. Interurban cars
920	General works
925	Car wiring and equipment
930	Controllers
935	Railway motors
940	Car lighting, headlights, etc.
945	Car heating
947	Safety devices
	Including car fenders
949	Details of car construction
949.A9	Axles
949.B7	Brakes
949.G4	Gear wheels
949.W5	Wheels
	Supplies
950	General works
951	Directories
952	Catalogs
	Operation and management
960	General works
962	General special
	Including cost of operation, car resistance
	Cf. TF552, Train resistance

	Electric railways
	Operation and management -- Continued
965	Motormen's manuals
	For airbrake instructions, see TF420+
	Service rules and regulations
967	General works
968	Special companies
970	Freight service
975	Electric locomotives
	Cf. TN337, Electric mine locomotives
980	Electro-diesel locomotives
1021-1127	Electric railways. Special countries (Table T1)
	Class here technical descriptions of special systems
	Add country number in tables to TF1000
	High speed ground transportation
1300	Periodicals, societies, serials, etc.
1305	Congresses
1315	History
1321-1427	Special countries (Table T1)
	Add country number in tables to TF1300
	Biography
1439	Collective
1440.A-Z	Individual, A-Z
1450	General works
1455	Juvenile works
1460	General special
	Construction (General)
1470	General works
1480	Power supply
1490	Guideways
	Operation and management (General)
1500	General works
1510	Signaling
1520	Communications
	Special systems
1540	Improved passenger train (IPT)
	Tracked levitated vehicle (TLV)
1560	General works
1580	Tracked air cushion vehicle (TACV)
1600	Magnetic levitation vehicle (MAGLVE)
1620	Tube vehicle system (TVS)

	Bridge engineering
	Periodicals and societies. By language of publication
1	English
2	French
3	German
4	Other languages (not A-Z)
5	Congresses
	Exhibitions. Museums
6.A1	General works
6.A2-Z	By region or country, A-Z
	Under each country:
	.x General works
	.x2A-Z Special. By city, A-Z
7	Collections
9	Dictionaries and encyclopedias
12	Directories
	History
15	General works
16	Ancient
17	Medieval
18	Modern
19	Nineteenth century
20	Twentieth century
21-127	Country divisions (Table T1)
	Class here special bridges
	e.g.
	Add country number in table to TG0
	United States
23	General works
24.A-W	States, A-W
25.A-Z	Special places and special bridges, A-Z
	e.g.
25.N5A2	New York. Report of Commissioner of Bridges
25.N53	New York. Brooklyn Bridge (Suspension)
25.N57	Niagara Falls. Suspension Bridge
25.N58	Niagara Falls. Cantilever Bridge
25.O43	Old Saybrook (Connecticut). New Baldwin Bridge
25.S15	St. Louis Bridge (Steel arch)
25.W31	Washington, D. C. Aqueduct Bridge
	Canada
26	General works
27.A-Z	Special places and special bridges, A-Z
	e.g.
27.M82	Montreal. Victoria Bridge (Tubular)
	Great Britain
64.A-Z	Special places and special bridges, A-Z
	e.g.
64.B86	Britannia Bridge, Menai Strait (Tubular)
(64.F7)	Forth Bridge
	see TG64.S68
64.L84	London. Tower Bridge
64.M65	Monmouth (Wales). Monnow Bridge
64.S68	South Queensferry (Scotland). Forth Bridge

	Country divisions -- Continued
	France
72.A-Z	Special places and special bridges, A-Z
	e.g.
72.P23	Paris. Alexander III Bridge
130.A-Z	Special companies (History, description, etc.), A-Z
	Biography
139	Collective
140.A-Z	Individual, A-Z
	General works
144	Early to 1800
145	1800-
147	Elementary textbooks
147.5	Popular works
148	Juvenile works
149	Pictorial works
151	Pocketbooks, tables, etc.
153	General special
155	Addresses, essays, lectures
157	Catalogs of bridge building companies
160	Atlases, plans, etc.
170	Study and teaching
(215-255)	Bridge legislation and laws
	see class K
	Structural analysis as applied to bridges
	Including loads, stresses, and strains
260	General works
265	Structural dynamics. Vibration
267	Tables, calculations, etc.
270	Graphic statics in bridge engineering
	Bridge design and drafting
	Cf. TG160, Plans
300	General works
301	Pin proportioning
303	Wind pressure
304	Snow and ice loads
305	Bridge testing
307	Models of bridges
310	Bridge specifications
313	Bridge estimates. Quantities and costs
315	Bridge erection, superintendence, maintenance and repair
320	Bridge foundations
325	Abutments and retaining walls for bridges
325.6	Floors
326	Bridge details
	Including bearings, etc.
	Special types of bridges
	Arched bridges
327	General works
330	Masonry bridges
	Concrete bridges
335	General works
340	Reinforced concrete bridges

Special types of bridges -- Continued
  Beam and girder bridges
    Including the use of beams and girders in bridges
350   General works
355   Continuous girders
      Cf. TG413+, Continuous girder bridges
360   Plate girders
362   Box girders
    Trestles
365   Wood
367   Concrete and stone
370   Iron
    Trussed bridges
375   Wood
380   Iron and steel
385   Cantilever bridges
390   Tubular bridges
400   Suspension bridges
405   Cable-stayed bridges
410   Metal arches and metal arch bridges
    Continuous girder bridges
413   General works
414   Reinforced concrete bridges
416   Metal bridges
418   Prefabricated bridges
      Cf. UG335, Military bridges
    Ice crossings, ice bridges, see TE247
  Bridges for special uses
420   Movable bridges. Drawbridges
425   Highway bridges
428   Footbridges
430   Park and ornamental bridges
435   Ferry bridges
445   Railway bridges
      Cf. TF282, Culverts, etc.
      For special places, see TG21+
450   Pontoon bridges
      Cf. UG335, Military bridges
    Military bridges, see UG335
470   Bridge accidents

TG

	Building construction
	Cf. TA630+, Structural engineering
	Periodicals and societies. By language of publication
1	English
2	French
3	German
4	Other languages (not A-Z)
5	Congresses
	Exhibitions. Museums
6.A1	General works
6.A2-Z	By region or country, A-Z
	Under each country:
	.x General works
	.x2A-Z Special. By city, A-Z
7	Collected works (nonserial)
9	Dictionaries and encyclopedias
11	Builders' and contractors' bulletins
	Including prices, permits, etc.
	Directories of building supply companies, builders, and contractors
12	General works
	United States
12.5	General works
13.A-Z	By region or state, A-Z
13.2.A-Z	Other regions or countries, A-Z
	History and description
15	General works
16	Ancient
	Including primitive construction
17	Medieval
18	Modern to 1800
19	1801-
21-127	Country divisions (Table T1)
	Add country number in table to TH0
	Biography
139	Collective
140.A-Z	Individual, A-Z
	General works
144	Early to 1850
145	1850-
146	Elementary works
148	Popular works
149	Juvenile works
151	Pocketbooks, tables, etc.
	Cf. TA151, Engineering pocketbooks
	Cf. TA685, Iron and steel construction
	Cf. TH434+, Estimates, quantities and costs
153	General special
	Including dangerous structures, safety of exit, moving of structures, cold weather conditions
155	Addresses, essays, lectures
159	Building as a profession
	Study and teaching

Study and teaching -- Continued
165   General works
166   Examinations, questions, etc.
                Special schools
                  United States
210   General works
211   Correspondence schools
213.A-Z   Other countries. By country and city, A-Z
                Research
213.5   General works
213.7.A-Z   By region or country, A-Z
                Communication of building information
215   General works
216   Information services
(219-255)   Building laws, legislation, etc.
                  see class K
257   Patents
350   Engineering of the subdivision
                  Cf. TD160 +, Planning and laying out of cities
                The building site
                  Cf. TK4399.B8, Electric lighting
                  Cf. NA2540.5, Site planning (Architecture)
375   General works
380   Landscape construction by builders
383   Prevention of soil erosion
385   Building layout
420   Building standards
425   Specifications (General)
                For specifications for special types of building, see
                  TH4311 +
431   Drawings
                Including how to read plans
                Cf. T379, Blueprint reading
                Cf. TH2031, General details
(432)   Bookkeeping, etc. for the builder
                see HF5686.B7
              Estimates. Measurements. Quantities and cost
                General works
434   Early to 1890
435   1890-
437   General special
                  Including data processing
              Management of the construction site. Superintendence of
                building construction
438   General works
438.2   Quality control
438.4   Scheduling
439   Building inspection
441   Building failures, errors, defects, etc.
                Cf. TH9025 +, Protection of buildings
443   Building accidents and their prevention
              Maintenance and repair, see TH3301 +
447   Wrecking
449   Salvaging

TH

451.A-Z   Building companies, A-Z
                       Including circulars, prospectuses, etc.
453   Building performance
455   Catalogs of building supplies (General)
                       Cf. TH1655, Metalwork
                       Cf. TH2055, Building fittings
                   Architectural engineering. Structural engineering of
                       buildings
                       Cf. TH1111, Wooden buildings
845   Treatises
846   Elementary textbooks
851   Pocketbooks, tables, etc.
860   Modular coordination
                       Cf. NA2685+, Drafting
                       Cf. NA2750+, Design
891   Wind pressure
893   Rain loads
895   Snow loads
                   Insulation, see TH1715+
                   Architectural acoustics, see NA2800
                       Soundproof construction, see TH1725
                   Construction equipment in building
                       Including machinery used in building construction
                       Cf. TJ793.2, Internal combustion engines for
                           construction equipment
900   General works
915   Tools and implements (General)
                       Cf. TH5618, Carpenters' tools
                       Cf. TH6299, Plumbers' tools
                   Systems of building construction
                       Cf. TA401+, Building materials
1000   Industrialized building
                       Cf. TH1098, Prefabricated and portable
                           buildings
                   Fire-resistive or fireproof building construction
                       Cf. TH9057+, Lightning rods
                       Cf. TH9111+, Fire prevention
                       Cf. TP265+, Chemistry of fire and fire
                           prevention
1061   Periodicals, societies, etc.
1065   General works
1069   General details
                       Including fire doors and shutters, wire glass
                           windows, etc.
                       For fire escapes, see TH2274
                   Systems of fireproofing and special materials
                       Including catalogs
1073   Wood and other organic material
                       Including impregnated wood, fire-retardant
                           coatings
1074   Fire resistant plastics
1074.5   Fire resistant polymers
1075   Asbestos

Systems of building construction
    Fire-resistive or fireproof building construction
        Systems of fireproofing
            and special materials -- Continued
            Earthenware, brick, tile, terra-cotta
                Including combinations with steel, etc.
1077   General and solid forms
1083   Hollow earthenware
1087   Cement and concrete
                    Including reinforced concrete
                    Cf. TH1461+, Concrete building construction
1088   Reinforcing materials
1088.5   Smoke control systems
1089   Tile-concrete combination systems
            Tests of fire-resistant construction (General).
                Fire testing
                    Including artificial tests
                    Cf. TH9446.3+, Fire-testing of materials
                    For tests of special systems, see TH1099
1091   General works
1092   Tests of building materials
1093   Tests in fires
                        General conflagrations, not artificial tests
        Earth movements and building. Subsidences, etc.
1094   General works
1095   Earthquakes and building
                    Cf. TA654.6, Earthquake engineering
                    Cf. TA658.44, Earthquake resistant design
1095.5   Construction on contaminated sites
1096   Stormproof construction
1097   Bombproof construction. Bombproof shelters. Fallout
                shelters
                    Cf. TH7392.A8, Heating and ventilation of
                        atomic bomb shelters
            Waterproof construction, see TH9031+
1098   Prefabricated and portable buildings
                Cf. NA8480, Architecture
1099   Air-supported structures
1100   Lightweight construction
1101   Wood building construction
                Cf. TA666+, Wooden construction (General)
                For carpentry and joinery, see TH5601+
                For centering and centers, see TH5591
                For floor framing, see TH2311
                For roof framing, see TH2393
                For scaffolding, see TH5281
1111   Architectural engineering of wooden buildings
            Architectural woodwork
                Cf. TH8581+, Decorative woodwork
1151   General works
1155   Catalogs

	Systems of building construction -- Continued
	Masonry building construction
	Cf. TA670+, Masonry construction (General)
	Cf. TH5311+, Practical masonry
1201	Stone building construction
	For artificial stone building construction, see TH1451
	For stone construction (General), see TA676
	For stonemasonry and stonecutting, see TH5401+
1301	Brick building construction
	For brick construction (General), see TA679
	For bricklaying, see TH5501+
(1375)	Terra-cotta and hollow tile building construction see TH1077-TH1083
1421	Pisé, earth-wall or pressed-earth building construction
1431	Ice and snow building construction
1451	Artificial stone building construction
	Concrete building construction. Cement and stucco
	For concrete construction (General), see TA680+
1461	General works
1465	Specifications
1491	Concrete-block building construction
1498	Precast concrete construction
1501	Reinforced concrete construction
	For reinforced concrete construction (General), see TA682.92+
	For reinforced concrete fireproof building construction, see TH1087
1550	Staff building construction. Papier mâché, etc.
1555	Fiber building boards
	Cf. TH1715+, Insulation
1560	Glass construction
	Cf. TA450, Glass (Structural material)
	Cf. TH8251+, Glazing
	Iron and steel building construction
	Cf. TH4818.S73, Steel house construction
	For iron and steel construction (General), see TA684+
	General works
1610	Before 1890
1611	1890-
1615	Juvenile works
1619	Estimates
1621	Pocketbooks, tables, etc.
1625	Catalogs of buildings
	Forms of construction
1635	Space frame structures
	Architectural metalwork. Sheet metal, castings, etc.
	For gratings, see TH2273
1651	General works
1655	Catalogs (General)
	Special materials

Systems of building construction
 Architectural metalwork.
  Sheet metal, castings, etc.
  Special materials -- Continued
1675   Metal sheathing. Metal lathing
          Reinforcing materials in fireproof building
           construction, see TH1088
 Insulation and insulating materials
  Including thermal properties of walls
  Cf. TJ163.26+, Energy conservation
  Cf. TP490+, Refrigeration
1715.A1   Periodicals, societies, etc.
1715.A2-Z General works
1718   Cellulose insulation
1719   Sealing. Airtight construction
1720   Sheathing papers
1725   Soundproof construction. Noise in buildings
          Cf. NA2800, Architectural acoustics
1727   Acoustical materials
Details in building design and construction
2025   General works
2031   Structural drawings
          Cf. TH431, Drawings (General)
2055   Catalogs of building fittings (General)
          Cf. TH1155, Architectural woodwork
          Cf. TH1655, Architectural ironwork
          Cf. TH6010+, Building fittings and their
           installation
2060   Joints in buildings
2101   Foundations
          Including works from the engineering standpoint
          Cf. TH2221, Foundation walls
          Cf. TH5201, Practical construction
2140   Piers
 Arches and vaults
2150   General works
2160   Vaults
 Domes
          Cf. TH2416+, Shell roofs
2170   General works
2170.5   Concrete domes
2170.7   Masonry
2180   Towers
 Walls
          Cf. TH5311+, Masonry
2201   General works
2221   Foundation walls
 Walls above surface
2231   General works
 Exterior walls
2235   General works
2238   Curtain walls. Cladding
2238.5   Siding

	Details in building design and construction
	Walls
	Walls above surface
	Exterior walls -- Continued
2238.7	Exterior insulation and finish systems
2239	Interior walls
	Special materials
2243	Brick walls
2244	Clapboard walls
2245	Concrete walls
2247	Sheet metal walls
	Cf. TH1651+, Architectural metalwork
2249	Stone walls
	Wall details
2251	General works
2251.2	Balconies
2251.5	Veneers
	Other special accessories
	Columns. Capitals
2252	General works
2253	Catalogs
2255	Abutments
	Building-integrated photovoltaic systems, see TK1087
2258	Fixed ladders
2259	Ramps
	Window and door openings and their fittings
	Including lintels, plate-bonds, sills, reveals, caps, trimmings
2261	General works
2264	Window openings
2265	Bay and bow windows
	Windows and doors and their fittings
	Cf. TH1069, Fire doors and shutters
	Cf. TH1155, Woodwork catalogs
	Cf. TH8251+, Glazing
	Cf. TH9720+, Burglar proof construction
2270	General works
2271	Catalogs of door and window fittings
2272	Sashes. Frames
2273	Gratings. Window guards
2274	Fire escapes and fittings
2275	Windows
	For skylights, see TH2486+
2276	Shutters, blinds, screens, and other window fittings
	Doors. Sliding and folding doors. Screen doors. Fire doors
2278	General works
2279	Door fittings. Locks, knobs, etc.
	Chimneys and flues
	Cf. TH4591, Chimneys for powerplants
	Cf. TJ330+, Boiler plant engineering
2281	General works

Details in building design and construction
Chimneys and flues -- Continued
2284   Smoky chimneys and their remedy
     Cf. TD884, Smoke prevention
2285   Soot removal
    Fireplaces, see TH7421+
2288   Mantelpieces
     Cf. TH1151+, Architectural woodwork
   Framing (House framing, etc.)
    Cf. TH1101, Wood building construction
    Cf. TH1610+, Iron and steel building
      construction
2301   General works
2311   Floor framing
    Cf. TH2521+, Floors and flooring
   Roof framing, roofs and roofing
    Cf. TH5619, Steel square and its uses
2391   General works
2392   Roof trusses
2393   Roof framing. Rafters, etc.
2397   Special tools and appliances
     Including rafter gages
2398   Rafter tables, etc.
   Roofs
2401   General works
2405   Mansard roofs
2407   Saddle roofs
2409   Flat roofs
    Shell roofs
2416.A1   Periodicals, societies, etc.
2416.A3-Z   General works
2417   Suspension roofs
    Roofs for special parts of the building
2421   General works
2423   Bay window roofs
2425   Porch and veranda roofs
   Roofing
2430   Periodicals, societies, congresses, etc.
2431   General works
2433   Catalogs of roofing (General)
2435   Thatch roofing
2438   Board roofing
2441   Shingle roofing
    Stone roofing
2444   General works
2445   Slate roofing
2446   Concrete roofing
2447   Plastic roofing
2448   Tile roofing
2449   Textile roofing
    Composition roofing
2450   General works

	Details in building design and construction
	Roof framing, roofs and roofing
	Roofing
	Composition roofing -- Continued
2451	General special
	Including tar, felt, gravel, slag, etc.
2452	Single-ply roofing
	Metal roofing
	Cf. TH1651+, Architectural woodwork
	Cf. TS600+, Roofing catalogs
2454	General works
2455	Tin roofing. Tin shingling
2457	Iron and steel roofing
2458	Lead and copper roofing
2459	Aluminum roofing
	Roof details
	Cf. TH1651+, Architectural woodwork
	Cf. TH2433, Roofing catalogs
2481	General works
	Cornices and moldings
	Cf. TH1151+, Architectural woodwork
	Cf. TH2553, Interior cornices and moldings
2482	General works
2483	Catalogs
	Skylights and ventilators
2486	General works
2487	Skylights
(2489)	Ventilators
	see TH7683.V4
2491	Hatchways. Scuttles
2493	Gutters, eave troughs, down spouts, and conductors
2495	Finials and bannerets. Vanes
	Floors and flooring
	Cf. TH2311, Floor framing
	Cf. TH8541+, Tile
	For floors and flooring in special types of
	buildings, see the type of building, e.g.
	TH4534, Packinghouses
2521	General works
	Flooring
	For carpets, rugs, etc., see TS1772+
2525	General works
2528	Maintenance and care
2529.A-Z	Special types. By material, A-Z
2529.C6	Concrete (Nonstructural)
	Linoleum, see TS1779.L5
2529.M4	Metal
2529.P5	Plastic
	Including asphalt and vinyl
2529.S7	Stone
	Tile (Ceramic), see TH8541+
2529.W6	Wood. Parquetry

	Details in building
	design and construction -- Continued
	Ceilings and centerpieces
	Cf. NA2950, Architecture
	Cf. TH8120+, Plastering
2531	General works
2533.A-Z	Special types, A-Z
2533.S88	Suspended
2533.W66	Wooden
	Partitions
2541	General works
2544	Shoji screens
2547	Wainscots
2553	Moldings and cornices (Interior)
	Cf. TH1155, Woodwork catalogs
	Cf. TH2482+, Exterior cornices
	Cf. TH8581+, Decorative woodwork
2555	Shelving
	For mantelpieces, see TH2288
3000.A-Z	Special rooms, A-Z
3000.A74	Areaways
3000.A86	Attics
3000.B36	Basements
3000.B38	Bathrooms
3000.C55	Closets
3000.C73	Crawl spaces
3000.L36	Lofts
3000.R43	Recreation rooms
3000.S85	Sunspaces
	Maintenance and repair
	Cf. TH4817+, Dwellings
	Cf. TH6013, Maintenance of equipment
	Cf. TX323, Care of the house (Home economics)
3301	General works
3311	General special
	Maintenance
3351	General works
3361	General special
	Repair. Rebuilding. Remodeling
3401	General works
3411	General special
	Buildings: Construction with reference to use
	Including specifications and construction of
	individual or named buildings
	Public buildings
	Cf. NA4170+, Architecture
4021	General works
(4161)	Monuments, memorial arches
	see NA9320-NA9425
(4171)	Mausoleums, etc.
	see NA6120-NA6199
4221	Churches
	Cf. NA4790+, Architecture

TH

	Buildings: Construction with reference to use
	Public buildings -- Continued
4224	Pagodas
	Other public buildings, see TH4755+
	Commercial buildings. Office buildings
	Cf. NA6210+, Architecture
4311	General works
4315	Estimates. Measurements. Quantities and costs
(4411)	Transportation buildings
	see NA6300-NA6370, TA1225
(4421)	Railway stations
	see NA6310-NA6317; TF300
(4431)	Dock buildings
	see TC355
(4441)	Ferry houses
	see NA6330
	Storage buildings
4451	Warehouses
	Cf. NA6340+, Architecture
4461	Grain elevators
	Cf. NA6350, Architecture
	Cf. TH4498, Bins (General)
	Cf. TJ1415+, Grain-handling machinery
4471	Coal-handling plants
	Cf. TH4498, Bins (General)
	Cf. TJ1405, Coal-handling machinery
4481	Icehouses (Commercial)
	Cf. NA6360, Architecture
4485	Lumberyards, sheds, etc.
4498	Bins (General)
	Cf. TH4461, Grain elevators
	Cf. TH4471, Coal-handling plants
4499	Other storage buildings
	Cf. NA6290+, Architecture
	Factories and mills. Industrial plants
	Cf. NA6396+, Architecture
	Cf. TN675.5+, Metallurgical plants and furnaces
	Cf. TS186, Factory buildings
4511.A1	Periodicals, societies, etc.
4511.A2-Z	General works
4516	General drawings of factory construction
4518	Underground factories
4521	Textile mills
4522	Clothing factories
4524	Chemical plants
4526	Food processing plants
4531	Breweries
4532	Distilleries
4533	Electronics plants
4534	Packinghouses
4536	Paper and pulp mills
4536.5	Printing plants
4537	Rolling mills

	Buildings: Construction with reference to use
	Factories and mills. Industrial plants -- Continued
4538	Water treatment plants
4541	Other special factories and mills
4561	Mine buildings and other structures
4571	Refineries
	Power plants
4581	General works
4591	Chimneys. Smokestacks
	Cf. TD884, Smoke prevention
	Cf. TH2281+, Chimneys (General)
	Cf. TJ330+, Boiler plant engineering
	Educational buildings
(4621)	Schools
	see LB3205-LB3227, NA6600-NA6605
(4631)	Libraries
	see Z679
(4641)	Art museums and galleries
	see N450-N4995
(4651)	Exhibition buildings
	see NA6750, T391-T995
4652	Research buildings. Laboratories
	Cf. NA6751, Architecture
4655	Radio stations
4656	Television stations
(4661)	Hospitals
	see RA960-RA993
	For psychiatric hospitals, see RC438.92+
4711	Recreation buildings. Park buildings
	Cf. NA6800+, Architecture
	Other public buildings
4755	Restaurants
	Cf. NA7855+, Architecture
4758	Embassy buildings
4761	Baths
	Cf. NA7010, Architecture
	Cf. RA605+, Public health
4763	Swimming pools
(4765)	Public comfort stations
	see RA607
4800	Clubhouses
	Cf. NA7910+, Architecture
	Houses. Dwellings
	Cf. NA7100+, Architecture
4805	Periodicals, societies, congresses, etc.
	History and description
4808	General works
4809.A-Z	By region or country, A-Z
4811	General works
4811.5	Juvenile works
4812	General special
4813	Handbooks, manuals, etc.
4814	Research

	Buildings: Construction with reference to use
	Houses. Dwellings -- Continued
4815	Amateur construction manuals
4815.4	House construction contracting
	Including hiring a contractor
4815.5	Standards. Specifications
4815.8	Estimates. Measurements. Quantities and costs
	Remodeling
4816	General works
4816.15	Access for the handicapped
4816.2	Additions
4816.3.A-Z	Special rooms, A-Z
4816.3.A77	Attics
4816.3.B35	Basements
4816.3.B37	Bathrooms
4816.3.B43	Bedrooms
4816.3.C45	Children's rooms
4816.3.K58	Kitchens
	Office decoration, see NK2195.O4
4816.3.O34	Offices
	Maintenance and repair
4817	General works
4817.3	Amateurs' manuals
4817.5	State of repair. House buyers' guides
	Cf. HD1379, Popular guides in real estate
	business
4818.A-Z	Construction in special materials, A-Z
4818.A3	Adobe. Earth
4818.B3	Bamboo
4818.B7	Brick
4818.C6	Concrete blocks
	Earth, see TH4818.A3
4818.M37	Masonry
4818.P3	Paperboard
4818.P53	Plaster
4818.P7	Precast concrete
4818.R4	Reinforced concrete
4818.S55	Sod
4818.S6	Soil cement
4818.S73	Steel
4818.S75	Stone
4818.S77	Straw
4818.T57	Tires
4818.W6	Wood
4819.A-Z	Special methods of construction, A-Z
4819.E27	Earth sheltered houses
4819.M6	Mobile homes
	Cf. TL297+, Trailers
	Cf. TX1100+, Mobile home living
4819.P7	Prefabricated
4819.S5	Slab-on-ground
	Special types of houses
	Cf. TH4920, Farmhouses

	Buildings: Construction with reference to use
	Houses. Dwellings
	Special types of houses -- Continued
4820	Apartment houses
4825	Terrace houses
4835	Summer homes
4840	Log cabins
4850	Country homes
4870	Yurts
4880	Fishing lodges
4885	Tree houses
4890	Other shelters (not A-Z)
	Farm buildings
	Cf. NA8200+, Architecture
	Cf. S770+, Agriculture
4911	General works
4916	Handbooks, tables, etc.
4920	Farmhouses
	Cf. NA8208+, Architecture
4930	Barns. Poultry houses
4935	Silos
4940	Machine-tractor stations
	Minor buildings. Fences, gates, etc.
4955	General works
4960	Garages. Carports
	Cf. NA8348, Architecture
	Garden structures
	Including building of structural elements for landscape construction
4961	General works
4962	Garden toolsheds
4963	Gazebos
4965	Fences, gates, etc.
4967	Playhouses, Children's
	Cf. TH4885, Tree houses
4970	Terraces, patios, decks, garden walks, etc.
	Cf. NA8375, Architecture
4975	Privies. Outhouses
	Cf. TD775, Sewage disposal
4977	Fountains
	Cf. NA9400+, Architecture
	Construction by phase of the work (Building trades)
	For works from the engineering standpoint, see TH1101-TH2101
5011	General works
5101	Earthwork and excavation in building
	Including operations, tools, etc.
5201	Foundation work in building
	Cf. TA775+, Foundations (General engineering)
	Temporary structures in building
5280	General works

127

Construction by phase of the work (Building trades)
Temporary structures in building -- Continued
5281 · · · · · · Scaffolding in building. Shoring. Staging
Cf. TA682.44, Formwork for concrete
construction
Cf. TH5591, Centering
Masonry in building
Class here practical methods, operations, tools,
etc.
Cf. TA425+, Masonry materials
Cf. TA670+, Masonry construction (General)
Cf. TH1199+, Masonry building construction
(Engineering)
5311 · · · · · · Treatises
5313 · · · · · · Elementary manuals
5317 · · · · · · Addresses, essays, lectures
5321 · · · · · · General special
5330 · · · · · · Estimates, quantities and cost measurements, etc.
5371 · · · · · · Pointing and stucco
Stonemasonry and stonecutting
For stone building construction, see TH1201
For walls, design, etc., see TH2201+
5401 · · · · · · General works
5411 · · · · · · Elementary manuals
5421 · · · · · · General special
5440 · · · · · · Tools for stonemasons and stonecutters
Bricklaying in building
For brick building construction, see TH1301
For walls, design, etc., see TH2201+
5501 · · · · · · General works
5511 · · · · · · Elementary manuals
5520 · · · · · · Cleaning of masonry, stone, brick, etc.
(5551) · · · · Cement and concrete work
see TA680-TA683.9
5591 · · · · · · Centering of arches
For scaffolding, see TH5281
Carpentry and joinery
Cf. TH1101, Wood building construction
Cf. TS840+, Woodworking
5601 · · · · · · Periodicals
General works
5603 · · · · · · Early to 1800
1800-
5604 · · · · · · General works
5605 · · · · · · Graphic treatises
Plates or drawings, with text subordinate
5606 · · · · · · Beginners' manuals. Elements
5607 · · · · · · Popular works. Home carpentry
5608 · · · · · · Pocketbooks and tables. Handbooks and
compilations of rules
5608.5 · · · · Examinations, questions, etc.
5608.7 · · · · General special
5608.8 · · · · Vocational guidance

Construction by phase of the work (Building trades)
　　Carpentry and joinery -- Continued
5609　　　　　Specifications
5611　　　　　Drawing and drawings for carpentry and joiner
　　　　　　Mathematics
5612　　　　　　General works
5613　　　　　　Slide-rule calculations in carpentry and joinery
　　　　　　Estimates, quantities and cost, measurements, etc.
5614　　　　　　Before 1850
5615　　　　　　1850-
5618　　　　　Tools for carpenters and joiners
　　　　　　　Including catalogs
5619　　　　　The steel square and its uses
　　　　　　Finish carpentry
5640　　　　　　General works
　　　　　　Joinery
5662　　　　　　General works
5663　　　　　　Elementary manuals
　　　　　　Stairbuilding
　　　　　　　Including iron, wood, and stone
5667　　　　　　General works
　　　　　　Stair and handrail joinery. Wooden
　　　　　　　stairbuilding
5670　　　　　　General works
　　　　　　Stair joinery
5671　　　　　　　General works
5673　　　　　　　Tables of treads and risers
　　　　　　Handrail joinery. Stair railings
5675　　　　　　　General works
5677　　　　　　　Tools and appliances for handrail joinery
5680　　　　　　Catalogs
5691　　　　　Mitering
　　　　　　　For exterior moldings, see TH2482 +
　　　　　　　For interior moldings, see TH2553
5695　　　　　Trim carpentry
　　　　　Metalworking
　　　　　　Cf. TH1651 +, Architectural metalwork
5701　　　　　General works
　　　　　　Steel-girder riveting, etc , see TA891
　　　Building fittings and their installation
　　　　　Including mechanical equipment
　　　　　Cf. TH2055, Catalogs of building fittings
　　　　　Cf. TK4001 +, Applications of electric power
6010　　　General works
6012　　　Building control systems
　　　　　　Cf. TH7466.5, Heating control
　　　　　　Cf. TH7687.7, Air conditioning systems and
　　　　　　　details
6013　　　Maintenance and repair

	Environmental engineering of buildings. Sanitary engineering of buildings
	Class here works on general and household plumbing, heating, lighting, air conditioning, soundproofing, etc., treated collectively
	Class special aspects with the subject, e. g. TH7201-TH7641, Heating; TH1725, Soundproofing
6014	Periodicals, societies, congresses, etc.
6014.5	Dictionaries and encyclopedias
6015	Directories
6021	General works
6024	Handbooks, manuals, etc.
6025	General special
6028	Addresses, essays, lectures
6031	Design of systems
6051	Specifications
6053	Building orientation
6057.A-Z	Installations in special classes of buildings. By class, A-Z
6057.A6	Apartment houses. Dwellings
6057.C6	Canneries
	Dwellings, see TH6057.A6
6057.F3	Factories
6057.F35	Farm buildings
6057.I53	Industrial buildings
6057.L3	Laundries, Public
6057.M87	Museum buildings
6057.O4	Office buildings
6057.P8	Public buildings
6057.R4	Restaurants, lunchrooms, etc.
6057.T23	Tall buildings
6057.T3	Theaters
6057.W55	Wineries
6059.A-Z	Installations within special buildings. By name, A-Z
	Sanitary crafts
	General works
6071	Early to 1875
6072	1875-
6073	Textbooks
6081	Study and teaching. Schools
(6085)	Legislation
	see class K
	Plumbing and pipefitting
	Including household plumbing
	Cf. TH6703+, Pipefitting
6101	Periodicals, societies, etc.
6107	Collected works (nonserial)
6109	Dictionaries and encyclopedias
6112	Directories
	History
6115	General works
	Special countries
	United States

	Plumbing and pipefitting
	History
	Special regions or countries
	United States -- Continued
6116	General works
6117.A-W	States, A-W
6118.A-Z	Cities, A-Z
6119.A-Z	Other regions or countries, A-Z
	General works
6121	Early to 1875
6122	1875-
6123	Textbooks
6124	Popular works. Juvenile works
6125	Pocketbooks, tables, etc.
6126	General special
6127	Addresses, essays, lectures
6128	Examinations, questions, etc.
6130	Vocational guidance
	Study and teaching
6131	General works
	By region or country
	Individual institutions are classed by state or country without further subdivision
	United States
6151	General works
6152.A-Z	By region or state, A-Z
6153.A-Z	Other regions or countries, A-Z
(6161-6175)	Laws and regulations
	see class K
	General special
6225	Specifications
6231	Drawing and drawings
	Bookkeeping for plumber and pipefitter, see HF5686.P7
	Estimates. Measurements. Quantities and costs
6234	Early to 1850
6235	1850-
6238	Superintendence
6239	Inspection
6241	Testing
	Cf. TH6617, Testing for leakage
	Plumbing fixtures and fitting supplies
6249	General works
6252	Standards
6255	Catalogs of plumbing and fitting supplies
	Cf. TH6299, Plumbers' tools
	Cf. TH6529, Catalogs of water-supply fixtures
	Cf. TH6589, Catalogs of drainage fixtures
	Cf. TH6729, Catalogs of pipefittings
(6280)	Systems of domestic water supply, drainage, etc.
	see TH6521-TH6675
6288.A-Z	Special installations. By name, A-Z

Plumbing and pipefitting -- Continued
Plumbing work
Cf. TH6681+, Maintenance work
6291 General works
Laying pipes. Joints. Pipefitting
Cf. TH6703+, Pipefitting (General)
6293 General works
6294 Pipe bending
6295 Joint-wiping
6297 Soldering, solder, and fluxes in plumbing
Cf. TH6691, Lead burning
6299 Plumbers' tools and apparatus
Cf. TH6255, Catalogs of plumbing fixtures, etc.
Plastics in plumbing
6325 General works
6330 Plastic tubes and pipes
Cf. TA448, Testing of plastic pipes
Cf. TP1185.P5, Manufacture of plastic pipes
Plumbing of special rooms and areas
Bathrooms. Toilet rooms. Lavatories
For public comfort stations, see TH6515.P9
6485 General works
6486 General special. Specifications, etc.
6487 Systems
Details. Fixtures
6488 General works
6489 Catalogs of bathroom fixtures
6490 Basins
Baths
Cf. TH6518.B3, Public baths
6491 General works
6492 Shower baths. Sprays
6493 Tubs
6494 Foot baths
6495 Sitz baths
6496 Bidets
6497 Soil fixtures
6498 Water closets. Toilets
6499 Urinals
6500 Flush tanks and auxiliary valves, etc.
6501 Hot tubs
Laundry plumbing
For public laundry plumbing, see TH6518.L3
6502 General works
6503 Systems
Details
6505 Washtubs
Kitchen and pantry plumbing
For kitchen and laundry drainage systems, see
TH6661
For kitchen boilers, see TH6563
For range water-heating, see TH6553+
For refrigerator plumbing, see TH6671.R3

	Plumbing and pipefitting
	Plumbing of special rooms and areas
	Kitchen and pantry plumbing -- Continued
6507	General works
6508	Catalogs
6509	Systems
	Details
6511	Sinks
6512	Grease traps
	For traps (General), see TH6631+
6515.A-Z	Plumbing of special buildings, A-Z
6515.A6	Apartment house plumbing
6515.F2	Factory plumbing
6515.F3	Farmhouses
	Hospitals and health facilities, see RA969.33
6515.H8	Hotel plumbing
6515.O3	Office building plumbing
6515.P9	Public comfort station plumbing
6515.S4	Schools, universities, etc.
6515.T35	Tall buildings
	Tenement house plumbing, see TH6515.A6
6518.A-Z	Plumbing for special establishments, A-Z
6518.B2	Bar (saloon) plumbing
6518.B3	Baths, Public
6518.C3	Carriage house plumbing
	Laundries, Domestic (Plumbing), see TH6502+
6518.L3	Laundries, Public
6518.S6	Soda fountain plumbing
	For soda water apparatus, see TP635
	Water supply
	For cold water supply, see TH6541+
	For hot water supply, see TH6551+
	For municipal water supply, see TD201+
	For pumps, see TJ899+
6521	General works
6523	General special. Specifications, etc.
(6525)	Rural domestic water supply
	see TD927
	Details
6527	General works
6528	Valves. Faucets
	For filters, see TD449
6529	Catalogs of water-supply fixtures
	Catalogs of pipefittings, see TH6729
6531	Theory
(6535)	Domestic means of supply
(6538)	Water measurement and meters
	see TD499-TD500
	Cold water supply
6541	General works
	Systems
6542	General works
6544	Flushing systems (Automatic, etc.)

TH

	Plumbing and pipefitting
	Cold water supply -- Continued
6545	Storage systems. Storage tanks
	For fire storage tanks or towers, see TH9332+
(6547)	Details
	see TH6527-TH6529
	Hot water supply. Water heaters
6551	General. Tank systems. Cylinder systems
	Systems of heating
	For systems of supply, see TH6567
6552	General works
	Range water heaters
	For kitchen plumbing (General), see TH6507+
	For range boilers, see TH6563
6553	General works
6554	Types
	Details
6555	Water backs
6556	Water heating coils
6557	Thermostats
	Steam water heaters
6558	General works
6559	Steam coil tanks
6560	Steam condensation heating tanks
6561	Gas water heaters
6561.5	Electric water heaters
6561.7	Solar water heaters
	Cf. TJ809+, Solar energy
	Storage of hot water
6562	General works
6563	Kitchen boilers and supports
6564	Hot water tanks (used with water heaters)
	Explosions and their prevention. Kitchen boiler explosions
6565	General works
6566	Valves and blow-off cocks
	Cf. TJ350+, Steam boilers - Safety appliances
6567	Systems of supply
	For systems of heating, see TH6552+
6568	Connections and circulation piping
6569.A-Z	Special applications of water supply, A-Z
	Cf. TH9332+, Connections for fire extinction
	Cf. TH9365, Connections for fire extinction
6569.D7	Drinking fountains
6569.F7	Fountains
6569.S7	Sprinklers
	House drainage
6571	General works
6581	General special

	Plumbing and pipefitting
	House drainage -- Continued
6589	Catalogs of drainage fixtures, traps, etc.
	For catalogs of closets, basins, etc., see TH6489
	For catalogs of pipefittings, see TH6729
	For catalogs of plumbing and fitting supplies, see
	TH6255
6591	Theory
	Including expansion of drainage system
	Systems
6602	One-pipe systems
6604	Two-pipe systems
6607	Mechanical discharge systems
6609.A-Z	Special systems. By name of patentee or
	manufacturer, A-Z
(6610)	Work
6613	Connections
6615	Roughing in
6617	Testing for leakage
	Testing with compressed air, water, smoke,
	peppermint, etc.
	Details. Fittings
	For catalogs of general drainage fittings, see
	TH6589
6625	General works
6628	Drain piping (General)
	For soil piping, see TH6653
	For vent piping, see TH6668
	For waste piping, see TH6658 +
	Traps and vents. Siphonage
	For drain traps, see TH6647
6631	General works
6633	Special types of traps
	For grease traps, see TH6512
6635	Cleanouts
	For drain cleanout ferrules, see TH6646
(6637)	Cesspools
	see TD775
(6638)	Septic tanks
	see TD778
	Elements of drainage system
6641	House sewer
	Outside of house, connecting house drain with
	main sewer
	House drain
	Horizontal piping in cellar, receiving all house
	drainage
6642	General works
6644	Supports for drains
6646	Cleanout ferrules
	For cleanouts (General), see TH6635
6647	Special drain types
	For traps (General), see TH6631 +

Plumbing and pipefitting
  House drainage
    Elements of drainage system
      House drain -- Continued
        Floor and area drains, see TH6671.C3

6649   Fresh air inlets
        Rain leaders, see TH2493
        Soil stack systems
          Class here draining sewage or sewage and wastes

6651   General works
6652   Soil stack
6653   Soil piping
        Waste stack systems
          Class here draining wastes

6655   General works
6656   Waste stack
          Waste piping

6658   General works
           Special waste systems
            Cf. TH6671.A+, Special drainage
              applications

6661   Kitchen and laundry wastes
              For kitchen plumbing, see TH6507+
              For laundry plumbing, see TH6502+

(6663)   Laving systems and fixtures
              see TH6485, TH6500
            Toilet room plumbing and fixtures, see TH6485+
        Vent stack systems

6665   General works
6666   Vent stack. Roof outlets
6668   Vent piping
           For drain piping (General), see TH6628
         Trap ventilation, see TH6631+

6671.A-Z   Special drainages, A-Z
6671.C3   Cellar or basement drainage
6671.F6   Floor and yard drainage
6671.R3   Refrigerator drainage
6675.A-Z   Special installations. By name, A-Z
        Cf. TH6059.A+, Special sanitary installations
    Maintenance and repair of plumbing

6681   General works
6685   Freezing and thawing of pipes
6691   Lead burning. Autogenous soldering
       For soldering in plumbing, see TH6297
  Pipefitting
     Class here the installation of piping and fixtures
       for heating, lighting, etc.
     For gas fitting, see TH6840
     For pipefitting for steam and hot water heating, see
       TH7467+
     For plumbing, see TH6293+

6703   General works
6706   Textbooks

	Plumbing and pipefitting
	Pipefitting -- Continued
6711	Pocketbooks, tables, rules
6715	General special
6721	Estimates of material and labor
6723	Prices of pipefittings
6729	Catalogs of pipefitting

Catalogs of drainage fixtures, see TH6589
Catalogs of gas fixtures, see TH6865
Catalogs of water supply fixtures, see TH6529
Catalogs of plumbing and fitting supplies, see TH6255

Gas in buildings. Building gas supply
Cf. TH6561, Gas water heating
Cf. TH7405+, Gas heating
Cf. TH7466.G3, Central heating with gas
Cf. TH7910+, Gas lighting
Cf. TX657.O6, Kitchen gas ovens
Cf. TX657.S6, Kitchen gas ranges

6800	Periodicals, societies, congresses, etc.
6810	General works
6820	General special
	Safety measures
6830	General works
6835	Venting for appliances
6840	Piping installation. Pipefitting
	Details
6850	General works
	Fixtures and appliances
6855	General works
6860	Maintenance and repair. Testing
6865	Catalogs
6870	Meters
6875	Governors. Regulators
6880	Burners
6882	Flame monitors
	Ignition devices
	Including electric ignitors
6885	General works
6887	Pilot lights

Heating and ventilation
Cf. TH7201+, Heating of buildings, including special aspects of both heating and ventilation
Cf. TH7647+, Ventilation only

7005	Periodicals, societies, congresses, etc.
7007	Dictionaries and encyclopedias
	General works
7010	Early to 1860
7011	1860-
7012	Textbooks
7015	General special
	Including climatic factors

                    Heating and ventilation -- Continued

(7081-7084)	Legislation
	see class K
	Heating engineering. Industrial heating
	Cf. TH6552+, Heating of water
	Cf. TJ255+, Engines using heat as a source of
	power
	Cf. TP363, Heating, drying, cooling, etc.
7121	General works
7124	Pocketbooks, tables, etc.
7135	Stoves, etc., for commercial kitchens
	Kitchen stoves and ranges, see TX657.S3+
	Kitchen boilers, see TH6563
	Stove heating, see TH7435+
	Stove manufacture, see TS425
	Industrial furnaces
	Class furnaces for special uses in the field of
	application
	Cf. TK4661, Electric furnaces
	Cf. TN677+, Metallurgical furnaces
	Cf. TP841+, Kilns
	Cf. TS231, Cupola furnaces
7140	General works
7145	Solar furnaces
	Cf. TJ809+, Solar energy
	Solar water heating, see TH6561.7
	Solar heating of buildings, see TH7413+
	Heating of buildings
	Including domestic heating
	Class here also works which discuss special aspects
	of both heating and ventilation of buildings
7201	Periodicals, societies, etc.
7205	Congresses
7207	Collected works (nonserial)
7209	Dictionaries and encyclopedias
	Directories
7212	General works
7213	Special localities
	History
7215	General works
7216.A-Z	Country divisions, A-Z
	General works
7221	Early to 1860
7222	1860-
7223	Textbooks
7224	Popular works. Juvenile works
7225	Pocketbooks, tables, rules, etc.
7226	General special
7227	Addresses, essays, lectures
7231	Study and teaching
7325	Specifications
7331	Drawings
	Estimates. Measurements. Quantities and costs

	Heating and ventilation
	Heating of buildings
	Estimates. Measurements.
	Quantities and costs -- Continued
7335	General works
7337	Schedules of prices
7338	Superintendence
7339	Inspection
7341	Testing
7345	Equipment and supplies
7355	Catalogs of heaters and fixtures (General)
7391.A-Z	Special rooms, A-Z
7392.A-Z	Special classes of building. By name, A-Z
	Cf. TH7684+, Ventilation of special classes
	of buildings
7392.A6	Apartment houses
7392.A8	Atomic bomb shelters
7392.A9	Automobile service stations
7392.C56	Chemical plants
7392.C6	Churches
	College buildings, see TH7392.S35
7392.C65	Commercial buildings
7392.C7	Creameries
	Dwellings, see TH7201+
	Factories, see TH7392.M6
7392.F3	Farm buildings
7392.F6	Foundries
7392.G37	Garages
	Hospitals, see RA969
7392.I53	Industrial buildings
7392.M2	Machine shops
7392.M6	Mills and factories
7392.O35	Office buildings
7392.P33	Packinghouses
7392.P8	Prisons
7392.P9	Public buildings
7392.R3	Railroad structures and buildings
7392.S35	School buildings. University and college
	buildings
7392.S65	Sports facilities
7392.T34	Tall buildings
7392.T47	Textile factories
7392.T5	Theaters
	University buildings, see TH7392.S35
7395.A-Z	Special installations. By name, A-Z
	Cf. TH7685.A+, Ventilating installations
	Heating by special fuels or forms of energy
	Cf. TH7424+, Wood heating in fireplaces
	Cf. TH7437+, Wood stove heating
7400	Coal heating
	Cf. TH7428+, Grate heating
	Cf. TH7443+, Coal stove heating

	Heating and ventilation
	Heating of buildings
	Heating by special
	fuels or forms of energy -- Continued
	Oil heating
	Cf. TH7447+, Oil stove heating
	Cf. TH7466.O6, Central heating by oil
7402	Periodicals, societies, congresses, etc.
7403	General works
	Gas heating
	Cf. TH7434, Gas fireplace heating
	Cf. TH7453+, Gas stove heating
	Cf. TH7466.G3, Central heating by gas
7405	Periodicals, societies, congresses, etc.
7406	General works
	Electric heating
	Cf. TH7434.5+, Electric radiant heating
	Cf. TH7638, Heat pump systems
7409	Periodicals, societies, congresses
7410	General works
	Solar heating
	Cf. TK1056, Solar powerplants
7413	General works
7413.5	Central solar heating plants with seasonal storage
7414	Solar houses
	Geothermal heating
7416	General works
7416.5	Geothermal district heating
7417	Geothermal space heating
7417.5	Ground source heat pump systems
	Local heating
	Cf. TH2055, Radiative heating (Open fires)
	Cf. TH7435+, Convective heating (Stoves)
7418	General works
7419	General special
7420	Theory
	For fuel heating, see TP315+
	Radiative heating. Open fires
7421	General works
7422	Catalogs of fireplace and grate fixtures
	Cf. TH2055, Building fittings
	For fireplaces, see TH7425+
	For grates, see TH7428+
7423	Charcoal fires. Braziers
	Fireplace heating with wood
7424	General works
	Fireplaces
7425	General works
7426.A-Z	Special fireplaces. By name of manufacturer, etc., A-Z
	Including catalogs
7427.A-Z	Details and fittings, A-Z

	Heating and ventilation
	Heating of buildings
	Local heating
	Radiative heating. Open fires
	Fireplace heating with wood
	Details and fittings, A-Z -- Continued
7427.A5	Andirons
	Grate heating with coal, etc.
7428	General works
	Grates
7429.A1	General works
7429.A2-Z	Special types of grate. By name, A-Z
7430	Catalogs (General)
7431.A-Z	Special grates. By name of manufacturer, etc., A-Z
	Details and fittings
7432	General works
7433	Grate frames. Summer pieces
7434	Gas fireplace heating. Gas logs
	Gas stove heating, see TH7453+
	Electric radiant heating. Radiant heaters
7434.5	General works
7434.7	Panel type installations
	Convective heating. Stoves
	Cf. TS425, Manufacture of stoves
	Cf. TX657.S3+, Kitchen stoves
7435	General works
7436.A-Z	Special types, other than by fuel, A-Z
7436.B3	Base-heating stoves
7436.D6	Double jacket stoves
	With air chamber for air heating
7436.E4	Earthenware stoves
7436.M37	Masonry stoves
7436.5	Biomass stove heating
	Wood stove heating
7437	General works
	Wood stoves
7438	General works
7439	Catalogs
7440.A-Z	Special wood stoves. By name of manufacture, etc., A-Z
7441	Details and fixtures, A-Z
	Coal and coke stove heating
7443	General works
7444	Catalogs
7445.A-Z	Special stoves. By name of manufacture, A-Z
7446.A-Z	Details and fixtures, A-Z
	Oil and gas stove and radiator heating
7447	General works
	Oil stove and radiator heating
7448	General works
	Oil stoves and radiators
7449	General works

TH

Heating and ventilation
Heating of buildings
Local heating
Convective heating. Stoves
Oil and gas stove and radiator heating
Oil stove and radiator heating
Oil stoves and radiators -- Continued

7450	Catalogs
7450.5	Kerosene heaters
7451.A-Z	Special oil stoves. By name of manufacturer, A-Z
7452.A-Z	Details and fixtures, A-Z

Gas stove heating
Cf. TH7434, Gas grate heating
Cf. TH7447 +, Oil and gas stove heating

7453	General works

Gas stoves

7454	General works
7455	Catalogs
7456.A-Z	Special gas stoves. By name of manufacturer
7457.A-Z	Details and fixtures, A-Z
7457.B8	Burners
7457.D7	Draft hoods
7458.A-Z	Stove heating with other fuels. By fuel, A-Z
7458.G7	Grass heating and stoves

Local heating of special classes of buildings, see
TH7392.A +
Central heating
Cf. TH7511 +, Hot water heating
Cf. TH7561 +, Steam heating
Cf. TH7601 +, Hot air heating
Cf. TH7641 +, Heating from central stations

7461	General works
7463	General special

Including gas heating

7465	Theory
7466.A-Z	Special fuels, A-Z
7466.G3	Gas
7466.O6	Oil
7466.W66	Wood
7466.5	Regulators. Thermostats

Cf. TH7687 +, Air conditioning
Hydronic systems
Class here works discussing both hot water and
steam heating combined
Cf. TH6703 +, Pipefitting

7467	General works

Details for hydronic systems

7469.A1	General works
7469.A2-Z	Special. By name of manufacturer, etc., A-Z

Including histories of manufacturing firms

	Heating and ventilation
	Heating of buildings
	Central heating
	Hydronic systems
	Details for hydronic systems -- Continued
	Furnaces and boilers for heating
	Cf. TH7538+, Hot water furnaces and boilers
	Cf. TH7588+, Steam furnaces and boilers
	Cf. TJ263.5, Boilers (General)
7470	General works
7471	Testing
7473	Stationary or bricked-in
7475	Movable or independent
7476.A-Z	Special furnaces and boilers. By name of manufacturer, etc., A-Z
7477	Door and damper regulators
7478	Piping, valves and other fittings
	Cf. TH6703+, Pipefitting
7479	Air vents, etc.
	Radiators
	Cf. TH7547, Radiators for hot water heating
	Cf. TH7597, Radiators for steam heating
7480	General works
	Direct radiators and coils
7481	General works
	Coils
7482	General works
7483	Flat coils
7484	Wall coils
	Radiators
7486	General works
7487	Sectional (cast iron)
7488	Tubular, etc.
7490	Direct-indirect radiators. Ventilating radiators
	Indirect radiators
7492	General works
7493	Box coil radiators
7495.A-Z	Special radiators. By name of manufacturer, etc., A-Z
	Hot water heating and fixtures
	Cf. TH6703+, Pipefitting
7511	General works
7512	Pocketbooks, tables, etc.
7513	Specifications, drawings, etc.
7515	Theory
	Low-pressure hot water heating (with dome boilers)
7518	General works

	Heating and ventilation
	Heating of buildings
	Central heating
	Hydronic systems
	Hot water heating and fixtures
	Low-pressure hot water heating (with dome boilers) -- Continued
7525	Distribution
	Including two-pipe system, one-pipe system, and overhead system
7529	Special details or fixtures (not A-Z)
	Including furnaces, boilers, and appurtenances
	High-pressure hot water heating (with coil boilers)
7530	General works
7533	Distribution
7534.A-Z	Special details or fixtures, A-Z
	Including furnaces, boilers, etc.
7535	Forced circulation systems
7535.5	Radiant floor heating
	Details or fixtures of hot water heating
7536	General works
7537.A-Z	Special. By name of manufacturer, etc., A-Z
	Furnaces and boilers
	Cf. TH7470+, Furnaces and boilers for both steam and hot water heating
7538.A1	General works
7538.A2-Z	Special. By name of manufacturer, etc, A-Z
7539	Stationary or bricked-in furnaces and boilers
7540	Movable furnaces and boilers
7541	Door and damper regulators
7542	Expansion tanks
7543	Special piping and valves
7545	Air vents and other fittings
7547	Radiators for hot water heating
	Cf. TH7480+, Radiators for steam and hot water heating
(7548)	Hot water heating of special classes of buildings
	see TH7392
(7549)	Hot water heating of special installations
	see TH7395
	Steam heating and fixtures
	Cf. TH6703+, Pipefitting
7561	General works
7562	Pocketbooks, tables, etc.
7563	Specifications, drawings, etc.
7565	Theory

	Heating and ventilation
	Heating of buildings
	Central heating
	Hydronic systems
	Steam heating and fixtures -- Continued
(7567)	Systems of distribution, etc.
	Including two-pipe system, one-pipe system, and overhead or drop system
	Low-pressure steam heating
7570	General works
7571	Gravity systems (water returned to boiler)
7575	Condense-waste systems (water discharge)
	Live steam systems (from engine boilers)
7576	General works
7577	Exhaust-steam utilization systems
7578.A-Z	Special details, A-Z
	Cf. TJ444, Oil separators (General)
7578.B3	Back pressure valves
7578.G7	Grease separators
7578.V3	Valves
(7580)	High-pressure steam heating
7583.A-Z	Special steam-heating systems. By name, A-Z
	Details or fixtures of steam heating
7586	General works
7587.A-Z	Special. By name of manufacturer, etc., A-Z
	Furnaces and boilers
7588.A1	General works
7588.A2-Z	Special. By name of manufacturer, etc., A-Z
7589	Stationary or bricked-in furnaces
7590	Movable furnaces
7591	Door and damper regulators
7593	Special piping and valves
7595	Air vents and other fittings
7597	Radiators for steam heating
(7598)	Steam heating for special classes of buildings see TH7392
(7599)	Steam heating for special installations see TH7395
	Warm-air heating and fixtures
7601	General works
7602	Specifications, drawings, etc.
	Theory
7603	General works
7608	Cold air supply, etc.
7609	Construction
	Cf. TS250, Sheet metalwork
	Cf. TS600 +, Tinsmithing
	Systems
7610	General works
7619.A-Z	Special. By name, A-Z
	Details
7621	General works

	Heating and ventilation
	Heating of buildings
	Central heating
	Warm-air heating and fixtures
	Details -- Continued
7622.A-Z	Special. By name of manufacturer, A-Z
	Furnaces and appurtenances
	Cf. TH7609, Construction
7623	General works
7624.A-Z	Special. By name of manufacturer, etc., A-Z
7625	Flues and piping
7626	Registers
7627	Pipe dampers and draft registers
(7631)	Warm air heating of special classes of buildings see TH7392
(7632)	Warm air heating of special installations see TH7395
	Special warm air heating
7633	Warm air heating with heated air not admitted to rooms but removed by convection through floors, etc.
7635	Combination systems
	Including warm air and steam systems
7638	Heat pump systems
	Cf. TH7687+, Air conditioning
	Cf. TJ262, Theory
	For ground source heat pump systems, see TH7417.5
	Heating for a community from a single plant
	For geothermal district heating, see TH7416.5
7641	General works
7643	Heating pipes and mains
	Ventilation of buildings
	Periodicals, societies, congresses, etc , see TH7005
	History
7647	General works
	Special regions or countries
	United States
7648	General works
7649.A-W	States, A-W
7650.A-Z	Cities, A-Z
7651.A-Z	Other regions or countries, A-Z
	General works
7652	Early to 1800
7653	1800-
7654	Textbooks
7655	Popular works. Juvenile works
7656	Pocketbooks, tables, and rules
7657	General special
	Including use of ozone
7658	Addresses, essays, lectures
	Natural ventilation
	Class here natural draft, without fans, etc.

	Heating and ventilation
	Ventilation of buildings
	Natural ventilation -- Continued
7674	General works
7675.A-Z	Special systems. By name of manufacturer, A-Z
	Artificial ventilation
	Including ventilators
7678	General works
7681	General special
7682.A-Z	Special systems, A-Z
7682.D45	Demand controlled ventilation systems
7682.D57	Displacement ventilation
7683.A-Z	Details, fixtures, etc., A-Z
7683.A25	Air curtains
7683.A3	Air filters. Air washers
7683.D8	Air ducts
7683.F3	Fans
7683.H42	Heat exchangers
7683.L7	Louvers
7683.P8	Punkas
7683.R4	Registers and flues
	Cf. TH7626, Heating
7683.V4	Ventilators and chimney tops
	Special ventilation
7684.A-Z	Special buildings and facilities, A-Z
7684.A6	Apartment houses
7684.B35	Basements
7684.C44	Chemical plants
7684.C6	Churches
7684.D9	Dwellings
7684.F2	Factories
7684.F3	Farm buildings
7684.F45	Flour mills
	Hospitals, see RA969
7684.K5	Kitchens
7684.M2	Machine shops
7684.N83	Nuclear facilities
7684.P7	Power plants
7684.P75	Printing plants
7684.P8	Public buildings
7684.R3	Railroad repair shops
	Schoolhouses, see LB3244
7684.S55	Slaughterhouses
7684.T25	Textile factories
7684.T3	Theaters
7685.A-Z	Special ventilating installations, A-Z
	e.g.
7685.G8	Great Britain. House of Commons
	Air conditioning, cooling, etc.
7687.A1	Periodicals, societies, etc.
7687.A2-Z	General works
7687.5	General special
	Including noise

TH

Heating and ventilation
  Ventilation of buildings
    Air conditioning, cooling, etc. -- Continued

7687.7	Systems and details
7687.8	Humidity control
7687.85	Gas air conditioning
7687.9	Solar air conditioning
7687.95	Variable air volume systems
7688.A-Z	Special classes of building, A-Z
7688.B3	Bakeries
7688.C64	Commercial buildings
	Factories
7688.F2	General
7688.F24	Food
7688.F27	Paper
7688.F3	Textile
7688.H6	Homes. Dwellings
7688.L3	Laboratories
7688.O4	Office buildings
7688.O44	Offshore structures. Artificial islands
7688.P3	Packinghouses
7688.P7	Printing plants
7688.P78	Public buildings
7688.P8	Public shelters
	School buildings, see LB3244
7688.W3	Warehouses
	Dust removal (by pneumatic suction, etc.)
7692	General works
7694	Clean rooms
7695.A-Z	Special systems. By name, A-Z
7695.E4	Electrostatic precipitation
7695.I52	Inertial separation
7695.S6	Sonic coagulation
7695.V2	Vacuum system
7695.V45	Venturi scrubber
7696	Details. Fixtures
7697.A-Z	In special buildings and operations. By type, A-Z
7697.A8	Asbestos industry
7697.B75	Brickworks
7697.B8	Building materials industry
7697.B82	Bulk solids handling
7697.C4	Cement industries
7697.C54	Chemical plants
7697.C58	Coal preparation plants
7697.C6	Compressor stations
7697.C7	Crushed stone industry
7697.E45	Electric power plants
7697.F2	Factories and workshops
7697.F55	Food processing plants
7697.F6	Foundries
7697.G67	Grain elevators
7697.G7	Granite plants
7697.I76	Iron industry

Heating and ventilation
  Ventilation of buildings
    Dust removal (by pneumatic suction, etc.)
      In special buildings
        and operations. By type, A-Z -- Continued

7697.M4	Metallurgical plants
	Mine dust control, see TN312
7697.M56	Mineral industries
7697.O7	Ore-dressing plants
7697.P5	Plastics plants
7697.Q37	Quarries
7697.R4	Refractories industry
7697.R6	Rolling mills
7697.S3	Sand and gravel industry
7697.T4	Textile factories
7697.T5	Tin industry
7697.W4	Welding shops
7697.W6	Woodworking industries
7698.A-Z	Special installations. By name, A-Z
	e.g.
7698.S7	Spokane Post Office
7699.A-Z	Other hygienic aspects, A-Z
7699.D4	Deodorization

Illumination. Lighting
  Cf. NK2115.5.L5, Lighting as an element in
    interior decoration
  Cf. TH7910+, Gas lighting
  Cf. TK4125+, Electric lighting

7700	Periodicals. Societies. Collections
7703	General works
7710	Pocketbooks, tables, etc.
7715	Standards. Specifications
7720	Safety measures
7723	Shadows
7725	General special
	Natural lighting
7791	General works
7792	Easement of light. Light rights. Ancient light
7795	Luxfer prisms
7799	Sidewalk lights
	Artificial lighting
7900	General works
	Gas lighting
7910	General works
7915	Popular works. Consumers' guides, etc.
	Incandescent gas lighting
7953	General works
7955.A-Z	Special systems, A-Z
7955.W3	Washington system
7955.W4	Welsbach system
	Lighting fixtures
	Cf. TK4198, Electric lighting fixtures
	Gas and electric

```
                    Illumination.  Lighting
                      Artificial lighting
                        Lighting fixtures
                          Gas and electric -- Continued
7960                        General works
7963                        Specifications
                            Catalogs
7965                          To 1880
7967                          1880-
7970.A-Z                    Other special, A-Z
7970.L35                      Lampposts
7970.R4                       Reflectors
7975.A-Z                  Special types of buildings, A-Z
7975.C65                    Commercial buildings
7975.D8                     Dwellings
7975.F2                     Factories and workshops
                            Hospitals, see RA969.5
7975.P82                    Public buildings
                              Cf. TK4399.P8, Electric lighting
                            Workshops, see TH7975.F2
                      Acoustics in buildings, see TH1725
                      Decoration and decorative furnishings
                          Class here technical works for the artisan
                          For artistic interior decoration, see NK1700+
8001                      Periodicals
                          General works
8024                        Early to 1800
8025                        1800-
8026                        Textbooks
8031                        Pocketbooks, tables, receipts, etc.
                          Plastering, calcimining, etc.
8120                        Periodicals, societies, etc.
8131                        General works
8132                        General special
                              Including drawings, estimates, ready reckoners
                            Plaster
                              Cf. TP888, Manufacture
8135                          General works
8137.A-Z                     Special plasters, A-Z
8137.G8                        Gypsum plasters
8139                          Plasterboard.  Gypsum wallboard.  Drywall
8161                        Calcimining
8181                        Whitewashing
                          Glazing, painting, wall decoration, etc.
8203                        General works
                            Glazing
                              Cf. TH2270+, Windows and doors and their
                                  fittings
                              Cf. TP812.A1+, Glazes, enamels, etc.
                              Cf. TP823, Technology of ceramic decoration
8251                          General works
                              Ornamental, stained, art, or leaded glass (Use)
                                Cf. NK5300+, Art
```

	Decoration and decorative furnishings
	Glazing, painting, wall decoration, etc.
	Glazing
	Ornamental, stained,
	art, or leaded glass (Use) -- Continued
8271	General works
8275	Catalogs
	House painting
	see TT300-TT324
(8303)	General works
	see TT320
(8321)	Exterior painting and material
	see TT320-TT324
(8351)	Interior painting and material
	see TT323
	Wall decoration
	Cf. NK1700+, Art industries
(8403)	General works
	see NK2119
	Paperhanging and wallpaper
	Cf. NK3375+, Art industries
8423	General works
8441	Paperhanging
	Wallpaper
	Prefer NK3375+
8461	General works
8463.A-Z	Special. By name of manufacturer, A-Z
8471	Hanging burlap, buckram, lincrusta, etc.
	Cf. NK3175+, Art industries
8481	Tapestrying and tapestry
	Cf. NK2975+, Art industries
	Cf. TS1780, Manufactures
	Cf. TT849, Tapestry (Handicrafts)
	Tilelaying and tile
8521	General works
8531	Tilelaying
	Tile. Decorative and ceramic tile
	Class here works on tile of all materials,
	including plastic tile, when used for wall and
	ceiling decoration. Class here only works on
	ceramic tile when used for flooring
	Cf. NA3705, Architectural decoration
	Cf. NK4670+, Ceramics
	Cf. TP837, Manufacture of tile
	For other flooring materials, see TH2529
8541	General works
8542.A-Z	Special. By name of manufacturer, A-Z
	Decorative woodwork
	Including fretwork, grilles, etc.
	Cf. NK9600+, Artistic woodwork
	Cf. TH1151+, Architectural woodwork
	Cf. TH2553, Interior moldings
8581	General works

TH

Decoration and decorative furnishings
  Decorative woodwork -- Continued
    Parquet floors, see TH2529.W6

(8601)   Draping and drapery
                  see TT390
                Carpets, rugs, etc , see TS1772 +
          Protection of buildings
9025   General works
            Against damage from natural causes
9031   From dampness. Waterproofing
                Cf. TH2493, Guttering
9039   Weathering
9041   Pest control in buildings. Fumigation
                Cf. TA423.6 +, Wood preservation
                Cf. TX325, Household pests
            Protection of buildings from lightning
              Cf. TH1061 +, Fireproof building construction
              General works
9057   Treatises
9058   Elementary textbooks
9061   Miscellaneous minor works, addresses, essays, etc.
              Systems of protection from lightning
9092.A-Z   Special systems. By name of manufacturer, A-Z
                    Including catalogs
            Earthquakes and building, see TH1095
            Bombproof construction, see TH1097
            Stormproof construction, see TH1096
          Protection from fire. Fire prevention and extinction
            Cf. TH1061 +, Fireproof building construction
            Cf. TH9057 +, Protection against lightning
9111   Periodicals, societies, etc.
              For local societies, see TH9500 +
9112   Congresses, conventions, etc.
              For annual conventions of societies, see TH9111
            Exhibitions. Museums
9114.A1   General works
9114.A2-Z   By region or country, A-Z
                Apply table at TH6.A2-Z
9115   Collected works (nonserial)
9116   Dictionaries and encyclopedias
9116.5   Directories
            History
9117   General works
              Special countries, see TH9500 +
            Biography
9118.A1   Collective
9118.A2-Z   Individual, A-Z
9119   Fire prevention as a profession
            Study and teaching
              Cf. TH9225 +, Engineering
9120   General works
              United States
9123   General works

	Protection from fire. Fire prevention and extinction
	Study and teaching
	United States -- Continued
9124.A-W	States, A-W
9125.A-Z	Cities, A-Z
9127.A-Z	Other countries, A-Z
9128	Physical training for fire fighters
9130	Research
	General works
9145	Treatises
9146	Elements
9148	Popular works. Juvenile works
9149	Miscellanea
9150	Pocketbooks, tables, etc.
	Cf. HG9715, Manuals for insurance inspectors
9151	Firemen's manuals
9155	Addresses, essays, lectures
9157	Examinations, questions, etc.
9158	Fire department management
	For special countries, see TH9503-TH9599
(9160)	Legislation
	see class K
9176	Inspection. Fire inspectors' handbooks
	Including National Board of Fire Underwriters' rules
	and requirements
	Cf. HG9711+, Fire insurance surveys
9180	Investigation of fires
	Cf. SD421.45.I58, Forest fire investigation
9182	Safety measures
	Theory of fire protection, etc.
(9190)	General works
	see TH9145
9195	Enclosure fires
9197	Smoking and fires
9198	Spontaneous combustion (in relation to fire)
9198.5	Static electricity and fires
	Cf. TH9445.E43, Fire prevention and
	extinction in electrical equipment
	Fire insurance engineering
	Cf. TH1061+, Fireproof construction, including
	tests
9201	Periodicals, societies, etc.
9210	General works
9215	Pocketbooks, tables, etc.
9220	Addresses, essays, lectures
	Study and teaching
9225	General works
	Special schools
9230	United States
9235.A-Z	Other regions or countries, A-Z
9237	Laboratories
	Fire prevention
	Cf. TH1061+, Fireproof building construction

TH

	Protection from fire. Fire prevention and extinction
	Fire prevention -- Continued
9241	General works
9245	Appliances, etc.
	Fire doors, see TH2278+
	Fire detection and alarms
9271	Fire detectors. Combustible gas detectors
9275	Electric thermostat fire detectors
9280	Communication systems
	Fire extinction
	Cf. TH9151, Firemen's manuals
(9310)	Theory
9310.5	General works
9310.8	Command and control
	Water supply
9311	General works
	Local, see TH9503+
9323	Fire streams, nozzle forms, etc.
	Cf. TC173, Hydraulic engineering
	Special methods of fire extinction
	Including special apparatus
	Water tower systems
9332	General works
9333	For communities
9334	For individual buildings
9336	Automatic systems. Automatic sprinkler systems
9338	Chemical systems
	Cf. TH1073+, Fireproof construction
	(Impregnation)
	Cf. TH9362, Fire extinguishers
	Cf. TP265+, Chemistry of fire and fire
	prevention
9339	Explosion systems, etc.
	General equipment and apparatus
	Class special equipment with special systems
9360	General works
9361	General catalogs of fire department supplies
9362	Fire extinguishers
9363	Fire pumps. Hand pumps (Portable)
	Cf. TJ903, Hand pumps (General)
9365	Fire hydrants
	Vehicles
9370	General works
	Fire engines
9371	General works
9372	Juvenile works
9373	Catalogs
9374	Hand fire engines
9375	Chemical fire engines
9376	Steam fire engines
9377	Gasoline fire engines
	Fire hose and carts
9378	General works

	Protection from fire. Fire prevention and extinction
	Fire extinction
	General equipment and apparatus
	Vehicles
	Fire hose and carts -- Continued
9379	Hose carts
9380	Hose and nozzles
	For fire stream tables, see TH9323
9383	Hook and ladder trucks
9391	Fireboats
	Protective clothing. Uniforms
9395	General works
9396	Breathing apparatus
	Lifesaving at fires. Rescue work
	Including drills, etc.
	For fire escapes, see TH2274
9402	General works
9410	Evacuation of buildings
	Systems and apparatus
9412	Scaling ladder systems
9414	Rope systems
9416	Tubular bag systems
9418	Net or sheet systems (jumping systems)
(9425)	Special classes of buildings
	see TH9445.A-Z
9431	Salvage of material during fires
	Including protection from water
9445.A-Z	Fire prevention and extinction in special classes of buildings and facilities, A-Z
9445.A4	Aged, Housing for. Nursing homes
9445.A5	Airports
9445.A62	Apartment houses
9445.A7	Archive buildings
9445.A8	Asylums
9445.A85	Atomic power plants
9445.B6	Bowling alleys
9445.B8	Building sites
	Cathedrals, see TH9445.C5
9445.C47	Chemical plants
9445.C48	Chimneys
9445.C5	Churches, cathedrals, shrines, etc.
9445.C6	Cleaning and dyeing plants
9445.C65	Computers and computer installations
	Cf. TH9445.E45, Electronic data processing departments
9445.C67	Conveying machinery
9445.C68	Correctional institutions
9445.C7	Cotton gins
9445.D5	Distilleries
9445.D6	Dormitories
9445.D75	Drilling platforms
9445.D9	Dwellings
9445.E4	Electric power plants

TH

	Protection from fire. Fire prevention and extinction
	Fire extinction
	Fire prevention and extinction in
	special classes of buildings
	and facilities, A-Z -- Continued
9445.E43	Electrical equipment
9445.E45	Electronic data processing departments
	Cf. TH9445.C65, Computers and computer
	installations
9445.E46	Electronic equipment
9445.E48	Elevators
9445.F35	Farms
9445.F6	Food industry
9445.F87	Furnaces
9445.G3	Garages
	Garden apartments, see TH9445.A62
9445.G54	Glass trade
9445.G7	Grain elevators
(9445.H3)	Hangers
	see TH9445.A5
	Health facilities, see TH9445.H7
9445.H4	Heating equipment
	Heliports, see TH9445.A5
	Historic buildings, see TH9445.M8
9445.H7	Hospitals. Health facilities
9445.H75	Hotels
	Industrial buildings, see TH9445.M4 +
9445.L5	Libraries
9445.L8	Lumberyards
	Lunchrooms, see TH9445.R44
	Mills and factory buildings
9445.M4	General works
9445.M45	Flour mills
9445.M5	Textile factories
9445.M6	Woodworking industries
	Mines and mining, see TN315
9445.M8	Museums, historic buildings, etc.
9445.N3	Navy yards and naval stations
9445.N83	Nuclear facilities
	Nuclear power plants, see TH9445.A85
	Nursing homes, see TH9445.A4
9445.O4	Office buildings
9445.O43	Offshore structures
9445.O55	Oil storage tanks
9445.P3	Paint shops
9445.P38	Petroleum pipelines
9445.P4	Petroleum refineries
9445.P5	Piers and other waterfront structures
9445.P55	Plastics plants
9445.P8	Public buildings
9445.R44	Restaurants, lunchrooms, etc.
9445.S3	School buildings
9445.S4	Service industries

Protection from fire. Fire prevention and extinction
  Fire extinction
    Fire prevention and extinction in
      special classes of buildings
      and facilities, A-Z -- Continued
    Shopping centers, see TH9445.S8
    Shrines, see TH9445.C5
    Skyscrapers, see TH9445.T18

9445.S8	Stores, shopping centers, etc.
	Cf. TH9445.U5, Underground shopping centers
9445.T18	Tall buildings. Skyscrapers
9445.T2	Tanneries
	Temples, see TH9445.C5
	Theaters
9445.T3	General works
9445.T4	Motion picture theaters
9445.T5	Motion picture films in storehouses, etc.
9445.T7	Transportation industries
9445.T8	Tunnels
9445.U5	Underground shopping centers
9445.W2	Warehouses
	Waterfronts, see TH9445.P5
9446.A-Z	Fire prevention and extinction in special materials, A-Z
9446.A37	Aerosols
9446.C5	Chemicals
9446.C6	Chlorine dioxide
9446.C65	Cleaning compounds
9446.C7	Cotton and cotton fabrics
9446.D86	Dust
9446.G3	Gasoline
9446.H38	Hazardous substances
9446.H9	Hydraulic fluids
9446.H96	Hydrogen
	Inflammable materials
9446.I47	General works
9446.I5	Inflammable liquids
9446.I55	Insecticides
9446.L57	Liquefied natural gas
9446.M3	Magnesium
9446.O95	Oxygen
9446.P38	Peat
9446.P4	Petroleum
9446.P55	Plastics
9446.P65	Polymers
9446.R3	Radioactive substances
9446.R8	Rubber
9446.S3	Salts
	Fire-testing of materials. Flammability of materials
9446.3	General works
9446.5.A-Z	Special materials, A-Z
9446.5.B44	Belts and belting

	Protection from fire. Fire prevention and extinction
	Fire extinction
	Fire-testing of materials.
	Flammability of materials
	Special materials, A-Z -- Continued
9446.5.E43	Electric insulators and insulation
9446.5.F87	Furniture
9446.5.P45	Plastics
9446.5.P65	Polymers
9446.5.U63	Upholstery
9447	Private fire departments for individual establishments
	Fires
9448	General works
	Including descriptions of the great conflagrations
9449.A-Z	Special fires. By city, A-Z
	Class here only technical reports
	For popular descriptions, see local history in classes D-F
	Fires in mines, see TN315
	Forest fires, see SD420.5+
	Grassland fires, see SD421.5
	Ground cover fires, see SD421.47+
	Wildfires, see SD420.5+
	Protection from fire in special countries and cities
	Including city fire departments and fire fighters's associations.
9500	General collections
9501	America
	North America (United States and Canada)
9502	General works
	United States
9503	General works
9504.A-W	Special states, A-W
	Under each state, apply Table T3a
	Including works on separate counties
	Individual Cutters listed below are provided as examples
9504.D6	District of Columbia (Table T3a)
9504.N7	New York (State) (Table T3a modified)
9504.N71	State fire marshal's report
9505.A-Z	Special cities, A-Z
	Under each city, apply Table T3b
	e.g.
9505.N5	New York (N.Y.) (Table T3b)
	Washington (D.C.), see TH9504.D6
	Canada
9506.A1-A6	General works
9506.A8-Z	Provinces, A-Z
9507.A-Z	Special cities, A-Z
	Other countries
9508	Mexico

Protection from fire. Fire prevention and extinction
Protection from fire in special countries and cities
Other countries -- Continued
Central America

9510.A1-A6	General works
9510.A8-Z	By country, A-Z
9511.A-Z	Special cities, A-Z
	West Indies
9512.A1-A6	General works
9512.A7-Z	Special islands, A-Z
9513.A-Z	Special cities, A-Z
	South America
9514	General works
9516	Argentina
9518	Bolivia
9521	Brazil
9523	Chile
9525	Colombia
9527	Ecuador
	Guiana
9528	Guyana
9529	Surinam
9530	French Guiana
9531	Paraguay
9532	Peru
9533	Uruguay
9534	Venezuela
	Europe
9535	General works
	Great Britain. England
9537	General works
9539.A-Z	England. Cities, A-Z
9541	Ireland
9543	Scotland
9544	Wales
	Austria
9545	General works
9546.A-Z	Special cities, A-Z
9547	Belgium
9549	Denmark
9551	France
	Germany
9553	General works
9554.A-Z	Special cities, A-Z
9555	Greece
9557	Holland
9559	Italy
9561	Norway
9563	Portugal
9565	Russia. Soviet Union. Russia (Federation)
9567	Spain
9569	Sweden
9571	Switzerland

	Protection from fire. Fire prevention and extinction
	Protection from fire in special countries and cities
	Other countries
	Europe -- Continued
9575.A-Z	Other regions or countries, A-Z
	Asia
9580	General works
9581	China
9583	India
9585	Japan
9587	Iran
9589	Asia Minor. Turkey
9591	Siberia
9593.A-Z	Other regions or countries, A-Z
	Africa
9594	General works
9596	Egypt
9597.A-Z	Other regions or countries, A-Z
	Australia
9598.A1	General works
9598.A6-Z	Local, A-Z
	New Zealand
9598.5.A1	General works
9598.5.A6-Z	Local, A-Z
	Pacific islands
9599.A1	General works
9599.A6-Z	Local, A-Z
	Protection from burglary, sabotage, etc. Security in
	buildings
	Cf. HV6646 + , Theft
	Cf. HV8290 + , Guards, watchmen, etc.
9701	Periodicals, societies, congresses, etc.
9705	General works
	Burglar proof construction
9720	General works
9725.A-Z	Details, A-Z
9725.W5	Window guards
	Protection equipment and devices
9730	General works
9732	Fences
9734	Safes and vaults
9735	Locks. Electronic locking devices
	Cf. TH2279, Door fittings
	Cf. TS519 + , Locksmithing
9737	Electronic security systems
9739	Detection and alarm equipment. Burglar alarms
9745.A-Z	Security of special buildings, A-Z
	Archives, see CD986
	Art museums, see N463
9745.D85	Dwellings
9745.F3	Factories
	Health facilities, see RA969.95
	Houses, see TH9745.D85

Protection from burglary,
    sabotage, etc. Security in buildings
  Protection equipment and devices
    Security of special buildings, A-Z -- Continued
      Libraries, see Z679.6
      Museums, see AM148

9745.S59   Skyscrapers
9745.S7   Stores, Retail

Mechanical engineering and machinery
    Periodicals and societies. By language of publication

1	English
2	French
3	German
4	Other languages (not A-Z)
5	Congresses

    Exhibitions. Museums

6.A1	General works
6.A2-Z	By region or country, A-Z

        Under each country:
        .x   *General works*
        .x2A-Z   *Special. By city, A-Z*

7	Collected works (nonserial)
9	Dictionaries and encyclopedias

    Directories
        For directories of makers and dealers in machinery
            tools, supplies, etc., see TJ1170

11	General and the United States
12.A-W	United States. By state, A-W

        Under each state:
        .x   *General works*
        .x2A-Z   *Local, A-Z*

13.A-Z	Other countries, A-Z
14	Philosophy of machinery

    History

15	General works
16	Ancient
17	Medieval
18	Modern
19	Nineteenth century
20	Twentieth century
21-127	Country divisions (Table T1)

        Add country number in table to TJ0

130.A-Z	Special companies (History, description, etc), A-Z

    Biography

139	Collective
140.A-Z	Individual, A-Z

    General works on mechanical engineering

144	Early to 1800
145	1800-
146	Elementary textbooks
147	Popular works. Juvenile works
148	Laboratory practice and student manuals. Testing

        Cf. TA416+, Engineering laboratories

151	Pocketbooks, rules, tables, etc.
153	General special

        Including data processing, costs, etc.

155	Addresses, essays, lectures
157	Mechanical engineering as a profession

    Study and teaching

158	General works
159	Problems, questions, etc.

	Research
159.5	General works
159.7.A-Z	By region or country, A-Z
	Communication in mechanical engineering
160	General works
160.5	Information centers
	Mechanical and electrical engineering combined
163	General works
163.12	Mechatronics
	For microelectromechanical systems, see TK7875
	Power resources
	Cf. TJ260, Heat as a source of power
	Cf. TJ807+, Renewable energy sources
	Cf. TN263.5, Energy minerals
	For special power resources, see the resources e.g.
	TP315+, Fuel; TK9001+, Atomic power; etc.
163.13	Periodicals. Societies. Serials
163.15	Congresses
	Exhibitions. Museums
163.155.A1	General works
163.155.A2-Z	By region or country, A-Z
	Apply table at TJ6.A2-Z
163.16	Dictionaries and encyclopedias
163.165	Directories
163.17	Information services
163.2	General works
163.23	Juvenile works
163.235	Handbooks, tables, etc.
163.24	Addresses, essays, lectures
163.245	Energy audits
163.25.A-Z	Special regions or countries, A-Z
	Energy conservation
	Cf. HD9502+, Economics of power resources and
	energy policy
	Cf. TN860+, Petroleum conservation
163.26	Periodicals. Societies. Serials
163.27	Congresses
163.28	Dictionaries and encyclopedias
163.3	General works
163.35	Juvenile works
163.4.A-Z	Special regions or countries, A-Z
	Biography
163.45	Collective
163.46.A-Z	Individual, A-Z
163.5.A-Z	Energy conservation or consumption in special
	industries, facilities, etc., A-Z
163.5.A37	Agriculture
	Air transport, see TJ163.5.T7
	Apartment houses, see TJ163.5.D86
163.5.B84	Buildings
163.5.C45	Cement industries
163.5.C54	Chemical industry
163.5.C57	Churches. Religious institutions

	Energy conservation
	Energy conservation or consumption
	in special industries,
	facilities, etc., A-Z -- Continued
	Colleges, see TJ163.5.U5
163.5.C65	Construction industry
163.5.D86	Dwellings
163.5.F3	Factories
163.5.F5	Finishing industry
163.5.F6	Food industry
	Foundries, see TJ163.5.M48
163.5.G55	Glass manufacture
	Health facilities and hospitals, see RA967
163.5.H4	Heating plants
163.5.H67	Hotels. Motels
163.5.M48	Metallurgical plants
163.5.M54	Military bases
163.5.M56	Mineral industries
163.5.M87	Museums
163.5.O35	Office buildings
163.5.P33	Package goods industry
163.5.P37	Paper and pulp mills
163.5.P47	Petroleum refineries
163.5.P68	Power plants
	Religious institutions, see TJ163.5.C57
163.5.R64	Rolling mills
163.5.R82	Rubber industry
	Schools, see TJ163.5.U5
163.5.S67	Sports facilities
163.5.S83	Steelworks
163.5.S85	Stores, Retail
163.5.S93	Sugar industry
	Supermarkets, see TJ163.5.S85
	Taverns, see TJ163.5.H67
163.5.T48	Textile industry
163.5.T7	Transportation
163.5.U5	Universities and colleges. Schools
163.5.W36	Waterworks
163.5.W66	Wood-using industries
	Power (Mechanics)
163.6	Periodicals. Societies. Serials
163.7	Congresses
163.8	Dictionaries and encyclopedias
163.9	General works
163.95	Juvenile works
164	Power plants (General)
	Cf. TJ395+, Steam
	Cf. TK1191+, Electric
	Cf. TK4399.P6, Electric lighting

165	Energy storage
	Cf. TJ260, Thermal energy storage
	Cf. TJ541, Flywheels
	Cf. TJ981+, Compressed air
	Cf. TK2980+, Electric energy storage
166	Safety measures and devices
	Cf. TJ1177, Machine shops
168	General catalogs of mechanical engineering equipment
	Mechanics applied to machinery. Dynamics
170	General works
173	General special
	Including work diagrams
175	Principles of mechanism. Kinematics of machinery
177	Vibration of machinery
177.5	Alignment of machinery
179	Noise in machinery
	Cf. TD893.6.M3, Noise in machine shops
	Mechanical movements
181	General works
	Special movements and devices
181.3	Perpetual motion
181.5	The wheel
181.6	Intermittent-motion mechanisms
181.7	Geneva mechanisms
181.8	Straight-line mechanisms
181.9	Pantograph
	Belt gearings, belts, pulleys, etc , see TJ1100+
	Links and link motion. Cranks
	Cf. TJ762.C73, Motors
182	General works
183	Hooke's and other link couplings
183.5	Rolling contact
	Toothed gears. Gearing
184	General works
185	Tables, lists, etc.
186	Laying out gear teeth. Odontographs
187	Gear-cutting machines
188	Catalogs
	Special gears
189	Spur gears
190	Racks (Racks and pinions)
191	Annular gears
192	Stepped, twisted, and helical gears
	Bevel gears
193	General works
194	Miter wheels
196	Screw bevel gears
	Screw gears, see TJ192
200	Worm gears
202	Other forms of gears
	Including internal gears, reduction gears
204	Transmission gears
	Cf. TL260+, Automobiles

TJ

	Mechanical movements
	Special movements and devices -- Continued
206	Cams
208	Vibrators
209	Gyroscopes
	Cf. QA862.G9, Analytic mechanics
	Cf. TL589.2.C58, Compass (Gyroscope)
	Cf. TL589.2.O6, Optical gyroscope
210	Springs
	Mechanical devices and figures. Automata. Ingenious mechanisms. Robots (General)
	Cf. ML1050, Automatic musical instruments
	Cf. S678.65, Robotics in agriculture
	Cf. TL1097, Space robotics
	For industrial robots, see TS191.8
210.2	Periodicals. Societies. Serials
210.3	Congresses
210.4	Dictionaries and encyclopedias
210.5	Directories
211	General works
211.15	Popular works
211.2	Juvenile works
211.25	Vocational guidance
211.26	Study and teaching
211.3	Robot vision
211.35	Control systems
211.37	Evolutionary robotics
211.4	Robot motion. Robot dynamics
211.412	Robot kinematics
211.415	Mobile robots
211.416	Personal robotics
211.417	Error detection and recovery
211.419	Calibration
211.42	Robot wrists
211.45	Programming
211.47	Computer simulation
211.49	Human factors
211.495	Autonomous robots
211.5	Specifications and standards
	Control engineering systems. Automatic machinery (General)
	Cf. HD6331+, Labor displacement
	Cf. T59.5, Automation
	Cf. TA165, Industrial instrumentation
	Cf. TJ1180+, Automatic machine tools
	Cf. TS156.8, Process control
212	Periodicals. Societies. Collected works
212.2	Congresses
212.5	Dictionaries and encyclopedias
213	General works
213.5	Popular works. Juvenile works
213.7	Addresses, essays, lectures
213.75	Study and teaching

	Control engineering systems.
	Automatic machinery -- Continued
213.8	Problems, exercises, etc.
213.9	Laboratory manuals
213.95	Reliability
	Control systems
214	Servomechanisms
214.5	Motion control devices
216	Feedback control systems
216.5	Feedforward control systems
217	Adaptive control systems
217.5	Intelligent control systems
217.6	Predictive control
217.7	Real-time control
218	Carrier control systems
218.5	Relay control systems
218.7	Binary control systems
219	Pneumatic control systems
220	Linear control systems
220.5	Sliding mode control
221	Passivity-based control
222	Supervisory control systems
223.A-Z	Special, A-Z
223.A25	Actuators
223.C45	Chattering control
223.C6	Counters
	Digital control, see TJ223.M53
223.E4	Electromagnets
223.E65	Equalizers
223.L5	Level indicators
223.M3	Magnetic devices
223.M53	Microprocessors. Microcomputers. Digital control
	Cf. QA76.6+, Computer programming
	Cf. TK7895.M5, Computer hardware
	Optoelectronic devices, see TJ223.P5
223.P4	Perceptrons
223.P5	Photoelectronic devices. Optoelectronic devices
223.P55	PID controllers
223.P76	Programmable controllers
223.R3	Radioactive measurements
223.S45	Semiconductors
223.S6	Solions
223.T4	Thermometers, etc.
223.T5	Timers
223.T75	Transducers
223.V3	Valves
225	Applications (General)
	For special applications, see field of application,
	e.g. TJ1225, Milling machines numerically
	controlled

TJ

Machine design and drawing
   Including construction if contained in the same works
   For the design of special machines, see below under
     each machine
   For mechanical drawing, see T351+

227	Drafting room practice
230	General works
233	General special
235	Graphic statics applied to machinery
240	Atlases and collections of designs and plans
241	Machinery manufacturing (General)

   Cf. HD9705+, Machinery trade and manufacture
   For special types of machinery and machine-building
     processes, see under each machine or process,
     e.g. TJ1125-TJ1345, Machine shop practice;
     TK2331, Electric machinery; TN345, Mining
     machinery; TS225-TS225.2, Forging;
     TS228.99-TS239, Founding; TS1525, Textile
     machinery

243	Machine parts
245	Specifications for machinery
245.5	Quality control of machinery
246	Packing. Gaskets. Sealing

   Cf. TJ529, Steam engine cyclinder packing

247	Diaphragms
247.5	Bellows
248	Mechanical models
249	Erecting work. Foundations
	Prime movers in general
250	General works
253	Testing
254	Governors and governing

   Cf. TJ550+, Steam engines
   Cf. TJ1055, Machinery exclusive of prime movers
Combustion engineering
   Cf. QD516, Thermochemistry
   Cf. TH7140+, Industrial furnace
   Cf. TJ324.7, Furnaces
   Cf. TJ756, Internal combustion engines
   Cf. TJ773, Explosion or ignition devices
   Cf. TJ797, Diesel engines
   Cf. TP315+, Fuel

254.5	General works
254.7	Combustion chambers

   Cf. TL709.5.C55, Jet engines
Heat engines
   Class here engines using heat as a source of power
   For hot-air engines, see TJ765

255	General works
255.5	Materials

   Including ceramic materials

	Heat engines -- Continued
260	Heat in its applications, as a source of power, etc
	Class here heat from the mechanical engineering standpoint
262	Heat pumps
	Cf. TH7638, Heating and air conditioning
	Heat exchangers
	For special applications, see under machine or process, e. g. TJ778, Gas turbines; TP363, Heating, drying, cooling, evaporating, etc.
263	General works
263.2	Thermosyphons
263.5	Boilers (General)
	Cf. TH7470+, Heating
	Cf. TJ281+, Steam boilers
264	Heat pipes
264.5	Vortex tubes
265	Theory of heat engines. Thermodynamics
	Turbines. Turbomachines (General)
	Cf. TJ735+, Steam turbines
	Cf. TJ778, Gas turbines
	Cf. TJ870+, Hydraulic turbines
	Cf. VM740, Marine turbines
266	General works
267	Theory of turbines. Fluid, aero- and hydrodynamics of turbomachinery
267.5.A-Z	Special topics, A-Z
267.5.B43	Bearings
267.5.B5	Blades
267.5.C3	Cascades
	Compressors
267.5.C5	General works
267.5.C6	Supersonic compressors
267.5.D4	Diffusers
267.5.D5	Disks
267.5.I6	Impellers
267.5.N5	Noise
267.5.N6	Nozzles
	Including supersonic nozzles, etc.
	Steam engineering
	Steam
	Including heated fluids
268	Properties, etc.
270	Tables, calculations, etc.
271	Flow in pipes, orifices, etc.
272	Superheated steam. Superheaters, etc.
	Cf. TJ693, Locomotives
275	Treatises, textbooks, etc.
277	Pocketbooks, tables, etc.
279	General special
	Including high pressure steam
	Study and teaching
280	General works

TJ

	Steam engineering
	Study and teaching -- Continued
280.5	Examinations, questions, etc.
280.7	Geothermal engineering
	Cf. TH7416+, Geothermal heating
	Cf. TK1055, Production of electric power from
	geothermal energy
	Steam boilers
	Cf. TJ263.5, Boilers (General)
281	Periodicals, societies, etc.
282	Dictionaries and encyclopedias
283	History
	General works
284	Early works to 1850
285	1850-
286	Elementary textbooks
288	General special
	Including boiler accessories
289	Handbooks, management and care of boilers
	Including firemen's manuals, catechisms, etc.
	Cf. VM749, Manuals for marine boiler attendants
	Construction (Boilermaking)
290	General works
291	Material of boilers, strength and testing
292	Settings
293	Supports
294	Manholes
295	Models
296	Catalogs
	For special types, see TJ310+
297	Testing. Heat transmission through boiler tubes
298	Safety measures. Inspection
	Steam boiler explosions
	Cf. TH6565+, Kitchen boiler explosions
299	General works
301	Reports of special boiler explosions
(302-308)	Law and legislation
	see class K
	Types of boilers
310	Early types
	Including Cornish, Lancashire, etc.
	Multitubular
311	General works
312	Vertical
	Locomotive boilers, see TJ642
	Water tube boilers
314	General works
315.A-Z	Special types, A-Z
316.A-Z	Combination and other forms, A-Z
318	Electrically heated steam boilers
319	Waste heat boilers
	Kitchen boilers, see TH6563
	Marine boilers, see VK588+

	Steam boilers -- Continued
	Boiler details and accessories
	Furnaces
320	General works
	Grates
322	General works
324.A-Z	Special types, A-Z
324.5	Fuel systems
324.7	Combustion
325	Gas burning installations
326	Oil burning installations
328	Air preheating
	Chimneys
	Cf. TH4591, Construction
330	General works
333	Draft
335	Forced draft. Mechanical draft
	Smoke prevention and consumers, see TD884
340	Fuel economizers
345	Mechanical stokers. Automatic stokers
347	Grate shakers
	Safety appliances
	Cf. TH6565+, Hot water supply
350	General works
	Safety valves
352	General works
354.A-Z	Special types, A-Z
356	Fusible plugs
357	Pressure regulators
358	Blowoffs
	Water gages
360	General works
363	Gage or try cocks
366	Water glasses
	Steam or pressure gages
370	General works
372.A-Z	Steam types, A-Z
	Feed apparatus
375	General works
377	Water supply for boilers
378	Wells, etc.
379	Feedwater purification. Water softeners, etc.
	Feedwater heaters
381	General works
383.A-Z	Special types, A-Z
385	Feed pumps
387	Injectors
	Boiler scale
	Including its prevention and removal
390	General works
392	Boiler compounds. Catalogs, circulars, etc.
393	Steam accumulators
	Steam powerplants. Boiler plants

	Steam powerplants. Boiler plants -- Continued
395	Plants for power, heating, etc.
	Plants for power alone
400	General works
403	General special
405	Operation and management
407	Special plants. Description, plans, drawings, testing, etc.
	Coal and ash handling, see TJ1405
411	Directories of manufacturers and dealers in equipment and supplies
412	Equipment and supplies
	Including catalogs
	Pipe and fittings
	Including standardization
	Cf. TH7478, Steam heating fittings
415	General works
(418)	Catalogs
	see TJ412
421	Pipe flanges
	Including standardization
424	Expansion joints
427	Steam pipe covering
	Steam valves
430	General works
432	Catalogs
433	Reducing valves
435	Steam packing
438	Steam traps
441	Steam separators
444	Oil separators
	Cf. TH7578.G7, Steam heating, grease separators
	Steam engines
461	History
464	Early works to 1850
465	1850-
466	Textbooks
467	Popular works. Juvenile works
469	General special
	Including curiosa
471	Handbooks, etc., for engine tenders
472	Addresses, essays, lectures
473	Catalogs (General)
	For special types, see below
474	Standards. Specifications
475	Tests and efficiencies
478	Indicators
480	Models
	Steam engines. Special types (Reciprocating)
	For early types see TJ461-TJ465
485.A-Z	Types. By inventor or maker, A-Z
	e.g.

	Steam engines
	Steam engines. Special types (Reciprocating)
	Types. By inventor or maker, A-Z -- Continued
485.C5	Corliss
	Types. By use of steam
	Simple
490	General works
492	Single acting
494	Double acting
495.A-Z	Special makes, A-Z
	Compound
497	General works
499.A-Z	Special makes, A-Z
	Triple expansion
501	General works
503.A-Z	Special makes, A-Z
505	Quadruple expansion
507	Other types (not A-Z)
	Steam engines (Design and construction)
515	General works
520	Balancing of engines
	Details
	Including description and parts
523	Foundations
525	Frame setting
	Cylinder
527	General works
529	Stuffing box. Packing
531	Steam jacket
533	Piston and piston rod. Piston rings
535	Crosshead and connecting rod
537	Crank and crankpin
539	Shaft and journals
541	Flywheel
543	Eccentric and eccentric-rod
545	Slide valve
546	Piston valve
	Valve gears
547	General works
548.A-Z	Special types, A-Z
	Governors
550	General works
551.A-Z	Special types, A-Z
551.C8	Corliss valve gears
	Steam engine accessories
555	General works
557	Condensers
559	Jet
561	Surface
563	Cooling towers
565	Wells
567	Exhausts

TJ

	Locomotives
	Cf. TF1+, Railroads
	History
	Cf. TJ625.A+, Special locomotive works
603	General works
	Special countries
	United States
603.2	General works
603.3.A-Z	Special railroad lines. By line, A-Z
	e.g.
603.3.S6	Southern Pacific Railroad
603.4.A-Z	Other regions or countries, A-Z
	Under each:
	.x General works
	.x2A-Z By special line, A-Z
	Biography of locomotive engineers
	For biography of inventors, designers,
	manufacturers, etc., of locomotives, see
	TJ140.A+
603.49	Collective
603.5.A-Z	Individual, A-Z
	General works
	Including dictionaries
604	Early to 1850
605	1850-
605.5	Juvenile works
606	Manuals, pocketbooks, etc. for the locomotive builder
607	Handbooks, manuals, etc. for locomotive engineers and firemen
608	General special
	Including boiler accessories
	Special types
609	General works
611	Simple
613	Compound
615	Other types. By use of steam
	Electric locomotives, see TF975
618	Oil burning steam locomotives
	Diesel locomotives
619	General works
	Special regions or countries
	United States
619.2	General works
619.3.A-Z	Special railroad lines. By line, A-Z
619.4.A-Z	Other regions or countries, A-Z
	Apply table at TJ603.4.A-Z
619.5	Engines
619.7	Electric equipment
	Electro-diesel locomotives, see TF980
621	Gasoline locomotives
622	Gas turbine locomotives
623	Nuclear locomotives

	Locomotives -- Continued
625.A-Z	Special locomotive works and companies, A-Z
	Including reports, histories, catalogs and descriptions of their locomotives
	e.g.
625.B2	Baldwin Locomotive Works
630	Models and miniature engines
635	Design and construction
	Repairs, see TJ675
	Details (Various motive powers)
640	Frames and running gear
642	Boilers
	Including regulation and inspection
	Fireboxes
646	General works
647	Ashpans
648	Fuel for locomotives. Coal, oil, etc.
	Cf. TJ690, Locomotive performance
649	Mechanical stokers
650	Draft appliances. Exhausts
653	Smoke prevention
656	Sparks and spark arresters
659	Cylinders, pistons, etc.
662	Connecting rods, etc.
665	Valves and valve gears
	Other special
668	Headlights
669.A-Z	Other, A-Z
669.B4	Bearings
669.B6	Boosters
669.B7	Brakes
669.C6	Compressors
669.C7	Cranks and crankshafts
669.E4	Electric equipment
669.S6	Speedometers
669.S7	Storage batteries
669.W54	Wheels
671	Locomotive tenders
675	Locomotive maintenance and repair. Lubrication
	Locomotive works and shops
680	General works
683	Shop practice
	Supervision and inspection of locomotives
	Cf. TJ642, Boiler inspection
	Documents
685.A1-A5	United States
685.A6A-Z	Other countries, A-Z
685.A7-Z	General works
690	Testing. Locomotive performance
	Cf. TF550+, Movement of trains
693	Superheated steam for locomotives

TJ

	Locomotives -- Continued
695	Locomotives for industrial purposes, logging, mining, etc.
	Cf. TN337, Electric mine locomotives
	Other steam engines
	Marine engines, see VM731 +
700	Traction engines, etc.
705	Steam wagons, trucks, etc.
	Cf. TL200 +, Steam automobiles
	Road rollers, see TE223 +
710	Portable engines
712	Farm engines
717	Reciprocating engines of unusual form
	Steam engines of other forms not reciprocating
720	General works
725	Eolipiles
727	Aerosteam engines
729	Rotary engines
731	Cycloidal engines
	Steam turbines
	Cf. VM740, Marine turbines
735	General works
737	General special
740	Special types, makes, etc. (not A-Z)
	Miscellaneous motors and engines
	Including internal combustion engines; air, gas, and oil engines, etc.
751	Periodicals, societies, etc.
752	Dictionaries and encyclopedias
753	History
755	General works
755.5	Juvenile works
756	Combustion. Thermodynamics
	Cf. TJ797, Diesel engines
758	Patents
759	General special
762.A-Z	Parts and systems, A-Z
762.B4	Bearings
762.C73	Cranks and crankshafts
	Cf. TJ669.C7, Locomotives
	Cf. TL210 +, Motor vehicles
762.C94	Cylinder blocks
762.F84	Fuel systems
762.S95	Superchargers
763	Adiabatic engines
765	Hot-air engines. Caloric engines
	Compressed air engines
766	General works
766.5	Air turbines
766.7	Air cooled engines
768	Gas powerplants
	Gas engines
770	General works

Miscellaneous motors and engines
Gas engines -- Continued

773	Explosion or ignition devices
774	Other details. Cylinders, pistons, etc.
775	Regulation devices
776	Special types
	Including catalogs
777.A-Z	Special applications, A-Z
777.F3	Farm engines
778	Gas turbines

Cf. TJ812.6, Solar gas turbines
Cf. VM740, Marine turbines

779	Free piston engines
780	Engines for utilization of furnace and waste gases and heat

Internal combustion engines, spark ignition
Cf. TJ621, Gasoline locomotives
Cf. TL210+, Automobile motors
Cf. TL701+, Airplane motors
Cf. VM771+, Marine engines

782	Periodicals, societies, congresses, etc.
785	General works
787	Carburetion, ignition, etc. Spark plugs. Magnetos
	Cf. TL213, Automobiles
788	Cylinders, pistons, and other parts
789	General special

Including lubrication, cooling, etc.
For automobile or airplane lubricants prefer
TL153.5, and TL702.L8

Special types

790	Small gasoline engines
	Including two-stroke engines
791	Stratified charge engines
792	Rotary combustion engines
	Including Wankel engine, Frasca engine

Special applications

793	Agricultural machinery
793.2	Construction equipment
793.3	Hoisting machinery

Diesel engines
Cf. TJ619.5, Diesel engines for locomotives
Cf. TK1075, Diesel engine electric plants
Cf. TL704.2, Diesel engines for aircraft
Cf. VM770, Marine diesel engines

795.A1	Periodicals, societies, etc.
795.A2-Z	General works
795.5	Special types, makes, etc. (not A-Z)
797	Fuel systems. Fuel injection systems. Combustion
	Cf. TP343+, Diesel fuels
798	Lubrication
798.5	Cylinders, pistons and other parts

TJ

	Miscellaneous motors and engines
	Diesel engines -- Continued
799	General special
	Including cooling, governors, exhaust systems, etc.
800	Alcohol motors
805	Engines or motors using other combustible liquids and vapors
	Renewable energy sources
	Cf. GB1199.5 +, Geothermal resources
	Cf. TC147, Water power
	Cf. TP360, Biomass energy
807	Periodicals. Societies. Serials
807.2	Congresses
807.4	Dictionaries and encyclopedias
807.6	Directories
807.8	Information services
807.9.A-Z	By region or country, A-Z
808	General works
808.2	Juvenile works
808.3	Handbooks, tables, etc.
808.5	Addresses, essays, lectures
	Research
808.6	General works
808.7.A-Z	By region or country, A-Z
	Solar energy
	Class here general works on solar energy. For applications in special fields, see the field, e.g. TH7413, Solar heating of buildings
	Cf. HD9681, Solar energy industry
	Cf. NA2542.S6, Architecture and solar radiation
	Cf. QC910.2 +, Solar radiation
	Cf. TH6561.7, Solar water heating
	Cf. TH7414, Solar houses
	Cf. TK1056, Production of electric power from solar energy
809	Periodicals. Societies. Serials
809.2	Congresses
	Exhibitions. Museums
809.4	General works
809.5.A-Z	By region or country, A-Z
	Apply table at TJ6.A2-Z
809.6	Dictionaries and encyclopedias
809.8	Directories
809.9	Information services
	By region or country
	United States
809.95	General works
809.96.A-Z	By region or state, A-Z
809.97.A-Z	Other regions or countries, A-Z
810	General works
810.3	Juvenile works
810.5	Handbooks, tables, etc.

	Renewable energy sources
	Solar energy -- Continued
810.7	Addresses, essays, lectures
810.9	Study and teaching
	Research
811	General works
811.5.A-Z	By region or country, A-Z
	Special topics
	Solar batteries. Solar cells, see TK2960
812	Solar collectors
812.5	Solar engines
812.6	Solar gas turbines
812.7	Solar materials
812.8	Solar ponds
	Wind power
820	General works
	Windmills
823	History
824	Early works to 1800
825	1800-
827	Trade catalogs
828	Wind turbines
	Wind pumps, see TJ926
830	Animal motors. Treadmills
	Hydraulic machinery
	Cf. TC1+, Hydraulic engineering
836	Periodicals. Societies. Serials
838	Congresses
839	Dictionaries and encyclopedias
	General works
840.A2	Early to 1800
840.A3-Z	1800-
843	Oil hydraulics and oil hydraulic machinery
844	Hydraulic fluids
	Hydraulic powerplants
	Cf. TK1081+, Hydroelectric plants
	Cf. TK1421+, Hydroelectric plants, by place
(845)	General works
	see TC147
847	Sluices, gates, etc.
849	Penstocks and pipelines
851	Wasteways, etc.
853	Fluidic devices
	Hydraulic motors
855	General works
857	General special
	Including regulators, etc.
859	Water mills
	Water wheels
860	General works
862	Overshot
864	Undershot
866	Tangential (Pelton, etc.)

Hydraulic machinery
　　Water wheels -- Continued
　　　Turbines
　　　　Cf. TJ735+, Steam turbines
870　　　　General works
873　　　　General special
875　　　　Special types
880　　　Hydraulic brakes
890　　Water-pressure engines
　　Conveying of gases, liquids and solids by means of
　　　steam, air, or water
898　　General works
898.5　　Coal slurry pipelines
　　　　Cf. TJ1405, Coal-handling machinery
　　Pumps and pumping engines
　　　Cf. TC929, Irrigation pumps
899　　Periodicals, societies, etc.
899.5　　Congresses
899.7　　Dictionaries and encyclopedias
900　　General works
901　　General special
　　　　Including ancient and primitive pumps
902　　Catalogs
　　　　Cf. TH6529, Water-supply fittings
902.5　　Standards. Specifications
903　　Hand pumps
　　　　Cf. TH9363, Fire pumps
905　　Hydraulic rams
　　Steam pumps
906　　　General works
908　　　Catalogs, etc.
910　　Electric pumping machinery
912　　Solar pumps
915　　Piston pumps. Reciprocating pumps
916　　Metering pumps
917　　Rotary pumps
919　　Centrifugal pumps (Kreiselpumpen)
921　　Pulsometers, steam syphons, etc.
925　　Pumping by compressed air. Airlift pumps
926　　Wind pumps
927　　Submersible pumps
　　Fire engines, see TH9371+
　Pipelines (General)
　　Cf. TA660.P55, Structural engineering
　　Cf. TC1800, Ocean engineering
　　Cf. TJ898.5, Coal slurry pipelines
　　Cf. TN879.5+, Petroleum pipelines
　　Cf. TN880.5, Natural gas pipelines
930　General works
930.5　Supports
933　Equipment and supplies
　　　Including catalogs
934　Double wall piping

935	Flow of fluids in pipes. Flowmeters
	Cf. TC174, Flow of water in pipes
	Vacuum technology
940	General works
940.5	Vacuum pumps
	Pneumatic machinery
950	General works
	Airbrakes, see TF420 +
955	Air pumps
	Blowers and fans. Exhausters
	Cf. TH7683.A +, Ventilation fixtures
960	General works
963	Piston blowers. Blast engines
966	Rotary blowers
969	Centrifugal blowers
	Compressed air
981	Periodicals, societies, etc.
985	General works
	Air compressors
990	General works
992	Catalogs and trade publications
1000	Distribution and transmission
	Pneumatic tools
1005	General works
1007	Catalogs
1009	Sandblast
	Cf. TP864, Glasswork
1015	Pneumatic tubes and carriers
	Flow of gases in pipes. Air meters
1025	General works
1030	Air jets
	Machinery exclusive of prime movers
	Including millwork, e.g., the shafting, gearing and
	other driving machinery of mills and factories
	Cf. TS191.3, Installation and maintenance of
	factory machinery
	For mills of specific places, see TS21 +
1040	General works
	Power and power transmission
1045	General works
1049	General special
1051	Power transmission machinery
	Including catalogs
1053	Measurement of power. Dynamometers
1053.5	Torquemeters
1054	Speed and revolution indicators
1055	Regulation and control of power. Governors
	For steam engine governors, see TJ550 +
1057	Shafting
1057.4	Axles
	Cf. TF386, Rail car axles
	Cf. TF949.A9, Electric railway car axles
	Cf. TL683.A8, Airplane axles

TJ

	Machinery exclusive of prime movers -- Continued
1058	Rotors
1059	Universal joints
1060	Brakes
	Cf. TF415+, Railroad brakes
	Cf. TF949.B7, Electric railway brakes
	Cf. TJ669.B7, Locomotive brakes
	Cf. TJ880, Hydraulic brakes
	Cf. TJ1377, Elevator brakes
	Cf. TK4081, Electric brakes
	Cf. TL269+, Automobile brakes
	Cf. TL683.B7, Airplane brakes
1060.2	Shock absorbers
	Cf. TF393, Railroads
	Cf. TL257.5, Motor vehicles
	Cf. TL683.S4, Airplanes
	Bearings
	Cf. TA660.B45, Structural engineering
	General and metallic bearings
1061	General works
1063	Plain bearings. Journal bearings
1065	Pillow blocks, hangers, brackets
1067	Pivot bearings
1069	Collar bearings
1071	Antifriction devices. Ball and roller bearings
	Nonmetallic bearings
	Including special types of bearings
1072	General works
1073.A-Z	Special materials, A-Z
1073.C45	Ceramic
1073.J4	Jewel
1073.P6	Plastic
1073.R8	Rubber
1073.W6	Wood
1073.5	Hydrodynamic and hydrostatic lubrication.
	Gas-lubricated bearings
1073.6	Oil mist lubrication
1073.7	Magnetic bearings
1074	Clutches. Friction clutches
	For automobile clutches, see TL261
	Tribology. Lubrication and friction
1075.A2	Periodicals, societies, etc.
1075.A3-Z	General works
	Lubricants
	Cf. TJ789, Lubrication of motors and engines
	Cf. TP669+, Oils, fats, etc.
1077	General works
1078	Solid lubricants
1079	Oil feeders, etc.
1081	Oil strainers, etc.
1095	Traction drives
	Belt gearing. Belt transmission
1100	General works

	Machinery exclusive of prime movers
	Belt gearing. Belt transmission -- Continued
1103	Pulleys
1105	Belting
1107	Belt shifters, etc.
1115	Rope transmission
1117	Chain gearing
1119	Link belting
	Toothed gearing, see TJ184+
	Machine shops and machine shop practice
	Cf. TS200+, Metal manufactures. Metal forming
1125	General works
1127	Film catalogs
	Building and arrangement of machine shops
1130	General works
1133	Plans for buildings and shops
	Management of machine shops
	Drafting-room practice, see TJ227+
1135	General works
	Accounting and bookkeeping, see HF5686.M2
1143	Production standards. Time and motion study
1146	Cost of production
1148	Estimating
	Including estimates
1150	Storerooms, stockrooms, supplies
	Machine shop practice
1160	General works
1165	Machinists' manuals. Shop kinks, shop mathematics, repairing, etc.
1166	Gages and gaging systems
1167	General special
	Including errors in workmanship, accuracy of fitting, etc.
1170	Directories of dealers in machinery and supplies
	Special companies (History, etc.), see TJ130.A+
1175	Catalogs of machinery (General)
1177	Safety appliances (General)
	For safety appliances for special types of machinery, see the machinery, e. g. TS850, Woodworking
	Machine tools and machining
	Including design, manufacture, and use
	Cf. TS215, Use of metal working machinery (General)
1180	Periodicals, societies, etc.
1183	Dictionaries and encyclopedias
1185	General works
1185.5	Automatic lines, indexing tables, transfer machines

TJ

Machine shops and machine shop practice
Machine tools and machining -- Continued
1186   Cutting tools
            Class here drill bits, milling cutters, reamers,
               broaches, etc., treated collectively
            For cutting tools treated individually, see the
               special numbers, e. g. TJ1263, Drills;
               TJ1270, Reamers
1187   Jigs and fixtures
1187.4   Spindles
1188   Machine tool drives
            For electric drives, see TK4059.M32
1189   Numerical control of machine tools
            For numerical control of special types of
               machinery, see the machinery, e. g. TJ1225,
               Milling machines
1190   Catalogs
1191   Special types of machining
            Including electric spark, ultrasonic, etc.
1191.5   Micromachining
        Materials used in machine and hand tools
1192   General works
         Special materials
1193   Diamonds and other precious stones
1194   Plastics. Other materials (not A-Z)
        Handtools
            Cf. TH5618, Carpentry tools
            Cf. TL1098, Space tools
            Cf. TT186, Woodworking tools
1195   General works
1200   Catalogs
1201.A-Z   Special handtools, A-Z
1201.A9   Axes
           Files, see TJ1285
1201.H3   Hammers
1201.N8   Nut runners and setters
1201.P55   Planes
           Pliers, see TJ1201.T64
           Saws, see TJ1235
1201.S3   Scrapers
1201.S34   Screwdrivers
           Shears, see TJ1240
1201.S68   Squares
1201.T64   Tongs. Pliers
1201.V5   Vises
1201.W44   Wedges
1201.W8   Wrenches
        Special tools
         Planing machines
1205   General works
1206   Planers
1208   Shapers. Routing tools
            Cf. TT203.5, Woodworking

Machine shops and machine shop practice
Machine tools and machining
Special tools
Planing machines -- Continued
1210   Slotting and grooving machines
Turning machines. Screw machines
Cf. TT207, Metal turning
1215   General works
Lathes
1218   General works
1219   Chucks
1220   Boring attachments
1222   Screw-cutting machines
Milling machines
For gear cutting machinery, see TJ187
1225   General works
1227   Milling cutters
Cutting and sawing machinery
Cf. TK4660.5, Electric cutting machinery
1230   General works
Saws
For sawmill machinery, see TS850
1233   General works
1235   Saw filing
Cf. TJ1285, Files and filing
1237   Saw sets
1240   Shears
Perforating machinery
1250   General works
Punching machinery
Cf. TS253, Punch and die work; press tool
work
1255   General works
1257   Multiple punches
Drilling machinery
1260   General works
Drills
Including making and tempering
1263   General works
1265   Catalogs
1270   Reamers
Abrading machinery. Grinding, lapping, etc.
Sharpening
Cf. TS654.5, Electrolyic polishing
1280   General works
1285   Files and filing
Cf. TJ1235, Saw filing
1287   Catalogs
1290   Emery wheels
1293   Grindstones
Abrasives and polishes
1296   General works
1298   Carborundum. Silicon carbide

	Machine shops and machine shop practice
	Machine tools and machining
	Special tools -- Continued
1300	Bending machines
	Including straightening and shaping
	Hammers. Steam hammers. Power hammers, etc.
1305	General works
1310	Riveting machines
1313	Measuring tools, rules, calipers, etc.
1315	Bench work and fitting
	Assembling machines
1317	General works
1317.5	Orienting mechanisms
	Fastenings
	Cf. TA492.A+, Special forms in metal
1320	General works
1325	Rivets
1327	Retaining rings
1328	Pins
1329	Keys and keyways. Splines
	Bolts and nuts
1330	General works
1333	Bolt cutters
1335	Taps and dies
	Screws and screw threads
1338	General works
1340	Standards
	Screw-cutting machines, see TJ1222
1345	Crushing and milling machinery
	Cf. TE239, Stonecrushers for road material
	Cf. TJ1225+, Milling machines
	Cf. TJ1280+, Abrading machinery
	Cf. TN496+, Ore-dressing, etc.
	Cf. TP937.5, Paint machinery
	Cf. TS2120+, Flour mills, etc.
	Hoisting and conveying machinery
	Cf. TS180.3, Materials handling machinery
1350.A1	Periodicals, societies, etc.
1350.A2-Z	General works
1353	Catalogs
1355	Excavators
	Cf. TA735+, Excavating machinery (Operation and use)
	Hoisting machinery
	Cf. TJ793.3, Internal combustion engines for hoisting machinery
1357	Blocks and falls
1359	Chain blocks
1360	Vacuum lifters
1361	Shear legs, etc.
1362	Winches
	Cranes and derricks
1363	General works

	Hoisting and conveying machinery
	Hoisting machinery
	Cranes and derricks -- Continued
1365	Travelling cranes
1366	Lifting magnets
1367	Details of construction
	Including girders and beams
	Elevators
1370	General works
1372	Specifications
1374	Electric elevators
1375	Hydraulic elevators
1376	Escalators
1377	Brakes and safety devices
1380	Elevator service in buildings
1382	Dumbwaiters
1383	Hoists
	For ashes, etc.
	Conveying machinery
	Cableways. Telpherage. Wire rope transportation
1385	General works
1387	Electric telpher systems
	Conveyors, belts, etc., for assembly line production. Endless carriers
1390	General works
1395	Catalogs
1398	Conveyors, chutes, etc., for letters, parcels, cash, etc.
1400	Passenger conveyors
1405	Coal-handling machinery
	Cf. TF294, Locomotive coaling plants
	Cf. TH4471, Coal-handling plants
	Cf. TJ898.5, Coal slurry pipelines
	Cf. TN815, Mining
1410	Ash-handling machinery
	Grain-handling machinery
	Cf. TH4461, Grain elevators
1415	General works
1417	Special systems, companies, etc.
1418	Dumping devices
	Lifting and pressing machinery
1425	General works
	Lifting jacks
1430	General works
1433	Screwjack
1435	Hydraulic jack
	Presses
1450	General works
1452	Catalogs
1455	Screw press
1460	Hydraulic presses
1465	Pneumatic presses
	Filter presses

TJ

	Lifting and pressing machinery
	Presses
	Filter presses -- Continued
1470	General works
1475	Catalogs
	Agricultural machinery. Farm machinery
	Cf. S671+, Utilization of agricultural machines
	Cf. S675.5, Maintenance and repair
	Cf. S677, Catalogs
1480.A1	Periodicals, societies, etc.
1480.A2-Z	General works
1482	Soil working machines: plows, harrows, cultivators, etc.
1483	Seeders, planters, etc.
1484	Machines for caring for plants
1485	Harvesters, reapers, etc.
1486	Threshing machines. Combines
1486.5	Lumbering machinery
1487	Other
	Farm gas engines, see TJ777.F3
	Farm steam engines, see TJ712
	Gasoline tractors, see TL233+
	Pumps and pumping engines, see TJ899+
	Trucks, see TL230+
1495.A-Z	By country, A-Z
1496.A-Z	By company, A-Z
	Sewing machines
	Cf. TT713, Sewing machine work
1501	Periodicals, societies, etc.
	Exhibitions
1503.A1	General works
1503.A2-Z	By region or country, A-Z
	Apply table at TJ6.A2-Z
1504	Dictionaries and encyclopedias
1505	Directories
1507	History
1510	General works
1512	Patents
1513	General special
1515	Manuals of instruction for users
1519	Trade catalogs
	Other special machinery
1530	Goffering machines
1535	Winding machines
1540	Screening machinery
(1545)	Packaging machinery
	see TS196.4
1550	Wrapping machines
1555	Sorting devices
	Coin operated machines
1557	General works
1560	Vending machines
1570	Amusement machines

	Electrical engineering. Electronics. Nuclear engineering
	For distribution or transmission of electric power, see TK3001+
	For dynamoelectric machinery and auxiliaries, see TK2000+
	For electricity in general, see QC501+
	For production of electric energy, see TK1001+
	For works combining mechanical and electrical engineering, see TJ163+
	Periodicals and societies
	Arrange by language of publication
1.A1	International or polyglot
1.A3-Z	English
2	French
3	German
4	Other languages (not A-Z)
5	Congresses
	Exhibitions. Museums
	For telegraphic exhibitions, see TK5107.5.A1+
6.A1	General works
6.A2-Z	By region or country, A-Z
	Under each country:
	.x *General works*
	.x2A-.x2Z *Special. By city, A-Z*
7	Collected works (nonserial)
9	Dictionaries and encyclopedias
	Cf. QC505, Electrical dictionaries
11	Electrotechnical readers
12	Directories of electrical industries
	For central station directories, see TK1194
13	Yearbooks
	History
15	General works
16	Early to 1830
17	Nineteenth century, 1830-1880
18	1880-
21-127	Country divisions (Table T1)
	Including general reports of government bureaus
	Add country number in table to TK0
	Biography
139	Collective
140.A-Z	Individual, A-Z
	General works
143	Before 1830
144	1830-1870
145	1870-
146	Elementary textbooks
147	Laboratory manuals, outlines, syllabi, etc.
	For standardizing, see TK275+
	For testing, see TK401
148	Juvenile works. Popular works
	For amateur's handbooks, see TK9900+
151	Pocketbooks, tables, etc.

TK

152	Safety measures (General)
153	General special
	Including electromechanical transducers
155	Addresses, essays, lectures
159	Electrical engineering as a profession
	For electrical engineering (Biography), see TK139+
	Study and teaching
165	General works
168	Problems, exercises, etc.
169	Examinations, questions, etc.
	America
171	General works
	United States
173	General works
174.A-W	States, A-W
175.A-Z	Cities, A-Z
	Canada
176	General works
177.A-Z	Special provinces, A-Z
178.A-Z	Special cities, A-Z
179	Latin America
180	Mexico
	Central America
182	General works
183.A-Z	Special countries, A-Z
	West Indies
185	General works
186.A-Z	Special islands, A-Z
	South America
188	General works
189.A-Z	Special countries, A-Z
	Europe
191	General works
192.A-Z	Special countries, A-Z
	Asia
194	General works
195.A-Z	Special countries, A-Z
	Africa
197	General works
199.A-Z	Special countries, A-Z
	Australia
201	General works
202.A-Z	Special states, A-Z
203	New Zealand
	Pacific islands
204	General works
205.A-Z	Special islands, A-Z
	Special schools
	United States
210.A-Z	By school, A-Z
211.A-Z	Correspondence schools, A-Z
213.A-Z	Other countries. By school, A-Z

(215-255)	Laws and legislation relating to applications of electricity
	see class K
257	Patents
260	Insurance requirements
	Cf. TK3275, Wiring
	Electric standards and measurements
	Class here works of a practical nature
	Cf. TK425, Specifications
	For testing of electric machinery, see TK401
	For works on the theory, experimental aspects and study of electrical measurements, see QC535+
	For standards of special machinery or material, see the subject, e.g. TK2311, Dynamoelectric machinery; TK3307, Wire and cable
275	General works
277	General special
	Electric meters
301	General treatises
	General catalogs
308	Manufacturers' catalogs
309	Supply companies' catalogs
	Meters for special measurements
311	Resistance meters and measurements
	Including galvanometers, ohmmeters, resistance boxes, Wheatstone's bridge, shunts
315	Impedance meters and measurements
321	Potential and voltage meters and measurements
	Including voltmeters, voltage detectors
325	Voltohmmeters
	For combined works on voltohmmeters and vacuum tube voltmeters, see TK7879.2
331	Intensity and current meters and measurements
	Including ammeters, coulometers, ampere-hour meters, voltameters
335	Capacitance meters and measurements
341	Quantity meters and measurements
	Including wattmeters
351	Energy and power meters and measurements
	Including watt-hour meters, power factor meters
381	Other meters and measurements
	Including frequency meters and measurements, oscillographs, phase meters, synchronizers
393	Recording meters (General). Process recorders
	For special types, see TK311+
396	Prepayment meters
399	Telemeter systems
401	Testing of electric machinery and appliances (General)
	Cf. TK147, Laboratory manuals
	Cf. TK275+, Electric measurement
	For the testing of special machinery or appliances, see the special subject, e.g. TK2316, Machinery testing

TK

	Electrical engineering and testing laboratories
411	General works
415.A-Z	Special laboratories, A-Z
425	Specifications (General)
	For specifications for special machinery, etc., see the special subject, e.g. TK2321, Dynamoelectric machinery
431	Drawings
435	Estimates
	Management and superintendence of electrical enterprises
	Cf. TK1811, Management of electric power plant central stations
441	General works
445	Business getting. Soliciting
	Interconnection of power systems
447	General works
448	Automation
	General electrical manufacturing and engineering companies
	For economic aspects, see HD9685+
451.A2	Collective
451.A3-Z	Individual, A-Z
	Electric apparatus and materials
452	General works
453	Materials (General)
	Electric circuits
	Cf. TK3226, Electric-power circuits
454	General works
454.15.A-Z	Special circuits, A-Z
454.15.A48	Alternating current
454.15.D57	Direct current
454.15.E65	Equivalent
454.15.P37	Parallel
454.15.S47	Series
454.2	Electric networks
	Cf. TK3226, Electric-power networks
454.4.A-Z	Special, A-Z
454.4.C6	Copper
454.4.E5	Electromagnets
454.4.E9	Explosionproof apparatus
	Insulation and insulating materials, see TK3401+
454.4.L3	Laminated metals
454.4.M3	Magnetic materials
454.4.M33	Magnetic shielding
	Meters, see TK301+
	Microelectromechanical systems, see TK7875
454.4.P5	Phosphors
454.4.P55	Plastics
	Cf. TK3441.P55, Plastics (Insulation)
454.4.P7	Protective coatings
454.4.S7	Steel
454.4.S93	Superconductors
	Cf. TK7872.S8, Superconductors (Electronics)

	Electric apparatus and materials
	Special, A-Z -- Continued
454.4.T3	Talc
455	Catalogs of electric machinery and supplies
	Theory
(500)	Theory (General)
	see TK143-TK145
	Theory of dynamoelectric machinery, see TK2211
	Theory of direct-current machinery, see TK2615
	Theory of alternating-current machinery, see TK2715
	Theory of the line, see TK3226
	Special
531	Current and voltage waveforms
541	Resonance in electrical engineering
	Production of electric energy or power
	For distribution of electric power, see TK3001 +
	For dynamoelectric machinery (General), see TK2000 +
	For powerplants, see TK1191 +
1001	General works
1005	General special
	Including rural plants, metropolitan plants
1007	Electric power systems control
1010	Electric power system stability
	Production from heat. Cogeneration of electric power and heat
	Cf. TK2950 +, Thermoelectricity (Applied)
1041	General works
1051	Production from steam (Coal)
1055	Production from geothermal energy
1056	Production from solar thermal energy
1061	Production from gas
1071	Production from other fuels
1073	Ocean thermal energy conversion
1075	Diesel engine electric plants
1076	Gas turbine power plants
1078	Production from atomic power
	Production from waterpower. Hydroelectric power production
	For special countries and plants, see TK1421 +
1081	General works
1083	Pumped storage power plants
	Production from windpower, see TK1541
	Direct production from chemical action, see TK2901 +
	Production from solar energy
1085	General works
1087	Photovoltaic power generation. Photovoltaic power systems
	Including building-integrated photovoltaic systems
	Cf. TK2960, Solar batteries. Solar cells
	Cf. TK8322, Photovoltaic cells
	Production from solar thermal energy, see TK1056

TK

	Production of electric energy or power -- Continued
	Production classified by character of the electric current
	For distribution of electric energy (classified by character of the electric current), see TK3101+
	General works, see TK1001+
	Direct-current engineering
	Cf. TK2611+, Direct-current dynamoelectric machinery
1111	General works
1121	Edison three-wire system
	Alternating-current engineering
	Cf. TK2711+, Alternating-current machinery
1141	General works
1145	Single-phase currents
1151	Two-phase currents
	Polyphase currents
	Cf. TK2745+, Polyphase-current machinery
1161	General works
1165	Three-phase currents
1168	Multiphase currents
	Electric power plants (General)
	Including light and powerplants
	Cf. TH4581+, Construction of powerplants
	For central stations wiring, see TK3281
	For dynamoelectric machinery and auxiliaries, see TK2000+
	For electric lighting stations, see TK4201+
	For special types, see TK1001+
	For telegraph power production, see TK5371
	For telephone power production, see TK6271+
1191	General works
1193	Special regions or countries, A-Z
1194	Directories
	Cf. TK12, Directories of electrical industries
	Special
1221-1327	Power plants utilizing heat energy (Table T1)
	Add country number in table to TK1200
	Cf. TK1041+, Production of electric energy from heat
	Power plants utilizing nuclear power
	Cf. TK1078, Production of electric energy from nuclear power
	America
1341	General works
	United States
1343	General works
1344.A-W	States, A-W
1345.A-Z	Cities, A-Z
	Canada
1346	General works

Production of electric energy or power
  Electric power plants (General)
    Special
      Power plants utilizing nuclear power
        America
          Canada -- Continued

1347.A-Z	Special provinces, A-Z
1348.A-Z	Special cities, A-Z
1349	Latin America
1350	Mexico
	Central America
1352	General works
1353.A-Z	Special countries, A-Z
	West Indies
1355	General works
1356.A-Z	Special islands, A-Z
	South America
1358	General works
1359.A-Z	Special countries, A-Z
	Europe
1361	General works
1362.A-Z	Special countries, A-Z
	Asia
1364	General works
1365.A-Z	Special countries, A-Z
	Africa
1367	General works
1369.A-Z	Special countries, A-Z
	Australia
1371	General works
1372.A-Z	Special states, A-Z
1373	New Zealand
	Pacific islands
1374	General works
1375.A-Z	Special islands, A-Z
1421-1527	Power plants utilizing waterpower (Table T1)
	Add country number in table to TK1400
	Cf. TK1081+, Production of electric energy
	from waterpower
1541	Power plants utilizing wind
	Power plants utilizing both heat and waterpower, see
	TK1221+
1545	Power plants utilizing solar energy
1560	Power plants utilizing other power
1751	Substations
1811	Central station management
	For electric lighting (Central station
	management), see TK4238
	For machine operators' manuals, see TK2184
1831	Central station testing
	Cf. TK2316, Testing of dynamoelectric
	machinery

TK

Production of electric energy or power
   Electric power plants (General) -- Continued
1841   Electric power rates
         Cf. HD9685+, Economic aspects
         Cf. TK21+, Special places
   Dynamoelectric machinery and auxiliaries
      Including motive power, machinery and auxiliaries
      For auxiliaries (General), see TK2811+
      For powerplants, see TK1191+
      For production of electric energy, see TK1001+
2000   General works
     Dynamoelectric machinery
        Including both direct and alternating-current
         generators, motors, etc.
2081   Special motive power and driving apparatus for
       dynamoelectric machinery
       General works
2181   Treatises
2182   Elementary textbooks
2184   Operators' manuals
        Amateurs' handbooks of generator and motor
         construction, see TK9911
2189   General special
2211   Theory
        For theory of alternating-current machinery, see
         TK2715
        For theory of direct-current machinery, see TK2615
2271   Eddy currents in electrical engineering
2281   Commutation and brush resistance
        Cf. TK2481, Commutation
2311   Standards
2313   Monitoring
2316   Testing
        For alternating-current machinery, see TK2723
        For central station testing, see TK1831
        For direct-current machinery, see TK2623
        For generators and motors, see TK2433
2321   Specifications
2325   Machine drawing for electrical engineers
2331   Design and construction
        For alternating-current machinery, see TK2725
        For direct-current machinery, see TK2625
        For generators and motors, see TK2435
2341   Types of dynamoelectric machinery
        For alternating-current machinery, see TK2731
        For direct-current machinery, see TK2631
        For generators, see TK2441
        For motors, see TK2537
2391   General special
        Including automata, coils, etc.

Dynamoelectric machinery and auxiliaries
Dynamoelectric machinery -- Continued
Generators (General) (D.C. and A.C.). Dynamos
Including works treating of both generators and
motors
For alternating-current generators, see TK2761+
For amateurs' handbooks of generator construction,
see TK9911
For direct-current generators, see TK2661+
For machinery for electric lighting, see TK4241

2411	General works
2433	Testing of generators and motors
2435	Design and construction of generators and motors

For design of alternating-current generators,
see TK2761+
For design of details, see TK2451+
For design of direct-current generators, see
TK2625

2441	Types of generators

For alternating-current generators, see TK2765
For direct-current generators, see TK2665
Details

2451	General works
	Special
	Mechanical details
2456	General works
2458.A-Z	Special, A-Z
2458.B4	Bearings
2458.F68	Foundation
2458.S5	Shafting
	Magnetic details
2461	General works
	Special
2464	Field yoke
2465	Field poles
2466	Field shoes
	Electrical details
2471	General works
	Special
	Winding
2474	General works
2475	Field winding and spools
2477	Armature winding and armatures
2481	Commutators and collectors

For commutation, see TK2281

2484	Brush holders and brushes
2487	Shunts. Leads
2488	Terminals
2491	General special

TK

Dynamoelectric machinery and auxiliaries
Dynamoelectric machinery -- Continued
Motors (General) (D.C. and A.C.)
For alternating-current motors, see TK2781+
For direct-current motors, see TK2681
For use of electric motors, see TK4055+
For works treating of generators and motors
together, see TK2411+

2511	Treatises
2514	Elementary textbooks
(2535)	Amateurs' handbooks
	see TK9911
2537	Types
	For railway motors, see TF935
2541	Details
	For details in common with generators, see
	TK2451+
2551	Transforming machinery (D.C. and A.C.)

For alternating-current transforming machinery,
see TK2791+
For amateurs' handbooks of transformer
construction, see TK9915
For direct-current transforming machinery, see
TK2691+
Direct-current machinery
For direct-current engineering, see TK1111+
General works

2611	Treatises
2612	Textbooks
2615	Theory
	Including short-circuited currents in
	armatures
2623	Testing of D.C. machinery
2625	Design and construction
2631	Types
	Details, see TK2451+
2644	General special
	Special direct-current machinery
	Direct-current generators
2661	General works
	Design, see TK2625
2665	Types

Including constant-potential generators, low
voltage generators, constant-current
generators, commutation pole generators
Details, see TK2451+

2681	Direct-current motors
	Direct-current transforming machinery
2691	General works
	Special
2692	Inverters
2693	Dynamotors
2695	Motor generators

Dynamoelectric machinery and auxiliaries
Dynamoelectric machinery
Direct-current machinery
Special direct-current machinery
Direct-current transforming machinery
Special -- Continued
2697 Boosters
2699 Other direct-current machinery
Alternating-current machinery
Cf. TK1141+, Alternating-current engineering
General works
2711 Treatises
2712 Textbooks
2715 Technique of alternating-current machinery
Including "hunting" fields, parallel driving
2723 Testing of alternating-current machinery
2725 Design and construction
2731 Types of alternating-current machinery
Including synchronous, polyphase, etc.
Details, see TK2451+
2744 General special
Special classes of alternating-current machinery
2745 Polyphase-current machinery
For polyphase currents, see TK1161+
Alternating-current generators
2761 General works
2765 Types
Alternating-current motors
2781 General works
Types
2785 Induction, asynchronous and polyphase
motors. Squirrel-cage motors
Starting compensators, see TK2851
2787 Synchronous motors
2789 Repulsion motors. Repulsion induction
motors. Commutator motors. Series-wound
motors
Alternating-current transforming machinery
D.C. to A.C. transforming machinery
2791 General works
A.C. transformers. Autotransformers or
compensators. "Current" transformers
2792 General works
2794 Types
A.C. to D.C. transforming machinery
2795 General works
2796 Converters. Rotaries
2797 Motor-generator sets (A.C. synchronous or
induction motors)
Including cascade converters (i.e.
induction motor-dynamo; secondary
winding of motor and armature of
generator in cascade)

TK

Dynamoelectric machinery and auxiliaries
  Dynamoelectric machinery
    Alternating-current machinery
      Special classes of alternating-current
        machinery
        Alternating-current transforming machinery
          A.C. to D.C. transforming
            machinery -- Continued

2798   Other A.C. to D.C. transformers. Aluminum
              cells
                Cf. TK7871.7+, Electron tubes

2799   Other alternating-current machinery
            Including frequency converters

2805   Condensers
    Apparatus auxiliary to dynamoelectric machinery
2811   General works
      Switchboards and accessories
        Including switchboard meters, switches, rheostats
        For switchboards for electric power for
          telephones, see TK6271+
        For switchboards for telephone line connections,
          see TK6391+
2821   General works
2822   Direct current
        Alternating current
2825   General works
2826   Low tension A.C.
2828   High tension A.C.
2831   Switches
        Circuit breakers and fuses
2841   General works
2842   Circuit breakers
2846   Fuses and "Cutouts"
         For fuses (General), see TK3511
2851   Rheostats. Regulators. Controllers. Starters
         For controllers or starters for electric cars, see
          TF930
2861   Relays
2891   Accumulators in central stations
      Devices for production of electricity by direct energy
      conversion
        Cf. TL783.54+, Rocket engine propulsion
2896   General works
      Production of electricity directly from chemical
      action
2901   General works
        Special apparatus
         For amateurs' manuals, see TK9917
2921   Primary cells
         For special types, see TK2945.A+
2931   Fuel cells

	Devices for production of
	electricity by direct energy conversion
	Production of electricity
	directly from chemical action
	Special apparatus -- Continued
2941	Storage batteries. Rechargeable batteries.
	Secondary cells
	For accumulators in central stations, see TK2891
	For special types, see TK2945.A +
2942	Solid state batteries
2943	Battery chargers
2945.A-Z	Other special batteries, A-Z
	Fuel cells, see TK2931
2945.L42	Lead-acid
2945.L58	Lithium
2945.N52	Nickel-cadmium
2945.N53	Nickel-hydrogen
2945.S63	Sodium sulphur
	Solid state batteries, see TK2942
	Thermal batteries, see TK2953
2945.Z55	Zinc
	Thermoelectricity (Applied)
2950	General works
	Special apparatus
2953	Thermal batteries
2955	Thermionic converters
2960	Solar batteries. Solar cells
	Cf. TJ812.5, Solar engines
	Cf. TK1056, Production of electric power form
	solar thermal energy
	Cf. TK1087, Photovoltaic power generation.
	Photovoltaic power systems
	Cf. TK8322, Photovoltaic cells
	Cf. TK9918, Amateur construction
	Cf. TL1100 +, Electric equipment on space
	vehicles
2965	Atomic batteries. Isotopic power generators
2970	Magnetohydrodynamic generators
	Cf. TL783.6, Plasma rockets
	Cf. TL1102.G4, Generators
2975	Electrohydrodynamic generators
	Electric energy storage
	Cf. TK1081 +, Pumped storage power plants
	Cf. TK2805, Condensers
	Cf. TK2891, Storage batteries
2980	General works
2985	Magnetic energy storage
2986	Pulsed power systems
	Distribution or transmission of electric power
	Including the electric-power circuit
	Cf. TK1001 +, Production of electric energy
3001	General works

TK

Distribution or transmission
of electric power -- Continued
3081   Testing of distribution systems
For the line and component parts, see TK3207
3085   Lightning protection
3091   General special
Systems
For electric lighting (Systems), see TK4303+
For overhead and underground systems, see TK3221+
3101   General works. Tapping of line for various uses
3107   Transformation of electricity (General)
For transforming machinery, see TK2551
3111   Direct-current systems
Cf. TK1111+, Direct-current engineering
Alternating-current systems
Cf. TK1141+, Alternating-current engineering
3141   General works
3142   Low tension A.C. systems (to 500 volts)
3143   Medium tension A.C. systems (500-10,000 volts)
3144   High tension A.C. systems (above 10,000 volts)
3148   Flexible AC transmission systems
3151   Single-phase current systems
3153   Two-phase current systems
Polyphase current systems
3155   General works
3156   Three-phase current systems
3158   Multiphase current systems
3159   Polycyclic systems
Class here combinations of single and two-phase
currents transmitted over single line and used
as single and two-phase current at point of
application
3171   Composite systems (A.C. and D.C.)
Wiring
Including central station, line and user's plant
For the line (General), see TK3221+
For special wiring, see the subject, e.g. TK4255,
Electric wiring; TK5441, Telegraph; TK6341,
Telephone
3201   General works
3205   Pocketbooks, tables, diagrams, etc.
For tables of properties and dimensions of wire,
see TK3305
3207   Testing of line and component parts
For distribution system testing, see TK3081
For wire, see TK3307
3211   General special
The line
3221   General works

Distribution or transmission of electric power
Wiring
The line -- Continued
3226   Technique of the line. Electric-power circuits
and networks
Including induction capacity, etc., of parallel
lines, heat losses of overhead lines and
underground lines
Cf. TK454+, Electric circuits (Apparatus)
Cf. TK454.2, Electric networks (Apparatus)
Cf. TK7872.T74, Electronic circuits
3227   Grounding
Aerial or overhead lines and component parts
For telegraph overhead lines, see TK5452+
For telephone overhead lines, see TK6352
3231   General works
3239   Catalogs
Details
3242   Poles, crossarms and towers
3243   Pole supports
3246   Line insulators. Testing of insulators
Cf. TK3431, Testing of insulating
material
3248   Lightning arresters (General)
Underground lines and component parts
For telegraph underground lines, see TK5465+
For telephone underground lines, see TK6365
3251   General works
3255   General special
Including electrolysis due to underground
systems
Cf. TF912, Stray currents from electric
traction
3258   Specifications
3261   Details
Including conduits, manholes
For cables, see TK3351
Interior or indoor wiring
3271   General works
3275   Insurance underwriters' requirements
3278   Specifications
3281   Central station wiring
3283   Factory wiring
3284   Commercial building wiring
3285   House wiring
Conductors. Wires. Cables
For telegraph wire and cable, see TK5481
For telephone wire and cable, see TK6381+
3301   General works
3305   Tables of properties and dimensions of wire
Cf. TK3205, Pocketbooks of wiring
3307   Standards and testing of wire and cable
For testing of the line (General), see TK3207

TK

	Distribution or transmission of electric power
	Conductors. Wires. Cables -- Continued
3311.A-Z	Conductors, A-Z
3311.A6	Aluminum
3311.C6	Copper
3311.G3	Gases
3311.P6	Polymers
3321	Bare wires
	Insulated wires
3331	General works
3335	Testing
	Cf. TK3431, Insulating material
3351	Cables
	For submarine cables, see TK5661+
	Insulation and insulating material
3401	General works
	Insulating material
3421	General works
3431	Testing
	For insulated wire and cables, see TK3335
	For insulators, see TK3246
3441.A-Z	Special insulating materials, A-Z
3441.C35	Cellulose
3441.C38	Ceramics
3441.E6	Epoxy resins
3441.F55	Fluorine organic compounds
3441.G3	Gases
3441.G5	Glass
3441.L5	Liquids
3441.M4	Metallic oxides
3441.O5	Oil
3441.P25	Paper
3441.P55	Plastics
3441.P58	Polymers
3441.S46	Silicon nitride
3441.S47	Silicon organic compounds
3441.S48	Siloxanes
3441.S5	Slate
3441.S8	Sulphur hexafluoride
3441.V3	Varnish
	Other details
3511	Fuses (General)
	For fuses for switchboards, see TK2846
3521	Connectors
	Applications of electric power
4001	General works
	Electric railways, see TF854.2+
4015	General special
	Special applications
4018	Agriculture and the farm
	Cf. HD9688, Rural electrification
4025	School building equipment
4035.A-Z	Other special, A-Z

	Applications of electric power
	Special applications
	Other special, A-Z -- Continued
4035.A35	Air conditioning
	Airplanes, see TL690 +
4035.A6	Apartment houses
4035.B83	Building materials industry
4035.C25	Cement industries
4035.C35	Chemical laboratories
4035.C37	Chemical plants
4035.C4	Clothing factories
4035.C47	Clubhouses
4035.C6	Coke industry
	Commercial buildings, see TK4035.M37
4035.F3	Factories (General)
4035.F6	Flour mills
4035.F67	Food industry
4035.H3	Harbors
	Health facilities and hospitals, see RA969.48
	Heating (Building construction), see TH7409 +, TK4601 +
4035.H6	Hoisting machinery
4035.H9	Hydraulic structures
4035.K58	Knit goods industry
4035.L4	Leather industry
4035.M37	Mercantile buildings. Commercial buildings
4035.M4	Metallurgical plants
4035.M6	Motion picture theaters
4035.N6	Nonferrous metal industries
4035.O7	Ore-dressing plants
4035.P3	Paper industry
4035.P33	Peat industry
4035.P35	Petroleum engineering
4035.P55	Pipelines
4035.R3	Railroad repair shops
4035.R4	Refrigeration and refrigerating machinery
4035.R46	Restaurants
4035.R6	Rolling mills
4035.R82	Rubber industry
4035.S4	Service industries
4035.S5	Shipyards
4035.S7	Steelworks
4035.S9	Sugar factories
4035.T4	Textile factories
	Mechanical applications of electric power
4050	General works
	Use of electric motors
4055	General works
4057	General special
	Including motor repairers' manuals
	Cf. TK3205, Wiring manuals, etc.
	Electric driving
4058	General works

Applications of electric power
Mechanical applications of electric power
Use of electric motors
Electric driving -- Continued

4059.A-Z	Special, A-Z
4059.C64	Compressors
4059.C65	Construction equipment
4059.C67	Conveying machinery
4059.D4	Deck machinery
4059.D73	Dredges
4059.E9	Excavating machinery
4059.F35	Fans
4059.H64	Hoisting machinery
4059.K55	Knitting machines
4059.M32	Machine tools
4059.M55	Mining machinery
4059.P74	Printing presses, machinery, etc.
4059.P85	Pumping machinery
4059.R64	Rolling mill machinery
4059.S55	Sluice gates
4059.T48	Textile machinery
4059.T87	Turbomachines
4059.W56	Winding machines
4081	Electric brakes
	Electric calculating machines
	Class here also works which discuss both electric calculating machines and computers
	Cf. HF5679, Machine methods in accounting
	Cf. QA71+, Calculating machines (Mathematics)
	For works on computers only, see TK7885+
4090	General works
	Special machines
	Accounting machines
4100	General works
4101.A-Z	Special. By make, A-Z
	e.g.
4101.I5	International Business Machines Corporation
4102	Billing machines
	Electric lighting
	Cf. TH7700+, Domestic illumination
4125	Periodicals, societies, etc.
4129	Dictionaries and encyclopedias
4131	History
	Special countries
	Including annual reports of electric lighting departments
	Cf. HD4486+, Municipal industries
	Cf. TK4220+, Special plants
	America
4134	General works
	United States

	Electric lighting
	Special countries
	America
	United States -- Continued
4135	General works
4136.A-W	States, A-W
4137.A-Z	Cities, A-Z
	Canada
4138	General works
4139.A-Z	Special provinces, A-Z
4140	Mexico
	Central America
4141	General works
4142.A-Z	Special countries, A-Z
	West Indies
4143	General works
4144.A-Z	Special islands, A-Z
	South America
4145	General works
4146.A-Z	Special countries, A-Z
	Europe
4147	General works
4148.A-Z	Special countries, A-Z
	Asia
4149	General works
4150.A-Z	Special countries, A-Z
	Africa
4151	General works
4152.A-Z	Special countries, A-Z
	Australia
4153	General works
4154.A-Z	Special states, A-Z
4154.5	New Zealand
	Pacific islands
4155	General works
4156.A-Z	Special islands, A-Z
	General works
4160	Early to 1870
4161	1870-
4162	Elementary textbooks
4164	Electricians' manuals
4166	Pocketbooks, tables, etc.
	Wiring for electric lighting, see TK4255
	Amateurs' handbooks, see TK9921
4169	General special
4175	Technique. Theory of electric lighting
	Including candlepower, light distribution
4181	Specifications
	For incandescent lighting, see TK4348
4186	Management of electric lighting enterprises
	For management of electric lighting plants, see TK4238

TK

Electric lighting -- Continued

4188   Special aspects of electric lighting
Including city or metropolitan lighting, rural
lighting, indirect lighting, lighting of roads
Lighting machinery and supplies
Including catalogs
Cf. TK455, Electric machinery and supplies

4195	General works
4198	Fixtures

For gas and electric fixtures combined, see
TH7960+
Central stations for lighting

4201	General works
4218	General special

Special lighting plants

4219	General works

Special lighting plants utilizing heat energy

4220	United States
4221	Canada
4223.A-Z	Other American countries, A-Z
4224	Other (Asia, Africa, Australia, and Oceania)

Special lighting plants utilizing waterpower

4225	United States
4226	Canada
4228.A-Z	Other American countries, A-Z
4229	Other (Asia, Africa, Australia, and Oceania)

Special lighting plants utilizing both heat and
waterpower

4230	United States
4231	Canada
4233.A-Z	Other American countries, A-Z
4234	Other (Asia, Africa, Australia, and Oceania)
4237	Substations
4238	Management of electric lighting plants

Cf. TK4186, Electric lighting enterprises

4241	Machinery for electric lighting

For electric generators, see TK2411+
For operators' manuals, see TK2184
Distribution in electric lighting

4251	General works
4255	Wiring for electric lighting. Installation

For insurance underwriters' requirements, see
TK3275
For pocketbooks and tables for electric lighting,
see TK4166
Systems of electric lighting
General and miscellaneous, see TK4160-TK4169

4303	Direct-current systems
4304	Alternating-current systems
4308	Composite systems (D.C. and A.C.)
4310	Electric lamps (General)

Arc lighting

4311	General works

<table>
<tbody>
<tr><td></td><td>Electric lighting</td></tr>
<tr><td></td><td> Systems of electric lighting</td></tr>
<tr><td></td><td>   Arc lighting -- Continued</td></tr>
<tr><td>4319</td><td>   General special</td></tr>
<tr><td></td><td>   Arc lamps and systems</td></tr>
<tr><td>4321</td><td>   General works</td></tr>
<tr><td>4322</td><td>   Types. Open and enclosed arcs</td></tr>
<tr><td></td><td>   Prefer TK4329</td></tr>
<tr><td>4329.A-Z</td><td>   Special lamps and systems. By name, A-Z</td></tr>
<tr><td></td><td>   Details</td></tr>
<tr><td>4331</td><td>   General works</td></tr>
<tr><td>4335</td><td>   Carbons</td></tr>
<tr><td></td><td>   For manufacture of carbons, see TK7725</td></tr>
<tr><td></td><td>   Incandescent lighting</td></tr>
<tr><td>4341</td><td>   General works. Handbooks. Pocketbooks</td></tr>
<tr><td>4348</td><td>   Specifications</td></tr>
<tr><td>4349</td><td>   General special</td></tr>
<tr><td></td><td>   Including safety measures</td></tr>
<tr><td></td><td>   Incandescent lamps and special systems</td></tr>
<tr><td>4351</td><td>   General works</td></tr>
<tr><td>4352</td><td>   Types. Carbon and metal filament lamps</td></tr>
<tr><td>4359.A-Z</td><td>   Special lamps and systems. By name, A-Z</td></tr>
<tr><td>4359.H34</td><td>   Halogen lamps</td></tr>
<tr><td>4359.N47</td><td>   Nernst lamps and systems</td></tr>
<tr><td>4359.T9</td><td>   Tungsten lamps</td></tr>
<tr><td></td><td>   Details. Wall plugs, sockets, etc.</td></tr>
<tr><td>4361</td><td>   General works</td></tr>
<tr><td>4365</td><td>   Filaments</td></tr>
<tr><td>4367</td><td>   Tests of efficiency of incandescent lamps</td></tr>
<tr><td></td><td>   Electric discharge lighting</td></tr>
<tr><td></td><td>   Cf. TK4311+, Arc lighting</td></tr>
<tr><td>4371</td><td>   General works</td></tr>
<tr><td>4381</td><td>   Vapor lamps and systems</td></tr>
<tr><td></td><td>   Including mercury vapor lamps</td></tr>
<tr><td>4383</td><td>   Neon lamps and tubes</td></tr>
<tr><td>4386</td><td>   Fluorescent lamps and systems</td></tr>
<tr><td>4391</td><td>   Other lamps and systems (not A-Z)</td></tr>
<tr><td>4395</td><td> Private electric-light plants for country houses, etc.</td></tr>
<tr><td>4399.A-Z</td><td> Special uses of electric lighting, A-Z</td></tr>
<tr><td>4399.A9</td><td>   Auditoriums</td></tr>
<tr><td>4399.B8</td><td>   Building sites</td></tr>
<tr><td>4399.C6</td><td>   Coal preparation plants</td></tr>
<tr><td></td><td>   Cf. TN309, Electric lighting of mines</td></tr>
<tr><td></td><td>   Dwellings, see TK4255</td></tr>
<tr><td>4399.E5</td><td>   Emergency lighting</td></tr>
<tr><td>4399.F2</td><td>   Factories. Workshops</td></tr>
<tr><td>4399.F3</td><td>   Farm buildings</td></tr>
<tr><td>4399.F55</td><td>   Floodlighting</td></tr>
<tr><td>4399.H7</td><td>   Hotels</td></tr>
<tr><td></td><td>   Interior decoration, Lighting as an element in, see
    NK2115.5.L5</td></tr>
<tr><td>4399.I7</td><td>   Iron and steel works</td></tr>
<tr><td>4399.M5</td><td>   Mills</td></tr>
</tbody>
</table>

TK

	Electric lighting
	Special uses of electric lighting, A-Z -- Continued
4399.O35	Office buildings
4399.P44	Pedestrian areas
4399.P5	Physical education facilities
4399.P6	Power plants
4399.P8	Public buildings
4399.R4	Recreation areas
4399.S4	Searchlights
	Ships, see VM493
4399.S5	Show windows
4399.S6	Signs
	Cf. TK4383, Neon lamps and tubes
4399.S63	Sports facilities
4399.S8	Stores, Retail
	Streets, see TK4188
4399.T6	Theaters
	Cf. PN2091.E4, Electric devices for the stage, and stage lighting
	Cf. TR891, Lighting for motion pictures
(4500)	Infrared technology
	see TA1570
	Electric heating
	For rheostats and controllers, see TK2851
4601	General works
4635	Infrared heating
	Special applications of electric heating
	Electric space heating, see TH7409+
	Electric cooking stoves, see TX657.S5
	Electric cooking, see TX827
	Thawing of water pipes, see TH6685
4660	Electric welding
4660.5	Electric cutting
4661	Electric furnaces
	Cf. QD157, Inorganic chemistry
	Cf. QD277, Organic chemistry
	Cf. TN687, Electric metallurgy
	Cf. TP841+, Ceramic industries
	Electric ignition devices for gas lighting in buildings, see TH6885+
	Electric ignition devices for automobiles, see TL213
	Telecommunication
	Class here general works only. For works on special systems, see the subject
	Cf. QA268, Coding theory
5101.A1	Periodicals, societies, congresses, etc.
5101.A3-Z	General works
	Exhibitions
5101.5.A1	General works
5101.5.A2-Z	By region or country, A-Z
	Apply table at TK6.A2-Z
5102	Dictionaries and encyclopedias
5102.2	History

	Telecommunication -- Continued
5102.3.A-Z	By region or country, A-Z
5102.4	Juvenile works
5102.5	General special
5102.6	Telecommunication as a profession
	Study and teaching. Research
5102.7	General works
5102.8.A-Z	By region or country, A-Z
5102.85	Security measures
5102.9	Signal processing
	Coding theory
	For application in special field, see the field
5102.92	General works
5102.94	Cryptographic techniques
5102.96	Error correction
5102.98	Echo suppression
	Apparatus and supplies
5103	General works
5103.12	Wiring
5103.15	Telecommunication lines
	Modems, see TK7887.8.M63
	Wireless communication systems
5103.2	General works
	Broadband communication systems
5103.4	General works
	Asynchronous transfer mode, see TK5105.35
5103.45	Spread spectrum communications
5103.452	CDMA
5103.48	CDPD (Standard)
5103.483	Global system for mobile communications
5103.485	Personal communication service systems
5103.486	TDMA
5103.487	Broadcast data systems
	Radio data systems, see TK6570.R27
	Teletext systems, see TK6679.7
5103.488	Trunked radio. TETRA
5103.5	Information display systems
5103.59	Optical communications
5103.6	Laser communications systems
	Cf. TA1671+, Lasers
	Digital communications
5103.7	General works
	Synchronous data transmission systems, see TK5105.4+
5103.75	Integrated services digital networks
5103.8	Switching systems
	Packet switching, see TK5105.3+
	Artificial satellites in telecommunication
	Cf. HE9719+, Economics
5104	General works
5104.2.A-Z	Special systems and projects, A-Z
5104.2.A72	'Arabsāt
5104.2.A75	ASTRA
5104.2.D5	Dioscures project

TK

	Telecommunication
	Artificial satellites in telecommunication
	Special systems and projects, A-Z -- Continued
5104.2.E29	ECS satellites
5104.2.H46	Hermes
5104.2.I25	INSAT
5104.2.O49	Olympus
5104.2.P33	PACSAT
5104.2.P35	Palapa project
5104.2.R4	Relay
5104.2.S5	Skynet Project
5104.2.T4	Telstar
5104.2.V74	VSATs
	Data transmission systems
5105	General works
	Wireless communication systems, see TK5103.2+
5105.2	Picture transmission systems. Image transmission
	Cf. TK5103.75, Integrated services digital
	networks
	Cf. TK6505, Video telephone
	Cf. TK6600, Phototelegraphy
	Cf. TK6710+, Facsimile transmission
	Packet switching
5105.3	General works
5105.35	Asynchronous transfer mode
5105.38	Frame relay
	Synchronous transfer systems
5105.4	General works
5105.415	SONET
5105.42	Synchronous digital hierarchy
5105.45	TMN
	Computer networks
	For application in special field, see the field
5105.5	General works
5105.543	Bridges. Routers. Gateways
	Computer network protocols. Standards
5105.55	General works
5105.555	BGP
5105.56	CEBus
5105.565	CGI
5105.567	IPSec
5105.572	L2TP
5105.577	Open Document Architecture
5105.58	Open Systems Interconnect
5105.582	PPP
5105.583	Simple Network Management Protocol (SNMP)
5105.585	TCP/IP
5105.586	TINA
5105.587	X.500
5105.59	Computer network security
5105.595	Directory services
5105.6	Telematics
	Local area networks

	Telecommunication
	Computer networks
	Local area networks -- Continued
5105.7	General works
5105.72	Ring networks
5105.73	Electronic mail systems
	Including systems which also connect outside the local network
	Cf. HE7551, Postal service
5105.8.A-Z	Special systems, A-Z
5105.8.A77	AppleTalk
	Banyan VINES, see TK5105.8.V56
5105.8.B57	BLEND
5105.8.E25	Econet
5105.8.E83	Ethernet
5105.8.I24	IBM Token-Ring Network
5105.8.I44	ILLINET
5105.8.L34	LAN Server
5105.8.N65	Novell Netware networks
5105.8.S65	SNA
5105.8.T65	TOPS
5105.8.V56	VINES
5105.83	Electronic villages
5105.85	Metropolitan area networks
	Wide area networks
5105.87	General works
5105.875.A-Z	Special networks and systems, A-Z
5105.875.B57	BITNET
5105.875.C45	CGNET
5105.875.D37	DDN
5105.875.E87	Extranets
5105.875.F55	Florida Information Resource Network
5105.875.I57	Internet
5105.875.I6	Intranets
5105.875.N37	National Research and Education Network
5105.875.S95	SURAnet
5105.875.S97	Switched multi-megabit data service
5105.875.U83	Usenet
	Specific aspects of, or services on, the Internet
	General works, see TK5105.875.I57
	Browsers
5105.882	General works
5105.883.A-Z	Special, A-Z
(5105.883.C66)	Communicator (Netscape)
	see TK5105.883.N49
5105.883.M53	Microsoft Internet Explorer
5105.883.N43	NetCruiser
5105.883.N48	Netscape. Netscape Navigator
5105.883.N49	Netscape Communicator
5105.883.N493	Netscape SuiteSpot
(5105.883.S85)	SuiteSpot (Netscape)
	see TK5105.883.N493
	Search engines

	Telecommunication
	Computer networks
	Wide area networks
	Specific aspects of, or services on, the Internet
	Search engines -- Continued
5105.884	General works
5105.885.A-Z	Special, A-Z
5105.885.A45	AltaVista
	Electronic mail systems, see TK5105.73
	Internet games, see GV1469.15+
5105.886	Internet Relay Chat
5105.8865	Internet telephony
5105.887	Webcasting. Push technology
5105.888	World Wide Web
	Web authoring software
	Including Web server software
	For HTML, see QA76.76.H94
5105.8883	General works
5105.8885.A-Z	Special, A-Z
5105.8885.A26	Active server pages
5105.8885.A28	ActiveX
5105.8885.A36	Adobe PageMill
5105.8885.C55	Claris Home page
(5105.8885.C66)	Composer (Netscape)
	see TK5105.8885.N49
(5105.8885.F76)	FrontPage (Microsoft)
	see TK5105.8885.M53
5105.8885.F87	FutureTense Texture
5105.8885.G64	GoLive CyberStudio
(5105.8885.L58)	LiveConnect (Netscape)
	see TK5105.8885.N5
5105.8885.L67	Lotus Domino
5105.8885.M53	Microsoft FrontPage
5105.8885.M54	Microsoft Office. Microsoft Office professional
5105.8885.M55	Microsoft Visual InterDev
5105.8885.N48	NetObjects Fusion
5105.8885.N49	Netscape Composer
5105.8885.N5	Netscape LiveConnect
(5105.8885.P34)	PageMill
	see TK5105.8885.A36
(5105.8885.T49)	FutureTense Texture
	see TK5105.8885.F87
5105.8885.T54	TK toolkit
(5105.8885.V58)	Visual InterDev (Microsoft)
	see TK5105.8885.M55
5105.8887	WebTV (Trademark)
5105.9	Communications software

	Telegraph
	Including works on the telegraph and telephone
	Cf. TK5601+, Submarine telegraph
	Cf. TK5700+, Radiotelegraph
	Cf. TK9941+, Construction for amateurs
	Cf. UG600+, Military telegraph
5107	Periodicals, societies, etc.
	Exhibitions
5107.5.A1	General works
5107.5.A2-Z	By region or country, A-Z
	Apply table at TK6.A2-Z
5108	Collected works (nonserial)
5110	Dictionaries and encyclopedias
	History
5115	General works
	Claims of inventors
5117	General works
5118.A-Z	Special. By name, A-Z
5118.B2	Claims of Bain
5118.C7	Claims of Cooke
5118.H5	Claims of Henry
5118.M7	Claims of Morse
5121-5227	Country divisions (Table T1)
	Add country number in table to TK5100
	For technical reports of telegraph companies, see
	TK5287.A+
	Biography
5241	Collective
5243.A-Z	Individual, A-Z
	Study and teaching
5250	General works
	Special schools
5255	United States
5257.A-Z	Other countries, A-Z
5261	Comprehensive treatises
5262	Elementary textbooks
5263	Telegraphers' manuals
5264	Beginners' primers
5265	Popular works
	Cf. TK9941+, Construction for amateurs
5266	Pocketbooks, tables, etc.
5269	General special
5275	Theory of telegraphy
5281	Specifications (General)
	Management of telegraph enterprises
	Cf. HE7661, Business administration of
	telegraph companies
	Cf. TK5381, Management of telegraph stations
5283	General works
	Office organization
5285	General works
5286	Records. Correspondence

Telegraph -- Continued

5287.A-Z	Technical reports of telegraph companies. By company, A-Z
	For financial and other non-technical reports, see HE7761+
5295	Catalogs of telegraph apparatus and supplies (General)
	Telegraph plants. Stations. The line
5301	General works
	Stations
5311	General works
	Central telegraph stations
5321	General works
5328.A-Z	Special. By country, A-Z
5341	Branch stations
5371	Power production and special machinery
5378	Electric cells
5381	Management of telegraph stations (Technical)
	Cf. TK5283+, Management of telegraph enterprises
	For telegraphers' manuals, see TK5263
5385	Testing of telegraph apparatus, lines and material
	Cf. TK5445, Inspectors' manuals
	Distribution. Construction. Connections
	Including works on telegraph and telephone lines
5401	General works
	Wiring of telegraph circuits
	Cf. TK6341+, Wiring of telephone circuits
5441	General works
5445	Telegraph wiremen's manuals. Inspectors' manuals. Diagrams of connections, etc.
	Cf. TK5266, Pocketbooks and tables for telegraph engineers
	The line
	Cf. TK6351+, Telephone lines
5451	General works
	Overhead lines
5452	General works
5454	Line material (General)
5455	Details
	Including poles and crossarms, guys and braces
	Underground lines
5465	General works
5467	Conduit material (General)
5468	Details
	Cables, see TK5481
5481	Telegraph wires and cables
	For submarine cables, see TK5671
5491	Switchboards and accessories (for line connections)
	For switchboards for electric power in telegraph, see TK5371
	Systems and instruments for telegraphing
	For systems and instruments for making connections, see TK5491

	Telegraph
	Systems and instruments
	for telegraphing -- Continued
5501	General works
5509	General special. Telegraph alphabets
(5511)	Early to 1830
	Claims of inventors, see TK5117-TK5118
5515	Optic systems. Dial telegraphs. Non-automatic
	electrolytic telegraphs
	Acoustic systems and instruments
5521	General works
5522	General special. Buzzer systems
5523	Simplex. Ordinary. High speed
5531	Duplex (two messages simultaneously, in opposite
	directions)
5535	Quadruplex or synchronous (four messages
	simultaneously, in two directions)
5538	Multiplex (more than four messages simultaneously)
	Automatic transmitting and receiving systems and
	instruments
5541	General works
5543	Printing
	Class here letters or characters printed
	directly
5545	Writing. Autographic
5546	Ink impression or inking receiving systems and
	instruments
5547	Perforating transmitting systems and instruments.
	Perforated paper-fillet in transmitter and ink
	impression in receiver. Synchronographs
5549	Chemical (Electrochemical. Photochemical)
	Cf. TK6600, Picture telegraph
5550	Induction systems
5569.A-Z	Telegraph systems. By application, A-Z
5569.T7	Train telegraph systems
	Cf. TK5550, Induction systems
	Instruments (General)
	Class special instruments with the system above
5571	General works
5575	Keys
	Sounders and relays
5581	General works
5585	Relays
	Submarine telegraph
5601	Periodicals, societies, etc.
	History
5605	General works
5607.A-Z	By country, A-Z
	Geographical subdivisions
5609	General works
5611	Atlantic submarine telegraph
	Including life and works of C.W. Field
5613	Pacific submarine telegraph

TK

	Telegraph
	Submarine telegraph
	Geographical subdivisions -- Continued
5615	Indian Ocean submarine telegraph
5621	Comprehensive treatises
5622	Elementary textbooks
5625	Popular works
5626	Pocketbooks, tables, etc.
5627	General special
5641	Stations. Construction. Component parts, etc.
	Cables and cable laying
5661	General works
	Cable laying and repairing
5662	General works
5671	The cable
	Cf. TK5481, Telegraph cables (General)
5681	Systems and instruments
	Radiotelegraph. Wireless telegraph
	Cf. HE8660+, Economics
	Cf. HJ6645+, Coast Guard service (U.S.)
	Cf. TK6540+, Wireless telephone
	Cf. UG610+, Military wireless telegraph
	Cf. VG76+, Naval wireless telegraph
5700	Periodicals, societies, etc.
5707	Collected works (nonserial)
5709	Dictionaries and encyclopedias
	Directories of wireless stations, see HE8663+
5711	History
	Special countries
	United States
5718	General works
5719.A-W	States, A-W
5720	Canada
5721	Latin America
5721.5	West Indies
	South America
5722.A1	General works
5722.A2-Z	By region or country, A-Z
	Europe
5723.A1	General works
5723.A2-Z	By region or country, A-Z
	Asia
5724.A1	General works
5724.A2-Z	By region or country, A-Z
	Africa
5725.A1	General works
5725.A2-Z	By region or country, A-Z
5726	Australia
5726.5	New Zealand
5727	Pacific Islands
5728	Arctic regions
	Biography
5733	Collective

	Telegraph
	Radiotelegraph. Wireless telegraph
	Biography -- Continued
5739.A-Z	Individual, A-Z
	Study and teaching. Schools
5740	General works
5740.5	Laboratory manuals
5741	Comprehensive treatises
5742	Elementary textbooks
5743	Operators' manuals
5745	Popular works
	For amateurs' manuals for construction, see TK9946
5746	Pocketbooks, tables, etc.
5747	General special
5751	Theory
5755	Patents
5771	Stations for radiotelegraph
	Special applications
5773	General works. Position finding, etc.
(5775)	Aeronautical
	see TL693-TL696
5777	General special
	Systems and instruments for radiotelegraph
	For general works, see TK5741-TK5747
5811	Special systems
	Instruments
5861	General works
5863	Coherers
5865	Other special
	Electroacoustics. Electroacoustic transducers
5981	General works
5982	Ultrasonic transducers
5983	Loudspeakers
5983.5	Headphones
5984	Magnetic tape and magnetic tape heads
	For data tapes, see TK7895.D3
5986	Microphones
	Cf. TK6478, Telephone transmitters
5987	Hydrophones
	Recorders and recording (Magnetic), see TK7881.6 +
	Sound systems (General), see TK7881.4 +
5990	Sirens
	Telephone
	For Internet telephony, see TK5105.8865
	For military telephone systems, see UG620.A +
	For mobile communication systems, see TK6570.M6
	For systems and standards used in wireless
	communication, including wireless telephone
	systems, see TK5103.2 +
	For telecommunications devices for the deaf, see
	HV2502.5
	For telephone plants, see TK6201 +
	For telephone systems and instruments, see TK6401 +

	Telephone -- Continued
6001	Periodicals, societies, etc.
6005	Congresses. Conventions
	Exhibitions. Museums
6005.5.A1	General works
6005.5.A2-Z	By region or country, A-Z
	Apply table at TK6.A2-Z
6006	Collected works (nonserial)
6007	Dictionaries and encyclopedias
6011	Directories of the telephone industry
	History
6015	General works
	Claims of inventors
6017	General works
6018.A-Z	Special. By name, A-Z
	e.g.
6018.B4	Claims of Bell
6018.P6	Claims of Pickering
6018.S8	Claims of Strong
6021-6127	Special countries (Table T1)
	Add country number in table to TK6000
	For technical reports of telephone companies, see TK6187.A +
	Biography
6141	Collective
6143.A-Z	Individual, A-Z
	Study and teaching
6150	General works
	Special schools
6155	United States
6157.A-Z	Other countries, A-Z
6161	Comprehensive treatises
6162	Elementary textbooks
6163	Operators' manuals
	Cf. TK6345, Telephone wiremen's manuals
6164	Beginners' primers
6165	Popular works. Juvenile works
	Cf. TK9951, Amateurs' manuals for construction
6167	Pocketbooks, tables, etc.
6168	Examinations, questions, etc.
6169	General special
	Including rural telephones, estimates
6175	Theory of the telephone
6181	Specifications (General)
	Management of telephone enterprises
	Cf. HE8761 +, Business administration of telephone companies
	Cf. TK6281, Management of telephone stations
6183	General works
	Office organization
6185	General works
6186	Records, correspondence, etc.

	Telephone -- Continued
6187.A-Z	Technical reports of telephone companies. By company, A-Z
	For financial and other non-technical reports, see HE8801 +
6188	General special
6195	Catalogs of telephone apparatus and supplies (General)
	Telephone plants. Stations. The line
6201	General works
	Stations. Central telephone stations. Exchanges
6211	General works
6241	Substations
	Power production and special machinery
	For central stations (General), see TK1191 +
6271	General works
6278	Batteries
6281	Management of telephone stations
	Cf. TK6183 +, Management of telephone enterprises
6285	Testing of telephone apparatus, line and material
	Distribution. Construction. Connections
6301	General works
	Wiring of telephone circuits
6341	General works
6343	General special
	Including phantom circuits
6345	Telephone wiremen's manuals. Inspectors' manuals
	Cf. TK3205, Wiring manuals for electricians
	Cf. TK5445, Telegraph wiremen's manuals
	Cf. TK6163, Telephone operators' manuals
	The line
	Cf. TK5451 +, Telegraph (The line)
6351	General works
6352	Overhead or aerial lines
	For telegraph overhead lines, see TK5452 +
6365	Underground lines
	Submarine telephone cables
	History
6370	General works
6372.A-Z	By country, A-Z
	Geographical subdivisions
6373	Atlantic Ocean
6375	Pacific Ocean
6377	Treatises
6379	Popular works. Juvenile works
	Telephone wires and cables
	For telegraph wires and cables, see TK5481
6381	General works
6383	Wiretapping
	Switchboards and accessories for line connections
	For switchboards for electric power for telephones, see TK6271 +
6391	General works

TK

Telephone
   Distribution. Construction. Connections
     Switchboards and accessories
       for line connections -- Continued

6392	General special
	Systems for making connections
6394	Manual systems
6397	Automatic systems
	Systems and instruments for transmitting sound
	For systems and instruments for making electric connections, see TK6391+
6401	General works
6418	Catalogs of instruments
	Cf. TK6195, Catalogs of apparatus and supplies
	Special systems and instruments
	Cf. TK6394+, Systems for making connections
6421	General works
6425	Multiplex systems
6430	Centrex systems and services
	Instruments
6471	General works
6473	Technique of telephone instruments
	Transmitters
6475	General works
6478	Microphones
6481	Receivers
6500	Telegraphones. Telephonographs. Recording telephones. Dictographs. Mechanical telephones
6505	Video telephones
6525	Simultaneous telegraph and telephone
	Radio
	Including wireless telephone
	Cf. QC660.5+, Electric waves
6540	Periodicals, societies, etc.
6541	Congresses
6542	Yearbooks
6543	Collected works (nonserial)
6544	Dictionaries and encyclopedias
	Biography
6545.A1	Collective
6545.A2-Z	Individual, A-Z
6547	History
6548.A-Z	By country, A-Z
6550	General works
	Cf. TK9956+, Amateur construction
6550.7	Popular works. Juvenile works
6550.8	Laboratory manuals
6552	Tables, calculations, etc.
6553	General special
	Including testing, standards, repairing, safety, two-way radio (Radiotelephone), etc.

	Radio -- Continued
6553.5	Addresses, essays, lectures
	Study and teaching. Research
6554	General works
6554.5	Examinations, questions, etc.
6555	Directories of radio stations
	Cf. TL695.5, Aircraft stations
6557	Trade directories
	Radio stations
	Cf. TH4655, Construction of radio station
	structures
6557.5	General works
6558.A-Z	Special radio stations. By place, A-Z
	e.g.
6558.P5	Pittsburgh, KDKA
6559	Patents
	Apparatus
6560.A1-Z4	General works
	Prefer TK6561-TK6565
6560.Z5	Trade publications
6561	Sending apparatus. Transmitters
6562.A-Z	Special, A-Z
6562.D54	Digital audio broadcasting
6562.F2	FM broadcasting
6562.P32	Packet transmission
6562.S5	Shortwave transmission
6562.S54	Single-sideband transmission
6562.S7	Stereophonic broadcasting
6562.W5	Wire broadcasting
	Radio receiving apparatus
	Including catalogs
6563	General works
6563.2	Collectors and collecting
6564.A-Z	Special, A-Z
6564.C79	Crystal sets
6564.F7	Frequency modulation radios
6564.M64	Monitoring receivers
6564.P35	Panoramic receivers
6564.P6	Portable radios
6564.S5	Shortwave radios
6564.T7	Transistor radios
6565.A-Z	Other radio apparatus, A-Z
6565.A55	Amplifiers
6565.A6	Antennas
6565.A8	Attenuators
6565.C3	Cathode ray tubes
6565.C6	Coils
6565.C65	Condensers
6565.D4	Detectors
6565.D5	Direction finders
(6565.E6)	Electron tubes
	see TK6565.V3
6565.F5	Filters

TK

	Radio
	Apparatus
	Other radio apparatus, A-Z -- Continued
6565.F7	Frequency changers
	Loudspeakers, see TK5983
6565.M35	Mains supply
	Microphones, see TK5986
6565.O7	Oscillators
6565.P3	Panels
6565.R32	Radio and television towers
	Receivers, see TK6563+
6565.R4	Recording apparatus
6565.R42	Rectifiers
6565.R426	Resistors
6565.R43	Resonators
6565.S9	Switchgear
	Television and radio towers, see TK6565.R32
6565.T7	Transformers
6565.T73	Transmission lines
6565.V3	Vacuum tubes. Electron tubes
6565.V6	Voltage regulators
6565.W25	Walkie-talkies
6565.W3	Waveguides
6570.A-Z	Special applications of radio, A-Z
	Aircraft, see TL692+
6570.A8	Automobiles
(6570.B7)	Broadcasting
	see PN1991-PN1991.9
6570.C5	Citizens band radio
6570.C6	Radio control
	Military radio systems, see UG610+
6570.M6	Mobile communication systems
	For systems and standards used in wireless
	communications, see TK5103.2+
	Naval radio systems, see VG76+
6570.P5	Pipelines
6570.P6	Police
6570.P8	Public safety radio service
6570.R27	Radio data systems
6570.R3	Railroads
6570.T76	Tropospheric scatter communication systems
	Wireless communication systems, see TK5103.2+
	Extraterrestrial radio communication
	For radio in astronautics, see TL3035
6571	General works
6571.5.A-Z	Special celestial bodies, A-Z
6571.5.M6	Moon
	Radar
6573	Periodicals, societies, congresses, etc.
6574	Dictionaries and encyclopedias
6574.2	History
6574.4.A-Z	By region or country, A-Z
6575	General works

	Radar -- Continued
6576	Popular works. Juvenile works
6578	Tables, calculations, etc.
6580	General special
	Apparatus
6585	General works
6587	Transmitting apparatus
	Including transmitter-receiver units
6588	Receiving apparatus
6590.A-Z	Other apparatus, A-Z
6590.A5	Amplifiers
6590.A6	Antennas
6590.C3	Cathode ray tubes
6590.I5	Indicators
6590.M5	Microwave lenses
6590.O67	Optical equipment
6590.O7	Oscillators
6590.R3	Radomes
6590.R4	Resonators
6590.S4	Servomechanisms
6590.T72	Transmit-receive tubes
6590.V6	Voltage regulators
6590.W3	Waveguides
6592.A-Z	Special types, A-Z
6592.A9	Automatic tracking
6592.B57	Bistatic radar
6592.C6	Coherent radar
6592.C65	Continuous wave radar
6592.D6	Doppler
6592.M6	Monopulse
6592.M67	Moving target indicator radar
6592.O6	Optical radar
6592.O94	Over-the-horizon
6592.P85	Pulse compression radar
6592.S4	Search radar
6592.S95	Synthetic aperture radar
6595.A-Z	Special applications of radar, A-Z
	To be classified here unless provided for elsewhere
	Aeronautics, see TL692+
6595.G4	Geodesy
	Military science, see UG610+
	Naval science, see VG76+
	Navigation, see VK560+
	Shipborne equipment and installations, see VM453, VM480+, VM480
6600	Phototelegraphy. Picture telegraphy
	Including radio photographs
	Cf. TK6710+, Facsimile transmissions
	Television
	Cf. GV1469.3+, Video games
	Cf. PN1992+, Television broadcasts
6630.A1	Periodicals, societies, etc.
6630.A2-Z	General works

TK

	Television -- Continued
6634	Dictionaries and encyclopedias
	Biography
6635.A1	Collective
6635.A2-Z	Individual, A-Z
6637	History
6638.A-Z	By country, A-Z
6640	Popular works. Juvenile works
	Cf. TK9960+, Television for amateurs
6641	Laboratory manuals
6642	Handbooks, manuals, etc.
6643	General special
6644	Television as a profession
6645	Directories of television stations
6646	Television stations
	Cf. TH4656, Construction of television station structures
	Television relay systems
6648	General works
6649.A-Z	Special systems and projects, A-Z
	Apparatus
	Cf. TK5105.8887, WebTV (Trademark)
6650	General works
6651	Transmitting apparatus
6653	Receiving apparatus
6655.A-Z	Other, A-Z
6655.A5	Amplifiers
6655.A6	Antennas
6655.C3	Camera tubes
	Cathode ray tubes, see TK6655.P5
6655.C5	Channel selectors
6655.D43	Deflection systems
	Electronic cameras, see TR882+
6655.O7	Oscillators
6655.P5	Picture tubes
6655.T7	Transformers
6655.T8	Tuners
6655.U6	Ultrahigh frequency apparatus (General)
6655.V5	Video tape recorders
	Cf. TR845+, Cinematography. Motion pictures. Video recording
	Cf. TR882.3, Camcorders
6670	Color television
6675	Community antenna television
6676	Master antenna television
6677	Direct broadcast satellite television
6678	Digital television
6679	High definition television
6679.3	Interactive television
6679.5	Underwater television
6679.7	Teletext systems
6680	Closed-circuit television
	Video telephones, see TK6505

	Digital video
6680.5	General works
	Multimedia computer systems, see QA76.575
6681	Video game equipment
	Cf. GV1469.3+, Video games
	Cf. TK9971, Amateur constructors' manuals
(6683)	Underwater television
	see TK6679.5
6685	Video discs and video disc equipment
6687	Interactive video
	Cf. LB1028.75, Education
	Facsimile transmission
6710	General works
6720	Ultrafax
	Installation of household appliances
	For electric space heating, see TH7409+
7018	Treatises
	Cf. TK9900+, Amateur constructors' manuals
7019	Popular works
7028	Catalogs
	Electric bells and buzzers
	For buzzer systems in telegraphy, see TK5522
7108	General works
7109	Popular works
7118	Catalogs of electric bells
	Electric annunciators and alarms
	Cf. TH9739, Security in buildings
7201	General works
7221	Annunciators
	Alarms
7241	General works
(7251)	Burglar alarms
	see TH9739
(7271)	Fire alarms
	see TH9271
(7291)	Electric ignition of gas
	see TH6885
(7301)	Electric clocks
	see TS544
	Miscellaneous electrical industries
(7611)	Electric train signaling
	see TF615-TF640
	Train telegraph systems, see TK5569.T7
7725	Manufacture of electrodes, carbons, etc.
	For use of carbons for arc lamps, see TK4335
	Electronics
	Cf. TK6540+, Radio
	Cf. TK6573+, Radar
	Cf. TK6630+, Television
7800	Periodicals, societies, yearbooks, etc.
7801	Congresses. Conventions
	Exhibitions
7802.A1	General works

TK

	Electronics
	Exhibitions -- Continued
7802.A2-Z	By region or country, A-Z
	Apply table at TK6.A2-Z
7803	Collected works (nonserial)
7804	Dictionaries and encyclopedias
7805	Directories
	Biography
7806	Collective
7807.A-Z	Individual, A-Z
7809	History
	By country
7811	United States
7812.A-Z	Other countries, A-Z
7815	Treatises
7816	Elementary textbooks
7817	Outlines, syllabi, etc.
7818	Laboratory manuals
7819	Popular works
7820	Juvenile works
7825	Handbooks, pocketbooks, tables, etc.
7828	Addresses, essays, lectures
7835	General special
7836	Electronic plants and equipment. Manufacture of electronic components and apparatus
7845	Electronics as a profession
	Patents
7850.A1	Periodicals, societies, etc.
7850.A2-Z	General works
7855	Research
	Study and teaching
7860	General works
7862	Problems, exercises, etc.
7863	Examinations, questions, etc.
7864	Mathematics
7866	Drawing. Diagrams, etc.
	Electronic circuits (General)
	For circuitry of special apparatus and components, see TK7871.2-TK7871.58, e. g., TK7871.2, Circuitry of amplifiers
7867	General works
7867.2	Electromagnetic interference and compatibility
7867.5	Noise
7867.8	Shielding
7868.A-Z	Special circuits (General)
7868.A79	Asynchronous
7868.B7	Bridge
7868.D5	Digital
	Integrated circuits, see TK7874 +
7868.I58	Interface circuits
7868.L6	Logic circuits
	Microwave circuits, see TK7876 +
7868.P6	Power supply

Electronics
  Electronic circuits (General)
    Special circuits (General) -- Continued

7868.P7   Printed circuits
7868.P8   Pulse
7868.S88   Switched capacitor circuits
7868.S9   Switching
7868.T5   Timing
7868.T7   Trigger
    Apparatus and materials
7869   Periodicals, societies, etc.
7870   General works
7870.15   Electronic packaging
7870.2   Maintenance and repair.   Electronic troubleshooting
7870.23   Reliability.   Failures
          Cf. TK7871.852, Semiconductor failures
7870.25   Cooling.   Thermal properties
7870.27   Contamination and decontamination
7870.28   Corrosion
7870.285   Effect of radiation on
7870.3   Catalogs
     Materials (General)
7871   General works
7871.15.A-Z   Special, A-Z
7871.15.B47   Berlinite crystals
7871.15.C33   Cadmium alloys
7871.15.C4   Ceramic materials
7871.15.D53   Diamonds
7871.15.F4   Ferrites
7871.15.F5   Films
7871.15.G3   Gallium arsenide
7871.15.G33   Gallium nitride
7871.15.G5   Glass
7871.15.I53   Indium phosphide
7871.15.M3   Magnetic materials
7871.15.N53   Nickel alloys
7871.15.N57   Nitrides
7871.15.O7   Organometallic compounds
7871.15.P4   Phosphors
7871.15.P5   Plastic materials
7871.15.P6   Polymers
7871.15.P65   Potting compounds
7871.15.Q3   Quartz
7871.15.S54   Silicides
7871.15.S55   Silicon
7871.15.S558   Silicon nitride
7871.15.S56   Silicon organic compounds
7871.15.T56   Titanium
7871.15.T85   Tungsten
    Amplifiers
7871.2   General works
          Including vacuum-tube and transistor amplifiers
7871.22   Dielectric

TK

	Electronics
	Apparatus and materials
	Amplifiers -- Continued
7871.23	Magnetic
	Cf. TK2851, Electric controllers
7871.24	Parametric
	Rotating, see TK2699
(7871.3-37)	Lasers
	see TA1671-TA1707
(7871.33)	Chemical lasers
	see TA1690
(7871.35)	Gas lasers
	see TA1695
(7871.37)	Solid-state lasers
	see TA1705
7871.4	Masers
	Cf. TA1671 +, Lasers
7871.58.A-Z	Other, A-Z
7871.58.A9	Audio
7871.58.B74	Broadband
7871.58.C75	Crossed-field
7871.58.D46	Differential
7871.58.D5	Direct current
7871.58.D54	Distributed
7871.58.F4	Feedback
7871.58.L57	Lock-in
7871.58.L6	Logarithmic
7871.58.O6	Operational
7871.58.P6	Power
7871.58.P8	Pulse
7871.58.T8	Tuned
7871.58.V5	Video amplifiers
	Antennas and waveguides
7871.6	Antennas
	Cf. TK6565.A6, Radio
	Cf. TK6590.A6, Radar
	Cf. TK6655.A6, Television
7871.65	Waveguides
7871.67.A-Z	Special, A-Z
7871.67.M53	Microwave antennas
	Electroluminescent devices
7871.68	General works
	Light-emitting diodes, see TK7871.89.L53
	Electroluminescent display systems, see TK7882.I6
	Electron tubes
7871.7	General works
	Vacuum tubes
7871.72	General works
7871.73	Cathode ray tubes
7871.74	Klystrons
7871.75	Magnetrons
7871.76	Storage tubes
7871.77	Traveling-wave tubes

	Electronics
	Apparatus and materials
	Electron tubes
	Vacuum tubes -- Continued
7871.79.A-Z	Other, A-Z
7871.79.G95	Gyrotrons
7871.79.K4	Kenotrons
7871.79.P4	Pentodes
7871.79.T7	Trochotrons
7871.79.X2	X-ray tubes
	Gas tubes
7871.8	General works
7871.82	Mercury-arc rectifiers
7871.83	Thyratrons
7871.84.A-Z	Other, A-Z
7871.84.C6	Cold cathode tubes
7871.84.N4	Neon tubes
	Semiconductors
	Class here works on semiconductor materials used in electronic engineering
	For general works on the physical properties of semiconductor materials, see QC610.9+
	For specific semiconductor materials used in electronic engineering, see TK7871.15.A+
	For specific semiconductors, see TK7871.86-89
7871.85	General works
7871.852	Failures (General)
	For specific semiconductors, see TK7871.86-89
7871.86	Diodes
7871.87	General works
7871.88	Tunnel diodes
7871.89.A-Z	Varactors
7871.89.A94	Other, A-Z
7871.89.G84	Avalanche diodes
7871.89.L53	Gunn diodes
7871.89.S35	Light-emitting diodes
7871.89.S95	Schottky-barrier diodes
7871.89.Z46	Switching diodes
	Zener diodes
	Electroluminescent devices, see TK7871.68+
	Integrated circuits, see TK7874+
7871.9	Transistors
7871.92	General works
7871.95	Junction
7871.96.A-Z	Field effect
7871.96.B55	Other, A-Z
7871.96.M53	Bipolar
7871.96.T45	Microwave
7871.98	Thin film
7871.99.A-Z	Thermistors
7871.99.A45	Other, A-Z
	Amorphous semiconductors
7871.99.C45	Cf. QC611.8.A5, Physics
7871.99.C65	Charge transfer devices. Charge coupled devices
	Compound semiconductors

TK

	Electronics
	Apparatus and materials
	Semiconductors
	Other, A-Z -- Continued
7871.99.M4	Metal insulator semiconductors
7871.99.M44	Metal oxide semiconductors
7871.99.T5	Thyristors
7871.99.V3	Varistors
	Optoelectronic devices, see TK8300+
7872.A-Z	Other, A-Z
	Apparatus and components to be classed here unless otherwise provided for in the field of application
	Capacitors, see TK7872.C65
	Charge transfer devices, see TK7871.99.C45
7872.C56	Coils
7872.C65	Condensers. Capacitors
7872.C67	Contactors
7872.C68	Contacts
7872.C7	Counters
7872.C77	Cryoelectronic devices
7872.C8	Current converters
7872.C83	Current regulators
7872.D37	Decoders
7872.D4	Delay lines
7872.D53	Dielectric devices
7872.E45	Electron gun
7872.E7	Equalizers
7872.F4	Ferrite devices
7872.F44	Ferroelectric devices
7872.F5	Filters (Electric)
7872.F7	Frequency changers
7872.F73	Frequency synthesizers
	Frequency-voltage converters, see TK7872.V54
7872.F85	Function generators
	Cf. TK7895.F8, Function generators (Computers)
7872.G8	Gunn effect devices
7872.G9	Gyrators
7872.H3	Hall effect devices
7872.H4	Heat sinks
7872.I63	Inductors
7872.I65	Inverters
7872.L56	Liquid crystal displays
7872.L64	Logic devices
7872.M25	Magnetic cores and devices
7872.M3	Masks
7872.M46	Membrane switches
7872.M5	Mixers
7872.M6	Modulators
7872.M8	Multiplexers
7872.N4	Negative-resistance devices
7872.N6	Noise generators

Electronics
  Apparatus and materials
    Other, A-Z -- Continued

7872.O7	Oscillators
7872.P38	Phase-locked loops
7872.P39	Phase shifters
7872.P54	Piezoelectric devices
7872.P6	Potentiometer
7872.P8	Pulse generators
7872.R35	Rectifiers
7872.R38	Relays
7872.R4	Resistors
7872.S5	Signal generators
7872.S8	Superconductors
7872.T55	Thin film devices
7872.T6	Transducers
7872.T7	Transformers
7872.T74	Transmission lines
7872.V53	Voltage dividers
7872.V54	Voltage-frequency converters
7872.V55	Voltage regulators

  Microelectronics. Integrated circuits

7874	General works
7874.5	Catalogs of microelectronic equipment
7874.6	Application specific integrated circuits
7874.65	Digital integrated circuits
7874.66	Low voltage integrated circuits
7874.7	Very high speed integrated circuits
7874.75	Very large scale integrated circuits
7874.76	Ultra large scale integrated circuits
7874.8	Molecular electronics
7874.85	Nanowires
7874.88	Quantum dots
7875	Microelectromechanical systems

      For devices applied to a specific field, see the
        field
  Microwaves
    Including microwave circuits

7876	General works

    Amplifiers, see TK7871.2 +
    Heating, see TK4601 +
    Transistors, see TK7871.96.M53
    Tubes, see TK7871.7 +
    Waveguides, see TK7871.65

7876.5	Millimeter waves
7877	Submillimeter waves
	Electronic measurements
7878	General works
7878.2	Time measurements
	Electronic instruments

      Cf. TK301 +, Electric meters

7878.4	General works
	Auxiliary equipment

	Electronics
	Electronic measurements
	Electronic instruments
	Auxiliary equipment -- Continued
7878.5	General works
7878.6	Probes
7878.7	Cathode ray oscillographs. Oscilloscopes
	Voltmeters
7879	General works
7879.2	Vacuum tube voltmeters
7879.4	Frequency meters
	Applications of electronics
7880	General works
7881	Industrial electronics
7881.15	Power electronics
	Special power supply circuits, see TK7868.P6
	Special applications
7881.2	Electronic control
7881.3	Home entertainment systems
	Cf. TK9961, Home video systems amateurs' manuals
	Sound systems. Sound recording. Sound reproduction
	For electroacoustics, see TK5981+
7881.4	General works
7881.5	Intercommunication systems
	Magnetic tape recorders and recording
7881.6	General works
	Cf. TK5981+, Electroacoustics
7881.65	Digital audiotape recorders and recording
7881.7	High fidelity systems
7881.75	Compact disc players
7881.78	Minidiscs and players
	Stereo high fidelity systems. Quadraphonic sound systems
7881.8	General works
7881.83	Surround-sound systems
7881.85	Automobile sound systems and equipment
7881.9	Theaters, auditoriums, etc.
7882.A-Z	Other, A-Z
	Class works here unless otherwise provided for in the field of application
7882.A37	Agriculture
7882.C56	Compact discs
7882.E2	Eavesdropping
	Facsimile transmission, see TK6710+
7882.G35	Games
7882.I6	Information display systems
7882.M4	Metal detectors
	Mobile communication systems, see TK6570.M6
7882.P3	Pattern recognition systems
	Cf. TA1650, Optical pattern recognition
7882.P7	Proximity detectors

Electronics
  Applications of electronics
    Other, A-Z -- Continued

7882.S3	Scanning systems
7882.S65	Speech processing systems
7882.S78	Stun guns
	Telecommunication, see TK5101+
7882.W44	Weighing systems

  Computer engineering. Computer hardware
    Including design and construction
      Cf. QA75.5+, Computers (General), electronic
        data processing, computer software,
        etc.
      Cf. QA267+, Machinery theory
      Cf. T58.6+, Industrial information systems
      Cf. TJ212+, Control engineering

7885.A1	Periodicals, societies, congresses, etc.
7885.A2	Dictionaries and encyclopedias
7885.A4	Directories
7885.A5	History
7885.A6-Z	General works
	Biography
7885.2	Collective
7885.22.A-Z	Individual, A-Z
7885.4	Popular works
	Amateurs' manuals for construction, see TK9969
7885.5	Juvenile works
	Computer engineering as a profession
7885.53	General
7885.54	Computer technicians
7885.6	Study and teaching
7885.7	Hardware description languages
7886	Computer manufacturing plants. Manufacturing of
	computers and computer components
	Including management
7887	Maintenance and repair
	Including upgrading
	Input-output equipment
7887.5	General works
	Special
7887.55	Data tape drives
7887.6	Analog-to-digital converters.
	Digital-to-analog converters
7887.7	Printout equipment
7887.8.A-Z	Other equipment, A-Z
7887.8.C6	Computer output microfilm devices
7887.8.D37	Data disk drives
7887.8.D5	Digital plotters
	Disk drives, Data, see TK7887.8.D37
7887.8.M63	Modems
7887.8.R4	Reading machines
7887.8.T4	Terminals
7887.8.X18	XY plotters

TK

Electronics
  Applications of electronics
    Computer engineering.
      Computer hardware -- Continued

7888	Analog computers
	Digital computers
7888.3	General works
7888.4	Circuits
	Including logic and switching circuits
7889.A-Z	Special computers. By name, A-Z
7889.A37	AIM 65
7889.A66	Apple II
7889.A663	Apple IIe
7889.A85	AT&T
7889.B3	BBC microcomputer
7889.B4	Besm
7889.C2	CDC 6600
7889.E5	ES 1020
7889.F44	FELIX C-256
7889.I26	IBM Personal Computer
7889.I5	Illiac
7889.M33	Macintosh
7889.M55	Minsk
7889.R4	Reac
7889.S4	Seac
7889.S7	Strela
7889.S8	Swac
7889.T77	TRS-80
7889.U6	Univac
7889.U7	Ural
7889.W47	Whirlwind
7889.Z54	Zilog Model Z-80
7895.A-Z	Special components and auxiliary equipment, A-Z
7895.A5	Amplifiers
7895.A65	Arithmetic units
7895.A8	Automatic check equipment
7895.B33	Backplanes. Motherboards
7895.B87	Buses
7895.C3	Cathode ray tube memory systems
7895.C39	CD-ROMs. CD-ROM drives
7895.C7	Cryotrons
7895.D3	Data tapes
7895.E42	Embedded computer systems
7895.E96	Expansion boards
7895.F8	Function generators
	Cf. TK7872.F85, Function generators
	(Electronic instruments)
7895.G36	Gate array circuits
	Input-output equipment, see TK7887.5 +
7895.M3	Magnetic memory
7895.M4	Memory systems
	Memory cards, see TK7895.S62

Electronics
  Applications of electronics
    Computer engineering. Computer hardware
      Special components and
        auxiliary equipment, A-Z -- Continued

7895.M5	Microprocessors
	Cf. TJ223.M53, Automatic control
	Motherboards, see TK7895.B33
7895.O6	Optical equipment
7895.P3	Parametrons
7895.P38	PCMCIA cards
7895.P68	Power supply
7895.S54	Shift registers
7895.S62	Smart cards. Memory cards
7895.S65	Speech recognition systems
7895.T73	Transputers

    Optoelectronic devices. Photoelectronic devices
      Including circuits manuals
      For general works on optoelectronics, see TA1750+
      For special applications, see the field of
        application, e.g. TR260.5, Electric eye
        cameras

8300	Periodicals, societies, congresses, etc.
8304	General works
	Photoemissive tubes. Phototubes
8308	General works
8312	Photodiodes
8314	Photomultipliers
	Imaging systems
8315	General works
8316	Image converters and intensifiers
	Cf. TK8334, Solid-state image
	intensifiers
	Semiconductor devices
8320	General works
8322	Photovoltaic cells
	For solar batteries, see TK2960
	Photoconductive cells
8330	General works
8331	Photoresistors
8332	Phototransistors
8334	Solid-state image intensifiers
8360.A-Z	Other devices, A-Z
8360.P5	Photopotentiometer
(8404)	Optical data processing systems
	see TA1630-TA1650

Nuclear engineering. Atomic power

9001	Periodicals, societies, etc.
9006	Congresses
	Exhibitions. Museums
9007.A1	General works

	Nuclear engineering. Atomic power
	Exhibitions. Museums -- Continued
9007.A2-Z	By region or country, A-Z
	Under each country:
	.x *General works*
	.x2A-Z *Special. By city, A-Z*
9008	Collected works (nonserial)
9009	Dictionaries and encyclopedias
9012	Directories
	Biography
9013	Collective
9014.A-Z	Individual, A-Z
9021-9127	Country divisions (Table T1)
	Add country number in table to TK9000
9145	General works
9146	Elements. Popular works
9148	Juvenile works
9149	Laboratory manuals
9151	Handbooks, tables, etc.
	Radiation environment procedures and equipment
	Cf. RA569, Radioactive substances and ionizing radiation in public health
	Cf. TK9210+, Shielding
9151.4	General works
	Remote handling
9151.6	General works
9151.7	Manipulators
	Accidents and their prevention. Nuclear safety
	For accidents or safety of nuclear power plants in specific places, see TK1341+
9152	General works
9152.13	Emergency planning
9152.14	Human factors
9152.15	Inspection
9152.16	Risk assessment
9152.165	Storage
	Including temporary storage of discarded materials
	For permanent disposal, see TD898.17+
9152.17	Transportation of radioactive substances
	Cf. TD897.85+, Radioactive waste disposal
9152.2	Decontamination. Decommissioning of facilities
	Cf. RA569, Public health
	Cf. S589.6, Agriculture
	Cf. TD427.R3, Water pollution
	Cf. TD887.R3, Air pollution
	Cf. TD898.15+, Radioactive waste sites
9152.5	Patents
9153	General special
9155	Addresses, essays, lectures
9155.5	Nuclear engineering as a profession
	Study and teaching
9165	General works
9165.5	Examinations, questions, etc.
	United States
9166	General works

	Nuclear engineering. Atomic power
	Study and teaching
	United States -- Continued
9167.A-Z	Special schools. By place, A-Z
9168.A-Z	Other countries, A-Z
9169.A-Z	Special schools. By place, A-Z
	Instruments. Nuclear reactor instrumentation
9178	General works
9180	Nuclear counters
	Cf. QC787.C6, Counters
9182	Neutron sources
9183.A-Z	Other special instrumentation, A-Z
9183.S24	Safety instrumentation
9183.T54	Thermometers
	Materials
	For radioisotopes, radioactive substances, see
	TK9400+
	For reactor fuels, enrichment, reprocessing, see
	TK9360+
9185.A1	Periodicals, societies, etc.
9185.A2-Z	General works
9185.2.A-Z	Special, A-Z
9185.2.G73	Graphite
9185.2.M66	Molybdenum
	Nuclear reactors
	For nuclear power plants for electricity, see
	TK1341+
	Fission reactors
9202	General works
9203.A-Z	Special types, A-Z
9203.B6	Boiling water reactors
9203.B7	Breeder reactors
9203.F3	Fast reactors
9203.F5	Fluid fuel reactors
9203.G3	Gas cooled reactors
9203.H4	Heavy water reactors
9203.L45	Light water reactors
9203.L5	Liquid metal-cooled reactors
9203.M65	Molten salt reactors
9203.O7	Organic moderated reactors
9203.P7	Pressurized water reactors
9203.P8	Pulsed reactors
9203.S6	Sodium graphite reactors
9203.S65	Solid fuel reactors
9203.S86	Superheating reactors
9203.W37	Water-cooled reactors
9204	Fusion reactors
9207	Fuel elements
9207.5	Fuel claddings
9209	Moderators
	Shielding
9210	General works
9211	Containment

TK

	Nuclear engineering. Atomic power
	Nuclear reactors -- Continued
9211.5	Nuclear pressure vessels
9212	Cooling
9220	Control rooms for nuclear facilities
9230	Nuclear reactors for propulsion
	Cf. TJ623, Nuclear locomotives
	Cf. TL704.1, Atomic engines for aircraft
	Cf. TL783.5, Nuclear rockets
	Cf. VM774+, Marine nuclear reactor plants
9340	Particle accelerators
9350	Chemical processes. Radiochemistry
	Reactor fuels. Enrichment. Reprocessing
9360	General works
9363	Uranium as fuel
9365	Plutonium as fuel
	Radioisotopes. Radioactive substances
9400	General works
9401	Catalogs, pricelists, etc.
	Electricity for amateurs. Amateur constructors' manuals
9900	Periodicals, societies, etc.
9901	General works
9909	Magnetoelectric machines
9911	Generators and motors
9915	Transformers
9917	Electric batteries
9918	Solar batteries. Solar cells
9921	Electric lighting and lamps
	Cf. TT197.5.L34, Woodwork
	Cf. TT897.2, Decorative crafts
	Electric bells, see TK7108+
	Telegraph
9941	General works
9946	Wireless telegraph
9951	Telephone
	Radio. Wireless telephone
9956	General works
9957	Microwave communication systems
	Television
9960	General works
9961	Video tape recorders. Video recording. Home video systems
	Cf. TR896+, Home video photography
9962	Satellite television. Home earth stations
	Electronics (General)
9965	General works
9966	Integrated circuits
9967	Magnetic recorders and recording
9968	Sound systems
	Including high fidelity and stereophonic systems
9969	Computers
9971	Electronic games and toys
	Including video games

	Motor vehicles. Aeronautics. Astronautics
	Motor vehicles
	Including automotive engineering
	Cf. GV1020 +, Automobile travel
	Periodicals and societies
	Arrange by language of publication
1	English
2	French
3	German
4	Other languages, not A-Z
5	Yearbooks
6	Congresses
	Exhibitions. Museums. Collectors and collecting
	Cf. TL152.2, Restoration of automobiles
7.A1	General works
7.A2-Z	By region or country, A-Z
	Under each country:
.x	*General works*
.x2A-Z	*Special. By city, A-Z*
8	Collected works (nonserial)
9	Dictionaries. Encyclopedias
	Communication of automotive information
10	General works
11	Computer network resources
	Including the Internet
12	Directories
15	History. Pictorial works
21-127	Special countries (Table T1)
	Including registers
	Add country number in table to TL0
	Biography
139	Collective
140.A-Z	Individual, A-Z
	General works
	Cf. TL200 +, Automobiles
144	Early to 1890
145	1890-
146	Elementary textbooks
146.5	Popular works
147	Juvenile works
151	Manuals, pocketbooks, etc.
	Motor vehicle operation. Automobile operation
	Cost of operation
151.5	General works
151.6	Fuel consumption
	Maintenance and repair
152	General works
152.2	Restoration

Motor vehicles
>Motor vehicle operation.
>>Automobile operation -- Continued
>Drivers
>>Including health and psychology
>>Cf. HD8039.A76, Automobile driving as an occupation
>>Cf. HE5613.5+, Traffic accidents, safety, etc.

152.3	General works
152.35	Medical and psychological examination
152.4	Drivers' tests
	Driving
152.5	General works
	Special countries
152.52	United States
152.55.A-Z	Other countries, A-Z
152.58	Stunt driving
	Driver education
152.6	General works
152.65	Elementary and secondary school courses
152.66.A-Z	By country, A-Z
152.7.A-Z	Special methods and equipment, A-Z
152.7.D7	Driving simulators
152.8	Automatic control
	Cf. TE228.3, Intelligent Vehicle Highway Systems
153	Service stations
153.5	Lubrication and lubricants
153.7	Towing
154	General special
155	Addresses, essays, lectures
156	Study and teaching. Automobile schools
157	Examinations, questions, etc.
158	Research
	Automobile equipment and supplies
	Including parts catalogs
	Cf. TL240+, Design, construction and equipment
159	General works
159.5	Safety appliances. Air bags. Child seats. Seat belts
	Cf. HE5620.S34, Seat belt use
	Cf. TL242, Safety factors. Safety standards
160	Catalogs of dealers
	For special motive powers, see TL200+
162	Automobile purchasing. Buyers' guides
165	Motor vehicle fleets
175	Parking facilities
	Including parking lots and parking garages
	Cf. HE336.P37, Parking
	Special automobiles. By power
200	Steam automobiles
	Steam wagons, trucks, etc , see TJ705

	Motor vehicles
	Special automobile, by power -- Continued
	Gasoline automobiles
	Where possible use TL144-TL165
205	General works
206	Popular works. Juvenile works
207	Manuals, pocketbooks, etc.
(208)	Maintenance and repair
	see TL152-TL152.2
209	General special
	Construction details
	Motors. Engines
	Cf. TJ782+, Internal combustion engines
210	General works
210.5	Two-stroke cycle engines
210.7	Wankel engines
212	Carburetors and carburetion
213	Ignition devices. Magnetos
214.A-Z	Other, A-Z
214.A4	Air filters
214.B43	Bearings
214.C35	Camshafts
214.C64	Control systems
	Cooling system, see TL214.R3
214.C73	Crankshafts
214.C93	Cylinders. Cylinder heads. Cylinder blocks
214.E93	Exhaust systems
214.F78	Fuel injection systems
214.F8	Fuel systems
	Low pollution combustion, see TL214.P6
214.O5	Oil system
214.P57	Pistons
214.P6	Pollution control devices. Low pollution combustion
	Cf. TD886.5, Automobile exhaust pollution
214.R3	Radiators. Cooling system
214.S8	Superchargers
214.T55	Timing belts. Timing chains
	Timing chains, see TL214.T55
214.T87	Turbochargers
214.V3	Valves
215.A-Z	Special makes, A-Z
	Including catalogs, handbooks, etc.
217	Alcohol automobiles
	Electric vehicles and their batteries, etc.
220	General works
221.13	Fuel cell for vehicles
221.15	Hybrid vehicles. Hybrid cars
222	Solar vehicles. Solar cars
223	Industrial vehicles and trucks
225	Compressed-air automobiles
	Gas turbine automobiles

TL

	Motor vehicles
	Special automobile, by power
	Gas turbine automobiles -- Continued
226	General works
227	Automotive gas turbines
228	Natural gas vehicles
	For gas producer automobiles, see TL229.G3
229.A-Z	Other, A-Z
229.A25	Acetylene
	Alcohol, see TL217
(229.A5)	Amphibious
	see TL235.63
(229.C66)	Compressed natural gas
	see TL228
229.D5	Diesel
229.G3	Gas producer
(229.G33)	Gases, Compressed
	see TL228
229.H9	Hydrogen
229.L56	Liquid nitrogen
(229.N38)	Natural gas
	see TL228
	Nitrogen, Liquid, see TL229.L56
	Automobiles for freight, etc. Trucks
	Including vans and sport utility vehicles
	Cf. TL297.6, Truck trailers
	For steam wagons, trucks, etc., see TJ705
	For truck-mounted campers and coaches, see TL298
230.A1	Periodicals, societies, etc.
230.A2-Z	General works
230.12	Pictorial works
230.15	Juvenile works
230.2	Maintenance and repair
230.3	Truck drivers, driver training and driving
	Cf. HD7269.A+, Industrial hygiene and welfare of truck drivers
	Cf. HD8039.A76, Automobile driving as an occupation
	Cf. HE5601+, Regulations and special problems
230.5.A-Z	Special types, makes, etc., A-Z
	e.g.
230.5.F6	Four Wheel Drive Vehicle
	Buses
	Cf. HE5601+, Automotive transportation (economic aspects)
232	General works
232.2	Maintenance and repair
232.3	Bus drivers, driver training, and driving
232.5	Taxicabs
232.7	Limousines

	Motor vehicles -- Continued
	Tractors
	Cf. S711+, Transportation and power
	transmission machinery (Use on farms)
	Cf. TJ700, Steam traction engines
233.A1	Periodicals, societies, etc.
233.A2-Z	General works
233.15	Juvenile works
233.2	Maintenance and repair
233.25	Conservation and restoration. Collectors and
	collecting
233.3	Tractor driving
233.6	Special types, makes, etc., A-Z
233.8	Models
	Tracklaying vehicles
	For military tanks, see UG446.5
234	General works
234.2	Snowmobiles
	Cf. GV856.4+, Snowmobiling
235	Automobile trains
	Off-road vehicles
	Including off-road trucks and all terrain vehicles
	For dune buggies, see TL236.7
	For snowmobiles, see TL234.2
	For trail bikes, see TL441
235.6	General works
235.63	Amphibious vehicles
235.65.A-Z	Special makes, A-Z
235.7	Off-road vehicle driving
	Including all terrain vehicle driving
235.8	Ambulances, hearses, etc.
	Cf. RA995+, Ambulance service
236	Racing automobiles. Sports cars
	Dragsters
236.2	General works
236.23	Funny cars
236.28	Stock cars
236.3	Hot rods. Street rods
236.5	Midget cars. Karts
236.7	Dune buggies
	Cf. GV1029.9.D8, Racing
	Models
	Cf. GV1570, Model car racing
237	General works
237.2	Collectors and collecting
	Design, construction and equipment
	Cf. TL210+, Motors
240	General works
240.2	Amateurs' manuals. Kit cars
240.5.A-Z	Special materials, A-Z
240.5.A46	Alloys
240.5.A48	Aluminum
240.5.C65	Composite materials

	Motor vehicles
	Design, construction and equipment
	Special materials, A-Z -- Continued
240.5.M33	Magnesium
240.5.P42	Plastics
241	Fires and fire prevention
242	Safety factors. Safety standards. Crashworthiness
	Dynamics
	Including effect of soil mechanics
	For traction, see TL295
243	General works
245	Aerodynamics
245.5	Handling characteristics
245.8	Stability
246	Vibration. Noise
250	Human engineering in design
	Including trucks, buses, etc.
253	Automotive drafting
	Special topics
	Motors, see TL210+
	Frame. Chassis. Carriage body
255	General works
255.2	Customizing. Decorating. Painting
255.6	Seats
256	Upholstery
256.5	Windows and windshields
	Springs and suspension
257	General works
257.3	Air suspensions
257.5	Shock absorbers
259	Steering gear
	Running gear. Power trains
260	General works
261	Clutches
	Transmission devices
262	General works
263	Automatic transmission devices
265	Transaxles
	Brakes
269	General works
269.2	Air brakes
269.3	Antilock brake systems
270	Wheels and tires
	Heating and ventilation equipment
271	General works
271.5	Air conditioning

Motor vehicles
　　Design, construction and equipment
　　　Special topics, not A-Z -- Continued
272　　　　　Electric equipment. Batteries
　　　　　　　Including starting, lighting and ignition
　　　　　　　　devices, etc.
　　　　　　　Cf. TK2921, Primary cells
　　　　　　　Cf. TK2941, Storage batteries
　　　　　　　Cf. TL213, Ignition
　　　　　　　Cf. TL220+, Batteries for electric
　　　　　　　　automobiles
　　　　　Electronic equipment
272.5　　　　General works
272.52　　　　Collision avoidance systems
272.53　　　　Computers
　　　　　　　For engine control modules, see TL214.C64
272.55　　　　Display systems
　　　　　Audio equipment, see TK7881.85
273　　　　　Automobile headlights
274　　　　　Automobile horns
275　　　　　Other details
278　　　　Manufacturing. Factory methods and equipment
278.5　　　Quality standards
　　　　　Including QS-9000
280　　Patents
285　　Testing (General)
　　　　　Including motor vehicle safety inspection. For
　　　　　　emissions inspection, see TL214.P6
　　　　　Cf. TL242, Safety factors in motor vehicle
　　　　　　design and construction
290　　Endurance tests
295　　Traction. Skidding. Traction tests
　　　　　Cf. TE450, Roads and pavements
296　　Industrial power trucks
296.5　　Loaders (Automotive)
　　　Trailers
　　　　　Cf. GV198.5+, Trailer camping
　　　　　Cf. TH4819.M6, Mobile home construction
　　　　　Cf. TX1100+, Mobile home living
297　　　General works
297.2　　　Boat trailers
297.6　　　Truck trailers
　　　　　　Including piggyback trailers
298　　Truck-mounted campers and coaches
390　　Cyclecars
　　　Cycles
　　　　　Cf. GV1040+, Cycling
400　　　General works
　　　　　Including history
405　　　Early forms
　　　　　Including velocipedes

	Cycles -- Continued
	Bicycles and tricycles
	Cf. HD9993.B54+, Bicycle industry
	Cf. HE5736+, Bicycle transportation
410	General works
412	Juvenile works
	Motor bicycles, see TL443
	Details. Parts
414	General works
415	Frame
420	Driving gear
422	Wheels
425	Tires
430	Repairs
435	Catalogs and other trade publications
	Including cycles
437	Patents
	Including cycles and motorcycles
437.5.A-Z	Special types, makes, etc., A-Z
438	Models
	Including cycles and motorcycles
	Motorcycles
439	Dictionaries
439.5.A-Z	By region or country, A-Z
440	General works
440.15	Juvenile works
440.2	Motorcyclists
440.5	Motorcycle riding
441	Trail bikes. Dirt bikes
442	Racing motorcycles
	Cf. GV1060+, Motorcycle racing
443	Motor bicycles
444	Maintenance and repair
444.2	Conservation and restoration. Collectors and collecting
445	Motors, etc.
448.A-Z	Special makes, A-Z
	e.g.
448.A47	Ariel
448.C54	Cleveland
	Motor scooters
450	General works
453.A-Z	Special makes, A-Z
460	Motor sledges
	Roving vehicles (Astronautics)
475	General works
480	Moon cars
482	Coaster cars
	Cf. GV1029.7, Soapbox racing, etc.
483	Pedal cars
484	Golf carts

	Aeronautics. Aeronautical engineering
	Cf. GV750+, Air sports
	Cf. HD9711.3, Lighter-than-air craft industry
	(Economic aspects)
	Cf. HD9711.5, Aerospace industry
	Cf. HE9761+, Air transportation
	Cf. UG622+, Military aeronautics. Air warfare
	Cf. VG90+, Naval aeronautics. Naval air warfare
	Periodicals, societies, yearbooks, etc.
	Cf. TL521+, Serial documents of special
	countries, e. g. TL521.A3-TL521.A35, U.S.
	National Advisory Committee for
	Aeronautics; TL526.G7A3-TL526.G7A4, Great
	Britain Aeronautical Research Council
	International
500	General
500.5	International Civil Aviation Organization
	Including technical material and general
	collections published by the organization
	which includes material of a technical nature
	For administrative material, see HE9762.5
501	English language
502	French language
503	German language
504	Other, not A-Z by language
505	Congresses
	Exhibitions. Museums. Collectors and collecting
506.A1	General works
506.A2-Z	By region or country, A-Z
	Apply table at TL7.A2-Z
507	Collected works (nonserial)
508	Scrapbooks
509	Dictionaries, encyclopedias, etc. Nomenclature.
	Symbols. Abbreviations
	Directories. Registers
512	General works
	Registers of aircraft, see HE9769.A+
512.7	Registers of pilots
513	Patents
514	Catalogs of materials and equipment (General)
	History
515	General works
516	Antiquities and legends
	Special regions or countries
	Cf. TL539+, Biography
	America. United States
521	General works
	U.S. National Aeronautics and Space Administration
	For NASA launch complexes, see TL4027.A+
	For special space research centers, see TL862.A+
521.3.A-Z	Serials and collected sets, A-Z
	e.g.
521.3.C6	Contractor report

TL

	Aeronautics. Aeronautical engineering
	Special regions or countries
	America. United States
	U.S. National Aeronautics
	and Space Administration -- Continued
521.312	Monographs
521.5	Regions
522.A-W	States, A-W
523	Canada and Newfoundland
524.A-Z	Latin America, Central America and West Indies. By country or island, A-Z
525.A-Z	South America, A-Z
526.A-Z	Europe, A-Z
	e.g.
526.G7	Great Britain
527.A-Z	Asia, A-Z
	e.g.
527.P4	Philippines
528.A-Z	Africa, A-Z
529	Australia
529.5	New Zealand
	Pacific Ocean and islands
530.A1	General works
530.A5-Z	Special islands, A-Z
531	Transoceanic flights
532	Arctic regions. Antarctica
537	Awards, prizes, etc. Competitions
	Cf. TL721.5+, Air meets
538	Badges, insignia, etc.
	Biography
539	Collective
540.A-Z	Individual, A-Z
	e.g.
540.L5	Lindbergh
	General works
544	Early to 1900
	Cf. TL516, Antiquities and legends
545	1900-
546	Textbooks
546.5	Examinations, questions, etc.
546.7	Popular works
547	Juvenile works
549	Pictorial works
551	Handbooks, pocketbooks, tables, etc.
551.5	High-speed aeronautics
	For hypersonic aerodynamics, see TL571.5
	For supersonic and transonic aerodynamics, see TL571
552	Civil aviation (Technology)
	Cf. HE9761+, Air transportation
	Cf. TL515+, History of aeronautics
	Cf. TL664+, Use of airships
	Cf. TL719.92+, Special uses of airplanes
	Miscellaneous aspects of the general subject

	Aeronautics. Aeronautical engineering
	Miscellaneous aspects
	of the general subject -- Continued
553	General works
553.5	Accidents and their prevention. Air safety
	Cf. HE9784+, Air transportation
	Cf. TL697.S3, Safety devices (General)
	Geography and aviation, see G142
	Aviation risks in life insurance, see HG8810
	Aviation insurance, see HG9972
553.55	Near misses
553.6	Human engineering in aeronautics
553.7	Survival after airplane accidents
553.8	Search and rescue
	Survival and rescue adventures and narratives
553.9.A1	Periodicals, societies, etc.
553.9.A2-Z	General works
	Aeronautics in art, see N8217.A4
(554)	Aeronautics in literature
	see class P
	Wit and humor, see PN6231.A4
555	Physical and mental requirements for pilots
	Including tests
	Cf. RA615.2, Public health aspects
	Cf. RA641.5, Transmission of disease
	Cf. RA655+, Quarantine
	For clinical aspects, see RC1050+
	Meteorology in aeronautics. Aeronautical
	meteorology
556	General works
556.5	Study and teaching
557.A-Z	Special, A-Z
557.A5	Air currents. Winds
	Atmospheric electricity, see TL557.S65
557.A8	Atmospheric temperature
	Cf. TL557.D4, Density altitude
557.C4	Charts
557.C6	Clouds
557.C7	Condensation trails
557.D4	Density altitude. Density altitude computers
	Density altitude computers, see TL557.D4
557.F6	Fog control
557.H3	Hail
557.I3	Ice prevention
557.R4	Reporting and forecasting
557.S65	Static electricity. Atmospheric electricity
557.S7	Storms
557.V5	Visibility
	Winds, see TL557.A5
558.A-Z	By country or region, A-Z
	e.g.
558.A1	General
558.A5	Antarctica

TL

	Aeronautics. Aeronautical engineering
	Miscellaneous aspects of the general subject
	Meteorology in aeronautics.
	Aeronautical meteorology
	By country or region, A-Z -- Continued
558.F8	France
558.G4	Germany
559	Addresses, essays, lectures
	Study and teaching
	Cf. LB1594.5, Elementary education
560	General works
	United States
560.1	General works
560.2.A-Z	Special schools, A-Z
	Employee training in factories
560.25.A1	General works
560.25.A2-Z	By company, A-Z
560.3.A-Z	Other countries, A-Z
560.4.A-Z	Special schools, A-Z
	Flying schools, see TL713.A +
561	Aeronautics as a vocation
563	Electronic data processing
	Communication of aeronautics informations
563.5	General works
564	Information services
564.5	Language. Authorship
	Aeronautical research
	Cf. UG640 +, Military aeronautical research
565	General works
	Research equipment. Laboratory construction and layout
566	General works
567.A-Z	Special, A-Z
567.B3	Balances
567.B33	Ballistic ranges
567.B4	Basins. Water channels
567.I6	Instruments
567.M6	Models for wind tunnel and water testing
567.N6	Nozzles
567.P6	Plane table
567.R47	Research aircraft
567.S4	Shock tubes
567.T6	Towing apparatus
	Water channels, see TL567.B4
567.W5	Wind tunnels
568.A-Z	Special institutions, A-Z
	Including research conducted by governments, universities or others
	For the research reports, transactions and other serial publications of such institutions, see TL500 +
	Mechanics of flight: Aerodynamics
570	General works

	Aeronautics. Aeronautical engineering
	Mechanics of flight: Aerodynamics -- Continued
570.3	Dictionaries and encyclopedias
571	Supersonic aerodynamics (General)
	Including transonic aerodynamics
	For special topics, see TL574.A+
571.5	Hypersonic aerodynamics (General)
	Cf. TL683.5, Hypersonic planes
	For special topics, see TL574.A+
573	General special
574.A-Z	Special topics, A-Z
574.A37	Aeroelasticity
574.A4	Aerofoils. "Profils d'ailes"
574.A45	Aerothermodynamics. Aerodynamic heating
	Aerodynamic heating, see TL574.A45
574.B3	Base flow
574.B6	Boundary layer
	Burbling, see TL574.T8
574.C3	Cascades
574.C4	Compressibility
574.C6	Control
	Damping, see TL574.S7
574.D6	Downwash
574.D7	Drag. Head resistance
574.F5	Flow
574.F6	Flutter
574.F7	Friction
	Ground cushion, see TL574.G7
574.G7	Ground effect. Ground cushion
	Head resistance, see TL574.D7
574.I5	Interference
574.L3	Laminar flow
574.L4	Leading edges
574.L5	Lift. Thrust
574.M3	Magnus effect
574.M6	Moments. Pitch. Yaw. Roll
574.N6	Noise
	Oscillations, see TL574.S7
	Pitch, see TL574.M6
574.P7	Pressure. Pressure distribution. Wing load
	Pressure distribution, see TL574.P7
	Resistance, see TL574.D7
	Resistance, Air, see TL570+
	Roll, see TL574.M6
574.S4	Shock waves
574.S55	Sonic boom
574.S6	Spinning
574.S7	Stability. Oscillations. Damping
574.S74	Stalling
	Thrust, see TL574.L5
574.T8	Turbulence. Burbling
574.U5	Unsteady flow
574.V5	Vibration

TL

	Aeronautics. Aeronautical engineering
	Mechanics of flight: Aerodynamics
	Special topics, A-Z -- Continued
574.V6	Vortex theory
574.W3	Wakes
	Wing load, see TL574.P7
	Yaw, see TL574.M6
575	Natural flight
	Cf. QL698.7, Flight of birds
576	Soaring
577	Hovering
578	Aerostatics
	Air navigation. Astronomy and navigation for air pilots
586	General works
587	Logbooks, maps, charts, tables, etc.
	Cf. QB7+, Ephemerides
	Special methods. Latitude and longitude
	Cf. VK565, Navigation
588	General works
588.5	Inertial navigation
	Instruments
589	General works
589.2.A-Z	Special, A-Z
589.2.A3	Accelerometers
589.2.A5	Air-speed indicators
589.2.A6	Altimeter
	Anemometer, see QC932
589.2.A78	Artificial horizons
589.2.A8	Autosyn indicator
589.2.B3	Barograph
589.2.C5	Cinemitrailleuse
589.2.C58	Compass (Gyroscope)
589.2.C6	Compass (Magnetic)
589.2.D7	Drift indicator
589.2.E2	Earth inductor compass
589.2.F5	Flight recorders
589.2.N3	Navigation computer
589.2.O6	Optical gyroscope
589.2.P7	Pressure instruments
(589.2.R2)	Radio compass
	see TL696.C7
589.2.R3	Rate of climb indicator
589.2.S4	Sextant
589.2.S7	Stall warning systems
589.2.T4	Tensionmeter
589.2.T5	Theodolite
589.2.T53	Thermometers
589.2.T8	Turn and bank indicator
	Display systems
589.3	General works
589.35.A-Z	Special, A-Z
589.35.G46	Geographical displays

	Aeronautics. Aeronautical engineering
	Instruments
	Display systems
	Special, A-Z -- Continued
589.35.H42	Head-up displays
589.35.H44	Helmet-mounted displays
	Guidance systems and automatic control
589.4	General works
589.5	Automatic pilots. Gyropilot
	Engine instruments
589.6	General works
589.7.A-Z	Special, A-Z
589.7.T3	Tachometer
	Sailing directions. Pilot guides, see TL726 +
	Aircraft (General)
	Including both lighter-than-air and heavier-than-air
600	General works
603	Identification marks and symbols
	Cf. TL694.I4, Identification of aircraft by
	radar signal (IFF equipment)
	Lighter-than-air. Aerostation
605	General works
	Balloons
	Including free spheric balloons
609	Periodicals, societies, etc.
610	General works
612	Accidents
615	General special
	History
616	General works
617	Invention and early history to 1800
	Including the Montgolfiers
618	1800-
	Special ascensions. Special aeronauts.
	Personal narratives
620.A1	Collections
620.A2-Z	By name of aeronaut, A-Z
	e.g.
620.B6	Blanchard
620.F6	Flammarion
620.G6	Goddard, Eugene
620.G7	Green, Charles
620.L8	Lunardi
620.O7	Orlandi
620.P5	Piccard
620.S55	Silberer
620.T5	Tissandier
620.T6	Tournachon
621.A-Z	Special balloons, A-Z
622	Design and construction
623	Rigging
625.A-Z	Parts and equipment, A-Z
625.A6	Anchor

TL

Aeronautics. Aeronautical engineering
Aircraft (General)
Lighter-than-air. Aerostation
Balloons
Parts and equipment, A-Z -- Continued

625.B2	Ballast
625.B3	Ballonet
625.B4	Basket
625.D7	Drag rope
625.E6	Envelope
	Instruments, see TL589 +
625.N4	Net
625.R5	Rip panel
625.V3	Valves

Operations of free balloons

626	Instructions and textbooks
626.5	Licensing of balloon pilots
627	Use of free balloons

Cf. GV762 +, Air sports and racing
Cf. QC879.3 +, Meteorology
Cf. UG640 +, Military aeronautics

630	Pilot balloons
631	Sounding balloons

Cf. QC879.3 +, Meteorology

632	Jumping balloons and balloon jumping
633	Toy and propaganda balloons

Captive balloons

634	General and spherical
635	Kite balloons
636	Equipment for captive balloons
637	Use of captive balloons

Use in war, see UG640 +

638	Hot air balloons

Early history, see TL616 +

639	Miscellaneous projects

Including balloon railways

Airships

650	General works
650.5	Juvenile works
651	General special

Including discussions of the possibility of
dirigibles, airships vs. airplanes,
controversial material, safety, etc.

654.A-Z	Special projects to 1900. By name of inventor, etc., A-Z

e.g.

654.D8	Dupuy de Lôme
654.G5	Giffard

Modern airships

655	General works

Pressure airships

656	General works
656.2	Nonrigid. Blimps

Aeronautics. Aeronautical engineering
  Aircraft (General)
    Lighter-than-air. Aerostation
      Airships
        Modern airships
          Pressure airships -- Continued

656.4	Semirigid
656.6	Metal-clad
657	Rigid airships
658.A-Z	Special makes, A-Z
	e.g.
658.Z4	Zeppelin
659.A-Z	Individual ships, A-Z. Special voyages. Personal narratives
	e.g.
659.A4	Akron
659.G7	Graf Zeppelin
659.H5	Hindenberg
660	Design and construction
660.1	Rigging
660.2	Strains and stresses
660.3	Performance. Performance calculation
	Testing
660.4	General works
660.5	Model testing
	Details and parts
661	General works
662.A-Z	Special, A-Z
662.B3	Ballast
662.B7	Bow caps
662.C3	Cars
662.C6	Control compartment
662.E6	Envelope
662.F7	Frame
662.G3	Gas cells
662.K4	Keel
	Motor, see TL701 +
	Propellers, see TL705 +
662.S7	Stabilizers
662.S8	Steering apparatus
663	Operation of airships
	Use of airships
664	General works
	Transportation, see HE9770.A4
664.2	War
664.3	Other
	Cf. G599, Polar exploration
	Materials and accessories for lighter-than-air craft
665	General works
666	Gas, hydrogen, helium. Inflation machinery
	Other special, see TL699.A +

TL

	Aeronautics. Aeronautical engineering
	Aircraft (General)
	Lighter-than-air. Aerostation -- Continued
	Lighter-than-air craft industry (Technical aspects)
	Cf. HD9711.3, Lighter-than-air craft industry (Economic aspects)
667	General works
668.A-Z	Special companies, A-Z
	Heavier-than-air craft
	Airplanes
	Periodicals, see TL500+
670	General works
	History
670.3	General works
670.5	Development of heavier-than-air craft before 1914
	Including models and gliders
670.7.A-Z	Special projects before 1914, A-Z
	e.g.
670.7.L3	Langley
670.7.M3	Maxim
	General special
671	General works
671.1	Airworthiness requirements. Specifications. Standards
	Collectors and collecting, see TL506.A1+
671.2	Design and construction
671.25	Drafting and blueprint reading
671.28	Manufacturing. Factory equipment and methods
	Cf. HD9711+, Airplane industry
	Cf. TL724+, Airplane industry (Technical aspects)
671.3	Monoplane, biplane, multiplane characteristics (Comparative)
671.4	Performance. Performance calculation. Handling characteristics
671.5	Rigging, bracing, welding, etc.
	Stability, see TL574.S7
671.6	Structural analysis and design of air frames
671.65	Noise
	Cf. TD893.6.A57, Noise control
671.7	Testing. Inspection
671.8	Model testing
671.85	Purchasing
671.9	Maintenance and repair
671.95	Conservation and restoration
	Details and parts
	Supporting surfaces
672	General works
673.A-Z	Special, A-Z
673.A6	Angle of incidence
673.C3	Camber

Aeronautics. Aeronautical engineering
Aircraft (General)
Heavier-than-air craft
Airplanes
Details and parts
Supporting surfaces
Special, A-Z -- Continued

.673.C35	Canard wings
673.C7	Cruciform wings
673.D4	Decalage
	Delta wings, see TL673.T7
673.D5	Dihedral angle
673.D8	Duct inlets
673.F6	Flaps
673.G3	Gap
673.O4	Ogee wings
673.O8	Overhang
673.R4	Rectangular wings
673.S4	Section
	Shielding, see TL673.T4
673.S6	Slotted wings
673.S7	Stagger
673.S9	Sweepback
	Taper, see TL673.T4
673.T4	Tips of wings. Taper. Shielding
673.T7	Triangular wings. Delta wings
673.W3	Washin and washout
674	Structural parts and details
	Including ribs, spars, struts, wires, etc.
675	Folding wings
	Control and stabilizing surfaces
676	General works
677.A-Z	Special, A-Z
677.A5	Ailerons
677.E6	Elevators
677.F5	Fins. Vertical stabilizer
677.R8	Rudder
677.S8	Stabilizer. Tailplane
	Tailplane, see TL677.S8
	Control apparatus. Control stick
678	General works
678.5	Fly-by-wire systems
	Fuselage
680	General works
681.A-Z	Special, A-Z
681.A5	Air conditioning
681.C3	Cabin
681.C6	Cockpit
681.C7	Cowling
681.F5	Firewall
681.H4	Heating
681.I6	Instrument board
	Instruments, see TL589+

TL

	Aeronautics. Aeronautical engineering
	Aircraft (General)
	Heavier-than-air craft
	Airplanes
	Details and parts
	Fuselage
	Special, A-Z -- Continued
681.L6	Longerons
681.P7	Pressurization
681.S6	Soundproofing
681.W5	Windshields
681.5	Nacelles
	Landing gear. Undercarriage
682	General works
683.A-Z	Special, A-Z
683.A35	Air cushion landing systems
683.A8	Axles
683.B7	Brakes
	Landing gear for use on snow, see TL683.S6
683.R4	Retractable landing gear
683.S4	Shock absorbers
683.S5	Skids. Wing and tail skids
683.S6	Skis. Landing gear for use on snow
683.T5	Tires
683.W5	Wheels
	Wing and tail skids, see TL683.S5
683.5	Hypersonic planes
	Seaplanes
	Cf. TL711.S43, Seaplane flying
684	General works
684.1	Amphibians
684.2	Flying boats. Hulls
684.3	Floatplanes. Floats
684.4	Biplanes
684.5	Triplanes
684.6	Tailless airplanes
684.8	Flying automobiles
685	Convertiplanes. Vertically rising aircraft
	Airplanes for special uses
685.1	Light (or sport). Private planes
	Cf. HE9795+, Economic aspects
	Cf. TL721.4, Private flying
685.15	Ultralight aircraft
685.2	Mailplanes
685.3	Military planes
	Class here works on the manufacture, testing, and restoration of military airplanes
	For markings, procurement, and use in warfare, see UG1240+
	Passenger planes
	Cf. HE9787+, Passenger service
685.4	General works

	Aeronautics. Aeronautical engineering
	Aircraft (General)
	Heavier-than-air craft
	Airplanes
	Airplanes for special uses
	Passenger planes -- Continued
685.5.A-Z	Special equipment, etc., A-Z
685.5.I6	Interior decoration
685.5.R4	Restaurant
685.5.S4	Seats
685.5.S6	Sleeping accommodations
685.6	Racing planes
685.7	Transport planes. Cargo planes
	Cf. HE9761+, Air transportation
	(Economic aspects)
686.A-Z	Special makes. By name of manufacturer, A-Z
	e.g.
686.A77	Auster aircraft
686.B65	Boeing Aircraft Company
686.B68	Bréguet
686.D4	De Havilland Aircraft Company
686.D65	Douglas Aircraft Company
686.L6	Lockheed Aircraft Corporation
686.R7	Rozhestvenskii
686.S7	Stearman
	Airplane materials and accessories
688	General works
	Special materials, see TL699.A+
	Flying machines other than airplanes
	see TL714-TL718
689	Radioisotope technology and components
	Electrical systems and equipment
690	General works
690.5	Electromagnetic interference in aeronautics
691.A-Z	Special, A-Z
691.A95	Auxiliary power supply
691.B3	Batteries
691.G4	Generators
691.L3	Landing lights
691.M3	Magnetic recorders
691.N3	Navigation lights
	Radio, see TL693+
	Radio, see TL695+
691.S4	Searchlights
691.W5	Wiring
	Communication methods and equipment
692	General special
	Including signaling, etc.
	Electronic methods and equipment. Telegraph.
	Radio. Radar. Television
693	General works
694.A-Z	Special, A-Z
694.A6	Antennas

TL

	Aeronautics. Aeronautical engineering
	Communication methods and equipment
	Electronic methods and
	equipment. Telegraph.
	Radio. Radar. Television
	Special, A-Z -- Continued
	Bonding, see TL694.I6
694.C6	Cipher and telegraph codes
694.I4	Identification
	Including IFF (Identification - Friend or Foe)
694.I5	Inspection
694.I6	Interference. Bonding. Shielding
694.R4	Receiving
	Shielding, see TL694.I6
694.T35	Telemetry
694.T4	Teletype
694.T7	Transmitting
	Electronic aids to navigation. Radio. Radar.
	Television
695	General works
695.5	Directories of radio stations
696.A-Z	Special, A-Z
	Altimeter, see TL696.H4
696.A77	Artificial satellites
696.B4	Beacons
696.B5	Beacon receiver
696.C6	Collision prevention
696.C7	Radio compass
696.C75	Control tower display systems
696.C8	Course computers. Course-line computers, etc.
696.D5	Direction finders
696.D6	Distance indicator
696.D65	Distance measuring equipment (Aircraft to ground
	station)
	Field and runway localizer, see TL696.L3
	Glide path systems, see TL696.L33
696.G7	Ground-speed indicator
696.H4	Height indicator. Altimeter
696.I5	Inspection
696.L3	Landing aids
696.L33	Instrument landing systems
	Including ground controlled approach, etc.
	Cf. TL711.B6, Blind flying
	Cf. TL711.L3, Landing
696.L65	Loran
696.M3	Markers
696.O5	Omnirange system
696.R2	Radar
696.R25	Radar air traffic control systems
696.R3	Range
696.T3	Tacan
	Miscellaneous equipment and apparatus
697.A1	General works

Aeronautics. Aeronautical engineering
  Miscellaneous equipment and apparatus -- Continued

697.A2-Z	Special, A-Z
697.A57	Air ducts
697.B4	Bearings
697.C6	Clothing for pilots
	Cf. TL697.G6, Goggles
	Cf. TL697.P7, Pressure suits
697.C65	Compressors
697.F5	Fire prevention
	Cf. TH9445.A5, Fire hazards of hangars
697.G6	Goggles
697.H4	Heat pipes
697.H44	Helmets
697.H9	Hydraulic equipment
	Ice prevention, see TL557.I3
697.L3	Landing flares
697.L34	Lasers
	Military equipment (General and Army), see UG1240+
	Military equipment (Navy), see VG90+
697.O65	Optical equipment
697.O8	Oxygen equipment
	Photographic equipment, see TR1+
697.P5	Pilot ejection seats
697.P6	Pneumatic equipment
697.P7	Pressure suits
697.S3	Safety devices (General)
	Cf. TL750+, Parachutes
697.S8	Stabilizing devices
	Materials of construction
698	General works
699.A-Z	Special, A-Z
699.A58	Alloys
699.A6	Aluminum
	Including alloys
699.A8	Asbestos
699.C44	Cellulose acetate
699.C46	Ceramic materials
699.C57	Composite materials
699.C6	Copper
	Including alloys
699.D6	Dopes
699.D9	Duralumin
699.F2	Fabrics
699.F5	Finishes
699.G6	Glue
699.G85	Gums and resins, Synthetic
699.L23	Laminated materials
	Laminated wood, see TL699.W7
699.L3	Lautal
699.M32	Magnesium
699.M4	Metals
699.P6	Plastics

TL

	Aeronautics. Aeronautical engineering
	Materials of construction
	Special, A-Z -- Continued
	Plywood, see TL699.W7
699.P7	Potting compounds
	Resins, Synthetic, see TL699.G85
699.R8	Rubber
699.S7	Spruce
699.S8	Steel
	Including alloys
	Timbers, see TL699.W6
699.T56	Titanium
699.T8	Tubes
699.W5	Wire
699.W6	Wood. Timbers
699.W7	Wood, Laminated. Plywood
	Motors. Aircraft engines
701	General works
701.1	General special
701.2	Influence of altitude
701.4	Installation
701.5	Maintenance and repair. Inspection
701.6	Performance
701.7	Specifications. Standards
701.8	Testing
702.A-Z	Details and parts, A-Z
702.A37	Actuators. Control systems
702.C3	Carburetors
702.C5	Connecting rods
	Cooling system, see TL702.R3
702.C6	Cowlings
702.C7	Crankshafts
702.C9	Cylinders
702.F8	Fuel feeding and tanks
702.G4	Gearing
702.I5	Ignition devices. Magnetos
702.L8	Lubrication
	Magnetos, see TL702.I5
702.M8	Mufflers
702.O55	Oil filters
	Opening and closing system, see TL702.V3
702.P5	Pistons
702.R3	Radiators. Cooling system
702.S7	Starting devices
702.S8	Superchargers
702.V3	Valves. Opening and closing system
703.A-Z	Special makes, A-Z
	e.g.
703.D4	De Havilland
703.H5	Hispano-Suiza
	Engines other than gasoline
704	General works
704.1	Atomic engines

	Aeronautics. Aeronautical engineering
	Motors. Aircraft engines
	Engines other than gasoline -- Continued
704.2	Diesel engines
704.4	Steam engines for aircraft
704.6	Model engines
704.7	Fuel for aircraft engines
	Cf. TL711.J4, Jettisoning of fuel
	Cf. TL711.R4, Refueling
	Propellers. Airscrews
705	General works
706.A-Z	Special, A-Z
706.A2	Abrasion
706.B3	Balancing. Flutter
706.E8	Etching
	Flutter, see TL706.B3
706.I6	Interference
706.N6	Noise
706.P4	Performance. Performance calculation
706.P8	Pusher vs. tractor
706.S4	Slip
706.S5	Slip stream
706.S6	Specifications. Standards
	Standards, see TL706.S6
706.S7	Strains and stresses
706.T4	Testing
706.T5	Thrust
706.V4	Vibration
707.A-Z	Details and parts, A-Z
707.B6	Blade section and form
707.B7	Boss
707.G4	Gear
707.H8	Hub
707.P5	Pitch, Adjustable and controllable
707.S6	Spinner
707.T5	Tipping
	Nuclear power plants. Nuclear propulsion for aircraft
	Cf. TL704.1, Atomic engines, propeller engine
	systems
	Cf. TL783.5, Nuclear rockets, propulsion
	systems
708.A1	Periodicals, societies, etc.
708.A2-Z	General works
708.3.A-Z	By country, A-Z
	Jet propulsion. Jet engines
	For rocket propulsion, see TL780 +
709	General works
709.3.A-Z	Special types, A-Z
709.3.R3	Ramjet engines
709.3.S37	Scramjet engines
709.3.T8	Turbine-propeller engines
709.3.T82	Turbofan engines
709.3.T83	Turbojet engines

TL

	Aeronautics. Aeronautical engineering
	Jet propulsion. Jet engines -- Continued
709.5.A-Z	Details and parts of jet engines, A-Z
	Air intakes or inlets, see TL709.5.I5
709.5.B4	Bearings
709.5.B6	Blades
709.5.C55	Combustion chambers
709.5.C56	Compressors
709.5.C57	Control systems
709.5.C6	Cooling systems
709.5.D5	Diffusers
709.5.F8	Fuel systems
709.5.H42	Heating regenerators
709.5.I5	Intakes or inlets for air
709.5.N68	Nozzles
	Roller bearings, see TL709.5.B4
709.5.S8	Starting devices
	Supersonic intakes or inlets, see TL709.5.I5
709.5.T5	Thrust reversers
709.5.T87	Turbines
	Operation of airplanes. Flying
710	General works
	Including textbooks and instruction books
711.A-Z	Special, A-Z
	Aerobatics, see TL711.S8
711.A5	Airspeed
711.A6	Altitude flying
	Cf. TL555, Physical and mental requirements
	for pilots
711.A7	Special altitude flights
	Arrange by date
711.B6	Blind flight. Instrument flying
711.B88	Bush flying
711.C64	Cold weather operation
	Cross-country flying, see TL711.L7
711.D4	Dispatching
711.D5	Ditching
711.D7	Dropping of cargo
711.E57	Emergency maneuvers
711.E6	Endurance flights
711.F47	Ferrying
	Formation flying, Military, see UG632.2 +
711.H65	Holding patterns
711.I47	Intercepting other aircraft
	Instrument flying, see TL711.B6
711.J38	Jet flying
711.J4	Jettisoning of fuel
711.L3	Landing
	Cf. TL696.L3, Radio
711.L6	Loading
711.L7	Long distance flying. Cross-country flying
711.M68	Mountain flying
	Multiengine flying, see TL711.T85

	Aeronautics. Aeronautical engineering
	Operation of airplanes. Flying
	Special, A-Z -- Continued
711.N5	Night flying
711.O26	Ocean flying. Overwater flying
	Overwater flying, see TL711.O26
711.R4	Refueling
711.S43	Seaplane flying
711.S5	Single heading
711.S8	Stunt flying. Aerobatics
711.T28	Taildragger flying
711.T3	Takeoff
711.T85	Twin-engine flying. Multiengine flying
	Flight training
712	General works
712.5	Flight simulators and trainers
712.8	Computer flight games
	Cf. GV1469.15+, Computer games
	Cf. TL1088, Space flight computer simulation
	For war games, see U310+
713.A-Z	Flying schools. By place, A-Z
713.5	Flying clubs
	Flying machines other than airplanes
	Including experimental models, but not toy models
713.7	Lifting bodies
	Rotor aircraft
714	General works
715	Autogiros
	Helicopters
	Cf. TL685, Convertiplanes. Vertical takeoff and landing aircraft
	Cf. UG1230+, Military helicopters
716.A1	Periodicals, societies, etc.
716.A2-Z	General works
716.2	Juvenile works
716.5	Operation of helicopters
716.9.A-Z	Special makes. By name of manufacturer, A-Z
717	Ornithopters. Winged flight
717.5	Personal propulsion units. Rocket belts. Jet belts
718	Other
	Special uses of airplanes
	Civil aviation (Technology), see TL552
	Transportation (Technology)
	For economic aspects, see HE9761+
720	General works
721.A-Z	Special flights, A-Z
	Cf. TL539+, Biography
	For collected flights over an individual country, see TL521+
	For collected flights overseas, see TL531
721.B3	Balbo
721.B5	Blériot

TL

	Aeronautics. Aeronautical engineering
	Special uses of airplanes
	Transportation (Technology)
	Special flights, A-Z -- Continued
721.B7	Bremen
721.B83	Buck
721.C5	Chichester
721.C6	Cobham
721.C65	Costes
721.E3	Earhart
	Gatty and Post, see TL721.P6
721.K5	Kingsford-Smith
	Lindbergh, see TL540.L5
	McIntosh and Parer, see TL721.P27
721.M35	McMillan-Kidby
721.M443	Miranda and Tejeda
721.P27	Parer and McIntosh
721.P6	Post and Gatty
721.R54	Rodgers
	Rutan and Yeager, see G445
721.S63	Smith, Dick
721.U6	U.S. Army world flight
	Yeager, see TL551.5
721.1	Exploration. Mountain climbing
	Cf. G599, Aircraft for polar exploration
	For special localities, see TL521+
(721.2)	Surveying and mapping
	see TA593
(721.3)	Aerial photography
	see TR810
721.4	Private flying
	For sports flying, see GV758+
	Air meets
721.5	General works
	Races, see GV759+
721.6.A-Z	Special meets, A-Z
	Use of airplanes in various industries
722	General works
(722.1)	Agriculture
	see S494.5.A3
722.2	Fisheries and whaling
(722.3)	Forestry, fire patrol
	see SD387.A3
722.4	Mining. Prospecting
722.5	Use of airplanes for advertising
	Including flying exhibits, flying signboards, voice of the air, skywriting, and distribution of literature
722.8	Use of airplanes for humanitarian purposes. Lifesaving at sea
	Cf. RA996.5+, Aeronautics and medicine
	Cf. TL553.8, Search and rescue

	Aeronautics. Aeronautical engineering
	Special uses of airplanes -- Continued
723	Government uses of airplanes
	For airmail (general), see HE6238
	For airmail (U.S.), see HE6496
	For war, see VG90+
	Airplane industry (Technical aspects)
	Including management
	Cf. TL671.28, Manufacturing. Factory equipment
	and methods
724	General works
	For trade directories, see TL512+
724.5.A-Z	Special companies, A-Z
	Airways (Routes). Airports and landing fields.
	Aerodromes
	Including air pilot guides
	Cf. HE9797+, Air transportation
	Cf. UG622+, Military aeronautics
	Cf. VG90+, Naval aeronautics
725.A1	Periodicals, societies, etc.
725.A2-Z	General works
725.15	Juvenile works
725.2	Specifications
725.3.A-Z	Special topics, A-Z
725.3.A2	Access to airports
725.3.A6	Areas, Danger
725.3.B5	Bird control
725.3.B8	Buildings
	Cf. TL725.3.R4, Repair shops
725.3.C3	Camouflage
725.3.C6	Cold weather conditions
725.3.C63	Communication systems
725.3.C64	Control towers
725.3.D35	Defense measures. War damage
725.3.D4	Dispatching of airplanes
	Cf. TL725.3.T7, Traffic control
725.3.D7	Drainage
725.3.E43	Electric equipment
725.3.E6	Equipment
	Fire prevention and extinction, see TH9445.A5
	Fog control, see TL557.F6
725.3.G6	Government operation and support
725.3.I6	Intra-airport transportation
725.3.L2	Landing aids
	Cf. TL691.L3, Landing lights (Aircraft)
	Cf. TL696.C75, Control tower display
	systems (Electronic)
	Cf. TL696.L3, Landing aids (Electronic)
	Cf. TL725.3.L5, Lighting (Airports)
	Cf. TL725.3.T7, Air traffic control
725.3.L3	Landing fees
725.3.L5	Lighting
725.3.L6	Location

TL

	Aeronautics. Aeronautical engineering
	Airways (Routes).
	Airports and landing fields. Aerodromes
	Special topics, A-Z -- Continued
725.3.M16	Maintenance and repair
725.3.M2	Management
725.3.M3	Marking
	Meteorology, see TL556 +
725.3.M63	Models
725.3.N6	Noise
725.3.P3	Passenger accommodations
725.3.P35	Pavements
725.3.P5	Planning
725.3.P55	Pneumatic equipment
725.3.P67	Power plants
725.3.P7	Private aircraft
725.3.R3	Radiation safety
725.3.R4	Repair shops
725.3.R8	Runways
725.3.S34	Safety measures
725.3.S44	Security measures
725.3.S47	Signs and signboards
725.3.S5	Size
725.3.S6	Soils
725.3.T5	Time schedules, etc., for making timetables
	For the timetables themselves, see HE9768
725.3.T7	Traffic control
	Cf. TL696.C75, Control tower display
	systems (Electronic)
	Cf. TL696.R25, Radar air traffic control
	systems
	War damage, see TL725.3.D35
725.3.Z6	Zoning
725.5	Heliports
	For special places, see TL726 +
725.6	Seaplane bases
	For special places, see TL726 +
725.7	Floating airports
	For special places, see TL726 +
725.8	Aircraft carriers
	Cf. V874 +, Vessels
	Special countries
726	General works
726.15	General special
	Including Plymouth to Basra, and transpacific
	routes, etc.
	United States
726.2	General works
726.3.A-W	States, A-W
726.4.A-Z	Cities, A-Z
	Other countries
	America (except United States)
726.5.A1	General works

	Aeronautics. Aeronautical engineering
	Airways (Routes).
	Airports and landing fields. Aerodromes
	Special countries
	Other countries
	America (except
	United States), A-Z -- Continued
726.5.A2-Z	Individual countries, A-Z
	Under each:
	.x *General works*
	.x2A-Z *Local, A-Z*
	Europe
726.6.A1	General works
726.6.A2-Z	Individual countries, A-Z
	Apply table at TL726.5.A2-Z
	Asia
726.7.A1	General works
726.7.A2-Z	Individual countries, A-Z
	Apply table at TL726.5.A2-Z
	Africa
726.8.A1	General works
726.8.A2-Z	Individual countries, A-Z
	Apply table at TL726.5.A2-Z
726.85	Australia
726.87	New Zealand
726.9	Pacific islands
	Beacons for aircraft
	Cf. TL725.3.L5, Airport lighting
727	General works
	Radio beacons, see TL696.B4
	Hangars
730	General works
	Cf. TH9445.A5, Fire prevention
730.1	General special
730.2	For airships
730.3	For airplanes
731	Mooring masts
732	Launching machinery. Catapults, etc.
733	Apparatus for picking up and delivering goods, etc., during flight
	Parachutes
	Historical and early works, including parachutes used from balloons for exhibition and other purposes
	For sport parachuting, see GV769.5+
750	General works
751.A-Z	Special jumpers, A-Z
	Modern parachutes
752	General works
752.5	Juvenile works
753	General special
754.A-Z	Special makes, A-Z
755	Personal narratives

TL

	Aeronautics. Aeronautical engineering
	Parachutes
	Modern parachutes -- Continued
758	Parachutes to carry airplanes
	Kites
	For sport and competitions, see GV769
759.A1	Periodicals, societies, etc.
759.A6-Z	General works
	History
759.3	General works
759.4.A-Z	By region or country, A-Z
759.5	Juvenile works
759.6.A-Z	Special types of kites, A-Z
759.6.F54	Fighter kites
759.6.P3	Parakites
759.7	Uses of kites (General)
	Cf. QC879.3 +, Meteorology
	Cf. TR810, Photography from kites
	Gliders. Gliding and soaring
760.A1	Periodicals, societies, etc.
	General works
760.A2	Early to 1903
760.A3-Z	1903-
760.4.A-Z	By region or country, A-Z
760.5	Air meets
761	General special
762	Design and construction
765	Operation of gliders. Launching. Gliding. Soaring
766	Equipment
769	Human powered aircraft
	Models
	Including model airplanes for hobbyists
	Cf. GV760 +, Flying and racing of model
	airplanes
	For experimental models prior to 1914, see TL670.5
770.A1	Periodicals, societies, etc.
770.A2-Z	General works
772	Collectors and collecting
	Model testing, see TL671.7
	Model rockets and space vehicles, see TL844
774	Model gliders
775	Model airships
776	Model helicopters
777	Details and parts of models
	Including propellers
778	Paper airplanes
	Rocket propulsion. Rockets
780	Periodicals, societies, etc.
780.5	Dictionaries and encyclopedias
	History
781	General works
781.5.A-Z	Special projects, A-Z
781.5.B55	Blue Streak

	Rocket propulsion. Rockets
	History
	Special projects, A-Z -- Continued
781.5.S3	Saturn
781.8.A-Z	By country, A-Z
	Biography
781.85.A1	Collective
781.85.A3-Z	Individual, A-Z
782	General works
782.5	Popular works. Juvenile works
782.55	Pictorial works
782.6	Handbooks, manuals, etc.
782.7	Amateurs' manuals, etc.
782.75	Addresses, essays, lectures
782.8	Rocketry as a profession
	Model rockets, see TL844
	Special types of rockets and propulsion
	Chemical rockets. Chemical propulsion systems
783	General works
783.3	Solid propellant rockets
783.4	Liquid propellant rockets
783.45	Hybrid propellant rockets
783.5	Nuclear rockets. Nuclear propulsion systems
	Electric rockets. Electric propulsion systems
783.54	General works
783.57	Photon rockets. Photon propulsion systems
783.6	Plasma rockets. Plasma propulsion systems
783.63	Ion rockets. Ion rocket propulsion
783.8	Hot water rockets. Hot water rocket propulsion
783.9	Solar sails
784.A-Z	Special topics, A-Z
784.C6	Combustion
784.C63	Controls. Guidance systems
784.C65	Cooling
784.E4	Electronics
784.E9	Expansion joints
784.F8	Fuel systems
784.L3	Launching
784.N65	Nozzles
784.P9	Pyrotechnics
784.R4	Reliability
784.S7	Stability
784.S74	Staging
784.T4	Thrust
784.T5	Telemetry
	Manufacturing. Factory methods
784.3	General works
784.5.A-Z	Special topics, A-Z
784.5.T4	Testing
784.5.W4	Welding
784.8	Materials
785	Fuel
	Rockets for special uses, A-Z

TL

	Rocket propulsion. Rockets
	Rockets for special uses, A-Z -- Continued
785.8.L3	Launch vehicles
785.8.S6	Sounding rockets
	Cf. QC879.4 +, Meteorology
	Spaceships, see TL795 +
	Astronautics. Space travel
	Cf. UG1500 +, Military astronautics. Space
	warfare
787	Periodicals, societies, etc.
787.5	Collected works (nonserial)
787.7	Abstracts
788	Dictionaries and encyclopedias
788.3	Directories
788.35	Patents
788.4	International cooperation
	History
788.5	General works
788.7	Imaginary voyages
	Unidentified flying objects. Flying saucers
	Cf. BF2050 +, Human-alien encounters
	Cf. BL65.U54, Religious aspects of unidentified
	flying objects
	Cf. CB156, Terrestrial evidence of
	interplanetary voyages
789.A1	Periodicals, societies, etc.
789.A2-Z	General works
789.16	Dictionaries
789.2	Juvenile works
789.3	Personal narratives
	Including personal sightings
	By region or country
	United States
789.4	General works
789.5.A-Z	By region or state, A-Z
789.6.A-Z	Other regions or countries, A-Z
789.8.A-Z	By country, region, etc., A-Z
	e.g.
	Under each country
.x	*General works*
.x2A-Z	*Special projects or programs, A-Z*
	United States
789.8.U5	General works
789.8.U6A-Z	Special projects or programs, A-Z
789.8.U6A5	Apollo
789.8.U6G4	Gemini
789.8.U6M3	Mariner
789.8.U6P56	Pioneer
789.8.U6R3	Ranger
789.8.U6S9	Surveyor
789.8.U6X5	X-15 program
789.85.A1-Z	Biography
789.85.A1	Collective

Astronautics. Space travel

Biography -- Continued

789.85.A3-Z	Individual, A-Z
790	General works
791	Textbooks
793	Popular works. Juvenile works
793.5	Pictorial works
793.7	Anecdotes, facetiae, etc.
794	Handbooks, pocketbooks, tables, etc.
794.3	Laboratory manuals. Amateur experiments
794.5	Addresses, essays, lectures

Space vehicles. Spaceships

For specific aspects, see TL874 +

795	General works
795.3	Space probes
795.4	Microspacecraft

Reusable space vehicles. Space shuttles

795.5	General works
795.515	Juvenile works
795.7	Space colonies. Space communities

Artificial satellites

Cf. TL1080, Artificial satellite orbits

796.A1	Periodicals, societies, etc.
796.A2-Z	General works
796.3	Juvenile works

Small satellites, see TL795.4

796.5.A-Z	By country, region, etc., A-Z

e.g.

For individual planets, etc., see TL796.6.A +

Under each country:

.x	*General works*
.x2A-Z	*Special projects or programs, A-Z*

United States

796.5.U5	General works
796.5.U6A-Z	Special projects or programs, A-Z

e.g.

796.5.U6V3	Vanguard
796.6.A-Z	By planet, etc., A-Z
796.6.E2	Earth
796.6.S8	Sun
796.8	Observers' handbooks

Space stations

797	General works
797.15	Juvenile works
798.A-Z	Special types by use, A-Z
798.G4	Geodetic satellites

Cf. QB343, Artificial satellites in geodesy

798.M4	Meteorological satellites

Cf. QC879.4 +, Meteorology

TL

	Astronautics. Space travel
	Artificial satellites
	Special types by use, A-Z -- Continued
798.N3	Navigation satellites
	Class here general works on navigation satellites, including the satellite component of the Global Positioning System. For special applications, see the subject, e. g. TA595.5, Satellite surveying; TL696.A77, Artificial satellites in air navigation; VK562, Artificial satellites in ship navigation
	For general works on the Global Positioning System, see G109.5
798.S3	Scientific satellites
	Cf. Q180.7, Astronautics in science
	Cf. QB500.267 +, Orbiting astronomical observatories
	Telecommunication satellites, see TK5104.2.A +
798.T47	Tethered satellites
799.A-Z	Flights to special planets, etc. By planet, A-Z
	Cf. QB600 +, Planets
799.J8	Jupiter
799.M3	Mars
799.M6	Moon
799.S86	Sun
799.V45	Venus
844	Model rockets. Model space vehicles
	Study and teaching
	Cf. TL1085, Space flight training
845	General works
	Audiovisual aids
845.5.A-Z8	General works
845.5.Z9	Catalogs of audiovisual materials
	United States
846	General works
847.A-Z	Special schools, A-Z
848.A-Z	Other countries, A-Z
849	Problems, exercises, etc.
	Astronautics as a profession
850	General works
	Qualifications for astronauts
855	General works
856	Physical and mental requirements for astronauts
	Including tests
	For clinical aspects, see RC1120 +
	Research
858	General works
	Equipment. Laboratories
859	General works
860.A-Z	Special, A-Z
862.A-Z	Special institutions, A-Z
865	Technology transfer. Space spinoffs
867	Accidents and their prevention. Space safety

	Astronautics. Space travel -- Continued
869	Specifications
	Systems engineering
870	General works
872	Estimates. Quantities. Costs
873	Manned space flight
	Specific aspects of space vehicles
(874)	General works
	see TL795
875	Design and construction
885	Reliability
900	Thermodynamics. Heat engineering
901	Fires and fire prevention
910	Structural dynamics
915	Maintenance and repair
917	Lubrication
920	Testing
940	Expandable space structures
943	Planetary quarantine
945	Sterilization
946	Contamination
	Materials
950	Periodicals, societies, etc.
953	General works
954.A-Z	Special, A-Z
	Coatings, see TL954.P35
954.M47	Metals. Metallurgy
954.P35	Paints and coatings
	Astrodynamics. Flight mechanics. Orbital mechanics
	Cf. QB349+, Astronomy
1050	General works
1055	Relativistic effects in astrodynamics. Relativistic rocket mechanics and dynamics
1060	Atmospheric entry phenomena
	Cf. TL3028, Reentry communications
	Space navigation
	Cf. TL3250+, Navigation systems. Guidance systems
1065	General works
1070	Astronautical charts, tables, etc. Logbooks
	Space trajectories. Orbital transfer
1075	General works
1078	Data processing
	Including computer programs
1080	Artificial satellite orbits
1082	Astronautical instruments
	For instruments of special systems, see the system; e.g. for navigation systems, see TL3250+
1085	Space flight training
1088	Space flight computer simulation
	Cf. TL712.8, Computer flight games
	Operation of space vehicles. Piloting
1090	General works

TL

	Astronautics. Space travel
	Operation of space vehicles. Piloting -- Continued
1095	Orbital rendezvous
1096	Extravehicular activity. Space walk
	Space mining, see TN291.3+
1097	Space robotics
	Space vehicle propulsion systems, see TL780+
1098	Space tools
	Electric equipment on space vehicles
1100	General works
1102.A-Z	Special, A-Z
1102.B3	Batteries
1102.G4	Generators
1102.I57	Insulators
1102.N8	Nuclear electric powerplants
	Including Project SNAP
	Project SNAP, see TL1102.N8
1102.T4	Thermoelectric devices
1102.W57	Wiring
1200	Optical equipment on space vehicles
	Environmental engineering in space. Space environment
1489	General works
1490	Radiation shielding on space vehicles
1492	Electrostatic charging
1495	Space simulators
1496	Flow of fluids. Fluid dynamics
1499	Space debris
	Life support systems. Human engineering. Human environment equipment and testing
1500	General works
1530	Cabin atmosphere
1550	Space suits
1555	Seats
1560	Food
1565	Water supply
	Test and training equipment
1570	General works
1572	Space cabin simulators
1575	Weightlessness simulators
	Astrionics. Electronic equipment on space vehicles
3000.A1	Periodicals, societies, etc.
3000.A3-Z	General works
	Telecommunication, guidance and control systems for space vehicles
	Communication methods and equipment
3025	General works
3026	Deep Space Network
3028	Reentry communications. Plasma sheath effects
3035	Radio
3040	Television
	Navigation systems. Guidance systems
3250	General works
	Theory of navigation, see TL1065+

	Astronautics. Space travel
	Astrionics. Electronic equipment on space vehicles
	Telecommunication, guidance
	and control systems for space vehicles
	Navigation systems.
	Guidance systems -- Continued
3252	Inertial navigation systems
3255	Star trackers
3260	Attitude control systems
3270	Pointing systems
3280	Command control systems
3285	Space-based radar
	Ground support systems, operations and equipment
4000	Periodicals, societies, etc.
4015	General works
	Launching bases. Launch complexes
	Including launch facilities
4020	General works
4024	Planning. Location
	By region or country
	United States
4026	General works
4027.A-Z	By region or state, A-Z
	Under each state:
.x	*General works*
.x2A-Z	*Special bases. By name, A-Z*
4028.A-Z	Other regions or countries, A-Z
4030	Space tracking
	Command control equipment
4040	General works
4045	Mobile facilities
4050	Ground transportation
	Extraterrestrial roving vehicles, see TL475 +

TL

	Mining engineering. Metallurgy
	Including mineral industries
	Periodicals and societies
	Arrange by language of publication
1.A1	International or polyglot
1.A2-Z	English
2	French
3	German
4	Other languages (not A-Z)
5	Congresses
	Exhibitions. Museums
6.A1	General works
6.A2-Z	By region or country, A-Z
	Under each country:
.x	*General works*
.x2A-Z	*Special. By city, A-Z*
7	Collected works (nonserial)
	Dictionaries and encyclopedias
9	General works
10	Polyglot dictionaries
12	Directories
13	Yearbooks
	For special countries, see TN21+
	History and description
15	General works
16	Ancient
17	Medieval
	Modern
18	To 1800
19	1800-
21-127	Special countries (Table T1)
	Including government reports on mineral resources and economic geology
	Add country number in table to TN0
	Biography
139	Collective
140.A-Z	Individual, A-Z
	General works
144	Early to 1800
145	1800-
146	Elementary works
147	Popular works
148	Juvenile works
151	Pocketbooks, tables, examinations, questions, etc.
153	General special
155	Addresses, essays, lectures
160	Mining engineering as a profession
	Study and teaching
165	General works
	America
171	General works
	United States
173	General works

	Study and teaching
	America
	United States -- Continued
174.A-W	States, A-W
175.A-Z	Cities, A-Z
	Canada
176	General works
177.A-Z	Special provinces, A-Z
179	Latin America (General)
	Mexico
180	General works
181.A-Z	Special divisions, A-Z
	Central America
182	General works
183.A-Z	Special countries, A-Z
	West Indies
185	General works
186.A-Z	Special islands, A-Z
	South America
188	General works
189.A-Z	Special countries, A-Z
	Europe
191	General works
192.A-Z	Special countries, A-Z
	Asia
194	General works
195.A-Z	Special countries, A-Z
	Africa
197	General works
198	South Africa
199.A-Z	Other countries, A-Z
	Australia
201	General works
202.A-Z	Special states, A-Z
203	New Zealand
	Pacific islands
204	General works
205.A-Z	Special islands, A-Z
207	Metallurgical research
	Special schools
	United States
210.A-Z	General schools. By name of school, A-Z
211	Correspondence schools
213.A-Z	Other countries. By place of school, A-Z
(215-255)	Mining laws and legislation
	See class K
(257)	Patents
	See class K
260	Economic or applied geology and mineralogy
	For special countries, see TN21 +

TN

263	Mineral deposits. Metallic ore deposits
	For metallic ore deposits of particular metals, see
	TN400+
	For nonmetallic mineral deposits of particular
	minerals, see TN799.5+
	For special countries, see TN21+
263.5	Energy minerals
	Cf. TJ163.13+, Power resources
264	Marine mineral resources
	For mining resources, see TN291.5
265	Metallic ores (General)
	Geophysical surveying
269	General works
	Electric logging
269.5	General works
269.55	Induction logging
269.7	Radioactive prospecting
	Seismic prospecting
269.8	General works
269.84	Seismic reflection method
269.85	Seismic refraction method
269.86	Vertical seismic profiling
269.88	Vibroseis
269.885	Water analysis. Sediment analysis
	Prospecting
	Cf. TN560, Ore sampling
270.A1	Periodicals, societies, congresses, etc.
270.A2-Z	General works
271.A-Z	Special minerals, etc., A-Z
271.A2	Rare metals. Rare earths (General)
271.A47	Aggregates
271.B3	Bauxite
271.B4	Beryllium
271.B6	Boron
271.C47	Chlorite
271.C5	Chromium
271.C53	Clay
271.C58	Coal
271.C6	Copper
271.D5	Diamonds
271.F6	Fluorspar (Fluorite)
271.G6	Gold
271.G7	Graphite
271.H43	Heavy minerals
271.I7	Iron
271.K2	Kaolin
271.K55	Kimberlite
271.L4	Lead
	Magnetite, see TN271.I7
271.M3	Manganese
271.M4	Mercury
271.M5	Mica
271.N5	Nickel

Prospecting
Special minerals, etc., A-Z -- Continued
271.N63   Nonmetallic minerals
271.P27   Peat
271.P3   Pegmatites
271.P4   Petroleum
271.P45   Phosphates
271.P56   Platinum
271.P6   Potassium
271.P9   Pyrites
271.Q4   Quartz
271.R33   Radioactive minerals
                 Rare metals, rare earths, see TN271.A2
271.S55   Silver
271.S88   Sulphides
271.S9   Sulphur
271.T3   Tantalum
271.T4   Thorium
271.T5   Tin
271.T55   Titanium
271.T8   Tungsten
271.U7   Uranium
271.Z5   Zinc
                 Mine examination and valuation. Mine selling
272   General works
272.7   Statistical methods. Kriging
273   Mine surveying. Mine maps
                 Construction of mine structures, buildings, etc , see
                     TH4561
274   Mine organization and management
                     For the organization and management of special types
                         of mines, see TN400 +
                 Practical mining operations
275.A1   Periodicals, societies, etc.
275.A2-Z   General works
276   Automation
277   Excavating and quarrying
278   Hydraulic mining
278.3   In situ processing (Mining)
                     Cf. TP759, Underground coal gasification
278.5   Solution mining
279   Drilling and blasting
                     For use of explosives in coal mines, see TN803
281   Deep boring
281.5   Borehole mining
283   Shaft sinking
285   Tunneling, drifting
286   Longwall mining
287   Stoping
                 Ground control. Ground support
288   General works
289   Timbering
289.3   Mine roof bolting

TN

	Practical mining operations
	Ground control. Ground support -- Continued
289.5	Concrete mine supports
289.8	Pillaring
290	Mine filling
291	Open working. Strip mining
	Cf. QH545.S84, Ecology
	Cf. TD195.S75, Environmental technology
	Mining in extreme environments
291.24	General works
291.26	Cold weather conditions
	Outer space. Space mining
291.3	General works
291.35	Lunar mining
291.5	Underwater mining. Ocean mining
	Cf. TD195.O25, Environmental technology
292	General special
295	Safety measures
	Cf. HD7269.A +, Labor hygiene
297	Rescue work, stations, first aid, etc.
300	Mine sanitation
	Ventilation of mines
301	General works
303	Ventilating appliances and machines
304	Stoppings
	Gases in mines. Firedamp
	Cf. TN844 +, Coalbed methane
305	General works
306	Gases resulting from use of explosives
	Lighting of mines
306.5	General works
307	Miners' lamps. Safety lamps
309	Electric lighting of mines
	Cf. TK4399.C6, Electric lighting of coal preparation plants
	Dangers and accidents in mines and quarries
	Cf. TN802 +, Coal mines and mining
311	General works
312	Mine dusts
313	Explosions
315	Fires
317	Falls of roof, etc.
318	Flooding
318.5	Spoil bank failures
319	Mine subsidences
319.5	Tailings dam failures
320	Machinery
	Mine drainage
321	General works
325	Mine pumps
	Mine transportation, haulage and hoisting
331	General works
333	Underground roads

	Mine transportation,
	haulage and hoisting -- Continued
335	Mechanical haulage
336	Mine railroads, tracks, etc.
337	Electric mine locomotives and their use
338	Gasoline engines
	Hoists and elevators
339	General works
340.A-Z	Special apparatus. By place, A-Z
341	Surface transportation
342	Mine and ore cars
343	Electrical engineering and equipment
	For electric lighting of mines, see TN309
344	Mine communication systems
	Mining machinery, tools, appliances, etc.
	Cf. TN320, Mining accidents
	For coal mining machinery, see TN813+
345	General works
347	Catalogs
380.A-Z	General mining and smelting companies, A-Z
	Ore deposits and mining of particular metals
	Including mining and smelting companies
	For prospecting, see TN270+
	For extraction of particular metals from their ores,
	see TN703-TN799
	Iron ore deposits and mining
400	General works
401	General special
402.A-Z	Individual ores, A-Z
	Prefer classification by country
402.H4	Hematite
402.M3	Magnetite
402.S5	Siderite
402.T3	Taconite
	Special countries
	America
403.A1	General works
	United States
403.A5	General works
403.A6-W	States, A-W
403.Z6A-Z	Special companies. By name, A-Z
404.A-Z	Other countries, A-Z
	Under each country, island, etc.:
	.x *General works*
	.x2A-Z *Local, A-Z*
	Europe
405.A1	General works
405.A4-Z	Special countries, A-Z
	Apply table at TN404.A-Z
	Asia
406.A1	General works
406.A4-Z	Special countries, A-Z
	Apply table at TN404.A-Z

	Ore deposits and mining of particular metals
	Iron ore deposits and mining
	Special countries -- Continued
	Africa
407.A1	General works
407.A4-Z	Special countries, A-Z
	Apply table at TN404.A-Z
	Australia, Oceania, etc.
408.A1	General works
408.A4-Z	Special countries or islands, A-Z
	Apply table at TN404.A-Z
409.A-Z	Companies outside of United States. By name of company, A-Z
	For special companies in the United States, see TN403.Z6A +
	Gold and silver ore deposits and mining. Precious metals
410	General works
411	General special
	Special countries
	America
413.A1	General works
	United States
413.A5	General works
413.A6-W	States, A-W
413.Z6A-Z	Special companies. By name, A-Z
414.A-Z	Other countries, A-Z
	Apply table at TN404.A-Z
	Europe
415.A1	General works
415.A4-Z	Special countries, A-Z
	Apply table at TN404.A-Z
	Asia
416.A1	General works
416.A4-Z	Special countries, A-Z
	Apply table at TN404.A-Z
	Africa
417.A1	General works
417.A4-Z	Special countries, A-Z
	Apply table at TN404.A-Z
	Australia, Oceania, etc.
418.A1	General works
418.A4-Z	Special countries or islands, A-Z
	Apply table at TN404.A-Z
419.A-Z	Companies outside of United States. By name of company, A-Z
	For special companies in the United States, see TN413.Z6A +
	Gold ore deposits and mining
420	General works
421	Hydraulic and placer mining
422	Other methods
	Including gold dredging

	Ore deposits and mining of particular metals
	Gold and silver ore deposits
	and mining. Precious metals
	Gold ore deposits and mining -- Continued
	Special countries
	America
423.A1	General works
	United States
423.A5	General works
423.A6-W	States, A-W
423.Z6A-Z	Special companies. By name, A-Z
424.A-Z	Other countries, A-Z
	Apply table at TN404.A-Z
	Europe
425.A1	General works
425.A4-Z	Special countries, A-Z
	Apply table at TN404.A-Z
	Asia
426.A1	General works
426.A4-Z	Special countries, A-Z
	Apply table at TN404.A-Z
	Africa
427.A1	General works
427.A4-Z	Special countries, A-Z
	Apply table at TN404.A-Z
	Australia, Oceania, etc.
428.A1	General works
428.A4-Z	Special countries or islands, A-Z
	Apply table at TN404.A-Z
429.A-Z	Companies outside of United States. By name of company, A-Z
	For special companies, United States, see TN423.Z6A +
	Silver ore deposits and mining
430	General works
431	General special
432.A-Z	Individual ores, A-Z
	Prefer classification by country
432.S7	Stephanite
	Special countries
	America
433.A1	General works
	United States
433.A5	General works
433.A6-W	States, A-W
433.Z6A-Z	Special companies. By name, A-Z
434.A-Z	Other countries, A-Z
	Apply table at TN404.A-Z
	Europe
435.A1	General works
435.A4-Z	Special countries, A-Z
	Apply table at TN404.A-Z
	Asia

	Ore deposits and mining of particular metals
	Gold and silver ore deposits
	and mining. Precious metals
	Silver ore deposits and mining
	Special countries
	Asia -- Continued
436.A1	General works
436.A4-Z	Special countries, A-Z
	Apply table at TN404.A-Z
	Africa
437.A1	General works
437.A4-Z	Special countries, A-Z
	Apply table at TN404.A-Z
	Australia, Oceania, etc.
438.A1	General works
438.A4-Z	Special countries or islands, A-Z
	Apply table at TN404.A-Z
439.A-Z	Companies outside of United States. By name of company, A-Z
	For special companies in the United States, see TN433.Z6A+
	Copper ore deposits and mining
440	General works
441	General special
442.A-Z	Individual ores, A-Z
	Prefer classification by country
442.C5	Chalcopyrite
	Special countries
	America
443.A1	General works
	United States
443.A5	General works
443.A6-W	States, A-W
443.Z6A-Z	Special companies. By name, A-Z
444.A-Z	Other countries, A-Z
	Apply table at TN404.A-Z
	Europe
445.A1	General works
445.A4-Z	Special countries, A-Z
	Apply table at TN404.A-Z
	Asia
446.A1	General works
446.A4-Z	Special countries, A-Z
	Apply table at TN404.A-Z
	Africa
447.A1	General works
447.A4-Z	Special countries, A-Z
	Apply table at TN404.A-Z
	Australia, Oceania, etc.
448.A1	General works
448.A4-Z	Special countries or islands, A-Z
	Apply table at TN404.A-Z

Ore deposits and mining of particular metals
Copper ore deposits and mining
Special countries -- Continued

449.A-Z   Companies outside of United States. By name of
company, A-Z
For special companies in the United States, see
TN443.Z6A +

Lead ore deposits and mining

450   General works
451   General special
452.A-Z   Individual ores, A-Z
Prefer classification by country
452.C4   Cerussite
452.G3   Galena

Special countries
America

453.A1   General works

United States

453.A5   General works
453.A6-W   States, A-W
453.Z6A-Z   Special companies. By name, A-Z
454.A-Z   Other countries, A-Z
Apply table at TN404.A-Z

Europe

455.A1   General works
455.A4-Z   Special countries, A-Z
Apply table at TN404.A-Z

Asia

456.A1   General works
456.A4-Z   Special countries, A-Z
Apply table at TN404.A-Z

Africa

457.A1   General works
457.A4-Z   Special countries, A-Z
Apply table at TN404.A-Z

Australia, Oceania, etc.

458.A1   General works
458.A4-Z   Special countries or islands, A-Z
Apply table at TN404.A-Z

459.A-Z   Companies outside of United States. By name of
company, A-Z
For special companies in the United States, see
TN453.Z6A +

Mercury ore deposits and mining

460   General works
461   General special
462.A-Z   Individual ores, A-Z
Prefer classification by country
462.C5   Cinnabar

Special countries
America

463.A1   General works
United States

TN

Ore deposits and mining of particular metals

Mercury ore deposits and mining

Special countries

America

United States -- Continued

463.A5	General works
463.A6-W	States, A-W
463.Z6A-Z	Special companies. By name, A-Z
464.A-Z	Other countries, A-Z
	Apply table at TN404.A-Z

Europe

465.A1	General works
465.A4-Z	Special countries, A-Z
	Apply table at TN404.A-Z

Asia

466.A1	General works
466.A4-Z	Special countries, A-Z
	Apply table at TN404.A-Z

Africa

467.A1	General works
467.A4-Z	Special countries, A-Z
	Apply table at TN404.A-Z

Australia, Oceania, etc.

468.A1	General works
468.A4-Z	Special countries or islands, A-Z
	Apply table at TN404.A-Z
469.A-Z	Companies outside of United States. By name of company, A-Z
	For special companies, United States, see TN463.Z6A +

Tin ore deposits and mining

470	General works
471	General special
472.A-Z	Individual ores, A-Z
	Prefer classification by country
472.C3	Cassiterite

Special countries

America

473.A1	General works

United States

473.A5	General works
473.A6-W	States, A-W
473.Z6A-Z	Special companies. By name, A-Z
474.A-Z	Other countries, A-Z
	Apply table at TN404.A-Z

Europe

475.A1	General works
475.A4-Z	Other countries, A-Z
	Apply table at TN404.A-Z

Asia

476.A1	General works
476.A4-Z	Other countries, A-Z
	Apply table at TN404.A-Z

Ore deposits and mining of particular metals
Tin ore deposits and mining
Special countries -- Continued
Africa
477.A1   General works
477.A4-Z   Other countries, A-Z
                    Apply table at TN404.A-Z
Australia, Oceania, etc.
478.A1   General works
478.A4-Z   Special countries or islands, A-Z
                    Apply table at TN404.A-Z
479.A-Z   Companies outside of United States. By name of
                    company, A-Z
                    For special companies in the United States, see
                      TN473.Z6A +
Zinc ore deposits and mining
480   General works
481   General special
482.A-Z   Individual ores, A-Z
                 Prefer classification by country
482.S6   Sphalerite
Special countries
America
483.A1   General works
United States
483.A5   General works
483.A6-W   States, A-W
483.Z6A-Z   Special companies. By name, A-Z
484.A-Z   Other countries, A-Z
                    Apply table at TN404.A-Z
Europe
485.A1   General works
485.A4-Z   Other countries, A-Z
                    Apply table at TN404.A-Z
Asia
486.A1   General works
486.A4-Z   Other countries, A-Z
                    Apply table at TN404.A-Z
Africa
487.A1   General works
487.A4-Z   Other countries, A-Z
                    Apply table at TN404.A-Z
Australia, Oceania, etc.
488.A1   General works
488.A4-Z   Special countries or islands, A-Z
                    Apply table at TN404.A-Z
489.A-Z   Companies outside of United States. By name of
                    company, A-Z
                    For special companies, United States, see
                      TN483.Z6A +
490.A-Z   Other metals, A-Z
                 Class individual ores of particular metals with the
                   metal

TN

	Ore deposits and mining of particular metals
	Other metals, A-Z -- Continued
490.A2	Rare metals. Rare earths (General)
490.A3	Radioactive minerals
490.A5	Aluminum. Bauxite
490.A6	Antimony
490.A8	Arsenic
490.B2	Barium
	Bauxite, see TN490.A5
490.B4	Beryllium
490.B6	Bismuth
490.C2	Cadmium
490.C4	Chromium
490.C6	Cobalt
490.G4	Germanium
490.I6	Indium
490.L5	Lithium
490.M2	Magnesium
490.M3	Manganese
490.M7	Molybdenum
490.N6	Nickel
490.N65	Niobium
490.P7	Platinum and platinum group
490.R3	Radium
	Rare earths and metals, see TN490.A2
490.R48	Rhenium
490.R8	Rubidium
490.S4	Scandium
490.S8	Strontium
490.T2	Tantalum
490.T5	Tellurium
490.T55	Thorium
490.T6	Titanium
490.T9	Tungsten (Wolfram)
490.U7	Uranium
	Cf. TN490.A3, Radioactive minerals
490.V2	Vanadium
490.Z5	Zirconium
495.A-Z	Metallic compounds, A-Z
495.S9	Sulphides
	Ore dressing and milling
	For specific ores prefer classification by ore; , see
	TN538.A +
496	Periodicals. Societies. Serials
497	Congresses
500	General works
501	Addresses, essays, lectures
502	Dictionaries and encyclopedias
504	Plants and equipment
	Milling machinery
	Cf. TJ1345, Mechanical engineering
505	General works
507	Trade catalogs

Ore deposits and mining of particular metals
Ore dressing and milling -- Continued

510	Crushing. Rolls, stamps, breakers
515	Screening and sorting. Screens, classifiers
	Concentrating. Jigs, tables, vanners
520	General works
523	Flotation
525	Slime treatment
530	Magnetic separation
531	Dielectric separation
535	General special
	Including dewatering
538.A-Z	Individual ores, A-Z
538.A55	Aluminum
538.A57	Antimony ores
538.C57	Chromium
538.C66	Copper
538.C9	Cyanite
538.G64	Gold
538.I7	Iron
538.M35	Manganese
538.N6	Nonferrous metals
538.P43	Phosphates
538.P53	Platinum
538.P6	Potassium
538.S84	Sulphides
538.T55	Tin
538.T74	Troilite
538.U7	Uranium
	Assaying
	Cf. HG325 +, Money
550	General works
555	General special
560	Sampling of ores
	Cf. TN272 +, Mine examination and valuation
565	Metallurgical analysis
	Metallurgical and assay laboratories
570	General works
571.A-Z	Special laboratories. By place, A-Z
575	Assaying apparatus
580.A-Z	Assaying of special substances, A-Z
	Including the analysis of ores
580.C5	Chromium
580.C64	Copper
580.G6	Gold and gold ores
580.H43	Heavy metals
580.I8	Iron and iron ores
580.M3	Manganese
580.M4	Mercury
580.N6	Nonferrous metals
580.P7	Platinum
580.P74	Precious metals
580.R48	Rhenium

TN

	Ore deposits and mining of particular metals
	Assaying
	Assaying of special substances, A-Z -- Continued
580.S5	Silver
580.T5	Tin ores
580.T73	Trace elements
	Metallurgy
	Cf. TA459+, Properties of metals
	Cf. TS200+, Metal manufactures
600	Periodicals, societies, etc.
605	Congresses
607	Collected works (nonserial)
609	Dictionaries and encyclopedias
	Communication of metallurgical information
610	General works
610.5	Metallurgical literature
612	Directories
	History
615	General works
616	Ancient
617	Medieval
618	Modern
619	19th century
620	20th century
	Special countries
621	America
	United States
623	General works
624.A-W	States, A-W
	Canada
626	General works
627.A-Z	Special divisions, A-Z
629	Latin America (General)
	Mexico
630	General works
631.A-Z	Special divisions, A-Z
	Central America
632	General works
633.A-Z	Special countries, A-Z
	West Indies
635	General works
636.A-Z	Special islands, A-Z
	South America
638	General works
639.A-Z	Special countries, A-Z
	Europe
641	General works
642.A-Z	Special countries, A-Z
	Asia
644	General works
645.A-Z	Special countries, A-Z
	Africa
647	General works

Metallurgy
  Special countries
    Africa -- Continued
648   South Africa
649.A-Z   Special countries, A-Z
    Australia
651   General works
652.A-Z   By state, A-Z
    Pacific islands
654   General works
655.A-Z   Special islands, A-Z
  General works
664   Early to 1800
665   1800-
667   Popular works. Juvenile works
669   Laboratory manuals
671   Pocketbooks, tables, etc.
672   Heat treatment of metals
673   General special
675   Addresses, essays, lectures
675.3   Study and teaching
          Cf. TN207, Metallurgical research
675.4   Information services
        Metallurgical plants
675.5   General works
675.7   Management
        Accidents and their prevention. Safety measures
          Cf. HD7269.A +, Labor hygiene
676.A1   General works
676.A3   United States
676.A5-Z   Other countries, A-Z
        Special equipment
          Metallurgical furnaces
677   General works
677.5   Refractory materials
678   Plasma jets
678.5   Reagents
    Electrometallurgy
        Cf. TS670 +, Electroplating
        For applications to special metals, see the metal,
          e.g. TN706, Iron and steel
681   Periodicals, societies, etc.
683   Congresses
685   General works
686   General special
686.5.A-Z   Special processes, A-Z
686.5.E4   Electroslag process
686.5.V3   Vacuum metallurgy
686.5.Z6   Zone melting
          Cf. TP156.Z6, Chemical engineering
687   Special equipment
          Including electric furnaces
    Hydrometallurgy

TN

	Metallurgy
	Hydrometallurgy -- Continued
688	General works
688.3.A-Z	Special processes, A-Z
688.3.B33	Biotechnology
	Including bacterial leaching
688.3.H4	Heap leaching
688.3.I65	Ion exchange process
688.5	Pyrometallurgy
	Metallography. Physical metallurgy
	Cf. QC176+, Solid state physics
	Cf. QD478, Solid state chemistry
	Cf. QD506+, Surface chemistry
	Cf. QD901+, Crystallography
	Cf. TA483+, General properties of alloys
	Cf. TS650, Manufacture of alloys
689	Periodicals, societies, etc.
689.2	Congresses
689.4	Dictionaries and encyclopedias
690	General works
690.2	Addresses, essays, lectures
690.4	Handbooks, manuals, etc.
	Study and teaching
690.6	General works
690.65	Field work
690.7	Metallographic specimens
693.A-Z	Special metals, A-Z
	Including alloys
693.A4	Alkali metals
693.A5	Aluminum
693.A54	Americium
693.B4	Beryllium
693.B5	Bismuth
693.B6	Boron alloys
693.C5	Chromium
693.C8	Cobalt
693.C9	Copper (Bronze)
693.F7	Friction metals
693.G6	Gold
693.H4	Heat resistant metals
693.I7	Iron and steel
693.L4	Lead
	Light metals and alloys, see TN693.N6
693.M3	Magnesium
693.M35	Manganese
693.M38	Metallic composites
693.M4	Metallic glasses
	Mischmetal, see TN693.R3
693.M64	Molybdenum
693.N5	Nickel
693.N6	Nonferrous metals
693.P3	Palladium
693.P55	Platinum

	Metallurgy
	Metallography. Physical metallurgy
	Special metals, A-Z -- Continued
693.P7	Precious metals
693.R3	Rare earth metal alloys
	Including Mischmetal
	Refractory transition metal compounds, see TN693.T7
693.R45	Rhenium
693.S5	Silver
693.S9	Superconductors
693.T34	Tantalum
693.T4	Tellurium
693.T45	Thorium
693.T5	Titanium
693.T7	Transition metal compounds
	Including refractory transition metal compounds
693.T94	Tungsten
693.U7	Uranium
693.V3	Vanadium
693.Z5	Zirconium
	Powder metallurgy
	Cf. TS245, Manufactures
695	General works
697.A-Z	Special metals, A-Z
697.A47	Aluminum
697.C65	Copper
697.H4	Heat resistant alloys
697.I7	Iron and steel
697.T5	Titanium
697.Z54	Zinc
698	Mechanical alloying
700	Metallurgy of heat resistant alloys
	Metallurgy of ferrous metals
	Iron and steel
	Cf. TA464 +, Properties
	Cf. TS300 +, Manufactures
	Periodicals and societies, see TS300
701.5	Congresses
702	Dictionaries and encyclopedias
	Directories, see TS301
703	History
704.A-Z	Special countries, A-Z
	Under each:
	.x *General works*
	.x2.A-Z *Local, A-Z*
705	General works
706	Electric processes
706.5	Pyrometallurgy
707	General special
	Including slag
708	Patents
	Cast iron. Pig iron
710	General works

TN

Metallurgy
 Metallurgy of ferrous metals
 Iron and steel
 Cast iron. Pig iron -- Continued
 Blast furnaces

713	General works
715	Hot blast. Dry-air blast
	Cf. TS231, Cupola furnaces
718	Utilization of waste heat, gas, etc.
719	Malleable cast iron
719.5	Nodular iron

 Wrought iron

720	General works
723	Direct processes
725	Refinery processes. Puddling and puddling furnaces
727	Sponge iron

 Steel

730	General works
731	General special
	Including temperature measurements
732	Popular works. Juvenile works

 Special processes

733	Direct processes
734	Cementation processes
735	Crucible process

 Bessemer process

736	General works
737	Acid Bessemer process
738	Basic Bessemer process

 Open hearth or Siemens process

740	General works
741	Acid open hearth process
742	Basic open hearth process
745	Electric furnace processes
746	Ladle metallurgy
747	Oxygen steelmaking
750	Other processes. Continuous ingot casting, etc.

 Heat treatment

751	General works
752.A-Z	Special processes, A-Z
752.A5	Annealing
752.C3	Case hardening. Nitriding
752.C5	Chromizing
752.F4	Flame hardening
752.I5	Induction hardening
	Nitriding, see TN752.C3
752.Q4	Quenching
752.S8	Surface hardening
752.T4	Tempering
752.T54	Thermomechanical treatment
755.A-Z	Special plants and works, A-Z

	Metallurgy
	Metallurgy of ferrous metals
	Iron and steel -- Continued
	Iron and steel alloys
	Class here production only
	For microscopic examination, see TN689 +
	For properties, strength, etc., see TA464 +
756	General works
757.A-Z	Special alloys, A-Z
	Aluminum, see TN775
757.B6	Boron steel
757.C35	Calcium steel
757.C48	Chrome-manganese steel
757.C49	Chrome-nickel steel
757.C5	Chrome steel. Stainless steel
757.F25	Ferrochromium
757.F3	Ferromanganese
757.F33	Ferronickel
757.F4	Ferrosilicon
757.M3	Manganese steel
757.M7	Molybdenum steel
757.N5	Nickel steel
757.N6	Nickel chromium alloys
757.N66	Nitrogen
757.S45	Semikilled steel
757.S7	Spiegel iron
	Stainless steel, see TN757.C5
757.T5	Titanium steel
757.T9	Tungsten steel
757.U7	Uranium steel
757.V3	Vanadium steel
	Metallurgy of nonferrous metals
758	General works
758.3	Heat treatment
758.4.A-Z	Individual plants and works, A-Z
	Precious metals
759	General works
	Gold and silver
760	General works
761	General special
761.5	Popular works
761.6	Juvenile works
762	Milling
	Special processes
763	Amalgamation
765	Chlorination
767	Cyanide process
768	Electric processes
769	Other special processes
770	Silver and lead
	For lead alone, see TN785
	Light metals
773	General works

TN

	Metallurgy
	Metallurgy of nonferrous metals
	Light metals -- Continued
775	Aluminum and its alloys
780	Copper
785	Lead
790	Mercury
793	Tin
796	Zinc
	Minor metals
798	Collectively
799.A-Z	Special metals, A-Z
799.A6	Antimony
799.B4	Beryllium
799.B5	Bismuth
799.C2	Cadmium
799.C25	Calcium
799.C4	Cesium
799.C5	Chromium
799.C6	Cobalt
799.G3	Gallium
799.G4	Germanium
799.I5	Indium
799.L57	Lithium
799.M2	Magnesium
799.M3	Manganese
799.M7	Molybdenum
799.N47	Neodymium
799.N5	Neptunium
799.N6	Nickel
799.N7	Niobium
799.P34	Palladium
799.P7	Platinum
799.P74	Plutonium
799.R37	Rare earth metal alloys
799.R45	Rhenium
799.R5	Rhodium
	Selenium, see TN948.S4
799.T3	Tantalum
799.T4	Thorium
799.T5	Titanium
799.T9	Tungsten
799.U7	Uranium
799.V3	Vanadium
799.Z5	Zirconium
	Nonmetallic minerals
	Including deposits and associated mining industries
	For prospecting, see TN270+
799.5	General works
	By region or country
	United States
799.6.A1	General works
799.6.A2-Z	By region or state, A-Z

Nonmetallic minerals
By region or country -- Continued
799.7.A-Z   Other regions or countries, A-Z
Under each country:
.x   *General works*
.x2A-Z   *Local, A-Z*
Coal
799.9   Periodicals, societies, etc.
799.95   Dictionaries and encyclopedias
800   General works
801   Elementary and popular works
Mines and mining
For lighting, see TN306.5+
For practical mining operations, see TN275+
For safety measures, see TN295
For ventilation, see TN301+
802   General works
803   General special
Including use of explosives
Special countries
Including geology of coal deposits in the region or country
America
805.A1   Periodicals, societies, etc.
805.A2   General works
United States
805.A3   Periodicals, societies, etc.
805.A4   Directories
805.A5   General works
805.A6-W   Individual states, A-W
805.Z6A-Z   Individual companies. By name, A-Z
806.A-Z   Other countries, A-Z
Apply table at TN404.A-Z
807.A-Z   American companies outside of United States, A-Z
Europe
808.A1   General works
808.A4-Z5   Special countries, A-Z
Apply table at TN404.A-Z
808.Z6A-Z   Special companies. By name, -Z
Asia
809.A1   General works
809.A4-Z5   Special countries, A-Z
Apply table at TN404.A-Z
809.Z6A-Z   Special companies. By name, A-Z
Africa
810.A1   General works
810.A4-Z5   Special countries, A-Z
Apply table at TN404.A-Z
810.Z6A-Z   Special companies. By name, A-Z
Australia, Oceania, etc.
811.A1   General works

TN

	Nonmetallic minerals
	Coal
	Mines and mining
	Special countries
	Australia, Oceania, etc. -- Continued
811.A4-Z5	Special countries, A-Z
	Apply table at TN404.A-Z
811.Z6A-Z	Special companies. By name, A-Z
812	Arctic regions and Antarctica
	Including Spitzbergen, Bear Island, etc.
	Coal mining machinery, etc.
813	General works
814	Catalogs
815	Coal-handling machinery for colliery purposes
	For machinery for handling coal commercially, see TJ1405
	Coal preparation, washing, screening, etc.
816.A1	Periodicals, societies, etc.
816.A3-Z	General works
817	Coal storage, weathering, etc.
	Underground gasification, see TP759
	Anthracite
820	General works
823.A-Z	Special countries, A-Z
	Bituminous coal
825	General works
	Special countries, see TN805 +
827	Cannel coal
	Lignite. Brown coal
831	General works
834.A-Z	Special countries, A-Z
	Peat
837	General works
840.A-Z	Special countries, A-Z
841	Peat machinery
842	Peat straw, peat mull, etc.
	Coalbed methane
	Cf. TN305 +, Mine safety
	Cf. TP761.M4, Gas industry
844	Periodicals, societies, etc.
844.5	General works
	By region or country
	United States
844.6	General works
844.62.A-Z	By region or state, A-Z
844.7.A-Z	Other regions or countries, A-Z
	Other natural carbons and hydrocarbons
845	Graphite
847	Schungite
850	Bitumen
851	Sapropel
853	Asphalt
	Including uses

	Nonmetallic minerals
	Other natural carbons and hydrocarbons -- Continued
857	Ozokerite, ceresin, natural paraffin
	Cf. TP695, Chemical technology
	Oil shales
	Cf. TP699, Chemical technology
858.A1	Periodicals, societies, etc.
858.A2-Z	General works
859.A-Z	Special countries, A-Z
	Apply table at TN404.A-Z
	Petroleum. Petroleum engineering
	Cf. HD9560 +, Petroleum trade
	Cf. TP690 +, Refining, etc.
860	Periodicals, societies, etc.
862	Yearbooks
863	Congresses
864	Collected works (nonserial)
865	Dictionaries and encyclopedias
867	Directories
	Biography
869	Collective
869.2.A-Z	Individual, A-Z
870	General works
870.3	Juvenile works
	Origin and composition. Petroleum geology
	For analysis and testing, see TP691
870.5	General works
870.515	Brines. Groundwater. Water chemistry
870.52	Capillarity
870.53	Mathematical modelling
870.54	Oil sands
870.55	Remote sensing
870.56	Rock mechanics
870.57	Traps. Reservoirs
	Prospecting, see TN271.P4
871	General special
	Including well testing, storage, diffusion, etc.
871.15	Addresses, essays, lectures
871.18	Reservoir oil pressure
	Well drilling
871.2	General works
871.215	Blowouts
871.22	Casing
871.23	Directional drilling
871.24	Formation damage
871.25	Horizontal well drilling
871.27	Muds. Fluids
871.3	Submarine well drilling
871.35	Well logging
871.37	Secondary recovery of oil
871.4	Mobile offshore structures
871.5	Petroleum and gas well supplies
	Including catalogs

TN

	Nonmetallic minerals
	Other natural carbons and hydrocarbons
	Petroleum. Petroleum engineering -- Continued
	Special countries
	America
872.A2	General works
	By region or country
	United States
872.A3-A34	Periodicals, societies, congresses, etc.
	Documents
872.A35-A44	Serials
872.A45	Monographs
	Arrange by date
	Directories, see TN867
872.A5	General works
872.A6-W	By state, A-W
872.Z6A-Z	Special companies. By name, A-Z
873.A-Z	Other regions or countries, A-Z
	Apply table at TN404.A-Z
	Europe
874.A1	General works
874.A4-Z	Special countries, A-Z
	Apply table at TN404.A-Z
875	Caspian, Baku, etc.
	Asia
876.A1	General works
876.A4-Z	Special countries, A-Z
	Apply table at TN404.A-Z
	Africa
877.A1	General works
877.A4-Z	Special countries, A-Z
	Apply table at TN404.A-Z
	Australia, Oceania, etc.
878.A1	General works
878.A6-Z	Special countries or islands, A-Z
	Apply table at TN404.A-Z
878.2	Arctic regions
	Including Greenland
879	Oil companies outside of United States
	Petroleum pipelines
	Cf. TH9445.P38, Fire prevention and
	extinction
879.5	General works
879.52	Control
879.53	Design and construction
879.54	Equipment and supplies
879.55	Failure. Accidents. Leaks. Reliability
879.56	Fluid dynamics
879.57	Insulation. Heat transmission
879.58	Maintenance and repair
879.59	Safety measures
879.6	Welding
	Natural gas

	Nonmetallic minerals
	Other natural carbons and hydrocarbons
	Natural gas -- Continued
880.A1	Periodicals, societies, etc.
880.A3-Z	General works
880.2	Gas well drilling
880.5	Natural gas pipelines
	Natural gas storage, see TP756, TP756.5
	United States
881.A1	General works
881.A2-W	Special states, A-W
882.A-Z	Other countries, A-Z
	Apply table at TN404.A-Z
883	Helium in natural gas
884	Hydrates in natural gas
885	Amber, fossil gums, etc.
890	Sulphur
	Alkalies
	Cf. TN919, Potassium salts
	Cf. TP222+, Chemical technology
895	General works
	United States
896.A1	General works
896.A6-W	States, A-W
897.A-Z	Other countries, A-Z
	Apply table at TN404.A-Z
	Sodium salts. Soda deposits
899	General works
	Salt
	Mining and manufacture
900	General works
	By region or country
	United States
902.A1	General works
902.A2-W	By state, A-W
903.A-Z	Other regions, countries, etc., A-Z
	Apply table at TN404.A-Z
	Manufacture
905	Sea water
907	Saline springs
909	Company prospectuses, etc.
	Sodium sulphate, see TN948.S7
911	Nitrates. Chile saltpeter
	Cf. TP237+, Chemical technology
	Phosphates
913	General works
914.A-Z	Special countries, A-Z
	Apply table at TN404.A-Z
917	Borax and other borates
919	Potassium salts. Potash-bearing rocks and plants.
	Kelp
	Cf. TP245.P8, Chemical technology

TN

	Nonmetallic minerals -- Continued
	Mineral waters
	Cf. GB1198+, Hot springs
	Cf. RA794, Health resorts, spas, etc.
	Cf. TP625, Artificial mineral waters
923	General works
	United States
925	General works
926.A-W	Special states, A-W
927.A-Z	Other American countries, A-Z
	Apply table at TN799.7.A-Z
	Europe
928.A1	General works
928.A3-Z	By country, island, or region, A-Z
	Apply table at TN799.7.A-Z
	Asia
929.1.A1	General works
929.1.A3-Z	By country, island, region, A-Z
	Apply table at TN799.7.A-Z
	Africa
929.3.A1	General works
929.3.A3-Z	By country, island, region, A-Z
	Apply table at TN799.7.A-Z
	Australia
929.5.A1	General works
929.5.A3-Z	Local, A-Z
	New Zealand
929.6.A1	General works
929.6.A3-Z	Local, A-Z
	Pacific islands
929.7.A1	General works
929.7.A3-Z	By country, island, region, A-Z
	Apply table at TN799.7.A-Z
930	Asbestos
933	Mica
936	Abrasives. Emery, corundum, etc.
939	Sand and gravel
	Clay
	Cf. TP785+, Ceramic industries
941	General works
942	United States
943.A-Z	Other countries, A-Z
	Apply table at TN799.7.A-Z
	Structural materials in general, see TN950+
945	Cement materials
946	Gypsum
	Cf. TP888, Plaster and other gypsum products
948.A-Z	Other specific nonmetallic minerals, A-Z
	Including minerals from which metals are not normally extracted
948.A5	Allanite
948.A6	Alunite
948.A65	Anhydrite

Nonmetallic minerals
Other specific nonmetallic
minerals, A-Z -- Continued

948.A7	Apatite
948.A76	Argillite
948.B18	Barite
948.B4	Bentonite
948.B45	Beryl
	Calcite, see TN967
948.C3	Carbonatites
948.C34	Carnallite
948.C5	Chalk. Whiting
948.C55	Chiolite
948.C6	Clinoptilolite
948.C72	Conglomerate
948.C73	Coprolites
948.C75	Cordierite
(948.C8)	Corundum
	see TN936
948.C95	Cyanite
948.D49	Diaspore
948.D5	Diatomaceous earth
948.D8	Dumortierite
948.F3	Feldspar
948.F45	Fillers
948.F5	Flint
948.F6	Fluorspar
948.F9	Fullers' earth
	Garnet, see TN997.G3
948.H3	Halloysite
948.L3	Laterite
948.L46	Lime
948.M2	Magnesite
948.M3	Marl
948.M5	Meerschaum
948.M7	Monazite
948.M72	Montmorillonite
	Mordenite, see TN948.Z4
948.M8	Mullite
948.M85	Muscovite
948.N37	Nepheline syenite
948.N4	Nephelite (Nepheline)
948.O2	Ocher
948.P25	Palygorskite
948.P38	Pegmatites
948.P4	Perlite
948.P5	Pigments
948.P74	Pumice
948.P8	Pyrite
948.P82	Pyrochlore
948.P85	Pyrophyllite
948.Q3	Quartz
948.R45	Rhodonite

TN

	Nonmetallic minerals
	Other specific nonmetallic minerals, A-Z -- Continued
948.S24	Saprolites
948.S4	Selenium
948.S45	Serpentine
948.S5	Shale
	Cf. TN858+, Oil shales
948.S6	Silica
948.S63	Sillimanite
948.S7	Sodium sulphate
948.S9	Syenite
948.T2	Talc and soapstone
948.T74	Tripoli
948.T76	Trona
948.T9	Tysonite
948.V4	Vermiculite
	Whiting, see TN948.C5
948.W6	Wollastonite
948.Z4	Zeolites. Mordenite
	Building and ornamental stones
	Cf. TA426+, General properties, testing, etc.
	Cf. TA670+, Stonemasonry and stonecutting
950.A1	Periodicals, societies, etc.
950.A5-Z	General works
	Special countries
	America
951.A1	General works
	United States
951.A5	General works
951.A6-W	Special states, A-W
952.A-Z	Other American countries, A-Z
	Europe
953.A1	General works
953.A3-Z	Special countries, A-Z
	Asia
954.A1	General works
954.A3-Z	Special countries, A-Z
	Africa
955.A1	General works
955.A3-Z	Special countries, A-Z
	Australia. Oceania
956.A1	General works
956.A3-Z	Special countries, A-Z
	Special stones
957	Sandstone
958	Slate
	Soapstone, see TN948.T2
967	Limestone. Marble
970	Granite
973	Other building stones
	Stones for roadmaking, see TE200+
	Ornamental stones. Gems

	Building and ornamental stones
	Ornamental stones. Gems -- Continued
980	General works
	Special countries
	America
981.A1	General works
	United States
981.A5	General works
981.A6-W	Special states, A-W
982.A-Z	Other American countries, A-Z
	Europe
983.A1	General works
983.A3-Z	Special countries, A-Z
	Asia
984.A1	General works
984.A3-Z	Special countries, A-Z
	Africa
985.A1	General works
985.A3-Z	Special countries, A-Z
	Australia. Oceania
986.A1	General works
986.A3-Z	Special countries, A-Z
989.A-Z	Special ornamental stones (other than gems), A-Z
989.A3	Alabaster
989.B55	Blue john
	Diamonds
990	General works
	South Africa
991	General works
992	Company reports, etc.
993	United States
994.A-Z	Other special countries, A-Z
997.A-Z	Other precious and semiprecious stones, A-Z
997.A35	Agates
997.E5	Emeralds
997.G3	Garnets
997.J3	Jade
997.M35	Malachite
997.O7	Opals
997.S24	Sapphires

TN

	Chemical technology
	Cf. HD9000+, Economics
1	Periodicals, societies, etc.
5	Congresses
	Exhibitions. Museums
6.A1	General works
6.A2-Z	By region or country, A-Z
	Under each country:
.x	*General works*
.x2A-Z	*Special. By city, A-Z*
7	Collected works (nonserial)
9	Dictionaries and encyclopedias
12	Directories
	History
15	General works
16	Ancient
17	Medieval
18	Modern
19	Nineteenth century
20	Twentieth century
21-127	Country divisions (Table T1)
	Add country number in table to TP0
130.A-Z	Special companies, A-Z
	Including history, description, etc.
	Biography
139	Collective
140.A-Z	Individual, A-Z
	General works
144	Early to 1900
145	1900-
146	Elementary works
147	Popular works
	Addresses, essays, lectures, see TP185
149	General special
	Including municipal chemistry, safety measures, etc.
150.A-Z	Special aspects of the subject as a whole, A-Z
150.A23	Accidents. Disasters
	For works on accidents in specific places, see TP21+
	Data processing, see TP184
	Disasters, see TP150.A23
151	Tables, pocketbooks, etc.
	Cf. T49, Technical receipts
	Chemical engineering
	For chemical engineering aspects of atomic power, see TK9350
155	General works
155.2.A-Z	Special aspects of the subject as a whole, A-Z
	Data processing, see TP184
155.2.M34	Markov processes
155.2.M36	Mathematics
	Chemical plants
	Cf. TH4524, Building construction
155.5	General works

	Chemical engineering
	Chemical plants -- Continued
155.6	Management
	Chemical processes
155.7	General works
155.75	Chemical process control
156.A-Z	Special processes and operations, A-Z
156.A3	Absorption of gases
156.A33	Acoustics. Ultrasonics
156.A35	Adsorption
156.B7	Briquetting
156.C3	Carbonization
156.C35	Catalysis
156.C38	Cavitation
156.C5	Chromatography
156.C57	Coating processes
	Cf. TA418.9.C57, Coatings
	Cf. TS670+, Electroplating
	Cf. TT300+, Industrial painting
156.C59	Compacting
156.C6	Condensation
156.C64	Controlled release technology
	Cooling, see TP363
156.C7	Crystallization
156.C8	Curing
	Dehydration, see TP363
156.D4	Dehydrogenation
156.D42	Demulsification
156.D43	Desulphuration
	Cf. TD885.5.S85, Air pollution control
156.D45	Dialysis
156.D47	Diffusion
156.D5	Distillation
(156.D7)	Drying
	see TP363
156.E5	Electrostatic separation
156.E6	Emulsion
156.E65	Equilibrium
156.E68	Etching
(156.E7)	Evaporation
	see TP363
156.E8	Extraction
156.F4	Fermentation, Industrial
	Cf. TP248.25.S64, Solid-state fermentation
156.F5	Filtration
156.F55	Flocculation
156.F6	Flow of liquids
156.F65	Fluidization
(156.G7)	Grinding
	see TP156.S5
	Heating, see TP363
156.H78	Hydrogen-ion concentration
156.H8	Hydrogenation

TP

Chemical engineering
  Special processes and operations, A-Z -- Continued

156.H82	Hydrolysis
156.H85	Hydroxylation
156.I6	Ion exchange
156.I7	Isotope separation
156.M26	Magnetic separation
	Cf. TN530, Ore dressing and milling
156.M3	Mass transfer
156.M45	Methanation
156.M5	Mixing
156.N5	Nitration
156.N8	Nucleation
156.O7	Osmosis. Reverse osmosis
156.O9	Oxidation
156.P3	Particle technology
156.P4	Pelletizing
156.P5	Plasma
156.P6	Polymerization
156.P7	Precipitation
156.P75	Pressure processes
156.P8	Pumping
156.P83	Purification
156.P9	Pyrolysis
156.R35	Rectification
156.R38	Recycle processes
156.R4	Reduction
	Reverse osmosis, see TP156.O7
156.R45	Rheology
156.S3	Screening
156.S32	Scrubber process
156.S4	Sedimentation
156.S45	Separation
	Cf. TP156.M26, Magnetic separation
	Cf. TP248.25.M46, Membrane separation
	(Biotechnology)
	Cf. TP248.25.S47, Biotechnology
156.S5	Size reduction. Grinding
156.S55	Solidification
156.S57	Sprouted bed processes
156.S6	Spraying
156.S8	Sterilization
156.S9	Sublimation
156.S95	Surface analysis
156.T7	Transport processes
	Ultrasonics, see TP156.A33
156.V3	Vacuum technology
156.W4	Weighing and measuring
156.W45	Wetting
156.Z6	Zone melting
	Apparatus and supplies
157	General works
158	Trade catalogs

	Apparatus and supplies -- Continued
159.A-Z	Special, A-Z
159.A47	Antifoaming agents
159.A5	Antioxidants
159.A85	Atomizers
159.A9	Autoclaves
159.C3	Catalysts
159.C4	Centrifuges
159.C46	Chemical detectors
159.C55	Coagulants
159.C57	Compressors
159.C6	Cooling towers
159.D4	Densimeters
	Detectors, Chemical, see TP159.C46
159.D5	Distillation apparatus
159.D7	Drying agents
159.E37	Electrochemical sensors
159.E39	Electrodes
159.E4	Electrolytic cells
159.E85	Evaporators
159.E9	Extractors
159.F4	Feeders
159.F52	Flare gas systems
159.F54	Flocculants
159.F87	Furnaces
159.H4	Heat transfer media
159.L4	Leaching equipment
159.M4	Membranes
	Cf. TP248.25.M46, Membrane separation (Biotechnology)
159.M6	Molecular sieves
159.N6	Nozzles
159.O9	Oxidizing agents
159.P3	Packed towers
159.P5	Pipe
159.P57	Plasma jets
159.P6	Plate towers
	Pressure vessels, see TS283
159.P8	Pumping machinery
159.S34	Scrubbers
	Sensors, Chemical, see TP159.C46
159.S4	Separators (Machine)
159.S6	Sorbents
159.S7	Steam-jacketed pans
159.S73	Steaming apparatus
159.V3	Vacuum tubes
159.V34	Valves
159.V52	Vibrators
161	Laboratory manuals
	Study and teaching
165	General works
168	Problems, exercise, etc.
	Country divisions

TP

Study and teaching
  Country divisions -- Continued
    America

170	General works
	United States
171	General works
172.A-W	By state, A-W
173	Canada
174	Latin America. West Indies
175	South America
176	Europe
177	Asia
178	Africa
179	Australia
179.5	New Zealand
180	Pacific islands
	Special schools
182	United States
183.A-Z	Other countries, A-Z
184	Data processing
185	Addresses, essays, lectures
	Chemical engineering as a profession
186	General works
186.5	Chemical technicians
	Communication in chemical engineering
186.7	General works
186.8	Computer network resources
	Including the Internet
	Government and industrial laboratories, etc.
187	General works
	Including organization, etc.
	Special countries
190	United States
191	Canada. British America
	Other American countries
192.A1	General works
192.A2-Z	By country, A-Z
	Europe
193.A1	General works
193.A2-Z	By country, A-Z
	Asia
194.A1	General works
194.A2-Z	By country, A-Z
	Africa
195.A1	General works
195.A2-Z	By country, A-Z
196	Australia
196.5	New Zealand
197	Pacific islands
	Chemicals
	Class here manufacture, use, etc.
	For purification, see TP156.P83
200	General works

	Chemicals -- Continued
201	General special
202	Catalogs, pricelists, etc.
	Cf. TK9401, Radioisotopes
	Directories, see TP12
210	Patents
	Special inorganic chemicals
	Acids
213	General works
215	Sulphuric acid
217.A-Z	Other acids, A-Z
	For organic acids, see TP248.A+
217.C5	Chromic
217.H8	Hydrochloric
217.H9	Hydrocyanic
217.H94	Hydrofluoric
217.N5	Nitric
217.P4	Perchloric
217.P5	Phosphoric
	Alkalies
	Cf. TN895+, Mineral industries
222	General works
223	Ammonia and its compounds
	Other special, see TP245.A+
	Salts
230	General works
233	Chlorides
	Nitrates
237	General works
238	Saltpeter. Niter
240	Sulphates and sulphites
	Gases
242	General works
243	Compressed and liquefied gases
	Including cylinders
244.A-Z	Special gases, A-Z
	Cf. TP750.2+, Gas industry
	For gaseous elements, see TP245.A+
244.A3	Aerosols
244.C1	Carbonic acid
244.R3	Rare gases
244.S83	Sulphur dioxide
245.A-Z	Other inorganic chemicals. By principal elements, A-Z
	Class here commercial products only
	For pure chemistry, see QD181.A+
245.A4	Aluminum
245.A6	Antimony
245.A7	Argon
245.A8	Arsenic
245.B2	Barium
245.B4	Beryllium
245.B5	Bismuth

TP

Chemicals
  Special inorganic chemicals
    Other inorganic chemicals.
      By principal elements, A-Z -- Continued

245.B6	Boron
245.B7	Bromine
245.C2	Cadmium
245.C25	Caesium
245.C3	Calcium
245.C4	Carbon
245.C45	Cerium
245.C5	Chlorine
245.C6	Chromium
245.C7	Cobalt
245.C8	Copper
245.E6	Erbium
245.F6	Fluorine
245.G2	Gadolinium
245.G4	Gallium
245.G5	Germanium
245.G6	Gold
245.H4	Helium
245.H9	Hydrogen
245.I5	Indium
245.I6	Iodine
245.I7	Iridium
245.I8	Iron
245.K6	Krypton
245.L2	Lanthanum
245.L4	Lead
245.L5	Lithium
245.M2	Magnesium
245.M3	Manganese
245.M5	Mercury
245.M7	Molybdenum
245.N4	Neodymium
245.N5	Neon
245.N6	Nickel
245.N7	Niobium
245.N8	Nitrogen
245.O7	Osmium
245.O9	Oxygen. Ozone
245.P2	Palladium
245.P5	Phosphorus
245.P7	Platinum
245.P8	Potassium
245.P9	Praseodymium
245.P94	Promethium
245.P95	Protoactinium
245.R2	Radium
245.S2	Samarium
245.S3	Scandium
245.S4	Selenium

	Chemicals
	Special inorganic chemicals
	Other inorganic chemicals.
	By principal elements, A-Z -- Continued
245.S5	Silicon
	Silicones, see TP248.S5
245.S6	Silver
245.S7	Sodium
245.S8	Strontium
245.S9	Sulphur
245.T2	Tantalum
245.T3	Tellurium
245.T4	Terbium
245.T5	Thallium
245.T6	Thorium
245.T7	Thulium
245.T8	Tin
245.T85	Titanium
245.T9	Tungsten
245.U7	Uranium
245.V2	Vanadium
245.V5	Victorium
245.X4	Xenium
245.Y8	Ytterbium
245.Y9	Yttrium
245.Z7	Zinc
245.Z8	Zirconium
	Organic chemicals and preparations
247.A1	Periodicals, societies, etc.
247.A2-Z	General works
247.2	Acids
247.5	Solvents
247.7	Plasticizers
248.A-Z	Special, A-Z
	For chemical technology of specific drugs, see
	RS431.A +
248.A17	Acetates
248.A18	Acetic acid
248.A2	Acetone
248.A28	Acridines
248.A4	Acrylic acid
248.A5	Alcohols
	Cf. TP593, Fermentation industries
248.A53	Aldehydes. Ketones
248.A555	Allene
248.A56	Allyl compounds
248.A6	Amino acids
248.A62	Antibiotics
	Antibodies, Monoclonal, see TP248.65.M65
248.A7	Aromatic compounds
248.A8	Ascorbic acid
248.A9	Aziridines
248.B4	Benzene

Chemicals
  Organic chemicals and preparations
    Special, A-Z -- Continued

248.B5	Benzoic acid
248.B55	Biomass chemicals
248.B57	Biosurfactants
248.B6	Boron organic compounds
248.B78	Butanediol
248.B8	Butanone
248.B87	Butylene
248.C15	Calcium gluconate
248.C2	Camphor
248.C27	Carbohydrates
248.C3	Carbolic acid
248.C34	Carbon disulphide
248.C38	Carboxymethyl cellulose
248.C4	Casein
248.C45	Cellulose acetate
248.C5	Chloroform
248.C6	Citric acid
248.C67	Cresols
248.C7	Cresylic acid
248.C9	Cyanides
248.C93	Cyanocobalamine
248.C94	Cyclodextrins
248.D5	Diolefins
248.E5	Enzymes
248.E62	Esters
248.E65	Ether
248.E68	Ethylcellulose
248.E72	Ethylene
248.F5	Fluoro-organic compounds
248.F6	Formaldehyde
248.F63	Formic acid
248.F79	Fungicides
248.F8	Furaldehyde
248.G6	Glucosides
248.G65	Glutamic acid
	Glycerin, see TP973
248.H3	Halogens
248.H36	Herbicides
248.H4	Hexachlorethane
248.H43	Hexone
248.H85	Hydrazine
248.H9	Hydrocarbons
	Cf. TP290.H9, Inflammable material
248.I57	Insecticides
248.I8	Isocyanates
248.I86	Isoprene
	Ketones, see TP248.A53
248.L27	Lactams
248.L3	Lactic acid
248.M4	Menthol

	Chemicals
	Organic chemicals and preparations
	Special, A-Z -- Continued
248.M43	Metal carbonyls
248.M45	Metallo-organic compounds
248.M48	Methyl sulphoxide
	Monoclonal antibodies, see TP248.65.M65
248.N7	Nitrocellulose
248.N8	Nitrogen compounds
248.N9	Nucleotides
248.O9	Oxalic acid
248.P4	Pectin
248.P44	Pentosan
248.P46	Peroxides
248.P47	Pesticides
248.P5	Phenol products
248.P55	Phosphatides
248.P6	Phthalic acid
248.P62	Phthalocyanins
248.P65	Picric acid
248.P67	Polymethylbenzenes
248.P68	Polysaccharides
248.P73	Proline
248.P75	Propylene
248.P77	Proteins
248.P8	Pyridine
(248.S3)	Saccharin
	see TP424
248.S5	Silicones
248.S6	Sorbitol
248.S7	Starch
	Cf. TP415+, Food industry
248.S76	Stearates
248.S8	Stearic acid
248.S9	Sugar esters
248.S93	Sulphur-organic compounds
248.T27	Tartaric acid
248.T3	Tartrates
248.T46	Terephthalic acid
248.T55	Tocopherol
248.T6	Toluene
248.T7	Trichloroethylene
248.U7	Urea
(248.W6)	Wood alcohol
	see TP594
248.X9	Xyloles
248.X95	Xylose
	Biotechnology
	Cf. QR183.5, Immunotechnology
	Cf. RS380, Pharmaceutical biotechnology
	Cf. S494.5.B563, Agricultural biotechnology
	Cf. TD192.5+, Environmental biotechnology
248.13	Periodicals, societies, serials

	Biotechnology -- Continued
248.14	Congresses
248.15	Collected works (nonserial)
248.16	Dictionaries and encyclopedias
248.162	Symbols, formulas, abbreviations
248.17	Directories
248.175	Patents
248.18	History
	By region or country
	United States
248.185	General works
248.19.A-Z	By region or state, A-Z
248.195.A-Z	Other regions or countries, A-Z
248.2	General works
248.215	Popular works
248.218	Juvenile works
248.22	Study and teaching
248.23	Social aspects
	Processes, operations, and techniques
248.24	General works
248.25.A-Z	Special, A-Z
248.25.A96	Automation. Computer simulation. Data processing
248.25.B53	Bilayer lipid membranes
248.25.B55	Bioreactor processes
248.25.C37	Capillary electrophoresis
248.25.C42	Cell adhesion
248.25.C44	Cell culture
	Computer simulation, see TP248.25.A96
	Control, see TP248.25.M65
248.25.C79	Cryopreservation
	Data processing, see TP248.25.A96
248.25.E88	Extraction
248.25.F55	Flocculation
248.25.G7	Granulation
248.25.H54	High performance liquid chromatography
248.25.H56	High pressure
248.25.I55	Immobilized cell processes
248.25.M34	Magnetic separation
248.25.M38	Mass spectrometry
248.25.M39	Mathematical models
248.25.M43	Measurement
248.25.M45	Membrane reactors
248.25.M46	Membrane separation
248.25.M58	Mixed culture
248.25.M65	Monitoring. Control
248.25.N35	Nanotechnology
248.25.P44	Pervaporation
248.25.P53	Phase partition
	Pressure, High, see TP248.25.H56
248.25.S47	Separation
248.25.S64	Solid-state fermentation
248.27.A-Z	Special biotechnologies, A-Z
248.27.A46	Algal biotechnology

	Biotechnology
	Special biotechnologies, A-Z -- Continued
248.27.A53	Animal cell biotechnology
248.27.F86	Fungal biotechnology
248.27.I56	Insect cell biotechnology
248.27.M37	Marine biotechnology
248.27.M47	Methylotrophic microorganisms
248.27.M53	Microbial biotechnology
	Cf. TN688.3.B33, Hydrometallurgy
248.27.P55	Plant biotechnology
	Cf. SB106.B56, Crops
248.27.P75	Protozoan biotechnology
248.27.Y43	Yeast biotechnology
248.3	Biochemical engineering. Bioprocess engineering
	Cf. TP156.F4, Industrial fermentation
	Cf. TP248.3, Hydrometallurgy
	Cf. TP500+, Fermentation industries
	For industrial applications of specific biomolecules or classes of biomolecules, see TP248.A+
248.6	Genetic engineering applications
	Cf. QH442+, Genetic engineering (Biology)
	Biotechnological production, modification, and applications of individual compounds or classes of compounds
248.65.A-Z	Special, A-Z
248.65.A39	Allergens
248.65.A43	Amino acids
248.65.A45	Amylodextrins
248.65.A57	Antibiotics
248.65.B56	Blood products
	Carbohydrates, see TP248.65.P64
248.65.C35	Carbon compounds
248.65.C44	Cellulase
248.65.C45	Cellulose
248.65.C55	Chitin
248.65.C92	Cyclodextrins
248.65.E35	Eggs
248.65.E59	Enzymes
248.65.F44	Feeds
248.65.F66	Food
248.65.G49	Glycoconjugates
248.65.H9	Hydrogen
248.65.H93	Hydrolases
248.65.I45	Immobilized enzymes
248.65.I47	Immobilized proteins
248.65.I49	Immunoglobulins
248.65.L54	Lignocellulose
248.65.L57	Lipids
248.65.M37	Materials
248.65.M53	Microbial exopolysaccharides
248.65.M54	Microbial proteins
248.65.M65	Monoclonal antibodies
248.65.O65	Optical isomers

TP

	Biotechnology
	Biotechnological production,
	modification, and applications of
	individual compounds or classes of ompounds
	Special, A-Z -- Continued
248.65.O73	Organic compounds
248.65.P53	Plant lipids
248.65.P58	Polyethylene glycol
248.65.P62	Polymers
248.65.P64	Polysaccharides. Carbohydrates
248.65.P76	Proteins
248.65.S55	Single cell lipids
248.65.S56	Single cell proteins
248.65.V32	Vaccines
248.65.V57	Vitamins
249	Industrial radiochemistry. Industrial radiation
	chemistry
249.5	Industrial photochemistry
	Industrial electrochemistry
	Cf. QD115+, Electrochemical analysis
	Cf. QD273, Electrochemistry of organic compounds
	Cf. QD551+, Chemistry
	Cf. TK4661, Electric furnaces
250	Periodicals, societies, etc.
251	Directories
252	History
253.A-Z	Special countries, A-Z
255	General works
256	General special
257	Addresses, essays, lectures
258	Study and teaching
	Special applications
259	Electrolysis of water
	Electroplating, see TS670+
	Electrotyping, see Z252
	Metallurgical processes (General), see TN681+
261.A-Z	Other special, A-Z
261.A1	Alloys
261.B7	Brine
	Calcium carbide, see TP770
261.C3	Carborundum
261.C5	Chlorates
261.C67	Corundum
261.G7	Graphite
261.H9	Hydrogen
261.N7	Nitrogen
261.O9	Oxygen
261.P48	Phosphorus
	Water in chemical industry
262	General works
263	Water softening
	Cf. TD466, Municipal water supply
	Cf. TJ379, Feedwater purification

	Chemistry of fire and fire prevention
	Cf. QD516, Heat of formation, combustion, flame, explosion
	Cf. TH9446.3+, Flammability of materials
265	General works
266	Fire extinguishing agents
	Cf. TH9338, Chemical systems of fire extinction
266.5	Fireproofing agents
267	Fireproofing of fabrics
	Explosives and pyrotechnics
267.5	General works
268	History
	Special topics, see TP272+
268.5.A-Z	Biography, A-Z
	e.g.
268.5.N7	Nobel
269	Early works to 1800
	Explosives
	Cf. UF860+, Military explosives and pyrotechnics
270.A1	Periodicals, societies, etc.
270.A2	Dictionaries and encyclopedias
270.A3-Z	General works
270.5	Popular works. Juvenile works
271	Study, testing, etc.
	Special explosives
272	Gunpowder
273	Smokeless powder
276	Nitrocellulose compounds. Guncotton
285	Nitroglycerine compounds. Dynamite
290.A-Z	Other, A-Z
290.A5	Ammonium nitrate fuel oil
290.B7	Bobbinite
290.C7	Compensating powder
290.C8	Cordite
290.C9	Cyclotetramethylene-tetranitramine
290.H9	Hydrocarbons
	Cf. TP248.H9, Organic preparations
290.L5	Liquid air or oxygen
290.L8	Lyddite. Melanite
290.N53	Nitrogen compounds
290.P5	Peroxides
290.T8	Trinitrotoluene (TNT)
290.V5	Vigorit
291	Additives
293	Fuses, caps, fulminates, etc.
295	Storage and handling. Powder magazines. Thaw houses
297.A-Z	Regulation, inspection, etc. By country, A-Z
(299)	Laws relating to explosives
	see class K
	Pyrotechnics
300	General works

	Explosives and pyrotechnics
	Pyrotechnics -- Continued
301	Catalogs of fireworks, etc.
310	Matches
	Fuel
	Cf. TH7201+, Heating of buildings
	Cf. TJ163.13+, Power resources
315	Periodicals, societies, congresses, etc.
316	Dictionaries and encyclopedias
317.A-Z	Special countries, A-Z
318	General works
318.3	Juvenile works
319	General special
	Including fuel for motor transport
	Cf. TP343+, Liquid and gaseous fuel
320	Minor works, pamphlets, etc.
320.5	Tables, calculations, etc.
	Analysis. Testing
	Cf. TP691, Oil inspection, analysis, testing,
	standards, etc.
	Cf. TP754, Analysis, tests, etc. in the gas
	industry
321	General works
322	Fuel testing plants
323	Briquets and briquetting (General)
	Cf. TP327, Coal briquets
	Cf. TP340, Peat
	For special kinds see the subject
324	Wood
	Coal
	Cf. TP352, Coal liquefaction
325	General works
326.A-Z	By region or country, A-Z
327	Coal briquets
328	Pulverized coal
329	Lignite
331	Charcoal
336	Coke. Carbonization of coal
339	Biomass
	Cf. TP324, Wood
340	Peat
	Liquid and gaseous fuel
	Cf. TL704.7, Fuel for aircraft engines
	Cf. TP750.2+, Gas industry
343	General works
	Gas
345.A1	Periodicals, societies, congresses, etc.
345.A2-Z	General works
350	Natural gas
	Cf. TP359.M4, Methane
352	Coal liquefaction
355	Petroleum
	Including synthetic petroleum

	Fuel
	Liquid and gaseous fuel -- Continued
358	Alcohol and alcohol mixtures. Gasohol
359.A-Z	Other special, A-Z
359.B4	Benzene (Benzol)
359.B48	Biogas
359.H8	Hydrogen
359.L5	Liquefied petroleum gas
359.M4	Methane
359.V44	Vegetable oils
360	Other
	Including colloidal fuel, mud fuel, artificial fuel
361	Inflammable liquids and gases
	Including production, storage, handling and transportation
	Cf. TH9446.I5, Fire prevention
362	Antifreeze solutions
363	Heating, drying, cooling, evaporating
	Cf. TP159.D7, Drying agents
	Cf. TP159.H4, Heat transfer media
365	By-products of combustion
	Food processing and manufacture
	Cf. TX341+, Nutrition
	Cf. TX641.2+, Cookery
	For beverages, see TP500+
368	Periodicals, societies, congresses
368.2	Dictionaries and encyclopedias
368.3	Directories
368.4	Catalogs
368.5	Patents
368.6	History
369.A-Z	By region or country, A-Z
	Biography
369.5	Collective
369.52.A-Z	Individual, A-Z
370	General works
370.2	Popular works
370.3	Juvenile works
370.4	Handbooks, tables, etc.
370.5	General special
370.6	Addresses, essays, lectures
370.7	Study and teaching
370.8	Research
	Special processes
	For biotechnology applied to food processing, see TP248.65.F66
	For processing of a special food, see TP375+
371	General works
	Preservation techniques
	For home preservation, see TX599+
371.2	General works
	Canning
371.3	General works

Food processing and manufacture
Special processes
Preservation techniques
Canning -- Continued

371.35	Sterilization of canned foods
	Chemical preservation
371.4	General works
	By use of additives
371.42	General works
371.44	Brining, pickling, fermenting, etc.
	Drying. Dehydration
371.5	General works
371.6	Freeze-drying
371.8	Irradiation
	Low temperature
372	General works
372.2	Cold storage
372.3	Freezing
372.4	Ultrasound
	Chemistry testing. Quality control
	Cf. TX501+, Nutrition
372.5	General works
372.55.A-Z	Special reactions, A-Z
372.55.E59	Enzymatic browning
372.55.M35	Maillard reaction
372.6	Standards
372.7	Production control
372.8	Automation
373	Food processing plants and equipment
	Cf. TH4526, Building construction
373.2	Transportation
373.3	Storage
	Including food storage pests
	Cf. SB937, Farm insect pests
373.5	Safety measures
373.6	Sanitation
373.8	By-products
	Packaging
374	General works
374.5	Labeling
	Special foods
	Sugars and syrups (General). Cane sugar. Sucrose
375	Periodicals, societies, congresses
375.3	Yearbooks
375.4	Dictionaries and encyclopedias
375.5	Directories
375.6	Patents
375.7	History
375.8.A-Z	By region or country, A-Z
	General works
376	Early through 1800
377	1801-
378	Popular works

Food processing and manufacture
Special foods
Sugars and syrups (General).
Cane sugar. Sucrose -- Continued
378.2   Juvenile works
379   Handbooks, tables, etc.
380   General special
Including production control, automation
381   Sugar-making machinery
381.5   Special methods
382   Analysis, testing. Saccharimetry
Special kinds of sugars and syrups
Beet
For periodicals, see TP375
390   General works
391   General special
Cane, see TP375 +
395   Maple
405   Sorghum and corn
413   Molasses
414   Other special kinds of sugar
Including glucose, lactose, dextrose, date,
Jerusalem artichoke
Sugar products
414.3   General works
414.4   Caramel
Confectionery, see TX780.2 +
414.5   Sugar byproducts
For bagasse, see TP996.B3
Starches. Cornstarch
415   General works
416.A-Z   Special starches and starch products, A-Z
416.D4   Dextrin
416.S3   Sago
416.T3   Tapioca. Cassava
Fats and oils, see TP669 +
Flavoring aids
418   General works
Essential oils, see TP958 +
419   Extracts
420   Spices, condiments
For soy sauce, see TP438.S6
Sweeteners
421   General works
Nonnutritive
422   General works
423   Cyclamates
424   Saccharin
426   Natural
For honey, see SF539
For sugar, see TP375 +
Vinegar
429   General works

TP

Food processing and manufacture
 Special foods
  Flavoring aids
   Vinegar -- Continued
429.5   Rice vinegar
   Leavening agents and baking aids
431   General works
432   Baking powder. Cream of tartar
433   Yeast. Compressed yeast
  Cereals and cereal products
434   General works
   Milling, see TS2120 +
435.A-Z   Special, A-Z
435.C4   Cereals, Prepared
435.C67   Corn products
    Feeds, see TS2284 +
    Flour, see TS2120 +
435.M3   Macaroni, spaghetti, etc. Pasta
435.O37   Oat products
     Including oat bran
435.R3   Rice products
435.S65   Sorghum products
435.W48   Wheat products
   Bakery goods, see TX761 +
   Confectionery, see TX780.2 +
  Seeds and seed products
    Cf. TS2120 +, Flours and other milled products
437   General works
438.A-Z   Special, A-Z
438.P4   Peanuts. Peanut butter
438.S6   Soybeans
     Including tofu, miso, natto and soy sauce
  Nuts and nut products
439   General works
439.5.A-Z   Special nuts and products, A-Z
439.5.C45   Chestnuts
439.5.C6   Coconuts
439.5.P42   Pecans
  Fruit and fruit products
440   General works
441.A-Z   Special fruits and products, A-Z
441.A6   Apples
441.B34   Bananas
441.B4   Berries
441.C45   Cherries
441.C5   Citrus products
441.J3   Jam. Jelly (General)
441.M36   Mangos
441.O4   Olives
441.P4   Peaches
441.P54   Pineapple
441.P55   Plums
441.P7   Prunes

	Food processing and manufacture
	Special foods -- Continued
	Vegetables and vegetable products
443	General works
444.A-Z	Special vegetables and products, A-Z
444.A8	Asparagus
444.B38	Beans, Dried
444.B4	Beets
444.C3	Cabbage
444.C8	Cucumbers
444.G37	Garlic
444.K65	Konnyaku
444.M8	Mushrooms
444.O5	Onions
444.P4	Peas
444.P6	Potatoes
444.S27	Sauerkraut
444.S65	Spinach
444.S94	Sweet potatoes
444.T6	Tomatoes
	Algae and algae products
445	General works
445.5.A-Z	Special algae and products, A-Z
445.5.A35	Agar
445.5.A45	Algin
445.5.C35	Carrageenan
	Animal foods
	Butchers' meats, see TS1950 +
	Dairy foods, see SF250.5 +
	Eggs, see SF490 +
	Poultry, see TS1968
	Seafood, see SH334.9 +
	Food substitutes
446	General works
447.A-Z	Special, A-Z
447.F37	Fat substitutes
	Margarine, see TP684.M3
447.M4	Meat substitutes
	Sugar substitutes, see TP422 +
	Special food forms and foods for special purposes
450	General works
451.A-Z	Special, A-Z
451.B38	Batters
	Beverages, see TP500 +
	Cereals, Prepared, see TP435.C4
451.C6	Convenience foods
451.D53	Dietetic food
451.E3	Edible coatings
	Gelatin, see TP965
451.L67	Low-fat foods
451.S57	Snack foods
451.S67	Soups
453.A-Z	Special food constituents, A-Z

TP

Food processing and manufacture
  Special foods
    Special food constituents, A-Z -- Continued

453.C65	Colloids
453.L43	Lecithin
453.L56	Lipids
453.P45	Phenols
453.P64	Polysaccharides
453.P7	Proteins
453.V5	Vitamins

    Food additives
        Cf. TP371.42+, Chemical preservation by use
           of additives
        Cf. TX553.A3, Nutrition

455	General works
456.A-Z	Special additives, A-Z
456.A2	Acids
456.B32	Bacterial starter cultures
456.C65	Colorants
456.E58	Enzymes
456.K64	Koji

Low temperature engineering. Cryogenic engineering
    Cf. TP243, Compressed and liquefied gases
    Cf. TP363, Heating, drying, cooling, evaporating,
        etc.

480	Periodicals, societies, congresses, etc.
482	General works

Refrigeration and icemaking

490	Periodicals, societies, congresses, etc.
490.4	Dictionaries and encyclopedias
490.5	Directories
	General works
491	Early to 1850
492	1850-
492.2	Juvenile literature
492.3	Study and teaching
492.5	Theory. Thermodynamics
492.6	Domestic refrigeration
	Cf. TP496+, Refrigerators
492.7	Miscellaneous special topics
	Refrigerants
492.8	General works
492.82.A-Z	Special refrigerants, A-Z
492.82.D78	Dry ice
492.82.H93	Hydrocarbons
492.9	Thermoelectric cooling

    Cf. QC621+, Thermoelectricity. Thomson effect.
        Peltier effect
Cold storage of food, see TP372.2
Freezing of food (Food processing industry), see TP372.3
Freezing of food (Home methods), see TX610
History

494.A1	General works

	Refrigeration and icemaking
	History -- Continued
494.A5-Z	Special countries, A-Z
495	Special machinery
	Including catalogs
	Refrigerators
496	General works
	Electric, gas, etc.
497.A1	Periodicals, societies, etc.
497.A2-Z	General works
498	Ice cutting and storage
	Cf. NA6360, Commercial icehouses
	Cf. NA8350, Private icehouses
	Fermentation industries. Beverages. Alcohol
	Cf. HD9350+, Economics
	Cf. TP371.44, Preserving food by fermentation
500	Periodicals, societies, etc.
500.5	Directories
501	Congresses
	Exhibitions
502.A1	General works
502.A2-Z	By region or country, A-Z
	Apply table at TP6.A2-Z
503	Dictionaries and encyclopedias
	General works
504	Early to 1800
505	1800-
506	General special
507	Popular works
510	Handbooks, tables, etc.
511	Analysis. Testing
515	Use of the microscope
	Cf. QR151+, Microorganisms of fermentation
517	Apparatus, instruments, tools, etc.
	Cf. TP659.A1+, Bottling supplies, containers,
	etc.
	History
	Cf. TP544+, Wines
	Cf. TP573.A1+, Brewing
520	General works
521	Ancient
522	Medieval
523	Modern
	America
526	General works
	United States
527	General works
528	Special states, A-W
529	Canada
530	West Indies
531	Mexico and Central America
532	South America
533.A-Z	Europe, A-Z

TP

	Fermentation industries. Beverages. Alcohol
	History -- Continued
534.A-Z	Asia, A-Z
535.A-Z	Africa, A-Z
536	Australia
536.5	New Zealand
537	Pacific islands
	Study and teaching
540	General works
543	Special schools
	Cf. TP574, Brewing and malting schools
	Wine and winemaking
	Cf. BM523.5.W5, Judaism
544	Periodicals, societies, congresses, etc.
546	Dictionaries and encyclopedias
546.5	Directories
	Biography
547.A1	Collective
547.A5-Z	Individual, A-Z
	General works
547.5	Early to 1800
548	1800-
548.2	Amateurs' manuals
548.5.A-Z	Special topics, A-Z
548.5.A38	Adulteration
548.5.A5	Analysis, testing, etc.
548.5.A6	Apparatus and supplies
548.5.B9	By-products
	Microbiology, see QR151+
548.5.P7	Preservatives
548.5.S35	Sanitation
548.5.S7	Sterilization
549	History
	Special countries
	France
553	General works
555	Champagne
557	United States
559.A-Z	Other regions and countries, A-Z
560	Unfermented grape juice. Must
561	Fruit wines. Flower wines
	Fruit juices
	Cf. TP636, Syrups
	Cf. TP656+, Noncarbonated fruit beverages
562.A1	Periodicals. Societies. Serials
562.A2	Congresses
562.A3-Z	General works
562.5.A-Z	Special fruit juices, A-Z
562.5.O73	Orange juice
	Cider
563	General works
564	Unfermented apple juice
564.5	Perry

	Fermentation industries.
	Beverages. Alcohol -- Continued
565	Fermented milk
	Including kefir and kumiss
	Brewing and malting
	Cf. TH4531, Brewery design and construction
568	Dictionaries and encyclopedias
	General works
569	Early to 1800
570	1800-
572	Directories
	History
573.A1	General works
573.A3-Z	Special countries, A-Z
	Biography
573.5.A1	Collective
573.5.A2-Z	Individual, A-Z
574	Schools
	General special
577	Beer. Beer and ale
578	Ale. Porter
579	Rice beer. Saké
	Yeast in brewing
580	General works
581	Pure-culture yeast
583	Water in brewing
585	Hops in brewing
587	Malting and malt
588.A-Z	Other fermented beverages, A-Z
588.G8	Guarapo
588.K86	Kvass
588.M4	Mead
588.P8	Pulque
	Distilling
	General works
589	Early to 1800
590	1800-
	History
590.5	General works
590.6.A-Z	Special regions or countries, A-Z
	Biography
591.A1	Collective
591.A2-Z	Individual, A-Z
592	General special
	Including fermentation of molasses
593	Alcohol (Ethanol)
	Including denatured alcohol
	Cf. HD9399, Economics
594	Wood alcohol (Methanol)
	Distilled liquors
	Cf. HD9390+, Economics
597	General works
599	Brandy

TP

Fermentation industries. Beverages. Alcohol
Distilling
Distilled liquors -- Continued

605	Whiskey
607.A-Z	Others, A-Z
607.A57	Apple brandy
607.A6	Aquavit
607.G4	Gin
607.K3	Kaoliang
607.K57	Kirsch
607.R9	Rum
607.S5	Shochu
607.T46	Tequila
607.V6	Vodka
609	Gaging and testing
	Including tables
	Cf. HF5716.L3+, Gaging of liquids in general
611	Liqueurs. Cordials
612	Compounding. Liquor-makers' receipts
617	Catalogs of liquors
(618)	Adulteration of liquors
	see TX597
	Nonalcoholic beverages
620	General works
625	Artificial mineral waters
	Carbonated beverages. Soda water
628	Periodicals, societies, etc.
629	Directories
630	General works
635	Apparatus. Soda fountains
	Including catalogs
636	Syrups
	Chocolate, coffee, tea, etc.
	Cf. TX583+, Adulterations
638	General works
640	Cacao. Chocolate. Cocoa
645	Coffee
	Cf. TD888.C6, Air pollution by coffee processing plants
650	Tea
655.A-Z	Others, A-Z
	Noncarbonated fruit beverages
	Cf. TP562+, Fruit juices
656	General works
657.A-Z	Special noncarbonated fruit beverages, A-Z
657.L46	Lemonade
658	Congelation of beverages
	Bottling. Bottler's machinery and supplies
	Including labeling
659.A1	Periodicals, societies, etc.
659.A2-Z	General works
660	Beverage containers

	Oils, fats, and waxes
	Cf. TJ1077+, Lubricants
	Cf. TP447.F37, Fat substitutes (Food processing
	and manufacture)
669	Periodicals, societies, etc.
669.5	Congresses
670	General works
671	Analysis, testing, etc.
673	Bleaching of oils, fats, waxes, etc.
675	Sulphonated oils
676	Animal fats, oils, etc.
	Cf. TS1980+, Lard, tallow, fish oils, etc.
	Insect waxes
677	General works
678	Beeswax
679.A-Z	Other waxes, A-Z
679.S8	Sugarcane wax
	Vegetable oils and fats
	Cf. TP958+, Essential oils
680	General works
	Cottonseed oil
681.A1	Periodicals, societies, etc.
681.A2-Z	General works
681.5	Tables, etc.
682	Linseed oil
683	Olive oil
684.A-Z	Other special oils and fats, A-Z
684.B3	Bati oil
684.C2	Cacao butter. Cocoa butter
684.C275	Cashew oil
684.C3	Castor oil
	Chinese wood oil, see TP684.T8
684.C6	Cnidoscolus oil
684.C7	Coconut oil
684.C8	Corn oil
684.I8	Isano oil
684.J64	Jojoba oil
684.M3	Margarine
	Cf. HD9330.M37+, Margarine industry
	Orange oil, see TP959.O7
684.P3	Palm oil
684.P4	Peanut oil
684.P47	Perilla oil
684.P85	Pumpkinseed oil
684.R23	Ragweed seed oil
684.R3	Rape oil
684.R5	Rice oil
684.R7	Rosin oil
684.R83	Rubber-seed oil
684.S2	Sal seed oil
684.S6	Soybean oil
684.S8	Sunflower seed oil
684.T3	Tall oil

	Oils, fats, and waxes
	Vegetable oils and fats
	Other special oils and fats, A-Z -- Continued
684.T8	Tung oil. Chinese wood oil
684.V36	Vanaspati
	Mineral oils and waxes
685	General works
686	Analysis, testing, etc.
687	Reclamation of oil
	Petroleum refining. Petroleum products
	Cf. TD888.P4, Air pollution by petroleum
	refineries
	Cf. TN860+, Petroleum extraction
690.A1	Periodicals, societies, etc.
690.A2-Z	General works
	Directories of the industry, see TN867
690.1	History
690.2.A-Z	By country, A-Z
690.25	Juvenile works
690.3	Refineries, refinery equipment, automatic control
	Cf. TH4571, Construction of refineries
690.4	Cracking process
690.45	Other special processes (not A-Z)
	Including alkylation, hydrogenation, etc.
690.5	Patents
690.6	Safety measures and equipment
	Cf. TH9445.P4, Fire prevention and
	extinction in petroleum refineries
690.8	General special
	Including corrosion
691	Oil inspection, analysis, testing, standards, etc.
692	Tables
	Special products
692.2	Gasoline
692.3	Chemicals
692.4.A-Z	Other products, A-Z
692.4.A8	Asphalts
692.4.B5	Bitumen
692.4.C6	Coke
692.4.H9	Hydrocarbons
692.4.K4	Kerosene
692.4.M3	Mazut
692.4.N3	Naphtha
692.4.O3	Oil gas
692.4.P3	Paraffins
692.4.S9	Sulphur compounds
692.4.T6	Toluene
692.5	Oil and gasoline handling and storage
693	Paraffin
695	Ozokerite, ceresin, etc. Natural paraffin
	Cf. TN857, Mineral resources, mining, etc.
698	Synthetic petroleum and its products

	Oils, fats, and waxes
	Mineral oils and waxes -- Continued
699	Shale oil and its products
	Cf. TN858+, Mineral industries
	Illuminating industries (Nonelectric)
	Cf. HD4486+, Municipal lighting industries
	Cf. TH7700+, Domestic illumination
	Cf. TK4125+, Electric lighting
700	Periodicals, societies, etc.
	Exhibitions
702.A1	General works
702.A2-Z	By region or country, A-Z
	Apply table at TP6.A2-Z
703	Congresses
704	Dictionaries and encyclopedias
705	General works
710	Tables, pocketbooks, etc.
713	General special
714	Directories
	Lighting fixtures, see TH7960+
	History
715	General works
716	Ancient
717	Medieval
718	Modern
719	Nineteenth century
720	Twentieth century
	Special countries
	Including regulation, inspection, etc.
721	America
722	North America
	United States
724.A-W	States, A-W
725.A-Z	Cities, A-Z
	Canada
726.A1-A4	General works
726.A5-Y	Special provinces, A-Y
727.A-Z	Cities, A-Z
	Mexico
728.A1-A4	General works
728.A5-Z	Special states, A-Z
	West Indies
729.A1-A4	General works
729.A5-Z	Special islands, A-Z
	South America
730	General works
731.A-Z	Special countries, A-Z
	Under each country:
	.x *General works*
	.x2A-Z *Local, A-Z*
	Europe
732	General works

TP

Illuminating industries (Nonelectric)
Special countries
Europe -- Continued
733.A-Z   Special countries, A-Z
Apply table at TP731.A-Z
Asia
734   General works
735.A-Z   Special countries, A-Z
Apply table at TP731.A-Z
Africa
736   General works
737.A-Z   Special countries, A-Z
Apply table at TP731.A-Z
738   Australia
738.5   New Zealand
739   Pacific islands
741   Street lighting
Cf. TK4188, Electric lighting
743   Torches
Candles, see TP993
746   Lamps
Ancient lamps, see NK4680
Gas industry
Periodicals, societies, etc , see TP700
Congresses, see TP703
Dictionaries and encyclopedias, see TP704
Directories, see TP714
History, see TP715+
Special countries, see TP721+
751   General works
751.1   General special
Including corrosion and its prevention
751.3   Business management
751.5   Popular works
751.6   Juvenile works
751.7   Coal, oil, shale, and other resources for gas
manufacture
752   Gasworks
For special plants, see TP721+
753   Tables, pocketbooks, etc.
754   Analysis, tests, recorders, purification, etc.
755   By-products
756   Gas storage. Gasholders
756.5   Underground storage
757   Distribution. Mains, pipes, etc.
758   Uses of gas
Cf. TH6800+, Gas in guildings
Cf. TP345.A1+, Gas as fuel
Natural gas (Mining engineering), see TN880+
Natural gas fuel, see TP350

	Gas industry -- Continued
759	Gasification of coal and oil
	Including underground gasification of coal
	Cf. TP336, Coke, carbonization of coal
	Cf. TP751.7, Coal and oil resources for gas manufacture
	Cf. TP762, Gas producers
760	Water gas
761.A-Z	Other special kinds, A-Z
761.B8	Butane
761.C65	Compressed gas
761.L5	Liquid gas
761.M4	Methane
761.M44	Methylpropene
761.M7	Mond gas
761.P4	Petroleum gas
761.P9	Producer gas
761.P94	Propane
	Sludge gas, see TD769.4
762	Gas producers for industrial purposes
	Acetylene industry
765	Periodicals, societies, etc.
767	General works
769	Apparatus
770	Manufacture from calcium carbide
	Clay industries. Ceramics. Glass
	Cf. HD9590+, Economics
	Cf. NK3700+, Ceramics (Art industries)
	Cf. NK5100+, Glass (Art industries)
	Cf. TA430, Ceramic materials
	Cf. TA450, Glass in engineering
	Cf. TN941+, Mineral industries
	Cf. TT919+, Pottery craft
785	Periodicals, societies, etc.
	For periodicals on glass alone, see TP845
786	Congresses
	Exhibitions. Museums
787.A1	General works
787.A2-Z	By region or country, A-Z
	Apply table at TP6.A2-Z
788	Dictionaries and encyclopedias
789	Directories
790	Collected works (nonserial)
	History
791	General works
792	Ancient
793	Medieval
794	Modern
	Country divisions
797	America
	United States
798	General works
799.A-W	States, A-W

TP

                     Clay industries. Ceramics. Glass
                       Country divisions
                         United States -- Continued

800.A-Z	Cities, A-Z
801	Canada
802.A-Z	Other American countries, A-Z
	Europe
802.95	General works
803.A-Z	By region or country, A-Z
804.A-Z	Other countries, A-Z
	Biography
805	General works
806.A-Z	Individual, A-Z
	Potters' marks, see NK4215
	Ceramic technology. Pottery
	General works
807.A2	Early to 1800
807.A3-Z	1800-
808	Popular works
	For pottery craft, see TT919+
808.2	Juvenile works
809	Tables, calculations, etc.
809.5	Equipment and supplies
	For kilns, see TP841+
810	Chemistry of pottery
810.5	Materials
811	Clay and clay analysis
	Cf. TN941+, Mineral industries - Clay
	Glazes, enamels, etc.
	Cf. NK4997+, Enamels (Art)
	Cf. TP823, Pottery decorating
812.A1	Periodicals, societies, etc.
812.A2-Z	General works
814	Technical processes
	Including finishing, cutting, machining, etc.
815	General special
	Including studies of clay, vitrification, dehydration, saggars
816	Study and teaching
817	Pottery machinery
818	Catalogs of pottery, stoneware, porcelain, glass, etc.
820	Earthenware. Stoneware
822	Porcelain
823	Technology of ceramic decoration. Glazes, engobes, colors
	Architectural ceramics
825	General works
	Bricks and brickmaking
	Cf. TA432+, Properties of bricks
	Special countries
826	United States
826.5.A-Z	Other countries, A-Z

	Clay industries. Ceramics. Glass
	Architectural ceramics
	Bricks and brickmaking -- Continued
	General works
827.A1	Early to 1800
827.A2-Z	1800-
828	General special
829	Brickmaking machinery, etc.
831	Pressed brick
832.A-Z	Other varieties. By name, A-Z
832.A35	Adobe brick
832.C5	Clinker brick
832.C6	Cob
832.F5	Firebrick
832.G6	Glazed brick
832.G7	Granite brick
832.H7	Hollow brick
832.L7	Lock-joint brick
832.S2	Sand-lime brick
833	General catalogs
835	Terra-cotta
	Cf. TA432 +, Properties of terra-cotta
837	Tiles
	Cf. NA3705, Architectural decoration
	Cf. NK4670 +, Art industries
	Cf. TA432 +, Properties of tile
	Cf. TH8521 +, Tile laying and tile decoration
	Cf. TT927, Tile craft
838	Fireclay products and other refractories
	Cf. TA418.26, Engineering properties of refractories
	Cf. TA455.F5, Engineering properties of fireclay
	Cf. TN677 +, Metallurgical plants. Metallurgical furnaces and refractory materials
	Cf. TP832.F5, Firebricks
839	Draintile. Sewer pipe
	Including those made of clay, cement, etc.
	Cf. TA447, Testing
	Cf. TD682, Sewers
	Cf. TP885.P5, Cement pipe
	Salt glazes, etc , see TP812.A1 +
	Kilns
	Cf. TT924, Pottery craft
841	General works
842.A-Z	Special, A-Z
842.H7	Hoffman's kiln
842.T8	Tunnel kilns
	Glass and glassmaking
	Cf. NK5100 +, Art industries
845	Periodicals, societies, etc.
	Cf. TP785, Ceramics and glass

Clay industries. Ceramics. Glass
    Glass and glassmaking -- Continued
        Exhibitions. Museums
846.A1   General works
846.A2-Z   By region or country, A-Z
                            Apply table at TP6.A2-Z
847   Directories
848   Collected works (nonserial)
                    History
849   General works
850   Ancient
851   Medieval
852   Modern
                        Special countries
                            United States
853.A1-A3   General works
853.A5-W   Special states, A-W
854.A-Z   Other countries, A-Z
855   Study and teaching
                    General works
856   Early to 1800
857   1800
857.3   Popular works. Juvenile works
857.5   Tables, calculations, etc.
858   General special
                        Including safety measures, patents, etc.
                    Analysis, see QD139.G5
859   Glassblowing, manipulation, etc.
                        Cf. QD63.G5, Chemical laboratory manipulation
                        Cf. TT298, Glass craft
859.5   Machinery, furnaces and other special equipment
859.7   Waste glass. Glass recycling
860   Plate glass
860.5   Glass fibers
                        Cf. TA450, Engineering materials
                        Cf. TS1549.G5, Textile industries
861   Cut glass
861.5   Colored glass
862   Other special varieties of glass
                    Ornamental glass used in buildings, etc.
                        Cf. NK5300 +, Decorative arts
                        Cf. TH8271 +, Decoration of buildings
                        Cf. TT298, Handicrafts
863   General works
864   Sand-blast process
                    Glassware. Articles made of glass
                        For early American pressed glass, see NK5112
865   General works
866   Bottles
                            Cf. TP659.A1 +, Bottling
867   Mirrors and mirror-frames
                        Optical glass, see QC375
867.3   Glass-ceramic pipe

Clay industries. Ceramics. Glass
  Glass and glassmaking -- Continued

868	General catalogs and trade publications
869	Soluble glass. Water glass
870	Artificial minerals
871	Artificial stone

Cf. TP832.G7, Granite brick
Cf. TP832.S2, Sand-lime brick
Cf. TP875+, Cement industries

Artificial gems

873	General works
873.5.A-Z	Special, A-Z
873.5.D5	Diamonds

Cement industries. Cement, lime, mortar, plaster, etc.
  Including industrial processes only
  For engineering properties and on-site preparation, see TA434+

875	Periodicals, societies, etc.
	Directories
876.A2	General works
876.A4-Z	By country, A-Z
877	General works
	Special countries
	United States
879.A1	General works
879.A2-W	States, A-W
880.A-Z	Other countries, A-Z

Cement manufacture
  Including concrete when used for the factory-made products provided for in TP885

881	General works
882	Plants and equipment
882.3	Analysis of cement
883	Portland cement
884.A-Z	Other special, A-Z
884.A3	Additives
884.A48	Alumina cement
884.A8	Asbestos cement
884.A85	Asphalt concrete
884.C5	Clinker concrete
884.L5	Lightweight concrete
884.M2	Magnesia cements
884.R7	Roman cement
884.S3	Sand-lime products
884.S6	Slag cement
884.S85	Sulphur cement

Articles of cement or concrete
  Class here factory made products only
  Cf. TT295, Handicrafts

885.A2	General works
885.A5-Z	Special. By name, A-Z

Cement industries. Cement, lime, mortar, plaster, etc.
Cement manufacture
Articles of cement or concrete
Special. By name, A-Z -- Continued

885.C7   Concrete blocks and slabs
Cf. TH1491, Concrete block building construction
885.F7   Fountains
885.G3   Garden furniture
885.L3   Lampposts
885.M7   Monuments
885.P5   Pipe and tile
Cf. TA447, Pipes of cement and clay
Cf. TP839, Draintile and sewer pipe
Sidewalks, curbs, see TE291
885.T7   Trusses
886   Lime and limekilns
Cf. TP841+, Kilns
887   Mortar
888   Plaster and other gypsum products
Cf. TH8135+, Building trades
889   Magnesia industries
Textile bleaching, dyeing, printing, etc.
Cf. TS1474.5, Textile chemistry
Cf. TT852+, Textile crafts
890   Periodicals, societies, etc.
890.5   Congresses
891   Directories
892   Theory
Including color combinations, etc.
893   General works
Bleaching, cleaning, scouring
894   General works
894.5   Bleaches
895   Cleaning
Cf. TP932+, Commercial garment cleaning
Cf. TP990+, Cleaning compounds
Dyeing
Cf. NK9500+, Textile decoration
897   General works
Dyeing of cotton, see TP930+
899   Dyeing of wool
901   Dyeing of silk
902   Dyeing of artificial silk
903   Dyeing of linen
904   Dyeing of synthetic textile fibers
Dyeing of fur, see TS1060+
Dyeing of leather, see TS967
Dyeing of paper, see TS1118.D9
907   Special colors. Effects, shades, not dyes
Including khaki, etc.
908   Dyeing of special articles
Garment dyeing, Commercial, see TP932+

	Textile bleaching, dyeing, printing, etc.
	Dyeing -- Continued
	Garment dyeing, Home, see TT853+
	Dyes
	Periodicals, societies, etc , see TP890
910	General works
	Artificial dyes
913	General works
914	Coal-tar colors. Aniline dyes. Azo dyes
915	Anthracene dyes
918.A-Z	Other special dyes, A-Z
918.A4	Alizarin
	Alizarin black, see TP918.N2
918.A5	Aniline black
918.A6	Anthraquinones
	Artificial indigo, see TP924
918.A9	Azo dyes
918.C37	Carbazoles
918.C9	Cyanines
918.I5	Induline
918.N2	Naphthazarin. Alizarin black
918.P65	Polymethines
918.S8	Sulphide dyes
918.V37	Vat dyes
	Natural dyes
919	General works
	Indigo
923	General works
924	Artificial indigo
925.A-Z	Other special dyes, A-Z
925.C38	Catechu
925.C63	Cochineal
925.K35	Kamala
925.P9	Purple
925.S23	Safflower
925.W8	Woad
927	Mordants
929	Miscellaneous
	Textile printing. Calico printing. Cotton dyeing
	Cf. NK9500+, Textile decoration
	Cf. TS1475, Textile design
930	General works
930.5	Machinery
931.A-Z	Special, other than cotton or calico, A-Z
931.C2	Carpet yarns
931.S6	Silk fabrics
	Commercial garment cleaning and dyeing
	Cf. TT853+, Textile crafts
	Cf. TT980+, Laundry
932	General works
932.3	Dry cleaning
932.5	Wet cleaning
932.6	Spotting

TP

	Textile bleaching,
	dyeing, printing, etc. -- Continued
933	Feather renovating, etc.
	Paints, pigments, varnishes, etc.
	Class here manufacture only
	Cf. ND1500+, Fine arts
	Cf. TT300+, Industrial painting
934	Periodicals, societies, congresses, etc.
934.3	Dictionaries and encyclopedias
934.5	Directories
	General works
	Documents
	United States
935.A2U4-A2U5	Serial
935.A2U6	Special. By date
935.A3A-W	By state, A-W
935.A4A-Z	Other countries, A-Z
935.A5-Z	Nonofficial works
	Paints and pigments. Zinc oxide. Iron oxide
	Cf. TP682, Linseed oil
	Cf. TP951, Blacks (Pigments)
	Cf. TP977+, Turpentine, etc.
936	General works
936.5	Paint analysis, testing, etc.
937	Catalogs
937.5	Paint machinery
	Including machines used for grinding, mixing, etc.
937.7	Driers, thinners, fillers, etc.
937.8	Paint removers
938	Varnishes. Shellac
939	Lacquers and enamels
940	Polishes
941	Putty
942	Japanning materials
944	Blacking materials
945	High solids coatings
	Ink manufacture
	Cf. Z45, History of writing materials
	Cf. Z112, Paleography
946	General works
947	History
948.A-Z	Particular inks. By name, A-Z
948.A8	Arnold's fluid
	Printers' ink
	Cf. Z247, Printing
949	General works
949.9	Catalogs of dealers
949.95	Other special inks
	Including inks for recording instruments
	Miscellaneous organic chemical industries
950	General works
951	Blacks
	Cf. TP245.C4, Carbon

	Miscellaneous organic
	chemical industries -- Continued
953	Coal products, coal tar, etc.
	Cf. TP914, Dyes
955	Dentifrices
	Essences, essential oils and ethers
	Cf. RS201.E7, Pharmacy
	Cf. TP680 +, Vegetable oils
958	General works
959.A-Z	Special substances, A-Z
	Attar of roses, see TP959.R6
959.B4	Bergamot oil
959.C5	Citronella oil
959.C54	Citrus oils
959.E9	Eucalyptus oils
959.L4	Lemongrass oils
959.M8	Mustard oil
959.O7	Orange oil
959.P4	Peppermint oil
959.P5	Pine oil
959.R6	Rose oil. Attar of roses
959.S2	Sassafras oil
	Fertilizers
	Cf. S631 +, Use of fertilizers
	Cf. TD772, Manufacture of fertilizer from
	sewage sludge
963	General works
963.4.A-Z	Special fertilizers, A-Z
963.4.A38	Ammonium phosphate
963.4.A4	Ammonium sulphate
963.4.C3	Calcium cyanamide
963.4.N5	Nitrogen
963.4.S9	Superphosphates
963.4.U7	Urea
965	Gelatin
	Glue and other adhesives
	Cf. TS857, Wood adhesives
967	Periodicals, societies, congresses, etc.
967.6	Directories
968	General works
970	Mucilage and pastes
973	Glycerin
	Gums and resins. Turpentine, etc.
	Cf. TP1101 +, Plastics
977	Periodicals
978	General works
979	Resinography
979.5.A-Z	Special, A-Z
979.5.B4	Benzoin
979.5.I6	Ion exchange resin
979.5.P6	Polysaccharides
	Perfumes, cosmetics, and other toilet preparations
983.A1-A5	Periodicals, societies, congresses, etc.

TP

	Miscellaneous organic chemical industries
	Perfumes, cosmetics, and
	other toilet preparations -- Continued
983.A55	Dictionaries and encyclopedias
983.A6	Directories
	Biography
983.A65	Collective
983.A66A-Z	Individual, A-Z
983.A7-Z4	General works
983.Z5	Trade publications
983.3	Cosmetic delivery systems
984	Hair preparations
	Including shampoos, hair conditioners, etc.
985	Antiperspirants, deodorants, etc.
(986-987)	Plastics
	see TP1101+
988	Sealing. Sealing compounds
	Soap, cleaning compounds, etc.
	Cf. TP895, Cleaning
990	General works
991	Soaps
992	Metallic soaps
992.5	Other cleaning compounds
993	Candles
	Cf. TP669+, Oils, fats, and waxes
	Cf. TS1980+, Lard, tallow, etc.
	Cf. TT896.5, Handicraft
994	Surface active agents
	Utilization of wastes
	Prefer field of application
	Cf. TS169, Waste control
995.A1	Periodicals, societies, etc.
995.A2-Z	General works
996.A-Z	Special, A-Z
996.B3	Bagasse
996.C6	Corncobs
996.C7	Cornstalks
996.C75	Cotton
996.F5	Fish
996.T5	Tin
996.W6	Wood
	Cf. TS875, Fiberboard, particle board, etc.
997	Wood distillation
	Cf. TS920+, Chemical processing of wood
	Polymers and polymer manufacture
	Cf. QD281.P6, Polymerization (Chemistry)
	Cf. QD380+, Polymer chemistry
	Cf. TA455.P58, Engineering materials
	Cf. TP156.P6, Polymerization (Chemical
	engineering)
1080	Periodicals, societies, etc.
1081	Congresses
1087	General works

	Polymers and polymer manufacture -- Continued
1088	Popular works
1089	Juvenile works
1091	Handbooks, tables, etc.
1092	General special
	Technical processes, see TP1150+
	Special polymers, see TP1180.A+
	Special forms, see TP1183.A+
	Special products, see TP1185.A+
	Elastomers, synthetic rubber, see TS1925
	Synthetic fibers, see TS1548.2+
	Plastics
	Cf. HD9661+, Economics
	Cf. TA455.P5+, Engineering materials
	Cf. TA668, Structural engineering
	Cf. TJ1194, Materials used in machine and hand tools
	Cf. TT297+, Plastic craft
1101	Periodicals, societies, etc.
1103	Yearbooks
1105	Congresses
	Exhibitions. Museums
1107.A1	General works
1107.A2-Z	By region or country, A-Z
	Apply table at TP6.A2-Z
1109	Collected works (nonserial)
1110	Dictionaries and encyclopedias
1111	Plastics literature
1112	Directories
1114	Patents
	History
1116	General works
	Special countries
1117	United States
1118.A-Z	Other countries, A-Z
	Biography
1119.A1	Collective
1119.A2-Z	Individual, A-Z
1120	General works
1122	General special
1124	Popular works
1125	Juvenile works
	Study and teaching
1127	General works
1129	Laboratory manuals
1130	Handbooks, manuals, tables, etc.
1132	Catalogs
1135	Plastics plants and equipment
1140	Technical chemistry of plastics (Analysis)
	For testing for mechanical properties, see TA455.P5+
	For use of plastics in fireproof construction, see TH1074

TP

	Polymers and polymer manufacture
	Plastics -- Continued
1142	Additives
	For plasticizers, see TP247.7
1145	Handling, packing, etc.
1148	Safety measures
	Technical processes
	For general works, see TP1120
1150	Molding and casting
1155	Machining and cutting
1160	Welding
1165	Joining and bonding
1170	Finishing and decorating
1175.A-Z	Other processes, A-Z
1175.C3	Calendering
1175.E9	Extrusion
1175.M4	Metal coating
1175.M5	Mixing
1175.P84	Pultrusion
1175.R43	Recycling
1175.S6	Spraying with plastics
	Reinforced plastics
1177	General works
1177.5.A-Z	Special reinforcement materials, A-Z
1177.5.A8	Asbestos
1177.5.G5	Glass
1180.A-Z	Special plastics, A-Z
1180.A15	ABS resins
1180.A33	Acetal resins
1180.A35	Acrylic resins
1180.A5	Aminoplastics
1180.B3	Bakelite
1180.C2	Casein
1180.C4	Cellophane
1180.C5	Celluloid
1180.C6	Cellulose
1180.D45	Dendrimers
1180.D5	Diallyl phthalate
1180.E6	Epoxy resins
1180.F5	Fiberloid
1180.F6	Fluorocarbons
1180.F8	Furans
1180.G8	Gum plastics
1180.I5	Indene resins
1180.L8	Lucite
	Nylon, see TP1180.P55
1180.P39	Phenolic resins
1180.P4	Phenolite
1180.P5	Plexiglas
1180.P53	Polyacetylenes
1180.P54	Polyacrylamides
1180.P55	Polyamides. Nylon
1180.P555	Polybishchloromethyloxetane

Polymers and polymer manufacture
  Plastics
    Special plastics, A-Z -- Continued

1180.P56	Polybutenes
1180.P57	Polycarbonates
1180.P6	Polyesters
1180.P65	Polyethylene
1180.P653	Polyethylene glycol
1180.P655	Polyethylenimine
1180.P66	Polyimides
1180.P67	Polyolefins
1180.P68	Polypropylene
1180.P685	Polysulphides
1180.P7	Polytetrafluorethylene
1180.P8	Polyurethanes
	Polyvinyl, see TP1180.V48
1180.S7	Styrene
1180.T4	Tenite
1180.T5	Thermoplastics
1180.T55	Thermosetting plastics
1180.U7	Urea-formaldehyde resins
1180.V42	Vinidur
1180.V48	Vinyl. Polyvinyl
1180.W37	Water-soluble polymers
1183.A-Z	Special forms, A-Z
1183.B3	Bars
1183.F5	Films
1183.F6	Foamed plastics
1183.L3	Laminated plastics
1183.M5	Microcrystalline polymers
1183.P68	Powders
	Reinforced plastics, see TP1177 +
1185.A-Z	Special products, A-Z
(1185.C6)	Containers
	see TS198.3.P5
(1185.E4)	Electric apparatus and appliances
	see TK454.4.P55
(1185.E5)	Electric insulators
	see TK3441.P55
1185.E9	Eye protectors
1185.F8	Furniture
1185.H4	Helmets
	Lenses for optical instruments, see TS517.5.P5
1185.M3	Machine parts
1185.P5	Pipe
	Cf. TA448, Testing of plastic pipe
	Cf. TH6330, Plastic pipes in plumbing
1185.S65	Sporting surfaces
1185.T3	Tanks
1185.T5	Tiles

	Photography
	Cf. BP190.5.A7, Islam and photography
1	Periodicals. Societies. Almanacs. Yearbooks
5	Congresses
	Exhibitions. Museums
	Cf. TR646.A+, Exhibitions of artistic photography
6.A1	General works
6.A2-Z	By region or country, A-Z
	Under each country:
	.x *General works*
	.x2A-Z *Special. By city, A-Z*
6.5	Collectors' manuals. Collections of old photographs and photographic equipment
7	Collected works (nonserial)
9	Dictionaries. Encyclopedias
	Communication of photography information
10	General works
11	Computer network resources
	Including the Internet
12	Directories. Bluebooks
15	History (General)
21-127	Country divisions (Table T1)
	Add country number in table to TR0
	Biography
	Prefer TR650-TR654, for collections of artistic photographs by one photographer where biographic material is slight
139	Collective
140.A-Z	Individual, A-Z
	General works
144	Early to 1850
145	1850-
146	Elementary works. Handbooks, manuals, etc.
147	General special
	Including manipulation, causes of failures, etc.
148	Photographic amusements. Trick photography. Special effects
149	Popular works. Juvenile works
150	Photographers' reference handbooks
151	Tables, formulas, etc.
154	Photography as a profession
161	Study and teaching
162	Examinations, questions, etc.
179	Composition
183	Psychology, aesthetics, etc.
	Cf. TR640+, Artistic photography
185	Addresses, essays, lectures
187	Photographic criticism
(193-195)	Law. Legislation
	see class K
	Materials, supplies, etc.
196	General works
	Including testing

	Materials, supplies, etc. -- Continued
196.5.A-Z	Special companies, A-Z
197	Catalogs of apparatus
198	Catalogs of materials and supplies
199	Catalogs of photographs (General)
	Cf. TR640 +, Artistic photography
	For catalogs of photographs treated as an information resource, see ZA4650 +
	For catalogs of photographs on specific subjects, see the subject
	Theory of photographic processes in general
200	General works
	Photographic chemistry and chemicals
210	General works
212	Photographic chemicals
	Photographic physics
215	General works
220	Photographic optics
222	Properties of the photographic image. Image science
225	Recovery of photographic waste
	Cameras
250	General works
	Prefer TR263, for special makes of cameras
	Motion picture cameras, see TR880
256	Digital cameras
257	Medium format cameras
257.5	Streak cameras
258	View cameras
259	Stereoscopic cameras
260	Hand cameras
260.5	Automatic cameras. Electric eye cameras
260.7	Autofocus cameras
261	Reflex cameras
262	Miniature cameras
263.A-Z	Special makes of cameras, A-Z
263.C5	Ciro-flex
263.E75	Ernemann
263.Y3	Yashica
265	Camera accessories
	Catalogs, see TR197
267	Digital photography
	Cf. TR502, Photo CDs
268	Pinhole photography
269	Instant photography
	Lenses
270	General works
271.A-Z	Special, A-Z
271.M33	Macro
	Cf. TR684, Macrophotography
271.T44	Telephoto
	Cf. TR770, Telephotography
271.W53	Wide-angle
	Cf. TR687, Wide-angle photography

TR

	Lenses
	Special, A-Z -- Continued
271.Z65	Zoom
272	Shutters
	Sensitive surfaces
	Including sensitometry
280	General works
281	Plates
283	Films
285	Papers
	Photographic processing. Darkroom technique (General)
287	General works
	Treatment of negatives
290	General works
295	Development
299	Intensification and reduction
305	Fixing and washing
310	Finishing, retouching
312	Contact prints
	Treatment of positives
320	General works
	Printing
330	General works
333	By electric or other artificial light
335	Fixing. Toning. Intensification
337	Finishing
340	Trimming, mounting and framing of prints
	Photographic processes
350	General works
	Direct positives
360	General works
365	Daguerreotype
370	Ambrotype
375	Ferrotype (Tintype)
	Processes with salts of silver
385	General works
390	Collodion process
395	Emulsion processes. Aristotypes, calotypes, etc.
400	Other processes. Salts of silver and other metals
	Including kallitype
	Processes with salts of iron
405	General works
415	Blueprints from photographic negatives.
	Cyanotypes
	Cf. TR921, Industrial blueprints
420	Processes with salts of platinum
	Processes with salts of metals
430	General works
433	Chromium. Ozotype, etc.
440	Carbon processes. Pigment processes
443	Oil processes. Bromoil
445	Gum-bichromate process. Photoaquatint

Photographic processing.
    Darkroom technique (General)
  Photographic processes -- Continued

453   Photography of colored objects. Orthochromatic, isochromatic, etc.
           Cf. TR510+, Color photography
455   Other processes
465   Conservation and restoration of photographs
470   Copying
           Cf. TR825, Reproductions (photocopying)
           Cf. TR835, Reproductions (microfilming)
           Cf. TR900+, Reproductions (industrial)
475   Enlargement and reduction
           Cf. TR905, Industrial reproduction
485   Coloring of prints. Airbrush work, etc.
487   Photo-oleographs
495   Photographs on metal, glass, cloth, leather, etc.
500   Photoenamels. Photoceramics
502   Photo CDs
    Transparencies. Diapositives
504   General works
505   Lantern slides
      Projectors
           Cf. TR890, Motion picture projectors
506   General works
507   Catalogs
508   Overhead projectors
    Color photography
        Cf. TR453, Photography of colored objects
510   General works
515   Materials, supplies, etc.
        Including testing
520   Tricolor
525   Interference. Lippmann's process
      General darkroom procedures. Processing of exposed film
530   General works
        Treatment of positives
540   General works
545   Printing
    Studio and laboratory
550   General works
560   Darkrooms
570   Accessories and apparatus
573   Studio lighting
      Portrait photography
           Cf. TR680+, Artistic photography
575   General works
577   Advice to sitters
581   Business methods
    Lighting
        Cf. TR573, Studio lighting
        Cf. TR891, Lighting for motion pictures

TR

Lighting -- Continued
Artificial and natural
590   General works
590.5   Light filters
     Exposures
591   General works
592   Instantaneous
         Including exposures of one thousandth of a second or longer
593   High speed
         Including exposures shorter than one thousandth of a second
595   Daylight
600   Artificial light
     Flashlight. Flash photography
605   General works
606   Electronic flash
610   Night views
615   Open air views
620   Interiors
     Applied photography
         Class here techniques for taking and using photographs in special fields
         Collections of photographs in special fields are normally classed with the field, e.g., pictorial works in natural history in QH46, views of modern Greece in DF719, pictorial works on North American Indians in E77.5
         For collections of artistic photographs, however, or collections where the artistic intent is more overriding than the actual subject content, see TR640 +
     Periodicals, exhibitions, dictionaries, etc. see TR1-TR15
624   General works
     Artistic photography
640   Periodicals, societies, congresses, etc.
642   General works
     Exhibitions
         Prefer TR650-TR654, for collections of photographs
     Works of more than one photographer
     United States
644   General works
645.A-Z   By city, A-Z
         Under each city:
         .x   *General works*
         .x2A-Z   *By museum, A-Z*
646.A-Z   Other regions or countries, A-Z
         Under each country:
         .x   *General works*
         .x2A-Z   *By city, A-Z*

	Applied photography
	Artistic photography
	Exhibitions -- Continued
647.A-Z	Works of individual photographers. By name of photographer, A-Z
	Under each photographer, arrange by date of exhibition
	Collections
650	General works
	By period
651	1800-1850
652	1851-1900
653	1901-1950
654	1951-
656	Abstract photography
656.5	Still life photography
	Cf. TR721+, Nature photography
	Photography of art
657	General works
658	Paintings
658.3	Sculpture
658.5	Photography of handicraft
659	Architectural photography
659.5	Outdoor photography
659.8	Street photography
	Landscape photography
660	General works
660.5	Collections
661	Panoramic views
662	Gardens
	Marines. Seashore photography. Water
670	General works
670.5	Ships, boats, etc.
672	Mines
	Human figures. Photography of the nude
674	General works
675	Collections
676	Erotic photography
678	Glamour photography
679	Fashion photography
679.5	Humorous photography
	Portraits
	Cf. TR575+, Portrait photography
680	Collections
681.A-Z	Special classes of persons, A-Z
681.A26	Acrobats
681.A35	Aged
681.A38	AIDS patients
681.A69	Artisans
681.A7	Artists
681.A75	Asians
681.A85	Authors
681.B35	Bald persons

TR

	Applied photography
	Artistic photography
	Portraits
	Special classes of persons, A-Z -- Continued
681.B37	Baseball players
681.B57	Bodybuilders
681.B6	Boys
681.C5	Children
681.C66	Cooks
	Dancers, see GV1785.A +
	Daughters and fathers, see TR681.F33
681.D43	Dead
681.E94	Exiles
681.F28	Families
681.F3	Famous persons
681.F32	Father and child
681.F33	Fathers and daughters
681.F34	Fathers and sons
	Foreign visitors, see TR681.V58
681.G5	Girls
681.G73	Grandmothers
681.G9	Gypsies
681.H35	Handicapped
681.H63	Homeless persons
681.H65	Homosexuals
681.I58	Indigenous peoples
681.I6	Infants
681.J35	Janitors
681.L44	Leisure class
681.L47	Letter carriers
681.M4	Men
681.M65	Monsters
681.M67	Mothers
681.M69	Motorcyclists
681.M86	Musicians
681.P56	Photographers
681.P6	Poor
681.P69	Prisoners
681.P73	Prostitutes
681.P76	Psychiatric hospital patients
681.P84	Punks
681.R44	Redheads
681.R48	Refugees
681.S36	Scholars
681.S6	Snapshooters
	Sons and fathers, see TR681.F34
681.S88	Swimmers
681.T47	Terminally ill
681.T7	Transvestites
681.T85	Twins
681.V58	Visitors, Foreign
681.W6	Women
681.W65	Working class

Applied photography
  Artistic photography
    Portraits
      Special classes of persons, A-Z -- Continued
681.Y6   Youth
682   Photographic patterns. Textures
      Close-up photography
683   General works
683.5   Table-top photography
684   Macrophotography
685   Composite photography. Photomontage
686   Photography of the grotesque
687   Wide-angle photography
688   Photograms
    Commercial photography
      Cf. TR550+, Studio and laboratory
690   General works
690.2   Freelance photography. Amateur photography for profit
      Cf. TR820, Photojournalism
690.4   Advertising photography
690.6   Stock photography
    Scientific and technical applications
692   General works
692.5   General special
      Photogrammetry
        Cf. TA592+, Photography in surveying
        Cf. TR810, Aerial applications
693   General works
695   Tables, formulas, etc.
696   Instruments, equipment, etc.
702   Photography in engineering
706   Industrial photography
708   Medical photography
710   Scientific expeditions
713   Space photography
714   Photography of airplanes
715   Photography of railroads
       Including model railroads
      Astronomical photography, see QB121+
      Photomicrography, see QH251
      Nature photography
       Cf. QH46, Pictorial works in natural history
721   General works
      Plants, flowers, etc.
724   General works
726.A-Z   Special subjects, A-Z
726.B3   Bark
726.F85   Fungi
726.O73   Orchids
726.R66   Roses
726.T7   Trees
      Animals

TR

	Applied photography
	Scientific and technical applications
	Nature photography
	Animals -- Continued
727	General works
729.A-Z	Special subjects, A-Z
729.B5	Birds
729.C3	Cats
729.D6	Dogs
729.F5	Fish
729.H6	Horses
729.I6	Insects
729.L5	Livestock
729.P74	Primates
729.R47	Reptiles
729.W54	Wildlife
732	Rocks
732.5	Minerals
733	Clouds
	Agricultural photography
739	General works
739.5	Farms
739.6	Grain elevators
750	Radiography
	Cf. QD945, X-ray crystallography
	Cf. RC78+, Medical radiography
	Cf. TA417.5, Radiographic examination
	Cf. TR896.8, Cinderradiography
755	Infrared photography
757	Polarized-light photography
760	Kirlian photography. High voltage photography
770	Telephotography
775	Archaeological photography
780	Stereophotography
	Cf. TR858, Stereoscopic motion pictures
(785)	Military photography
	see UG476
	Geographical applications
786	General works
787	Mountain photography
788	Subterranean photography. Cave photography
	Cf. TR672, Photography of mines
790	Travel photography
792	Cold weather photography
795	Tropical photography
800	Underwater photography
	Cf. GC10.4.P5, Photography in oceanography
810	Aerial photography. Photographic interpretation
	Cf. G70.4, Remote sensing in geography
	Photography in library science, see Z681+
816	Audiovisual photography. Photography in education
817	Stage photography. Theater photography

	Applied photography -- Continued
817.5	Dance photography
	Cf. GV1596, Pictorial works
	Cf. GV1785.A +, Portraits of dancers
818	School photography
819	Wedding photography
	Cf. HF5439.W4, Salesmanship
820	Photojournalism
820.5	Documentary photography
	Cf. D16.155, Photography in historiography
820.6	War photography
821	Sports photography
822	Photography in criminology and law
	Cf. KF8968, Photographic evidence (U.S.)
	Photographic reproduction. Photocopying processes
	Cf. Z265 +, Printing
824	General works
824.4	Dictionaries. Encyclopedias
824.6	Directories
	Industrial reproduction, see TR900 +
	Map reproduction, see GA150.7
	Photomechanical processes, see TR925 +
	Photography of art objects, see TR657 +
825	Photography of manuscripts, historic documents, etc.
835	Microfilming. Microphotography
	Including standards
	Class here works on the operation and use of
	equipment to make microforms or other images too
	small to be seen by the naked eye
	For microforms used in preservation and storage of
	library collections, see Z681.3.M53
	For micropublishing, see Z286.M5
	For works on the design and use of books,
	documents, computer-output data, etc., in a
	microform format, see Z265.5.M53
840	Chronophotography
	Cf. TR857, Time lapse cinematography
	Cinematography. Motion pictures. Video recording
	Cf. NC1765 +, Cartoons
	Cf. PN1993 +, Drama
	Cf. TR592, Instantaneous photography
	Cf. UF840, Photochronograph in ballistics
845	Periodicals and societies. Yearbooks. Collections
846	Congresses
847	Dictionaries and encyclopedias
847.5	Directories
848	History
	Biography
	Including inventors, projectionists, etc.
	For actors and actresses, see PN2287.A +
	For producers, directors, etc., see PN1998.3.A +
849.A1	Collective
849.A2-Z	Individual, A-Z

TR

	Cinematography. Motion
	pictures. Video recording -- Continued
850	Treatises
851	Elementary and juvenile works
851.8	Tables, calculations, etc.
852	Study and teaching
	Special photographic processes
853	Color cinematography
854	3-D films. Stereoscopic motion pictures
	Including true 3-D and simulated 3-D
855	Wide-screen processes
857	Time-lapse photography
858	Trick cinematography. Special effects
859	Front-screen projection
	Motion picture machines
878	General works
880	Motion picture cameras. Cinematograph
	Electronic cameras. Television cameras
882	General works
882.3	Camcorders
	Cf. TK6655.V5, Television equipment
	Cf. TR896+, Home video photography
882.5	Television camera operation
883.A-Z	Special makes of motion picture cameras, A-Z
	e.g.
883.B6	Bolex
885	Other special machines
	Including kinetoscope, photochronograph, etc.
	Motion picture film
886	General works
886.2	Processing of exposed film
886.3	Preservation
886.5	Splicing
886.7	Dubbing
886.9	Titling
	Cf. PN1995.9.C65, Credit titles
	Cf. PN1995.9.T57, Titles of motion pictures
887	Catalogs, etc.
889	Classification
890	Projection
891	Lighting for motion pictures
	Including lighting for video recording
	Cf. TR590+, Lighting
	For lighting for television broadcasting, see
	PN1992.8.L5
	Applied cinematography
892	General works
892.4	Artistic cinematography
892.7	Educational cinematography
	Cf. LB1044, Audiovisual education
	Scientific cinematography
893	General works
	Microcinematography, see QH46

	Cinematography. Motion pictures. Video recording
	Applied cinematography
	Scientific cinematography -- Continued
(893.2)	Medical cinematography
	Nature cinematography
893.4	General works
893.5	Wildlife cinematography
893.8	Underwater cinematography
894	Industrial cinematography
	Commercial cinematography
894.3	General works
894.4	Freelance cinematography
894.6	Advertising cinematography
895	Newsreel cinematography
	Cf. PN4784.M6, Motion-picture journalism
895.4	Documentary cinematography
	Cf. PN1995.9.D6, Drama
895.6	Sports cinematography
	Family cinematography. Amateur cinematography.
	Home video photography
896	General works
896.5	Vacation and travel cinematography
896.8	Cineradiography
897 *we use for*	Sound motion pictures
recording sound	Animated motion pictures
on motion pictures	Cf. NC1765 +, Motion picture cartoons
897.5	General works
	Computer animation
897.7	General works
897.75	Morphing
898	Motion pictures for television
	Cf. PN1992.63, Drama
	Cf. PN1992.8.F5, Films in television
	programming
	Editing of motion pictures
899	General works
899.5	Time code
	Industrial reproduction
900	General works
905	Englargements
910	Reductions
	Direct reproductions on same scale
915	General works
	Processes for reproducing working drawings, plans,
	etc.
920	General works
921	Blue processes. Blueprints
923	Black processes
	Photomechanical processes
925	General works
927	Special applications. Book illustration, etc.
	Collotype processes
930	General works

TR

	Photomechanical processes
	Collotype processes -- Continued
933	Albertype
935	Autotype
937	Heliotype
	Photolithography
940	General works
950	Aluminium process
955	Photozincography
960	Photoxylography
970	Photoengraving. Relief processes
975	Halftone process
976	Mezzograph
977	Color processes
	Cf. TR510+, Color photography
980	Photogravure. Heliogravure. Intaglio process
	Gelatine relief processes
990	Photogalvanography
995	Woodburytype. Photoglyptie
997	Stannotype
(1010)	Phototypesetting
	see Z253.2
	Electrophotography
1035	General works
	Electrostatic printing
1042	General works
1045	Xerography
1050	Ferromagnetography

	Manufactures
	Cf. HD9000+, Economics
	Cf. HF5686.M3, Accounting
	Cf. TP1+, Chemical technology
	Cf. TT1+, Handicrafts
1	Periodicals, societies, etc.
5	Congresses
	Museums and local exhibitions, see T180+
	Exhibitions, national and international, see T391+
7	Collected works (nonserial)
9	Encyclopedias and dictionaries
	Directories, see T11.95+
15	History
21-127	Country divisions (Table T1)
	Add country number in table to TS0
	Cf. T21+, Technology (General)
	Biography
139	Collective
140.A-Z	Individual, A-Z
	General works
144	Early to 1800
145	1800-
146	Juvenile works. Popular works
147	Pictorial works
	Workshop manuals, etc , see TT153+
	Machinists' manuals, see TJ1165
	Tables, receipts, etc , see T49
148	Addresses, essays, lectures
149	General special
	Production management. Operations management
	Including factory management
155.A1	Periodicals, societies, etc.
155.A2-Z	General works
	Study and teaching, see T56.4+
	Manufacturing personnel
	Cf. HF5549+, Personnel management
	Cf. T55+, Plant safety
	Cf. TA158+, Industrial technicians
155.4	Plant supervisors
155.5	Foremen
	Data processing. CAD/CAM systems
155.6	General works
155.63	Computer integrated manufacturing systems
155.65	Flexible manufacturing systems
155.67	Parallel kinematic machines
155.7	Environmental aspects
	Control of production systems
155.8	General works
	Quality control
	Cf. TJ245.5, Quality control of machinery
156.A1	Periodicals, societies, etc.
156.A2-Z	General works
	Inspection

TS

	Production management. Operations management
	Control of production systems
	Quality control
	Inspection -- Continued
156.2	General works
156.25	Grading
156.4	Acceptance sampling
156.6	Quality assurance
156.8	Process control
	Cf. TP155.75, Chemical process control
	Production control
	Cf. HF5415.2, Market research
	Cf. TS176+, Production planning
157.A1	Periodicals, societies, etc.
157.A2-Z	General works
157.4	Just-in-time systems
	Scheduling
	Cf. HD69.T54, Industrial management
157.5	General works
157.7	Gantt charts
158	Critical path analysis
158.2	PERT
158.4	Line of balance technique
158.6	Automatic data collection systems
	Inventory control
	Cf. HD39.5, Industrial procurement
	Cf. HD40, Inventory policy
	Cf. HD40.7, Surplus property
	Cf. HF5484+, Warehousing and storage
160	General works
161	Materials management. Industrial ecology
162	Economic lot size. Economic order quantity
163	Stockkeeping
	Cf. TS189.6, Storerooms. Warehouses
	Cost control
	Cf. HD47.3, Economics
	Cf. TA177.4+, Engineering economy
165	General works
166	Estimating
167	Manufacturing costs
(167.5)	Break-even point
	see HD47.25
168	Value analysis. Value engineering
169	Waste control
	Product engineering
	Cf. T59+, Standardization
	Cf. TS195+, Packaging
170	General works
	Industrial research, see T175+
170.5	Environmental aspects
	Product design. Industrial design
171.A1	Periodicals, societies, congresses, etc.
	Museums, exhibitions of local societies, see T179+

	Production management. Operations management
	Product engineering
	Product design. Industrial design -- Continued
	Exhibitions, national and international, see T391+
	Special countries and designers, see TS21+
171.A5-Z	General works
171.4	General special
171.6	Pictorial works
172	Tolerances
	Cf. T50, Technical metrology
173	Reliability of industrial products
	Cf. TA169+, Systems reliability
174	Maintainability
175	Product safety. Safety of consumer products
	Cf. T55+, Industrial safety. Industrial accident prevention
	Cf. TA169.7, System safety
175.5	Product testing
	Manufacturing engineering. Process engineering
	Including manufacturing planning, production planning
	Cf. HD58, Plant location
176	General works
177	Plant design. Factory planning
177.3	Plant size. Factory size
	Plant layout
178	General works
178.2	Batch production
	Production lines. Assembly line processes
178.4	General works
178.5	Line balancing
178.7	Operation sequence analysis
	Materials handling
180	General works
180.3	Machinery
180.5	Loading and unloading
	In-plant transportation
180.6	General works
180.8.A-Z	Special materials, A-Z
180.8.B8	Bulk solids
	Planning for machinery. Equipment analysis
	Cf. TS191.3, Installation of machinery
181	General works
181.3	Selection
181.4	Tool life
181.6	Replacement
	Manufacturing processes
	Cf. TJ1180+, Tool engineering
183	General works
	Process planning
183.3	General works
183.6	Make-or-buy decisions
183.8	Remanufacturing

TS

	Production management.
	Operations management -- Continued
	Plant engineering
	Cf. T55+, Plant safety
	Cf. T59.77, Working environment
	Cf. TD895+, Factory sanitation
	Cf. TD896+, Factory waste disposal
	Cf. TH9445.M4+, Fire prevention in factories
	Cf. TH9745.F3, Plant protection
184	General works
186	Factory buildings. Industrial buildings
	Cf. NA6396+, Architecture
	Cf. TH4511+, Factory construction
187	Plant utilities
	For specific utilities, see the utility, e.g.
	TH7392.M6, Heating of mills and factories
188	Employee facilities and buildings
	Plant service facilities
189	General works
189.3	Toolrooms and cribs
189.6	Storerooms. Storage facilities. Warehouses
	Plant grounds
190	General works
190.5	Industrial landscape architecture
	Machinery and equipment
191	General works
191.3	Installation
191.6	Catalogs
191.8	Industrial robots
	Cf. TJ210.2+, Robots (General)
192	Plant maintenance
193	Plant housekeeping
194	Plant performance monitoring
	Packaging
	Cf. HF5770.A1+, Shipping of merchandise
	Cf. TA1215, Containerization of freight
	For packaging of special products, see the product,
	e.g. TP374, Packaging of food
195.A1	Periodicals, societies, congresses, etc.
195.A2	Dictionaries and encyclopedias
195.A3	Directories
195.A4A-Z	Special companies. By name, A-Z
195.A5-Z	General works
195.2	General special
195.4	Design
195.6	Standards and specifications
195.8	Testing
	Management
196	General works
196.2	Costs
196.4	Machinery
	Labeling
196.6	General works

	Packaging
	Labeling -- Continued
196.7	Printing
197	Handling
197.5	Containers (General)
198.A-Z	Special containers and packaging methods, A-Z
198.A3	Aerosols
198.B3	Bags
198.B6	Boxes
	Cf. TS900, Box making
198.C3	Cans
198.C33	Capsules
198.C46	Child-resistant packaging
198.F55	Flexible packaging
198.I58	Insect-resistant packaging
198.P7	Pressure packaging
198.W7	Wrapping
	Materials
198.2	General works
198.3.A-Z	Special materials, A-Z
	Prefer TS198
198.3.A3	Adhesives. Tapes
198.3.C6	Coatings
198.3.F5	Films. Foils
198.3.G5	Glass
198.3.M4	Metal (non-foil)
198.3.P3	Paper. Paperboard
198.3.P5	Plastics (non-foil)
	Tapes, see TS198.3.A3
198.3.T5	Textile fabrics
198.3.W6	Wood
	Packaging for protection from mechanical damage
	Including packing for shipment
198.5	General works
198.6.A-Z	Special protective materials and shipping containers, A-Z
	Prefer TS198
198.6.B3	Barrels
198.6.C6	Conex containers
198.6.C7	Crates
198.6.C8	Cushioning
198.6.D7	Drums
198.6.E9	Excelsior
198.6.P3	Pallets
	Packaging for protection from exposure to harmful environments
198.7	General works
198.8.A-Z	Special environments, A-Z
198.8.C6	Corrosion
198.8.F8	Fungi
198.8.M6	Moisture
199	General catalogs

TS

	Metal manufactures. Metalworking
	Including metal forming and working
200	Periodicals, societies, etc.
203	Directories
204	Dictionaries and encyclopedias
205	General works
207	Cold working
209	Heating of metals
	Cf. TS325, Heating of steel
209.5	Hot working
210	Handbooks, tables, etc.
213	General special
214	Scrap metals
215	Metalworking machinery
	Cf. TJ1180+, Machine and hand tools
	Machining, see TJ1180+
	Forging. Drop-forging
	Cf. TT218+, Blacksmithing
225	General works
	History
225.2.A1	General works
225.2.A5-Z	By region or country, A-Z
	Joining of metals
226	General works
	Bonding (Metal finishing), see TS718
	Brazing (Handicrafts), see TT267
	Fastenings, see TJ1320+
	Riveting (Iron and steel work), see TA891
	Riveting (Machine shop practice), see TJ1325
	Sealing (Machinery), see TJ246
	Soldering (Tinsmithing), see TS610
	Soldering (Handicrafts), see TT267
	Welding
	Cf. TA492.W4, Welded joints
	Cf. TT211, Welding in mechanical arts
227.A1	Periodicals, societies, etc.
227.A3-Z	General works
227.2	General special
227.3	Hard-facing
227.4	Directories
227.5	Dictionaries and encyclopedias
227.55	Examinations, questions, etc.
227.6	Research
227.7	Vocational guidance
227.8	Safety measures
	Gas welding. Oxyacetylene welding
228.A1	Periodicals, societies, etc.
228.A2-Z	General works
228.2	Oxygen cutting
(228.4-7)	Electric welding, arc welding, resistance welding
	see TK4660
(228.8)	Electric cutting
	see TK4660.5

Metal manufactures. Metalworking
  Joining of metals
    Welding -- Continued

228.9	Pressure welding
228.92	Ultrasonic welding
228.95	Laser welding
228.96	Explosive welding

  Casting. Foundry work
    Including general foundry work, and iron and steel
      founding
    For the founding of nonferrous metals, see TS375
    For the founding of other special metals see TS551-
      TS640

228.99	Periodicals, societies, etc.
229	Directories of foundries
229.3	Dictionaries and encyclopedias
	History
229.5.A1	General works
229.5.A5-Z	By region or country, A-Z
230	General works
230.5	Addresses, essays, lectures
231	Cupola furnaces
	Cf. TN715, Blast furnaces
233	General special
	Including automation
234	Specifications
235	Handbooks, tables, etc.
236	Castings
237	Foundry equipment and supplies. Catalogs
238	Foundry management. Estimating, etc.
	Including safety measures
239	Diecasting
240	Patternmaking
	For patternmaking for copper, see TS620+
	For patternmaking for sheet metals, see TS250
	For patternmaking for tin, see TS600+
	Molding. Coremaking
243	General works
243.5	Molding materials. Molding sand
245	Powder metallurgy processes and manufactures
	Cf. TN695+, Metallurgy
247	Rapid solidification processing
250	Sheet metalwork
	For coppersmithing, see TS620+
	For tinsmithing, see TS600+
253	Metal stamping
	Including punch and die work, press-tool work,
	diemaking, etc.
	Cf. TJ1255+, Punching machinery
255	Extrusion of metals
256	High energy forming
257	Explosive forming
260	Leaf metals

TS

Metal manufactures. Metalworking -- Continued
  Wiremaking
    Cf. TS1787, Wire rope

270.A1	Periodicals, societies, etc.
270.A2-Z	General works
271	Barbed wire

        Cf. S790+, Fences

273	Wire screens

        Cf. TH2276, Screens

275	Sieves
277	Valves (General)

        For special applications, see the field of
           application, e.g. TD491, Water distribution
           systems; TJ352-TJ354, Steam boiler safety
           valves; TL625.V3, Balloon valves

  Pipes and tubes

280	General works
282	Catalogs
283	Pressure vessels

        Cf. TA660.T34, Tanks. Pressure vessels
           (Structural engineering)

285	General catalogs of metal manufactures

  Iron and steel
    Cf. HD9510+, Economics

300	Periodicals, societies, etc.

    Exhibitions

300.5.A1	General works
300.5.A2-Z	By region or country, A-Z

         Under each country:
      .x   *General works*
      .x2A-Z   *Special. By city, A-Z*

301	Directories
302	Dictionaries and encyclopedias

    History, see TN703
    Special countries
      Cf. TN704.A+, Metallurgy
      United States

303	General works
303.5	Biography
304.A-Z	Other countries, A-Z
305	General works
307	General special

        Including patents

309	Catalogs

    Specifications, see TA466

320	Steelworking. Tool steel
325	Heating of steel
330	Steel plants

        Including technical descriptions, histories, etc.

330.A1	Collective
330.A2-Z	Individual, A-Z
340	Rolling of metals. Rolling mills and machinery

	Metal manufactures. Metalworking
	Iron and steel -- Continued
350	Structural iron and steel
	Cf. TA685, Pocketbooks, tables, etc.
360	Sheet iron and steel
	Steel pens, see TS1263
	Nonferrous metals (General)
370.A1	Periodicals, societies, etc.
370.A2-Z	General works
371	General special
372	Catalogs
375	Founding. Casting
	Special plants
377.A1	Collective
377.A2-Z	Individual, A-Z
	Cutlery
380	General works
	Biography
380.3	Collective
380.4.A-Z	Individual, A-Z
381	Scissors and shears (Hand)
	Hardware
	Cf. HD9745, Economics
	Cf. TH5618, Carpenters' tools
	Cf. TH6299, Plumbers' tools
	Periodicals, see TS200
400	General works
403	Directories
405	Catalogs
408	Furniture
	Including steel, iron, other metal
	Cf. TS879.2 +, Lumber and woodwork
410	Scales (Weighing instruments)
420	Safes
	Cf. TH9735, Security in buildings
425	Stoves and ranges
	Cf. TX657.S3 +, Home economics
	Miscellaneous articles of iron and steel
	Including chains, nails, etc.
440	General works
445	Catalogs
	Instrument manufacture
	Cf. Q184 +, Scientific instruments and apparatus
	Cf. TA165, Engineering instruments
500	General works
	Optical instruments
510	Periodicals, societies, congresses, etc.
511.A-Z	By region or country, A-Z
	Under each country:
.x	*General works*
.x2A-Z	*Local, A-Z*
512.A-Z	Special companies, A-Z
513	General works

TS

	Metal manufactures. Metalworking
	Instrument manufacture
	Optical instruments -- Continued
514	General special
515	Standards and specifications
516	Catalogs
517	Preparation of optical surfaces
	Including grinding and polishing
517.2	Optical coatings
	Lenses
517.3	General works
517.5.A-Z	Special types of lenses, A-Z
517.5.A86	Aspheric lenses
517.5.C38	Catadioptric systems
	Mirror lenses, see TS517.5.C38
517.5.P5	Plastic lenses
518	Liquid crystal devices
	Locksmithing
	Cf. TH9737, Building protection equipment
519	Periodicals, societies, etc.
519.5	History
520	General works
521	General special
525	Lock picking
529	Catalogs of locks
530	Catalogs of keys
531	Handcuffs and other metal restraints
531.5	Padlocks
	Firearms. Guns
	Cf. NK6900+, Decorative arts
532	Periodicals, societies, etc.
532.15	Dictionaries and encyclopedias
	Museums. Exhibitions
532.2.A1	General works
532.2.A2-Z	By region or country, A-Z
	Apply table at TS300.5.A2-Z
532.4	Collectors and collecting
	History
533	General works
	Special countries
	United States
533.2	General works
533.3.A-W	By state, A-W
533.4.A-Z	Other regions or countries, A-Z
	Biography
533.6	Collective
533.62.A-Z	Individual, A-Z
534	General works
534.5	General special
534.7	Catalogs

	Metal manufactures. Metalworking
	Firearms. Guns -- Continued
	Gunsmithing
	Cf. HD9743, Economics
	Cf. SK274+, Hunting
	Cf. UD380+, Military rifles, etc.
535	General works
535.2.A-Z	Special features and equipment, A-Z
535.2.G8	Gunstocks
535.2.H64	Holsters
535.2.L6	Locks
535.2.S46	Sights
	For telescopic sights, see TS535.2.T4
535.2.S5	Silencers
535.2.T4	Telescopic sights
535.4	Maintenance and repair
535.8	Muzzle-loading firearms
	Cf. TS536.6.M8, Rifles
	Types of guns
536	Repeating firearms
	Rifles
536.4	General works
536.6.A-Z	Special types, A-Z
536.6.B6	Bolt action
536.6.F34	Falling block
536.6.G37	Garand rifle
536.6.K4	Kentucky rifle
536.6.L48	Leveraction
536.6.M8	Muzzle-loading
536.6.R44	Remington rifle
536.6.R84	Ruger rifle
536.6.S3	Schuetzen rifles
536.6.S5	Single shot
536.6.S64	Spencer rifle
536.6.W55	Winchester rifle
536.8	Shotguns
536.9	Submachine guns
537	Handguns
	Including pistols and revolvers
537.5	Air guns
	Ammunition
	Cf. UF700, Military science
538	General works
538.3	Handloading
538.4	Pinfire
538.5	Teargas munitions
	Watches and clocks
	Cf. HD9999.C58+, Economics
	Cf. NK7480+, Decorative art
540	Periodicals, societies, etc.
540.7	Dictionaries and encyclopedias
	Museums. Exhibitions
541.A1	General works

Metal manufactures. Metalworking
  Watches and clocks
    Museums. Exhibitions -- Continued

541.A2-Z	By region or country, A-Z
	Apply table at TS300.5.A2-Z
	History
542	General works
542.5	Juvenile works
543.A-Z	By country, A-Z
543.5.A-Z	Special clocks. By place, A-Z
544	Standard clock systems. Electric clocks
544.5	Specifications
544.8.A-Z	Biography, A-Z
545	General works
545.8	Study and teaching. Schools
545.9	Vocational guidance
546	Watchmakers' lathes and other machinery
547	Repairing and adjusting
548	General special
	Including testing, reading the clock
549	Catalogs
	Sundials, see QB215
	Light metals
551	Periodicals, societies, etc.
552	General works
	Aluminum
	Cf. TN775, Metallurgy
554	Periodicals, societies, etc.
555	General works
556	Aluminum plants
557	Catalogs
560	Magnesium
562	Titanium
	Brass and bronze
564	Periodicals, societies, etc.
565	General works
570	Bronze
573	Catalogs
	Bells
	For history and antiquities, see CC200+
	General works
583	Early to 1800
585	1800-
588	General catalogs, etc.
	For lists of the products of individual
	foundries and makers, see CC206.A+
589	Doorbells
	Cf. TK7108+, Electric bells
	Tinplate
	Cf. HD9539.T5+, Economics
590	General works
597	Tables, calculations, etc.
	Cf. HF5716.T4, Economics

	Metal manufactures. Metalworking
	Tinplate -- Continued
599	Catalogs
	Tinsmithing
	Cf. TT266 +, Handicraft
600	General works
610	Soldering
619	Tinware and tinsmiths' supplies
	Coppersmithing. Copper founding
620	General works
625	Catalogs
640	Zinc
650	Alloys
	Cf. TA483 +, General properties of alloys
	Cf. TN689 +, Metallography
	Metal finishing and surface treatment (General)
	Cf. TT382 +, Handicrafts
653.A1	Periodicals, societies, etc.
653.A2-Z	General works
653.5	General special
	Including safety measures
654	Cleaning and pickling
654.5	Electrolytic polishing
655	Metallizing. Metal spraying
657	Calorizing
660	Galvanizing and tinning
662	Electroless plating
	Electroplating. Electrometallurgy
670.A1	Periodicals, societies, etc.
670.A2-Z	General works
671	Pulse plating
672	Plating baths
675	Electroplated ware. Catalogs
678	Gold plating
680	Silver plating
690	Nickel plating
692.A-Z	Other metals, A-Z
692.A5	Aluminum
692.C18	Cadmium
692.C4	Chromium
692.C57	Cobalt
692.C6	Copper
692.I7	Iron
692.P55	Platinum
692.P56	Platinum group
692.R5	Rhodium
692.T5	Titanium
692.T8	Tungsten
692.Z5	Zinc
693	Alloys
	Anodic oxidation
694	General works
694.2	Aluminum

TS

	Metal manufactures. Metalworking
	Metal finishing and surface
	treatment (General) -- Continued
	Vapor-plating. Chemical vapor deposition
695	General works
695.15	Plasma-enhanced chemical vapor deposition
695.2	Ion plating
695.25	Ion implantation
695.3	Boriding
695.5	Siliconizing
695.7	Sulphonitriding
695.9	Refractory coating
696	Phosphate coating
698	Painting and lacquering
	Enameling
	Cf. TT382.6, Handicrafts
700	General works
705	Catalogs of enameled ware
710	Coloring
715	Gilding. Silvering. Bronzing
	Cf. TT380, Mechanic trades
718	Bonding
	Including rubber to metal bonding
719	Printing
	Precious metals. Gold and silver work. Jewelry
	Cf. HD9536, Economics
	Cf. NK7100+, Decorative art
	Cf. NK7210, Hallmarks
720	Periodicals, societies, etc.
722	Dictionaries and encyclopedias
723	History
725	General works
729	General special
	Including alloys, tables, calculations, recovery
	of wastes
	Silversmithing
730	General works
735	Silverware, etc. Catalogs
	Jewelry
	Cf. HD9747, Jewelry industry
	Cf. TS759, Jewelers' catalogs
	Cf. TS760, Jewelers' supplies
	Cf. TT212, Jewelry craft
740	General works
	Precious stones. Gems
	Biography
747	Collective
748	Individual, A-Z
	General works
750	Early to 1800
752	1800-
752.5	Gem cutting
	Special

	Metal manufactures. Metalworking
	Precious metals. Gold and silver work. Jewelry
	Jewelry
	Precious stones. Gems
	Special -- Continued
	Diamonds
753	General works
753.5	Diamond cutting
755.A-Z	Other special, A-Z
755.A5	Amber
755.E5	Emeralds
755.J34	Jade
755.O73	Opals
	Pearls
755.P3	General works
755.P4	Cultured pearls
755.R82	Rubies
755.T8	Turquoise
756	General special
757	Trade publications
758	Directories
759	Jewelers' catalogs
760	Jewelers' supplies
761	Emblems, badges, etc.
770	Platinum
	Stonework
	Cf. NK8700 +, Decorative arts
780	General works
788	Monuments, tombstones, tablets, etc.
	Glass manufacture, see TP845 +
	Plastic manufactures, see TP1101 +
	Wood technology. Lumber
	Cf. HD9750 +, Economics
	Cf. SD1 +, Forestry
	Cf. TA419 +, Engineering materials
800	Periodicals
801	Societies
802	Congresses
803	Directories
804	Dictionaries and encyclopedias
	History
	United States
805	General works
806.A-W	Special states, A-W
810.A-Z	Other countries, A-Z
815.A-Z	Special corporations, mills, etc., A-Z
820	General works
821	Juvenile works
825	Inspection, grading, etc. Handbooks
835	General special
	Including utilization, handling, standards, etc.
836	Catalogs
837	Drying of lumber. Lumber kilns. Seasoning

TS

Wood technology. Lumber -- Continued
Lumberyards and sheds, see TH4485
Wood products. Furniture
　　Including industrial woodworking
　　Cf. HD9773, Economics
　　Cf. TT180+, Arts and crafts

840	Periodicals, societies, etc.
842	Directories
	History and special countries, see TS805+
843	General works
847	Tables, calculations, etc.
850	Machinery. Sawmills. Planing mills
851	Care of saws, saw sharpening, etc.
	Cf. TJ1235, Saw sharpening, etc.
852	General special
853	Catalogs
857	Bonding. Wood adhesives
858	Formaldehyde release
868	Compressed wood
869	Laminated wood
870	Veneers and veneering. Plywood
875	Fiberboard, particle board, etc.
	Cf. TH1555, Fiberboard
878	Millwork. Planing-mill products
	Cf. TH1151+, Architectural woodwork
	Furniture
	Cf. NK2200+, Decorative arts
	Cf. TP1185.F8, Plastic furniture
	Cf. TS408, Metal furniture
	Cf. TT194+, Arts and crafts
	Periodicals, see TS840
880	General works
	Juvenile works, see TS821
	Exhibitions
882.A1	General works
882.A2-Z	By region or country, A-Z
	Apply table at TS300.5.A2-Z
	Directories, see TS842
885	General special
886	Finishing
	Cf. TT199.4, Handicrafts
886.5.A-Z	Special types of furniture, A-Z
886.5.B4	Beds and bedsteads
886.5.C45	Chairs
	Including rocking chairs
886.5.C74	Cribs
886.5.T3	Tables
887	Catalogs
889	Fixtures for stores, etc.
890	Cooperage. Barrels. Staves
900	Box making
	Cf. TS198.B6, Packaging
903	Miscellaneous manufactures of wood

	Wood technology. Lumber
	Wood products. Furniture -- Continued
905	General catalogs of woodwork
908	Cork industry
	Cf. TP659.A1+, Bottling
910	Willowware. Basketmaking
	Cf. NK3649.5+, Decorative arts
	Cf. TT879.B3, Handicrafts
913	Miscellaneous hand-woven products
	Including baskets, trays, lampshades, etc.
915	Wire-grass industry
	Including Crex Carpet Company products
	Cf. TS1747+, Fiber industries
	Chemical processing of wood
	Including wood from trees and other woody plants
920	Periodicals. Societies. Collections
921	Congresses
922	Dictionaries and encyclopedias
	Special countries
924	United States
926.A-Z	Other countries, A-Z
928	General works
930	General special
	Wood composition and chemistry
932	General works
933.A-Z	Individual components, A-Z
933.C4	Cellulose
933.L5	Lignin
933.S2	Salt
934.A-Z	Chemical properties of individual timbers and woods, A-Z
936	Processing methods
	Cf. TP997, Destructive distillation of wood
937	Management
	Special products
	Charcoal, see TP331
	Fiberboard, particle board, etc , see TS875
	Paper, see TS1080+
	Rayon, see TS1544.R3
	Tannins, see TS985
	Turpentine, see TP977+
	Woodpulp, see TS1171+
	Leather industries. Tanning
	Cf. HD9780, Economics
	Cf. TT290, Handicraft
940	Periodicals, societies, etc.
	Exhibitions
943.A1	General works
943.A2-Z	By region or country, A-Z
	Apply table at TS300.5.A2-Z
945	Directories
947	Dictionaries and encyclopedias
	History

TS

	Leather industries. Tanning
	History -- Continued
950	General works
951	Origins
952	Medieval
954	Modern
	Special regions or countries
	United States
955	General works
956.A-W	States, A-W
957.A-Z	Europe, A-Z
959.A-Z	Other regions or countries, A-Z
965	General works
965.5	Juvenile works
967	General special
	Including chemistry, testing, hides and skins
968	Study and teaching. Schools
970	Patent leather
980.A-Z	Other special kinds of leather, A-Z
980.B82	Buckskin
980.R8	Russia leather
980.S6	Sole leather
980.U6	Upholstery leather
980.U7	Uppers
980.V6	Vici kid
985	Tanning materials. Tannins
	Boot and shoemaking
	Cf. HD9787, Economics
	Cf. TT678.5, Handicraft
	For local, see TS955 +
989	Periodicals, societies, etc.
	Directories, see TS945
	Dictionaries, see TS947
990	General works
1000	History
	Cf. GT2130, Footwear (Costume)
1005	Machinery
1007	Finishing processes
1015	Hygienic shoes
	Cf. RD757.S45, Orthopedic shoes
1017	Athletic shoes
1020	General special
	Repairing
1023.A1	Periodicals, societies, etc.
1023.A2-Z	General works
1025	Catalogs
	Harness. Saddles
1030	Periodicals, societies, etc.
1032	General works
1033	Catalogs
1035	Saddlery hardware. Harness hardware
	Including catalogs

	Leather industries. Tanning -- Continued
1040	Other kinds of leatherwork
	Cf. NK6200+, Leather (Decorative arts)
	For luggage, see TS2301.L8
1043	Leatherwork machinery. Catalogs
	Imitation leathers
1045	General works
1047.A-Z	Special, A-Z
1050	Articles of horn, ivory, bone, etc.
	Cf. NK5800+, Ivory (Decorative art)
	Cf. NK6020+, Horn and bone (Decorative art)
	Cf. TT288, Bone and horn craft
	Furs
	Cf. HD9944, Economics
	Cf. TT525, Fur garments
1060	Periodicals, societies, etc.
1061	General works
1063	Quality control, grading, etc.
1066	Directories
1067	Catalogs
1070	Artificial fur
	Animal fibers, see TS1545+
	Paper manufacture and trade
	Cf. HD9820+, Economics
	Cf. Z45, Writing instruments, including paper
	Cf. Z112, Paleography materials
	Cf. Z237, Watermarks
	Cf. Z247, Practical printing
1080	Periodicals, societies, congresses, etc.
	Exhibitions
1083.A1	General works
1083.A2-Z	By region or country, A-Z
	Apply table at TS300.5.A2-Z
1085	Dictionaries and encyclopedias
1088	Directories
	History
1090	General works
	Ancient (Papyrus, etc.), see Z105+
1091	Origins (Arab, Chinese, etc.)
	Medieval
1092	General works
1093.A-Z	Special countries, A-Z
	Modern
1094	General works
1095.A-Z	Special countries, A-Z
1096.A-Z	Special companies, A-Z
	Cf. TS1210+, Catalogs
1098.A-Z	Biography, A-Z
	General works
1104	Early to 1800
1105	1800-
1105.5	Juvenile works
1107	Quality control

TS

	Paper manufacture and trade -- Continued
1109	General special
	Including testing, waste prevention, use of cornstalks, hemp, etc.
1111	Study and teaching. Schools
1115	Watermarks, trademarks, etc. (Modern)
	Cf. Z237, Watermarks of early printers
	Papermills and their management
1116	General works
1116.2	Water supply
1116.6	Paper handling. Transportation
	Machinery
1117	General works
1117.6	Automation
1118.A-Z	Special manufacturing processes and equipment, A-Z
1118.C34	Calenders and calendering
	Coloring, see TS1118.D9
1118.C8	Cutting and cutting machinery
1118.D42	Deacidification
1118.D7	Drying and drying machinery
1118.D9	Dyes and dyeing. Coloring
1118.F4	Felts
1118.F5	Finishing. Coatings
	Folding, see Z261
1118.P74	Pressing
1118.P85	Pulp consistency transmitters
1118.R4	Refining
1118.S5	Sizing
1118.S85	Stock preparation
1120	Chemistry of paper manufacture
1120.5	Paper recycling
1121	Paper characteristics, properties, etc.
	Paper types. Special papers
1124	General works
1124.5	Handmade
1125	Papyrus
	Cf. Z45, Calligraphy materials
	Cf. Z112, History of writing
1130	Japanese paper
	Paperboard
	Including cardboard, pasteboard
1135	General works
1138	Corrugated paperboard
1155	Papier mâché
	Cf. TT871, Papier-mâché craft
1160	Newsprint
1165	Parchment
1167	Reproduction paper
1168	Tissue paper
	Woodpulp industry. Pulping processes
	Cf. HD9750+, Economics
1171	Periodicals, societies, congresses, etc.
1172	Annuals. Directories

	Paper manufacture and trade
	Woodpulp industry. Pulping processes -- Continued
1173	United States
1174.A-Z	Other countries, A-Z
1175	General works
1176	General special
1176.4.A-Z	Special pulps, A-Z
1176.4.A8	Aspen
1176.4.B3	Bamboo
1176.4.E9	Eucalyptus
1176.4.H3	Hardwoods
1176.4.K44	Kenaf
1176.4.L3	Larch
1176.4.P5	Pine
1176.4.S7	Spruce
1176.4.T7	Tropical woods
1176.6.A-Z	Special aspects, A-Z
1176.6.A5	Analysis of pulp
1176.6.B56	Biotechnology
1176.6.B6	Bleaching of pulp
1176.6.E7	Equipment and supplies
	Kraft processes, see TS1176.6.S9
1176.6.M4	Mechanical process
1176.6.S5	Smelt-water explosions
1176.6.S6	Soda process
1176.6.S9	Sulphate process
1176.6.S915	Sulphate waste liquor
1176.6.S92	Sulphite liquor
1176.6.S93	Sulphite process
1176.6.T4	Testing of pulp
1176.6.W36	Washing
1176.6.W6	Wood chips
1177	Articles manufactured from woodpulp
	Cf. TS1155, Papier mâché
	Artificial flowers, see TT890+
	Other articles of paper
	Including bags, paper boxes, etc.
	For folding and folding machinery, see Z261
1200.A1	Periodicals, societies, etc.
1200.A2-Z	General works
	Catalogs of paper and pulp mill equipment and supplies
	Including bags, paper boxes, etc.
1205.A1	Periodicals, societies, etc.
1205.A2-Z	General works
	Catalogs of paper manufacturers
	Cf. TS1090+, History
1210	General works
1220	Sample books
	Stationery
1228	Periodicals, societies, etc.
	Directories, see TS1088
(1229)	Biography
	see TS1098

TS

	Paper manufacture and trade
	Stationery -- Continued
1230	General works
1233	General special
	Including history and antiquities
1238	Trade publications other than catalogs
1240	Catalogs
1250	Blank books
1251	Copybooks
1260	Ruling-machinery
	Pens
	Including catalogs
1262	General works
1263	Steel pens
1265	Gold pens
1266	Fountain pens
1267	Ball-point pens
1268	Pencils
	Textile industries
	Cf. HD9850+, Economics
	Cf. SB241+, Fiber plant culture
1300	Periodicals, societies, conferences, etc.
1301	Yearbooks
	Museums. Exhibitions
1306.A1	General works
1306.A2-Z	By region or country, A-Z
	Apply table at TS300.5.A2-Z
1309	Dictionaries and encyclopedias
1312	Directories
	History
1315	General works
1316	Ancient
1317	Medieval
1318	Modern
1321-1424.5	Special countries (Table T1 modified)
	Add country number in table to TS1300
	Arctic regions
1424.2	General works
1424.25	Greenland
1424.3	Antarctica
1424.4	Tropics
1424.5	Developing countries
1425.A-Z	Special corporations, mills, etc., A-Z
	Biography
1439	Collective
1440.A-Z	Individual, A-Z
	General works
1444	Early to 1800
1445	1800-
1446	Elementary works
1449	General special
	Including microscopy, testing, safety measures, yarn

	Textile industries -- Continued
1450	Standardization
	Including thread numbers
1450.5	Production standards
1451	Handbooks, tables, etc.
1463	Vocational guidance
	Study and teaching
1465	General works
1465.5	Problems, exercises, etc.
	By region or country
	For individual institutions, see the state or country without further subdivision
	United States
1471	General works
1472.A-Z	By region or state, A-Z
1473.A-Z	Other regions or countries, A-Z
1474	Information services
1474.5	Textile chemistry
	Cf. TP890 +, Bleaching, dyeing, printing of textiles (Chemical technology)
1475	Textile design
	Cf. NK8800 +, Decorative arts
	Cf. TT851 +, Textile decoration (Arts and crafts)
	Spinning
	Including preliminary processes
	Cf. TS1577, Cotton spinning
	Cf. TS1628, Woolen spinning
	Cf. TS1727, Hand spinning
1480	General works
1483	Machinery
1484	Spinning wheel, distaff, etc.
	Carding and combing
	Cf. TS1578, Cotton carding
	Cf. TS1628, Wool carding
	Cf. TS1727, Flax spinning
1485	General works
1487	Machinery
1487.5	Twisting and twisting machinery
1487.7	Crimping
	Sizing
1488	General works
	Cotton sizing, see TS1580
	Weaving (Industrial)
	Cf. TT848 +, Hand weaving
1490	General works
1493	Machinery. Looms
1500	Jacquard weaving
	Including jacquard looms
1510	Finishing
1511	Setting of textiles
1512	Coating of fabrics

TS

	Textile industries -- Continued
1512.5	Electrostatic flocking
	Cf. TS1828, Nonwoven fabrics
1513	Crease-resisting process
1514	Drying. Drying equipment
1515	Mercerization
1517	Mothproofing
1520	Waterproofing
	Fireproofing, see TP267
1525	Textile machinery (General)
	Textile mills (Design and construction), see TH4521
	Textile supplies
1529	General works
1530	Catalogs
1535	Directories
	Textile fibers
1540	General works
	Vegetable
1541	General works
1542	Cotton
1543	Linen
1544.A-Z	Others, A-Z
1544.A5	Ambary hemp. Kenaf
1544.B3	Bast
1544.C4	Cellulose
1544.C6	Coconut fiber
1544.H4	Hemp
	Cf. TS1733, Hemp manufactures
	Kenaf, see TS1544.A5
1544.M3	Marine fiber
1544.P55	Piña cloth
1544.R2	Ramie
	Cf. SB259, Plant culture
1544.R3	Rayon
	Cf. TS1688.A1+, Rayon manufactures
	Animal
1545	General works
1546	Silk
1547	Wool
1548.A-Z	Others, A-Z
1548.C3	Camel's hair
1548.H6	Horsehair
1548.M6	Mohair
1548.V5	Vicuna
	Synthetic textile fibers
1548.2	Dictionaries and encyclopedias
1548.5	General works
1548.7.A-Z	Special, A-Z
1548.7.A25	Acrylic
1548.7.P57	Polyamide
1548.7.P58	Polyesters
1548.7.P6	Polypropylene
1548.7.P63	Polyurethanes

	Textile industries
	Textile fibers
	Synthetic textile fibers
	Special, A-Z -- Continued
1548.7.V5	Vinyl
	Inorganic fibers
1549.A1	General works
1549.A3-Z	Special, A-Z
1549.A7	Asbestos
1549.G5	Glass
1549.G6	Gold
	Cotton manufactures
	Cf. HD9870+, Economics
	Cf. SB245+, Cotton culture
1550	Periodicals, societies, etc.
1551	Yearbooks
1555	Directories
	Exhibitions
1557.A1	General works
1557.A2-Z	By region or country, A-Z
	Apply table at TS300.5.A2-Z
	History
1560	General works
1561	Ancient
1562	Medieval
1564	Modern
1565.A-Z	Special regions and countries, A-Z
1566.A-Z	Special companies. By name, A-Z
1570	Biography
1575	General works
1576	Elementary works
1577	Spinning
	Including preliminary processes
1578	Carding. Combing. Lapping
1579	Weaving
1580	General special
	Including finishing processes
1581	Handbooks, tables, calculations, etc.
1582	Cotton fabrics
1583	Cotton machinery
1585	Ginning, baling, etc.
1587	Cotton waste products
	Cf. TP996.C75, Chemical technology
	Cotton baling, see TS1585
1590	Thread manufacture
	Woolen manufactures
	Cf. HD9890+, Economics
	Cf. SF371+, Sheep culture
1600	Periodicals, societies, etc.
1601	Yearbooks
1603	Directories
	Exhibitions
1606.A1	General works

TS

	Textile industries
	Woolen manufactures
	Exhibitions -- Continued
1606.A2-Z	By region or country, A-Z
	Apply table at TS300.5.A2-Z
	History
1610	General works
1611	Ancient
1612	Medieval
1614	Modern
1615.A-Z	Special regions or countries, A-Z
1620	Biography
1625	General works
1626	Elementary works
	Spinning and other preliminary processes
1627	General works
1628	Carding. Combing
1629	Weaving
1630	General special
	Including finishing processes, wool substitutes, etc.
1631	Handbooks, tables, calculations, etc.
1633	Woolen and worsted machinery
1634	Catalogs of woolen goods
1635	Artificial wool
	Silk manufactures
	Cf. HD9910+, Economics
	Cf. SF541+, Sericulture
1640	Periodicals, societies, congresses, etc.
1641	Yearbooks
1643	Directories
	Exhibitions
1646.A1	General works
1646.A2-Z	By region or country, A-Z
	Apply table at TS300.5.A2-Z
	History
1650	General works
1651	Ancient
1652	Medieval
1654	Modern
1655.A-Z	Special regions or countries, A-Z
1660	Biography
1665	General works
1667	Spinning and other preliminary processes
1669	General special
1671	Handbooks, tables, etc.
1672	Silk machinery
1673	Catalogs
1675	Velvets
1676	Brocade
1677	Crepe
1680	Plush
1687	Cords, trimmings, passementerie, gimp, braids, etc.

	Textile industries
	Silk manufactures -- Continued
	Artificial silk. Rayon. Celanese
1688.A1	Periodicals, societies, etc.
1688.A2	Directories
1688.A3-Z	General works
	Flax, hemp and jute industries
	Cf. TS1540+, Fibers
	Cf. TS1784+, Cordage
	Cf. TS1795, Twine
1700	Periodicals, societies, etc.
1705	General works
1707	Tables, calculations, etc.
	Flax industries. Linen, etc.
	Cf. HD9930, Economics
1710	History
1715.A-Z	Special regions or countries, A-Z
1725	General works
1727	Spinning and other preliminaries
1728	Machinery
1730	Tables, calculations, etc.
1731	Catalogs of linen goods
1733	Hemp industries
1735	Jute industries, burlap, etc.
	Other fiber industries
1747.A-Z	Special, A-Z
1747.C6	Coir
1747.D3	Date palm fiber
1747.E8	Esparto
1747.H6	Horsehair
1747.K3	Kapok
1747.O3	Oakum
1747.R2	Raffia
1747.R3	Ramie
1747.R6	Roselle
1747.S5	Sisal
1747.S7	Straw plaiting
	Wire grass, see TS915
1750	General special
	Textile fabrics. Dry goods
	Cf. TT490+, Clothing manufacture
1760	Periodicals, societies, etc.
1763	Directories
1765	General works
1767	General special
1768	Catalogs
1770.A-Z	Special kinds of fabrics, A-Z
1770.I53	Industrial fabrics
1770.S54	Sheer fabrics
	Knit goods, hosiery, etc , see TT679+
	Carpets, rugs, etc.
	Cf. NK2775+, Decorative art
1772	Periodicals, societies, etc.

TS

	Textile industries
	Carpets, rugs, etc. -- Continued
1773	Directories
	Exhibitions
1774.A1	General works
1774.A2-Z	By region or country, A-Z
	Apply table at TS300.5.A2-Z
	History
1774.4	General works
1774.6.A-Z	Special regions or countries, A-Z
1775	General works
1775.5	General special
1776	Catalogs, etc.
	Rugs
	Cf. NK2775+, Art
1777	General works
1778	Oriental rugs
	Cf. NK2808+, Art
1779.A-Z	Other floor coverings, A-Z
1779.G7	Grass rugs
1779.L5	Linoleum
1779.M2	Matting. Straw, etc.
1779.O5	Oilcloth
1779.5	Carpet measuring, cutting, laying, etc.
1780	Tapestry
	Cf. NK2975+, Art
	Cf. TT849, Hand weaving
1781	Miscellaneous textile articles and products
	Including bagging, shawls, towels, etc.
	For artificial fur, see TS1070
	For flags, see TS2301.F6
1782	Lace (Machine made)
	Cf. HD9933, Trade
	Cf. NK9400+, Decorative art
	Cf. TT800+, Needlework
1782.5	Braid (Machine made)
1783	Embroidery (Machine made)
	Cf. NK9200+, Decorative art
	Cf. TT769+, Needlework
	Miscellaneous fiber products
	Cordage
1784	Periodicals, societies, etc.
1784.5	Directories
1785	General works
1787	Wire rope
1795	Twine
1825	Felt
1828	Nonwoven fabrics
1850	Other fiber products
1860	Tent and awning making
1865	Umbrellas and parasols

	Rubber industry
	Cf. HD9161, Economics
	Cf. SB289+, Agriculture
1870	Periodicals, societies, etc.
1871	Congresses
	Exhibitions
1872.A1	General works
1872.A2-Z	By region or country, A-Z
	Apply table at TS300.5.A2-Z
1875	Dictionaries and encyclopedias
1877	Directories
	History
1880	General works
1885.A-Z	Special countries, A-Z
1890	General works
1891	Vulcanizing
1891.5	Machinery
1892	General special. Examination, testing, etc.
1893	Catalogs and other trade publications
1910	Rubber boots and shoes
1912	Rubber tires
1920	Other articles of rubber
	Including hand stamps, rubber bands, tubes, etc.
1925	Synthetic rubber. Elastomers
1927.A-Z	Special, A-Z
1927.C92	Cyclized rubber
1927.E86	Ethylene-propylene rubber
1927.S55	Silicone rubber
1930	Gutta-percha
1935	Balata
	Miscellaneous industries
	Animal products
	Cf. SK283.8, Field dressing and skinning of game
1950	Periodicals, societies, etc.
1953	Dictionaries and encyclopedias
1955	General works
	Butchering. Slaughterhouses. Meat curing
	Class here technical works only
	Cf. HD9410+, Animal industry
	Cf. RA578.A6, Slaughterhouses
	For Judaism, see BM720.S6
1960	General works
1962	Minor works
	Special countries
	United States
1963	General works
1964.A-W	States, A-W
1965.A-Z	Cities, A-Z
1966.A-Z	Other countries, A-Z
1967.A-Z	Other cities, A-Z
1968	Poultry processing
	Fish processing, see SH334.9+

TS

	Miscellaneous industries
	Animal products -- Continued
	Furs, see TS1060+
	Leather, see TS940+
	Meat-packing industries
	Cf. HD9410+, Economics
	Cf. TS2284+, Pet food industry
1970	General works
1971.A-Z	By region or country, A-Z
	Apply table at TS511.A-Z
1973	Packinghouse equipment, etc.
1974.A-Z	Special topics, A-Z
1974.B3	Bacon
1974.C67	Corned beef
1974.F5	Flavoring, seasoning, etc.
1974.S3	Sausages
1975	Meat inspection
	Lard, tallow, etc.
	Cf. TP669+, Oils, fats, and waxes
1980	General works
1981	Rendering apparatus
1982	Bone products
	Carriage and wagonmaking
	Cf. HD9709.5, Economics
2001	Periodicals, societies, etc.
	Exhibitions. Museums
2003.A1	General works
2003.A2-Z	By region or country, A-Z
	Apply table at TS300.5.A2-Z
2005	Directories
2010	History
2020	General works
2025	General special
	Carriage painting
2030	General works
2032	Scrolls and designs for carriage painters
2033	Catalogs of carriagemakers
2035	Carriage hardware
	Automobiles, see TL1+
	Cereals and grain. Milling industry
	Including flour
	Cf. HD9056, Economics
2120	Periodicals, societies, etc.
	Exhibitions
2123.A1	General works
2123.A2-Z	By region or country, A-Z
	Apply table at TS300.5.A2-Z
2129	Directories
	History
2130	General works

Miscellaneous industries
Cereals and grain. Milling industry
History -- Continued

2135.A-Z   By country, A-Z
Under each country:
.x   *General works*
.x2A-Z   *By state, province, etc., A-Z*
General works
2144   Early to 1800
2145   1800-
2149   General special
          Including moisture in grain
2155   Catalogs
          Cereal products, see TP434 +
          Feeds and feed mills, see TS2284 +
2159.A-Z   Milling and processing of individual cereals, A-Z
2159.C2   Corn
2159.R5   Rice
2159.S65   Sorghum
          Wheat, see TS2120 +
2160   Gloves
          Cf. HD9947, Economics
     Hats
          Cf. HD9948, Economics
          Cf. TT650 +, Millinery
2180   Periodicals, societies, etc.
          Exhibitions
2181.A1   General works
2181.A2-Z   By region or country, A-Z
            Apply table at TS300.5.A2-Z
2182   Directories
2185   General works
2190   General special
2193   Renovating, cleaning, etc.
     Tobacco industry
          Cf. HD9130 +, Economics
2220   Periodicals, societies, etc.
2225   Dictionaries and encyclopedias
2228   Directories
          History
2230   General works
2234   Modern
2235.A-Z   Special places, A-Z
2240   General works
2249   General special
          Including machinery, curing, testing, facts for
            smokers, enjoyment of smoking
2251   Tables, calculations, etc.
2255   Nicotine (Preparation, use, etc.)
2260   Cigars and cigarettes
2270   Pipes for smoking
2280   Smoking paraphernalia
          Including lighters

TS

	Miscellaneous industries
	Tobacco industry -- Continued
2283	Catalogs of cigars, smoking paraphernalia, etc.
	Animal feeds and feed mills. Pet food industry
	Cf. SF94.5+, Animal nutrition
	Cf. SF414, Pet feeding
2284	Periodicals, societies, etc.
2285	Congresses
2286	General works
2286.5	General special
2287	Patents
2288.A-Z	Special foods. Foods for special animals, A-Z
2288.C36	Cat food
2288.C45	Cereals
2288.D63	Dog food
2288.M4	Meat
2301.A-Z	Other industries, A-Z
	Class here primarily catalogs of wares, especially
	articles not made of any one material
	Audiovisual equipment
2301.A7	General works
	Phonographs, see TS2301.P3
	Sound recording instruments, see TS2301.S6
	Baggage, see TS2301.L8
2301.B4	Beads
	Cf. TT860, Beadwork
2301.B5	Belts
2301.B8	Brushes and brooms
2301.B9	Buttons
2301.C3	Canes
2301.C4	Catgut
2301.C5	Church supplies
	Cf. NK1657, Trade catalogs, etc.
2301.C75	Combs
	Containers, see TS195+
2301.D4	Decalcomania
	Dolls, see TS2301.T7
2301.F4	Feathers
2301.F6	Flags, banners, etc.
2301.H7	Hose
	Cf. TH9380, Firehose
2301.I6	Insignia
2301.I8	Isinglass
2301.L8	Luggage
2301.M3	Marking devices
(2301.M8)	Monuments, tombstones, tables, etc.
	see TS788
2301.N5	Notions
2301.N55	Novelties
2301.P2	Page turners
2301.P24	Palm products
2301.P3	Phonographs
2301.P5	Pins and needles

	Miscellaneous industries
	Other industries, A-Z -- Continued
2301.S5	Skates
2301.S6	Sound recording instruments
	Cf. TK7881.4+, Electronic sound systems
	Cf. TS2301.P3, Phonographs
2301.S7	Sporting goods
2301.T5	Time stamps
2301.T7	Toys, etc.
	Cf. GV1218.5+, Games and amusements
	Cf. NK4891.3+, Dolls and dollhouses
	(Decorative arts)
	Cf. NK9509+, Toys (Decorative arts)
	Cf. TT174+, Handicrafts
2301.T9	Transfer pictures, etc.
2301.U5	Undertakers' supplies, etc.
2301.W3	Wax figures
2301.W5	Window shades

TS

	Handicrafts. Arts and crafts
	Including mechanic trades
	Cf. NK1+, Decorative arts
	Cf. NK1135+, Arts and crafts movements
	Cf. TH5011+, Building trades
	Cf. TP1+, Industrial products (Chemical technology)
	Cf. TS1+, Manufactures
1	Periodicals, societies, etc.
	Exhibitions. Museums
6.A1	General works
6.A2-Z	By region or country, A-Z
	Under each country:
.x	*General works*
.x2A-Z	*Special. By city, A-Z*
7	Collected works (nonserial)
9	Dictionaries and encyclopedias
	Communication of handicraft information
10	General works
11	Computer network resources
	Including the Internet
12	Directories
15-127	History and country divisions (Table T1)

15-127: Class here general works on the crafts as practiced in particular regions or countries. Also class here manuals on how to duplicate craft articles of particular regions or countries, including craft articles of particular ethnic groups. For example, class manuals on duplicating crafts of the Indians of North America in TT22

Add country number in table to TT0

For ethnological works about crafts of North American Indians, see E98.I5

For ethnological works on the crafts as practiced by the ethnic groups of particular regions, see GN575-GN681, or the class numbers for particular groups in classes D-F

	Biography
139	Collective
140.A-Z	Individual, A-Z
	General works
144	Early to 1800
145	1800-
149	General special
150	Study and teaching
151	Mending and repairing
	Cf. NK4233, Ceramics
	Cf. TH4817+, Home maintenance and repair
	Cf. TX323, Care of the home
152	Workshops: Planning and maintenance
	Workshop practice
	Including use of workshop tools
153	General works
153.5	Power tools

153.7	Craft materials and supplies
	Models and modelmaking
	Cf. TT178, Miniature crafts
154	General works
154.5	Radio control systems
155	Handbooks, manuals, etc.
157	Special crafts treated collectively
	Including general works on craft projects and items to make
	Cf. SF413.5, Craft items for pets
	Cf. TT180+, Special crafts, by material
	Cf. TT699+, Textile arts and crafts
	Cf. TT855+, Decorative crafts
	Juvenile works. Projects for boys
	Cf. TT171, Handicraft for girls
159	Periodicals, societies, etc.
160	General works
	Manual training. Industrial arts training. School shops
	Cf. LB1594+, Industrial arts training in elementary schools
	Cf. LC1081+, Industrial education (Theory)
	Cf. LC2780.5, Industrial education of Blacks and Afro-Americans
	Cf. T61+, Technology - Study and teaching
161	Periodicals, societies, etc.
	Exhibitions
162.A1	General works
162.A2-Z	By region or country, A-Z
	Under each country:
	.x *General works*
	.x2A-Z *Special. By city, A-Z*
163	Directories
165	Textbooks
166.A-Z	Special countries, A-Z
167.A-Z	Special cities, A-Z
	Including special schools
	Teaching methods
168	General works
169	General special
	School shops
170	General works
170.4	Safety measures
170.7	Equipment and supplies
	Including catalogs
171	Handicrafts for girls
	Articles for children
	Cf. TT197.5.C5, Children's furniture
	Toys
	Cf. GV1218.5+, Games and amusements
	Cf. LB1029.T6, Educational toys
	Cf. NK9509+, Decorative arts
	Cf. TS2301.T7, Toy manufacture

TT

	Articles for children
	Toys -- Continued
174	General works
174.3	Soft toys
174.5.A-Z	Other special, A-Z
174.5.P3	Paper toys
174.5.S35	Scooters, skateboards, etc.
174.5.V43	Vehicles
174.5.W6	Wooden toys
174.7	Puppets
	For general works on puppetry, including manipulation of puppets, puppet plays, etc., see PN1972+
	Dolls
	Including paper dolls
	Cf. GV1218.5+, Games and amusements
	Cf. NK4891.3+, Decorative arts
	Cf. TS2301.T7, Doll manufacture
175	General works
175.3	Dollhouses
175.5	Doll furniture
175.7	Doll clothes
176	Playground equipment
	Playhouses, see TH4967
178	Miniature craft
	Cf. TT154+, Models and modelmaking
	Woodworking
	Cf. TH5601+, Carpentry and joinery
	Cf. TS840+, Manufactures of wood
180	General works
185	Elementary works, outline, syllabi, etc.
	Including amateurs' manuals
186	Tools and supplies
	Cf. TH5618, Carpentry tools
	Sloyd
187	General works
	Special schools, see TT167.A+
188	Models
189	Balsa craft
190	Bamboo work
190.5	Cork craft
191	Plywood working
	Scroll saw work, see NK9930
192	Marquetry
	Furniture
	Cf. TP1185.F8, Plastic furniture manufacture
	Cf. TS879.2+, Furniture manufacture
	Cf. TT175.5, Doll furniture
	Cf. TT213, Metal furniture
	Cf. TT297.5, Plastic furniture craft
194	General works
195	Amateurs' manuals
196	Furniture design. Drawings

	Woodworking
	Furniture -- Continued
197	Box furniture. Cabinetwork
197.5.A-Z	Special, A-Z
197.5.B3	Bars
197.5.B4	Bedroom furniture
197.5.B6	Bookcases
197.5.B8	Built-in furniture
197.5.C45	Chairs
197.5.C5	Children's furniture
197.5.C62	Coffins
197.5.C65	Computer furniture
197.5.C68	Counter tops
197.5.D4	Desks
197.5.D5	Dining room furniture
197.5.E57	Entertainment centers
197.5.K57	Kitchen cabinets, kitchen furniture, etc.
197.5.L34	Lamps. Lighting devices
	Including candlesticks, chandeliers, sconces, etc.
	Cf. TK9921, Electricity for amateurs
	Cf. TT897.2, Decorative crafts
	Lighting devices, see TT197.5.L34
197.5.L5	Living room furniture
197.5.L6	Loudspeaker cabinets
197.5.O9	Outdoor furniture
197.5.T3	Tables
197.5.T65	Toolboxes
197.5.W6	Workbenches
197.7	Wicker furniture
197.8	Rattan furniture
198	Upholstering
199	Repairing. Restoring
199.4	Finishing. Refinishing
	Carving and whittling
	Cf. NK9700+, Decorative art
199.7	General works
199.75	Decoys
	Including painting
199.8	Pyrography. Woodburning
	Cf. NK8600+, Decorative art
200	General special
	Including rustic works
	Picture framing, see N8550+
	Wood staining, see TT345
	Lathework. Turning
	Cf. TJ1215+, Machine tools
	Cf. TS546, Watchmakers' lathes
	Cf. TT207, Metal turning
201	General works
202	Elementary textbooks of woodturning
203	Ornamental, geometric, eccentric, etc.
203.5	Routing. Routers

TT

	Metalworking
	Cf. NK6400+, Decorative art
	Cf. TS720+, Precious metals. Jewelry
205.A1	Periodicals
205.A2-Z	General works
206	Metal spinning
207	Metal turning
209	Milling
211	Welding
	Cf. TK4661, Electric welding
	Cf. TS227+, Manufacturing processes
212	Jewelry craft
213	Other special metal products (not A-Z)
	Including home furnishings in metal
213.6	Nail craft
214	Scrapmetal craft
214.3	Wire craft
	Ironworking. Forging
	Cf. TS225+, Manufacturing processes
215	General works
	Blacksmithing
	Cf. SF907+, Horseshoeing
218	Periodicals, societies, etc.
220	General works
221	Amateurs' manuals
223	Tables, calculations, etc.
224	Equipment and supplies
240	Bent iron work. Wrought-iron work
	Cf. NK8200+, Decorative art
242	Aluminum work. Aluminum foil craft
250	Copperwork
	Cf. NK8100+, Decorative art
265	Leadwork
	Cf. NK8350, Decorative art
	Tinwork. Tin can craft
	Cf. NK8425, Decorative art
	Cf. TS600+, Metal manufactures
266	General works
266.3	Pewter craft
	Cf. NK8400+, Decorative art
267	Soldering and brazing
	Cf. TH6297, Plumbing
	Stencil cutting. Stencil work
	Cf. NK8650+, Decorative stencil work
270	General works
273	Screen process work. Silk-screen printing
	Cf. TT852+, Textile printing
	For serigraphy, see NE2236+
288	Bone and horn craft
	Cf. NK6020+, Decorative art
	Cf. TS1050, Manufactures

290	Leatherwork
	Cf. NK6200+, Decorative art
	Cf. TS1030+, Manufactures
	Cf. TT666, Gloves
	Cf. TT667, Handbags
293	Rock craft
	Including flintknapping
295	Cement work, plaster craft, etc.
	Including sand casting, earth casting, etc.
	Cf. NB1190, Sculpture
	Plastic craft
	Including use of plastic foam
297	General works
297.5	Plastic furniture
297.8	Fiberglass craft
298	Glass craft
	Including glass engraving, glass painting, glass
	constructions, glass forming, etc.
	Cf. NB1270.G4, Glass sculpture
	Cf. NE2690, Glass engravings
	Cf. NK5100+, Decorative arts
	Cf. TH8271+, Decoration in buildings
	Painting, varnishing, gilding, etc.
	Including industrial painting
	Cf. ND1.2+, Fine arts
	Cf. NK2140+, Decorative painting
	Cf. TP934+, Paint manufacture
	Cf. TS698, Metal painting
	Cf. TS2030+, Carriage painting
	Cf. TT851, Textile painting
300	Periodicals, societies, etc.
301	Collected works (nonserial)
303	Directories
304	History
	General works
305.A2	Early to 1800
305.A3-Z	1800-
305.3	Paint shops and equipment
310	Paintmixing
315	Spray painting
317	Electrocoating. Electrophoretic deposition
	House painting. Painting of buildings and structures
	Cf. TH8001+, Decoration of buildings
320	General works
323	Interior painting
	Including decorative finishes, frescoing, etc.
324	Painters' materials (General)
	Cf. TP934+, Paint manufacture
	Wood finishing
	Cf. TS886, Furniture manufacture
	Cf. TT199.4, Furniture in woodworking crafts
325	General works
330	Graining and marbling

TT

Painting, varnishing, gilding, etc.

Wood finishing -- Continued

340   Varnishing

345   Wood staining

Sign painting and lettering. Show cards

Cf. NC1800 +, Posters

360.A1   Periodicals, societies, etc.

360.A6-Z   General works

365   House numbers

370   Coloring of bone, stone, etc.

378   Lacquering, crackle

380   Gilding, bronzing, etc.

Metal finishing

Cf. TS653 +, Industrial manufactures

382   General works

382.2   Coloring

382.4   Painting and lacquering

382.6   Enameling

Including cloisonné and champlevé

Cf. NK4997 +, Decorative arts

382.8   Gilding, bronzing, silvering

385   Decorative painting on various materials. Tole painting

Cf. NK5312, Folk art in the United States

Cf. NK5313 +, Folk art in other countries

386   Felt marker decoration

Soft home furnishings

Cf. TT198, Upholstering

Cf. TT849, Tapestry

Cf. TT850, Rugs, carpets, etc.

387   General works

390   Curtain making. Drapes

395   Slipcovers

Bedding

Cf. TX315, Home furnishings

399   General works

403   Bedspreads

Cf. TT835, Quilts

405   Blankets

406   Sheets

408   Pillowcases

410   Pillows and cushions

Clothing manufacture

Including the garment industry

490   Periodicals, societies, etc.

494   Dictionaries and encyclopedias

495   Directories

496.A-Z   By region or country, A-Z

Under each country:

.x   *General works*

.x2A-Z   *Local, A-Z*

497   General works

	Clothing manufacture -- Continued
498	Clothing factories
	Cf. TH4522, Building construction
499	Tables, calculations, etc.
	Dressmaking and women's tailoring. Fashion
	Cf. GT500+, History of dress and costume
	Cf. NK4700+, Decorative arts
	Cf. TR679, Fashion photography
500.A1	History and criticism of periodicals
500.A2-Z	Periodicals and societies. Fashion magazines
	Cf. PN4784.F33, Journalism
502	Fashion shows, exhibitions, etc.
503	Dictionaries and encyclopedias
	Directories, see TT495
503.5	Fashion writing
504	History of dressmaking and tailoring
	Special countries
504.4	United States
504.6.A-Z	Other countries, A-Z
	Biography
505.A1	Collective
505.A2-Z	Individual, A-Z
	e.g.
505.P6	Poiret
505.W6	Worth
506	Pictorial works
507	Art of dress. Theory. Aesthetics. Costume design
508	Study and teaching
509	Fashion drawing
	General works
510	Early to 1800
	1800-
515	General works
518	Textbooks
519	Addresses, essays, lectures
	Women's tailoring
519.5	General works
520	Patternmaking and design
	Including cutting, drafting, measuring and grading
522	Blank forms
523	Dress forms
524	Leather garments
525	Fur garments
530	Coats and capes
535	Jackets
540	Skirts
542	Slacks. Trousers
	For men's slacks, or men's and women's slacks, see TT605
545	Blouses
546	Smocks
	Cf. TT840.S66, Smocking

TT

Clothing manufacture
  Dressmaking and women's
      tailoring. Fashion -- Continued
546.5   Aprons
547   Maternity clothes
550   Alterations. Restyling
552   Trimming
             Catalogs and pricelists
555   General works
556   Catalogs of patterns
                 For catalogs issued periodically, see TT500+
557   Special fabrics and materials
               Including buttons, zippers, lining
560   General special
562   Clothing for girls
565   Dress reform
  Tailoring. Men's clothing
    Periodicals, societies, etc.
570   Tailoring
572   Furnishing goods, etc.
    Directories, see TT495
574   Dictionaries and encyclopedias
    Tailoring
      General works
575   Early to 1800
580   1800-
583   Repairing, pressing, etc.
585   General special
590   Patternmaking and design
               Including cutting, drafting, measuring, and
                 grading
593   Study and teaching
595   Coats
600   Overcoats
603   Sleeves
605   Trousers. Slacks
610   Breeches
612   Shirts
615   Vests
616   Neckties
617   Men's fashions
618   Correct dress
           Catalogs and pricelists
620   General works
625   Uniforms
626   Livery
627   Furnishings
628   Sample books
630   Clothing for boys
633   Costumes for special occasions
         Children's clothing
           Cf. TT562, Clothing for girls
635   General works

```
                         Clothing manufacture
                         Children's clothing -- Continued
637                          Baby clothes.  Layettes
640                          Patterns, etc.
645                          Catalogs and pricelists
647                          Ecclesiastical vestments
                                 Cf. BV167, Religion (General)
                                 Cf. BX1925, Catholic Church
                                 Cf. BX5180, Church of England
                                 Cf. NK4850, Art industries
648                          Clothing for the handicapped
649                          Other special types of clothing
                                 Including work clothes, sport clothes
                             Millinery
                                 Cf. TS2180+, Hats
650                              Periodicals, societies, etc.
                                 Biography
653.A1                               Collective
653.A2-Z                             Individual, A-Z
655                              General works
657                              General special
660                              Illustrations and styles
665                              Catalogs and pricelists
666                          Gloves
                                 Cf. TS2160, Glove industry
667                          Handbags.  Tote bags
667.5                        Kerchiefs.  Bandannas
668                          Belts
                             Underwear.  Lingerie
669                              Periodicals, societies, etc.
670                              General works
                                 Special
675                                  Undershirts
677                                  Foundation garments
                                         Including corsets, girdles, brassieres, etc.
678                                  Other special
678.5                        Footwear
                                 Cf. TS989+, Boot and shoemaking
                             Knit goods, hosiery, sweaters, etc.  Machine knitting
                                 Cf. TS2160, Gloves
                                 Cf. TT819+, Hand knitting and crocheting
679                              Periodicals, societies, etc.
679.5                            Dictionaries and encyclopedias
680                              General works
681                              Hosiery
682                              Other special
683                              Trade publications
685                              Knitting and crocheting machinery
687                              Domestic machines
688                              Knit goods specifications
690                              General special
695                              Directories
```

TT

	Home arts. Homecrafts
	Including home arts for women
	Cf. GT480+, Manners and customs
697	Periodicals, societies, etc.
698	General works
	Textile arts and crafts
	Cf. TT387+, Soft home furnishings
	Cf. TT490+, Clothing manufacture
	Cf. TT925, Soft sculpture
699	General works
	Sewing. Needlework
	Cf. TT845, Needlework tools
700	Periodicals, societies, etc.
705	General works
708	Study and teaching
710	Textbooks
712	Juvenile works
713	Sewing by machine
	Cf. TJ1501+, Sewing machine construction
715	General special
	Mending
720	General works
730	Darning
	Decorative needlework. Fancy work
	Cf. NK9100+, Decorative work
740	Periodicals, societies, etc.
750	General works
751	General special
	Patterns
753	General works
755	Stamping
760	Stitches
	Embroidery
	Cf. NK9200+, Decorative art
	Cf. TS1783, Manufacture
769.A-Z	By region or country, A-Z
	Apply table at TT496.A-Z
770	General works
770.5	Juvenile works
771	General patterns
772	Machine embroidery
773	Classes of designs
	e.g. alphabets, birds, flowers
775	Articles embroidered
	e.g. doilies, table covers
777	Materials
	e.g. embroidery silk, gold thread
778.A-Z	Types of embroidery, A-Z
778.A87	Assisi
778.B5	Blackwork embroidery
778.B73	Brazilian dimensional embroidery
778.C24	Candlewicking
778.C3	Canvas embroidery

	Home arts. Homecrafts
	Textile arts and crafts
	Decorative needlework. Fancy work
	Embroidery
	Types of embroidery, A-Z -- Continued
778.C63	Couching
778.C65	Counted thread embroidery
778.C7	Crewelwork
778.C76	Cross-stitch
778.F33	Fagoting
778.H83	Huckaback
778.M47	Metal thread embroidery
778.S55	Shisha mirror embroidery
778.S64	Silk ribbon embroidery
778.S75	Stump work
778.W55	White work
779	Appliqué
	Drawnwork
785	General works
	Special kinds
787	Hardanger
791.A-Z	Other, A-Z
	Lacemaking
	Cf. NK9400+, Decorative art
	Cf. TS1782, Machine-made lace
800	General works
805.A-Z	Special laces, A-Z
805.B36	Battenberg lace
805.B63	Bobbin lace
805.H34	Hairpin lace
805.I74	Irish crochet lace
805.K54	Knitted lace
805.N43	Needlepoint lace
810	Lace craft
	Knitting and crocheting
	Cf. RM735.7.K54, Therapeutic use
	Cf. TT679+, Machine knitting
819.A-Z	By region or country, A-Z
	Apply table at TT496.A-Z
820	General works
825	Shawls, sweaters, socks and other articles
829	Toy-knitting. Spool-knitting for children
833	Locker hooking
	Class here general works on the technique of hooking. For works on making specific items, see the item, e.g. TT850, Rugs; TT850.2, Wall hangings
	Cf. TT850, Rugs
835	Quilting and patchwork
	Including quilts, coverlets, etc. made by this technique
	Cf. TT779, Appliqué
840.A-Z	Other kinds of fancy work, A-Z

TT

	Home arts. Homecrafts
	Textile arts and crafts
	Other kinds of fancy work, A-Z -- Continued
840.M33	Macramé
840.N48	Netting
840.R66	Ropework
840.S66	Smocking
840.S68	Sprang
840.T38	Tatting
845	Tools and supplies
	Including catalogs
847	Hand spinning
	Including use of the spinning wheel
	Cf. TS1480+, Industrial spinning
	Hand weaving
	Including hand weaving not requiring looms, e. g.
	card weaving
	Cf. TS1490+, Industrial weaving
848	General works
848.5	Handlooms
849	Tapestry
	Cf. NK2975+, Decorative art
	Cf. TH8481, Tapestrying (Wall decoration)
	Cf. TS1780, Machine-made tapestry
849.2	Hammocks
	Cf. GN415.3.H35, Ethnology
	Cf. TS1781, Textile manufacture
849.5	Felting
849.7	Textile finishing
850	Hand-made rugs, carpets, etc.
	Including those made by hooking
850.2	Flags. Banners. Wall hangings
850.5	Ribbon work
	Including paper ribbon work
	Textile decoration
	Cf. NK9500+, Decorative arts
	Cf. TP890+, Chemical industries
851	Textile painting
	Textile printing. Block printing
852	General works
852.5	Batik
	Cf. NK9503+, Decorative arts
852.6	Stencil printing
852.7	Transfer printing. Iron-on transfer work
	Cf. NK9510, Art industries
	Textile dyeing
	Including the dyeing of garments
853	General works
853.5	Tie-dyeing
	Dyes
854	General works
854.3	Natural
854.5	Synthetic

	Home arts. Homecrafts -- Continued
	Decorative crafts
	Cf. BM729.H35, Jewish handicraft
	Cf. TT205+, Metal crafts
855	Periodicals, societies, etc.
857	General works
860	Beadwork
	Cf. NK3650+, Decorative art
	Cf. TS2301.B4, Manufactures
	Cf. TT890.2, Bead flowers
862	Shellcraft
865	Sand craft
	Cf. NB1270.S3, Sand sculpture
	Cf. TT295, Sand casting
866	Wax craft
	Cf. NK9580+, Wax modeling
	Cf. TT894, Wax flowers
867	Rubber stamp printing
868	Potato printing
869	Typewriter art
869.5	Computer art. Computer craft
	Cf. N7433.8+, Visual arts
	Paperwork
	Including the use of cardboard, corrugated paper, etc.
	Cf. TL778, Paper airplanes
	Cf. TT175+, Paper dolls
	Cf. TT850.5, Paper ribbon work
	Cf. TT892, Paper flowers
870	General works
870.5	Box craft
	Including box making
871	Papier-mâché craft
	Cf. TS1155, Manufactures
872	Greeting card craft
	Including making Christmas cards, birthday cards, etc.
	Vegetable-fiber work
873	General works
873.5	Gourd craft
874	Pine needle crafts
874.5	Pine cone craft
875	Raffia and bast work
	Cf. LB1543, Primary education
876	Straw work
876.3	Grasswork
876.5	Rattan work
	Cf. TT197.8, Rattan furniture
877	Rush work
877.5	Palm frond weaving. Lauhala weaving
877.8	Water hyacinth craft
878	Cornhusk craft
879.A-Z	Special articles, A-Z

	Home arts. Homecrafts
	Decorative crafts
	Vegetable-fiber work
	Special articles, A-Z -- Continued
879.B3	Baskets
	Cf. NK3649.5+, Decorative arts
	Cf. TS910, Industrial basketmaking
879.J3	Jackets for bottles, etc.
	Wicker furniture, see TT197.7
880	Work in miscellaneous materials
	Including felt, string, braid
	Fancy articles
	Artificial flowers
890	General works
890.2	Bead flowers
890.3	Bread flowers
890.4	Ceramic flowers
	Fabric flowers
890.5	General works
890.7	Silk flowers
	Cf. SB449.3.S44, Flower arrangement
891	Feather flowers
892	Paper flowers
894	Wax flowers
896	Artificial fruits
896.5	Candles
	Cf. TP993, Chemical technology of candles
896.55	Chessmen
	Cf. NK4696, Decorative art
896.7	Decorated eggs. Eggshell craft
	Cf. NK4900, Decorative art of Easter eggs
896.8	Decorative balls
	Jewelry, see TT212
897	Lampshades
897.2	Lamps
	Cf. TK9921, Electricity for amateurs
	Cf. TT197.5.L34, Woodwork
898	Masks
	For theatrical masks, see PN2071.M37
898.2	Merry-go-round art
898.3	Mirrors
	Cf. NK8440+, Decorative arts
899	Mobiles
	Cf. NB1272, Sculpture
899.3	Pincushions
	Cf. NK4660, Pincushion dolls
899.4	Potpourris (Scented floral mixtures)
899.5	Tassels
899.7	Windchimes
899.73	Door harps
899.74	Tabletop fountains
	Plant containers and container gardening equipment, see SB418.4

	Home arts. Homecrafts
	Decorative crafts
	Fancy articles -- Continued
899.75	Wreaths
	Cf. SB449.5.W74, Flower arrangement
900.A-Z	Decorations for special events, A-Z
900.C4	Christmas
	Cf. GT4988, Manners and customs
900.E2	Easter
900.H32	Halloween
900.H34	Hanukkah
900.H6	Holidays
900.K92	Kwanzaa
900.P3	Parties
900.S25	Saint Patrick's Day
900.T5	Thanksgiving
900.V34	Valentine's Day
	Other special techniques
910	Collage, assemblage, constructions, etc. in miscellaneous materials
	Cf. N6494.A8, Assemblage (Art)
	Cf. N6494.C6, Collage (Art)
	Cf. TR685, Composite photography
911	Face painting (Handicrafts)
912	Rubbing craft
	Cf. NB1840+, Sculpture
	Cf. NC915.R8, Graphic arts
916	Modeling in clay, etc.
	Cf. NB1180, Sculpture
	Pottery craft
	Cf. NK3700+, Ceramics (Art industries)
	Cf. TP807+, Ceramic technology
	Cf. TT890.4, Ceramic flowers
919	Periodicals, societies, etc.
919.5	Dictionaries and encyclopedias
919.7.A-Z	By region or country, A-Z
	Apply table at TT496.A-Z
920	General works
921	Juvenile works
	Equipment and supplies
921.5	General works
922	Glazes
924	Kilns
925	Soft sculpture
	Cf. NB1203, Sculpture
926	Balloon sculpture. Balloon decorations
927	Tile craft
	Hairdressing, barbering, beauty culture, cosmetology, etc.
	Including beauty shop practice
950	Periodicals, societies, collections, etc.
951	Dictionaries and encyclopedias
	Documents

Hairdressing, barbering,
    beauty culture, cosmetology, etc.
    Documents -- Continued
      United States

952	General works
953.A-W	States, A-W
954.A-Z	Other countries, A-Z
954.5	Directories
	Biography
955.A1	Collective
955.A2-Z	Individual, A-Z
	General works
956	Before 1800
957	1800-
958	General special
	Including vocational guidance
958.3	Nail care. Manicuring

        Class here works on nail care as practiced by
          professionals and beauty operators
        For nail care as practiced by individuals, see RL94

958.5	Skin care

        Class here works on skin care as practiced by beauty
          operators
        For skin care as practiced by individuals, see RL87

959	Permanent makeup
960	Barbers' manuals
963	Hair styles for men
964	Shaving
	Shop management
965	General works
	Equipment and supplies
966	General works
	Catalogs, see TT979
967	Razors
968	Other special
969	Materials
	Including dyes, oils, soaps, etc.
970	Haircutting (General)
	Cf. TT960, Barber's manuals
971	Study and teaching
	Hairdressing for women
972	General works
973	Hair tinting and bleaching
	Hairwork
975	Braids, wigs, toupees, etc.
976	Ornaments, jewelry, etc.
977	Receipts for barbers
979	Catalogs of equipment and supplies
	Laundry work
	Cf. GT482, Laundering customs
	Cf. TP932 +, Dry cleaning
980	Periodicals, societies, etc.
983	Directories

Laundry work -- Continued
985	General and domestic
990	Commercial. Steam-laundry work
991	Blueing and bleaching
993	Starching
995	Ironing
997	Materials. Machinery
998	General special
999	Catalogs, etc.

TT

	Home economics
1	Periodicals, societies, etc.
5	Congresses
	Exhibitions. Museums
6.A1	General works
6.A2-Z	By region or country, A-Z
	Under each country:
.x	*General works*
.x2A-Z	*Special. By city, A-Z*
	Collected works (nonserial)
7	Collections by several authors
8	Collected works of individual authors
9	Minor collections: Papers, essays, etc.
11	Dictionaries and encyclopedias
13	Theory. Philosophy
	History and antiquities
	Including manners and customs, gastronomy, etc.
	Cf. GT1+, Manners and customs
	For modern works on gastronomy, see TX631+
15	General works
16	Ancient
17	Medieval
18	17th-18th centuries
19	19th-20th centuries
21-127	Special countries (Table T1)
	Add country number in table to TX0
	Biography
139	Collective
140.A-Z	Individual, A-Z
	General works
144	Early to 1800
145	1800-
	Textbooks, see TX167
147	General special
	Including economics of daily life for men, institutional administration
148	Juvenile works
149	Household science (Chemistry, physics, etc.)
150	Home accidents and their prevention
	Pocketbooks, tables, receipts, etc.
	Class here works which emphasize household economics
151	16th-18th century
	19th century
153	American
154	English
155	French
156	German
157	Other (not A-Z)
	20th century
158	American
159	English
160	French
161	German

	Pocketbooks, tables, receipts, etc.
	20th century -- Continued
162	Other (not A-Z)
164	Home economics as a profession
	Study and teaching
165.A1	Periodicals, societies, etc.
165.A3-Z	General works
167	Textbooks
170	Examinations, questions, etc.
170.7	Laboratory manuals
171-277	Special countries (Table T1)
	Add country number in table to TX150
	Special schools
285.A-Z	United States. By school, A-Z
286.A-Z	Other countries. By school, A-Z
295	Essays, light literature, fiction, etc.
	Household apparatus and utensils
	Cf. TX656 +, Kitchen utensils
298	General works
299	Catalogs
	The house
	Cf. NA7120, Domestic architecture (Popular works)
	Cf. TH4805 +, House construction
	Cf. TX653 +, Kitchens
	Cf. TX855 +, Dining rooms
301	General works
303	General special
	Location
305	General works
307	Household moving
309	Arrangement
	Furnishing
	Cf. TT387 +, Soft home furnishings (Handicraft)
311	General works
315	General special
	Including sheets and pillowcases
(317)	Decoration and ornament
	see NK1700-NK3505
	Administration
321	General works
323	Care of the house
	Cf. TH2528, Flooring
	Cf. TH4817 +, Home maintenance and repair
324	Cleaning
	Including silver cleaning
325	Household pests
	Cf. RA639 +, Insects and disease
	Cf. SB818 +, Economic entomology
	Cf. SB992 +, Noxious and useful animals
	Cf. TA423.7, Termite control
	Finance, budgets, bookkeeping, accounts
	Cf. HD6977 +, Cost of living
	For early works, see TX15 +

TX

	The house
	Administration
	Finance, budgets,
	bookkeeping, accounts -- Continued
326.A1	Periodicals. Societies. Serials
326.A3-Z	General works
	Servants
331	General works
333	General special. Morals, conduct, etc.
	Biography
334	Collective
334.1.A-Z	Individual, A-Z
	Shopping. Consumer education
	Including shopping guides and directories of
	discount and outlet stores
	Cf. TX356, Marketing for food
	For economic aspects of discount and outlet
	stores, see HF5429.2 +
335	General works
335.5	Juvenile works
	By region or country
	United States
336	General works
336.5.A-Z	By region or state, A-Z
	Under each state:
	.x *General works*
	.x2A-Z *Local, A-Z*
337.A-Z	Other regions or countries, A-Z
	Under each country:
	.x *General works*
	.x2A-Z *Local, A-Z*
339	Janitor service
	Cf. LB3235, Schoolhouse service
	Cf. TX957 +, Apartment house service
340	Clothing
	Cf. TT490 +, Clothing manufacture
	Cf. TT700 +, Sewing
	Cf. TT980 +, Laundry work
	Nutrition. Foods and food supply
	Cf. HD9000 +, Provision trade
	Cf. TP368 +, Food processing industry
	Cf. TP500 +, Beverage industry
	Cf. TS1950 +, Butchering, packinghouse industries
	Cf. TS1975, Meat inspection
	Cf. TS2120 +, Cereal and grain milling industry
	Periodicals, societies, etc. Food research institutes
	Cf. PN4784.F55, Journalism
341	General periodicals
343	Grocery trade periodicals
	Periodicals relating to adulteration and
	inspection, see TX501
345	Congresses
	Directories of grocers, see HD9320 +

	Nutrition. Foods and food supply -- Continued
	Exhibitions. Pure food shows, etc.
346.A1	General works
346.A2-Z	Special. By city, A-Z
	Apply table at TX6.A2-Z
	Dictionaries and encyclopedias
	Including dictionaries of cookery
349	General works
350	Bilingual and polyglot
	Biography
350.7	Collective
350.8.A-Z	Individual, A-Z
	General works. Sources, supply, etc.
351	Early to 1800
353	1800-
354	Textbooks
354.5	Grocers' catalogs
355	Popular works. Juvenile works
	Cf. TX149, Household science
	Cf. TX533, Food adulteration, etc.
355.5	Addresses, essays, lectures
356	Marketing for food. Economy. Thrift
357	General special
	Including dietitians, food economy in war time
359	Nutrition policy
	Prefer classification by country in TX360.A-TX360.Z
	Cf. HD9000.6, Food products industry
	Diet, food supply, nutrition policy of special
	countries
360.A-Z	By region or country, A-Z
	e.g.
	Under each country:
.x	*General works*
.x2A-Z	*By state, province, etc., A-Z*
.x3A-Z	*Special. By city, A-Z*
	United States
360.U6	General works
360.U62A-W	By state, A-W
360.U63A-Z	By city, A-Z
360.5	Developing countries
361.A-Z	Diet and nutrition of special classes and groups, A-Z
361.A27	Afro-Americans
361.A3	Aged
361.A4	Agricultural laborers
361.A8	Athletes
361.B64	Bodybuilders
361.C5	Children
361.C6	College students
361.C94	Cyclists
361.E93	Executives
361.F37	Farmers
361.F5	Fishers
361.H35	Handicapped

Nutrition. Foods and food supply
   Diet and nutrition of
      special classes and groups, A-Z -- Continued
361.H57   Hispanic Americans
361.H65   Homeless
      Low-income groups, see TX361.P66
361.M47   Middle aged persons
361.M48   Migrant laborers
361.M5   Miners
361.P66   Poor. Low-income groups
361.R86   Runners
361.T45   Tennis players
361.W55   Women
361.W6   Workers
361.W7   Working women
361.Y6   Youth
     Study and teaching
364   General works
365.A-Z   Special schools, A-Z
367   Research
        For food research institutes, see TX341+
     Markets, see HF5469.7+
     Grocery business, see HD9320+
369   Natural foods
370   Junk food. Convenience foods
     Animal foods
        Cf. TS1960+, Butchering, packinghouse
           industries, etc.
        Cf. TS1975, Meat inspection
371   General works
373   Butchers' meats
375   Poultry and game
        Cf. SF481+, Poultry culture
     Dairy foods
        Cf. SF221+, Dairying
377   General works
379   Milk
380   Yogurt
381   Butter
382   Cheese
383   Eggs
        Cf. SF481+, Poultry culture
385   Fish
        Cf. SH1+, Fisheries
387   Shellfish
        Cf. SH365+, Fisheries
        Cf. SH380+, Lobster fisheries
388.A-Z   Other natural products, A-Z
388.I5   Insects
388.T8   Turtles
388.W4   Whales
389   Prepared foods, meat extracts, etc.
       Including trade publications

	Nutrition. Foods and food supply -- Continued
	Vegetable foods
391	General works
	Vegetarianism
	Cf. BL65.V44, Religious aspects
	Cf. TX837 +, Cookery
392.A1-A4	Periodicals, societies, etc.
392.A5-Z	General works
	Biography
392.7	Collective
392.8.A-Z	Individual, A-Z
	Cereals
393	General works
394	Bread
394.5	Pasta products
395	Prepared cereals
	Cf. TP435.C4, Food processing industry
396	Flowers
397	Fruits
399	Nuts
	Vegetables
401	General works
401.2.A-Z	Special, A-Z
401.2.P67	Potatoes
401.2.S69	Soybeans and soybean products
	Including soy sauce
402	Algae as food
	Including marine algae
	Condiments, spices, etc.
406	General works
407.A-Z	Special, A-Z
407.M38	Mayonnaise
407.O34	Oils and fats, Edible
407.S69	Soy sauce
409	Baking powders, etc.
	Beverages
	Cf. TP620 +, Chemical technology
412	General works
415	Tea, coffee, cocoa, etc.
	Examination and analysis. Composition. Adulteration
	For food processing, see TP372.5 +
	For foods and public health, see RA601 +
	For meat inspection, see TS1975
501	Periodicals, societies, etc.
	Including those relating to adulteration and inspection
	Cf. TX341 +, Nutrition
511	Congresses
	For pure food congresses, see HD9000.9.A1 +
515	History
	Biography
517	Collective

TX

Nutrition. Foods and food supply
   Examination and analysis.
      Composition. Adulteration
      Biography -- Continued

518.A-Z	Individual, A-Z
	e.g.
518.W5	Wiley, H. W.
531	General works
533	Popular works
535	General special. Pamphlets
537	Food standards, etc.
	Analysis (Methods)
541	General works
542	Magnetic resonance imaging
543	Microscopic
544	Thermal
545	Chemical
546	Sensory evaluation
	Spectrum analysis
547	General works
547.2.A-Z	Special methods, A-Z
547.2.I53	Infrared spectroscopy
	Chromatography
548	General works
548.2.A-Z	Special methods, A-Z
548.2.G36	Gas
548.2.L55	Liquid
548.2.T48	Thin layer
549	Immunoassay
	Dietary studies, food values, experiments, tests,
	etc.
	Cf. RM214 +, Therapeutics
	Cf. TX341 +, Food supply
	Cf. TX361.A +, Foods for special classes
551	General works
552	Canned foods
552.15	Baked products
553.A-Z	Special constituents, A-Z
553.A3	Additives
553.A5	Amino acids
553.A7	Antibiotics
553.A73	Antioxidants
553.A8	Ascorbic acid
553.C23	Calcium
553.C28	Carbohydrates
553.C3	Carotinoids
553.C43	Cholesterol
553.C45	Choline
553.E6	Enzymes
553.F53	Fibers
553.G47	Gluten
553.I75	Iron
553.L5	Lipids

Nutrition. Foods and food supply
Examination and analysis.
Composition. Adulteration
Dietary studies, food values,
experiments, tests, etc.
Special constituents, A-Z -- Continued

553.M55	Minerals
553.P4	Pectic substances
553.P45	Phosphorus
553.P65	Polysaccharides
553.P7	Proteins
553.S65	Sodium
553.S8	Sugar
553.T7	Trace elements
553.U5	Unsaturated fatty acids
553.V5	Vitamins
553.W3	Water

Special foods
Animal foods

555	General works
556.A-Z	Special, A-Z
556.B4	Beef
556.B8	Buffalo
	Dairy products, see TX556.M5
556.E4	Eggs
556.H8	Horsemeat
556.L3	Lamb
556.M4	Meat
556.M43	Meat, Precooked
556.M5	Milk and milk products
556.P6	Pigeons
556.P8	Pork
556.P9	Poultry
556.V4	Venison
556.5	Fish. Seafood

Vegetables, cereals, fruits, etc.

557	General works
558.A-Z	Special, A-Z
558.A3	Acorns
558.A6	Apples
558.B3	Bananas
558.B35	Barley
	Bean curd, see TX558.T57
558.B4	Beans
558.B6	Bran
558.B7	Bread
558.C2	Cabbage
558.C35	Cassava
558.C38	Chia
558.C4	Chickpea
558.C5	Citrus fruits
558.C57	Corn. Cornmeal. Maize
558.C6	Cowpea

TX

Nutrition. Foods and food supply
Examination and analysis.
Composition. Adulteration
Dietary studies, food values,
experiments, tests, etc.
Special foods
Vegetables, cereals, fruits, etc.
Special, A-Z -- Continued

558.D3	Dasheen
558.D35	Date
	Flour, see TX558.W5
558.F7	Fruit (General)
558.G6	Grapes
558.G67	Groats
558.H2	Hay
558.L4	Legumes (General)
558.L5	Lemon
558.L6	Logan blackberry
	Maize. Corn, cornmeal, see TX558.C57
558.M5	Millet
558.M9	Mushrooms and other fungi
558.N6	Nori
558.N8	Nuts
558.O3	Oats
558.O5	Olives
558.O7	Oranges
558.P3	Peaches
558.P35	Peas
558.P8	Potatoes
558.R4	Rhubarb
558.R5	Rice
558.R9	Rye
558.S6	Sorghum
558.S7	Soybean
558.S75	Sprouts
558.S8	Starches
558.S94	Sweet potatoes
558.T39	Tempeh
558.T57	Tofu
558.T6	Tomatoes
558.T7	Triticale
558.V4	Vegetable juices
558.W5	Wheat. Flour
	Miscellaneous products
559	General works
560.A-Z	Special, A-Z
560.A3	Alcohol
560.B8	Bread
560.C2	Cacao
	Cocoa-butter, see TP684.C2
560.C63	Coffee
560.C65	Confectionery
560.C7	Cottonseed products

Nutrition. Foods and food supply
Examination and analysis.
Composition. Adulteration
Dietary studies, food values,
experiments, tests, etc.
Special foods
Miscellaneous products
Special, A-Z -- Continued

560.D68	Dough
560.F3	Fats (Animal and vegetable)
560.F47	Fermented food
560.H7	Honey
560.M2	Macaroni
560.M3	Maple sugar. Maple syrup
560.M35	Mate (Tea)
560.N7	Nut oils
560.O3	Oils (General)
560.O4	Olive oil
560.P6	Pollen
560.S4	Seed oils
560.S9	Sugar
560.Y4	Yeast

Adulterants and adulteration, impurities, etc.
Cf. QP501+, Physiological effects of
chemicals
Cf. RA601+, Public hygiene - Foods
General works, see TX531

563	Detection of adulterants
567	Microscopic analysis
569	Chemical analysis

Special adulterants and impurities

571.A-Z	By classes, A-Z

Cf. TX599+, Preservatives

571.A58	Antibiotic residues
571.C7	Coloring matter
571.G3	Gases, Asphyxiating and poisonous
571.M48	Metals
571.P4	Pesticide residues
571.P63	Plastics. Urethanes
571.R3	Radioactivity
571.S65	Solvents
571.S9	Sweeteners, Artificial

Urethanes, see TX571.P63

571.V48	Veterinary drug residues
571.X45	Xenobiotics
572.A-Z	By chemical composition, A-Z
572.A6	Aluminum
572.A77	Arsenic
572.C4	Cadmium
572.C6	Calcium sulphate
572.H4	Heavy metals
572.L4	Lead
572.M4	Mercury

TX

Nutrition. Foods and food supply
  Examination and analysis.
    Composition. Adulteration
     Adulterants and adulteration, impurities, etc.
      Special adulterants and impurities
       By chemical composition, A-Z -- Continued

572.N5	Nitrates, nitrites
572.P65	Polychlorinated biphenyls
572.S79	Styrene
572.S9	Sulphurous acid
572.T6	Tin

     Special foods
      Including methods of analysis

583	Coffee
585	Tea
	Milk, see SF254.A1 +
	Spices
587	General works
588.A-Z	Special, A-Z
589	Flavoring extracts
595.A-Z	Other foods, A-Z
595.F47	Fish
595.F5	Flour
595.R37	Rape oil
595.T6	Tomatoes
	Beverages
596	General works
597	Alcoholic beverages

       Cf. TP612, Compounding

Preservation and storage of foods in the home. Food
  handling in the home
    Cf. HD9320 +, Grocery trade
    Cf. RA601 +, Public hygiene
    Cf. SB129 +, Farm produce
    Cf. SF250.5 +, Dairy products
    Cf. SH334.9 +, Fishery products
    Cf. TP371.2 +, Food processing industry
    Cf. TS1968, Poultry processing

599	Periodicals, societies, yearbooks, etc.
600	Directories
601	General works
602	Study and teaching. Research
603	Canning
	Cold storage, see TP372.2
	Chemical treatment. Preservatives, see TP371.4 +
609	Drying, smoking, etc.
	Cf. TX835, Smoked foods cookery
610	Freezing
	Sterilization, see TP371.35
	Radiation sterilization, see TP371.8
612.A-Z	Special foods and condiments, A-Z
612.A6	Apples
612.B4	Berries

Nutrition. Foods and food supply
  Preservation and storage of
    foods in the home. Food handling in the home
    Special foods and condiments, A-Z -- Continued

612.C5	Cherries
612.E4	Eggs
612.F5	Fish (General)
612.F7	Fruit (General)
	Game dressing and skinning, see SK36.2
612.J3	Jam (General)
612.J4	Jelly (General)
612.M37	Marmalade
612.M4	Meat
612.M8	Mushrooms
612.T7	Tomatoes
612.V4	Vegetables (General)
	Cf. SB324.85, Storage for market

Gastronomy, pleasures of the table, dining, etc.

631	General works
633	American
635	English
637	French
639	German
641	Other (not A-Z)

Cookery
  Periodicals, see TX1
  Exhibitions. Museums, see TX6.A1+

642	Collectors and collecting. Collectibles
	Dictionaries and encyclopedias, see TX349+

Communication of cookery information

643	General works
644	Language. Authorship
645	History
648	Awards, prizes, etc. Competitions
	Biography
649.A1	Collective
649.A2-Z	Individual, A-Z
650	Directories
	For directories of restaurants, etc., see TX907+
	General works
651	Treatises
	Class here works emphasizing technique of cookery, with or without recipes
	Cf. TX714, General recipe collections
652	General special
652.5	Juvenile works
652.7	Minor works, tables, etc.
652.9	Essays, lectures, etc.
	Kitchen
653	General works
655	Arrangement
	Equipment, appliances, utensils, etc.
	Cf. NK6140, Kitchen collectibles

TX

Cookery
    Equipment, appliances, utensils, etc. -- Continued

656	General works
657.A-Z	Special, A-Z
657.A66	Apple parers
657.B34	Baking pans
	Chafing dishes, see TX825
657.C67	Coffee making paraphernalia
657.C7	Cookers
657.C72	Cookie molds. Cookie cutters
	Cookware
657.C74	General works
	Baking pans, see TX657.B34
	Kettles, see TX657.K4
657.C76	Corkscrews
657.D6	Dishwashing machines
657.E35	Eggbeaters
	Fireless cookers, see TX831
657.F7	Fryers
657.I24	Ice cream scoops
657.K4	Kettles
657.K54	Knives
657.M85	Muffin pans
657.N87	Nutcrackers
	Ovens
657.O57	Brick. Clay
657.O6	Gas
657.O64	Microwave
657.P6	Potato peeling machines
657.S28	Spoons
	Stoves and ranges
	Cf. TS425, Stove manufacture
657.S3	General
657.S4	Coal
657.S5	Electric
657.S6	Gas
657.S7	Gasoline
657.S8	Oil
657.S9	Wood
657.T43	Tea making paraphernalia
	Toasters
657.T58	Electric
657.T6	Gas
658	Catalogs of miscellaneous articles
	Study and teaching
661	General works
663	Textbooks, etc.
	Special schools
667	American
669.A-Z	Other countries, A-Z
	Cooking processes
681	General works
683	Baking

	Cookery
	Cooking processes -- Continued
685	Boiling
686	Braising
687	Broiling
	Frying
689	General works
689.4	Sautéing
689.5	Stir frying
690	Roasting
691	Steaming
693	Stewing. Cooking en casserole
	Cookbooks
	Early to 1800
703	American. Canadian
705	English
707	French
709	German
711	Italian
713	Other (not A-Z)
	1800-
714	General recipe collections
	Class here works consisting of collected recipes not primarily of a regional, ethnic, or international nature, nor using a specific ingredient or method of cooking, in which the technique of cookery is not emphasized
	For ethnic or regional cookery, see TX714+
	For international cookery, see TX725.A1
	For treatises, see TX651
	American
	For French, German, etc., cookbooks published in America, see TX719, TX721, etc.
715	General works
715.2.A-Z	By style of cookery, A-Z
715.2.C34	California style
	Hawaiian style, see TX724.5.H3
715.2.L68	Louisiana style
715.2.M53	Midwestern style
715.2.N48	New England style
715.2.P32	Pacific Northwest style
	Pennsylvania Dutch style, see TX721
715.2.S68	Southern style
715.2.S69	Southwestern style
715.2.W47	Western style
715.6	Canadian
715.8	Greenlandic
	Latin American
716.A1	General works
716.A3-Z	By country, A-Z
717	English
717.2	Celtic
717.3	Scottish

TX

	Cookery
	Cookbooks
	1800- -- Continued
717.5	Irish
717.7	Welsh
	French
719	General works
719.2.A-Z	By style of cookery, A-Z
719.2.A45	Alsatian
719.2.B74	Brittany
719.2.B87	Burgundy
719.2.F73	Franche-Comté
719.2.G37	Gascony
719.2.N67	Normandy
719.2.P75	Provençal
721	German. Austrian
	Including Pennsylvania-Dutch cookbooks
	Scandinavian
722.A1	General works
722.A3-Z	By country, A-Z
	Italian
723	General works
723.2.A-Z	By style of cookery, A-Z
723.2.N65	Northern
723.2.S55	Sicilian
723.2.S65	Southern
723.2.T86	Tuscan
	Russian
723.3	European
723.4	Asiatic
	Including Caucasian
	Other European
723.5.A1	General works
723.5.A3-Z	By country, A-Z
724	Jewish. Israeli
	Cf. TX739.2.H35, Hanukkah
	Cf. TX739.2.P37, Passover
	Oriental
	Including East Asian, South Asian, Southeast Asian, and Polynesian
	For Asiatic Russian, see TX723.4
	For Middle Eastern, see TX725.M628
724.5.A1	General works
724.5.A3-Z	By region or country, etc., A-Z
	e. g.
724.5.C5	Chinese
724.5.H3	Hawaiian
724.5.I4	India
724.5.I5	Indonesia
724.5.J3	Japan
724.5.K65	Korea
724.5.T5	Thailand
724.5.V5	Vietnam

	Cookery
	Cookbooks
	1800- -- Continued
	Other
725.A1	International
725.A3-Z	By region or country, A-Z
	Including Africa, Australia, Middle East, etc.
725.M628	Middle East
(725.N36)	Near East
	see TX725.M628
	Cookery using alcoholic beverages
726	Wine. Liquors
726.2	Cider
726.3	Beer
	Menus, bills of fare, kitchen almanacs, etc.
	Cf. TX911.3.M45, Hotels, clubs, restaurants,
	etc.
727	Early to 1800
728	1800-
731	Entertaining, dinner-giving, etc.
	For entertaining in which food is not primary, see
	GV1+
	Special meals
	For individual foods or ingredients, see TX743+
	For special methods of cookery, see TX820.2+
733	Breakfasts. Brunches
735	Luncheons
	Including lunchbox cookery
736	Afternoon teas
	Cf. GT2905+, Tea customs
	Cf. TX817.T3, Beverages
737	Dinners
738	Suppers
738.5	Buffets
	Special occasions. Holidays
739	General works
739.2.A-Z	By occasion or holiday, A-Z
739.2.C45	Christmas
739.2.E37	Easter
	Fast day, see TX837+
739.2.H34	Halloween
739.2.H35	Hanukkah
	Lent, see TX837+
739.2.P37	Passover
	Picnics, see TX823
739.2.T45	Thanksgiving
739.2.V34	Valentine's Day
740	Miscellaneous recipes. Canapes, hors d'oeuvres,
	salads, etc.
	For vegetable salads, see TX807
740.5	Food presentation. Garnishes
741	Natural foods
	Animal food

TX

	Cookery
	Animal food -- Continued
743	General works
745	Eggs
746	Insects
746.2	Earthworms
	Fish. Seafood
747	General works
748.A-Z	Special, A-Z
748.A53	Anchovies
748.B37	Bass
748.B55	Bluefish
748.B67	Bowfin
748.B85	Burbot
748.C35	Carp
748.C36	Catfish
748.C63	Codfish
748.C73	Crappie
748.D64	Dogfish
748.E32	Eels
748.F83	Fugu
(748.G7)	Grayfish
	see TX748.D64
748.G74	Groupers
748.H33	Haddock
748.H45	Herring
748.M32	Mackerel
748.M84	Mullet
748.P54	Pike
748.P64	Pollock
748.S24	Salmon
748.S26	Sardines
748.S5	Sharks
748.S58	Skates (Fishes)
748.S68	Squid
748.S75	Striped bass
748.T54	Tilefish
748.T74	Trout
748.T84	Tuna
748.W48	Whale meat
	Meat
749	General works
749.5.A-Z	Special, A-Z
749.5.B43	Beef
	Game, see TX751
749.5.H35	Ham
749.5.H67	Horsemeat
749.5.L35	Lamb and mutton
749.5.P67	Pork
	Poultry, see TX750 +
749.5.R32	Rabbit
749.5.S28	Sausages
749.5.V37	Variety meats

	Cookery
	Animal food -- Continued
	Poultry
750	General works
750.5.A-Z	Special, A-Z
750.5.C45	Chicken
750.5.D82	Duck
750.5.E45	Emu
750.5.O77	Ostrich
750.5.P45	Pheasant
750.5.Q34	Quail
750.5.T87	Turkey
751	Game
	Shellfish
753	General works
754.A-Z	Special, A-Z
754.C53	Clams
754.C83	Crabs
754.C84	Crayfish
754.L63	Lobsters
754.M98	Mussels
754.O98	Oysters
754.S58	Shrimp
754.S63	Snails
757	Soups
	Dairy products
759	General works
759.5.A-Z	Special, A-Z
759.5.B87	Butter
759.5.C48	Cheese
	Evaporated milk, see TX759.5.M54
759.5.M54	Milk
759.5.S68	Sour cream and milk
759.5.Y63	Yogurt
	Baking. Confectionery
	Cf. GT5960.B34+, Manners and customs
761	Periodicals, societies, etc.
763	General works
765	Minor works, recipe books, etc.
767.A-Z	Recipes for special food products, A-Z
767.A65	Apple butter
767.C5	Chocolate
767.H7	Honey
767.M3	Maple sugar and syrup
767.W48	White chocolate
	Bread
769	General works
770.A-Z	Special breads, A-Z
770.B35	Bagels
770.B55	Biscuits. Scones
770.C72	Crackers
	Crepes, see TX770.P34
770.C74	Croissants

TX

                                    Cookery
                                      Baking.   Confectionery
                                        Bread
                                          Special breads, A-Z -- Continued
770.D67   Doughnuts
770.F55   Filo dough
770.F63   Focaccia
770.F73   French toast
770.M83   Muffins
770.P34   Pancakes.   Waffles.   Crepes
770.P56   Pita bread
770.P58   Pizza
770.P73   Pretzels
                                              Scones, see TX770.B55
770.S66   Sourdough bread
770.T65   Tortillas
                                              Waffles, see TX770.P34
                                        Cakes
771   General works
771.2   Cake decorating
772   Cookies
773   Desserts, pies, and puddings.   Pastry
775   Directories of bakers, etc.
776   Bakers' trade publications
778   Bakers' and confectioners' supplies
                                              Including catalogs
                                              Cf. TX657.B34, Baking pans
                                        Confectionery
                                          Periodicals, see TX761
783   General works
                                          Candy
784   History of candy manufacture
791   General works
792   Juvenile works
793   Candymakers' tools, etc.
                                          Desserts, see TX773
                                          Ice creams and ices
795.A1   Periodicals, societies, etc.
795.A2-Z   General works
799   General special
                                    Vegetables (Preparation)
                                        Cf. TX392+, Vegetarianism
801   General works
803.A-Z   Special vegetables, A-Z
803.A7   Artichokes
803.A8   Asparagus
                                           Bean curd, see TX814.5.T63
803.B4   Beans
803.B66   Broccoli
803.B7   Brussels sprouts
803.C3   Cabbage
803.C35   Carrots
803.C37   Cassava

Cookery
  Vegetables (Preparation)
    Special vegetables, A-Z -- Continued

803.C68	Cowpeas
803.D34	Dandelions
803.E4	Eggplant
803.F85	Fungi
803.G74	Greens
803.L4	Leeks
803.O37	Okra
803.O5	Onions
803.P35	Peanuts
	Cf. TX814.5.P38, Peanut butter
803.P4	Peas
803.P46	Peppers
803.P8	Potatoes
803.P93	Pumpkin
803.R33	Radishes
803.R58	Rhubarb
803.S6	Soybeans
803.S63	Spaghetti squash
803.S67	Squash
803.S94	Sweet potatoes
803.T6	Tomatoes
	Cf. TX814.5.T65, Tomato paste
	Vegetable spaghetti, see TX803.S63
803.Z82	Zucchini
804	Mushrooms
	Including specific types of mushrooms
804.5	Truffles
805	Pickles
806	Kimch'i
807	Salads

  Cereals (Preparation)

808.A1	Periodicals, societies, etc.
808.A2-Z	General works
809.A-Z	Special, A-Z
	Cf. TX395, Prepared cereals
	Cf. TX803.A+, Special vegetables
809.B75	Brown rice
809.B8	Buckwheat
809.B85	Bulgur
	Corn, see TX809.M2
809.G55	Gluten
809.G7	Granola
809.M17	Macaroni. Pasta
809.M2	Maize. Corn
809.N65	Noodles
809.O22	Oat bran
809.O23	Oats
	Pasta, see TX809.M17
809.P67	Porridge
809.R5	Rice

TX

Cookery
Cereals (Preparation)
Special, A-Z -- Continued
809.R52   Rice flour
809.S64   Spelt
809.W45   Wheat
809.W453   Wheat germ
809.W55   Wild rice
Fruits (Preparation)
811   General works
813.A-Z   Special fruits, A-Z
813.A6   Apples
813.A64   Apricots
813.A9   Avocados
813.B3   Bananas
813.B4   Berries
813.B5   Blueberries
813.C4   Cherries
813.C5   Citrus fruits
813.C7   Cranberries
813.C87   Currant grapes
813.D3   Dates
813.F5   Figs
813.G73   Grapefruit
813.H83   Huckleberries
813.K55   Kiwifruit
813.L4   Lemons
813.L55   Limes
813.M35   Mangos
813.O4   Olives
813.O6   Oranges
813.P3   Papaya
813.P38   Peach palm
813.P4   Peaches
813.P43   Pears
813.P45   Persimmons
813.P5   Pineapples
813.P55   Plums
813.P78   Prunes
813.R34   Raisins
813.R37   Raspberries
813.S9   Strawberries
Nuts (Preparation)
814   General works
814.2.A-Z   Special nuts, A-Z
814.2.A25   Acorns
814.2.A44   Almonds
814.2.C48   Chestnuts
814.2.C63   Coconuts
814.2.H39   Hazelnuts
814.2.M33   Macadamia
814.2.P4   Pecans
814.2.W3   Walnuts

	Cookery -- Continued
814.5.A-Z	Other, A-Z
	Bean curd, see TX814.5.T63
814.5.C35	Carob
814.5.F5	Flowers
814.5.G4	Gelatin
814.5.H45	Hemp
814.5.J35	Jam
814.5.K83	Kudzu
814.5.P38	Peanut butter
814.5.P66	Popcorn
814.5.R58	Roselles
814.5.R6	Roses
814.5.S34	Sago
814.5.S44	Seeds
814.5.S47	Sesame
814.5.T45	Tempeh
814.5.T48	Textured soy protein
814.5.T63	Tofu
814.5.T64	Tomato juice
814.5.T65	Tomato paste
	Beverages
	Cf. TP500+, Technology
	Cf. TX726+, Cookery using alcoholic beverages
	Cf. TX951, Bartenders' manuals
815	General works
817.A-Z	Special beverages, A-Z
	Beer, see TX726.3
817.C4	Chocolate
817.C5	Cocoa
817.C6	Coffee
817.M5	Milkshakes. Malted milk
817.T3	Tea
818	Sandwiches
	Condiments, sauces, etc.
819.A1	General works
819.A3-Z	Special, A-Z
	Cf. TX740, Canapes, hor d'oeuvres, etc.
	Cf. TX805, Pickles
819.B37	Basil
819.C53	Cinnamon
819.C6	Coffee (as a flavor)
819.C65	Coriander
819.C9	Curry
819.F78	Fructose
819.G3	Garlic
819.G53	Ginger
819.G55	Glutamate
819.H4	Herbs
	Cf. GT5164, Manners and customs
819.H66	Hot peppers
819.K48	Ketchup
819.L38	Lavender

TX

	Cookery
	Condiments, sauces, etc.
	Special, A-Z -- Continued
819.M25	Marijuana
819.M26	Marinades
819.M3	Mayonnaise
819.M56	Mint
819.M57	Miso
819.M65	Molasses
819.M87	Mustard
819.O4	Olive butter
819.O42	Olive oil
819.P3	Pepper
819.P45	Pestos
819.S24	Saffron
819.S27	Salad dressing
819.S29	Salsas
819.S58	Soy sauce
819.S75	Stevia
819.S8	Stocks
819.S94	Sugar
819.S96	Syrups
819.V35	Vanilla
819.V5	Vinegar
819.W5	White sauce
819.W65	Worcestershire sauce
820	Cookery for large numbers. Institutional cookery
	For communal kitchens, see TX946
	Other special varieties of cookery
	For individual foods or ingredients, see TX743+
	Army, see UC720+
821	Canned foods, etc.
823	Camp and picnic. Outdoor cookery
	Casserole cookery, see TX693
825	Chafing dish cookery
825.5	Clay pot cookery
826	Cold-storage foods
	Cookery for sick soldiers, see UH487+
	Cookery for the sick, see RM219+
	Diabetic cookery, see RC662
826.5	Dried foods
827	Electric cooking
	Cf. TX657.S5, Electric stoves
	Cf. TX832, Microwave cookery
	Fast day, see TX837+
828	Frozen food
829	Hot weather
830	Cold dishes
831	Fireless cookers. Hayboxes, etc.
832	Microwave cookery
	Navy, see VC350+
833	Paper-bag cookery
833.5	Quick and easy cookery

	Cookery
	Other special varieties of cookery -- Continued
834	Skewer cookery. Kabobs
835	Smoked foods
	Cf. TX609, Smoking of foods
835.5	Solar cookery
836	Stuffed foods
	Vegetarian. Lenten. Fast day
	Cf. TX391+, Vegetables
837	General works
838	Meat substitutes
840.A-Z	Other special, A-Z
840.B3	Barbecue cookery
840.B5	Blender recipes
840.C65	Convection oven cookery
840.D88	Dutch oven cookery
840.F5	Fireplace cookery
840.F6	Food processor recipes
840.J84	Juicer recipes
	Lunchbox cookery, see TX735
840.M35	Mandoline recipes
	Marine cookery, see TX840.M7
840.M5	Mixer recipes
840.M6	Mobile home cookery
840.M7	Motorboat cookery. Marine cookery
840.P7	Pressure cooker recipes
840.S55	Skillet cookery
840.T63	Toaster oven cookery
	Trailer cookery, see TX840.M6
840.W65	Wok cookery
	Cf. TX724.5.C5, Chinese cookery
	Dining-room service
851	General works
	Dining room
855	General works
857	Arrangement
859	Decoration
	Table
871	General works
873	Arrangement
877	Furnishings
879	Decoration
881	Serving
885	Carving
	Hospitality industry. Hotels, clubs, restaurants, etc.
	Food service
	Cf. GT3770+, Manners and customs
	Cf. GV198.945+, Farm vacations, dude ranches, etc.
	Cf. GV854.35+, Ski resorts
	Cf. NA7800+, Architecture
	Cf. RA794, Health resorts
	Cf. SH405, Fishing resorts

TX

	Hospitality industry.
	Hotels, clubs, restaurants,
	etc. Food service -- Continued
901	Periodicals, societies, etc.
905	Dictionaries and encyclopedias
	Directories
	Including restaurant and hotel guidebooks, etc.
	For directories of chefs, see TX650
907	General works
	By region or country
	United States
907.2	General works
907.3.A-Z	By region or state, A-Z
	Apply table at TX336.5.A-Z
907.5.A-Z	Other regions or countries, A-Z
	Apply table at TX337.A-Z
	History
908	General works
	Special countries
	United States
909.A1	Periodicals, societies, etc.
909.A2-Z	General works
	Other countries
910.A1	Europe
910.A2-Z	By country, A-Z
	Special hotels, see TX941.A +
	Special restaurants, see TX945.5.A +
	Special taverns, barrooms, etc , see TX950 +
	Biography
910.3	Collective
910.5.A-Z	Individual, A-Z
911	General works
911.2	General special
911.3.A-Z	Special topics, A-Z
	Accounting, see HF5686.H75
	Appraisal, see TX911.3.V34
	Bookkeeping, see HF5686.H75
911.3.C3	Cashiering
911.3.C6	Commercial correspondence
	Concierge services, see TX911.3.C63
911.3.C63	Concierges and concierge service
911.3.C65	Cost control
911.3.C8	Customer relations
911.3.E4	Electronic data processing
911.3.E45	Energy consumption
	Equipment and supplies, see TX912
911.3.E84	Ethics
911.3.F5	Finance
	Fires and fire prevention in hotels, see TH9445.H75
	Fires and fire prevention in restaurants, see
	TH9445.R44
	Food service, see TX943 +
911.3.F75	Front desk

	Hospitality industry.
	Hotels, clubs, restaurants, etc. Food service
	Special topics, A-Z -- Continued
	Housekeeping, see TX928
911.3.I5	Inventory control
911.3.J65	Job descriptions
911.3.L27	Labor productivity
911.3.L3	Labor turnover
911.3.L62	Location
	Maintenance and repair, see TX928
911.3.M27	Management
911.3.M3	Marketing
911.3.M33	Mathematics
911.3.M45	Menus. Wine lists
911.3.P4	Personnel management
911.3.P46	Planning
911.3.P7	Prices
911.3.P77	Public relations
911.3.P8	Purchasing
911.3.Q34	Quality control
911.3.R3	Rates
911.3.R47	Reservations
911.3.R57	Risk management
	Room service, see TX943+
911.3.S24	Safety measures
911.3.S3	Sanitation
911.3.S4	Security
	Site selection, see TX911.3.L62
911.3.S73	Statistical methods
911.3.S8	Stockroom keeping
911.3.T32	Table setting and decoration
911.3.T73	Training
911.3.V34	Valuation and appraisal
911.3.V62	Vocational guidance
	Wine lists, see TX911.3.M45
911.5	Study and teaching
912	Furnishings, equipment, etc.
(913-917)	Law and legislation. Inspectors' reports
	see class K
921	Stewards' manuals. Caterers' manuals. Kitchen
	control
925	Dining room service. Table service. Wine service
	Including manuals for waiters, waitresses, bussing
	attendants, etc.
926	Bellmen, doormen, elevator operators
928	Housekeeping, maintenance, repair
930	Social executives, hostesses, etc.
931	General special
	Including youth hostels
941.A-Z	Special hotels and hotel chains. By name, A-Z

TX

                      Hospitality industry.
                           Hotels, clubs, restaurants,
                           etc. Food service -- Continued
                       Food service
                           Including room service
                           For food service in the transportation industry, see
                                 TA1227
                           For special topics, see TX911.3.A +

943	General works
	Restaurants, cafeterias, tearooms, etc.
	Cf. HE7581.5, Cybercafes
	Cf. TP635, Soda fountains
945	General works
945.2	School lunchrooms, cafeterias, etc.
945.5.A-Z	Special restaurants. By name, A-Z
946	Mass feeding, communal kitchens, canteens, etc.
	Industrial feeding. Factory canteens
946.5.A1	Periodicals, collections, congresses
946.5.A3-Z	General works
	Taverns, barrooms, saloons
950	Periodicals, societies, etc.
	Biography of bartenders, saloonkeepers, etc.
950.5.A1	Collective
950.5.A2-Z	Individual, A-Z
950.53	Directories
	History
950.54	General works
	By region or country
	United States
950.56	General works
950.57.A-Z	By region or state, A-Z
950.59.A-Z	Other regions or countries, A-Z
950.7	General works
951	Bartenders' manuals and recipes
	Cf. TX815 +, Non-alcoholic beverages
	Furnishings, equipment, etc. Housekeeping
952	General works
953	Bars and bar supplies
	Building operation and housekeeping
955	General works
	Apartment houses
957	General works
958	Janitor service
	Cf. TX339, Household janitor service
959	Other services
	Including elevator service
960	Housing developments
980	Office buildings
985	Public buildings
	Mobile home living
	Cf. GV198.5 +, Mobile home living
1100	Periodicals, societies, etc.
1105	General works

	Mobile home living -- Continued
1106	Juvenile works
	By region or country
	United States
1107	General works
1107.2.A-Z	By region or state, A-Z
1107.4.A-Z	Other regions or countries, A-Z
1110	Recreational vehicle living

	History
15	General works
16	Ancient
17	Medieval
18	Modern
19	19th century
20	20th century
	Special countries

The special provision for local or special subdivision does not apply to single number or Cutter number countries, which remain undivided

The numbers for "Cities or other special," "Local or special," "Province or special" may be used in some cases for local subdivision, and in other cases for special canals, rivers, harbors, railroads, or bridges, as appropriate for the subject matter to which the table is applied

		America
21		General works
		North America
22		General works
		United States
23		General works
23.1		Eastern states. Atlantic coast
23.15		New England
23.2		Appalachian region
23.3		Great Lakes region
23.4		Midwest. Mississippi Valley
23.5		South. Gulf states
23.6		West
23.7		Northwest
23.8		Pacific coast
23.9		Southwest
24.A-W		States, A-W
		e.g.
24.A4		Alaska
24.H3		Hawaii
25.A-Z		Cities (or other special), A-Z
		Canada
26		General works
27.A-Z		Provinces (or other special), A-Z
27.5		Latin America
		Mexico
28		General works
29.A-Z		Local or special, A-Z
		Central America
30		General works
31.A-Z		Special countries, A-Z
		West Indies
32		General works
33.A-Z		Special islands, A-Z
		South America
34		General works

TABLES

445

	Special countries
	America
	South America -- Continued
	Argentina
36	General works
37.A-Z	Local or special, A-Z
	Bolivia
38	General works
39.A-Z	Local or special, A-Z
	Brazil
41	General works
42.A-Z	Local or special, A-Z
	Chile
43	General works
44.A-Z	Local or special, A-Z
	Colombia
45	General works
46.A-Z	Local or special, A-Z
47	Ecuador
48	Guyana
49	Surinam
50	French Guiana
51	Paraguay
52	Peru
53	Uruguay
54	Venezuela
	Europe
55	General works
	Great Britain. England
57	General works
58.A-Z	English counties or regions, A-Z
	Ireland
59	General works
59.2	Irish Free State. Ireland (Eire)
59.3	Northern Ireland
60.A-Z	Special counties, A-Z
	Scotland
61	General works
62.A-Z	Special counties, A-Z
63	Wales
64.A-Z	Cities or other special, A-Z
	Austria
65	General works
65.2.A-Z	Local, or special, A-Z
	Czechoslovakia
65.3	General works
65.4.A-Z	Local, or special, A-Z
	Hungary
65.5	General works
65.9.A-Z	Special counties, A-Z
66.A-Z	Cities (or other special), A-Z
	Belgium
67	General works

	Special countries
	Europe
	Belgium -- Continued
68.A-Z	Local or special, A-Z
	Denmark
69	General works
70.A-Z	Local or special, A-Z
	France
71	General works
72.A-Z	Local, or special, A-Z
72.5	Colonies (Collectively)
	Germany
73	General works
73.1	East Germany. Eastern Germany
73.2	Baden-Württemburg
73.3	Bavaria
73.4	Hesse
73.5	Prussia
73.6	Saxony
73.7	North Rhine-Westphalia
73.9.A-Z	Other states, A-Z
74.A-Z	Cities (or other special), A-Z
74.5	Colonies (Collectively)
	Greece
75	General works
76.A-Z	Local or special, A-Z
	Netherlands
77	General works
78.A-Z	Local or special, A-Z
	Italy
79	General works
80.A-Z	Local or special, A-Z
80.5	Malta
	Norway
81	General works
82.A-Z	Local or special, A-Z
	Portugal, Azores, etc.
83	General works
84.A-Z	Local or special, A-Z
84.5	Colonies (Collectively)
	Russia in Europe
85	General works
86.A-Z	Local or special, A-Z
	Spain
87	General works
88.A-Z	Local or special, A-Z
88.5	Scandinavia
	Sweden
89	General works
90.A-Z	Local, or special, A-Z
	Switzerland
91	General works
92.A-Z	Local or special, A-Z

TABLES

	Special countries
	Europe -- Continued
95.A-Z	Other regions and countries, A-Z
95.A2	Balkan Peninsula
95.A38	Albania
95.A44	Alps
95.B3	Baltic Sea
95.B45	Benelux countries
95.B9	Bulgaria
95.C37	Carpathian Mountains
95.D35	Danube River
95.F5	Finland
95.I43	Iceland
95.L285	Lapland
95.L37	Latvia
95.L78	Lithuania
95.L9	Luxemburg
95.M4	Mediterranean Region
95.N67	North Sea
95.P7	Poland
95.P75	Pomerania (Poland and Germany)
95.R48	Rhine River
95.R6	Romania
95.S55	Slovenia
95.T48	Thrace
95.U95	Ukraine
95.Y8	Yugoslavia
	Asia
99	General works
	China
101	General works
102.A-Z	Local or special, A-Z
	Taiwan
102.5	General works
102.6.A-Z	Local or special, A-Z
	South Asia
102.9	General works
	India
103	General works
104.A-Z	Local or special, A-Z
	Pakistan
104.5	General works
104.6.A-Z	Local or special, A-Z
	Bangladesh
104.65	General works
104.66.A-Z	Local or special, A-Z
	Sri Lanka. Ceylon
104.7	General works
104.8.A-Z	Local or special, A-Z
	Japan
105	General works
106.A-Z	Local or special, A-Z

	Special countries
	Asia -- Continued
	Korea
	Including South Korea
106.5	General works
106.6.A-Z	Local or special, A-Z
	North Korea
106.7	General works
106.8.A-Z	Local or special, A-Z
	Iran. Persia
107	General works
108.A-Z	Local or special, A-Z
	Russia in Asia. Siberia
109	General works
110.A-Z	Local or special, A-Z
	Turkey. Asia Minor
111	General works
112.A-Z	Local or special, A-Z
113.A-Z	Other divisions of Asia
113.A3	Afghanistan
113.B54	Borneo
113.B7	Brunei
113.B8	Burma
113.C16	Cambodia
113.C9	Cyprus
113.G39	Gaza Strip
113.H85	Hong Kong
113.I55	Indonesia
113.I7	Iraq
113.I75	Israel
113.J6	Jordan
113.K85	Kuwait
113.L28	Laos
113.L4	Lebanon
113.M2	Macao
113.M318	Malaya
113.M32	Malaysia
113.M45	Mekong River Valley
113.N4	Nepal
113.P6	Philippines
113.Q36	Qatar
113.S33	Saudi Arabia
113.S53	Singapore
113.S6	Southeast Asia
113.S94	Syria
113.T48	Thailand
113.U54	United Arab Emirates
113.V5	Vietnam
113.W48	West Bank
113.Y45	Yemen (People's Democratic Republic)
113.5	Middle East. Near East
114	Arab countries
114.5	Islamic countries

TABLES

	Special countries -- Continued
	Africa
115	General works
	Egypt
117	General works
118	Local or special, A-Z
119.A-Z	Other divisions of Africa, A-Z
119.A4	Algeria
119.A5	Angola
119.B57	Botswana
119.B85	Burundi
119.C17	Cameroon
119.C42	Central Africa
119.C43	Central African Republic
119.C75	Congo (Brazzaville)
	Congo (Democratic Republic), see 119.Z3
119.D3	Dahomey
119.D55	Djibouti
119.E18	East Africa
119.E19	Eastern Africa
119.E8	Ethiopia
119.F82	French-speaking Equatorial Africa
119.F83	French-speaking West Africa
119.G23	Gabon
119.G45	Ghana
119.G92	Guinea
119.G94	Guinea-Bissau
119.I9	Ivory Coast
119.K4	Kenya
119.L45	Lesotho
119.L49	Liberia
119.L74	Libya
119.M28	Madagascar
119.M3	Malawi
119.M34	Mali
119.M39	Mauritania
119.M6	Morocco
119.M85	Mozambique
	Namibia, see 119.S68
119.N53	Niger
119.N54	Nigeria
119.N6	Nile River Valley
119.R45	Rhodesia, Southern. Zimbabwe
119.R9	Rwanda
119.S18	Sahel
119.S38	Senegal
119.S5	Sierra Leone
119.S59	Somalia
119.S6	South Africa
119.S64	Southern Africa
119.S68	Southwest Africa. Namibia
119.S73	Sub-Saharan Africa
119.S74	Sudan

	Special countries
	Africa
	Other divisions
	of Africa, A-Z -- Continued
119.S87	Swaziland
119.T35	Tanzania
119.T64	Togo
119.T8	Tunisia
119.U4	Uganda
119.U66	Upper Volta
119.W48	West Africa
119.Z3	Zaire. Congo (Democratic Republic)
119.Z34	Zambia
	Zimbabwe, see 119.R45
	Indian Ocean islands
120	General works
120.5.A-Z	Special islands, A-Z
120.5.M38	Mauritius
120.5.R48	Réunion
	Australasia
120.7	General works
	Australia
121	General works
122.A-Z	Local or special, A-Z
	New Zealand
122.5	General works
122.6.A-Z	Local or special, A-Z
122.7	Papua New Guinea
	Pacific Islands
123	General works
124.A-Z	By island, A-Z
	Arctic regions
125	General works
125.5	Greenland
126	Antarctica
126.5	Tropics
127	Developing countries

TABLES

	Special exhibitions
	Guidebooks
.A1	Official
.A2A-Z	Others, A-Z
	Histories and descriptions
.B1	General works
.B2	General special
.C1	Collections of pictures, views, etc.
	Official publications
	Acts of incorporation, rules, organization, etc.
.D1	General works
.D13	Translations of acts
	Rules, regulations, etc.
.D15	General works
.D17	Translations of rules, regulations, etc.
.D2	General reports, proceedings, etc., of governing board
.D25	Reports of national (government) commission
.D3	General reports of special boards, commissions, etc.
.D4	Congressional hearings and reports of national government on appropriations, etc. By date
.D5	Special reports. By date
	General catalogs
.D6	Official. By date
.D7	Nonofficial
	Subarranged by author
.D8	Reports and awards of jurors
.D9	Miscellaneous printed matter
.E1	Official comprehensive reports on the exhibits by editorial commissions, etc. By date
.E1A-Z	General official reports of other countries on exhibitions
	For their own exhibits, see .G1
	Exhibits of the country in which the exhibition is held
.F1	Collective
	Class here general only special with subject
.F2	Government exhibit
.F3	State exhibits, etc.
.G1	Exhibits of other countries
	Cf. .E1A-.E1Z, General official reports on exhibitions
.H1	Parts of the exposition
	Works on various exhibits which cannot well be classified with any one subject, e. g. a work on an educational exhibit goes in class L, Education, subdivision Exhibits, but a work on Machinery hall is classed here

	Special exhibitions -- Continued
.K1	Exhibits arranged by names of exhibitors
	Works on various exhibits which cannot well be classified with any one subject, e. g. a work on an educational exhibit goes in class L, Education, subdivision Exhibits, but a work on Machinery hall is classed here
.L1	Miscellaneous
	Other than .A1--.K1
.N1	Congresses. General reports

	General works, histories, etc.
.xA2-.xA5	Official works
.xA6-.xZ	By author, A-Z
.x1	Regular reports of the fire department or fire commissioner, chief engineer, superintendent, fire marshall, etc.
.x2	Special bureau reports. Fire patrol bureau reports
.x3	Special reports and petitions. By date
.x4	Reports of commissions, committees, investigations. By date
	Laws, ordinances, regulations
	see KFA-W
.x6	Manuals and lists of alarm stations or boxes
.x65	Examinations. Admission to fire service (Civil service, etc.)
.x68	Pensions, relief, etc.
	Fire companies. Conventions, etc.
.x7	General works
.x71	Paid companies. History, etc.
.x74	Volunteer companies. Constitution, by-laws, history, etc.
.x77	Veteran associations
.x8	Local fire equipment. Engines, enginehouses, etc.
.x9	Various unofficial publications

	General works, histories, etc.
.xA2-.xA5	Official works
.xA6-.xZ	By author, A-Z
.x01	Regular reports of the fire department or fire commissioner, chief engineer, superintendent, fire marshall, etc.
.x02	Special bureau reports. Fire patrol bureau reports
.x03	Special reports and petitions. By date
.x04	Reports of commissions, committees, investigations. By date
	Laws, ordinances, regulations
	see KFX
.x06	Manuals and lists of alarm stations or boxes
.x065	Examinations. Admission to fire service (Civil service, etc.)
.x068	Pensions, relief, etc.
	Fire companies. Conventions, etc.
.x07	General works
.x071	Paid companies. History, etc.
.x074	Volunteer companies. Constitution, by-laws, history, etc.
.x077	Veteran associations
.x08	Local fire equipment. Engines, enginehouses, etc.
.x09	Various unofficial publications

TABLES

.A1	General works
.A3-.Z	Special regions or countries, A-Z
	Under each country:
	General works
2A-Z	*Special divisions, A-Z*
3A-Z	*Special cities, A-Z*

NUMERALS

3-D films: TR854

A

Abbreviations
  Industrial engineering: T55.52
  Technology: T8
Abrading machinery
  Machine shops: TJ1280+
Abrasion
  Aircraft propellers: TL706.A2
Abrasives
  Abrading machinery: TJ1296+
  Engineering materials: TA455.A3
  Mining engineering: TN936
ABS resins
  Plastics: TP1180.A15
Absorption of gases
  Chemical engineering: TP156.A3
Abstract photography: TR656
Abutments
  Bridges: TG325
  Buildings: TH2255
Accelerometers
  Aeronautical instrument:
    TL589.2.A3
Acceptance sampling
  Production management: TS156.4
Access for the handicapped
  House remodeling: TH4816.15
Access to airports: TL725.3.A2
Accident prevention
  Building construction: TH443
Accident prevention,
  Industrial: T55+
Accidents
  Aeronautics: TL553.5
  Balloons: TL612
  Chemical technology: TP150.A23
  Metallurgical plants: TN676.A1+
  Nuclear engineering: TK9152+
  Petroleum pipelines: TN879.55
Accidents, Bridge: TG470
Accounting machines: TK4100+
Accounts, Household: TX326.A1+
Accumulators in central
  stations
  Dynamoelectric machinery:
    TK2891

Accuracy of fitting
  Machine shop practice: TJ1167
Acetal resins
  Plastics: TP1180.A33
Acetates
  Chemical technology: TP248.A17
  Environmental pollutants:
    TD196.A2
Acetic acid
  Chemical technology: TP248.A18
  Environmental pollutants:
    TD196.A22
Acetone
  Chemical technology: TP248.A2
Acetylene automobiles:
  TL229.A25
Acetylene industry: TP765+
Acid Bessemer process
  Steel metallurgy: TN737
Acid deposition
  Environmental pollution:
    TD195.4+
  Water pollutants: TD427.A27
Acid mine drainage
  Water pollutants: TD427.A28
Acid open hearth process
  Steel metallurgy: TN741
Acid precipitation
  Environmental pollution:
    TD195.4+
Acid rain
  Environmental pollution:
    TD195.4+
Acids: TP213+
  Chemical technology: TP247.2
  Food additives: TP456.A2
Acorns
  Cookery: TX814.2.A25
  Food values: TX558.A3
Acoustic systems and
  instruments
  Telegraph: TK5521+
Acoustical engineering: TA365+
Acoustical materials
  Building construction: TH1727
Acoustical properties and tests
  Engineering materials: TA418.84
Acoustics
  Chemical engineering: TP156.A33
Acoustics in engineering:
  TA365+
Acoustooptical devices: TA1770

Acoustooptics, Applied: TA1770
Acridines
  Chemical technology: TP248.A28
Acrobats
  Photographic portraits:
    TR681.A26
Acrylic acid
  Chemical technology: TP248.A4
Acrylic resins
  Plastics: TP1180.A35
Acrylic textile fibers:
  TS1548.7.A25
Acrylonitrile
  Air pollutants: TD887.A37
Activated sludge
  Sewage treatment: TD767.7
Activated sludge method
  Sewage treatment: TD756
Active server pages
  Web authoring software:
    TK5105.8885.A26
ActiveX
  Web authoring software:
    TK5105.8885.A28
Actuators
  Aircraft engines: TL702.A37
  Control engineering: TJ223.A25
Adaptive control systems
  Mechanical engineering: TJ217
Additions
  House remodeling: TH4816.2
Additives
  Cement manufacture: TP884.A3
  Explosives: TP291
  Food constituent: TX553.A3
  Plastics: TP1142
Adhesive joints, Metal
  Engineering and construction:
    TA492.A3
Adhesives
  Engineering materials:
    TA455.A34
  Organic chemical industries:
    TP967+
  Packaging materials: TS198.3.A3
Adhesives, Wood: TS857
Adiabatic engines: TJ763
Adjustable pitch aircraft
  propellers: TL707.P5
Adjustment tables
  Freight: TF666

Adobe
  Housing material: TH4818.A3
Adobe brick
  Chemical technology: TP832.A35
Adobe PageMill
  Web authoring software:
    TK5105.8885.A36
Adsorption
  Chemical engineering: TP156.A35
  Sewage purification: TD753.5
  Water purification: TD449.5
Adulterants
  Food: TX562.2+
Adulterants, Detection of
  Food: TX563
Adulteration
  Food: TX562.2+
  Food supply: TX501+
  Wine and winemaking:
    TP548.5.A38
Advertising
  Use of airplanes: TL722.5
Advertising cinematography
  Photography: TR894.6
Advertising photography:
  TR690.4
Advice to sitters
  Portrait photography: TR577
Aerated package treatment
  systems
  Sewage disposal systems: TD779
Aeration
  Food processing: TP371.15
  Sewage disposal: TD758
  Water purification: TD458
Aerial lines
  Electric power: TK3231+
  Telephone connections: TK6352
Aerial photography: TR810
Aerial photography in railroad
  surveying: TF213.5
Aerial surveying: TA592+
Aerial surveys
  Location engineering: TE209.5
Aerobatics: TL711.S8
Aerodromes: TL725+
Aerodynamic heating: TL574.A45
Aerodynamics
  Aeronautics: TL570+
  Motor vehicle dynamics: TL245
  Turbomachinery: TJ267
  Vehicles: TA359

Aerodynamics in engineering:
  TA358
Aeroelasticity
  Aerodynamics: TL574.A37
Aerofoils
  Aerodynamics: TL574.A4
Aeronautical engineering:
  TL500+
Aeronautical instruments:
  TL589+
Aeronautical laboratories:
  TL566+
Aeronautical meteorology:
  TL556+
Aeronautics: TL500+
  Environmental effects:
    TD195.A27
Aeronautics as a vocation:
  TL561
Aeronauts
  Balloons: TL620.A1+
Aerosols
  Chemical technology: TP244.A3
  Fire prevention and
    extinction: TH9446.A37
  Packaging: TS198.A3
Aerospace industries
  Air pollution: TD888.A53
Aerostatics: TL578
Aerostation
  Aircraft: TL605+
Aerosteam engines: TJ727
Aerothermodynamics: TL574.A45
Aesthetics
  Dress: TT507
  Photography: TR183
Afro-Americans
  Nutrition: TX361.A27
Afternoon teas
  Cookery: TX736
Agar
  Food processing and
    manufacture: TP445.5.A35
Agates
  Mineral industries: TN997.A35
Aged
  Nutrition: TX361.A3
  Photographic portraits:
    TR681.A35
Aggregate industry
  Environmental effects:
    TD195.A33

Aggregates
  Masonry materials: TA441
  Prospecting: TN271.A47
Agricultural chemicals
  Environmental pollutants:
    TD196.A34
  Soil pollutants: TD879.A35
  Water pollutants: TD427.A35
Agricultural laborers
  Nutrition: TX361.A4
Agricultural machinery
  Internal combustion engines:
    TJ793
  Mechanical engineering: TJ1480+
Agricultural photography:
  TR739+
Agricultural wastes
  Disposal and drainage: TD930+
Agriculture
  Electric power: TK4018
  Electronics: TK7882.A37
  Energy conservation:
    TJ163.5.A37
  Environmental effects:
    TD195.A34
  Water pollution: TD428.A37
AIDS patients
  Photographic portraits:
    TR681.A38
Ailerons
  Airplanes: TL677.A5
AIM 65 computer: TK7889.A37
Air bags
  Automobiles: TL159.5
Air brakes
  Automobiles: TL269.2
Air compressors
  Pneumatic machinery: TJ990+
Air conditioning
  Airplanes: TL681.A5
  Buildings: TH7687+
  Electric power: TK4035.A35
  Motor vehicles: TL271.5
  Railroad cars: TF453
Air conditioning equipment
  Transportation engineering:
    TA1280
Air cooled engines: TJ766.7
Air currents
  Aeronautical meteorology:
    TL557.A5

Air curtains
  Ventilation of buildings:
    TH7683.A25
Air cushion landing systems
  Airplanes: TL683.A35
Air ducts
  Airplanes: TL697.A57
  Ventilation of buildings:
    TH7683.D8
Air filters
  Gasoline automobiles: TL214.A4
  Ventilation of buildings:
    TH7683.A3
Air frames
  Airplanes: TL671.6
Air guns
  Manufactures: TS537.5
Air inlets
  Jet engines: TL709.5.I5
Air intakes
  Jet engines: TL709.5.I5
Air jets
  Pneumatic machinery: TJ1030
Air meets
  Airplanes: TL721.5+
  Gliders: TL760.5
Air meters
  Pneumatic machinery: TJ1025+
Air navigation: TL586+
Air pilot guides: TL725+
Air pollution control: TD881+
Air pollution control
  equipment: TD889
Air pollution sources: TD888.A+
Air pollution, Indoor: TD883.17
Air preheating
  Furnaces: TJ328
Air pumps
  Pneumatic machinery: TJ955
Air quality, Indoor: TD883.17
Air safety: TL553.5
Air sampling and analysis:
    TD890
Air-speed indicators
  Aeronautical instrument:
    TL589.2.A5
Air-supported structures
  Building construction: TH1099
Air suspensions
  Motor vehicles: TL257.3

Air transportation
  Environmental effects:
    TD195.A27
  Technological aspects: TL720+
Air turbines: TJ766.5
Air vents
  Hot water heating: TH7545
  Hydronic systems: TH7479
  Steam heating: TH7595
Air washers
  Ventilation of buildings:
    TH7683.A3
Air, Compressed
  In plumbing testing: TH6617
Airbrakes
  Railroad cars: TF420+
Airbrush work
  Photographic processing: TR485
Aircraft: TL600+
Aircraft carriers: TL725.8, TL726+,
    V874+
Aircraft engines: TL701+
Aircraft exhaust emissions
  Air pollutants: TD886.7
Aircraft, Human powered: TL769
Airlift pumps
  Hydraulic machinery: TJ925
Airplane accessories: TL688+
Airplane industry
  Technical aspects: TL724+
Airplane materials: TL688+
Airplanes: TL669.2+
  Government use: TL723
  Humanitarian uses: TL722.8
  Noise control: TD893.6.A57
  Photography: TR714
Airplanes in industry: TL722+
Airport buildings
  Aeronautics: TL725.3.B8
Airports
  Access: TL725.3.A2
  Aeronautics: TL725+
  Environmental effects:
    TD195.A36
  Fire prevention and
    extinction: TH9445.A5
  Government operation and
    support: TL725.3.G6
  Intra-airport transportation:

Airports
TL725.3.I6
Size: TL725.3.S5
Airscrews
Aeronautical engineering:
TL705+
Airships: TL650+
Airspeed
Airplanes: TL711.A5
Airtight construction
Building construction: TH1719
Airways (Routes): TL725+
Airworthiness requirements
Airplanes: TL671.1
Akron (Airship): TL659.A4
Alabaster
Mineral industries: TN989.A3
Alarm equipment
Security in buildings: TH9739
Alarms
Installation in houses: TK7241+
Albertype
Photography: TR933
Alcohol
Chemical technology: TP500+
Distilling: TP593
Food values: TX560.A3
Alcohol and alcohol mixtures
Fuel: TP358
Alcohol automobiles: TL217
Alcohol motors: TJ800
Alcoholic beverages
Adulteration: TX597
Cookery: TX726+
Alcohols
Chemical technology: TP248.A5
Aldehydes
Chemical technology: TP248.A53
Ale
Brewing and malting: TP578
Algae and algae products
Food processing and
manufacture: TP445+
Algae as food
Nutrition: TX402
Algae control by copper
sulphate
Water purification: TD465
Algal biotechnology:
TP248.27.A46

Algin
Food processing and
manufacture: TP445.5.A45
Alignment of machinery
Mechanical engineering: TJ177.5
Alizarin
Textile dyes: TP918.A4
Alizarin black
Textile dyes: TP918.N2
Alkali metals
Metallography: TN693.A4
Alkalies: TP222+
Mining engineering: TN895+
Alkylation
Petroleum refining: TP690.45
All terrain vehicle driving:
TL235.7
All terrain vehicles: TL235.6+
Allanite
Mining engineering: TN948.A5
Allene
Chemical technology: TP248.A555
Allergens
Chemical biotechnology:
TP248.65.A39
Allocation method
Linear programming: T57.77
Allowances, Time
Industrial engineering: T60.45
Alloys
Aeronautics: TL699.A58
Electroplating: TS693
Engineering materials: TA483+
Industrial electrochemistry:
TP261.A1
Manufactures: TS650
Metallography: TN693.A+
Motor vehicle construction
materials: TL240.5.A46
Precious metals: TS729
Allyl compounds
Chemical technology: TP248.A56
Almonds
Cookery: TX814.2.A44
Alpha-bearing wastes
Radioactive waste disposal:
TD898.7.A46
Alphabets
Embroidery: TT773
Alsatian cookery: TX719.2.A45
AltaVista: TK5105.885.A45

461

INDEX

Alterations
  Women's tailoring: TT550
Alternating current
  Dynamoelectric machinery:
    TK2825+
  Electrical engineering:
    TK454.15.A48
Alternating-current engineering
  Electrical engineering: TK1141+
Alternating-current
  generators: TK2761+
Alternating-current machinery
  Dynamoelectric machinery:
    TK2711+
Alternating-current motors
  Dynamoelectric machinery:
    TK2781+
Alternating-current systems
  Electric lighting: TK4304
  Electrical engineering: TK3141+
Alternating-current
  transforming machinery:
    TK2791+
Altimeter
  Aeronautical instrument:
    TL589.2.A6
  Aeronautical navigation:
    TL696.H4
Altitude flights, Special
  Airplanes: TL711.A7
Altitude flying
  Airplanes: TL711.A6
Alumina cement
  Cement manufacture: TP884.A48
Aluminium process
  Photolithography: TR950
Aluminum
  Aeronautics: TL699.A6
  Chemical technology: TP245.A4
  Effect on food: TX572.A6
  Electroplating: TS692.A5
  Engineering materials: TA480.A6
  Manufactures: TS554+
  Metal finishing: TS694.2
  Metallography: TN693.A5
  Metallurgy: TN775
  Mining: TN490.A5
  Motor vehicle construction
    materials: TL240.5.A48
  Ore dressing and milling:
    TN538.A55

Aluminum
  Powder metallurgy: TN697.A47
  Structural engineering: TA690
  Waste disposal: TD812.5.A48
  Water pollutants: TD427.A45
Aluminum alloys
  Aeronautics: TL699.A6
  Metallurgy: TN775
  Structural engineering: TA690
Aluminum conductors
  Electric power: TK3311.A6
Aluminum foil craft: TT242
Aluminum industry
  Environmental effects:
    TD195.A37
  Waste control: TD899.A44
Aluminum mines and mining
  Water pollution: TD428.A48
Aluminum plants
  Air pollution: TD888.A56
  Manufactures: TS556
Aluminum roofing
  Building construction: TH2459
Aluminum work
  Handicrafts: TT242
Alunite
  Mining engineering: TN948.A6
Amalgamation
  Gold and silver metallurgy:
    TN763
Amateur cinematography: TR896+
Amateur experiments
  Astronautics: TL794.3
Amateur photography for
  profit: TR690.2
Amateurs' manuals
  Electricity: TK9900+
  House construction: TH4815
  House repair: TH4817.3
Ambary hemp
  Textile fiber: TS1544.A5
Amber
  Jewelry work: TS755.A5
  Mining engineering: TN885
Ambrotype
  Photography: TR370
Ambulances: TL235.8
Americium
  Metallography: TN693.A54

Amino acids
  Biotechnology: TP248.65.A43
  Chemical technology: TP248.A6
  Food constituent: TX553.A5
Aminoplastics
  Plastics: TP1180.A5
Ammeters: TK331
Ammonia
  Air pollutants: TD887.A66
  Alkalies: TP223
Ammonia compounds
  Alkalies: TP223
Ammonia industry
  Environmental effects:
    TD195.A44
Ammonium nitrate fuel oil
  Explosives: TP290.A5
Ammonium phosphate
  Fertilizers: TP963.4.A38
Ammonium sulphate
  Fertilizers: TP963.4.A4
Ammunition
  Manufactures: TS538+
Amorphous semiconductors:
  TK7871.99.A45
Amorphous substances
  Engineering: TA418.9.A58
Ampere-hour meters: TK331
Amphibians
  Seaplanes: TL684.1
Amphibious vehicles: TL235.63
Amplifiers
  Computer engineering: TK7895.A5
  Electronics: TK7871.2+
  Radar: TK6590.A5
  Radio: TK6565.A55
  Television: TK6655.A5
Amusement machines
  Mechanical engineering: TJ1570
Amylodextrins
  Biotechnology: TP248.65.A45
Analog computers: TK7888
Analog-to-digital converters
  Computer engineering: TK7887.6
Analogs
  Mathematical models: TA343
Analysis
  Food composition: TX541+
  Gas industry: TP754
  Pollution measurement: TD193+
  Sewage: TD735

Analysis
  Water: TD380+
  Wine and winemaking: TP548.5.A5
  Woodpulp: TS1176.6.A5
Analysis of food: TX501+
Analysis, Chemical
  Food adulterants: TX569
Analysis, Microscopic
  Food adulterants: TX567
Anchor
  Balloons: TL625.A6
Anchorage
  Structural engineering: TA772
Anchors, Guy: TA777
Anchovies
  Cookery: TX748.A53
Ancient light
  Natural lighting: TH7792
Ancient pumps
  Hydraulic machinery: TJ901
Andirons
  Building construction:
    TH7427.A5
Anechoic chambers: TA365.5
Angle measurement
  Surveying: TA603
Angle of incidence
  Airplanes: TL673.A6
Angles
  Structural engineering:
    TA660.A53
Angles, Metal
  Engineering materials: TA492.A6
Anhydrite
  Mining engineering: TN948.A65
Aniline black
  Textile dyes: TP918.A5
Aniline dyes: TP914
Animal cell biotechnology:
  TP248.27.A53
Animal fats
  Chemical technology: TP676
Animal feeds and feed mills:
  TS2284+
Animal fibers
  Textile industries: TS1545+
Animal food
  Cookery: TX743+
Animal foods
  Food values: TX555+
  Nutrition: TX371+

Animal motors: TJ830
Animal oils
  Chemical technology: TP676
Animal products
  Manufactures: TS1950+
Animal waste
  Rural engineering: TD930.2
Animals
  Nature photography: TR727+
Animated motion pictures
  Cinematography: TR897.5+
Annealing
  Steel metallurgy: TN752.A5
Annular gears
  Toothed gears: TJ191
Annunciators
  Installation in houses: TK7221
Anodic oxidation
  Metal finishing: TS694+
Antennas
  Aircraft communication
    equipment: TL694.A6
  Electronics: TK7871.6+
  Radar: TK6590.A6
  Radio: TK6565.A6
  Television: TK6655.A6
Anthracene dyes: TP915
Anthracite
  Mining: TN820+
Anthraquinones
  Textile dyes: TP918.A6
Antibiotic residues
  Effect on food: TX571.A58
Antibiotics
  Biotechnology: TP248.65.A57
  Food constituent: TX553.A7
Antifoaming agents
  Chemical technology: TP159.A47
Antifreeze solutions
  Chemical technology: TP362
Antifriction devices
  Machinery: TJ1071
Antilock brake systems
  Motor vehicles: TL269.3
Antimony
  Chemical technology: TP245.A6
  Metallurgy: TN799.A6
  Ore deposits and mining:
    TN490.A6
  Ore dressing and milling:
    TN538.A57

Antioxidants
  Chemical technology: TP159.A5
  Food constituent: TX553.A73
Antiperspirants: TP985
Antiquities
  Aeronautical engineering: TL516
  Astronautics: TL516
  Railroad engineering: TF16
Antobiotics
  Chemical technology: TP248.A62
Apartment houses
  Construction: TH4820
  Electric power: TK4035.A6
  Fire prevention and
    extinction: TH9445.A62
  Heating and ventilation:
    TH7392.A6
  Housekeeping: TX957+
  Plumbing: TH6515.A6
  Sanitary engineering: TH6057.A6
  Ventilation: TH7684.A6
Apatite
  Mining engineering: TN948.A7
Apollo project: TL789.8.U6A5
Apparatus
  Acetylene industry: TP769
  Radar: TK6585+
  Television: TK6650+
Apparatus and materials
  Electronics: TK7869+
Apparatus and supplies
  Chemical engineering: TP157+
  Wine and winemaking: TP548.5.A6
Apparatus for delivering goods
  during flight: TL733
Apparatus for picking up goods
  during flight: TL733
Apparatus, instruments, tools
  Fermentation industries: TP517
Apple brandy
  Distilled liquors: TP607.A57
Apple butter
  Cookery: TX767.A65
Apple II computer: TK7889.A66
Apple IIe computer: TK7889.A663
Apple juice, Unfermented: TP564
Apple parers
  Cookery: TX657.A66
Apples
  Cookery: TX813.A6
  Food processing: TP441.A6
  Food values: TX558.A6
  Preservation and storage:
    TX612.A6

AppleTalk: TK5105.8.A77
Appliances
  Cookery: TX656+
  Fire prevention and
    extinction: TH9245
  Street cleaning: TD860
Application specific integrated
  circuits
  Electronics: TK7874.6
Applications of astronomy
  Surveying: TA597
Applied acoustooptics: TA1770
Applied cinematography: TR892+
Applied dynamics: TA352+
Applied electrooptics: TA1750+
Applied fiber optics: TA1800+
Applied fluid mechanics: TA357+
Applied forces, Behavior of
  materials under: TA404.8+
Applied geology: TN260
Applied holography: TA1540+
Applied mathematics
  Industrial engineering: T57+
Applied mechanics: TA349+
Applied mineralogy: TN260
Applied neutron optics: TA1773
Applied optics: TA1501+
Applied photography: TR623.2+
Applied plasma dynamics:
  TA2001+
Applied statics: TA351
Applied X-ray optics: TA1775
Appliqué
  Decorative needlework: TT779
Appraisal
  Hotels, clubs, restaurants,
    etc.: TX911.3.V34
Approach channels
  Harbor engineering: TC352
Approximations
  Engineering mathematics: TA335
Appurtenances
  Low-pressure hot water
    heating: TH7529
  Warm-air heating: TH7623+
Apricots
  Cookery: TX813.A64
Aprons
  Women's tailoring: TT546.5
Aquaculture
  Water pollution: TD428.A68

Aquatic pests
  Water pollution: TD427.A68
Aquavit
  Distilled liquors: TP607.A6
Aqueducts
  Water supply: TD398
Aquifer storage recovery of
  groundwater: TD404.5
'Arabsāt (Artificial
  satellite): TK5104.2.A72
Arc lamps and systems: TK4321+
Arc lighting, Electric: TK4311+
Archaeological photography:
  TR775
Arched bridges: TG327+
Arches
  Structural engineering:
    TA660.A7
Arches and vaults
  Building design and
    construction: TH2150+
Arches, Centering of
  Building construction: TH5591
Architectural ceramics
  Chemical technology: TP825+
Architectural engineering
  Building construction: TH845+
  Wooden buildings: TH1111
Architectural metalwork
  Building construction: TH1651+
Architectural photography:
  TR659
Architectural woodwork
  Building construction: TH1151+
Archive buildings
  Fire prevention and
    extinction: TH9445.A7
Archives, Technical: T11.9
Areaways
  Building design and
    construction: TH3000.A74
Argillite
  Mining engineering: TN948.A76
Argon
  Chemical technology: TP245.A7
Ariel motorcycle: TL448.A47
Aristotypes
  Photographic process: TR395
Arithmetic units
  Computer engineering:
    TK7895.A65

Armature winding and armatures
  Generators: TK2477
Armed Forces
  Environmental effects:
    TD195.A75
Arnold's fluid
  Ink manufacture: TP948.A8
Aromatic compounds
  Chemical technology: TP248.A7
  Environmental pollutants:
    TD196.A75
Arrangement
  Dining room: TX857
  Kitchen: TX655
  Table: TX873
  The house: TX309
Arsenals
  Waste control: TD899.A76
Arsenic
  Chemical technology: TP245.A8
  Effect on food: TX572.A77
  Environmental pollutants:
    TD196.A77
  Ore deposits and mining:
    TN490.A8
  Water pollutants: TD427.A77
Arsenic wastes
  Waste disposal: TD898.8.A76
Art glazing
  Decorative furnishings: TH8271 +
Art of dress: TT507
Artesian wells
  Water supply: TD410
Artichokes
  Cookery: TX803.A7
Articles for children
  Handicrafts: TT174 +
Articles made of glass: TP865 +
Artificial diamonds: TP873.5.D5
Artificial dyes: TP913 +
Artificial fire testing
  Building construction: TH1091 +
Artificial flowers
  Decorative crafts: TT890 +
Artificial fruits
  Decorative crafts: TT896
Artificial fuel: TP360
Artificial fur
  Manufactures: TS1070
Artificial gems
  Chemical technology: TP873 +

Artificial horizons
  Aeronautical instrument:
    TL589.2.A78
Artificial indigo
  Dyes: TP924
Artificial islands
  Air conditioning: TH7688.O44
Artificial light
  Photographic processing: TR333
  Photography: TR600
Artificial lighting
  Building construction: TH7900 +
  Photography: TR590 +
Artificial materials
  Masonry materials: TA431 +
Artificial mineral waters:
    TP625
Artificial minerals
  Chemical technology: TP870
Artificial recharge
  Groundwater: TD404
Artificial satellite orbits:
    TL1080
Artificial satellites: TL796 +
  Aeronautical navigation:
    TL696.A77
  Earth: TL796.6.E2
  Sun: TL796.6.S8
Artificial satellites in
  telecommunication
  Electrical engineering: TK5104 +
Artificial silk
  Dyeing: TP902
  Silk manufactures: TS1688.A1 +
Artificial stone
  Chemical technology: TP871
Artificial stone building
  construction: TH1451
Artificial sweeteners
  Effect on food: TX571.S9
Artificial ventilation
  Ventilation of buildings:
    TH7678 +
Artificial wool
  Woolen manufactures: TS1635
Artisans
  Photographic portraits:
    TR681.A69
Artistic cinematography:
    TR892.4
Artistic photography: TR640 +

Artists
  Photographic portraits:
    TR681.A7
Arts and crafts: TT1+
Asbestos
  Aeronautics: TL699.A8
  Air pollutants: TD887.A8
  Engineering materials: TA455.A6
  Environmental pollutants:
    TD196.A78
  Fireproofing materials: TH1075
  Mining engineering: TN930
  Reinforced plastics:
    TP1177.5.A8
Asbestos cement
  Cement manufacture: TP884.A8
Asbestos fiber: TS1549.A7
Asbestos industry
  Dust removal: TH7697.A8
Asbestos substitutes
  Engineering materials:
    TA455.A62
Ascensions, Balloon: TL620.A1+
Ascorbic acid
  Chemical technology: TP248.A8
  Food constituent: TX553.A8
Ash-handling machinery
  Conveying machinery: TJ1410
Ashes
  Nonmetallic materials:
    TA455.A63
  Waste disposal: TD797
Ashpans
  Locomotives: TJ647
Ashpits
  Railway structures: TF272
Asians
  Photographic portraits:
    TR681.A75
Asparagus: TP444.A8
  Cookery: TX803.A8
Aspen
  Woodpulp industry: TS1176.4.A8
Asphalt
  Bituminous pavements: TE275
  Cementing substance: TA443.A7
  Engineering materials: TA455.A7
  Mining engineering: TN853
  Sidewalks: TE293
Asphalt block
  Bituminous pavements: TE276

Asphalt concrete
  Cement manufacture: TP884.A85
Asphalt flooring: TH2529.P5
Asphalt mixing machinery
  Bituminous pavements: TE273
Asphalt plants
  Air pollution: TD888.A86
Asphalts
  Petroleum products: TP692.4.A8
Aspheric lenses: TS517.5.A86
Assay laboratories: TN570+
Assaying
  Metallurgy: TN550+
Assaying apparatus: TN575
Assemblage
  Crafts: TT910
Assembling machines
  Machine shops: TJ1317+
Assembly line processes
  Manufacturing engineering:
    TS178.4+
Assessment, Technology: T174.5
Assisi
  Embroidery: TT778.A87
ASTRA (Artificial satellite):
    TK5104.2.A75
Astrionics: TL3000+
Astrodynamics: TL1050+
Astronautical instruments:
    TL1082
Astronautics: TL787+
  Accidents: TL867
  Research: TL858+
Astronautics as a profession:
    TL850+
Astronautics research
  Equipment: TL859+
  Laboratories: TL859+
Astronauts
  Mental requirements: TL856
  Physical requirements: TL856
  Qualifications: TL855+
Astronomical charts
  Space navigation: TL1070
Astronomy for air pilots:
    TL586+
Astronomy, Applications of
  Surveying: TA597
Aswan High Dam: TC558.E5A8
Asylums
  Fire prevention and
    extinction: TH9445.A8

Asynchronous electronic
  circuits: TK7868.A79
Asynchronous motors
  Alternating-current motors:
  TK2785
Asynchronous transfer mode
  Packet switching: TK5105.35
AT&T computer: TK7889.A85
Athletes
  Nutrition: TX361.A8
Athletic shoes
  Boot and shoemaking: TS1017
Atlantic submarine telegraph:
  TK5611
Atmospheric deposition
  Water pollution: TD427.A84
Atmospheric electricity
  Aeronautical meteorology:
  TL557.S65
Atmospheric entry phenomena
  Astronautics: TL1060
Atmospheric railways: TF692
Atmospheric temperature
  Aeronautical meteorology:
  TL557.A8
Atomic batteries
  Electrical engineering: TK2965
Atomic bomb shelters
  Heating and ventilation:
  TH7392.A8
Atomic engines
  Aircraft engines: TL704.1
Atomic power
  Nuclear engineering: TK9001+
Atomic power plants
  Environmental effects: TD195.E4
  Fire prevention and
  extinction: TH9445.A85
  Waste control: TD899.A8
  Water pollution: TD428.A86
Atomizers
  Chemical technology: TP159.A85
Atrato Canal: TC788
Atrazine
  Water pollutants: TD427.A86
Attar of roses
  Organic chemical industries:
  TP959.R6
Attenuators
  Radio: TK6565.A8

Attics
  Building design and
  construction: TH3000.A86
  House remodeling: TH4816.3.A77
Attitude control systems
  Space vehicles: TL3260
Audio amplifiers: TK7871.58.A9
Audiovisual equipment
  industry: TS2301.A7+
Audiovisual photography: TR816
Auditing, Environmental:
  TD194.7
Auditoriums
  Electric lighting: TK4399.A9
  Electric sound control:
  TK7881.9
Austenitic steel
  Engineering materials:
  TA479.A88
Auster aircraft: TL686.A77
Authors
  Photographic portraits:
  TR681.A85
Authorship
  Aeronautics: TL564.5
  Cookery: TX644
  Safety manuals: T55.3.A87
Autoclaves
  Chemical technology: TP159.A9
Autofocus cameras
  Photography: TR260.7
Autogenous soldering
  Plumbing: TH6691
Autogiros: TL715
Autographic
  Telegraph: TK5545
Automata
  Mechanical engineering:
  TJ210.2+
Automatic cameras
  Photography: TR260.5
Automatic check equipment
  Computer engineering: TK7895.A8
Automatic control
  Aeronautical instruments:
  TL589.4+
  Motor vehicle operation:
  TL152.8
  Petroleum refining: TP690.3
Automatic data collection
  systems
  Production control: TS158.6

Automatic flushing systems
  Cold water supply plumbing:
  TH6544
Automatic lines
  Machine tools: TJ1185.5
Automatic machinery
  Mechanical engineering: TJ212+
Automatic pilots
  Aeronautical instruments:
  TL589.5
Automatic receiving instruments
  Telegraph: TK5541+
Automatic sprinkler systems
  Fire extinction: TH9336
Automatic stokers
  Furnaces: TJ345
Automatic systems
  Telephone connections: TK6397
Automatic tracking
  Radar: TK6592.A9
Automatic train control
  Railway operation: TF638
Automatic transmission
  devices: TL263
Automatic transmitting systems
  Telegraph: TK5541+
Automation
  Biotechnology: TP248.25.A96
  Electrical engineering: TK448
  Food processing and
    manufacture: TP372.8
  Foundry work: TS233
  Industrial engineering: T59.5
  Mining: TN276
  Papermills: TS1117.6
  Sugar processing: TP380
  Transportation engineering:
  TA1230
Automobile equipment and
  supplies: TL159+
Automobile exhaust
  Air pollutants: TD886.5
Automobile graveyards
  Municipal refuse: TD795.4
Automobile headlights: TL273
Automobile horns: TL274
Automobile operation: TL151.5+
Automobile purchasing: TL162
Automobile radios: TK6570.A8
Automobile related wastes
  Waste disposal: TD797.5+

Automobile repair shops
  Waste control: TD899.A96
Automobile schools: TL156
Automobile service stations
  Heating and ventilation:
  TH7392.A9
Automobile sound systems
  Electronics: TK7881.85
Automobile trains: TL235
Automotive drafting: TL253
Automotive engineering: TL1+
Automotive gas turbines: TL227
Autonomous robots
  Mechanical engineering:
  TJ211.495
Autosyn indicator
  Aeronautical instrument:
  TL589.2.A8
Autotype
  Photography: TR935
Auxiliary equipment
  Electronic measurements:
  TK7878.5+
Auxiliary power supply
  Aircraft: TL691.A95
Auxiliary valves
  Plumbing: TH6500
Avalanche control
  Engineering: TA714
Avalanche diodes
  Semiconductors: TK7871.89.A94
Aviation climatology: TL556+
Avocados
  Cookery: TX813.A9
Awards
  Cookery: TX648
Awards programs
  Industrial safety: T55.3.A93
Awning making
  Textile industries: TS1860
Axes
  Machine shops: TJ1201.A9
Axles
  Airplanes: TL683.A8
  Electric railways: TF949.A9
  Machinery: TJ1057.4
  Railroad cars: TF386
Axonometric projection
  Mechanical drawing: T363
Azimuth observations: TA597
Aziridines
  Chemical technology: TP248.A9

Azo dyes: TP914
  Textile dyes: TP918.A9

B

Babbitt metal
  Engineering materials: TA480.T5
Baby clothes: TT637
Back pressure valves
  Low-pressure steam heating:
    TH7578.B3
Backplanes
  Computer engineering:
    TK7895.B33
Bacon
  Meat-packing industries:
    TS1974.B3
Bacteria
  Water pollutants: TD427.B37
Bacterial leaching
  Hydrometallurgy: TN688.3.B33
Bacterial purification
  Sewage: TD755+
Bacterial starter cultures
  Food additives: TP456.B32
Bacteriological analysis
  Water: TD384
Bacteriology
  Sewage: TD736
Badges
  Aeronautics: TL538
  Metal manufactures: TS761
Bagasse
  Utilization of waste: TP996.B3
Bagels
  Cookery: TX770.B35
Baggage
  Railway operation: TF656
Baggage cars
  Railway equipment: TF463
Bagging
  Textile industries: TS1781
Bags
  Packaging: TS198.B3
  Paper manufacture: TS1200.A1+
Baked products
  Food values: TX552.15
Bakelite
  Plastics: TP1180.B3
Bakeries
  Air conditioning: TH7688.B3
Bakers' supplies: TX778

Bakers' trade publications:
  TX776
Baking
  Cookery: TX761+
  Cooking process: TX683
Baking aids: TP431+
Baking pans
  Cookery: TX657.B34
Baking powder
  Food processing: TP432
  Nutrition: TX409
Balances
  Aeronautical research: TL567.B3
Balancing
  Aircraft propellers: TL706.B3
  Steam engines: TJ520
Balata
  Rubber industry: TS1935
Balconies
  Wall details: TH2251.2
Bald persons
  Photographic portraits:
    TR681.B35
Baldwin Locomotive Works:
  TJ625.B2
Baling
  Cotton manufactures: TS1585
Ball and roller bearings
  Machinery: TJ1071
Ball-point pens
  Stationery: TS1267
Ballast
  Airships: TL662.B3
  Balloons: TL625.B2
  Railway construction: TF250
Ballistic missile defenses
  Environmental effects:
    TD195.B34
Ballistic ranges
  Aeronautical research:
    TL567.B33
Ballonet
  Balloons: TL625.B3
Balloon ascensions: TL620.A1+
Balloon decorations
  Decorative crafts: TT926
Balloon jumping: TL632
Balloon pilots, Licensing of:
  TL626.5
Balloon railways: TL639
Balloon sculpture
  Decorative crafts: TT926

Balloons
  Aeronautics: TL609 +
Balls, Metal
  Engineering and construction:
    TA492.B3
Balsa craft
  Woodworking: TT189
Bamboo
  Engineering materials: TA455.B3
  Housing material: TH4818.B3
  Woodpulp industry: TS1176.4.B3
Bamboo work
  Woodworking: TT190
Bananas
  Cookery: TX813.B3
  Food processing and
    manufacture: TP441.B34
  Food values: TX558.B3
Bandannas
  Clothing manufacture: TT667.5
Bannerets
  Building construction: TH2495
Banners
  Textile arts: TT850.2
Banners industry: TS2301.F6
Banyan VINES: TK5105.8.V56
Barbecue cookery: TX840.B3
Barbed wire: TS271
Barbering: TT950 +
Barbers' manuals: TT960
Barbers, Receipts for: TT977
Bare wires
  Electric power: TK3321
Barite
  Mining engineering: TN948.B18
Barium
  Chemical technology: TP245.B2
  Ore deposits and mining:
    TN490.B2
Bark
  Nature photography: TR726.B3
Barley
  Food values: TX558.B35
Barns
  Building construction: TH4930
Barograph
  Aeronautical instrument:
    TL589.2.B3
Barrages
  Hydraulic engineering: TC540 +

Barrels
  Manufactures: TS890
  Packaging: TS198.6.B3
Barrooms: TX950 +
Bars
  Furniture: TT197.5.B3
  Plastics: TP1183.B3
  Plumbing: TH6518.B2
  Structural engineering:
    TA660.B3
  Taverns, barrooms, saloons:
    TX953
Bars, Reinforcing
  Reinforced concrete
    construction: TA683.42
Bartenders' manuals and
  recipes: TX951
Base course
  Highway engineering: TE212
Base flow
  Aerodynamics: TL574.B3
Base-heating stoves
  Convective heating: TH7436.B3
Baseball players
  Photographic portraits:
    TR681.B37
Basements
  Building design and
    construction: TH3000.B36
  Drainage: TH6671.C3
  House remodeling: TH4816.3.B35
  Ventilation: TH7684.B35
Basic Bessemer process
  Steel metallurgy: TN738
Basic open hearth process
  Steel metallurgy: TN742
Basil
  Cookery: TX819.B37
Basins
  Aeronautical research: TL567.B4
  Plumbing: TH6490
Basketmaking
  Manufactures: TS910
Baskets
  Balloons: TL625.B4
  Decorative crafts: TT879.B3
  Wood products: TS913
Bass
  Cookery: TX748.B37
Bast
  Textile fiber: TS1544.B3

Bast work
  Decorative crafts: TT875
Batch production
  Manufacturing engineering:
    TS178.2
Bathroom fixtures, Catalogs of
  Plumbing: TH6489
Bathrooms
  Building design and
    construction: TH3000.B38
  House remodeling: TH4816.3.B37
  Plumbing: TH6485+
Baths
  Plumbing: TH6491+
Baths, Public
  Building construction: TH4761
  Plumbing: TH6518.B3
Bati oil
  Chemical technology: TP684.B3
Batik
  Textile decoration: TT852.5
Battenberg lace: TT805.B36
Batteries
  Aircraft: TL691.B3
  Electric vehicles: TL220+
  Household
    Waste disposal: TD799.8
  Motor vehicles: TL272
  Space vehicles: TL1102.B3
  Telephone plants: TK6278
Batters
  Food processing and
    manufacture: TP451.B38
Battery chargers
  Electrical engineering: TK2943
Bauxite
  Mining: TN490.A5
  Prospecting: TN271.B3
Bauxite industry
  Environmental effects:
    TD195.A37
Bauxite mines and mining
  Water pollution: TD428.A48
Bay and bow windows
  Building design and
    construction: TH2265
Bay window roofs
  Building construction: TH2423
BBC microcomputer: TK7889.B3
Beach nourishment: TC332

Beacon receiver
  Aeronautical navigation:
    TL696.B5
Beacons
  Aeronautical navigation:
    TL696.B4
Beacons for aircraft: TL727+
Bead flowers
  Decorative crafts: TT890.2
Beads industry: TS2301.B4
Beadwork
  Decorative crafts: TT860
Beam and girder bridges: TG350+
Beams
  Bridge engineering: TG350+
  Hoisting machinery: TJ1367
  Reinforced concrete
    construction: TA683.5.B3
  Structural engineering:
    TA660.B4
  Wooden construction:
    TA666.5.B43
Beams, Castellated
  Structural engineering:
    TA660.C37
Beams, Continuous
  Structural engineering:
    TA660.B43
Beams, Flitch
  Structural engineering:
    TA660.F57
Beams, Steel
  Structural engineering:
    TA660.S66
Beans
  Cookery: TX803.B4
  Food values: TX558.B4
Beans, Dried: TP444.B38
Bearing pads
  Cement and concrete
    construction: TA682.445
Bearings
  Airplanes: TL697.B4
  Bridge engineering: TG326
  Gasoline automobiles: TL214.B43
  Generators: TK2458.B4
  Jet engines: TL709.5.B4
  Locomotives: TJ669.B4
  Machinery: TJ1061+
  Miscellaneous motors and
    engines: TJ762.B4

Bearings
  Railroad cars: TF389
  Structural engineering:
    TA660.B45
  Turbines: TJ267.5.B43
Beartrap dams: TC549
Beauty culture: TT950+
Beauty shop practice: TT950+
Bedding
  Handicrafts: TT399+
Bedroom furniture
  Woodworking: TT197.5.B4
Bedrooms
  House remodeling: TH4816.3.B43
Beds
  Wood manufactures: TS886.5.B4
Bedspreads
  Handicrafts: TT403
Bedsteads
  Wood manufactures: TS886.5.B4
Beef
  Cookery: TX749.5.B43
  Food values: TX556.B4
Beer
  Brewing and malting: TP577
  Cookery: TX726.3
Beeswax
  Chemical technology: TP678
Beet
  Sugars and syrups: TP390+
Beetles
  Deterioration of wood: TA423.63
Beets
  Food processing and
    manufacture: TP444.B4
Behavior modification
  Industrial safety: T55.3.B43
Behavior of materials under
  applied forces: TA404.8+
Belgian stone blocks: TE263
Bellmen
  Hotels, clubs, restaurants,
    etc.: TX926
Bellows
  Machinery: TJ247.5
Bells
  Manufactures: TS583+
Belt gearing
  Mechanical engineering: TJ1100+
Belt shifters
  Mechanical engineering: TJ1107

Belt transmission
  Mechanical engineering: TJ1100+
Belting
  Fire-testing: TH9446.5.B44
  Mechanical engineering: TJ1105
Belts
  Clothing manufacture: TT668
  Fire-testing: TH9446.5.B44
Belts for assembly line
  production
  Conveying machinery: TJ1390+
Belts industry: TS2301.B5
Bench fitting
  Machine shops: TJ1315
Bench work
  Machine shops: TJ1315
Bending
  Iron and steel work: TA890+
Bending machines
  Machine shops: TJ1300
Bending moments
  Structural analysis: TA648.4
Benefits-to-costs ratios
  Engineering economy: TA177.7
Bent iron work
  Handicrafts: TT240
Bentonite
  Mining engineering: TN948.B4
Benzene
  Air pollutants: TD887.B43
  Chemical technology: TP248.B4
  Environmental pollutants:
    TD196.B38
  Fuel: TP359.B4
Benzoic acid
  Chemical technology: TP248.B5
Benzoin
  Gums and resins: TP979.5.B4
Benzol
  Fuel: TP359.B4
Benzpyrene
  Air pollutants: TD887.B45
  Environmental pollutants:
    TD196.B4
Bergamot oil
  Organic chemical industries:
    TP959.B4
Berlinite crystals
  Electronic materials:
    TK7871.15.B47

Berries
  Cookery: TX813.B4
  Food processing: TP441.B4
  Preservation and storage:
    TX612.B4
Beryl
  Mining engineering: TN948.B45
Beryllium
  Chemical technology: TP245.B4
  Engineering materials: TA480.B4
  Metallography: TN693.B4
  Metallurgy: TN799.B4
  Ore deposits and mining:
    TN490.B4
  Prospecting: TN271.B4
Besm computer: TK7889.B4
Bessemer process
  Steel metallurgy: TN736+
Bevel gears
  Mechanical movements: TJ193+
Beverage container industry
  Waste control: TD899.B48
Beverage containers: TP660
Beverages
  Adulteration: TX596+
  Chemical technology: TP500+
  Cookery: TX815+
  Nutrition: TX412+
BGP
  Computer network protocols:
    TK5105.555
Bicycle paths and tracks
  Highway engineering: TE301
Bidets
  Plumbing: TH6496
Bilayer lipid membranes
  Biotechnology: TP248.25.B53
Billing machines: TK4102
Bills of fare
  Cookery: TX727+
Binary control systems
  Mechanical engineering: TJ218.7
Bins
  Building construction: TH4498
Biochemical engineering:
  TP248.3
Biochemical oxygen demand
  Sewage: TD737
Biodegradation
  Hazardous substance disposal:
    TD1061
  Industrial and factory wastes:
    TD897.842
  Radioactive waste disposal:

Bioengineering: TA164
Biogas
  Fuel: TP359.B48
Biological purification
  Sewage: TD755+
Biological treatment
  Pollution control methods:
    TD192.5+
  Water treatment: TD475
Biomanipulation
  Environmental technology:
    TD365.5
Biomass
  Fuel: TP339
Biomass chemicals
  Chemical technology: TP248.B55
Biomass energy
  Environmental effects:
    TD195.B56
Biomass stove heating
  Convective heating: TH7436.5
Bioprocess engineering: TP248.3
Bioreactor processes
  Biotechnology: TP248.25.B55
Bioremediation
  Pollution control methods:
    TD192.5+
Biorhythms
  Industrial accidents: T55.3.B56
Biosurfactants
  Chemical technology: TP248.B57
Biotechnological production
  Compounds: TP248.65+
Biotechnology: TP248.13+
  Environmental effects:
    TD195.B58
  Hydrometallurgy: TN688.3.B33
  Woodpulp industry: TS1176.6.B56
Biplane characteristics:
  TL671.3
Biplanes: TL684.4
Bipolar transistors:
  TK7871.96.B55
Bird control
  Airports: TL725.3.B5
Birds
  Embroidery: TT773
  Nature photography: TR729.B5
Birthday cards
  Decorative crafts: TT872
Biscuits
  Cookery: TX770.B55

Bismuth
  Chemical technology: TP245.B5
  Metallography: TN693.B5
  Metallurgy: TN799.B5
  Ore deposits and mining:
    TN490.B6
Bistatic radar: TK6592.B57
BITNET
  Computer networks:
    TK5105.875.B57
Bits
  Machine tools: TJ1186
Bitumen
  Mining engineering: TN850
  Petroleum products: TP692.4.B5
  Soil stabilization: TE210.5.B5
Bituminization
  Radioactive waste disposal:
    TD898.173
Bituminous coal
  Mining: TN825+
Bituminous materials
  Air pollutants: TD887.B58
  Engineering materials: TA455.B5
  Highway engineering: TE221
Bituminous pavements
  Highway engineering: TE266+
Black processes
  Industrial photography: TR923
Blackboard drawing
  Technical education: T65.5.B5
Blackboard drawing, Technical:
  T361
Blacking materials
  Chemical technology: TP944
Blacks (Pigments)
  Organic chemical industries:
    TP951
Blacksmithing: TT218+
Blackwork embroidery: TT778.B5
Blades
  Aircraft propellers: TL707.B6
  Jet engines: TL709.5.B6
  Turbines: TJ267.5.B5
Blank books
  Stationery: TS1250
Blank forms
  Dressmaking: TT522
Blankets
  Handicrafts: TT405
Blast engines
  Pneumatic machinery: TJ963

Blast furnaces
  Metallurgy: TN713+
  Noise control: TD893.6.B58
Blast loads
  Structural engineering: TA654.7
Blast resistant design
  Structural engineering:
    TA658.42
Blasting
  Excavations: TA748
  Mining: TN279
Bleaches
  Textiles: TP894.5
Bleaching
  Laundry work: TT991
  Oils, fats, waxes: TP673
Bleaching of pulp
  Woodpulp industry: TS1176.6.B6
BLEND: TK5105.8.B57
Blender recipes
  Cookery: TX840.B5
Blimps: TL656.2
Blind flight
  Airplanes: TL711.B6
Blinds
  Window fittings: TH2276
Block adjustment
  Photographic triangulation:
    TA593.83
Block printing
  Textile arts and crafts: TT852+
Block systems
  Railway operation: TF630
Blocks
  Hoisting machinery: TJ1357
Blood products
  Biotechnology: TP248.65.B56
Blouses
  Women's tailoring: TT545
Blow-off cocks
  Plumbing explosion prevention:
    TH6566
Blowers and fans
  Pneumatic machinery: TJ960+
Blowoffs
  Furnaces: TJ358
Blowouts
  Well drilling: TN871.215
Blue john
  Mineral industries: TN989.B55
Blue processes
  Industrial reproduction: TR921

Blueberries
  Cookery: TX813.B5
Bluefish
  Cookery: TX748.B55
Blueing
  Laundry work: TT991
Blueprint reading
  Airplanes: TL671.25
  Mechanical drawing: T379
Blueprints
  Industrial reproduction: TR921
Blueprints from photographic
  negative
  Photographic processes: TR415
Board roofing
  Building construction: TH2438
Boat railways: TC771+
Boat trailers
  Motor vehicles: TL297.2
Boating
  Environmental effects:
    TD195.B63
Boats
  Environmental effects:
    TD195.B63
  Seashore photography: TR670.5
Bobbin lace: TT805.B63
Bobbinite
  Explosives: TP290.B7
Bodybuilders
  Nutrition: TX361.B64
  Photographic portraits:
    TR681.B57
Boeing Aircraft Company:
  TL686.B65
Bogs
  Reclamation: TC975
Boiler accessories: TJ288
Boiler compounds
  Steam boilers: TJ392
Boiler details and
  accessories: TJ320+
Boiler plants
  Mechanical engineering: TJ395+
Boiler scale
  Steam boilers: TJ390+
Boilermaking
  Steam boilers: TJ290+
Boilers
  Central heating: TH7470+
  High-pressure hot water
    heating: TH7534.A+
  Hot water heating: TH7538+

Boilers
  Locomotives: TJ642
  Low-pressure hot water
    heating: TH7529
  Machinery: TJ263.5
  Steam heating: TH7588+
Boiling
  Cooking process: TX685
Boiling water reactors
  Nuclear engineering: TK9203.B6
Bolex motion picture camera:
  TR883.B6
Bolt action rifle: TS536.6.B6
Bolt cutters
  Fastenings: TJ1333
Bolts
  Railway construction: TF261
Bolts and nuts
  Fastenings: TJ1330+
Bolts, Metal
  Engineering materials:
    TA492.B63
Bombproof construction
  Building construction: TH1097
Bombproof shelters
  Building construction: TH1097
Bonding
  Aircraft communication
    equipment: TL694.I6
  Metal finishing: TS718
  Plastics: TP1165
  Wood products: TS857
Bone craft: TT288
Bone products
  Manufactures: TS1982
Bone, Articles of
  Manufactures: TS1050
Bone, Coloring of
  Painting: TT370
Book illustration
  Photomechanical processes:
    TR927
Bookcases
  Woodworking: TT197.5.B6
Bookkeeping, Household:
  TX326.A1+
Boosters
  Dynamoelectric machinery:
    TK2697
  Locomotives: TJ669.B6

Bootmaking
Leather industries: TS989+
Bopp's signaling system: TF628
Borates
Mining engineering: TN917
Borax
Mining engineering: TN917
Borehole mining: TN281.5
Borides
Engineering materials:
TA455.B65
Boriding
Metal finishing: TS695.3
Boring attachments
Machine shops: TJ1220
Boring machinery
Wells: TD414
Boron
Chemical technology: TP245.B6
Prospecting: TN271.B6
Water pollutants: TD427.B67
Boron alloys
Metallography: TN693.B6
Boron organic compounds
Chemical technology: TP248.B6
Boron steel
Engineering and construction:
TA479.B6
Metallurgy: TN757.B6
Boss
Aircraft propellers: TL707.B7
Bottle jackets
Decorative crafts: TT879.J3
Bottler's machinery and
supplies: TP659.A1+
Bottles
Glassware: TP866
Bottling: TP659.A1+
Bottling plants
Noise control: TD893.6.B68
Boundary layer
Aerodynamics: TL574.B6
Boundary value problems
Engineering mathematics:
TA347.B69
Bow caps
Airships: TL662.B7
Bowfin
Cookery: TX748.B67
Bowling alleys
Fire prevention and
extinction: TH9445.B6

Box coil radiators
Hydronic systems: TH7493
Box craft
Decorative crafts: TT870.5
Box furniture
Woodworking: TT197
Box girder bridges: TG362
Box making
Decorative crafts: TT870.5
Manufactures: TS900
Boxes
Packaging: TS198.B6
Boxes, Paper
Manufactures: TS1200.A1+
Boys
Photographic portraits:
TR681.B6
Boys, Projects for
Handicrafts: TT159+
Bracing
Airplanes: TL671.5
Brackets
Machinery: TJ1065
Braid
Decorative crafts: TT880
Braid (Machine made)
Textile industries: TS1782.5
Braids
Hairwork: TT975
Silk manufactures: TS1687
Braising
Cooking process: TX686
Brake gear
Railroad cars: TF415+
Brakes
Airplanes: TL683.B7
Electric railways: TF949.B7
Elevators: TJ1377
Locomotives: TJ669.B7
Machinery: TJ1060
Motor vehicles: TL269+
Bran
Food values: TX558.B6
Brandy: TP599
Brass
Engineering materials: TA480.C7
Manufactures: TS564+
Brassieres
Clothing manufacture: TT677
Braziers
Radiative heating: TH7423

Brazilian dimensional
  embroidery: TT778.B73
Brazing
  Handicrafts: TT267
Bread
  Cereals: TX394
  Cookery: TX769+
  Food values: TX558.B7, TX560.B8
Bread flowers
  Decorative crafts: TT890.3
Breakers
  Ore dressing and milling: TN510
Breakfasts
  Cookery: TX733
Breakwaters
  Coast protective works: TC333
Breathing apparatus
  Fire prevention and
    extinction: TH9396
Breeches
  Men's tailoring: TT610
Breeder reactors
  Nuclear engineering: TK9203.B7
Bréguet (Aircraft
  manufacturer): TL686.B68
Breweries
  Building construction: TH4531
Brewing
  Beverages: TP568+
Brick
  Fire-resistive building
    construction: TH1077+
  Housing material: TH4818.B7
  Masonry construction: TA679
  Masonry materials: TA432+
  Pavements: TE255
  Sewer design and construction:
    TD680
  Sidewalks: TE287
Brick building construction:
  TH1301
Brick ovens
  Cookery: TX657.O57
Brick walls
  Building design and
    construction: TH2243
Bricked-in boilers
  Hot water heating: TH7539
Bricked-in furnaces
  Hot water heating: TH7539
  Hydronic systems: TH7473
  Steam heating: TH7589

Bricklaying
  Building construction: TH5501+
Brickmaking
  Chemical technology: TP826+
Brickmaking machinery: TP829
Bricks
  Chemical technology: TP826+
Brickworks
  Dust removal: TH7697.B75
Bridge accidents: TG470
Bridge approaches
  Highway engineering: TE216
Bridge circuits
  Electronic circuits: TK7868.B7
Bridge design: TG300+
Bridge details: TG326
Bridge drafting: TG300+
Bridge engineering: TG1+
Bridge erection: TG315
Bridge estimates: TG313
Bridge foundations: TG320
Bridge testing: TG305
Bridges
  Computer networks: TK5105.543
  Engineering: TG1+
  Environmental effects:
    TD195.B74
  Models: TG307
Bridges, Small
  Highway engineering: TE213
Brine
  Industrial electrochemistry:
    TP261.B7
Brines
  Petroleum geology: TN870.515
Brining
  Food preservation: TP371.44
Briquets and briquetting
  Fuel: TP323
Briquetting
  Chemical engineering: TP156.B7
Brittany cookery: TX719.2.B74
Brittle fracture
  Structural analysis: TA656.4
Brittle states
  Plastic properties and tests:
    TA418.16+
Broaches
  Machine tools: TJ1186
Broadband amplifiers:
  TK7871.58.B74

Broadband communication
  systems: TK5103.4+
Broadcast data systems
  Wireless communication
    systems: TK5103.487
Brocade
  Silk manufactures: TS1676
Broccoli
  Cookery: TX803.B66
Broiling
  Cooking process: TX687
Broken stone
  Unpaved roads: TE235+
Bromate
  Water pollutants: TD427.B75
Bromine
  Chemical technology: TP245.B7
Bromoil
  Photography: TR443
Bronze
  Engineering materials: TA480.C7
  Manufactures: TS564+
  Metallography: TN693.C9
Bronzing
  Metal arts and crafts: TT382.8
  Metal finishing: TS715
  Painting: TT380
Broom and brush industry
  Manufactures: TS2301.B8
Brown coal
  Mining: TN831+
Brown rice
  Cookery: TX809.B75
Browsers
  Internet: TK5105.882+
Brunches
  Cookery: TX733
Brush holders
  Generators: TK2484
Brush industry
  Manufactures: TS2301.B8
Brushes
  Generators: TK2484
Brussels sprouts
  Cookery: TX803.B7
Buckling
  Structural analysis: TA656.2
Buckram
  Wall decoration: TH8471
Buckskin
  Leather: TS980.B82

Buckwheat
  Cookery: TX809.B8
Budgets, Household: TX326.A1+
Buffalo
  Food values: TX556.B8
Buffets
  Cookery: TX738.5
Builders
  Building construction: TH12+
Builders' and contractors'
  bulletins: TH11
Building accidents: TH443
Building as a profession: TH159
Building construction: TH1+
Building construction systems:
    TH1000+
Building control systems:
    TH6012
Building defects: TH441
Building details
  Building construction: TH2025+
Building errors: TH441
Building failures: TH441
Building fittings: TH6010+
Building fittings, Catalogs
  of: TH2055
Building gas supply
  Plumbing: TH6800+
Building-integrated
  photovoltaic systems
  Solar energy: TK1087
Building layout: TH385
Building materials
  Environmental pollutants:
    TD196.B85
  Fire-testing: TH1092
Building materials industry
  Dust removal: TH7697.B8
  Electric power: TK4035.B83
  Environmental effects:
    TD195.B84
Building of structural elements
  for landscape construction:
    TH4961+
Building operation and
  housekeeping: TX955+
Building orientation
  Environmental engineering of
    buildings: TH6053
Building performance
  Building construction: TH453

Building sites
  Building construction: TH375+
  Electric lighting: TK4399.B8
  Fire prevention and
    extinction: TH9445.B8
Building standards: TH420
Building stones
  Mining engineering: TN950+
Building supplies catalogs:
  TH455
Building supply companies:
  TH12+
Building trades
  Construction: TH5011+
Buildings
  Airports: TL725.3.B8
  Energy conservation:
    TJ163.5.B84
  Painting: TT320+
  Protection from lighting:
    TH9057+
Buildings, Protection of
  Building construction: TH9025+
Built-in furniture
  Woodworking: TT197.5.B8
Bulgur
  Cookery: TX809.B85
Bulk solids
  In-plant transportation:
    TS180.8.B8
Bulk solids handling
  Dust removal: TH7697.B82
Buoys
  Lighthouses: TC380
Burbling
  Aerodynamics: TL574.T8
Burbot
  Cookery: TX748.B85
Burglar alarms
  Security in buildings: TH9739
Burglar proof construction
  Building construction: TH9720+
Burglary, Protection from
  Building construction: TH9701+
Burgundy cookery: TX719.2.B87
Burial
  Sewage disposal: TD771
Burlap
  Jute industries: TS1735
Burners
  Building gas supply: TH6880
  Gas stove heating: TH7457.B8

Bus driving: TL232.3
Buses: TL232+
  Computer engineering:
    TK7895.B87
Bush flying: TL711.B88
Business getting
  Electrical engineering: TK445
Business management
  Gas industry: TP751.3
Business methods
  Portrait photography: TR581
Bussing attendants
  Hotels, clubs, restaurants,
    etc.: TX925
Butane
  Gas industry: TP761.B8
Butanediol
  Chemical technology: TP248.B78
Butanone
  Chemical technology: TP248.B8
Butchering
  Manufactures: TS1960+
Butchers' meats
  Nutrition: TX373
Butter
  Cookery: TX759.5.B87
  Nutrition: TX381
Button industry
  Manufactures: TS2301.B9
Buttons
  Women's tailoring: TT557
Butylene
  Chemical technology: TP248.B87
Buyers' guides
  Motor vehicles: TL162
Buzzer systems
  Telegraph: TK5522
By-products
  Food processing and
    manufacture: TP373.8
  Gas industry: TP755
  Wine and winemaking: TP548.5.B9
By-products of combustion
  Chemical technology: TP365

C

Cabbage
  Cookery: TX803.C3
  Food processing and
    manufacture: TP444.C3
  Food values: TX558.C2
Cabin
  Airplanes: TL681.C3
Cabin atmosphere
  Space environment: TL1530
Cabinet projection
  Mechanical drawing: T365
Cabinetwork
  Woodworking: TT197
Cable
  Mountain railways: TF682
  Submarine telegraph: TK5671
Cable laying and repairing
  Submarine telegraph: TK5662+
Cable laying systems
  Submarine telegraph: TK5681
Cable railways: TF835
Cable-stayed bridges: TG405
Cable structures
  Structural engineering:
    TA660.C3
Cables
  Electric power: TK3301+
  Standards and testing: TK3307
  Structural engineering:
    TA660.C3
  Submarine telegraph: TK5661+
  Telegraph: TK5481
Cableways
  Conveying machinery: TJ1385+
Cabooses
  Railway equipment: TF485
Cacao
  Chemical technology: TP640
  Food values: TX560.C2
Cacao butter
  Chemical technology: TP684.C2
Cachuma Dam: TC557.C3C2
CAD/CAM systems
  Production management: TS155.6+
Cadmium
  Air pollutants: TD887.C34
  Chemical technology: TP245.C2
  Effect on food: TX572.C4
  Electroplating: TS692.C18

Cadmium
  Environmental pollutants:
    TD196.C28
  Metallurgy: TN799.C2
  Ore deposits and mining:
    TN490.C2
  Soil pollutants: TD879.C33
Cadmium alloys
  Electronics: TK7871.15.C33
Cadmium industry
  Waste control: TD899.C25
Caesium
  Chemical technology: TP245.C25
Cafeterias
  Food service: TX945+
Caissons
  Hydraulic engineering: TC199
Cake decorating
  Cookery: TX771.2
Cakes
  Cookery: TX771+
Calcimining
  Building decoration: TH8161
Calcium
  Chemical technology: TP245.C3
  Food constituent: TX553.C23
  Metallurgy: TN799.C25
Calcium carbide
  Acetylene industry: TP770
Calcium chloride
  Soil stabilization: TE210.5.C3
Calcium cyanamide
  Fertilizers: TP963.4.C3
Calcium gluconate
  Chemical technology: TP248.C15
Calcium oxide
  Environmental pollutants:
    TD196.L55
Calcium steel
  Metallurgy: TN757.C35
Calcium suplhate
  Effect on food: TX572.C6
Calculus of variations
  Engineering mathematics:
    TA347.C3
Calendering
  Paper manufacture: TS1118.C34
  Plastics: TP1175.C3
Calenders
  Paper manufacture: TS1118.C34

Calibration
  Mechanical engineering:
    TJ211.419
Calico printing: TP930+
California style cookery:
    TX715.2.C34
Calipers
  Machine shops: TJ1313
Caloric engines: TJ765
Calorizing
  Metal finishing: TS657
Calotypes
  Photographic process: TR395
Camber
  Airplanes: TL673.C3
Camcorders
  Photography: TR882.3
Camel's hair
  Textile fiber: TS1548.C3
Camera accessories
  Photography: TR265
Camera tubes
  Television: TK6655.C3
Cameras
  Photography: TR250+
Camouflage
  Airports: TL725.3.C3
Camp cooking: TX823
Camp sites, facilities, etc.
  Waste control: TD899.C27
Campgrounds
  Sanitary engineering: TD931
Camphor
  Chemical technology: TP248.C2
Cams
  Mechanical engineering: TJ206
Camshafts
  Gasoline automobiles: TL214.C35
Can privies
  Sewage disposal: TD780
Canal aqueducts: TC764
Canal embankments: TC759
Canal gates: TC762
Canal locks: TC761
Canalboats: TC765
Canals
  Hydrodynamics: TC175+
  Inland navigation: TC601+
Canapes
  Recipes: TX740
Canard wings
  Airplanes: TL673.C35

Candlepower: TK4175
Candles
  Chemical technology: TP993
  Decorative crafts: TT896.5
Candlesticks
  Woodworking: TT197.5.L34
Candlewicking
  Embroidery: TT778.C24
Candy
  Cookery: TX784+
Candymakers' tools
  Cookery: TX793
Cane sugar
  Chemical technology: TP375+
Canes
  Manufactures: TS2301.C3
Canned foods
  Cookery: TX821
  Food values: TX552
Cannel coal
  Mining: TN827
Canneries
  Sanitary engineering: TH6057.C6
  Waste control: TD899.C3
Canning
  Food processing: TP371.3+
  Storage of foods: TX603
Cans
  Packaging: TS198.C3
Canteens
  Food service: TX946
Canteens, Factory
  Food service: TX946.5.A1+
Cantilever bridges: TG385
Canvas embroidery: TT778.C3
Capacitance meters and
    measurements
  Electrical engineering: TK335
Capacitors
  Electronics: TK7872.C65
Capes
  Women's tailoring: TT530
Capillarity
  Petroleum geology: TN870.52
Capillary electrophoresis
  Biotechnology: TP248.25.C37
Capitals (of columns)
  Building design and
    construction: TH2252+

Caps
  Explosives: TP293
  Window and door openings:
    TH2261+
Capsules
  Packaging: TS198.C33
Captive balloons: TL634+
Car bodies
  Railroad cars: TF400
Car building
  Railway equipment: TF371+
Car construction
  Electric railways: TF949
  Railroads: TF380+
Car fenders
  Electric railways: TF947
Car heating
  Electric railways: TF945
Car interchange systems
  Trains: TF605+
Car lighting
  Electric railways: TF940
Car resistance
  Electric railways: TF962
Car sanitation
  Railway equipment: TF445+
Car service associations
  Trains: TF605+
Car trucks, Railroad: TF380+
Car wiring and equipment
  Electric railways: TF925
Caramel
  Sugar products: TP414.4
Carbazoles
  Textile dyes: TP918.C37
Carbohydrates
  Biotechnology: TP248.65.P64
  Chemical technology: TP248.C27
  Food constituent: TX553.C28
Carbolic acid
  Chemical technology: TP248.C3
  Environmental pollutants:
    TD196.C33
Carbon
  Chemical technology: TP245.C4
  Engineering materials: TA455.C3
Carbon compounds
  Biotechnology: TP248.65.C35
Carbon dioxide
  Air pollutants: TD885.5.C3
  Water pollution: TD427.C37

Carbon disulphide
  Air pollutants: TD887.C37
  Chemical technology: TP248.C34
Carbon lamps: TK4352
Carbon monoxide
  Air pollutants: TD885.5.C33
Carbon processes
  Photography: TR440
Carbon steel
  Engineering and construction:
    TA479.C37
Carbonated beverages: TP628+
Carbonatites
  Mining engineering: TN948.C3
Carbonic acid
  Chemical technology: TP244.C1
Carbonization
  Chemical engineering: TP156.C3
Carbonization of coal
  Fuel: TP336
Carbons
  Electric lighting: TK4335
  Manufacture: TK7725
Carbons, Natural
  Metallurgy: TN845+
Carborundum
  Abrasive: TJ1298
  Industrial electrochemistry:
    TP261.C3
Carboxymethyl cellulose
  Chemical technology: TP248.C38
Carburetion
  Gasoline automobiles: TL212
  Internal combustion engines:
    TJ787
Carburetors
  Aircraft engines: TL702.C3
  Gasoline automobiles: TL212
Card weaving
  Textile arts: TT848+
Cardboard: TS1135+
  Decorative crafts: TT870+
Carding
  Cotton manufactures: TS1578
  Textile manufactures: TS1485+
  Woolen manufactures: TS1628
Carding machines: TS1487
Care of the house: TX323
Cargo planes: TL685.7
Carnallite
  Mining engineering: TN948.C34

Carob
  Cookery: TX814.5.C35
Carotinoids
  Food constituent: TX553.C3
Carp
  Cookery: TX748.C35
Carpentry
  Building construction: TH5601+
Carpet yarns
  Textile dyeing: TP931.C2
Carpets
  Measuring, cutting, laying:
    TS1779.5
  Textile manufactures: TS1772+
Carpets, Hand-made
  Textile arts: TT850
Carports
  Building construction: TH4960
Carrageenan
  Food processing and
    manufacture: TP445.5.C35
Carriage body
  Motor vehicles: TL255+
Carriage hardware: TS2035
Carriage houses
  Plumbing: TH6518.C3
Carriage making
  Manufactures: TS2001+
Carriage painters, Scrolls and
  designs for: TS2032
Carriage painting: TS2030+
Carrier control systems
  Mechanical engineering: TJ218
Carrots
  Cookery: TX803.C35
Carrying
  Industrial safety: T55.3.L5
Cars
  Airships: TL662.C3
  Electric railways: TF920+
Carving
  Woodworking: TT199.7+
Carving, Table
  Dining-room service: TX885
Cascades
  Aerodynamics: TL574.C3
  Turbines: TJ267.5.C3
Case hardening
  Steel metallurgy: TN752.C3
Case method
  Technical education: T65.5.C3

Casein
  Chemical technology: TP248.C4
  Plastics: TP1180.C2
Cashew oil
  Chemical technology: TP684.C275
Cashiering
  Hotels, clubs, restaurants,
    etc.: TX911.3.C3
Casing
  Well drilling: TN871.22
Cassava
  Cookery: TX803.C37
  Food values: TX558.C35
  Starch: TP416.T3
Cassiterite
  Ore deposits and mining:
    TN472.C3
Cast iron
  Engineering materials: TA474+
  Metallurgy: TN710+
Cast iron radiators
  Hydronic systems: TH7487
Castellated beams
  Structural engineering:
    TA660.C37
Castigliano's theorem: TA650+
Casting
  Metal manufactures: TS228.99+
  Nonferrous metals: TS375
  Plastics: TP1150
Castings
  Building construction: TH1651+
  Foundry work: TS236
Castor oil
  Chemical technology: TP684.C3
Cat food: TS2288.C36
Catadioptric systems
  Lenses: TS517.5.C38
Catalogs
  Abrading machinery: TJ1287
  Conveying machinery: TJ1395
  Drills: TJ1265
  Electronics: TK7870.3
  Filter presses: TJ1475
  Gas engines: TJ776
  Handtools: TJ1200
  Hoisting machinery: TJ1353
  Hydraulic machinery: TJ902
  Instruments for transmitting
    sound: TK6418
  Lighting machinery and
    supplies: TK4195+
  Liquors: TP617

Catalogs
  Machine shop machinery: TJ1175
  Machine tools: TJ1190
  Machinery exclusive of prime
    movers: TJ1051
  Mechanical engineering
    equipment: TJ168
  Mechanical movements: TJ188
  Motor vehicle dealers: TL160
  Pipelines: TJ933
  Presses: TJ1452
  Radio apparatus: TK6563+
  Steam boilers: TJ296
  Steam engines: TJ473
  Steam powerplants: TJ412
  Steam pumps: TJ908
  Telegraph apparatus and
    supplies: TK5295
  Telephone apparatus and
    supplies: TK6195
  Wind power: TJ827
Catalysis
  Chemical engineering: TP156.C35
  Environmental pollution:
    TD192.3
Catalysts
  Chemical technology: TP159.C3
Catapults
  Airports: TL732
Catechisms
  Steam boilers: TJ289
Catechu
  Textile dyes: TP925.C38
Caterers' manuals
  Hotels, clubs, restaurants,
    etc.: TX921
Catfish
  Cookery: TX748.C36
Catgut industry: TS2301.C4
Cathedrals
  Fire prevention and
    extinction: TH9445.C5
Cathode ray oscillographs
  Electronic instruments:
    TK7878.7
Cathode ray tube memory systems
  Computer engineering: TK7895.C3
Cathode ray tubes
  Electronics: TK7871.73
  Radar: TK6590.C3
  Radio: TK6565.C3

Cats
  Nature photography: TR729.C3
Cattle guards
  Railway structures: TF277
Cattle passes
  Railway structures: TF282
Cavalier projection
  Mechanical drawing: T365
Cave photography: TR788
Cavitation
  Applied fluid mechanics:
    TA357.5.C38
  Chemical engineering: TP156.C38
CD-ROM drives
  Computer engineering:
    TK7895.C39
CD-ROMs
  Computer engineering:
    TK7895.C39
CDC 6600 computer: TK7889.C2
CDMA (Wireless communication
  systems): TK5103.452
CDPD (Standard)
  Wireless communication
    systems: TK5103.48
CEBUS
  Computer networks: TK5105.56
Ceilings
  Building design and
    construction: TH2531+
Celanese
  Silk manufactures: TS1688.A1+
Cell adhesion
  Biotechnology: TP248.25.C42
Cell culture
  Biotechnology: TP248.25.C44
Cellars
  Drainage: TH6671.C3
Cellophane
  Plastics: TP1180.C4
Cellulase
  Biotechnology: TP248.65.C44
Celluloid
  Plastics: TP1180.C5
Cellulose
  Aeronautics: TL699.C44
  Biotechnology: TP248.65.C45
  Insulating material: TK3441.C35
  Plastics: TP1180.C6

Cellulose
  Textile fiber: TS1544.C4
  Wood composition: TS933.C4
Cellulose acetate
  Chemical technology: TP248.C45
Cellulose insulation
  Building construction: TH1718
Cement
  Analysis: TP882.3
  Building construction: TH1461+
  Chemical technology: TP875+
  Fire-resistive building
    construction: TH1087
  Masonry construction: TA680+
  Masonry materials: TA434+
  Sewer design and construction:
    TD682
  Sidewalks: TE291
Cement composites: TA438
Cement-guns: TA446
Cement industries
  Chemical technology: TP875+
  Dust removal: TH7697.C4
  Electric power: TK4035.C25
  Energy conservation:
    TJ163.5.C45
Cement manufacture: TP881+
Cement materials
  Mining engineering: TN945
Cement pipes
  Engineering materials: TA447
Cement plants: TP882
  Air pollution: TD888.C4
Cement work
  Handicrafts: TT295
Cementation processes
  Steel metallurgy: TN734
Centering of arches
  Building construction: TH5591
Centerpieces
  Building design and
    construction: TH2531+
Central heating
  Building construction: TH7461+
Central solar heating plants
  Building construction: TH7413.5
Central station management
  Electric power plants: TK1811
Central station testing
  Electric power plants: TK1831

Central station wiring
  Electric power: TK3281
Central stations
  Electrical engineering: TK3201+
Central stations for lighting:
  TK4201+
Centralized industrial waste
  treatment facilities:
    TD897.6
Centrex telephone systems and
  services: TK6430
Centrifugal blowers
  Pneumatic machinery: TJ969
Centrifugal pumps
  Hydraulic machinery: TJ919
Centrifuges
  Chemical technology: TP159.C4
Ceramic bearings
  Mechanical engineering:
    TJ1073.C45
Ceramic decoration: TP823
Ceramic flowers
  Decorative crafts: TT890.4
Ceramic industries
  Environmental effects:
    TD195.C42
Ceramic materials
  Aeronautics: TL699.C46
  Electronics: TK7871.15.C4
  Engineering materials: TA430,
    TA455.C43
  Heat engines: TJ255.5
Ceramic metals
  Engineering materials: TA479.6
Ceramic technology: TP807+
Ceramic tile
  Building construction: TH8541+
Ceramics
  Chemical technology: TP785+
  Insulating material: TK3441.C38
Cereal products
  Food processing and
    manufacture: TP434+
Cereals
  Cookery: TX808+
  Food processing and
    manufacture: TP434+
  Food values: TX557+
  Manufactures: TS2120+
  Nutrition: TX393+
  Pet food industry: TS2288.C45

Cereals, Prepared
  Food processing and
    manufacture: TP435.C4
Ceresin
  Mineral oils and waxes: TP695
  Mining engineering: TN857
Cerium
  Chemical technology: TP245.C45
Cerussite: TN452.C4
Cesium
  Metallurgy: TN799.C4
  Water pollutants: TD427.C48
Cesspools
  Sewage disposal: TD775
CGI
  Computer network protocols:
    TK5105.565
CGNET
  Computer networks:
    TK5105.875.C45
Chafing dish cookery: TX825
Chain blocks
  Hoisting machinery: TJ1359
Chain gearing
  Mechanical engineering: TJ1117
Chains
  Metal manufactures: TS440+
Chains, Metal
  Engineering and construction:
    TA492.C6
Chairs
  Wood manufactures: TS886.5.C45
  Woodworking: TT197.5.C45
Chalcopyrite
  Mining and metallurgy: TN442.C5
Chalk
  Mining engineering: TN948.C5
Champlevé
  Handicrafts: TT382.6
Chandeliers
  Woodworking: TT197.5.L34
Channel improvement
  Hydraulic engineering: TC529
Channel selectors
  Television: TK6655.C5
Channels
  Structural engineering:
    TA660.C47
Channels, Approach
  Harbor engineering: TC352
Character recognition, Optical
  Optical data processing: TA1640

Charcoal
  Fuel: TP331
Charcoal fires
  Radiative heating: TH7423
Charge coupled devices
  Semiconductors: TK7871.99.C45
Charge transfer devices
  Semiconductors: TK7871.99.C45
Chariots transbordeurs
  Railway structures: TF276
Charts
  Air navigation: TL587
Chassis
  Motor vehicles: TL255+
Chattering control
  Control engineering: TJ223.C45
Cheese
  Cookery: TX759.5.C48
  Nutrition: TX382
Chemical analysis
  Food: TX545
  Food adulterants: TX569
Chemical detectors
  Chemical technology: TP159.C46
Chemical engineering: TP155+
Chemical engineering as a
  profession: TP186+
Chemical fire engines
  Fire prevention and
    extinction: TH9375
Chemical industry
  Energy conservation:
    TJ163.5.C54
  Waste control: TD899.C5
Chemical laboratories
  Electric power: TK4035.C35
Chemical lasers
  Applied optics: TA1690
Chemical plants: TP155.5+
  Air pollution: TD888.C5
  Building construction: TH4524
  Dust removal: TH7697.C54
  Electric power: TK4035.C37
  Environmental effects:
    TD195.C45
  Fire prevention and
    extinction: TH9445.C47
  Heating and ventilation:
    TH7392.C56
  Management: TP155.6
  Noise control: TD893.6.C45
  Ventilation: TH7684.C44

Chemical precipitation
  Sewage purification: TD751
  Water purification: TD455
Chemical preservation
  Food processing: TP371.4+
Chemical process control:
  TP155.75
Chemical processes: TP155.7+
  Nuclear engineering: TK9350
Chemical processing
  Wood: TS920+
Chemical propulsion systems:
  TL783+
Chemical rockets: TL783+
Chemical systems
  Fire prevention and
    extinction: TH9338
Chemical technicians: TP186.5
Chemical technology: TP1+
Chemical telegraph system:
  TK5549
Chemical treatment
  Pollution control methods:
    TD192.2+
  Water purification: TD451+
Chemical vapor deposition
  Metal finishing: TS695+
Chemical weapons
  Water pollutants: TD427.C54
Chemicals
  Chemical technology: TP200+
  Environmental pollutants:
    TD196.C45
  Fire prevention and
    extinction: TH9446.C5
  Petroleum products: TP692.3
Chemicals, Agricultural
  Environmental pollutants:
    TD196.A34
  Soil pollutants: TD879.A35
Chemistry
  Home economics: TX149
  Leather industries: TS967
  Paper manufacture: TS1120
Chemistry testing
  Food processing: TP372.5+
Chemistry, Environmental:
  TD193+
Chemistry, Textile: TS1474.5

Cherries
  Cookery: TX813.C4
  Food processing and
    manufacture: TP441.C45
  Preservation and storage:
    TX612.C5
Chessmen
  Decorative crafts: TT896.55
Chestnuts
  Cookery: TX814.2.C48
  Food processing and
    manufacture: TP439.5.C45
Chia
  Food values: TX558.C38
Chicken
  Cookery: TX750.5.C45
Chickpea
  Food values: TX558.C4
Child-resistant packaging:
  TS198.C46
Child seats
  Automobiles: TL159.5
Children
  Nutrition: TX361.C5
  Photographic portraits:
    TR681.C5
Children, Articles for
  Handicrafts: TT174+
Children's clothing: TT635+
Children's furniture
  Woodworking: TT197.5.C5
Children's playhouses
  Building construction: TH4967
Children's rooms
  House remodeling: TH4816.3.C45
Chile saltpeter
  Mining engineering: TN911
Chimney tops
  Ventilation of buildings:
    TH7683.V4
Chimneys
  Boiler furnaces: TJ330+
  Building construction: TH2281+
  Fire prevention and
    extinction: TH9445.C48
Chimneys, Powerplant
  Building construction: TH4591
Chinese wood oil
  Chemical technology: TP684.T8
Chiolite
  Mining engineering: TN948.C55

Chitin
  Biotechnology: TP248.65.C55
Chlorates
  Industrial electrochemistry:
  TP261.C5
Chlorides
  Salts: TP233
Chlorination
  Gold and silver metallurgy:
  TN765
  Sewage disposal: TD747.7
  Water purification: TD462+
Chlorine
  Air pollutants: TD885.5.C47
  Chemical technology: TP245.C5
  Sewage treatment: TD758.5.C45
Chlorine dioxide
  Fire prevention and
  extinction: TH9446.C6
Chlorine organic compounds
  Environmental pollutants:
  TD196.C5
Chlorite
  Prospecting: TN271.C47
Chlorofluorocarbons
  Air pollutants: TD887.C47
Chlorofluoromethane
  Air pollutants: TD885.5.C5
Chloroform
  Chemical technology: TP248.C5
Chocolate
  Nonalcoholic beverages: TP638+
  Recipes: TX767.C5
Chocolate beverages
  Cookery: TX817.C4
Chocolate, White
  Cookery: TX767.W48
Cholesterol
  Food constituent: TX553.C43
Choline
  Food constituent: TX553.C45
Christmas
  Cookery: TX739.2.C45
Christmas cards
  Decorative crafts: TT872
Christmas decorations
  Decorative crafts: TT900.C4
Chromatography
  Chemical engineering: TP156.C5
  Food analysis: TX548+
Chrome-manganese steel
  Metallurgy: TN757.C48

Chrome-nickel steel
  Metallurgy: TN757.C49
Chrome steel
  Metallurgy: TN757.C5
Chromic acid: TP217.C5
Chromic materials
  Engineering materials:
  TA455.C45
Chromium
  Assaying: TN580.C5
  Chemical technology: TP245.C6
  Electroplating: TS692.C4
  Engineering materials: TA480.C5
  Environmental pollutants:
  TD196.C53
  Metallography: TN693.C5
  Metallurgy: TN799.C5
  Ore deposits and mining:
  TN490.C4
  Ore dressing and milling:
  TN538.C57
  Photography: TR433
  Prospecting: TN271.C5
  Water pollutants: TD427.C57
Chromium steel
  Engineering and construction:
  TA479.C5
Chromizing
  Steel metallurgy: TN752.C5
Chronophotography: TR840
Chucks
  Machine shops: TJ1219
Church facilities
  Environmental effects:
  TD195.C47
Church supplies industry:
  TS2301.C5
Churches
  Building construction: TH4221
  Energy conservation:
  TJ163.5.C57
  Fire prevention and
  extinction: TH9445.C5
  Heating and ventilation:
  TH7392.C6
  Ventilation: TH7684.C6
Chutes for letters, parcels,
  cash, etc.: TJ1398
Cider
  Beverages: TP563+
  Cookery: TX726.2

Cigarettes
  Tobacco industry: TS2260
Cigars
  Tobacco industry: TS2260
Cinder
  Sidewalks: TE283
Cinematograph: TR880
Cinematography: TR845+
Cinemitrailleuse
  Aeronautical instrument:
    TL589.2.C5
Cineradiography
  Cinematography: TR896.8
Cinnabar
  Ore deposits and mining:
    TN462.C5
Cinnamon
  Cookery: TX819.C53
Cipher codes
  Aircraft: TL694.C6
Circuit breakers: TK2842
  Dynamoelectric machinery:
    TK2841+
Circuits
  Computer engineering: TK7888.4
Circuits manuals
  Electronics: TK8300+
Circulation piping
  Plumbing: TH6568
Ciro-flex cameras
  Photography: TR263.C5
Citizen participation
  Environmental protection:
    TD171.7
  Hazardous substance disposal:
    TD1050.C57
Citizens band radio: TK6570.C5
Citric acid
  Chemical technology: TP248.C6
Citronella oil
  Organic chemical industries:
    TP959.C5
Citrus fruits
  Cookery: TX813.C5
  Food values: TX558.C5
Citrus oils
  Organic chemical industries:
    TP959.C54
Citrus processing plants
  Waste control: TD899.C55, TD899.C57

Citrus products
  Food processing and
    manufacture: TP441.C5
City planning
  Municipal engineering: TD160+
City surveying
  City planning: TD167
Civil aviation: TL552
Civil engineering: TA1+
  Environmental effects:
    TD195.C54
Cladding
  Exterior walls: TH2238
Claims of inventors
  Telegraph: TK5117+
  Telephone: TK6017+
Clams
  Cookery: TX754.C53
Clapboard walls
  Building design and
    construction: TH2244
Claris Home page
  Web authoring software:
    TK5105.8885.C55
Classification
  Motion picture film: TR889
Classifiers
  Ore dressing and milling: TN515
Clay
  Ceramic technology: TP811
  Mining engineering: TN941+
  Prospecting: TN271.C53
  Sewer design and construction:
    TD682
Clay analysis
  Ceramic technology: TP811
Clay industries
  Chemical technology: TP785+
Clay minerals
  Engineering materials:
    TA455.C55
Clay modeling
  Decorative crafts: TT916
Clay ovens
  Cookery: TX657.O57
Clay pipe
  Engineering materials: TA447
  Sewer design and construction:
    TD684
Clay pot cookery: TX825.5
Clean rooms
  Dust removal: TH7694

Cleaning
  Brick: TH5520
  Hats: TS2193
  Masonry: TH5520
  Metal finishing: TS654
  Sewers: TD719
  Stone: TH5520
  Textiles: TP895
  The house: TX324
Cleaning compounds
  Chemical technology: TP990+
  Fire prevention and
    extinction: TH9446.C65
Cleaning industry, Waste from
  Environmental technology:
    TD899.C58
Cleaning plants
  Fire prevention and
    extinction: TH9445.C6
Cleanout ferrules
  House drainage: TH6646
Cleanouts
  House drainage: TH6635
Cleveland motorcycle: TL448.C54
Climatic factors
  Heating and ventilating
    systems: TH7015
Clinker brick
  Brickmaking: TP832.C5
Clinker concrete
  Cement manufacture: TP884.C5
Clinkers
  Masonry materials: TA441
Clinoptilolite
  Mining engineering: TN948.C6
Clocks
  Manufactures: TS540+
Cloisonné
  Handicrafts: TT382.6
Close-up photography: TR683+
Closed-circuit television:
  TK6680
Closed circular ring problems
  Engineering mathematics:
    TA347.C54
Closets
  Building design and
    construction: TH3000.C55
Clothing
  Home economics: TX340

Clothing factories: TT498
  Building construction: TH4522
  Electric power: TK4035.C4
Clothing for boys: TT630
Clothing for girls: TT562
Clothing for pilots: TL697.C6
Clothing for the handicapped:
  TT648
Clothing manufacture: TT490+
Clouds
  Meteorological aeronautics:
    TL557.C6
  Nature photography: TR733
Clubhouses
  Building construction: TH4800
  Electric power: TK4035.C47
Clubs: TX901+
Clutches
  Mechanical engineering: TJ1074
  Motor vehicles: TL261
Cnidoscolus oil
  Chemical technology: TP684.C6
Coagulants
  Chemical technology: TP159.C55
Coagulation
  Water purification: TD455
Coagulation, Sedimentation with
  Sewage purification: TD751
Coal
  Environmental pollutants:
    TD196.C63
  Fuel: TP325+
  Gas manufacture: TP751.7
  Mining engineering: TN799.9+
  Prospecting: TN271.C58
Coal briquets
  Fuel: TP327
Coal cars
  Railway equipment: TF479
Coal computations: TF555
Coal-fired power plants
  Water pollution: TD428.C58
Coal gasification: TP759
Coal-handling machinery
  Collieries: TN815
  Conveying machinery: TJ1405
Coal-handling plants
  Building construction: TH4471
Coal heating of buildings:
  TH7400

Coal industry
  Environmental effects:
    TD195.C58
Coal liquefaction
  Fuel: TP352
  Waste control: TD899.C585
Coal mines and mining: TN802+
  Water pollution: TD428.C6
Coal mining machinery: TN813+
Coal preparation: TN816.A1+
Coal preparation plants
  Dust removal: TH7697.C58
  Electric lighting: TK4399.C6
  Waste control: TD899.C588
Coal products
  Organic chemical industries:
    TP953
Coal screening: TN816.A1+
Coal slurry pipelines: TJ898.5
Coal storage: TN817
Coal stove heating
  Convective heating: TH7443+
Coal stoves
  Cookery: TX657.S4
Coal tar
  Organic chemical industries:
    TP953
Coal-tar colors
  Textile dyeing: TP914
Coal washing: TN816.A1+
Coal weathering: TN817
Coalbed methane: TN844+
Coaling plants
  Railway structures: TF294
Coaling stations
  Air pollution: TD888.C58
Coalsheds
  Railway structures: TF294
Coast protective works
  Harbors: TC203+
  Hydraulic engineering: TC330+
Coastal engineering: TC203+
Coaster cars: TL482
Coating of fabrics
  Textile industries: TS1512
Coating processes
  Chemical engineering: TP156.C57
Coatings
  Engineering materials:
    TA418.9.C57
  Packaging materials: TS198.3.C6
  Paper manufacture: TS1118.F5
  Space vehicles: TL954.P35

Coats
  Men's tailoring: TT595
  Women's tailoring: TT530
Cob
  Brickmaking: TP832.C6
Cobalt
  Chemical technology: TP245.C7
  Electroplating: TS692.C57
  Engineering materials: TA480.C6
  Metallography: TN693.C8
  Metallurgy: TN799.C6
  Ore deposits and mining:
    TN490.C6
  Soil pollutants: TD879.C63
Cobalt mines and mining
  Environmental effects:
    TD195.C59
Cobblestone
  Pavements: TE259
Cochineal
  Textile dyes: TP925.C63
Cockpit
  Airplanes: TL681.C6
Cocoa
  Chemical technology: TP640
  Cookery: TX817.C5
  Nutrition: TX415
Cocoa butter
  Chemical technology: TP684.C2
Coconut fiber
  Textile fiber: TS1544.C6
Coconut oil
  Chemical technology: TP684.C7
Coconuts
  Cookery: TX814.2.C63
  Food processing and
    manufacture: TP439.5.C6
Coded centralized traffic
  control
  Railway operation: TF639
Codfish
  Cookery: TX748.C63
Coding theory
  Electrical engineering:
    TK5102.92+
Coffee
  Adulteration: TX583
  Chemical technology: TP645
  Cookery: TX817.C6
  Food values: TX560.C63

Coffee
  Nonalcoholic beverages: TP638+
  Nutrition: TX415
Coffee (as a flavor)
  Cookery: TX819.C6
Coffee making paraphernalia
  Cookery: TX657.C67
Coffee processing plants
  Air pollution: TD888.C6
Cofferdams
  Hydraulic engineering: TC198
Coffins
  Woodworking: TT197.5.C62
Coherent radar: TK6592.C6
Coherers
  Radiotelegraph: TK5863
Coil boilers
  Hot water heating: TH7530+
Coils
  Electronics: TK7872.C56
  Radiators: TH7482+
  Radio: TK6565.C6
Coin operated machines
  Mechanical engineering: TJ1557+
Coir
  Textile fiber: TS1747.C6
Coke
  Fuel: TP336
  Petroleum products: TP692.4.C6
Coke industry
  Electric power: TK4035.C6
Cold air supply
  Warm-air heating: TH7608
Cold cathode tubes:
    TK7871.84.C6
Cold dishes
  Cookery: TX830
Cold resistant materials:
    TA418.28
Cold storage
  Food preservation: TP372.2
Cold-storage foods
  Cookery: TX826
Cold water supply
  Building construction: TH6541+
Cold weather conditions
  Airports: TL725.3.C6
  Building construction: TH153
  Cement and concrete
    construction: TA682.43
  Mining: TN291.26

Cold weather operation
  Airplanes: TL711.C64
  Railway operation: TF506
Cold weather photography: TR792
Cold working of metals
  Manufactures: TS207
Collage
  Crafts: TT910
Collar bearings
  Machinery: TJ1069
Collectibles
  Cookery: TX642
Collecting
  Firearms: TS532.4
Collecting reservoirs
  Sewers: TD722
Collection of municipal refuse
  Environmental technology:
    TD785+
Collectors
  Firearms: TS532.4
Collectors and collecting
  Cookery: TX642
  Model airplanes: TL772
  Model motor vehicles: TL237.2
  Motorcycles: TL444.2
  Radio receiving apparatus:
    TK6563.2
  Tractors: TL233.25
College buildings
  Heating and ventilation:
    TH7392.S35
College students
  Nutrition: TX361.C6
Colleges
  Energy conservation: TJ163.5.U5
Collision avoidance systems
  Motor vehicles: TL272.52
Collision prevention
  Aeronautical navigation:
    TL696.C6
Collodion process
  Photographic process: TR390
Colloidal concrete
  Cementing substance: TA443.C64
Colloidal fuel: TP360
Colloids
  Food constituents: TP453.C65
Collotype processes
  Photography: TR930+
Color as a safety measure
  Industrial safety: T55.3.C6

Color blindness
   Railway operation: TF620
Color cinematography: TR853
Color combinations
   Textile dyeing: TP892
Color photography
   Photographic processing: TR510+
Color processes
   Photography: TR977
Color removal
   Sewage disposal: TD758.5.C65
   Water treatment and
      conditioning: TD468
Color television: TK6670
Colorants
   Food additives: TP456.C65
Colored glass
   Glassmaking: TP861.5
Coloring
   Metal finishing: TS710, TT382.2
   Paper manufacture: TS1118.D9
Coloring matter
   Effect on food: TX571.C7
Coloring of bone
   Painting: TT370
Coloring of prints
   Photographic processing: TR485
Coloring of stone
   Painting: TT370
Colors
   Ceramic decoration: TP823
   Dyeing: TP907
Columbian Exposition, 1893:
   T500
Columns
   Building design and
      construction: TH2252+
   Reinforced concrete
      construction: TA683.5.C7
   Structural engineering:
      TA660.C6
Columns, Metal
   Engineering and construction:
      TA492.C7
Comb industry
   Manufactures: TS2301.C75
Combination warm-air heating
   systems: TH7635
Combinatorial analysis
   Engineering mathematics:
      TA347.C6

Combined purpose desalination
   plants: TD479.5
Combined sewerage system: TD662
Combines
   Agricultural machinery: TJ1486
Combing
   Cotton manufactures: TS1578
   Textile manufactures: TS1485+
   Woolen manufactures: TS1628
Combing machines: TS1487
Combustible gas detectors
   Fire prevention and
      extinction: TH9271
Combustion
   Diesel engines: TJ797
   Furnaces: TJ324.7
   Rockets: TL784.C6
Combustion chambers
   Jet engines: TL709.5.C55
   Machinery: TJ254.7
Combustion engineering:
   TJ254.5+
Combustion gases
   Air pollutants: TD885.5.C66
Combustion, Spontaneous
   Fire prevention: TH9198
Command
   Fire extinction: TH9310.8
Command control equipment
   Astronautics: TL4040+
Command control systems
   Space vehicles: TL3280
Commercial buildings
   Air conditioning: TH7688.C64
   Artificial lighting: TH7975.C65
   Construction: TH4311+
   Electric wiring: TK3284
   Heating and ventilation:
      TH7392.C65
Commercial cinematography
   Photography: TR894.3+
Commercial correspondence
   Hotels, clubs, restaurants,
      etc.: TX911.3.C6
Commercial garment cleaning and
   dyeing: TP932+
Commercial laundry work: TT990
Commercial photography: TR690+
Communal kitchens
   Food service: TX946
Communication equipment
   Aircraft: TL692+

Communication in chemical
  engineering: TP186.7+
Communication in materials
  engineering: TA404.25
Communication in mechanical
  engineering: TJ160+
Communication methods
  Aircraft: TL692+
  Space vehicles: TL3025+
Communication of aeronautics
  information: TL563.5+
Communication of automotive
  information: TL10+
Communication of building
  information: TH215+
Communication of cookery
  information: TX643+
Communication of handicraft
  information: TT10+
Communication of metallurgical
  information: TN610+
Communication of photography
  information: TR10+
Communication of technical
  information: T10.5+
Communication of water supply
  information: TD209+
Communication systems
  Airports: TL725.3.C63
  Fire prevention and
    extinction: TH9280
  Highway engineering: TE228.3
Communications
  High speed ground
    transportation: TF1520
Communications software
  Electrical engineering:
    TK5105.9
Communicator (Netscape):
  TK5105.883.N49
Community antenna television:
  TK6675
Community water tower systems
  Fire prevention and
    extinction: TH9333
Commutation and brush
  resistance
  Dynamoelectric machinery:
    TK2281
Commutation pole generators
  Dynamoelectric machinery:
    TK2665

Commutators and collectors
  Generators: TK2481
Compact disc players
  Electronics: TK7881.75
Compact discs
  Electronics: TK7882.C56
Compacting
  Chemical engineering: TP156.C59
Compagnie nouvelle du canal de
  Panama: TC779+
Compagnie universelle du canal
  interocéanique de Panama:
    TC778+
Compass
  Surveying instruments: TA563
Compass (Gyroscope)
  Aeronautical instrument:
    TL589.2.C58
Compass (Magnetic)
  Aeronautical instrument:
    TL589.2.C6
Compass surveying: TA595+
Compensating powder
  Explosives: TP290.C7
Competitions
  Cookery: TX648
Complex analysis
  Engineering mathematics:
    TA347.C64
Compliant platforms
  Ocean engineering: TC1700+
Composer (Netscape)
  Web authoring software:
    TK5105.8885.N49
Composite materials
  Aeronautics: TL699.C57
  Engineering materials:
    TA418.9.C6
  Motor vehicle construction
    materials: TL240.5.C65
  Structural engineering: TA664
  Testing: TA417.7.C6
Composite photography: TR685
Composite systems (A.C. and
  D.C.)
  Electrical engineering: TK3171
Composite systems (D.C. and
  A.C.)
  Electric lighting: TK4308
Composition
  Photography: TR179
Composition of food: TX501+

Composition roofing
  Building construction: TH2450+
Composting
  Municipal refuse: TD796.5
Compound semiconductors
  Electronics: TK7871.99.C65
Compounding
  Distilling: TP612
Compressed-air automobiles:
    TL225
Compressed air engines: TJ766+
Compressed air machinery:
    TJ981+
Compressed air railways: TF838
Compressed gas
  Chemical technology: TP243
  Gas industry: TP761.C65
Compressed natural gas
  automobiles: TL228
Compressed wood: TS868
Compressed yeast
  Leavening agents and baking
    aids: TP433
Compressibility
  Aerodynamics: TL574.C4
Compression
  Testing of materials:
    TA417.7.C65
Compressor stations
  Dust removal: TH7697.C6
Compressors
  Aeronautics: TL697.C65
  Chemical technology: TP159.C57
  Electric driving: TK4059.C64
  Jet engines: TL709.5.C56
  Locomotives: TJ669.C6
  Turbines: TJ267.5.C5+
Computation of areas
  Surveying: TA613+
Computational methods
  Structural engineering: TA640+
Computer-aided engineering
  Engineering mathematics: TA345+
Computer animation
  Cinematography: TR897.7+
Computer art
  Decorative crafts: TT869.5
Computer-assisted instruction
  Technical education: T65.5.C65
Computer components
  Manufacturing: TK7886
Computer engineering: TK7885+

Computer engineering as a
  profession: TK7885.53+
Computer flight games
  Airplanes: TL712.8
Computer furniture
  Woodworking: TT197.5.C65
Computer graphics: T385
Computer hardware: TK7885+
Computer installations
  Fire prevention and
    extinction: TH9445.C65
Computer integrated
  manufacturing systems:
    TS155.63
Computer manufacturing plants:
    TK7886
Computer network protocols:
    TK5105.55+
Computer network resources:
    TA158.7
  Chemical engineering: TP186.8
  Handicrafts: TT11
  Motor vehicles: TL11
  Photography: TR11
Computer network security:
    TK5105.59
Computer networks
  Electrical engineering:
    TK5105.5+
Computer output microfilm
  devices: TK7887.8.C6
Computer programs
  Orbital transfer: TL1078
  Space trajectories: TL1078
Computer simulation
  Biotechnology: TP248.25.A96
  Civil engineering: TA404.23
  Mechanical engineering:
    TJ211.47
Computer technicians
  Electronics: TK7885.54
Computer vision: TA1634
Computers
  Amateurs' manuals: TK9969
  Fire prevention and
    extinction: TH9445.C65
  Manufacturing: TK7886
  Motor vehicles: TL272.53
Concentrating
  Ore dressing and milling:
    TN520+

Concierge service
  Hotels, clubs, restaurants,
    etc.: TX911.3.C63
Concierges
  Hotels, clubs, restaurants,
    etc.: TX911.3.C63
Concrete
  Fire-resistive building
    construction: TH1087
  Masonry construction: TA680+
  Masonry materials: TA439+
  Sewer design and construction:
    TD682
  Sidewalks: TE291
Concrete (Nonstructural)
  Floors and flooring: TH2529.C6
Concrete and stone
  Bridge engineering: TG367
Concrete and timber
  Masonry materials: TA442
Concrete-block building
  construction: TH1491
Concrete blocks
  Cement manufacture: TP885.C7
  Housing material: TH4818.C6
Concrete bridges: TG335+
Concrete building
  construction: TH1461+
Concrete construction,
  Reinforced
  Structural engineering:
    TA682.92+
Concrete corrosion: TA440
Concrete dams: TC547
Concrete domes
  Building design and
    construction: TH2170.5
Concrete mine supports
  Mining: TN289.5
Concrete piling
  Foundations: TA787
Concrete pipes
  Engineering materials: TA447
Concrete roads and pavements:
  TE278+
Concrete roofing
  Building construction: TH2446
Concrete slabs
  Cement manufacture: TP885.C7
Concrete walls
  Building design and
    construction: TH2245

Condensation
  Chemical engineering: TP156.C6
Condensation trails
  Aeronautical meteorology:
    TL557.C7
Condense-waste systems
  Low-pressure steam heating:
    TH7575
Condensers
  Dynamoelectric machinery:
    TK2805
  Electronics: TK7872.C65
  Radio: TK6565.C65
Condiments
  Cookery: TX819.A1+
  Flavoring aids: TP420
  Nutrition: TX406+
Conduct
  Household servants: TX333
Conductivity, Thermal
  Thermal properties: TA418.54
Conductors
  Building construction: TH2493
  Electric power: TK3301+
Conduit material
  Telegraph: TK5467
Conduits
  Hydrodynamics: TC174
  Water supply: TD398
Conex containers
  Packaging: TS198.6.C6
Confectioners' supplies: TX778
Confectionery
  Cookery: TX761+
  Food values: TX560.C65
Congelation of beverages: TP658
Conglomerate
  Mining engineering: TN948.C72
Connecting rods
  Aircraft engines: TL702.C5
  Locomotives: TJ662
Connections
  House drainage: TH6613
  Telegraph: TK5401+
  Telephone: TK6301+
Connections piping
  Plumbing: TH6568
Connectors
  Electric power transmission:
    TK3521

Conservation
  Airplanes: TL671.95
  Motorcycles: TL444.2
  Photographs: TR465
  Tractors: TL233.25
Conservation, Water: TD388+
Consolidation
  Soils: TA710+
Constant-current generators
  Dynamoelectric machinery:
    TK2665
Constant-potential generators
  Dynamoelectric machinery:
    TK2665
Constructed wetlands
  Sewage treatment: TD756.5
Construction
  Airships: TL660
  Balloons: TL622
  Boilermaking: TJ290+
  Electric railways: TF863+
  High speed ground
    transportation: TF1470+
  Lighthouses: TC375+
  Locomotives: TJ635
  Petroleum pipelines: TN879.53
  Radioactive waste sites:
    TD898.155.D47
  Sewers: TD678+
  Telegraph: TK5401+
  Telephone: TK6301+
  Warm-air heating: TH7609
Construction details
  Gasoline automobiles: TL210+
  Highway engineering: TE210+
Construction equipment
  Building construction: TH900+
  Electric driving: TK4059.C65
  Internal combustion engines:
    TJ793.2
Construction industry
  Air pollution: TD888.C63
  Energy conservation:
    TJ163.5.C65
  Noise control: TD893.6.C6
  Waste control
    Environmental technology:
    TD899.C5885
  Water pollution: TD428.C64

Construction methods
  Cement and concrete
    construction: TA682.4+
  Reinforced concrete
    construction: TA683.4+
Construction on contaminated
  sites: TH1095.5
Construction, Precast
  Reinforced concrete
    construction: TA683.7
Construction, Prestressed
  concrete: TA683.9+
Consulting engineering:
  TA215.22+
Consumer education
  Household administration:
    TX335+
Consumer products, Safety of
  Product engineering: TS175
Consumers' guides
  Gas lighting: TH7915
Contact mechanics
  Applied dynamics: TA353
Contact prints
  Photography: TR312
Contactors
  Electronics: TK7872.C67
Contacts
  Electronics: TK7872.C68
Containerization
  Transportation engineering:
    TA1215
Containers
  Packaging: TS197.5
Containment
  Nuclear reactors: TK9211
Contaminated sites,
  Construction on: TH1095.5
Contamination
  Electronics: TK7870.27
  Space vehicles: TL946
Continuous beams
  Structural engineering:
    TA660.B43
Continuous frames
  Structural engineering:
    TA660.F72
Continuous girder bridges:
  TG413+
Continuous girders: TG355
Continuous ingot casting
  Steel metallurgy: TN750

Continuous rails
  Railway construction: TF262
Continuous systems
  Structural analysis: TA651
Continuous wave radar:
  TK6592.C65
Contracting: TA201+
Contractor, Hiring a
  House construction: TH4815.4
Contractors
  Building construction: TH12+
Contractors' operations and
  equipment: TA201+
Contracts
  Engineering economy: TA180+
Control
  Aerodynamics: TL574.C6
  Biotechnology: TP248.25.M65
  Environmental pollution: TD172+
  Fire extinction: TH9310.8
  Petroleum pipelines: TN879.52
Control apparatus
  Airplanes: TL678+
Control compartment
  Airships: TL662.C6
Control engineering systems
  Mechanical engineering: TJ212+
Control of production systems
  Production management: TS155.8+
Control rooms for nuclear
  facilities: TK9220
Control stick
  Airplanes: TL678+
Control surfaces
  Airplanes: TL676+
Control systems
  Aircraft engines: TL702.A37
  Gasoline automobiles: TL214.C64
  Jet engines: TL709.5.C57
  Mechanical engineering:
    TJ211.35, TJ214+
Control tower display systems
  Aeronautical navigation:
    TL696.C75
Control towers
  Airports: TL725.3.C64
Controllable pitch aircraft
  propellers: TL707.P5
Controlled release technology
  Chemical engineering: TP156.C64

Controllers
  Dynamoelectric machinery:
    TK2851
  Electric railways: TF930
Controls
  Rockets: TL784.C63
Convection
  Applied fluid mechanics:
    TA357.5.C65
Convection oven cookery:
  TX840.C65
Convective heating
  Building construction: TH7435+
Convenience foods: TP451.C6
  Nutrition: TX370
Converters
  Dynamoelectric machinery:
    TK2796
Convertiplanes: TL685
Convex programming
  Industrial engineering: T57.815
Conveying machinery
  Electric driving: TK4059.C67
  Fire prevention and
    extinction: TH9445.C67
  Mechanical engineering: TJ1350+
Conveying of gases, liquids and
  solids by means of steam,
  air, or water: TJ898+
Conveyors for assembly line
  production
  Conveying machinery: TJ1390+
Conveyors for letters, parcels,
  cash, etc.: TJ1398
Cookbooks: TX703+
Cookers
  Cookery: TX657.C7
Cookery
  Home economics: TX641.2+
Cookery for large numbers:
  TX820
Cookery information,
  Communication of: TX643+
Cookery using alcoholic
  beverages: TX726+
Cookie cutters
  Cookery: TX657.C72
Cookie molds
  Cookery: TX657.C72
Cookies
  Cookery: TX772
Cooking en casserole: TX693

Cooking processes: TX681+
Cooks
  Photographic portraits:
    TR681.C66
Cookware
  Cookery: TX657.C74+
Cooling
  Buildings: TH7687+
  Chemical technology: TP363
  Diesel engines: TJ799
  Electronic apparatus and
    materials: TK7870.25
  Internal combustion engines:
    TJ789
  Nuclear reactors: TK9212
  Rockets: TL784.C65
Cooling systems
  Aircraft engines: TL702.R3
  Gasoline automobiles: TL214.R3
  Jet engines: TL709.5.C6
Cooling towers
  Chemical technology: TP159.C6
  Environmental effects: TD195.C6
  Steam engines: TJ563
Cooperage
  Manufactures: TS890
Coordinate measuring machines:
    TA165.5
Copper
  Aeronautics: TL699.C6
  Assaying: TN580.C64
  Chemical technology: TP245.C8
  Electrical engineering:
    TK454.4.C6
  Electroplating: TS692.C6
  Engineering materials: TA480.C7
  Metallography: TN693.C9
  Metallurgy: TN780
  Ore deposits and mining: TN440+
  Ore dressing and milling:
    TN538.C66
  Powder metallurgy: TN697.C65
  Prospecting: TN271.C6
  Waste disposal: TD812.5.C66
  Water pollutants: TD427.C66
Copper alloys: TL699.C6
Copper conductors
  Electric power: TK3311.C6
Copper founding
  Manufactures: TS620+
Copper industry
  Waste control: TD899.C59

Copper mines and mining
  Water pollution: TD428.C66
Copper roofing
  Building construction: TH2458
Copper steel
  Engineering and construction:
    TA479.C7
Copper sulphate
  Algae control: TD465
Coppersmithing
  Manufactures: TS620+
Copperwork
  Handicrafts: TT250
Coprolites
  Mining engineering: TN948.C73
Copybooks
  Stationery: TS1251
Copying
  Photography: TR470
Cordage
  Textile fiber: TS1784+
Cordials
  Distilling: TP611
Cordierite
  Mining engineering: TN948.C75
Cordite
  Explosives: TP290.C8
Cords
  Silk manufactures: TS1687
Coremaking
  Metal manufactures: TS243+
Coriander
  Cookery: TX819.C65
Cork
  Engineering materials: TA455.C6
Cork craft
  Woodworking: TT190.5
Cork industry
  Manufactures: TS908
Corkscrews
  Cookery: TX657.C76
Corliss steam-engine: TJ485.C5
Corliss valve gears: TJ551.C8
Corn
  Cookery: TX809.M2
  Food values: TX558.C57
  Milling: TS2159.C2
  Sugars and syrups: TP405
Corn oil
  Chemical technology: TP684.C8

Corn products
  Food processing and
    manufacture: TP435.C67
Corncobs
  Utilization of waste: TP996.C6
Corned beef
  Meat-packing industries:
    TS1974.C67
Cornhusk craft
  Decorative crafts: TT878
Cornices (Exterior)
  Building construction: TH2482+
Cornices (Interior)
  Building construction: TH2553
Cornish steam boiler
  Mechanical engineering: TJ310
Cornmeal
  Food values: TX558.C57
Cornstalks
  Paper manufacture: TS1109
  Utilization of waste: TP996.C7
Cornstarch: TP415+
Correct dress
  Men's tailoring: TT618
Correctional institutions
  Fire prevention and
    extinction: TH9445.C68
Correspondence, Technical:
  T11.3
Corrosion
  Electronics: TK7870.28
  Gas industry: TP751.1
  Iron and steel: TA467
  Metals: TA462
  Ocean engineering: TC1670
  Packaging protection:
    TS198.8.C6
  Petroleum refining: TP690.8
  Properties of materials:
    TA418.74+
  Reinforcing bars: TA445.5
  Sewers: TD691
  Underwater structures: TC200
Corrosion-resistant alloys
  Engineering and construction:
    TA486
Corrosion-resistant materials
  Engineering materials: TA418.75
Corrosive wastes
  Waste disposal: TD898.8.C67
Corrugated paper
  Decorative crafts: TT870+

Corrugated paperboard: TS1138
Corsets
  Clothing manufacture: TT677
Corundum
  Engineering materials:
    TA455.C65
  Industrial electrochemistry:
    TP261.C67
  Mining engineering: TN936
Cosmetic delivery systems:
  TP983.3
Cosmetics
  Organic chemical technology:
    TP983+
Cosmetology: TT950+
Cost control
  Hazardous substances and their
    disposal: TD1050.C67
  Hotels, clubs, restaurants,
    etc.: TX911.3.C65
  Production management: TS165+
Cost effectiveness
  Engineering economy: TA177.7
Cost measurements
  Masonry construction: TH5330
Cost of operation
  Electric railways: TF962
  Motor vehicles: TL151.5+
Cost of production
  Machine shops: TJ1146
Costs
  Cement and concrete
    construction: TA682.26
  Engineering economy: TA183
  Heating of buildings: TH7335+
  Municipal refuse and solid
    wastes: TD793.7
  Packaging: TS196.2
  Plumbing: TH6234+
  Railroad engineering: TF193
  Saline water conversion:
    TD479.3
  Sewage collection and disposal
    systems: TD653
Costume design: TT507
Cotton
  Fire prevention and
    extinction: TH9446.C7
  Textile fiber: TS1542
  Utilization of waste: TP996.C75
Cotton dyeing: TP930+

Cotton fabrics
  Cotton manufactures: TS1582
  Fire prevention and
    extinction: TH9446.C7
Cotton gins
  Air pollution: TD888.C65
  Fire prevention and
    extinction: TH9445.C7
Cotton gins and ginning: TS1585
Cotton industry
  Waste control: TD899.C6
Cotton machinery
  Cotton manufactures: TS1583
Cotton manufactures: TS1550+
Cotton waste products
  Cotton manufactures: TS1587
Cottonseed oil
  Chemical technology: TP681.A1+
Cottonseed products
  Food values: TX560.C7
Couching
  Embroidery: TT778.C63
Coulometers: TK331
Counted thread embroidery:
  TT778.C65
Counter tops
  Woodworking: TT197.5.C68
Counters
  Control engineering: TJ223.C6
  Electronics: TK7872.C7
Country homes
  Construction: TH4850
Country roads
  Highway engineering: TE229+
Coupled problems
  Engineering mathematics:
    TA347.C68
Couplers
  Railroad cars: TF410
Course computers
  Aeronautical navigation:
    TL696.C8
Course-line computers
  Aeronautical navigation:
    TL696.C8
Coverlets
  Handicrafts: TT835
Cowling
  Airplanes: TL681.C7
Cowlings
  Aircraft engines: TL702.C6

Cowpeas
  Cookery: TX803.C68
  Food values: TX558.C6
Crabs
  Cookery: TX754.C83
Crackers
  Cookery: TX770.C72
Cracking process
  Petroleum refining: TP690.4
Crackle
  Painting: TT378
Craft materials and supplies
  Handicrafts: TT153.7
Cranberries
  Cookery: TX813.C7
Cranes
  Hoisting machinery: TJ1363+
  Hydraulic engineering: TC370
  Railway structures: TF290
Crankpin
  Steam engines: TJ537
Cranks
  Locomotives: TJ669.C7
  Mechanical engineering: TJ182+
  Miscellaneous motors and
    engines: TJ762.C73
  Steam engines: TJ537
Crankshafts
  Aircraft engines: TL702.C7
  Gasoline automobiles: TL214.C73
  Locomotives: TJ669.C7
  Miscellaneous motors and
    engines: TJ762.C73
Crappie
  Cookery: TX748.C73
Crashworthiness
  Motor vehicles: TL242
Crates
  Packaging: TS198.6.C7
Crawl spaces
  Building design and
    construction: TH3000.C73
Crayfish
  Cookery: TX754.C84
Cream of tartar
  Food processing: TP432
Creameries
  Heating and ventilation:
    TH7392.C7
Crease-resisting process
  Textile industries: TS1513

Creep behavior
  Plastic properties and tests:
    TA418.22
Creosote
  Preservation of wood:
    TA424.6.C7
Crepe
  Silk manufactures: TS1677
Crepes
  Cookery: TX770.P34
Cresols
  Chemical technology: TP248.C67
Cresylic acid
  Chemical technology: TP248.C7
Crewelwork
  Embroidery: TT778.C7
Crex products
  Wood technology: TS915
Cribs
  Plant service facilities:
    TS189.3
  Wood manufactures: TS886.5.C74
Cribwork
  Hydraulic engineering: TC197
Crimping
  Textile industries: TS1487.7
Critical path analysis
  Management of engineering
    works: TA194
  Production control: TS158
Crocheting
  Decorative needlework: TT819+
Crocheting machinery
  Clothing manufacture: TT685
Croissants
  Cookery: TX770.C74
Crop residues
  Rural engineering: TD930.3
Cross-country flying
  Airplanes: TL711.L7
Cross-media pollution
  Measurement of pollution:
    TD193.3
Cross method: TA650+
Cross-stitch
  Embroidery: TT778.C76
Crossarms
  Electric power: TK3242
Crossed-field amplifiers:
    TK7871.58.C75
Crosshead and connecting rod
  Steam engines: TJ535

Crossings
  Railway construction: TF263
Crucible process
  Steel metallurgy: TN735
Cruciform wings
  Airplanes: TL673.C7
Crushed stone industry
  Dust removal: TH7697.C7
  Noise control: TD893.6.C78
Crushing
  Ore dressing and milling: TN510
Crushing and milling machinery
  Mechanical engineering: TJ1345
Cryoelectronic devices
  Electronics: TK7872.C77
Cryogenic engineering: TP480+
Cryopreservation
  Biotechnology: TP248.25.C79
Cryotrons
  Computer engineering: TK7895.C7
Cryptographic techniques
  Coding theory: TK5102.94
Cryptosporidium
  Water pollutants: TD427.C78
Crystal sets
  Radio receiving apparatus:
    TK6564.C79
Crystalline solids
  Materials of engineering and
    construction: TA418.9.C7
Crystallization
  Chemical engineering: TP156.C7
Cucumbers
  Food processing and
    manufacture: TP444.C8
Cultivators
  Agricultural machinery: TJ1482
Cultured pearls
  Jewelry work: TS755.P4
Culverts
  Highway engineering: TE213
  Railway structures: TF282
Culverts, Cement: TA447
Cupola furnaces
  Foundry work: TS231
Curbs
  Highway engineering: TE298
Curbstones
  Highway engineering: TE298
Curing
  Chemical engineering: TP156.C8
  Tobacco industry: TS2249

Currant grapes
  Cookery: TX813.C87
Current and voltage waveforms
  Electrical engineering: TK531
Current converters
  Electronics: TK7872.C8
Current meters and measurements
  Electrical engineering: TK331
Current regulators
  Electronics: TK7872.C83
Curry
  Cookery: TX819.C9
Curtain making
  Handicrafts: TT390
Curtain walls
  Building design and
    construction: TH2238
Curves
  Railroad surveying: TF216
  Railway construction: TF264
Cushioning
  Packaging: TS198.6.C8
Cushioning materials
  Packaging waste
    Disposal: TD797.92
Cushions
  Handicrafts: TT410
Customer relations
  Hotels, clubs, restaurants,
    etc.: TX911.3.C8
Customizing
  Motor vehicles: TL255.2
Cut glass
  Glassmaking: TP861
Cutlery
  Metal manufactures: TS380+
Cutouts
  Dynamoelectric machinery:
    TK2846
Cutting
  Ceramic technology: TP814
  Dressmaking: TT520
  Iron and steel work: TA890+
  Men's tailoring: TT590
  Paper manufacture: TS1118.C8
  Plastics: TP1155
Cutting machinery
  Machine shops: TJ1230+
  Paper manufacture: TS1118.C8
Cutting tools
  Machine tools: TJ1186

Cyanide process
  Gold and silver metallurgy:
    TN767
Cyanides
  Chemical technology: TP248.C9
  Environmental pollutants:
    TD196.C93
  Sewage treatment: TD758.5.C93
  Soil pollutants: TD879.C93
  Water pollutants: TD427.C9
Cyanines
  Textile dyes: TP918.C9
Cyanite
  Mining engineering: TN948.C95
  Ore dressing and milling:
    TN538.C9
Cyanocobalamine
  Chemical technology: TP248.C93
Cyanotypes
  Photographic processes: TR415
Cyclamates
  Sweeteners: TP423
Cyclecars: TL390
Cycles
  Vehicles: TL400+
Cyclists
  Nutrition: TX361.C94
Cyclized rubber
  Manufactures: TS1927.C92
Cyclodextrins
  Biotechnology: TP248.65.C92
  Chemical technology: TP248.C94
Cyclohexane
  Environmental pollutants:
    TD196.C95
Cycloidal engines: TJ731
Cyclotetramethylene-tetranitr
  amine
  Explosives: TP290.C9
Cylinder blocks
  Gasoline automobiles: TL214.C93
  Miscellaneous motors and
    engines: TJ762.C94
Cylinder heads
  Gasoline automobiles: TL214.C93
Cylinder systems
  Cold water supply plumbing:
    TH6551
Cylinders
  Aircraft engines: TL702.C9
  Diesel engines: TJ798.5
  Gas engines: TJ774
  Gasoline automobiles: TL214.C93

Cylinders
  Internal combustion engines:
  TJ788
  Locomotives: TJ659
  Steam engines: TJ527+
  Structural engineering:
  TA660.C9
Cylinders, Metal
  Engineering and construction:
  TA492.C9

D

Daguerreotype
  Photography: TR365
Daily life for men, Economics
  of: TX147
Dairy foods
  Nutrition: TX377+
Dairy plants
  Waste control: TD899.D3
Dairy products
  Cookery: TX759+
Dairy waste
  Rural engineering: TD930.4
Dam failures
  Hydraulic engineering: TC550.2
Dam geology
  Hydraulic engineering: TC542
Dam safety
  Hydraulic engineering: TC550
Dam types: TC543+
Damage by natural disasters
  Railway operation: TF539
Damper regulators
  Hot water heating: TH7541
  Hydronic systems: TH7477
  Steam heating: TH7591
Damping
  Aerodynamics: TL574.S7
Dampness in buildings
  Protection from: TH9031
Dams
  Civil engineering: TA760+
  Environmental effects:
  TD195.D35
  Hydraulic engineering: TC540+
  Hydrostatics: TC167
Damsite selection
  Hydraulic engineering: TC542+
Dance photography: TR817.5

Dandelions
  Cookery: TX803.D34
Danger areas
  Airports: TL725.3.A6
Dangerous structures
  Building construction: TH153
Dangers in mines and quarries:
  TN311+
Darien Canal: TC788
Darkroom procedures
  Photographic processing: TR530+
Darkroom technique
  Photography: TR287+
Darkrooms
  Photography: TR560
Darning
  Textile arts: TT730
Dasheen
  Food values: TX558.D3
Data disk drives
  Computer engineering:
  TK7887.8.D37
Data processing
  Applied fluid mechanics:
  TA357.5.D37
  Biotechnology: TP248.25.A96
  Building construction
  estimates: TH437
  Chemical technology: TP184
  Civil engineering: TA404.23
  Hydraulic engineering: TC157.8
  Industrial engineering: T57.5
  Mechanical engineering: TJ153
  Orbital transfer: TL1078
  Photography in surveying:
  TA593.5
  Production management: TS155.6+
  Space trajectories: TL1078
  Structural analysis: TA647
Data processing, Optical:
  TA1630+
Data storage, Optical: TA1635
Data tape drives
  Computer engineering: TK7887.55
Data tapes
  Computer engineering: TK7895.D3
Data transmission systems
  Electrical engineering: TK5105+
Date
  Food values: TX558.D35
  Sugars and syrups: TP414

Date palm fiber
  Textile fiber: TS1747.D3
Dates
  Cookery: TX813.D3
Daylight
  Photography: TR595
DDN
  Computer network:
    TK5105.875.D37
DDT (Insecticide)
  Water pollutants: TD427.D34
De Havilland Aircraft Company:
    TL686.D4
De Havilland aircraft engines:
    TL703.D4
Deacidification
  Paper manufactures: TS1118.D42
Dead
  Photographic portraits:
    TR681.D43
Dead loads
  Structural engineering: TA648.2
Decalage
  Airplanes: TL673.D4
Decalcomania industry:
    TS2301.D4
Decay
  Deterioration of wood: TA423.2+
Decision making
  Environmental protection:
    TD171.8
Decision support systems
  Industrial engineering: T58.62
Decision theory
  Industrial engineering: T57.95
Deck machinery
  Electric driving: TK4059.D4
Decks
  Building construction: TH4970
Decoders
  Electronics: TK7872.D37
Decommissioning of facilities
  Nuclear engineering: TK9152.2
Decontamination
  Electronics: TK7870.27
  Nuclear engineering: TK9152.2
Decorated eggs
  Decorative crafts: TT896.7
Decorating
  Motor vehicles: TL255.2
  Plastics: TP1170

Decoration
  Building construction: TH8001+
  Dining room: TX859
Decoration, Table
  Dining-room service: TX879
Decorative balls
  Decorative crafts: TT896.8
Decorative crafts: TT855+
Decorative finishes
  Painting: TT323
Decorative furnishings
  Building construction: TH8001+
Decorative needlework
  Textile arts: TT740+
Decorative painting on various
    materials: TT385
Decorative tile
  Building construction: TH8541+
Decorative woodwork
  Building construction: TH8581+
Decoys
  Carving and whittling: TT199.75
Deep boring
  Mining: TN281
Deep Space Network: TL3026
Deep-well injection
  Disposal of sewage effluent:
    TD761
Defense measures
  Airports: TL725.3.D35
Deflection systems
  Television: TK6655.D43
Deflections
  Structural analysis: TA648.5
Deformation of materials under
    stress: TA417.6
Dehydration
  Ceramic technology: TP815
  Food preservation: TP371.5+
Dehydrogenation
  Chemical engineering: TP156.D4
Delay lines
  Electronics: TK7872.D4
Delta wings
  Airplanes: TL673.T7
Demand controlled ventilation
    systems
  Building construction:
    TH7682.D45
Demulsification
  Chemical engineering: TP156.D42

Denatured alcohol
  Distilling: TP593
Dendrimers
  Plastics: TP1180.D45
Dense nonaqueous phase liquids
  Hazardous substances and their
    disposal: TD1066.D45
Denseness and porosity
  Engineering materials: TA418.82
Densimeters
  Chemical technology: TP159.D4
Density altitude
  Aeronautical meteorology:
    TL557.D4
Density altitude computers
  Aeronautical meteorology:
    TL557.D4
Dentifrices
  Organic chemical industries:
    TP955
Deodorants: TP985
Deodorization
  Sewage treatment: TD747+
  Ventilation of buildings:
    TH7699.D4
Depreciation
  Engineering economy: TA178
Derrick cars
  Railway equipment: TF490
Derricks
  Hoisting machinery: TJ1363+
Desalination plants: TD479.4+
Desalting, Ion exchange
  Saline water conversion:
    TD480.7
Design
  Airplanes: TL671.2
  Airships: TL660
  Balloons: TL622
  Dressmaking: TT520
  Locomotives: TJ635
  Machine tools: TJ1180+
  Men's tailoring: TT590
  Packaging: TS195.4
  Petroleum pipelines: TN879.53
  Radioactive waste sites:
    TD898.155.D47
  Sewerage systems: TD658
  Sewers: TD678+
DesignCAD
  Electronic computer system:
    TA345.5.D47

Designs
  Highway engineering: TE175
  Patents: T324
Desks
  Woodworking: TT197.5.D4
Desserts
  Cookery: TX773
Desulphuration
  Chemical engineering: TP156.D43
Detailing
  Reinforced concrete
    construction: TA683.28
Details
  Dynamoelectric machinery:
    TK2541
  Locomotives: TJ640+
  Telegraph: TK5455
Details of the permanent way
  Railway construction: TF250+
Detection equipment
  Security in buildings: TH9739
Detection of adulterants
  Food: TX563
Detectors
  Radio: TK6565.D4
Detergents
  Environmental pollutants:
    TD196.D48
  Water pollutants: TD427.D4
Deterioration
  Properties of materials:
    TA418.74+
  Underwater structures: TC200
Deterioration of wood: TA422+
Determinants
  Engineering mathematics:
    TA347.D4
Development
  Photographic negatives: TR295
  Technology: T175+
Dewatering
  Ore dressing and milling: TN535
  Sewage treatment: TD769.7
Dextrin
  Starch: TP416.D4
Dextrose
  Sugars and syrups: TP414
Diagrams of connections
  Telegraph: TK5445
Dial telegraphs: TK5515
Diallyl phthalate
  Plastics: TP1180.D5

Dialysis
  Chemical engineering: TP156.D45
Diamond cutting
  Jewelry manufacture: TS753.5
Diamond mines and mining
  Environmental effects: TD195.D5
Diamonds
  Artificial gems: TP873.5.D5
  Electronics: TK7871.15.D53
  Jewelry manufacture: TS753+
  Machine tools: TJ1193
  Mineral industries: TN990+
  Prospecting: TN271.D5
Diaper industry
  Environmental effects:
    TD195.D53
Diaphragms
  Machinery: TJ247
  Structural engineering:
    TA660.D52
Diapositives
  Photography: TR504+
Diaspore
  Mining engineering: TN948.D49
Diatomaceous earth
  Mining engineering: TN948.D5
Diatomaceous earth filtration
  Water purification: TD446
Dibromochloropropane
  Water pollutants: TD427.D52
Dibutyltin
  Water pollutants: TD427.D47
Dictographs: TK6500
Die work
  Metal manufactures: TS253
Diecasting
  Foundry work: TS239
Dielectric amplifiers:
  TK7871.22
Dielectric devices
  Electronics: TK7872.D53
Dielectric separation
  Ore dressing and milling: TN531
Diemaking
  Metal manufactures: TS253
Diesel automobiles: TL229.D5
Diesel engine electric plants:
  TK1075
Diesel engines: TJ795+
  Aircraft engines: TL704.2
Diesel exhaust
  Air pollutants: TD886.8

Diesel locomotives: TJ619+
Diesel motorcars
  Railway equipment: TF498
Diet
  Nutrition: TX360+
Dietary studies
  Examination and analysis of
    food: TX551+
Dietetic food: TP451.D53
Dietitians: TX357
Differential amplifiers:
  TK7871.58.D46
Differential equations
  Engineering mathematics:
    TA347.D45
Diffusers
  Jet engines: TL709.5.D5
  Turbines: TJ267.5.D4
Diffusion
  Chemical engineering: TP156.D47
  Petroleum engineering: TN871
Digestion tanks
  Sewage sludge treatment: TD769+
Digital audio broadcasting
  Radio: TK6562.D54
Digital audiotape recorders and
  recording
  Electronics: TK7881.65
Digital cameras
  Photography: TR256
Digital communications
  Electrical engineering:
    TK5103.7+
Digital computers: TK7888.3+
Digital control
  Control engineering: TJ223.M53
Digital electronic circuits:
  TK7868.D5
Digital integrated circuits
  Electronics: TK7874.65
Digital photography: TR267
Digital plotters
  Computer engineering:
    TK7887.8.D5
Digital television: TK6678
Digital-to-analog converters
  Computer engineering: TK7887.6
Digital video: TK6680.5+
Dihedral angle
  Airplanes: TL673.D5
Dikes
  Coast protective works: TC337

Dilution, Disposal by
  Sewage effluent: TD763+
Dimensional analysis
  Engineering mathematics:
    TA347.D5
Dimensionless numbers
  Engineering mathematics:
    TA347.D52
Dining
  Nutrition: TX631+
Dining car service
  Railway operation: TF668.A1+
Dining cars
  Railway equipment: TF461
Dining room: TX855+
Dining room furniture
  Woodworking: TT197.5.D5
Dining room service
  Etiquette: TX851+
  Hotels, clubs, restaurants,
    etc.: TX925
Dinner-giving
  Cookery: TX731
Dinners
  Cookery: TX737
Diodes
  Semiconductor: TK7871.86+
Diolefins
  Chemical technology: TP248.D5
Dioscures project
  Artificial satellites:
    TK5104.2.D5
Dioxins
  Air pollutants: TD887.D56
Dipatching
  Airplanes: TL711.D4
Direct broadcast satellite
  television: TK6677
Direct coils
  Hydronic systems: TH7481+
Direct current
  Dynamoelectric machinery:
    TK2822
  Electrical engineering:
    TK454.15.D57
Direct current amplifiers:
  TK7871.58.D5
Direct-current engineering:
  TK1111+

Direct-current generators
  Dynamoelectric machinery:
    TK2661+
  Types: TK2665
Direct-current machinery
  Dynamoelectric machinery:
    TK2611+
  Types: TK2631
Direct-current motors
  Dynamoelectric machinery:
    TK2681
Direct-current systems
  Electric lighting: TK4303
  Electrical engineering: TK3111
Direct-current transforming
  machinery
  Dynamoelectric machinery:
    TK2691+
Direct energy conversion
  devices: TK2896+
Direct filtration
  Mechanical treatment of water
    purification: TD442
Direct-indirect radiators
  Hydronic systems: TH7490
Direct positives
  Photographic processes: TR360+
Direct processes
  Steel metallurgy: TN733
  Wrought iron: TN723
Direct radiators
  Hydronic systems: TH7481+
Direct reproductions on same
  scale
  Industrial photography: TR915+
Direction finders
  Aeronautical navigation:
    TL696.D5
  Radio: TK6565.D5
Directional drilling: TN871.23
Directories, Industrial:
  T11.95+
Directory services
  Computer networks: TK5105.595
Dirigibles: TL651
Dirt bikes: TL441
Disasters
  Chemical technology: TP150.A23
Disasters and engineering:
  TA495

Discharge into streams, etc.
Sewage disposal: TD771.5
Sewage effluent: TD763+
Discount stores
Consumer education: TX335+
Dishwashing machines
Cookery: TX657.D6
Disinfection
Sewage treatment: TD747+
Water purification: TD459+
Disks
Turbines: TJ267.5.D5
Dispatching of airplanes
Airports: TL725.3.D4
Displacement ventilation
Building construction:
TH7682.D57
Display systems
Aeronautical instruments:
TL589.3+
Motor vehicles: TL272.55
Display techniques
Exhibitions: T396+
Disposal
Sewage effluent: TD759+
Disposal in the ground
Radioactive waste: TD898.2
Disposal in the water
Radioactive waste: TD898.4
Disposal of municipal refuse
Environmental technology:
TD785+
Disposal under the seabed
Radioactive waste: TD898.6
Dissolved minerals, Removal of
Water purification: TD466
Distaff
Spinning
Textile industries: TS1484
Distance indicator
Aeronautical navigation:
TL696.D6
Distance measurement
Surveying: TA601
Distance measuring equipment
Aircraft to ground station:
TL696.D65
Distillation
Chemical engineering: TP156.D5
Distillation apparatus
Chemical technology: TP159.D5

Distillation methods
Saline water conversion: TD480
Distilled liquors: TP597+
Distilleries
Building construction: TH4532
Fire prevention and
extinction: TH9445.D5
Waste control: TD899.D5
Distilling
Fermentation industries: TP589+
Distributed amplifiers:
TK7871.58.D54
Distribution
Electric lighting: TK4251+
Gas industry: TP757
Telegraph: TK5401+
Telephone: TK6301+
Distribution and transmission
Pneumatic machinery: TJ1000
Distribution of electric power
Electrical engineering: TK3001+
Ditches
Railway operation: TF548
Ditching
Airplanes: TL711.D5
Docks
Harbor engineering: TC355
Documentary cinematography
Photography: TR895.4
Documentary photography:
TR820.5
Dog food: TS2288.D63
Dogfish
Cookery: TX748.D64
Dogs
Nature photography: TR729.D6
Doilies
Embroidery: TT775
Doll clothes: TT175.7
Doll furniture: TT175.5
Dollhouses: TT175.3
Dolls
Handicrafts: TT175+
Dome boilers
Hot water heating: TH7518+
Domes
Building design and
construction: TH2170+
Structural engineering:
TA660.D6
Domestic filters
Water purification: TD449

Domestic heating
  Buildings: TH7201+
Domestic laundry work: TT985
Domestic machines
  Knitting: TT687
Domestic refrigeration: TP492.6
Domestic water supply: TD201+
Door fittings
  Building design and
    construction: TH2270+
Door harps
  Decorative crafts: TT899.73
Door knobs
  Building construction: TH2279
Door openings
  Fittings: TH2261+
Door regulators
  Hot water heating: TH7541
  Hydronic systems: TH7477
  Steam heating: TH7591
Doorbells
  Manufactures: TS589
Doormen
  Hotels, clubs, restaurants,
    etc.: TX926
Doors
  Building design: TH2278+
Dopes
  Aeronautics: TL699.D6
Doppler radar: TK6592.D6
Dormitories
  Fire prevention and
    extinction: TH9445.D6
Double jacket stoves
  Building construction:
    TH7436.D6
Double wall piping
  Mechanical engineering: TJ934
Dough
  Food values: TX560.D68
Doughnuts
  Cookery: TX770.D67
Douglas Aircraft Company:
  TL686.D65
Down spouts
  Building construction: TH2493
Downwash
  Aerodynamics: TL574.D6
Draft
  Furnaces: TJ333
Draft appliances
  Locomotives: TJ650

Draft gear
  Railroad cars: TF413
Draft hoods
  Gas stove heating: TH7457.D7
Draft registers
  Warm-air heating: TH7627
Drafting
  Airplanes: TL671.25
  Dressmaking: TT520
  Men's tailoring: TT590
Drafting room practice
  Mechanical engineering: TJ227
Drag
  Aerodynamics: TL574.D7
Drag rope
  Balloons: TL625.D7
Dragsters: TL236.2+
Drain piping
  Plumbing: TH6628
Drain supports
  Plumbing: TH6644
Drain tiles
  Architectural ceramics: TP839
  Engineering materials: TA447
Drainage
  Airports: TL725.3.D7
  Highway engineering: TE215
  Houses: TH6571+
  Hydraulic engineering: TC970+
  Railway construction: TF245
Drainage system
  Houses: TH6591
  Plumbing: TH6641+
Draining sewage
  Plumbing: TH6651+
Draining wastes
  House drainage: TH6655+
Drapes
  Handicrafts: TT390
Drawbridges: TG420
Drawing instruments: T375+
Drawing materials: T375+
Drawing-room management and
  practice
  Mechanical drawing: T352
Drawing, Fashion: TT509
Drawing, Structural
  Mechanical drawing: T355
Drawings
  Building construction: TH431
  Carpentry and joinery: TH5611
  Electrical engineering: TK431
  Engineering: TA175

Drawings
  Furniture design: TT196
  Heating of buildings: TH7331
  Highway engineering: TE175
  Hot water heating: TH7513
  Plastering: TH8132
  Plumbing: TH6231
  Reinforced concrete
    construction: TA683.28
  Steam heating: TH7563
  Warm-air heating: TH7602
Drawnwork
  Decorative needlework: TT785+
Dredges
  Electric driving: TK4059.D73
  Hydraulic engineering: TC188
Dredging
  Environmental effects:
    TD195.D72
  Hydraulic engineering: TC187+
Dress forms
  Dressmaking: TT523
Dress reform
  Women's tailoring: TT565
Dressmaking: TT500+
Dried foods
  Cookery: TX826.5
Driers
  Paints: TP937.7
Drift indicator
  Aeronautical instrument:
    TL589.2.D7
Drifting
  Mining: TN285
Drill cores
  Rock mechanics: TA706.3
Drilling
  Mining: TN279
Drilling machinery
  Machine shops: TJ1260+
Drilling platforms
  Fire prevention and
    extinction: TH9445.D75
Drills
  Fire extinction: TH9402+
  Machine shops: TJ1263+
Drinking fountains
  Water supply: TH6569.D7
Drinking water
  Railroad cars: TF451

Driver education
  Motor vehicle operation:
    TL152.6+
Driver training
  Buses: TL232.3
  Trucks: TL230.3
Drivers
  Buses: TL232.3
  Motor vehicles: TL152.3+
  Trucks: TL230.3
Drivers' tests
  Motor vehicle operation:
    TL152.4
Driveways
  Engineering: TE279.3
Driving
  All terrain vehicle: TL235.7
  Buses: TL232.3
  Motor vehicle operation:
    TL152.5+
  Off-road vehicle: TL235.7
  Tractors: TL233.3
  Trucks: TL230.3
Driving gear
  Cycles: TL420
Driving simulators
  Driver education: TL152.7.D7
Drop-forging
  Metal manufactures: TS225+
Drop system
  Steam heating: TH7567
Dropping of cargo
  Airplanes: TL711.D7
Drug factories
  Environmental effects:
    TD195.D78
Drums
  Packaging: TS198.6.D7
Dry-air blast
  Blast furnaces: TN715
Dry cleaning
  Commercial garment cleaning:
    TP932.3
Dry cleaning industry
  Water pollution: TD428.D78
Dry docks
  Harbor engineering: TC361
Dry goods
  Textile industries: TS1760+
Dry ice
  Refrigerants: TP492.82.D78

Dry rot
  Deterioration of wood: TA423.3
Drydocks
  Harbor engineering: TC361
Drying
  Chemical technology: TP363
  Food preservation: TP371.5+
  Lumber: TS837
  Paper manufacture: TS1118.D7
  Preservation of foods: TX609
  Sewage treatment: TD769.7
  Textile industries: TS1514
Drying agents
  Chemical technology: TP159.D7
Drying equipment
  Textile industries: TS1514
Drying machinery
  Paper manufacture: TS1118.D7
Drywall
  Decorative furnishings: TH8139
Dubbing
  Motion picture film: TR886.7
Duck
  Cookery: TX750.5.D82
Duct inlets
  Airplanes: TL673.D8
Ductile states
  Plastic properties and tests:
    TA418.16+
Dumbwaiters
  Hoisting machinery: TJ1382
Dumortierite
  Mining engineering: TN948.D8
Dumping devices
  Conveying machinery: TJ1418
Dune buggies: TL236.7
Dunes
  Coast protective works: TC339
Duplex telegraph system: TK5531
Duralumin
  Aeronautics: TL699.D9
  Engineering materials: TA480.A6
Dust
  Air pollutants: TD884.5
  Fire prevention and
    extinction: TH9446.D86
Dust control
  Highway maintenance: TE220.63
Dust preventives for unpaved
  roads: TE221

Dust removal
  Ventilation of buildings:
    TH7692+
Dutch oven cookery: TX840.D88
Dwellings
  Air conditioning: TH7688.H6
  Artificial lighting: TH7975.D8
  Building construction: TH4805+
  Energy conservation:
    TJ163.5.D86
  Fire prevention and
    extinction: TH9445.D9
  Sanitary engineering: TH6057.A6
  Security in buildings:
    TH9745.D85
  Ventilation: TH7684.D9
Dye lasers
  Applied optics: TA1690
Dyeing
  Textiles: TP897+
Dyeing industry, Waste from
  Environmental technology:
    TD899.C58
Dyeing of garments
  Textile decoration: TT853+
Dyeing plants
  Fire prevention and
    extinction: TH9445.C6
Dyes
  Hairdressing: TT969
  Textile decoration: TT854+
  Textile dyeing: TP909.2+
Dyes and dyeing
  Paper manufacture: TS1118.D9
Dynamic control
  Structural engineering: TA654.9
Dynamic loading conditions
  Structural analysis: TA654+
Dynamic loads
  Structural design: TA658.4+
Dynamic programming
  Industrial engineering: T57.83
Dynamic properties
  Time-dependent properties and
    tests: TA418.32+
Dynamics
  Mechanical engineering: TJ170+
  Motor vehicles: TL243+
Dynamite
  Explosives: TP285
Dynamoelectric machinery and
  auxiliaries: TK2000+

Dynamometers
  Machinery exclusive of prime
    movers: TJ1053
Dynamos: TK2411+
Dynamotors
  Dynamoelectric machinery:
    TK2693

E

Earth
  Housing material: TH4818.A3
  Sidewalks: TE283
Earth and sand
  Unpaved roads: TE230
Earth casting
  Handicrafts: TT295
Earth closets
  Sewage disposal: TD776
Earth inductor compass
  Aeronautical instrument:
    TL589.2.E2
Earth movements and building
  Building construction: TH1094+
Earth pressure
  Embankments: TA765
Earth sheltered houses
  Construction: TH4819.E27
Earth-wall building
  construction: TH1421
Earthen dams: TC543
Earthenware
  Ceramic technology: TP820
  Fire-resistive building
    construction: TH1077+
Earthenware stoves
  Convective heating: TH7436.E4
Earthmoving machinery: TA725
Earthquake engineering: TA654.6
Earthquake forces
  Structural engineering: TA654.6
Earthquake resistant design
  Structural engineering:
    TA658.44
Earthquakes and building
  Building construction: TH1095
Earthquakes and dams
  Hydraulic engineering: TC542.5
Earthquakes and hydraulic
  structures: TC181

Earthwork
  Building construction: TH5101
  Engineering: TA715+
  Railroad construction: TF220+
Earthworms
  Cookery: TX746.2
Easement of light
  Natural lighting: TH7792
Easter
  Cookery: TX739.2.E37
Easter decorations
  Decorative crafts: TT900.E2
Eave troughs
  Building construction: TH2493
Eavesdropping
  Electronics: TK7882.E2
Eccentric and eccentric-rod
  Steam engines: TJ543
Eccentric lathework: TT203
Ecclesiastical vestments
  Clothing manufacture: TT647
Echo suppression
  Coding theory: TK5102.98
Econet: TK5105.8.E25
Economic aspects
  Acid precipitation:
    TD195.56.E35
  Radioactive waste disposal:
    TD898.14.E36
Economic development
  Environmental effects:
    TD195.E25
Economic geology: TN260
Economic lot size
  Inventory control: TS162
Economic mineralogy: TN260
Economic order quantity
  Inventory control: TS162
Economics of daily life for
  men: TX147
Economy
  Foods and food supply: TX356
ECS satellites: TK5104.2.E29
Eddy currents in electrical
  engineering: TK2271
Edible coatings
  Food processing: TP451.E3
Edible oils and fats
  Condiments: TX407.O34
Edison three-wire system
  Electrical engineering: TK1121
Editing, Technical: T11.4

Education, Consumer
  Household administration:
    TX335+
Education, Technical
  Industrial engineering: T61+
Educational buildings
  Building construction: TH4621+
Educational cinematography
  Photography: TR892.7
Eels
  Cookery: TX748.E32
Effect of radiation on
  electronics: TK7870.285
Efficiency
  Industrial engineering: T58.8
Eggbeaters
  Cookery: TX657.E35
Eggplant
  Cookery: TX803.E4
Eggs
  Biotechnology: TP248.65.E35
  Cookery: TX745
  Food values: TX556.E4
  Nutrition: TX383
  Preservation and storage:
    TX612.E4
Eggshell craft: TT896.7
Elastic analysis
  Structural analysis: TA653
Elastic properties and tests:
  TA418+
Elastomers
  Engineering materials: TA455.E4
  Manufactures: TS1925
Electric alarms: TK7201+
Electric analysis
  Testing of materials: TA417.35
Electric annunciators: TK7201+
Electric apparatus and
  materials: TK452+
Electric batteries
  Amateurs' manuals: TK9917
Electric bells and buzzers:
  TK7108+
Electric brakes: TK4081
Electric calculating machines:
  TK4090+
Electric cells
  Telegraph: TK5378
Electric circuits
  Electric engineering: TK454+

Electric clocks
  Manufactures: TS544
Electric cooking: TX827
Electric cutting
  Electric heating: TK4660.5
Electric discharge lighting:
  TK4371+
Electric driving: TK4058+
Electric elevators: TJ1374
Electric energy storage
  Electrical engineering: TK2980+
Electric equipment
  Aircraft: TL690+
  Airports: TL725.3.E43
  Diesel locomotives: TJ619.7
  Fire prevention and
    extinction: TH9445.E43
  Locomotives: TJ669.E4
  Motor vehicles: TL272
  Railways: TF368
  Space vehicles: TL1100+
Electric eye cameras
  Photography: TR260.5
Electric furnace processes
  Steel metallurgy: TN745
Electric furnaces
  Electric heating: TK4661
  Electrometallurgy: TN687
Electric generators
  Amateurs' manuals: TK9911
Electric heating
  Electrical engineering: TK4601+
  Heating of buildings: TH7409+
Electric household appliances
  Installation: TK7018+
Electric ignitors
  Building gas supply: TH6885+
Electric insulators
  Fire-testing: TH9446.5.E43
Electric lamps: TK4310
Electric light
  Photographic processing: TR333
Electric lighting
  Electrical engineering: TK4125+
  Mines: TN309
  Railroad cars: TF449
  Theory: TK4175
Electric lighting and lamps
  Amateurs' manuals: TK9921
Electric lighting enterprises,
  Management of: TK4186

Electric lighting fixtures
  Artificial lighting: TH7960+
Electric lighting plants
  Management: TK4238
Electric lines
  Environmental effects:
  TD195.E37
  Noise control: TD893.6.E4
Electric locomotives: TF975
Electric logging: TN269.5+
Electric measurements: TK275+
Electric meters: TK301+
Electric mine locomotives:
  TN337
Electric motors
  Amateurs' manuals: TK9911
Electric networks: TK454.2
Electric power
  Distribution and transmission:
  TK3001+
Electric-power circuits: TK3226
Electric-power networks: TK3226
Electric power plants
  Air pollution: TD888.E43
  Dust removal: TH7697.E45
  Electrical engineering: TK1191+
  Environmental effects: TD195.E4
  Fire prevention and
  extinction: TH9445.E4
Electric power rates: TK1841
Electric power system
  stability: TK1010
Electric power systems
  control: TK1007
Electric power, Applications
  of: TK4001+
Electric processes
  Gold and silver metallurgy:
  TN768
  Metallurgy: TN706
Electric propulsion systems:
  TL783.54+
Electric pumping machinery:
  TJ910
Electric radiant heating
  Local heating: TH7434.5+
Electric railways: TF854.2+
Electric refrigerators:
  TP497.A1+
Electric rockets: TL783.54+
Electric spark machining
  Machine tools: TJ1191

Electric standards: TK275+
Electric stoves
  Cookery: TX657.S5
Electric systems
  Aircraft: TL690+
Electric telpher systems
  Conveying machinery: TJ1387
Electric thermostat fire
  detectors
  Fire prevention and
  extinction: TH9275
Electric toasters
  Cookery: TX657.T58
Electric vehicles: TL220+
Electric water heaters
  Plumbing: TH6561.5
Electric welding
  Electrical engineering: TK4660
Electric wiring
  Telecommunication: TK5103.12
Electrical engineering: TK1+
  Insurance requirements: TK260
  Systems: TK3101+
Electrical engineering and
  equipment
  Mines: TN343
Electrical engineering as a
  profession: TK159
Electrical manufacturing and
  engineering companies,
  General: TK451.A2+
Electrical motive power
  Canals: TC769
Electrically heated steam
  boilers: TJ318
Electricians' manuals: TK4164
Electricity for amateurs:
  TK9900+
Electricity in ocean
  engineering: TC1657
Electrification of steam
  railroads: TF858+
Electro-diesel locomotives:
  TF980
Electroacoustic transducers:
  TK5981+
Electroacoustics: TK5981+
Electrochemical sensors
  Chemical technology: TP159.E37
Electrochemical telegraph
  system: TK5549

Electrochemistry, Industrial
  Environmental effects:
    TD195.E43
Electrocoating
  Painting: TT317
Electrodes
  Chemical technology: TP159.E39
  Manufacture: TK7725
Electrodialysis
  Saline water conversion:
    TD480.5
Electrohydrodynamic generators
  Electrical engineering: TK2975
Electroless plating
  Metal finishing: TS662
Electroluminescent devices:
    TK7871.68+
Electroluminescent display
  systems: TK7882.I6
Electrolysis of water: TP259
Electrolytic cells
  Chemical technology: TP159.E4
Electrolytic polishing
  Metal finishing: TS654.5
Electrolytic treatment
  Sewage disposal: TD757
Electromagnetic compatibility:
    TK7867.2
Electromagnetic interference:
    TK7867.2
  Aeronautics: TL690.5
Electromagnets
  Control engineering: TJ223.E4
  Electrical engineering:
    TK454.4.E5
Electromechanical transducers:
    TK153
Electrometallurgy: TN681+
  Metal finishing: TS670+
Electron gun
  Electronics: TK7872.E45
Electron tubes
  Electronics: TK7871.7+
  Radio: TK6565.V3
Electronic apparatus
  Waste disposal: TD799.85
Electronic appliances
  Waste disposal: TD799.85
Electronic cameras
  Cinematography: TR882+
Electronic circuits: TK7867+

Electronic components and
  apparatus, Manufacture of:
    TK7836
Electronic computer methods
  Structural engineering: TA641
Electronic control: TK7881.2
Electronic data processing
  Aeronautics: TL563
  Engineering mathematics: TA345+
  Hotels, clubs, restaurants,
    etc.: TX911.3.E4
Electronic data processing
  departments
  Fire prevention and
    extinction: TH9445.E45
Electronic equipment
  Aircraft communication: TL693+
  Fire prevention and
    extinction: TH9445.E46
  Motor vehicles: TL272.5+
  Space vehicles: TL3000+
Electronic flash
  Photography: TR606
Electronic games and toys
  Amateurs' manuals: TK9971
Electronic instruments:
    TK7878.4+
Electronic locking devices
  Security in buildings: TH9735
Electronic mail systems
  Local area networks: TK5105.73
Electronic measurements:
    TK7878+
Electronic methods
  Aircraft communication: TL693+
Electronic packaging: TK7870.15
Electronic plants and
  equipment: TK7836
Electronic security systems
  Security in buildings: TH9737
Electronic troubleshooting:
    TK7870.2
Electronic villages
  Electrical engineering:
    TK5105.83
Electronics: TK7800+
  Amateurs' manuals: TK9965+
  Rockets: TL784.E4
Electronics as a profession:
    TK7845
Electronics in transportation:
    TA1235

Electronics plants
  Building construction: TH4533
Electronics, Applications of:
  TK7880+
Electronics, Effect of
  radiation on: TK7870.285
Electrooptical devices: TA1750+
Electrooptics, Applied: TA1750+
Electrophoretic deposition
  Painting: TT317
Electrophotography
  Photomechanical processes:
  TR1035+
Electroplated ware: TS675
Electroplating
  Environmental effects:
  TD195.E45
  Metal finishing: TS670+
Electroslag process
  Electrometallurgy: TN686.5.E4
Electrostatic charging
  Space environment: TL1492
Electrostatic flocking
  Textile industries: TS1512.5
Electrostatic precipitation
  Dust removal: TH7695.E4
Electrostatic printing
  Phtomechanical processes:
  TR1042+
Electrostatic separation
  Chemical engineering: TP156.E5
Elementary school courses
  Driver education: TL152.65
Elevated railways: TF840+
Elevator operators
  Hotels, clubs, restaurants,
  etc.: TX926
Elevator service
  Apartment houses: TX959
  Buildings: TJ1380
Elevators
  Airplanes: TL677.E6
  Fire prevention and
  extinction: TH9445.E48
  Hoisting machinery: TJ1370+
  Mine transportation: TN339+
Embankments
  Civil engineering: TA760+
  Coast protective works: TC337
Embassy buildings
  Building construction: TH4758

Embedded computer systems
  Computer engineering:
  TK7895.E42
Emblems
  Metal manufactures: TS761
Embroidery
  Decorative needlework: TT769+
Embroidery (Machine made)
  Textile industries: TS1783
Embroidery silk: TT777
Embroidery, Machine: TT772
Emeralds
  Jewelry work: TS755.E5
  Mineral industries: TN997.E5
Emergency lighting
  Electric lighting: TK4399.E5
Emergency maneuvers
  Airplanes: TL711.E57
Emergency planning
  Nuclear engineering: TK9152.13
Emery
  Mining engineering: TN936
Emery wheels
  Abrading machinery: TJ1290
Emissions from motor vehicles
  Air pollutants: TD886.5
Employee facilities and
  buildings
  Plant engineering: TS188
Employee training in factories
  Aeronautics: TL560.25.A1+
Emu
  Cookery: TX750.5.E45
Emulsion
  Chemical engineering: TP156.E6
Emulsion processes
  Photographic process: TR395
Enameled ware, Catalogs of
  Metal finishing: TS705
Enameling
  Handicrafts: TT382.6
  Metal finishing: TS700+
Enamels: TP939
  Ceramic technology: TP812.A1+
  Engineering materials: TA455.E5
Enclosure fires
  Fire prevention: TH9195
Endless carriers
  Conveying machinery: TJ1390+
Endurance flights
  Airplanes: TL711.E6

Endurance properties and
tests: TA418.36 +
Endurance tests
Motor vehicles: TL290
Energy conservation
Mechanical engineering:
TJ163.26 +
Energy consumption
Hotels, clubs, restaurants,
etc.: TX911.3.E45
Energy development
Environmental effects:
TD195.E49
Energy facilities
Environmental effects: TD195.E5
Energy meters and measurements
Electrical engineering: TK351
Energy minerals
Mining engineering: TN263.5
Energy storage
Mechanical engineering: TJ165
Engine instruments
Aeronautical engineering:
TL589.6 +
Engineering: TA1 +
Engineering analysis: TA329 +
Engineering design: TA174
Engineering economy: TA177.4 +
Engineering geology: TA703 +
Engineering graphics: T351 +
Engineering implements: TA213 +
Engineering instruments,
meters, etc.: TA165
Engineering laboratories:
TA416 +
Engineering machinery: TA213 +
Engineering mathematics: TA329 +
Engineering meteorology: TA197 +
Engineering models: TA177
Engineering tools: TA213 +
Engineering, Hydraulic
Environmental effects:
TD195.H93
Engineers
Accounting: TA185
Enginehouses
Railway structures: TF296
Engines
Gasoline automobiles: TL210 +
Engines for utilization of
furnace and waste gases and
heat: TJ780

Engobes
Ceramic decoration: TP823
Enjoyment of smoking
Tobacco industry: TS2249
Enlargement
Photographic processing: TR475
Enlargements
Industrial photography: TR905
Enrichment
Nuclear engineering: TK9360 +
Entertaining
Cookery: TX731
Entertainment centers
Woodworking: TT197.5.E57
Envelope
Airships: TL662.E6
Balloons: TL625.E6
Environmental aspects
Hazardous substances and their
disposal: TD1050.E58
Industries: TD194 +
Plants: TD194 +
Product engineering: TS170.5
Production management: TS155.7
Radioactive waste disposal:
TD898.14.E58
Environmental auditing: TD194.7
Environmental chemistry: TD193 +
Environmental effects, Space
Engineering materials: TA418.59
Environmental engineering:
TA170 +
Buildings: TH6014 +
Space: TL1489 +
Environmental forensics
Measurement of pollution:
TD193.4
Environmental geotechnology:
TD171.9
Environmental hydraulics:
TC163.5
Environmental impact analysis
Environmental effects of
industries and plants:
TD194.6 +
Environmental impact statements
Environmental effects of
industries and plants:
TD194.5 +
Environmental laboratories:
TD178.8.A1 +

Environmental pollutants,
  Special: TD195.4+
Environmental pollution: TD172+
Environmental protection:
  TD169+
Environmental technology: TD1+
Environmental testing: TA171
Enzymatic browning
  Food processing: TP372.55.E59
Enzymes
  Biotechnology: TP248.65.E59
  Chemical technology: TP248.E5
  Food additives: TP456.E58
  Food constituent: TX553.E6
Eolipiles: TJ725
Epichlorohydrin
  Air pollutants: TD887.E64
Epoxy resins
  Engineering materials: TA455.E6
  Insulating material: TK3441.E6
  Plastics: TP1180.E6
Equalizers
  Control engineering: TJ223.E65
  Electronics: TK7872.E7
Equations, Differential
  Engineering mathematics:
    TA347.D45
Equations, Integral
  Engineering mathematics:
    TA347.I5
Equestrian roads
  Highway engineering: TE303
Equilibrium
  Chemical engineering: TP156.E65
Equipment
  Airports: TL725.3.E6
  Blacksmithing: TT224
  Cookery: TX656+
  Heating of buildings: TH7345
  Petroleum pipelines: TN879.54
  Petroleum refining: TP690.6
  Photogrammetry: TR696
  Plant engineering: TS191+
  Pollution control methods:
    TD192
Equipment analysis
  Manufacturing engineering:
    TS181+
Equipment and supplies
  Ceramic technology: TP809.5
  Pipelines: TJ933
  Woodpulp industry: TS1176.6.E7

Equipment, Contractors': TA201+
Equivalent circuit
  Electrical engineering:
    TK454.15.E65
Erbium
  Chemical technology: TP245.E6
Erecting work
  Machinery: TJ249
Erie Canal
  Inland navigation: TC625.E6
Ernemann cameras
  Photography: TR263.E75
Erotic photography: TR676
Error correction
  Coding theory: TK5102.96
Error detection and recovery
  Mechanical engineering:
    TJ211.417
Errors
  Photography in surveying:
    TA593.9.E75
Errors in workmanship
  Machine shop practice: TJ1167
ES 1020 computer: TK7889.E5
Escalators: TJ1376
Esparto
  Textile fiber: TS1747.E8
Essences
  Organic chemical industries:
    TP958+
Essential oils
  Organic chemical industries:
    TP958+
Esters
  Chemical technology: TP248.E62
Estimates
  Building construction: TH434+
  Carpentry and joinery: TH5614+
  Cement and concrete
    construction: TA682.26
  Commercial buildings: TH4315
  Earthwork: TA721
  Electrical engineering: TK435
  Engineering economy: TA183
  Heating of buildings: TH7335+
  Houses: TH4815.8
  Machine shops: TJ1148
  Masonry construction: TH5330
  Municipal refuse and solid
    wastes: TD793.7

Estimates
  Plastering: TH8132
  Plumbing: TH6234+
  Railroad engineering: TF193
  Reinforced concrete
    construction: TA683.26
  Saline water conversion:
    TD479.3
Estimates of labor
  Pipefitting: TH6721
Estimates of material
  Pipefitting: TH6721
Estimating
  Cost control: TS166
  Foundry work: TS238
  Machine shops: TJ1148
Estimation of value
  Hydraulic engineering: TC409
Etching
  Aircraft propellers: TL706.E8
  Chemical engineering: TP156.E68
Ethanol
  Distilling: TP593
Ether
  Chemical technology: TP248.E65
Ethernet: TK5105.8.E83
Ethers
  Organic chemical industries:
    TP958+
Ethics
  Hotels, clubs, restaurants,
    etc.: TX911.3.E84
Ethylcellulose
  Chemical technology: TP248.E68
Ethylene
  Chemical technology: TP248.E72
Ethylene dibromide
  Water pollutants: TD427.E83
Ethylene dichloride
  Air pollutants: TD887.E83
Ethylene oxide
  Environmental pollutants:
    TD196.E86
Ethylene-propylene rubber
  Manufactures: TS1927.E86
Eucalyptus
  Woodpulp industry: TS1176.4.E9
Eucalyptus oils
  Organic chemical industries:
    TP959.E9

Evaluation
  Radioactive waste disposal:
    TD898.14.E83
  Radioactive waste sites:
    TD898.155.E83
Evaporating
  Chemical technology: TP363
Evaporation control
  Reservoirs: TD397
Evaporators
  Chemical technology: TP159.E85
Evolutionary robotics: TJ211.37
Examination
  Water: TD380+
Examination of food: TX501+
Examinations
  Building construction: TH166
Excavating
  Mining: TN277
Excavating machinery: TA735+
  Electric driving: TK4059.E9
  Railroad construction: TF225+
Excavation
  Building construction: TH5101
Excavations
  Engineering: TA730+
Excavators
  Hoisting machinery: TJ1355
Excelsior
  Packaging: TS198.6.E9
Exchanges
  Telephone: TK6211+
Executives
  Nutrition: TX361.E93
Exhaust emissions, Aircraft
  Air pollutants: TD886.7
Exhaust-steam utilization
  systems
  Low-pressure steam heating:
    TH7577
Exhaust systems
  Diesel engines: TJ799
  Gasoline automobiles: TL214.E93
Exhaust, Automobile
  Air pollutants: TD886.5
Exhaust, Diesel
  Air pollutants: TD886.8
Exhausters
  Pneumatic machinery: TJ960+
Exhausts
  Locomotives: TJ650
  Steam engines: TJ567

Exhibitions
  Technology: T391+
Exiles
  Photographic portraits:
    TR681.E94
Expandable space structures
  Space vehicles: TL940
Expansion boards
  Computer engineering:
    TK7895.E96
Expansion joints
  Rockets: TL784.E9
  Steam powerplants: TJ424
  Structural engineering:
    TA660.E9
Expansion tanks
  Hot water heating: TH7542
Expansion, Thermal
  Properties of materials:
    TA418.56+
Experimental design
  Industrial engineering: T57.37
Experiments
  Examination and analysis of
    food: TX551+
Exploration
  Airplanes: TL721.1
Explosion or ignition devices
  Gas engines: TJ773
Explosion prevention and
  protection
  Industrial safety: T55.3.E96
Explosion systems
  Fire prevention and
    extinction: TH9339
Explosionproof apparatus
  Electrical engineering:
    TK454.4.E9
Explosions
  Mines: TN313
  Sewers: TD690
  Water heaters: TH6565+
Explosive forming
  Metal manufactures: TS257
Explosive welding: TS228.96
Explosives
  Chemical technology: TP270+
  Coal mining: TN803
Explosives and pyrotechnics
  Chemical technology: TP267.5+

Exposed film
  Cinematography: TR886.2
  Photographic processing: TR530+
Exposure to harmful
  environments, Packaging for
  protection from: TS198.7+
Exposures
  Photography: TR591+
Express
  Railway operation: TF659
Exterior insulation and finish
  systems
  Building design and
    construction: TH2238.7
Exterior walls
  Building design and
    construction: TH2235+
Extraction
  Biotechnology: TP248.25.E88
  Chemical engineering: TP156.E8
Extractors
  Chemical technology: TP159.E9
Extracts
  Flavoring aids: TP419
Extranets
  Computer networks:
    TK5105.875.E87
Extraterrestrial radio
  communication: TK6571+
Extravehicular activity
  Space travel: TL1096
Extrusion
  Plastics: TP1175.E9
Extrusion of metals
  Metal manufactures: TS255
Eye protectors
  Plastic: TP1185.E9

F

Fabric flowers
  Decorative crafts: TT890.5+
Fabrics
  Aeronautics: TL699.F2
Fabrics, Coating of
  Textile industries: TS1512
Face painting (Handicrafts)
  Decorative crafts: TT911
Facsimile transmission
  Television: TK6710+

Factories
  Air conditioning: TH7688.F2+
  Air pollution: TD888.F3
  Artificial lighting: TH7975.F2
  Building construction: TH4511+
  Design: TS177
  Dust removal: TH7697.F2
  Electric lighting: TK4399.F2
  Electric power: TK4035.F3
  Energy conservation: TJ163.5.F3
  Environmental effects: TD194+
  Fire prevention and
    extinction: TH9445.M4+
  Heating and ventilation:
    TH7392.M6
  Plant engineering: TS186
  Plumbing: TH6515.F2
  Sanitary engineering: TH6057.F3
  Security in buildings:
    TH9745.F3
  Size: TS177.3
  Ventilation: TH7684.F2
Factory canteens
  Food service: TX946.5.A1+
Factory construction, Drawings
  of: TH4516
Factory equipment and methods
  Airplanes: TL671.28
Factory management: TS155+
Factory methods
  Motor vehicles: TL278
  Rockets: TL784.3+
Factory planning
  Manufacturing engineering:
    TS177
Factory sanitation: TD895+
Factory wastes: TD896+
Factory wiring
  Electric power: TK3283
Facts for smokers
  Tobacco industry: TS2249
Fagoting
  Embroidery: TT778.F33
Failure
  Dams: TC550.2
  Petroleum pipelines: TN879.55
Failure of materials: TA409
Failure of structures: TA656+
Failures
  Electronics: TK7870.23
Falling block rifle:
  TS536.6.F34

Fallout shelters
  Building construction: TH1097
Families
  Photographic portraits:
    TR681.F28
Family cinematography
  Photography: TR896+
Famous persons
  Photographic portraits:
    TR681.F3
Fancy articles
  Decorative crafts: TT890+
Fancy work
  Textile arts: TT740+
Fans
  Electric driving: TK4059.F35
  Ventilation of buildings:
    TH7683.F3
Faolite
  Engineering materials: TA455.F3
Far infrared lasers
  Applied optics: TA1696
Farm buildings
  Construction: TH4911+
  Electric lighting: TK4399.F3
  Heating and ventilation:
    TH7392.F3
  Sanitary engineering:
    TH6057.F35
  Ventilation: TH7684.F3
Farm engines: TJ712
  Gas engines: TJ777.F3
Farm machinery
  Mechanical engineering: TJ1480+
Farm roads
  Highway engineering: TE229.2
Farm sanitary engineering:
  TD920+
Farmers
  Nutrition: TX361.F37
Farmhouses
  Building construction: TH4920
  Plumbing: TH6515.F3
Farms
  Electric power: TK4018
  Fire prevention and
    extinction: TH9445.F35
  Photography: TR739.5
Fashion: TT500+
Fashion drawing: TT509
Fashion exhibitions: TT502
Fashion magazines: TT500.A2+

Fashion photography: TR679
Fashion shows: TT502
Fashion writing: TT503.5
Fast day cookery: TX837+
Fast express trains: TF573
Fast reactors
  Nuclear engineering: TK9203.F3
Fastenings
  Machine shops: TJ1320+
Fat substitutes: TP447.F37
Father and child
  Photographic portraits:
    TR681.F32
Fathers and daughters
  Photographic portraits:
    TR681.F33
Fathers and sons
  Photographic portraits:
    TR681.F34
Fatigue
  Man-machine systems: T59.72
  Psychological aspects: T59.72
  Structural analysis: TA656.3
Fatigue behavior
  Endurance properties and
    tests: TA418.38
Fats
  Chemical technology: TP669+
Fats (Animal and vegetable)
  Food values: TX560.F3
Faucets
  Water supply plumbing: TH6528
Feather flowers
  Decorative crafts: TT891
Feather industry: TS2301.F4
Feather renovating
  Chemical technology: TP933
Feed apparatus
  Steam boilers: TJ375+
Feed pumps
  Steam boilers: TJ385
Feedback amplifiers:
    TK7871.58.F4
Feedback control systems
  Mechanical engineering: TJ216
Feeders
  Chemical technology: TP159.F4
Feedforward control systems
  Mechanical engineering: TJ216.5
Feedlots
  Waste control: TD899.F4

Feeds
  Biotechnology: TP248.65.F44
Feedwater heaters
  Steam boilers: TJ381+
Feedwater purification
  Steam boilers: TJ379
Feldspar
  Mining engineering: TN948.F3
FELIX C-256 computer:
    TK7889.F44
Felt
  Composition roofing: TH2451
  Decorative crafts: TT880
  Textile fiber: TS1825
Felt marker decoration: TT386
Felting
  Textile arts: TT849.5
Felts
  Paper manufacture: TS1118.F4
Fences
  Building construction: TH4955+,
    TH4965
  Railway structures: TF277
  Security in buildings: TH9732
Fenders
  Hydraulic engineering: TC373
Fermentation industries
  Chemical technology: TP500+
Fermentation of molasses: TP592
Fermentation, Industrial
  Chemical engineering: TP156.F4
Fermented food
  Food values: TX560.F47
Fermented milk
  Beverages: TP565
Fermenting
  Food preservation: TP371.44
Ferrite devices
  Electronics: TK7872.F4
Ferrites
  Electronics: TK7871.15.F4
Ferrochromium
  Metallurgy: TN757.F25
Ferroelectric devices
  Electronics: TK7872.F44
Ferromagnetography
  Photography: TR1050
Ferromanganese
  Metallurgy: TN757.F3
Ferronickel
  Metallurgy: TN757.F33

Ferrosilicon
  Metallurgy: TN757.F4
Ferrotype
  Photography: TR375
Ferrous metals
  Metallurgy: TN701.482+
Ferry bridges: TG435
Ferrying
  Airplanes: TL711.F47
Fertilization
  Pollution control methods:
    TD192.6
Fertilizer industry
  Air pollution: TD888.F45
  Environmental effects:
    TD195.F46
  Waste control: TD899.F47
Fertilizer, Sewage disposal
  as: TD774+
Fertilizers
  Environmental pollutants:
    TD196.F47
  Organic chemical industries:
    TP963+
  Water pollutants: TD427.F45
Fiber building boards
  Building construction: TH1555
Fiber optics, Applied: TA1800+
Fiber strengthened composites
  Engineering and construction:
    TA481.5
Fiberboard
  Wood products: TS875
Fiberglass craft: TT297.8
Fiberloid
  Plastics: TP1180.F5
Fibers
  Air pollutants: TD887.F48
  Engineering materials:
    TA418.9.F5
  Food constituent: TX553.F53
Fibrous composites
  Engineering materials:
    TA418.9.C6
Field and runway localizer:
  TL696.L3
Field effect transistors:
  TK7871.95
Field poles
  Generators: TK2465
Field shoes
  Generators: TK2466

Field winding and spools
  Generators: TK2475
Field work
  Metallography: TN690.65
Field yoke
  Generators: TK2464
Field, C.W.: TK5611
Fighter kites: TL759.6.F54
Figs
  Cookery: TX813.F5
Filaments
  Electric lighting: TK4365
Files and filing
  Machine shops: TJ1285
Fillers
  Mining engineering: TN948.F45
  Paints: TP937.7
Fillets, Metal
  Engineering and construction:
    TA492.F4
Fills and embankments
  Highway engineering: TE210.8
Film catalogs
  Machine shops: TJ1127
Films
  Electronics: TK7871.15.F5
  Packaging materials: TS198.3.F5
  Plastics: TP1183.F5
  Sensitive surfaces
    Photography: TR283
Filo dough
  Cookery: TX770.F55
Filter basins and plants
  Mechanical treatment of water
    purification: TD447
Filter presses
  Lifting machinery: TJ1470+
Filters
  Radio: TK6565.F5
Filters (Electric)
  Electronics: TK7872.F5
Filtration
  Chemical engineering: TP156.F5
  Sewage purification: TD753
  Water purification: TD441+
Finance
  Hotels, clubs, restaurants,
    etc.: TX911.3.F5
Finance, Household: TX326.A1+
Finials
  Building construction: TH2495
Finish carpentry: TH5640+

Finishes
  Aeronautics: TL699.F5
Finishing
  Ceramic technology: TP814
  Paper manufacture: TS1118.F5
  Photographic processing: TR310
  Plastics: TP1170
  Textile industries: TS1510
  Treatment of positives
    Photographic processing: TR337
  Woodworking: TT199.4
Finishing industry
  Energy conservation: TJ163.5.F5
Finishing processes
  Boot and shoemaking: TS1007
  Cement and concrete
    construction: TA682.49
  Cotton manufactures: TS1580
  Woolen manufactures: TS1630
Finite element method
  Engineering mathematics:
    TA347.F5
Fins
  Airplanes: TL677.F5
Fire alarms: TH9271+
Fire and fire prevention
  Chemical technology: TP265+
Fire carts: TH9378+
Fire clay
  Engineering materials: TA455.F5
Fire department management
  Building construction: TH9158
Fire departments, City: TH9500+
Fire detection: TH9271+
Fire detectors: TH9271
Fire doors
  Building design: TH2278+
  Fire-resistive building
    construction: TH1069
Fire drills: TH9402+
Fire engines
  Fire extinction: TH9371+
Fire escapes
  Building construction: TH2274
Fire extinction
  Building construction: TH9111+,
    TH9310+
Fire extinction equipment:
  TH9360+
Fire extinguishers: TH9362
Fire extinguishing agents:
  TP266

Fire fighters
  Physical training: TH9128
Fire hose: TH9378+
Fire hydrants: TH9365
Fire inspectors' handbooks:
  TH9176
Fire insurance engineering
  Fire prevention and
    extinction: TH9201+
Fire investigation: TH9180
Fire prevention
  Aeronautics: TL697.F5
  Airports: TH9445.A5
  Building construction: TH9111+
    TH9241+
  Motor vehicles: TL241
  School buildings: TH9445.S3
  Space vehicles: TL901
Fire prevention as a
  profession: TH9119
Fire pumps: TH9363
Fire-resistant construction,
  Tests of: TH1091+
Fire resistant plastics: TH1074
Fire resistant polymers:
  TH1074.5
Fire-resistive building
  construction: TH1061+
Fire-retardant coatings
  Building construction: TH1073
Fire shutters
  Fire-resistive building
    construction: TH1069
Fire streams
  Fire extinction: TH9323
Fire testing
  Building construction: TH1091+
Fire testing of materials
  Fire prevention: TH9446.3+
Firearms
  Manufactures: TS532+
Firearms, Muzzle-loading
  Manufactures: TS535.8
Firearms, Repeating
  Manufactures: TS536
Fireboats
  Fire prevention and
    extinction: TH9391
Fireboxes
  Locomotives: TJ646+
Firebrick
  Brickmaking: TP832.F5

Fireclay products
   Architectural ceramics: TP838
Firedamp
   Mining engineering: TN305+
Fireless cookers
   Cookery: TX831
Firemen's associations: TH9500+
Firemen's manuals: TH9151
   Steam boilers: TJ289
Fireplace cookery: TX840.F5
Fireplace heating with wood
   Radiative heading: TH7424+
Fireplaces
   Radiative heating: TH7425+
Fireproof building
   construction: TH1061+
Fireproofing
   Building construction: TH1073+
Fireproofing agents: TP266.5
Fireproofing of fabrics: TP267
Fires
   Fire prevention and
      extinction: TH9448+
   Mines: TN315
   Motor vehicles: TL241
   Space vehicles: TL901
Fires and smoking
   Fire prevention: TH9197
Fires and static electricity
   Fire prevention: TH9198.5
Fires, Tests in
   Fire-resistive-building
      construction: TH1093
Firewall
   Airplanes: TL681.F5
First aid
   Mining engineering: TN297
Fish
   Adulteration: TX595.F47
   Cookery: TX747+
   Food values: TX556.5
   Nature photography: TR729.F5
   Nutritional value: TX385
   Preservation and storage:
      TX612.F5
   Utilization of waste: TP996.F5
Fisheries
   Use of airplanes: TL722.2
   Waste control: TD899.F5
Fishers
   Nutrition: TX361.F5

Fishery processing industries
   Environmental effects:
      TD195.F52
   Waste control: TD899.F57
Fishing lodges
   Construction: TH4880
Fishplates
   Railway construction: TF261
Fission reactors: TK9202+
Fittings
   Steam heating: TH7595
Fixed ladders
   Building design and
      construction: TH2258
Fixing
   Photographic negatives: TR305
   Photographic positives: TR335
Flagging
   Pedestrian facilities: TE280+
Flags
   Textile arts: TT850.2
Flags industry: TS2301.F6
Flame hardening
   Steel metallurgy: TN752.F4
Flame monitors
   Building gas supply: TH6882
Flammability of materials
   Fire prevention: TH9446.3+
Flanges, Metal
   Engineering and construction:
      TA492.F5
Flaps
   Airplanes: TL673.F6
Flare gas systems
   Chemical technology: TP159.F52
Flash photography: TR605+
Flashlight
   Photography: TR605+
Flat coils
   Radiators: TH7483
Flat roofs
   Building construction: TH2409
Flavoring
   Meat-packing industries:
      TS1974.F5
Flavoring aids: TP418+
Flavoring extracts
   Adulteration: TX589
Flax industry: TS1700+
Flexible AC transmission
   systems
      Electrical engineering: TK3148

Flexible manufacturing systems
  Manufactures: TS155.65
Flexible packaging: TS198.F55
Flexible structures
  Structural engineering:
    TA660.F53
Flexure
  Testing of materials:
    TA417.7.F5
Flight mechanics: TL1050 +
Flight recorders
  Aeronautical instrument:
    TL589.2.F5
Flight simulators
  Airplanes: TL712.5
Flight trainers
  Airplanes: TL712.5
Flight training
  Airplanes: TL712 +
Flint
  Mining engineering: TN948.F5
Flintknapping
  Handicrafts: TT293
Flitch beams
  Structural engineering:
    TA660.F57
Floating airports: TL725.7
Floating docks
  Harbor engineering: TC363
Floating harbors
  Harbor engineering: TC363
Floating piers
  Harbor engineering: TC363
Floatplanes: TL684.3
Floats
  Seaplanes: TL684.3
Flocculants
  Chemical technology: TP159.F54
Flocculation
  Biotechnology: TP248.25.F55
  Chemical engineering: TP156.F55
  Sewage purification: TD751
  Water purification: TD455
Flocking, Electrostatic
  Textile industries: TS1512.5
Flood control
  Hydraulic engineering: TC530 +
Flood control channels
  Hydraulic engineering: TC531
Flooding
  Deserts and wastelands: TC950 +
  Mines: TN318

Floodlighting
  Electric lighting: TK4399.F55
Floor drainage
  Plumbing: TH6671.F6
Floor framing
  Building construction: TH2311
Flooring
  Building: TH2521 +
Floors
  Bridge engineering: TG325.6
  Building: TH2521 +
  Structural engineering:
    TA660.F6
Florida Information Resource
Network
  Computer networks:
    TK5105.875.F55
Flotation
  Ore dressing and milling: TN523
Flour
  Adulteration: TX595.F5
  Food values: TX558.W5
Flour mills
  Electric power: TK4035.F6
  Fire prevention and
    extinction: TH9445.M45
  Noise control: TD893.6.F58
  Ventilation: TH7684.F45
Flow
  Aerodynamics: TL574.F5
Flow of fluids
  Space environment: TL1496
Flow of fluids in pipes
  Hydraulic machinery: TJ935
Flow of gases in pipes
  Pneumatic machinery: TJ1025 +
Flow of liquids
  Chemical engineering: TP156.F6
Flow theory
  Sewers: TD675 +
Flow visualization
  Applied fluid mechanics:
    TA357.5.F55
Flow, Unsteady
  Applied fluid mechanics:
    TA357.5.U57
Flow, Viscous
  Applied fluid mechanics:
    TA357.5.V56
Flower wines
  Beverages: TP561

Flowers
  Cookery: TX814.5.F5
  Embroidery: TT773
  Nature photography: TR724+
  Nutrition: TX396
Flowmeters
  Hydraulic machinery: TJ935
Flue gases
  Air pollutants: TD885+
Flues
  Building construction: TH2281+
  Ventilation of buildings:
    TH7683.R4
  Warm-air heating: TH7625
Fluid dynamics
  Engineering: TA357+
  Petroleum pipelines: TN879.56
  Space environment: TL1496
  Turbomachinery: TJ267
Fluid fuel reactors
  Nuclear engineering: TK9203.F5
Fluid mechanics, Applied:
  TA357+
Fluid-structure interaction
  Applied fluid mechanics:
    TA357.5.F58
Fluidic devices: TJ853
Fluidization
  Chemical engineering: TP156.F65
Fluids
  Well drilling: TN871.27
Flumes
  Hydrodynamics: TC175+
Fluorescent lamps and systems:
  TK4386
Fluoridation
  Water purification: TD467
Fluorides
  Air pollutants: TD887.F63
Fluorine
  Air pollutants: TD885.5.F57
  Chemical technology: TP245.F6
Fluorine compounds
  Environmental pollutants:
    TD196.F54
Fluorine organic compounds
  Insulating material: TK3441.F55
Fluorite
  Prospecting: TN271.F6
Fluoro-organic compounds
  Chemical technology: TP248.F5

Fluorocarbons
  Air pollutants: TD887.F67
  Environmental pollutants:
    TD196.F55
  Plastics: TP1180.F6
Fluorspar
  Mining engineering: TN948.F6
  Prospecting: TN271.F6
Flush tanks
  Plumbing: TH6500
Flushing apparatus
  Sewer appurtenances: TD698
Flushing systems
  Cold water supply plumbing:
    TH6544
Flutter
  Aerodynamics: TL574.F6
  Aircraft propellers: TL706.B3
Fluxes in plumbing: TH6297
Fly ash
  Engineering materials:
    TA455.F55
  Soil stabilization: TE210.5.F55
  Water pollutants: TD427.F58
Fly-by-wire systems
  Airplanes: TL678.5
Flying
  Aeronautics: TL710+
Flying automobiles
  Airplanes: TL684.8
Flying boats
  Seaplanes: TL684.2
Flying clubs
  Airplanes: TL713.5
Flying exhibits: TL722.5
Flying machines
  (Non-airplanes): TL713.7+
Flying saucers: TL789+
Flying schools
  Airplanes: TL713.A+
Flying signboards
  Airplane advertising: TL722.5
Flywheel
  Steam engines: TJ541
FM broadcasting
  Radio: TK6562.F2
Foam flotation
  Sewage purification: TD754.5
  Water purification: TD473
Foam fractionation
  Sewage purification: TD754.5
  Water purification: TD473

Foamed materials
  Engineering materials:
    TA418.9.F6
Foamed plastics: TP1183.F6
Focaccia
  Cookery: TX770.F63
Fog control
  Aeronautical meteorology:
    TL557.F6
Fog-pollutant mixtures
  Air pollutants: TD884.3
Foils
  Packaging materials: TS198.3.F5
Folded plates
  Structural engineering:
    TA660.P63
Folding
  Paper manufacture and trade:
    TS1200.A1+
Folding machinery
  Paper manufacture and trade:
    TS1200.A1+
Folding wings
  Airplanes: TL675
Food
  Biotechnology: TP248.65.F66
  Space environment: TL1560
Food additives
  Food processing: TP455+
Food economy in war time: TX357
Food handling in the home:
    TX599+
Food industry
  Electric power: TK4035.F67
  Energy conservation: TJ163.5.F6
  Environmental effects:
    TD195.F57
  Fire prevention and
    extinction: TH9445.F6
  Noise control: TD893.6.F64
  Waste control: TD899.F585
Food manufacturing
  Chemical technology: TP368+
Food presentation
  Cookery: TX740.5
Food processing
  Chemical technology: TP368+
Food processing plants
  Air conditioning: TH7688.F24
  Building construction: TH4526
  Chemical technology: TP373
  Dust removal: TH7697.F55

Food processor recipes
  Cookery: TX840.F6
Food research institutes
  Nutrition: TX341+
Food service: TX901+
  Business mathematics:
    TX911.3.M33
  Hotels, clubs, restaurants,
    etc.: TX943+
  Transportation engineering:
    TA1227
Food standards
  Examination and analysis: TX537
Food storage pests: TP373.3
Food substitutes
  Food processing and
    manufacture: TP446+
Food supply
  Home economics: TX341+
Food values
  Examination and analysis of
    food: TX551+
Foods
  Home economics: TX341+
Foods for special purposes:
    TP450+
Foot baths
  Plumbing: TH6494, TH6495
Footbridges: TG428
Footpaths
  Pedestrian facilities: TE280+
Footwear
  Clothing manufacture: TT678.5
Forced circulation systems
  Hot water heating: TH7535
Forced draft
  Furnaces: TJ335
Forecasting, Technological:
    T174
Foreign visitors
  Photographic portraits:
    TR681.V58
Foremen
  Manufacturing personnel:
    TS155.5
Forensic engineering: TA219
Forest roads
  Highway engineering: TE229.5
Forestry
  Water pollution: TD428.F67
Forge shops
  Noise control: TD893.6.F65

Forging
  Handicrafts: TT215+
  Metal manufactures: TS225+
Formaldehyde
  Chemical technology: TP248.F6
  Environmental pollutants:
    TD196.F65
Formaldehyde release
  Wood products: TS858
Formation damage
  Well drilling: TN871.24
Formic acid
  Chemical technology: TP248.F63
Formwork
  Cement and concrete
    construction: TA682.44
  Reinforced concrete
    construction: TA683.44
Fossil fuels
  Air pollutants: TD887.F69
  Environmental pollutants:
    TD196.F67
Fossil gums
  Mining engineering: TN885
Fouling organisms
  Water pollutants: TD427.F68
Foundation
  Generators: TK2458.F68
Foundation garments
  Clothing manufacture: TT677
Foundation work
  Building construction: TH5201
Foundations
  Building design and
    construction: TH2101
  Engineering: TA775+
  Highway engineering: TE210+
  Machinery: TJ249
  Steam engines: TJ523
  Walls: TH2221
Founding
  Nonferrous metals: TS375
Foundries
  Air pollution: TD888.F6
  Dust removal: TH7697.F6
  Environmental effects: TD195.F6
  Heating and ventilation:
    TH7392.F6
  Waste control: TD899.F6
Foundry equipment and
  supplies: TS237
Foundry management: TS238

Foundry work
  Metal manufactures: TS228.99+
Fountain pens
  Stationery: TS1266
Fountains
  Building construction: TH4977
  Cement manufacture: TP885.F7
  Water distribution systems:
    TD482
  Water supply: TH6569.F7
Four Wheel Drive Vehicles:
  TL230.5.F6
Fracture
  Strength of materials: TA409
Fracture, Brittle
  Structural analysis: TA656.4
Frame
  Airships: TL662.F7
  Cycles: TL415
  Motor vehicles: TL255+
Frame relay
  Packet switching: TK5105.38
Frame setting
  Steam engines: TJ525
Frames
  Reinforced concrete
    construction: TA683.5.F8
  Structural engineering:
    TA660.F7
  Window and door: TH2272
Frames and running gear
  Locomotives: TJ640
Frames, Continuous
  Structural engineering:
    TA660.F72
Frames, Multistory
  Structural engineering:
    TA660.F73
Framing
  Building construction: TH2301+
Framing of prints
  Photographic processing: TR340
Franche-Comté cookery:
  TX719.2.F73
Frasca engines
  Internal combustion engines:
    TJ792
Free balloons, Operation of:
  TL626+
Free electron lasers
  Applied optics: TA1693

Free lance cinematography
  Photography: TR894.4
Free piston engines: TJ779
Freehand drawing, Technical:
  T359
Freelance photography: TR690.2
Freeze-drying
  Food preservation: TP371.6
Freezing
  Food preservation: TP372.3
  Home preservation of foods:
    TX610
Freezing methods
  Saline water conversion:
    TD480.2
Freezing of pipes
  Plumbing: TH6685
Freight
  Railway operation: TF662 +
  Transportation engineering:
    TA1210 +
Freight cars
  Railway equipment: TF470 +
Freight service
  Electric railways: TF970
Freight subways: TF850 +
Freight trains: TF580 +
Freight yards and terminals
  Railway structures: TF305 +
French toast
  Cookery: TX770.F73
Frequency changers
  Electronics: TK7872.F7
  Radio: TK6565.F7
Frequency meters
  Electronics: TK7879.4
Frequency meters and
  measurements
  Electrical engineering: TK381
Frequency modulation radios:
  TK6564.F7
Frequency synthesizers
  Electronics: TK7872.F73
Frequency-voltage converters
  Electronics: TK7872.V54
Frescoing
  Painting: TT323
Fresh air inlets
  House drainage: TH6649
Fretwork
  Building construction: TH8581 +

Friction
  Aerodynamics: TL574.F7
  Mechanical engineering: TJ1075 +
Friction clutches
  Mechanical engineering: TJ1074
Friction metals
  Metallography: TN693.F7
Frogs
  Railway construction: TF266 +
Front desk
  Hotels, clubs, restaurants,
    etc.: TX911.3.F75
Front-screen projection
  Cinematography: TR859
Frontage roads
  Highway engineering: TE228.7
FrontPage (Microsoft)
  Web authoring software:
    TK5105.8885.M53
Frozen food
  Cookery: TX828
Frozen ground construction
  Engineering: TA713
Fructose
  Cookery: TX819.F78
Fruit
  Food processing: TP440 +
  Food values: TX558.F7
  Nutrition: TX397
  Preparation (Cookery): TX811 +
  Preservation and storage:
    TX612.F7
Fruit juices
  Beverages: TP562 +
Fruit processing plants
  Waste control: TD899.F7
Fruit products
  Food processing: TP440 +
Fruit wines
  Beverages: TP561
Fryers
  Cookery equipment: TX657.F7
Frying
  Cooking process: TX689 +
Fuel
  Aircraft engines: TL704.7
  Chemical technology: TP315 +
  Locomotives: TJ648
  Rockets: TL785
Fuel cells
  Electrical engineering: TK2931
  Vehicles: TL221.13

Fuel claddings
  Nuclear reactors: TK9207.5
Fuel consumption
  Motor vehicle operation:
    TL151.6
Fuel economizers
  Furnaces: TJ340
Fuel elements
  Nuclear reactors: TK9207
Fuel feeding
  Aircraft engines: TL702.F8
Fuel injection systems
  Diesel engines: TJ797
  Gasoline automobiles: TL214.F78
Fuel reprocessing plants,
  Reactor
  Environmental effects: TD195.R4
Fuel systems
  Diesel engines: TJ797
  Furnaces: TJ324.5
  Gasoline automobiles: TL214.F8
  Jet engines: TL709.5.F8
  Miscellaneous motors and
    engines: TJ762.F84
  Rockets: TL784.F8
Fuel testing plants: TP322
Fugu
  Cookery: TX748.F83
Fullers' earth
  Mining engineering: TN948.F9
Fulminates
  Explosives: TP293
Fumes
  Air pollutants: TD884.5
Fumigants
  Environmental pollutants:
    TD196.F85
Fumigation
  Protection of buildings: TH9041
Function generators
  Computer engineering: TK7895.F8
  Electronics: TK7872.F85
Functional analysis
  Engineering mathematics:
    TA347.F86
Functionally gradient materials
  Engineering materials:
    TA418.9.F85
Functions of complex variables
  Engineering mathematics:
    TA347.C64

Fungal biotechnology:
  TP248.27.F86
Fungi
  Cookery: TX803.F85
  Deterioration of wood: TA423.2+
  Nature photography: TR726.F85
  Packaging protection:
    TS198.8.F8
Fungicides
  Chemical technology: TP248.F79
  Preservation of wood:
    TA424.6.F8
Funny cars: TL236.23
Fur garments
  Women's tailoring: TT525
Furaldehyde
  Chemical technology: TP248.F8
Furans
  Plastics: TP1180.F8
Furnaces
  Central heating: TH7470+
  Chemical technology: TP159.F87
  Fire prevention and
    extinction: TH9445.F87
  Glassmaking: TP859.5
  High-pressure hot water
    heating: TH7534.A+
  Hot water heating: TH7538+
  Low-pressure hot water
    heating: TH7529
  Steam boilers: TJ320+
  Steam heating: TH7588+
  Warm-air heating: TH7623+
Furnaces, Cupola
  Foundry work: TS231
Furnishing
  The house: TX311+
Furnishings
  Hotels, clubs, restaurants,
    etc.: TX912
  Men's clothing: TT627
  Taverns, barrooms, saloons:
    TX952+
Furnishings, Table
  Dining-room service: TX877
Furniture
  Finishing: TS886
  Fire-testing: TH9446.5.F87
  Manufactures: TS840+
  Metal manufactures: TS408

Furniture
 Wood manufactures: TS879.2 +
 Woodworking: TT194 +
Furniture design
 Woodworking: TT196
Furniture, Plastic
 Plastic technology: TP1185.F8
Furs
 Manufactures: TS1060 +
Fuselage
 Airplanes: TL680 +
Fuses
 Dynamoelectric machinery:
  TK2841 +
 Electric power transmission:
  TK3511
 Explosives: TP293
Fusible plugs
 Furnaces: TJ356
Fusion reactors: TK9204
FutureTense Texture
 Web authoring software:
  TK5105.8885.F87

G

Gadolinium
 Chemical technology: TP245.G2
Gage
 Steam boilers: TJ363
Gages
 Machine shop practice: TJ1166
Gaging and testing
 Distilling: TP609
Gaging systems
 Machine shop practice: TJ1166
Galena: TN452.G3
Gallium
 Chemical technology: TP245.G4
 Metallurgy: TN799.G3
Gallium arsenide
 Electronics: TK7871.15.G3
Gallium nitride
 Electronics: TK7871.15.G33
Galvanizing
 Metal finishing: TS660
Galvanometers
 Electric meters: TK311
Game
 Cookery: TX751
 Nutrition: TX375

Game theory
 Industrial engineering: T57.92
Games
 Electronics: TK7882.G35
Gamma ray lasers
 Applied optics: TA1694
Gantt charts: TS157.7
Gap
 Airplanes: TL673.G3
Garages
 Building construction: TH4960
 Fire prevention and
  extinction: TH9445.G3
 Heating and ventilation:
  TH7392.G37
Garand rifle: TS536.6.G37
Garbage
 Waste disposal: TD801 +
Garden furniture
 Cement manufacture: TP885.G3
Garden structures
 Construction: TH4961 +
Garden toolsheds
 Building construction: TH4962
Garden walks
 Building construction: TH4970
Gardens
 Artistic photography: TR662
Garlic
 Cookery: TX819.G3
 Food processing and
  manufacture: TP444.G37
Garment industry: TT490 +
Garments, Dyeing of
 Textile decoration: TT853 +
Garnets
 Mineral industries: TN997.G3
Garnishes
 Cookery: TX740.5
Gas
 Blast furnaces: TN718
 Fuel: TP345.A1 +
 Lighter-than-air craft fuel:
  TL666
Gas air conditioning: TH7687.85
Gas appliances
 Building construction: TH6855 +
Gas burning installations
 Furnaces: TJ325
Gas cells
 Airships: TL662.G3

Gas chromatography
  Food analysis: TX548.2.G36
Gas cooled reactors
  Nuclear engineering: TK9203.G3
Gas engines: TJ770 +
Gas fireplace heating
  Local heating: TH7434
Gas fixtures
  Building construction: TH6855 +
Gas fuels
  Central heating: TH7466.G3
Gas heating
  Central heating: TH7463
  Heating of buildings: TH7405 +
Gas in buildings
  Plumbing: TH6800 +
Gas industry
  Chemical technology: TP750.2 +
  Environmental effects: TD195.G3
  Waste control: TD899.G3
Gas lasers
  Applied optics: TA1695
Gas lighting
  Building construction: TH7910 +
Gas lighting fixtures
  Artificial lighting: TH7960 +
Gas logs
  Local heating: TH7434
Gas-lubricated bearings
  Mechanical engineering:
    TJ1073.5
Gas manufacture and works
  Air pollution: TD888.G37
Gas masks
  Industrial safety: T55.3.G3
Gas meters
  Building construction: TH6870
Gas ovens
  Cookery: TX657.O6
Gas powerplants: TJ768
Gas producer automobiles:
  TL229.G3
Gas producers for industrial
  purposes: TP762
Gas recorders
  Gas industry: TP754
Gas refrigerators: TP497.A1 +
Gas storage: TP756
Gas stove heating
  Building construction: TH7453 +

Gas stoves
  Convective heating: TH7454 +
  Cookery: TX657.S6
Gas toasters
  Cookery: TX657.T6
Gas tubes: TK7871.8 +
Gas turbine automobiles: TL226 +
Gas turbine locomotives: TJ622
Gas-turbine motorcars
  Railway equipment: TF499
Gas turbine power plants:
  TK1076
Gas turbines: TJ778
Gas water heaters
  Plumbing: TH6561
Gas welding: TS228 +
Gas well drilling: TN880.2
Gas well supplies
  Petroleum engineering: TN871.5
Gas, Sewer: TD690
Gascony cookery: TX719.2.G37
Gaseous fuel
  Chemical technology: TP343 +
Gases
  Air pollutants: TD885 +
  Chemical technology: TP242 +
  Insulating material: TK3441.G3
Gases as conductors
  Electric power: TK3311.G3
Gases from explosives
  Mines: TN306
Gases in mines: TN305 +
Gases, Asphyxiating
  Effect on food: TX571.G3
Gases, Compressed
  Automobiles: TL228
Gases, Poisonous
  Effect on food: TX571.G3
Gasholders: TP756
Gasification of coal: TP759
Gasification of oil: TP759
Gaskets
  Machinery: TJ246
Gasohol
  Fuel: TP358
Gasoline
  Fire prevention and
    extinction: TH9446.G3
  Petroleum products: TP692.2
Gasoline automobiles: TL205 +
Gasoline engines
  Mine transportation: TN338

Gasoline fire engines: TH9377
Gasoline handling and storage: TP692.5
Gasoline locomotives: TJ621
Gasoline motorcars
  Railway equipment: TF497
Gasoline stoves
  Cookery: TX657.S7
Gastronomy: TX15+
  Nutrition: TX631+
Gasworks
  Gas industry: TP752
  Noise control: TD893.6.G37
Gate array circuits
  Computer engineering: TK7895.G36
Gates
  Building construction: TH4955+, TH4965
  Dams: TC553
  Hydraulic powerplants: TJ847
  Hydrostatics: TC169
  Irrigation engineering: TC937
Gateways
  Computer networks: TK5105.543
Gauges
  Railway construction: TF244
Gazebos
  Building construction: TH4963
Gear
  Aircraft propellers: TL707.G4
Gear-cutting machines
  Mechanical movements: TJ187
Gear wheels
  Electric railways: TF949.G4
Gearing
  Aircraft engines: TL702.G4
  Mechanical engineering: TJ184+
Gelatin
  Cookery: TX814.5.G4
  Organic chemical industries: TP965
Gelatine relief processes
  Photography: TR990+
Gem cutting: TS752.5
Gemini project: TL789.8.U6G4
Gems
  Jewelry manufacture: TS747+
  Mining: TN980+

Generators: TK2411+
  Aircraft: TL691.G4
  Design and construction: TK2435
  Details: TK2451+
  Electrical details: TK2471+
  Magnetic details: TK2461+
  Mechanical details: TK2456+
  Space vehicles: TL1102.G4
  Testing: TK2433
  Types: TK2441
Genetic engineering
  Biotechnology: TP248.6
Geneva mechanisms
  Mechanical engineering: TJ181.7
Geochemistry
  Radioactive waste disposal: TD898.14.G46
Geodesy
  Radar: TK6595.G4
Geodetic satellites: TL798.G4
Geographical applications
  Applied photography: TR786+
Geographical displays
  Aeronautical instruments: TL589.35.G46
Geographical subdivisions
  Telegraph: TK5609+
Geology
  Radioactive waste disposal: TD898.14.G47
Geology of coal deposits
  Coal mining: TN805+
Geology, Applied: TN260
Geology, Economic: TN260
Geology, Engineering: TA703+
Geometric lathework: TT203
Geometric programming
  Industrial engineering: T57.825
Geophysical surveying: TN269+
Geosynthetics
  Engineering materials: TA455.G44
Geothermal district heating of buildings: TH7416.5
Geothermal engineering: TJ280.7
Geothermal heating
  Heating of buildings: TH7416+
Geothermal power plants
  Environmental effects: TD195.G46
Geothermal space heating of buildings: TH7417

Germanium
  Chemical technology: TP245.G5
  Engineering materials: TA480.G4
  Metallurgy: TN799.G4
  Ore deposits and mining:
    TN490.G4
Gilding
  Handicrafts: TT300+
  Metal arts and crafts: TT382.8
  Metal finishing: TS715
Gimp
  Silk manufactures: TS1687
Gin
  Distilled liquors: TP607.G4
Ginger
  Cookery: TX819.G53
Ginning
  Cotton manufactures: TS1585
Girders
  Bridge engineering: TG350+
  Hoisting machinery: TJ1367
Girders, Metal
  Engineering and construction:
    TA492.G5
Girders, Plate
  Structural engineering:
    TA660.P59
Girdles
  Clothing manufacture: TT677
Girls
  Clothing: TT562
  Handicrafts: TT171
  Photographic portraits:
    TR681.G5
Glamour photography: TR678
Glass
  Chemical technology: TP785+
  Electronics: TK7871.15.G5
  Engineering materials: TA450
  Insulating material: TK3441.G5
  Packaging materials: TS198.3.G5
  Reinforced plastics:
    TP1177.5.G5
  Waste disposal: TD799
Glass and glassmaking: TP845+
Glass-ceramic pipe
  Glassware: TP867.3
Glass construction
  Building construction: TH1560
Glass craft: TT298
Glass engraving
  Handicrafts: TT298

Glass fiber: TS1549.G5
Glass fiber industry
  Waste control: TD899.G47
Glass fibers
  Glassmaking: TP860.5
Glass forming
  Handicrafts: TT298
Glass manufacture
  Energy conservation:
    TJ163.5.G55
  Environmental effects:
    TD195.G57
Glass objects
  Glassmaking: TP865+
Glass painting
  Handicrafts: TT298
Glass recycling
  Glassmaking: TP859.7
Glass trade
  Fire prevention and
    extinction: TH9445.G54
Glassblowing
  Glassmaking: TP859
Glassware
  Glassmaking: TP865+
Glazed brick
  Brickmaking: TP832.G6
Glazes
  Ceramic decoration: TP823
  Ceramic technology: TP812.A1+
  Pottery craft: TT922
Glazing
  Building construction: TH8251+
Gliders: TL760+
  Design and construction: TL762
  Equipment: TL766
  Heavier-than-air craft: TL670.5
  Launching: TL765
  Operation: TL765
Gliders, Model: TL774
Gliding: TL760+
Global Positioning System,
  Satellite component of the:
    TL798.N3
Global system for mobile
  communications
  Wireless communication
    systems: TK5103.483
Gloves
  Clothing manufacture: TT666
  Manufactures: TS2160

Glucose
  Sugars and syrups: TP414
Glucosides
  Chemical technology: TP248.G6
Glue
  Aeronautics: TL699.G6
  Organic chemical industries:
    TP967+
Glutamate
  Cookery: TX819.G55
Glutamic acid
  Chemical technology: TP248.G65
Gluten
  Cookery: TX809.G55
  Food constituent: TX553.G47
Glycerin
  Organic chemical industries:
    TP973
Glycoconjugates
  Biotechnology: TP248.65.G49
Glycols
  Hazardous substance disposal:
    TD1066.G48
Glyphosate
  Water pollutants: TD427.G55
Goffering machines: TJ1530
Goggles for air pilots:
  TL697.G6
Gold
  Assaying: TN580.G6
  Chemical technology: TP245.G6
  Metallography: TN693.G6
  Ore dressing and milling:
    TN538.G64
  Prospecting: TN271.G6
Gold and silver
  Metallurgy: TN760+
  Ore deposits and mining: TN410+
Gold dredging: TN422
Gold fiber: TS1549.G6
Gold industry
  Environmental effects:
    TD195.G64
  Waste control: TD899.G63
Gold mines and mining
  Water pollution: TD428.G64
Gold ore deposits and mining:
  TN420+
Gold ores
  Assaying: TN580.G6
Gold pens
  Stationery: TS1265

Gold plating
  Electroplating: TS678
Gold thread
  Embroidery: TT777
Gold work
  Manufactures: TS720+
Golf carts: TL484
Golf courses
  Environmental effects:
    TD195.G66
GoLive CyberStudio
  Web authoring software:
    TK5105.8885.G64
Gourd craft
  Decorative crafts: TT873.5
Government and industrial
  laboratories
  Chemical technology: TP187+
Government operation of
  airports: TL725.3.G6
Government policy
  Radioactive waste disposal:
    TD898.14.G68
Governors
  Building gas supply: TH6875
  Diesel engines: TJ799
  Machinery: TJ254
  Machinery exclusive of prime
    movers: TJ1055
  Steam engines: TJ550+
Grades
  Railway construction: TF243
Grading
  Dressmaking: TT520
  Lumber: TS825
  Men's tailoring: TT590
  Production management: TS156.25
Graf Zeppelin (Airship):
  TL659.G7
Grain
  Manufactures: TS2120+
  Moisture: TS2149
Grain elevators
  Building construction: TH4461
  Dust removal: TH7697.G67
  Fire prevention and
    extinction: TH9445.G7
  Noise control: TD893.6.G7
  Photography: TR739.6
Grain-handling machinery
  Conveying machinery: TJ1415+

Graining
  Wood finishing: TT330
Grandmothers
  Photographic portraits:
    TR681.G73
Granite: TN970
Granite brick
  Brickmaking: TP832.G7
Granite plants
  Dust removal: TH7697.G7
Granola
  Cookery: TX809.G7
Granulation
  Biotechnology: TP248.25.G7
Grape juice
  Unfermented: TP560
Grapefruit
  Cookery: TX813.G73
Grapes
  Food values: TX558.G6
Graphic analysis
  Industrial engineering: T57.4
Graphic methods
  Engineering mathematics: TA337+
Graphic statics
  Bridge engineering: TG270
  Machinery: TJ235
  Structural engineering: TA640.6
Graphics, Engineering: T351+
Graphite
  Engineering materials: TA455.G7
  Industrial electrochemistry:
    TP261.G7
  Mining engineering: TN845
  Nuclear engineering:
    TK9185.2.G73
  Prospecting: TN271.G7
Grass heating
  Convective heating: TH7458.G7
Grass rugs
  Floor covering: TS1779.G7
Grass stoves
  Convective heating: TH7458.G7
Grasswork
  Decorative crafts: TT876.3
Grate frames
  Building construction: TH7433
Grate heating with coal:
    TH7428+
Grate shakers
  Furnaces: TJ347

Grates
  Furnaces: TJ322+
  Local heating: TH7429+
Gratings
  Building design and
    construction: TH2273
Gravel
  Composition roofing: TH2451
  Engineering materials:
    TA455.G73
  Mining engineering: TN939
  Sidewalks: TE283
  Unpaved roads: TE233
Gravel industry
  Dust removal: TH7697.S3
  Environmental effects: TD195.S3
Gravity
  Mountain railways: TF686
Gravity environments, Reduced
  Applied fluid mechanics:
    TA357.5.R44
Gravity systems
  Low-pressure steam heating:
    TH7571
Grease separators
  Low-pressure steam heating:
    TH7578.G7, TH7578.V3
Grease traps
  Kitchen plumbing: TH6512
Greenhouse gases
  Air pollutants: TD885.5.G73
Greens
  Cookery: TX803.G74
Greeting card craft
  Decorative crafts: TT872
Grillages
  Structural engineering:
    TA660.G7
Grilles
  Building construction: TH8581+
Grinding
  Chemical technology: TP156.S5
  Optical instruments: TS517
Grinding tools
  Machine shops: TJ1280+
Grindstones
  Abrading machinery: TJ1293
Groats
  Food values: TX558.G67
Grooving machines
  Machine shops: TJ1210

Grotesque
  Photography: TR686
Ground control
  Mining: TN288+
Ground controlled approach
  Aeronautical navigation
    equipment: TL696.L33
Ground cushion
  Aerodynamics: TL574.G7
Ground effect
  Aerodynamics: TL574.G7
Ground source heat pump
  systems: TH7417.5
Ground-speed indicator
  Aeronautical navigation:
    TL696.G7
Ground support
  Mining: TN288+
Ground support systems
  Astronautics: TL4000+
Ground transportation
  Astronautics: TL4050
Grounding
  Electric power: TK3227
Groundwater
  Petroleum geology: TN870.515
  Pollution: TD426+
  Recharge: TD765
  Water supply: TD403+
Groupers
  Cookery: TX748.G74
Grouting
  Earthwork: TA755
Guarapo
  Fermented beverage: TP588.G8
Guardrails
  Railway construction: TF268
Guidance and control systems
  Space vehicles: TL3025+
Guidance systems
  Aeronautical instruments:
    TL589.4+
  Rockets: TL784.C63
  Space vehicles: TL3250+
Guideways
  High speed ground
    transportation: TF1490
Gum-biochromate
  Photography: TR445
Gum plastics: TP1180.G8

Gums and resins
  Organic chemical industries:
    TP977+
Gums and resins industry
  Waste control: TD899.G85
Gums and resins, Synthetic
  Aeronautics: TL699.G85
Guncotton
  Explosives: TP276
Gunite: TA446
Gunn diodes
  Semiconductors: TK7871.89.G84
Gunn effect devices
  Electronics: TK7872.G8
Gunpowder: TP272
Guns
  Manufactures: TS532+
Gunsmithing: TS535+
Gunstocks
  Gunsmithing: TS535.2.G8
Gutta-percha
  Rubber industry: TS1930
Gutters
  Building construction: TH2493
Guy anchors: TA777
Gypsies
  Photographic portraits:
    TR681.G9
Gypsum
  Engineering materials: TA455.G9
  Mining engineering: TN946
Gypsum plasters
  Decorative furnishings:
    TH8137.G8
Gypsum products
  Chemical technology: TP888
Gypsum wallboard
  Decorative furnishings: TH8139
Gyrators
  Electronics: TK7872.G9
Gyropilot
  Aeronautical instruments:
    TL589.5
Gyroscopes
  Mechanical engineering: TJ209
Gyrotrons: TK7871.79.G95

H

Haddock
  Cookery: TX748.H33
Hail
  Aeronautical meteorology:
  TL557.H3
Hair bleaching
  Women: TT973
Hair conditioners: TP984
Hair preparations: TP984
Hair styles
  Men: TT963
Hair tinting
  Women: TT973
Haircutting: TT970
Hairdressing: TT950+
Hairdressing for women: TT972+
Hairpin lace: TT805.H34
Hairwork: TT975+
Halftone process
  Photography: TR975
Hall effect devices
  Electronics: TK7872.H3
Halloween
  Cookery: TX739.2.H34
Halloween decorations
  Decorative crafts: TT900.H32
Halloysite
  Mining engineering: TN948.H3
Halocarbons
  Air pollutants: TD887.H3
Halogen lamps
  Electric lighting: TK4359.H34
Halogen organic compounds
  Environmental pollutants:
  TD196.H35
Halogenated hydrocarbons
  Water pollutants: TD427.H93
Halogens
  Chemical technology: TP248.H3
Ham
  Cookery: TX749.5.H35
Hammers
  Machine shops: TJ1201.H3
Hammers, Power
  Machine shops: TJ1305+
Hammocks
  Hand weaving: TT849.2
Hand cameras
  Photography: TR260

Hand fire engines
  Fire prevention and
  extinction: TH9374
Hand-made carpets
  Textile arts: TT850
Hand-made rugs
  Textile arts: TT850
Hand pumps
  Fire extinction: TH9363
  Hydraulic machinery: TJ903
Hand shears
  Metal manufactures: TS381
Hand signals
  Railway operation: TF625
Hand spinning
  Textile arts: TT847
Hand stamps
  Manufactures: TS1920
Hand weaving
  Textile arts: TT848+
Hand-woven products
  Wood products: TS913
Handbags
  Clothing manufacture: TT667
Handcuffs
  Locksmithing: TS531
Handguns
  Manufactures: TS537
Handicapped
  Clothing: TT648
  Nutrition: TX361.H35
  Photographic portraits:
  TR681.H35
Handicrafts: TT1+
Handicrafts for girls: TT171
Handling characteristics
  Airplanes: TL671.4
  Motor vehicle dynamics: TL245.5
Handloading ammunition: TS538.3
Handlooms
  Hand weaving: TT848.5
Handmade
  Paper types: TS1124.5
Handrail joinery
  Building construction: TH5675+
Handtools: TJ1195+
Hangars
  Airports: TL730+
Hangers
  Machinery: TJ1065
Hanging burlap
  Wall decoration: TH8471

Hanukkah
  Cookery: TX739.2.H35
Hanukkah decorations
  Decorative crafts: TT900.H34
Harbor engineering: TC352+
Harbors
  Electric power: TK4035.H3
  Hydraulic engineering: TC203+
Hard-facing
  Welding: TS227.3
Hard materials
  Hardness properties and tests:
    TA418.45
Hard water: TD374
Hardanger
  Drawnwork: TT787
Hardness
  Water quality: TD374
Hardness properties and tests:
    TA418.42
Hardware
  Metal manufactures: TS399.2+
Hardware description languages
  Electronics: TK7885.7
Hardwoods
  Woodpulp industry: TS1176.4.H3
Harmful environments, Packaging
  for protection from:
    TS198.7+
Harness
  Leather industries: TS1030+
Harness hardware
  Manufactures: TS1035
Harrows
  Agricultural machinery: TJ1482
Harvesters
  Agricultural machinery: TJ1485
Hatchways
  Building construction: TH2491
Hats
  Manufactures: TS2180+
Hauling tests
  Highway engineering: TE450
Hay
  Food values: TX558.H2
Hayboxes
  Cookery: TX831
Hazardous substances
  Disposal: TD1020+
  Fire prevention and
    extinction: TH9446.H38
  Industrial safety: T55.3.H3

Hazardous substances
  Soil pollutants: TD879.H38
  Water pollutants: TD427.H3
Hazardous waste management
  industry
  Environmental effects:
    TD195.H39
Hazardous waste sites: TD1052
Hazardous waste treatment
  facilities: TD1054
Hazardous wastes
  Sewage disposal: TD758.5.H39
  Soil pollutants: TD879.H38
Hazelnuts
  Cookery: TX814.2.H39
Head resistance
  Aerodynamics: TL574.D7
Head-up displays
  Aeronautical instruments:
    TL589.35.H42
Headlights
  Electric railways: TF940
  Locomotives: TJ668
Headphones
  Electroacoustics: TK5983.5
Health
  Motor vehicle drivers: TL152.3+
Health facilities
  Fire prevention and
    extinction: TH9445.H7
Heap leaching
  Hydrometallurgy: TN688.3.H4
Hearses: TL235.8
Heat
  Environmental pollutants:
    TD196.H4
  Mechanical engineering: TJ260
  Power source: TJ260
Heat engines: TJ255+
  Theory: TJ265
Heat exchangers: TJ263+
  Ventilation of buildings:
    TH7683.H42
Heat pipes: TJ264
  Airplanes: TL697.H4
Heat pollution
  Water pollutants: TD427.H4
Heat pump systems
  Central heating: TH7638
Heat pumps
  Mechanical engineering: TJ262

Heat resistant alloys
  Engineering materials: TA485
  Metallurgy: TN700
  Powder metallurgy: TN697.H4
Heat resistant materials:
  TA418.26
Heat resistant metals
  Metallography: TN693.H4
Heat resistant steel
  Engineering and construction:
  TA479.H43
Heat sinks
  Electronics: TK7872.H4
Heat transfer media
  Chemical technology: TP159.H4
Heat transmission
  Petroleum pipelines: TN879.57
Heat transmission through
  boiler tubes: TJ297
Heat treatment
  Metallurgy: TN758.3
  Steel metallurgy: TN751+
Heat treatment of metals: TN672
Heat utilization, Waste
  Municipal refuse: TD796.2
Heating
  Airplanes: TL681.H4
  Buildings: TH7201+
  Chemical technology: TP363
  Prisons: TH7392.P8
  Railway equipment: TF445+
  Transportation engineering:
  TA1280
Heating and ventilation
  Building construction: TH7005+
  Motor vehicles: TL271+
Heating engineering
  Building construction: TH7121+
Heating equipment
  Fire prevention and
    extinction: TH9445.H4
Heating from central stations
  Building construction: TH7641+
Heating mains
  Building construction: TH7643
Heating of metals
  Manufactures: TS209
Heating pipes
  Building construction: TH7643
Heating plants
  Air pollution: TD888.H43
  Energy conservation: TJ163.5.H4

Heating regenerators
  Jet engines: TL709.5.H42
Heating systems
  Hot water supply plumbing:
  TH6552+
Heating, Local
  Heating and ventilation:
  TH7418+
Heavier-than-air craft: TL669+
Heavy elements
  Environmental pollutants:
  TD196.H43
Heavy metals
  Air pollutants: TD887.H4
  Assaying: TN580.H43
  Effect on food: TX572.H4
  Environmental pollutants:
  TD196.M4
  Sewage disposal: TD758.5.H43
  Soil pollutants: TD879.H4
  Water pollutants: TD427.M44
Heavy minerals
  Prospecting: TN271.H43
Heavy water reactors
  Nuclear engineering: TK9203.H4
Height indicator
  Aeronautical navigation:
  TL696.H4
Helical gears
  Mechanical movements: TJ192
Helicopters: TL716+
Heliogravure
  Photography: TR980
Heliotype
  Photography: TR937
Helium
  Chemical technology: TP245.H4
  Lighter-than-air craft fuel:
  TL666
Helium in natural gas: TN883
Hell Gate
  Hydraulic engineering: TC192
Helmet-mounted displays
  Aeronautical instruments:
  TL589.35.H44
Helmets
  Aeronautics: TL697.H44
  Plastic: TP1185.H4
Helmets, Safety
  Industrial safety: T55.3.S23

Hematite
  Ore deposits and mining:
    TN402.H4
Hemp
  Cookery: TX814.5.H45
  Paper manufacture: TS1109
  Textile fiber: TS1544.H4
Hemp industry: TS1700+
Herbicides
  Chemical technology: TP248.H36
  Environmental pollutants:
    TD196.H47
  Soil pollutants: TD879.H47
  Water pollutants: TD427.H46
Herbs
  Cookery: TX819.H4
Hermes (Artificial satellite):
  TK5104.2.H46
Herring
  Cookery: TX748.H45
Heuristic programming
  Industrial engineering: T57.84
Hexachlorethane
  Chemical technology: TP248.H4
Hexazinone
  Water pollutants: TD427.H49
Hexone
  Chemical technology: TP248.H43
Hexylene glycol
  Air pollutants: TD887.H48
Hides
  Leather industries: TS967
High definition television:
  TK6679
High energy forming
  Metal manufactures: TS256
High fidelity systems
  Amateurs' manuals: TK9968
  Electronics: TK7881.7
High gravity
  Testing of materials:
    TA417.7.H53
High performance liquid
  chromatography
  Biotechnology: TP248.25.H54
High pressure
  Biotechnology: TP248.25.H56
High-pressure hot water heating
  (with coil boilers): TH7530+
High solids coatings
  Chemical technology: TP945
High-speed aeronautics: TL551.5

High speed ground
  transportation
  Railroad engineering: TF1300+
High-speed photography: TR593
High speed telegraph system:
  TK5523
High technology industries
  Environmental effects:
    TD195.H54
High temperature
  Testing of materials:
    TA417.7.H55
High tension A.C.
  Dynamoelectric machinery:
    TK2828
High tension A.C. systems
  Electrical engineering: TK3144
High voltage photography: TR760
Highway bridges: TG425
Highway design: TE175
Highway engineering: TE1+
Highway engineering
  management: TE195
Highway research: TE192
Hindenberg (Airship): TL659.H5
Hinges
  Cement and concrete
    construction: TA682.3
Hiring a contractor
  House construction: TH4815.4
Hispanic Americans
  Nutrition: TX361.H57
Hispano-Suiza aircraft
  engines: TL703.H5
Historic buildings
  Fire prevention and
    extinction: TH9445.M8
Historic documents
  Photography: TR825
Hoffman's kiln: TP842.H7
Hoisting machinery
  Electric driving: TK4059.H64
  Electric power: TK4035.H6
  Internal combustion engines:
    TJ793.3
  Mechanical engineering: TJ1350+
Hoists
  Hoisting machinery: TJ1383
  Mine transportation: TN339+
Holding patterns
  Airplanes: TL711.H65

INDEX

Holidays
  Cookery: TX739+
  Decorations: TT900.H6
Hollow brick
  Brickmaking: TP832.H7
Hollow earthenware
  Fire-resistive building
    construction: TH1083
Holographic interferometry:
  TA1555
Holographic testing
  Testing of materials: TA417.45
Holography, Applied: TA1540+
Holography, Microwave: TA1552
Holsters
  Gunsmithing: TS535.2.H64
Home accidents and their
  prevention: TX150
Home arts
  Handicrafts: TT697+
Home arts for women: TT697+
Home carpentry
  Building construction: TH5607
Home earth stations
  Amateurs' manuals: TK9962
Home economics: TX1+
  Elementary education: TX1+
  Secondary education: TX1+
Home economics as a
  profession: TX164
Home educators
  Technology: T47
Home entertainment systems
  Electronics: TK7881.3
Home furnishings in metal:
  TT213
Home video photography: TR896+
Home video systems
  Amateurs' manuals: TK9961
Homecrafts: TT697+
Homeless persons
  Nutrition: TX361.H65
  Photographic portraits:
    TR681.H63
Homes
  Air conditioning: TH7688.H6
Homosexuals
  Photographic portraits:
    TR681.H65
Honey
  Cookery: TX767.H7
  Food values: TX560.H7

Honeycomb structure
  Structural engineering:
    TA660.H66
Hook and ladder trucks
  Fire prevention and
    extinction: TH9383
Hooke's coupling: TJ183
Hooking
  Hand-made carpets: TT850
  Hand-made rugs: TT850
Hooks
  Engineering forms: TA492.H6
Hops
  Brewing and malting: TP585
Horizontal well drilling
  Petroleum engineering: TN871.25
Horn craft: TT288
Horn, Articles of
  Manufactures: TS1050
Hors d'oeuvres
  Recipes: TX740
Horse railroads
  Railroad antiquities: TF16
Horse railways
  Municipal railways: TF830
Horsehair
  Textile fiber: TS1548.H6
  Textile industry: TS1747.H6
Horsemeat
  Cookery: TX749.5.H67
  Food values: TX556.H8
Horses
  Nature photography: TR729.H6
Hose carts
  Fire prevention and
    extinction: TH9379
Hose industry
  Manufactures: TS2301.H7
Hose, Fire
  Fire extinction: TH9380
Hosiery
  Clothing manufacture: TT679+
Hospitality industry: TX901+
Hospitals
  Building construction: TH4661
  Fire prevention and
    extinction: TH9445.H7
Hostesses
  Hotels, clubs, restaurants,
    etc.: TX930
Hot air balloons: TL638
Hot-air engines: TJ765

545

Hot blast
  Blast furnaces: TN715
Hot peppers
  Cookery: TX819.H66
Hot rods: TL236.3
Hot tubs
  Plumbing: TH6501
Hot water fixtures of
  buildings: TH7511+
Hot water heating of
  buildings: TH7511+
Hot water rockets: TL783.8
Hot water supply
  Building construction: TH6551+
Hot water supply systems
  Plumbing: TH6567
Hot water tanks
  Plumbing: TH6564
Hot weather conditions
  Cement and concrete
    construction: TA682.48
Hot weather cooking: TX829
Hot working of metals
  Manufactures: TS209.5
Hotels: TX901+
  Business mathematics:
    TX911.3.M33
  Electric lighting: TK4399.H7
  Energy conservation:
    TJ163.5.H67
  Environmental effects:
    TD195.H67
  Fire prevention and
    extinction: TH9445.H75
  Plumbing: TH6515.H8
  Waste control: TD899.H65
House
  Home economics: TX301+
House buyers' guides
  Technical aspects: TH4817.5
House construction
  contracting: TH4815.4
House drain
  Plumbing: TH6642+
House drainage
  Plumbing: TH6571+
House framing
  Building construction: TH2301+
House numbers
  Painting: TT365
House painting: TT320+

House sewer
  Plumbing: TH6641
House wiring
  Electric power: TK3285
Household accounts: TX326.A1+
Household apparatus: TX298+
Household appliances
  Waste disposal: TD799.7
Household batteries
  Waste disposal: TD799.8
Household bookkeeping:
    TX326.A1+
Household budgets: TX326.A1+
Household economics: TX151+
Household finance: TX326.A1+
Household moving: TX307
Household pests: TX325
Household plumbing
  Building construction: TH6101+
Household science
  Home economics: TX149
Household utensils: TX298+
Housekeeping
  Hotels, clubs, restaurants,
    etc.: TX928
  Taverns, barrooms, saloons:
    TX952+
Houses
  Building construction: TH4805+
Housing developments
  Building operation and
    housekeeping: TX960
Housing for the aged
  Fire prevention: TH9445.A4
Hovering
  Aeronautics: TL577
How to invent
  Patents: T212
Hub
  Aircraft propellers: TL707.H8
Huckaback
  Embroidery: TT778.H83
Huckleberries
  Cookery: TX813.H83
Hulls
  Seaplanes: TL684.2
Human engineering: TA166+
  Aeronautics: TL553.6
  Space environment: TL1500+
Human engineering in design
  Motor vehicles: TL250

Human engineering in industry:
T59.7+
Human environment equipment and
testing
Space environment: TL1500+
Human factors
Mechanical engineering:
TJ211.49
Nuclear engineering: TK9152.14
Human figure
Artistic photography: TR674+
Human powered aircraft: TL769
Humanitarian use of airplanes:
TL722.8
Humidity control
Air conditioning: TH7687.8
Humorous photography: TR679.5
Humus
Water pollutants: TD427.H85
Hunting fields
Alternating-current machinery:
TK2715
Hybrid cars: TL221.15
Hybrid propellant rockets:
TL783.45
Hybrid vehicles: TL221.15
Hydrate process
Saline water conversion:
TD480.3
Hydrates in natural gas: TN884
Hydraulic brakes: TJ880
Hydraulic elevators: TJ1375
Hydraulic engineering: TC1+
Environmental effects:
TD195.H93
Hydraulic equipment
Airplanes: TL697.H9
Hydraulic filling
Earthwork: TA750
Hydraulic fluids: TJ844
Fire prevention and
extinction: TH9446.H9
Hydraulic instruments: TC177
Hydraulic jack
Lifting machinery: TJ1435
Hydraulic laboratories: TC158
Hydraulic machinery: TJ836+
Hydraulic measurements: TC177
Hydraulic mining: TN278
Gold mining: TN421
Hydraulic models: TC164+
Hydraulic motors: TJ855+

Hydraulic power plants
Hydraulic engineering: TC147
Mechanical engineering: TJ845+
Hydraulic presses
Lifting machinery: TJ1460
Hydraulic rams: TJ905
Hydraulic structures: TC180
Earthquake effects: TC181
Electric power: TK4035.H9
Hydraulic surveying
Engineering: TA623
Hydraulics, Environmental:
TC163.5
Hydrazine
Chemical technology: TP248.H85
Hydrocarbons
Air pollutants: TD887.H93
Chemical technology: TP248.H9
Explosives: TP290.H9
Metallurgy: TN845+
Petroleum products: TP692.4.H9
Refrigerants: TP492.82.H93
Water pollutants: TD427.H93
Hydrocarbons, Halogenated
Water pollutants: TD427.H93
Hydrocarbons, Polycyclic
aromatic
Water pollutants: TD427.H93
Hydrochloric acid
Chemical technology: TP217.H8
Hydrochloric acid plants
Air pollution: TD888.H9
Hydrocyanic acid
Chemical technology: TP217.H9
Hydrodynamic lubrication
Mechanical engineering:
TJ1073.5
Hydrodynamics
Hydraulic engineering: TC171+
Turbomachinery: TJ267
Hydroelectric power
production: TK1081+
Hydrofluoric acid: TP217.H94
Hydrogen
Biotechnology: TP248.65.H9
Chemical technology: TP245.H9
Fire prevention and
extinction: TH9446.H96
Fuel: TP359.H8
Industrial electrochemistry:
TP261.H9
Lighter-than-air craft fuel:
TL666

Hydrogen automobiles: TL229.H9
Hydrogen-ion concentration
    Chemical engineering: TP156.H78
Hydrogen sulphide
    Air pollutants: TD885.5.H9
Hydrogenation
    Chemical engineering: TP156.H8
    Petroleum refining: TP690.45
Hydrolases
    Biotechnology: TP248.65.H93
Hydrolysis
    Chemical engineering: TP156.H82
Hydrometallurgy: TN688+
Hydronic systems
    Building construction: TH7467+
Hydrophones
    Electroacoustics: TK5987
Hydrostatic lubrication
    Mechanical engineering:
        TJ1073.5
Hydrostatics
    Hydraulic engineering: TC165+
Hydroxylation
    Chemical engineering: TP156.H85
Hygienic shoes
    Boot and shoemaking: TS1015
Hypersonic aerodynamics:
    TL571.5
Hypersonic planes: TL683.5
Hypochlorite treatment
    Water purification: TD463
Hypochlorites
    Environmental pollutants:
        TD196.H94

I

I-Beams, Steel-wood
    Structural engineering:
        TA660.S67
IBM Personal Computer:
    TK7889.I26
IBM Token-Ring Network:
    TK5105.8.I24
Ice bridges
    Highway engineering: TE247
Ice building construction:
    TH1431
Ice control
    Streets: TD868+
Ice cream scoops
    Cookery: TX657.I24

Ice creams and ices
    Cookery: TX795.A1+
Ice crossings
    Highway engineering: TE247
Ice cutting and storage: TP498
Ice loads
    Structural analysis: TA654.4
Ice mechanics: TA714.5
Ice prevention
    Aeronautical meteorology:
        TL557.I3
Ice roads
    Highway engineering: TE247
Icehouses (Commercial)
    Building construction: TH4481
Icemaking
    Chemical technology: TP490+
Identification
    Aircraft communication
        equipment: TL694.I4
Identification marks
    Aircraft: TL603
Identification symbols
    Aircraft: TL603
IFF
    Aircraft communication
        equipment: TL694.I4
Ignition
    Internal combustion engines:
        TJ787
Ignition devices
    Aircraft engines: TL702.I5
    Building gas supply: TH6885+
    Gasoline automobiles: TL213
    Motor vehicles: TL272
Illiac computer: TK7889.I5
ILLINET: TK5105.8.I44
Illuminating industries
    (Nonelectric): TP700+
Illumination
    Building construction: TH7700+
Illustration, Technical: T11.8
Image converters and
    intensifiers
    Electronics: TK8316
Image processing
    Optical data processing: TA1637
Image science
    Photography: TR222
Image transmission
    Electrical engineering:
        TK5105.2

Imaginary voyages
  Astronautics: TL788.7
Imaging systems
  Electronics: TK8315+
Imhof tanks
  Sewage purification: TD750
Imitation leathers
  Manufactures: TS1045+
Immobilized cell processes
  Biotechnology: TP248.25.I55
Immobilized enzymes
  Biotechnology: TP248.65.I45
Immobilized proteins
  Biotechnology: TP248.65.I47
Immunoassay
  Food analysis: TX549
Immunoglobulins
  Biotechnology: TP248.65.I49
Impact loading
  Structural analysis: TA654.2
Impact strength
  Time-dependent properties and
    tests: TA418.34
Impedance meters and
  measurements
  Electric meters: TK315
Impellers
  Turbines: TJ267.5.I6
Impregnated wood
  Fire-resistive building
    construction: TH1073
Improved passenger train (IPT)
  High speed ground
    transportation: TF1540
Impurities
  Food: TX562.2+
In-plant transportation
  Materials handling: TS180.6+
In situ processing (Mining):
    TN278.3
In situ remediation
  Environmental pollution:
    TD192.8
Incandescent electric
  lighting: TK4341+
Incandescent gas lighting
  Building construction: TH7953+
Incandescent lamps: TK4351+
  Tests of efficiency: TK4367

Incineration
  Environmental effects:
    TD195.I52
  Hazardous substances and their
    disposal: TD1062
  Industrial and factory wastes:
    TD897.843
  Municipal refuse: TD796+
  Radioactive waste disposal:
    TD898.175
  Sewage disposal: TD770+
Incinerators
  Municipal refuse: TD796+
  Waste disposal: TD803
Indene resins
  Plastics: TP1180.I5
Independent furnaces
  Hydronic systems: TH7475
Indexing tables
  Machine tools: TJ1185.5
Indian Ocean submarine
  telegraph: TK5615
Indicators
  Radar: TK6590.I5
  Steam engines: TJ478
Indicators, Technology: T174.2
Indigenous peoples
  Photographic portraits:
    TR681.I58
Indigo
  Dyes: TP923+
Indirect radiators
  Hydronic systems: TH7492+
Indium
  Chemical technology: TP245.I5
  Engineering materials:
    TA480.I53
  Metallurgy: TN799.I5
  Mining and metallurgy: TN490.I6
Indium phosphide
  Electronics: TK7871.15.I53
Indoor air pollution: TD883.17
Indoor air quality: TD883.17
Indoor wiring: TK3271+
Induction
  Alternating-current motors:
    TK2785
Induction hardening
  Steel metallurgy: TN752.I5
Induction logging: TN269.55
Induction telegraph systems:
    TK5550

Inductors
  Electronics: TK7872.I63
Induline
  Textile dyes: TP918.I5
Industrial accident
  prevention: T55+
Industrial accidents and
  biorhythms
  Industrial safety: T55.3.B56
Industrial archaeology
  Technology: T37
Industrial arts training
  Handicrafts: TT161+
Industrial buildings
  Heating and ventilation:
    TH7392.I53
  Plant engineering: TS186
  Sanitary engineering:
    TH6057.I53
Industrial cinematography
  Photography: TR894
Industrial design
  Product engineering: TS171+
Industrial design coordination
  Patents: T342
Industrial directories: T11.95+
Industrial districts
  Environmental effects:
    TD195.I54
Industrial ecology
  Inventory control: TS161
Industrial education
  Secondary education: T61+
Industrial electrochemistry:
    TP250+
  Environmental effects:
    TD195.E43
Industrial electronics: TK7881
Industrial engineering: T55.4+
Industrial engineers: T56.3
Industrial fabrics
  Manufactures: TS1770.I53
Industrial feeding
  Food service: TX946.5.A1+
Industrial furnaces
  Heating engineering: TH7140+
Industrial heating
  Building construction: TH7121+
Industrial instrumentation:
    TA165

Industrial landscape
  architecture
  Plant grounds: TS190.5
Industrial painting
  Handicrafts: TT300+
Industrial photochemistry:
    TP249.5
Industrial photography: TR706
Industrial plants
  Building construction: TH4511+
Industrial power trucks: TL296
Industrial radiation
  chemistry: TP249
Industrial radiochemistry:
    TP249
Industrial railways: TF677
Industrial reproduction
  Photography: TR900+
Industrial research: T175+
Industrial robots: TS191.8
Industrial safety: T55+
Industrial sanitation: TD895+
Industrial vehicles and
  trucks: TL223
Industrial wastes: TD896+
Industrial water supply: TD201+
Industrial weaving
  Manufactures: TS1490+
Industrial woodworking
  Manufactures: TS840+
Industrialized building
  Building construction: TH1000
Industries
  Environmental effects: TD194+
Industry and meteorology: TA198
Inelastic properties and
  tests: TA418.14+
Inertial navigation
  Air navigation: TL588.5
Inertial navigation systems
  Space vehicles: TL3252
Inertial separation
  Dust removal: TH7695.I52
Infants
  Photographic portraits:
    TR681.I6
Inflammable liquids
  Chemical technology: TP361
  Fire prevention and
    extinction: TH9446.I5

Inflammable materials
  Fire prevention and
    extinction: TH9446.I47 +
Inflation machinery
  Lighter-than-air craft: TL666
Influence lines
  Structural engineering: TA640.8
Influence of altitude
  Aircraft engines: TL701.2
Information centers
  Mechanical engineering: TJ160.5
  Technology: T10.6
Information display systems
  Electrical engineering:
    TK5103.5
  Electronics: TK7882.I6
Information services
  Aeronautics: TL564
  Building construction: TH216
  Environmental protection:
    TD169.5
  Metallurgy: TN675.4
  Textile industries: TS1474
  Water supply: TD211
Information systems
  Industrial technology: T58.5 +
Information technology
  Industrial engineering: T58.5 +
Infrared examinations
  Testing of materials: TA417.5
Infrared heating
  Electric heating: TK4635
Infrared lasers
  Applied optics: TA1696
Infrared photography: TR755
Infrared spectroscopy
  Food analysis: TX547.2.I53
Infrared technology
  Applied optics: TA1570
Ingenious mechanisms
  Mechanical engineering:
    TJ210.2 +
Inhomogeneous materials
  Engineering materials:
    TA418.9.I53
Injectors
  Steam boilers: TJ387
Ink impression
  Telegraph: TK5546
Ink manufacture
  Chemical technology: TP946 +

Inking receiving systems and
  instruments
  Telegraph: TK5546
Inks for recording
  instruments: TP949.95
Inland navigation
  Hydraulic engineering: TC601 +
Inlets for air
  Jet engines: TL709.5.I5
Innovations, Technological:
  T173.8
Inorganic chemicals
  Chemical technology: TP213 +
Inorganic compounds
  Soil pollutants: TD879.I55
  Water pollutants: TD427.I55
Inorganic fibers
  Testile fibers: TS1549.A1 +
Input-output equipment
  Computer engineering: TK7887.5 +
INSAT (Artificial satellite):
  TK5104.2.I25
Insect cell biotechnology:
  TP248.27.I56
Insect pests in wood: TA423.6 +
Insect-resistant packaging:
  TS198.I58
Insect waxes
  Chemical technology: TP677 +
Insecticides
  Chemical technology: TP248.I57
  Fire prevention and
    extinction: TH9446.I55
Insects
  Cookery: TX746
  Nature photography: TR729.I6
  Nutrition: TX388.I5
Inserts
  Reinforced concrete
    construction: TA683.45
Insignia
  Aeronautics: TL538
Insignia industry: TS2301.I6
Inspection
  Aeronautical navigation
    equipment: TL696.I5
  Aircraft communication
    equipment: TL694.I5
  Aircraft engines: TL701.5
  Airplanes: TL671.7
  Fire prevention and
    extinction: TH9176
  Heating of buildings: TH7339

Inspection
  Locomotives: TJ685+
  Lumber: TS825
  Nuclear engineering: TK9152.15,
    TK9152.16
  Plumbing: TH6239
  Production management: TS156.2+
  Railway equipment: TF361
  Railway operation: TF537
  Sewers: TD719
  Steam boilers: TJ298
Inspection of workmanship
  Management of engineering
    works: TA191
Inspectors' manuals
  Telegraph wiring: TK5445
  Telephone wiring: TK6345
Installation
  Aircraft engines: TL701.4
  Electric lighting: TK4255
  Industrial equipment: TS191.3
Instant photography: TR269
Instantaneous photography:
  TR592
Institutional cookery: TX820
Instrument board
  Airplanes: TL681.I6
Instrument flying
  Airplanes: TL711.B6
Instrument landing systems
  Aeronautical navigation
    equipment: TL696.L33
Instrument manufacture: TS500+
Instruments
  Aeronautical engineering:
    TL589+
  Aeronautical research: TL567.I6
  Nuclear engineering: TK9178+
  Photogrammetry: TR696
  Surveying: TA562+
  Telegraph: TK5571+
  Telegraphing: TK5501+
Instruments for transmitting
  sound
  Telephone: TK6401+
Insulated wires
  Electric power: TK3331+
  Testing: TK3335
Insulating material
  Electric power: TK3401+
  Testing: TK3431

Insulating materials
  Building construction: TH1715+
Insulation
  Building construction: TH1715+
  Electric power: TK3401+
  Petroleum pipelines: TN879.57
Insulators
  Space vehicles: TL1102.I57
Intaglio process
  Photography: TR980
Intakes for air
  Jet engines: TL709.5.I5
Integral equations
  Engineering mathematics:
    TA347.I5
Integrated circuits
  Amateurs' manuals: TK9966
  Electronics: TK7874+
Integrated optics: TA1660
Integrated services digital
  networks
  Telecommunication: TK5103.75
Integrated solid waste
  management: TD794.2
  Local: TD788+
Intelligent control systems
  Mechanical engineering: TJ217.5
Intelligent Vehicle Highway
  Systems
  Highway engineering: TE228.3
Intensification
  Photographic negatives: TR299
  Treatment of photographic
    positives: TR335
Intensity meters and
  measurements
  Electrical engineering: TK331
Interactive television:
  TK6679.3
Interactive video
  Electronics: TK6687
Intercepting other aircraft:
  TL711.I47
Intercepting sewers: TD711
Interchanges
  Highway engineering: TE176+
Intercommunication systems
  Electronics: TK7881.5
Interconnection of power
  systems
  Electrical engineering: TK447+

Interface circuits
  Electronic circuits: TK7868.I58
Interference
  Aerodynamics: TL574.I5
  Aircraft communication
    equipment: TL694.I6
  Aircraft propellers: TL706.I6
  Photographic processing: TR525
Interferometry, Holographic:
  TA1555
Interior decoration
  Passenger planes: TL685.5.I6
Interior painting: TT323
Interior walls
  Building design and
    construction: TH2239
Interior wiring: TK3271+
Interiors
  Photographic lighting: TR620
Interlocking systems
  Railway operation: TF635
Intermittent-motion mechanisms
  Mechanical engineering: TJ181.6
Internal combustion engines:
  TJ782+
Internal gears
  Mechanical movements: TJ202
International Business Machines
  Corporation: TK4101.I5
International cooperation
  Astronautics: TL788.4
  Industrial engineering
    education: T65.3
  Radioactive waste disposal:
    TD898.14.I57
  Technology: T49.5
Internet
  Chemical engineering: TP186.8
  Engineering: TA158.7
  Handicrafts: TT11
  Motor vehicles: TL11
  Photography: TR11
Internet (Computer network):
  TK5105.875.I57
  Aspects or services:
    TK5105.8812+
Internet Relay Chat: TK5105.886
Internet telephony: TK5105.8865
Intersections
  Highway engineering: TE176+
Interurban cars
  Electric railways: TF920+

Interurban railways: TF701+
Intra-airport transportation:
  TL725.3.I6
Intranets (Computer networks)
  Electronics: TK5105.875.I6
Inventions
  History: T14.7+
  Patents: T212
Inventors
  Biography: T39+
  Patents: T212
Inventors' manuals: T339
Inventory control
  Hotels, clubs, restaurants,
    etc.: TX911.3.I5
  Production management: TS160+
Inverters
  Dynamoelectric machinery:
    TK2692
  Electronics: TK7872.I65
Iodine
  Chemical technology: TP245.I6
Ion exchange
  Chemical engineering: TP156.I6
  Sewage disposal: TD757.5
Ion exchange desalting
  Saline water conversion:
    TD480.7
Ion exchange process
  Hydrometallurgy: TN688.3.I65
Ion exchange resin
  Gums and resins: TP979.5.I6
Ion implantation
  Metal finishing: TS695.25
Ion plating
  Metal finishing: TS695.2
Ion rocket propulsion: TL783.63
Ion rockets: TL783.63
IPSec
  Computer network protocols:
    TK5105.567
IPT
  High speed ground
    transportation: TF1540
Iridium
  Chemical technology: TP245.I7
Irish crochet lace: TT805.I74
Iron
  Assaying: TN580.I8
  Bridge engineering: TG370
  Chemical technology: TP245.I8
  Electroplating: TS692.I7

Iron
 Food constituent: TX553.I75
 Metal manufactures: TS300+
 Ore dressing and milling:
  TN538.I7
 Prospecting: TN271.I7
 Stairbuilding: TH5667+
 Structural engineering: TA684+
Iron alloys
 Engineering materials: TA478+
 Metallurgy: TN756+
Iron and steel
 Building construction: TH1610+
 Engineering materials: TA464+
 Founding: TS228.99+
 Metal manufactures: TS440+
 Metallography: TN693.I7
 Metallurgy: TN701.482+
 Powder metallurgy: TN697.I7
 Railway construction: TF255
 Trussed bridges: TG380
Iron furniture
 Manufactures: TS408
Iron industry
 Dust removal: TH7697.I76
Iron mines and mining
 Water pollution: TD428.I74
Iron-on transfer work
 Textile decoration: TT852.7
Iron ore deposits and mining:
  TN400+
Iron ores
 Assaying: TN580.I8
Iron oxide
 Chemical technology: TP936+
Iron pipe
 Sewers: TD686
Iron roofing
 Building construction: TH2457
Iron salts
 Photographic processes: TR405+
Iron work
 Engineering: TA890+
Ironing
 Laundry work: TT995
Ironworking
 Handicrafts: TT215+
Ironworks
 Electric lighting: TK4399.I7
 Environmental effects:
  TD195.I76

Irradiation
 Food preservation: TP371.8
 Sewage treatment: TD769.8
 Water purification: TD476
Irrigation canals: TC930
Irrigation engineering: TC801+
Irrigation flumes and
 conduits: TC933
Irrigation projects
 Management: TC812
Irrigation pumps: TC929
Isano oil
 Chemical technology: TP684.I8
Isinglass industry: TS2301.I8
Isochromatic photography: TR453
Isocyanates
 Chemical technology: TP248.I8
Isometric projection
 Mechanical drawing: T363
Isopren
 Chemical technology: TP248.I86
Isotope separation
 Chemical engineering: TP156.I7
Isotopic power generators
 Electrical engineering: TK2965
Ivory, Articles of
 Manufactures: TS1050

J

Jackets
 Women's tailoring: TT535
Jackets for bottles
 Decorative crafts: TT879.J3
Jacquard looms
 Textile industries: TS1500
Jacquard weaving
 Textile industries: TS1500
Jade
 Jewelry work: TS755.J34
 Mineral industries: TN997.J3
Jam
 Cookery: TX814.5.J35
 Food processing and
  manufacture: TP441.J3
 Preservation and storage:
  TX612.J3
Janitor service
 Apartment houses: TX958
 Household administration: TX339

Janitors
  Photographic portraits:
  TR681.J35
Japanese paper: TS1130
Japanning materials
  Chemical technology: TP942
Jelly
  Food processing and
    manufacture: TP441.J3
  Preservation and storage:
    TX612.J4
Jerusalem artichoke
  Sugars and syrups: TP414
Jet
  Steam engines: TJ559
Jet belts: TL717.5
Jet engines
  Aeronautics: TL709+
Jet flying: TL711.J38
Jet propulsion
  Aeronautics: TL709+
Jets
  Hydrodynamics: TC173
Jetties
  River protective works: TC535
Jettisoning of fuel
  Airplanes: TL711.J4
Jewel bearings
  Mechanical engineering:
    TJ1073.J4
Jewelers' catalogs: TS759
Jewelers' supplies: TS760
Jewelry
  Hairwork: TT976
  Manufactures: TS720+
Jewelry craft
  Metalworking: TT212
Jigs
  Ore dressing and milling:
    TN520+
Jigs and fixtures
  Machine tools: TJ1187
Job descriptions
  Hotels, clubs, restaurants,
    etc.: TX911.3.J65
Job design
  Industrial engineering: T60.8
Joinery
  Building construction: TH5601+
  Finish carpentry: TH5662+

Joining
  Metals: TS226+
  Plastics: TP1165
Joint-wiping
  Building construction: TH6295
Joints
  Building construction: TH2060
  Cement and concrete
    construction: TA682.3
  Concrete roads: TE278.2
  Pipefitting: TH6293+
  Reinforced concrete
    construction: TA683.3
  Structural engineering:
    TA660.J64
  Wooden construction:
    TA666.5.J64
Joints, Expansion
  Structural engineering:
    TA660.E9
Joints, Welded (Metal)
  Engineering materials: TA492.W4
Jojoba oil
  Chemical technology: TP684.J64
Journal bearings
  Machinery: TJ1063
Juicer recipes
  Cookery: TX840.J84
Jumping balloons: TL632
Jumping systems
  Fire prevention and
    extinction: TH9418
Junction transistors: TK7871.92
Junk food
  Nutrition: TX370
Junkyards
  Municipal refuse: TD795.4
Jupiter (Planet)
  Flight to: TL799.J8
Just-in-time systems
  Production control: TS157.4
Jute industry: TS1700+

K

Kabobs
  Cookery: TX834
Kallitype
  Photographic processes: TR400
Kamala
  Textile dyes: TP925.K35

Kaoliang
  Distilled liquors: TP607.K3
Kaolin
  Prospecting: TN271.K2
Kapok
  Textile fiber: TS1747.K3
Karts: TL236.5
Keel
  Airships: TL662.K4
Kefir
  Beverages: TP565
Kelp
  Mining engineering: TN919
Kenaf
  Textile fiber: TS1544.A5
  Woodpulp industry: TS1176.4.K44
Kenotrons: TK7871.79.K4
Kentucky rifle: TS536.6.K4
Kerchiefs
  Clothing manufacture: TT667.5
Kerosene
  Petroleum products: TP692.4.K4
Kerosene heaters
  Convective heating: TH7450.5
Ketchup
  Cookery: TX819.K48
Ketones
  Chemical technology: TP248.A53
Kettles
  Cookery: TX657.K4
Keys
  Locksmithing: TS530
  Telegraph: TK5575
Keys and keyways
  Fastenings: TJ1329
Khaki
  Dyeing: TP907
Kilns
  Clay industries: TP841+
  Pottery craft: TT924
Kilns, Lumber: TS837
Kimberlite
  Prospecting: TN271.K55
Kimch'i
  Cookery: TX806
Kinematics of machinery
  Mechanical engineering: TJ175
Kinetoscope
  Cinematography: TR885
Kirlian photography: TR760
Kirsch
  Distilled liquors: TP607.K57

Kit cars: TL240.2
Kitchen
  Cookery: TX653+
Kitchen almanacs
  Cookery: TX727+
Kitchen arrangement
  Cookery: TX655
Kitchen boiler explosions
  Plumbing: TH6565+
Kitchen boilers
  Plumbing: TH6563
Kitchen cabinets
  Woodworking: TT197.5.K57
Kitchen control
  Hotels, clubs, restaurants,
    etc.: TX921
Kitchen furniture
  Woodworking: TT197.5.K57
Kitchen plumbing
  Building construction: TH6507+
Kitchen supports
  Plumbing: TH6563
Kitchen wastes
  House drainage: TH6661
Kitchens
  House remodeling: TH4816.3.K58
  Ventilation: TH7684.K5
Kite balloons: TL635
Kites
  Aeronautics: TL759+
Kiwifruit
  Cookery: TX813.K55
Klystrons: TK7871.74
Knit goods
  Clothing manufacture: TT679+
Knit goods industry
  Electric power: TK4035.K58
Knitted lace: TT805.K54
Knitting
  Decorative needlework: TT819+
Knitting machinery
  Clothing manufacture: TT685
Knitting machines
  Electric driving: TK4059.K55
Knives
  Cookery: TX657.K54
Koji
  Food additives: TP456.K64
Konnyaku
  Food processing and
    manufacture: TP444.K65

Kreiselpumpen
 Hydraulic machinery: TJ919
Kriging
 Mining engineering: TN272.7
Krypton
 Chemical technology: TP245.K6
Kudzu
 Cookery: TX814.5.K83
Kumiss
 Beverages: TP565
Kvass
 Fermented beverage: TP588.K86
Kwanzaa decorations
 Decorative crafts: TT900.K92

L

L2TP (Computer network
 protocols): TK5105.572
Labeling
 Bottling: TP659.A1+
 Food processing and
  manufacture: TP374.5
 Packaging: TS196.6+
Labor productivity
 Hotels, clubs, restaurants,
  etc.: TX911.3.L27
 Industrial engineering: T60.35
Labor turnover
 Hotels, clubs, restaurants,
  etc.: TX911.3.L3
Laboratories
 Aeronautics: TL566+
 Air conditioning: TH7688.L3
 Building construction: TH4652
 Fire insurance engineering:
  TH9237
 Photography: TR550+
 Waste control: TD899.L32
Laboratories, Assay: TN570+
Laboratories, Engineering:
 TA416+
Laboratories, Metallurgical:
 TN570+
Laboratories, Testing
 Engineering: TA416+
Laboratory machines
 Testing of materials: TA412
Laboratory manuals
 Astronautics: TL794.3
 Chemical technology: TP161

Lace (Machine made)
 Textile industries: TS1782
Lace craft: TT810
Lacemaking
 Decorative needlework: TT800+
Lacquering
 Metal finishing: TS698
 Metal finishing arts: TT382.4
 Painting: TT378
Lacquers: TP939
Lactams
 Chemical technology: TP248.L27
Lactic acid
 Chemical technology: TP248.L3
Lactose
 Sugars and syrups: TP414
Ladder trucks
 Fire prevention and
  extinction: TH9383
Ladle metallurgy
 Steel: TN746
Lagoons
 Sewage treatment: TD746.5
Lake engineering: TC401+
Lakes
 Reclamation: TC975
 Sewage effluent discharge
  into: TD763+
 Water supply source: TD392
Lamb
 Cookery: TX749.5.L35
 Food values: TX556.L3
Laminar flow
 Aerodynamics: TL574.L3
Laminated materials
 Aeronautics: TL699.L23
 Engineering materials:
  TA418.9.L3
Laminated metals
 Electrical engineering:
  TK454.4.L3
Laminated plastics: TP1183.L3
Laminated wood
 Aeronautics: TL699.W7
 Manufactures: TS869
Lampposts
 Cement manufacture: TP885.L3
 Lighting fixtures: TH7970.L35
Lamps
 Decorative crafts: TT897.2
 Lighthouses: TC377
 Nonelectric illuminating
  industries: TP746
 Woodworking: TT197.5.L34

Lampshades
  Decorative crafts: TT897
  Wood products: TS913
LAN Server (Computer network
  systems): TK5105.8.L34
Lancashire steam boiler
  Mechanical engineering: TJ310
Land disposal
  Hazardous substances: TD1064
Land use
  Soil pollution: TD880.L35
  Water pollution: TD428.L35
Landfill gases
  Air pollutants: TD885.5.L35
Landfills, Sanitary
  Municipal refuse: TD795.7
  Sewage disposal: TD771
Landing
  Airplanes: TL711.L3
Landing aids
  Aeronautical navigation
    equipment: TL696.L3
  Airports: TL725.3.L2
Landing fees
  Airports: TL725.3.L3
Landing fields: TL725+
Landing flares
  Aeronautics: TL697.L3
Landing gear
  Airplanes: TL682+
Landing gear for use on snow
  Airplanes: TL683.S6
Landing lights
  Aircraft: TL691.L3
Landscape construction by
  builders: TH380
Landscape photography: TR660+
Landscaping: TE177+
Language
  Aeronautics: TL564.5
  Cookery: TX644
Language, Technical: T11+
Lantern slides
  Photography: TR505
Lanthanum
  Chemical technology: TP245.L2
Lapping
  Cotton manufactures: TS1578
Lapping tools
  Machine shops: TJ1280+
Larch
  Woodpulp industry: TS1176.4.L3

Lard
  Manufactures: TS1980+
Laser ablation
  Applied optics: TA1715
Laser communications systems
  Engineering: TK5103.6
Laser welding: TS228.95
Lasers
  Aeronautics: TL697.L34
  Applied optics: TA1671+
Lasers in engineering: TA367.5
Laterite
  Engineering materials: TA455.L3
  Mining engineering: TN948.L3
Lathes
  Machine shops: TJ1218+
Lathework
  Handicrafts: TT201+
Latitude
  Air navigation: TL588+
Latrines
  Sewage disposal: TD775
Lauhala weaving
  Decorative crafts: TT877.5
Launch complexes
  Location: TL4024
Launch facilities
  Astronautics: TL4020+
Launch vehicles
  Rockets: TL785.8.L3
Launching
  Rockets: TL784.L3
Launching bases
  Astronautics: TL4020+
  Location: TL4024
Launching complexes
  Astronautics: TL4020+
Launching machinery
  Airports: TL732
Laundries
  Plumbing: TH6502+
  Waste control: TD899.L37
Laundries, Public
  Plumbing: TH6518.L3
  Sanitary engineering: TH6057.L3
Laundry wastes
  House drainage: TH6661
Laundry work: TT980+
Lautal
  Aeronautics: TL699.L3
Lavatories
  Plumbing: TH6485+

Lavender
Cookery: TX819.L38
Layettes
Children's clothing: TT637
Laying out cities
Municipal engineering: TD160+
Laying out gear teeth
Mechanical movements: TJ186
Laying pipes
Building construction: TH6293+
Layout
Sewerage systems: TD659
Leaching equipment
Chemical technology: TP159.L4
Lead
Air pollutants: TD887.L4
Chemical technology: TP245.L4
Effect on food: TX572.L4
Engineering materials: TA480.L4
Environmental pollutants:
TD196.L4
Metallography: TN693.L4
Metallurgy: TN785
Ore deposits and mining: TN450+
Prospecting: TN271.L4
Soil pollutants: TD879.L43
Lead-acid batteries
Electricity production:
TK2945.L42
Lead and silver
Metallurgy: TN770
Lead burning
Plumbing: TH6691
Lead roofing
Building construction: TH2458
Leaded glass
Decorative furnishings: TH8271+
Leading edges
Aerodynamics: TL574.L4
Leads
Generators: TK2487
Leadwork
Handicrafts: TT265
Leaf metals
Metal manufactures: TS260
Leakage, Testing for
House drainage: TH6617
Leaks
Petroleum pipelines: TN879.55
Leather garments
Women's tailoring: TT524

Leather industry
Electric power: TK4035.L4
Environmental effects: TD195.L4
Manufactures: TS940+
Leatherwork
Handicrafts: TT290
Machinery: TS1043
Leavening agents
Food processing and
manufacture: TP431+
Lecithin
Food constituents: TP453.L43
Leeks
Cookery: TX803.L4
Left-turn lanes
Highway engineering: TE176.3
Legends
Aeronautical engineering: TL516
Astronautics: TL516
Legumes
Food values: TX558.L4
Leisure class
Photographic portraits:
TR681.L44
Lemonade: TP657.L46
Lemongrass oils
Organic chemical industries:
TP959.L4
Lemons
Cookery: TX813.L4
Food values: TX558.L5
Lenses
Lighthouses: TC379
Optical instruments: TS517.3+
Photography: TR270+
Lenten cookery: TX837+
Letter carriers
Photographic portraits:
TR681.L47
Lettering
Mechanical drawing: T371
Levees
Coast protective works: TC337
River protective works: TC533
Level indicators
Control engineering: TJ223.L5
Leveling
Surveying: TA606+
Levels
Surveying instruments: TA565
Leveraction rifle: TS536.6.L48

Libraries
  Fire prevention and
    extinction: TH9445.L5
Liernur sewerage system: TD666
Life support systems
  Space environment: TL1500+
Lifesaving at fires
  Fire extinction: TH9402+
Lifesaving at sea
  Use of airplanes: TL722.8
Lift
  Aerodynamics: TL574.L5
Lifting
  Industrial safety: T55.3.L5
Lifting bodies
  Aeronautics: TL713.7
Lifting jacks
  Mechanical engineering: TJ1430+
Lifting machinery
  Mechanical engineering: TJ1425+
Lifting magnets
  Hoisting machinery: TJ1366
Lifts and inclines
  Canals: TC763
Light
  Electrical engineering: TK1191+
Light airplanes: TL685.1
Light distribution: TK4175
Light-emitting diodes
  Semiconductors: TK7871.89.L53
Light filters
  Photography: TR590.5
Light metals
  Manufactures: TS551+
  Metallurgy: TN773+
Light railways: TF670+
Light rights
  Natural lighting: TH7792
Light water reactors
  Nuclear engineering: TK9203.L45
Lighter-than-air craft: TL605+
Lighter-than-air craft industry
  Technical aspects: TL667+
Lighters for smokers
  Manufactures: TS2280
Lighthouses
  Hydraulic engineering: TC375+
Lighting
  Airports: TL725.3.L5
  Building construction: TH7700+
  Cinematography: TR891
  Mines: TN306.5+

Lighting
  Photography: TR590+
  Railroad cars: TF447+
  Railway equipment: TF445+
  Railway tunnels: TF236
  Tunneling: TA814
Lighting devices
  Motor vehicles: TL272
  Woodworking: TT197.5.L34
Lighting fixtures
  Artificial lighting: TH7960+
Lighting fixtures catalogs:
  TK4198
Lighting for video recording
  Cinematography: TR891
Lighting plants: TK4219+
Lightning arresters
  Electric power: TK3248
Lightning protection
  Building construction: TH9057+
  Electric power distribution
    system: TK3085
Lightning protection systems:
  TH9092
Lights
  Lighthouses: TC377
Lightweight alloys
  Engineering and construction:
    TA484
Lightweight concrete
  Cement manufacture: TP884.L5
Lightweight construction
  Building construction: TH1100
  Structural engineering: TA663
Lignin
  Wood composition: TS933.L5
Lignite
  Fuel: TP329
  Mining: TN831+
Lignite industry
  Environmental effects:
    TD195.L53
Lignocellulose
  Biotechnology: TP248.65.L54
Lime
  Chemical technology: TP886
  Environmental pollutants:
    TD196.L55
  Masonry materials: TA434+

Lime
  Mining engineering: TN948.L46
  Soil stabilization: TE210.5.L5
Lime treatment
  Pollution control methods:
    TD192.4
Limekilns
  Chemical technology: TP886
Limes
  Cookery: TX813.L55
Limestone: TN967
  Masonry materials: TA428.L5
Limestone industry
  Environmental effects:
    TD195.L55
Limit analysis
  Structural analysis: TA652
Limit design
  Structural engineering: TA658.6
Limousines: TL232.7
Lincrusta
  Wall decoration: TH8471
Line
  Electric power: TK3201+
  Technique of: TK3226
  Telegraph: TK5451+
  Telephone: TK6201+
Line balancing
  Manufacturing engineering:
    TS178.5
Line insulators
  Electric power: TK3246
Line material
  Telegraph: TK5454
Line of balance technique
  Production control: TS158.4
Linear algebras
  Engineering mathematics:
    TA347.L5
Linear control systems
  Mechanical engineering: TJ220
Linear programming
  Industrial engineering: T57.74+
Linen
  Dyeing: TP903
  Flax industries: TS1710+
  Textile fiber: TS1543
Lingerie
  Clothing manufacture: TT669+
Lining
  Women's tailoring: TT557

Link belting
  Mechanical engineering: TJ1119
Link couplings
  Mechanical engineering: TJ183
Link motion
  Mechanical engineering: TJ182+
Links
  Mechanical engineering: TJ182+
Linoleum
  Floor covering: TS1779.L5
Linseed oil
  Chemical technology: TP682
Lintels
  Window and door openings:
    TH2261+
Lipids
  Biotechnology: TP248.65.L57
  Food constituent: TX553.L5
  Food constituents: TP453.L56
Lippmann's process
  Photographic processing: TR525
Liquefied gas
  Chemical technology: TP243
Liquefied natural gas
  Fire prevention and
    extinction: TH9446.L57
Liquefied petroleum gas
  Fuel: TP359.L5
Liqueurs
  Distilling: TP611
Liquid air
  Explosives: TP290.L5
Liquid chromatography
  Food analysis: TX548.2.L55
Liquid crystal devices
  Optical instruments: TS518
Liquid crystal displays
  Electronics: TK7872.L56
Liquid crystals
  Engineering materials:
    TA418.9.L54
Liquid fuel
  Chemical technology: TP343+
Liquid gas
  Gas industry: TP761.L5
Liquid metal-cooled reactors
  Nuclear engineering: TK9203.L5
Liquid metals
  Engineering materials: TA463
Liquid nitrogen automobiles:
  TL229.L56

Liquid propellant rockets:
TL783.4
Liquids
Insulating material: TK3441.L5
Liquor-makers' receipts: TP612
Liquors
Cookery: TX726
Literature distribution by
airplane: TL722.5
Lithium: TN490.L5
Chemical technology: TP245.L5
Engineering and construction:
TA480.L5
Hazardous substances and their
disposal: TD1066.L57
Metallurgy: TN799.L57
Lithium batteries
Electricity production:
TK2945.L58
Litter and litter removal:
TD813+
Live loads
Structural analysis: TA654.3
Live steam systems
Low-pressure steam heating:
TH7576+
LiveConnect (Netscape)
Web authoring software:
TK5105.8885.N5
Livery
Men's clothing: TT626
Livestock
Nature photography: TR729.L5
Living room furniture
Woodworking: TT197.5.L5
Loaders (Automotive): TL296.5
Loading
Airplanes: TL711.L6
Loading and unloading
Materials handling: TS180.5
Loading conditions, Dynamic
Structural analysis: TA654+
Loading conditions, Static
Structural analysis: TA648+
Loads
Bridge engineering: TG260+
Loads, Blast
Structural engineering: TA654.7
Loads, Dynamic
Structural design: TA658.4+
Loads, Ice
Structural analysis: TA654.4

Loads, Live
Structural analysis: TA654.3
Loads, Moving
Structural analysis: TA654.3
Loads, Snow
Structural analysis: TA654.4
Loads, Water wave
Structural analysis: TA654.55
Loads, Wind
Structural analysis: TA654.5
Lobsters
Cookery: TX754.L63
Local area networks (Computer
networks)
Computer engineering: TK5105.7+
Local railways: TF670+
Location
Airports: TL725.3.L6
Hotels, clubs, restaurants,
etc.: TX911.3.L62
Railroad engineering: TF190
Railroad surveying: TF215+
Railway construction: TF200
Location engineering: TE206+
Lock-in amplifiers:
TK7871.58.L57
Lock-joint brick
Brickmaking: TP832.L7
Lock picking: TS525
Locker hooking
Handicrafts: TT833
Lockheed Aircraft Corporation:
TL686.L6
Locks
Building construction: TH2279
Gunsmithing: TS535.2.L6
Locksmithing: TS529
Security in buildings: TH9735
Locksmithing
Manufactures: TS519+
Locomotive tenders: TJ671
Locomotive works and shops:
TJ680+
Locomotives
Industrial use: TJ695
Maintenance: TJ675
Mechanical engineering: TJ603+
Loess
Engineering materials: TA455.L6
Lofts
Building design and
construction: TH3000.L36

Log cabins
  Construction: TH4840
Logan blackberry
  Food values: TX558.L6
Logarithmic amplifiers:
  TK7871.58.L6
Logbooks
  Air navigation: TL587
  Space navigation: TL1070
Logging railways: TF678
Logic circuits
  Computer engineering: TK7888.4
  Electronic circuits: TK7868.L6
Logic devices
  Electronics: TK7872.L64
Long distance flying
  Airplanes: TL711.L7
Longerons
  Airplanes: TL681.L6
Longitude
  Air navigation: TL588+
Longwall mining: TN286
Looms
  Weaving (Industrial): TS1493
Loran
  Aeronautical navigation
    equipment: TL696.L65
Losses in transmission
  Electric railways: TF912
Lost arts
  Technology: T33
Lotus Domino
  Web authoring software:
    TK5105.8885.L67
Loudspeaker cabinets
  Woodworking: TT197.5.L6
Loudspeakers
  Electroacoustics: TK5983
Louisiana style cookery:
  TX715.2.L68
Louvers
  Ventilation of buildings:
    TH7683.L7
Low-fat foods: TP451.L67
Low income groups
  Nutrition: TX361.P66
Low pollution combustion
  Gasoline automobiles: TL214.P6
Low-pressure hot water heating
  (with dome boilers): TH7518+
Low-pressure steam heating
  Hydronic systems: TH7570+

Low temperature
  Food preservation: TP372+
Low temperature engineering:
  TP480+
Low temperature sanitary
  engineering: TD940+
Low tension A.C.
  Dynamoelectric machinery:
    TK2826
Low tension A.C. systems
  Electrical engineering: TK3142
Low voltage generators
  Dynamoelectric machinery:
    TK2665
Low voltage integrated circuits
  Electronics: TK7874.66
Low-volume roads
  Highway engineering: TE228.5
Lubricants
  Motor vehicles: TL153.5
  Tribology: TJ1077+
Lubrication
  Aircraft engines: TL702.L8
  Diesel engines: TJ798
  Internal combustion engines:
    TJ789
  Locomotives: TJ675
  Mechanical engineering: TJ1075+
  Motor vehicles: TL153.5
  Railroad cars: TF389
  Space vehicles: TL917
Lucite
  Plastics: TP1180.L8
Luggage industry
  Manufactures: TS2301.L8
Lumber
  Manufactures: TS800+
Lumber industry
  Air pollution: TD888.W6
Lumber kilns: TS837
Lumber sheds
  Building construction: TH4485
Lumbering machinery
  Agricultural machinery:
    TJ1486.5
Lumberyards
  Building construction: TH4485
  Fire prevention and
    extinction: TH9445.L8
Lunar mining: TN291.35
Lunchbox cookery: TX735

Luncheons
  Cookery: TX735
Lunchrooms
  Fire prevention and
    extinction: TH9445.R44
  Sanitary engineering: TH6057.R4
Luxfer prisms
  Natural lighting: TH7795
Lyddite
  Explosives: TP290.L8

M

Macadam roads
  Unpaved roads: TE243
Macadamia
  Cookery: TX814.2.M33
Macaroni
  Cookery: TX809.M17
  Food processing and
    manufacture: TP435.M3
  Food values: TX560.M2
Machine assignments
  Industrial engineering: T60.74
Machine design
  Mechanical engineering: TJ227+
Machine drawing
  Mechanical engineering: TJ227+
Machine drawing for electrical
  engineers
  Dynamoelectric machinery:
    TK2325
Machine embroidery: TT772
Machine knitting
  Clothing manufacture: TT679+
Machine parts
  Plastic: TP1185.M3
Machine sewing
  Textile arts: TT713
Machine shops: TJ1125+
  Construction: TJ1130+
  Heating and ventilation:
    TH7392.M2
  Noise control: TD893.6.M3
  Ventilation: TH7684.M2
Machine tool drives
  Machine tools: TJ1188
Machine tools: TJ1180+
  Electric driving: TK4059.M32
Machine-tractor stations
  Building construction: TH4940

Machinery
  Boot and shoemaking: TS1005
  Engineering: TA213+
  Flax industries: TS1728
  Glassmaking: TP859.5
  Highway engineering: TE223+
  Laundry work: TT997
  Leatherwork: TS1043
  Materials handling: TS180.3
  Mine danger: TN320
  Packaging: TS196.4
  Papermills: TS1117+
  Plant engineering: TS191+
  Rubber industry: TS1891.5
  Spinning
    Textile industries: TS1483
  Telegraph: TK5371
  Textile printing: TP930.5
  Tobacco industry: TS2249
  Weaving (Industrial): TS1493
  Wood products: TS850
Machinery and auxiliaries
  Dynamoelectric machinery:
    TK2000+
Machinery exclusive of prime
  movers: TJ1040+
Machinery for electric
  lighting: TK4241
Machinery industry
  Air pollution: TD888.M26
  Waste control: TD899.M2
Machinery manufacturing: TJ241
Machinery, Planning for
  Manufacturing engineering:
    TS181+
Machines for caring for
  plants: TJ1484
Machining
  Ceramic technology: TP814
  Mechanical engineering: TJ1180+
  Plastics: TP1155
Machinists' manuals
  Machine shop practice: TJ1165
Macintosh (Computer)
  Electronics: TK7889.M33
Mackerel
  Cookery: TX748.M32
Macramé
  Textile arts: TT840.M33
Macro lenses
  Photography: TR271.M33
Macrophotography: TR684

Magazines, Fashion: TT500.A2+
Magazines, Powder
  Explosives: TP295
MAGLVE
  High speed ground
    transportation: TF1600
Magnesia cements
  Cement manufacture: TP884.M2
Magnesia industries
  Chemical technology: TP889
Magnesite
  Mining engineering: TN948.M2
Magnesium
  Aeronautics: TL699.M32
  Chemical technology: TP245.M2
  Engineering and construction:
    TA480.M3
  Fire prevention and
    extinction: TH9446.M3
  Manufactures: TS560
  Metallography: TN693.M3
  Metallurgy: TN799.M2
  Motor vehicle construction
    materials: TL240.5.M33
  Ore deposits and mining:
    TN490.M2
Magnesium industry and trade
  Environmental effects:
    TD195.M33
Magnetic amplifiers: TK7871.23
Magnetic analysis
  Testing of materials: TA417.3
Magnetic bearings
  Mechanical engineering:
    TJ1073.7
Magnetic cores and devices
  Electronics: TK7872.M25
Magnetic devices
  Control engineering: TJ223.M3
Magnetic energy storage
  Electrical engineering: TK2985
Magnetic levitation vehicle
  High speed ground
    transportation: TF1600
Magnetic materials
  Electrical engineering:
    TK454.4.M3
  Electronics: TK7871.15.M3
Magnetic memory
  Computer engineering: TK7895.M3

Magnetic recorders
  Aircraft: TL691.M3
  Amateurs' manuals: TK9967
Magnetic resonance imaging
  analysis of food: TX542
Magnetic separation
  Biotechnology: TP248.25.M34
  Chemical engineering: TP156.M26
  Ore dressing and milling: TN530
Magnetic shielding
  Electrical engineering:
    TK454.4.M33
Magnetic tape
  Electroacoustics: TK5984
Magnetic tape heads
  Electroacoustics: TK5984
Magnetic tape recorders and
  recording
  Electronics: TK7881.6+
Magnetite
  Ore deposits and mining:
    TN402.M3
Magnetoelectric machines
  Amateurs' manuals: TK9909
Magnetohydrodynamic devices
  Plasma engineering: TA2040
Magnetohydrodynamic generators
  Electrical engineering: TK2970
Magnetohydrodynamics
  Plasma engineering: TA2040
Magnetos
  Aircraft engines: TL702.I5
  Gasoline automobiles: TL213
  Internal combustion engines:
    TJ787
Magnetrons
  Electronics: TK7871.75
Magnus effect
  Aerodynamics: TL574.M3
Mail cars
  Railway equipment: TF467
Mail chutes: TJ1398
Maillard reaction
  Food processing: TP372.55.M35
Mailplanes: TL685.2
Mains
  Gas industry: TP757
Mains supply
  Radio: TK6565.M35
Maintainability
  Product engineering: TS174

Maintenance
  Airplanes: TL671.9
  Building construction: TH3351+
  Building gas supply: TH6860
  Buses: TL232.2
  Floors and flooring: TH2528
  Hotels, clubs, restaurants,
    etc.: TX928
  Houses: TH4817+
  Motor vehicle operation: TL152+
  Motorcycles: TL444
  Petroleum pipelines: TN879.58
  Plumbing: TH6681+
  Railway permanent way: TF530+
  Railway tunnels: TF234+
  Sewers: TD716+
  Tractors: TL233.2
  Trucks: TL230.2
Maintenance and repair
  Aircraft engines: TL701.5
  Airports: TL725.3.M16
  Bridge engineering: TG315
  Building construction: TH3301+
  Building fittings: TH6013
  Computer engineering: TK7887
  Electronics: TK7870.2
  Gunsmithing: TS535.4
  Highway engineering: TE220+
  Space vehicles: TL915
Maize
  Cookery: TX809.M2
  Food values: TX558.C57
Make-or-buy decisions
  Manufacturing engineering:
    TS183.6
Making up trains: TF593
Malachite
  Mineral industries: TN997.M35
Malleable cast iron
  Metallurgy: TN719
Malt
  Brewing and malting: TP587
Malted milk
  Cookery: TX817.M5
Malting
  Beverages: TP568+
Man-machine systems: TA167
  Industrial engineering: T59.7+
Management
  Airports: TL725.3.M2
  Chemical processing of wood:
    TS937
  Computer manufacturing plants:

Management
  TK7886
  Construction sites: TH438+
  Electrical enterprises: TK441+
  Engineering works: TA190+
  Hotels, clubs, restaurants,
    etc.: TX911.3.M27
  Industrial research: T175.5
  Irrigation projects: TC812
  Metallurgical plants: TN675.7
  Packaging: TS196+
  Radioactive waste disposal:
    TD898.14.M35
Management consultants
  Industrial engineering: T56.3
Management engineering: T55.4+
Management information systems
  Industrial engineering: T58.6+
Management of information
  systems
  Industrial engineering: T58.64
Management science: T55.4+
Managerial control systems
  Industrial engineering: T58.4
Mandoline recipes
  Cookery: TX840.M35
Manganese: TN490.M3
  Air pollutants: TD887.M34
  Assaying: TN580.M3
  Chemical technology: TP245.M3
  Engineering and construction:
    TA480.M35
  Metallography: TN693.M35
  Metallurgy: TN799.M3
  Ore dressing and milling:
    TN538.M35
  Prospecting: TN271.M3
Manganese steel
  Metallurgy: TN757.M3
Mangos
  Cookery: TX813.M35
  Food processing and
    manufacture: TP441.M36
Manholes
  Boilermaking: TJ294
  Sewer appurtenances: TD696
Manicuring
  Professional operators: TT958.3
Manipulation
  Glass and glassmaking: TP859
  Photography: TR147

Manipulators
  Industrial safety: T55.3.M35
  Nuclear engineering: TK9151.7
Manned space flight: TL873
Mansard roofs
  Building construction: TH2405
Mantelpieces
  Building construction: TH2288
Manual systems
  Telephone connections: TK6394
Manual training
  Handicrafts: TT161 +
Manufacture
  Machine tools: TJ1180 +
  Salt: TN905 +
Manufactures: TS1 +
  Waste control: TD899.M29
Manufacturing
  Airplanes: TL671.28
  Military airplanes: TL685.3
  Motor vehicles: TL278
  Rockets: TL784.3 +
Manufacturing capacity
  Industrial engineering: T58.7 +
Manufacturing costs
  Cost control: TS167
Manufacturing engineering
  Production management: TS176 +
Manufacturing personnel:
    TS155.4 +
Manufacturing planning
  Production management: TS176 +
Manufacturing processes
  Manufacturing engineering:
    TS183 +
Manuscripts
  Photography: TR825
Maple sugar
  Cookery: TX767.M3
  Food processing: TP395
  Food values: TX560.M3
Maple syrup
  Cookery: TX767.M3
  Food processing: TP395
  Food values: TX560.M3
Maps
  Air navigation: TL587
Marble: TN967
  Masonry materials: TA428.M3
Marbling
  Wood finishing: TT330

Margarine
  Chemical technology: TP684.M3
Marijuana
  Cookery: TX819.M25
Marinades
  Cookery: TX819.M26
Marinas
  Environmental effects:
    TD195.M37
  Hydraulic engineering: TC328
Marine algae
  Nutrition: TX402
Marine biotechnology:
    TP248.27.M37
Marine cookery: TX840.M7
Marine debris
  Water pollutants: TD427.M35
Marine fiber
  Textile fiber: TS1544.M3
Marine mineral resources: TN264
Marine terminals
  Environmental effects:
    TD195.M39
Mariner project: TL789.8.U6M3
Marines
  Artistic photography: TR670 +
Markers
  Aeronautical navigation
    equipment: TL696.M3
Marketing
  Hotels, clubs, restaurants,
    etc.: TX911.3.M3
Marketing for food
  Nutrition: TX356
Marking
  Airports: TL725.3.M3
  Industrial safety: T55.3.M37
Marking devices industry:
    TS2301.M3
Markov processes
  Chemical engineering:
    TP155.2.M34
Marl
  Mining engineering: TN948.M3
Marmalade
  Preservation and storage:
    TX612.M37
Marquetry
  Woodworking: TT192
Mars (Planet)
  Flight to: TL799.M3
Masers amplifiers: TK7871.4

567

INDEX

Masks
  Decorative crafts: TT898
  Electronics: TK7872.M3
Masonry
  Building design and
    construction: TH2170.7
  Housing material: TH4818.M37
Masonry bridges: TG330
Masonry building construction:
  TH1199 +
Masonry construction
  Structural engineering: TA670 +
Masonry dams: TC547
Masonry in building
  construction: TH5311 +
Masonry materials: TA425 +
Masonry stoves
  Convective heating: TH7436.M37
Mass feeding
  Food service: TX946
Mass spectrometry
  Biotechnology: TP248.25.M38
Mass transfer
  Chemical engineering: TP156.M3
Master antenna television:
  TK6676
Matches: TP310
Mate (Tea)
  Food values: TX560.M35
Material of boilers
  Boilermaking: TJ291
Materials
  Biotechnology: TP248.65.M37
  Ceramic technology: TP810.5
  Color photography: TR515
  Electronics: TK7871 +
  Hairdressing: TT969
  Laundry work: TT997
  Lighter-than-air craft: TL665 +
  Machine and hand tools: TJ1192 +
  Nuclear engineering: TK9185 +
  Packaging: TS198.2 +
  Photography: TR196 +
  Roadmaking material: TE200 +
  Rockets: TL784.8
  Space vehicles: TL950 +
Materials databases
  Materials engineering: TA404.25
Materials handling
  Manufacturing engineering:
    TS180 +
  Noise control: TD893.6.M35

Materials management
  Inventory control: TS161
Materials of engineering and
  construction: TA401 +
Materials science as a
  profession: TA403.9
Materials, Residual
  Engineering: TA709.5
Maternity clothes
  Women's tailoring: TT547
Mathematical modelling
  Petroleum geology: TN870.53
Mathematical models
  Biotechnology: TP248.25.M39
  Chemical engineering:
    TP155.2.M35
  Engineering mathematics: TA342 +
  Photography in surveying:
    TA593.5
Mathematics
  Carpentry and joinery: TH5612 +
  Chemical engineering:
    TP155.2.M36
  Electronics: TK7864
  Hotels, clubs, restaurants,
    etc.: TX911.3.M33
  Surveying: TA556.M38
Matrices
  Engineering mathematics:
    TA347.D4
Matrix methods
  Structural engineering: TA642
Matting
  Floor covering: TS1779.M2
Mayonnaise
  Condiments: TX407.M38
  Cookery: TX819.M3
Mazut
  Petroleum products: TP692.4.M3
Mead
  Fermented beverage: TP588.M4
Measurement
  Air pollution: TD890
  Biotechnology: TP248.25.M43
Measurement of angles
  Surveying: TA603
Measurement of distances
  Surveying: TA601
Measurement of noise: TD894
Measurement of pollution:
  TD193 +

568

Measurement of power
  Machinery exclusive of prime
    movers: TJ1053
Measurements
  Applied fluid mechanics:
    TA357.5.M43
  Building construction: TH434+
  Carpentry and joinery: TH5614+
  Commercial buildings: TH4315
  Heating of buildings: TH7335+
  Houses: TH4815.8
  Plumbing: TH6234+
  Soil mechanics: TA710.5
Measuring
  Dressmaking: TT520
  Men's tailoring: TT590
Measuring tools
  Machine shops: TJ1313
Meat
  Cookery: TX749+
  Food values: TX556.M4
  Pet food industry: TS2288.M4
  Preservation and storage:
    TX612.M4
Meat curing
  Manufactures: TS1960+
Meat extracts
  Nutrition: TX389
Meat industry
  Noise control: TD893.6.M43
  Waste control: TD899.M4
Meat inspection
  Manufactures: TS1975
Meat packing industries
  Manufactures: TS1970+
Meat substitutes: TP447.M4
  Cookery: TX838
Meat, Precooked
  Food values: TX556.M43
Mechanic trades: TT1+
Mechanical alloying: TN698
Mechanical applications of
  electric power: TK4050+
Mechanical damage, Packaging
  for protection from:
    TS198.5+
Mechanical devices and figures
  Mechanical engineering:
    TJ210.2+
Mechanical discharge systems
  House drainage: TH6607

Mechanical draft
  Furnaces: TJ335
Mechanical drawing: T351+
Mechanical engineering: TJ1+
Mechanical engineering and
  electrical engineering:
    TJ163+
Mechanical engineering as a
  profession: TJ157
Mechanical equipment
  Building fittings: TH6010+
Mechanical equipment of docks
  for cargo handling: TC370
Mechanical haulage
  Mines: TN335
Mechanical machinery: TJ1+
Mechanical models
  Machinery: TJ248
Mechanical motive power
  Canals: TC769
Mechanical movements
  Machinery: TJ181+
Mechanical process
  Woodpulp industry: TS1176.6.M4
Mechanical properties
  Materials: TA404.8+
Mechanical stokers
  Furnaces: TJ345
  Locomotives: TJ649
Mechanical telephones: TK6500
Mechanical treatment
  Water purification: TD437+
Mechanical wear
  Endurance properties and
    tests: TA418.4
Mechanics applied to machinery
  Mechanical engineering: TJ170+
Mechanics of engineering:
    TA349+
Mechanics of flight: TL570+
Mechanics of materials: TA405+
Mechanization
  Industrial engineering: T59.4
Mechatronics: TJ163.12
Medical examination
  Drivers: TL152.35
Medical photography: TR708
Medium format cameras
  Photography: TR257
Medium tension A.C. systems
  Electrical engineering: TK3143

Meerschaum
  Mining engineering: TN948.M5
Melanite
  Explosives: TP290.L8
Membrane filtration
  Water purification: TD442.5
Membrane methods
  Saline water conversion:
    TD480.4+
  Sewage purification: TD754
Membrane reactors
  Biotechnology: TP248.25.M45
Membrane separation
  Biotechnology: TP248.25.M46
Membrane switches
  Electronics: TK7872.M46
Membranes
  Chemical technology: TP159.M4
Memory cards
  Computer engineering:
    TK7895.S62
Memory systems
  Computer engineering: TK7895.M4
Men
  Hair styles: TT963
  Photographic portraits:
    TR681.M4
Mending
  Handicrafts: TT151
  Textile arts: TT720+
Men's clothing
  Tailoring: TT570+
Men's fashions: TT617
Mensuration, Technical: T50
Mental requirements
  Air pilots: TL555
Menthol
  Chemical technology: TP248.M4
Menus
  Cookery: TX727+
  Hotels, clubs, restaurants,
    etc.: TX911.3.M45
Mercantile buildings
  Electric power: TK4035.M37
Mercerization
  Textile industries: TS1515
Mercury
  Air pollutants: TD887.M37
  Assaying: TN580.M4
  Chemical technology: TP245.M5
  Effect on food: TX572.M4

Mercury
  Engineering and construction:
    TA480.M4
  Environmental pollutants:
    TD196.M38
  Metallurgy: TN790
  Ore deposits and mining: TN460+
  Prospecting: TN271.M4
  Water pollutants: TD427.M4
Mercury-arc rectifiers
  Electronics: TK7871.82
Mercury vapor lamps: TK4381
Merry-go-round art
  Decorative crafts: TT898.2
Metal
  Waste disposal: TD799.5
Metal (non-foil)
  Packaging materials: TS198.3.M4
Metal arch bridges: TG410
Metal bridges
  Continuous girder bridges:
    TG416
Metal carbonyls
  Chemical technology: TP248.M43
Metal-clad airships: TL656.6
Metal coating
  Plastics: TP1175.M4
Metal coatings
  Engineering and construction:
    TA491
Metal construction
  Structural engineering: TA684+
Metal detectors
  Electronics: TK7882.M4
Metal filament lamps: TK4352
Metal finishing
  Manufactures: TS653+
  Painting: TT382+
Metal finishing industry
  Waste control: TD899.M45
Metal flooring: TH2529.M4
Metal forming: TS200+
Metal furniture
  Manufactures: TS408
Metal insulator
  semiconductors: TK7871.99.M4
Metal lathing
  Building construction: TH1675
Metal manufactures: TS200+
Metal oxide semiconductors:
    TK7871.99.M44

Metal restraints
  Locksmithing: TS531
Metal roofing
  Building construction: TH2454 +
Metal salts
  Photographic processes: TR430 +
Metal sheathing
  Building construction: TH1675
Metal spinning
  Handicrafts: TT206
Metal spraying
  Metal finishing: TS655
Metal stamping
  Metal manufactures: TS253
Metal thread embroidery:
  TT778.M47
Metal turning
  Handicrafts: TT207
Metal wastes
  Waste disposal: TD898.8.M47
Metallic bearings
  Machinery: TJ1061 +
Metallic composites
  Engineering and construction:
    TA481 +
  Metallography: TN693.M38
Metallic glasses
  Metallography: TN693.M4
Metallic ore deposits: TN263
Metallic ores
  Mining engineering: TN265
Metallic oxides
  Insulating material: TK3441.M4
Metallic soaps: TP992
Metallizing
  Metal finishing: TS655
Metallo-organic compounds
  Chemical technology: TP248.M45
Metallographic specimens:
  TN690.7
Metallography: TN689 +
Metallurgical analysis
  Assaying: TN565
Metallurgical furnaces: TN677 +
Metallurgical information,
  Communication of: TN610 +
Metallurgical laboratories:
  TN570 +
Metallurgical literature:
  TN610.5

Metallurgical plants: TN675.5 +
  Air pollution: TD888.M4
  Dust removal: TH7697.M4
  Electric power: TK4035.M4
  Energy conservation:
    TJ163.5.M48
  Waste control: TD899.M43
  Water pollution: TD428.M47
Metallurgical research: TN207
Metallurgy: TN1 +, TN600 +
  Ferrous metals: TN701.482 +
  Nonferrous metals: TN758 +
  Space vehicles: TL954.M47
Metals
  Aeronautics: TL699.M4
  Air pollutants: TD887.M4
  Effect on food: TX571.M48
  Engineering materials: TA459 +
  Environmental pollutants:
    TD196.M4
  Hazardous substance disposal:
    TD1066.M46
  Heat treatment: TN672
  Joining: TS226 +
  Rolling: TS340
  Soil pollutants: TD879.M47
  Space vehicles: TL954.M47
  Surface treatment: TS653 +
  Water pollutants: TD427.M44
Metals, Extrusion of
  Metal manufactures: TS255
Metals, Heavy
  Air pollutants: TD887.H4
  Soil pollutants: TD879.H4
Metals, Radioactive
  Air pollutants: TD887.R3
Metalwork
  Noise control: TD893.6.M45
Metalworking
  Building construction: TH5701 +
  Handicrafts: TT205 +
  Manufactures: TS200 +
Metalworking industry
  Waste control: TD899.M45
Metalworking machinery
  Manufactures: TS215
Meteorological satellites:
  TL798.M4
Meteorology in aeronautics:
  TL556 +
Metering pumps
  Hydraulic machinery: TJ916

Meters
Electric meters: TK311+
Hydrodynamics: TC177
Methanation
Chemical engineering: TP156.M45
Methane
Air pollution: TD885.5.M48
Fuel: TP359.M4, TP360
Gas industry: TP761.M4
Methane industry
Water pollution: TD428.M49
Methanol
Distilling: TP594
Methods engineering
Industrial engineering: T60+
Methods time measurement
Industrial engineering: T60.52
Methyl sulphoxide
Chemical technology: TP248.M48
Methylotrophic microorganisms:
TP248.27.M47
Methylpropene
Gas industry: TP761.M44
Metric system
Industrial applications: T50.5
Metropolitan area networks
Electrical engineering:
TK5105.85
Metropolitan transportation
systems: TA1205+
Mezzograph
Photography: TR976
Mica
Engineering materials: TA455.M5
Mining engineering: TN933
Prospecting: TN271.M5
Microbial biotechnology:
TP248.27.M53
Microbial exopolysaccharides
Biotechnology: TP248.65.M53
Microbial proteins
Biotechnology: TP248.65.M54
Microcomputers
Control engineering: TJ223.M53
Microcrystalline polymers
Plastics: TP1183.M5
Microelectromechanical
systems: TK7875
Microelectronics: TK7874+
Microfilming
Photographic reproduction:
TR835

Micromachining: TJ1191.5
Microoganisms
Water pollutants: TD427.M53
Microphones
Electroacoustics: TK5986
Telephone: TK6478
Microprocessors
Computer engineering: TK7895.M5
Control engineering: TJ223.M53
Microscopic analysis
Food: TX543
Food adulterants: TX567
Water: TD384
Microscopy
Fermentation industries: TP515
Testing of materials: TA417.23
Textile industries: TS1449
Microsoft FrontPage
Web authoring software:
TK5105.8885.M53
Microsoft Internet Explorer:
TK5105.883.M53
Microsoft Office
Web authoring software:
TK5105.8885.M54
Microsoft Office professional
Web authoring software:
TK5105.8885.M54
Microsoft Visual InterDev
Web authoring software:
TK5105.8885.M55
Microspacecraft: TL795.4
Microwave antennas:
TK7871.67.M53
Microwave circuits
Electronics: TK7876+
Microwave communication systems
Amateurs' manuals: TK9957
Microwave cookery: TX832
Microwave holography: TA1552
Microwave lenses
Radar: TK6590.M5
Microwave ovens
Cookery: TX657.O64
Microwave transistors:
TK7871.96.M53
Microwaves
Electronics: TK7876+
Middens
Sewage disposal: TD775
Middle aged persons
Nutrition: TX361.M47

Middlesex Canal
  Inland navigation: TC625.M6
Midget cars: TL236.5
Midwestern style cookery:
  TX715.2.M53
Migrant laborers
  Nutrition: TX361.M48
Military aeronautics
  Environmental effects:
  TD195.M45
Military bases
  Energy conservation:
  TJ163.5.M54
Military planes: TL685.3
Milk
  Cookery: TX759.5.M54
  Food values: TX556.M5
  Nutrition: TX379
Milk plants
  Waste control: TD899.D3
Milk products
  Food values: TX556.M5
Milkshakes
  Cookery: TX817.M5
Millet
  Food values: TX558.M5
Millimeter waves
  Electronics: TK7876.5
Millinery
  Clothing manufacture: TT650+
Milling
  Gold and silver metallurgy:
  TN762
  Metalworking: TT209
Milling cutters
  Machine shops: TJ1227
  Machine tools: TJ1186
Milling industry: TS2120+
Milling machinery
  Mining: TN505+
Milling machines
  Machine shops: TJ1225+
Mills
  Building construction: TH4511+
  Electric lighting: TK4399.M5
  Fire prevention and
    extinction: TH9445.M4+
  Heating and ventilation:
  TH7392.M6
Millwork
  Manufactures: TS878
Mine accidents: TN311+

Mine buildings
  Building construction: TH4561
Mine cars: TN342
Mine communication systems:
  TN344
Mine drainage: TN321+
Mine dusts: TN312
Mine examination and
  valuation: TN272+
Mine explosions: TN313
Mine filling: TN290
Mine fires: TN315
Mine haulage: TN331+
Mine hoisting: TN331+
Mine maps: TN273
Mine organization and
  management: TN274
Mine pumps: TN325
Mine railroads: TN336
Mine roof bolting: TN289.3
Mine roof falls: TN317
Mine sanitation: TN300
Mine selling: TN272+
Mine subsidences: TN319
  Environmental effects:
  TD195.M48
Mine surveying: TN273
Mine tracks: TN336
Mine transportation: TN331+
Mineral deposits: TN263
Mineral industries: TN1+
  Dust removal: TH7697.M56
  Energy conservation:
  TJ163.5.M56
  Environmental effects: TD195.M5
  Noise control: TD893.6.M5
  Waste control: TD899.M47
  Water pollution: TD428.M56
Mineral oils
  Chemical technology: TP685+
Mineral waters
  Mining engineering: TN923+
Mineralogy, Applied: TN260
Mineralogy, Economic: TN260
Minerals
  Food constituent: TX553.M55
  Nature photography: TR732.5
Miners
  Nutrition: TX361.M5
Miners' lamps: TN307

Mines
  Dangers and accidents: TN311+
  Photography: TR672
  Waste control: TD899.M5
Mines, Lighting of: TN306.5+
Mines, Ventilation of: TN301+
Miniature cameras
  Photography: TR262
Miniature craft
  Handicrafts: TT178
Miniature engines
  Locomotives: TJ630
Minidisc players
  Electronics: TK7881.78
Minidiscs
  Electronics: TK7881.78
Mining
  Use of airplanes: TL722.4
Mining appliances: TN345+
Mining companies: TN400+
Mining engineering: TN1+
Mining engineering as a
  profession: TN160
Mining in extreme
  environments: TN291.24+
Mining machinery: TN345+
  Electric driving: TK4059.M55
Mining machinery accidents:
  TN320
Mining tools: TN345+
Mining, Ocean
  Environmental effects:
  TD195.O25
Mining, Salt: TN900+
Minsk computer: TK7889.M55
Mint
  Cookery: TX819.M56
Mirror-frames
  Glassware: TP867
Mirrors
  Decorative crafts: TT898.3
  Glassware: TP867
Mischmetal
  Metallography: TN693.R3
Miso
  Cookery: TX819.M57
  Food processing: TP438.S6
Mississippi River
  Jetties: TC425.M65
Mists
  Air pollutants: TD884.5

Miter wheels
  Mechanical movements: TJ194
Mitering
  Building construction: TH5691
Mixed culture
  Biotechnology: TP248.25.M58
Mixer recipes
  Cookery: TX840.M5
Mixers
  Electronics: TK7872.M5
Mixing
  Applied fluid mechanics:
  TA357.5.M59
  Chemical engineering: TP156.M5
  Concrete: TA439+
  Plastics: TP1175.M5
Mobile communication systems:
  TK6570.M6
Mobile home cookery: TX840.M6
Mobile home living: TX1100+
Mobile homes
  Construction: TH4819.M6
Mobile offshore structures
  Petroleum engineering: TN871.4
Mobile robots
  Mechanical engineering:
  TJ211.415
Mobiles
  Decorative crafts: TT899
Mocrophotography
  Photographic reproduction:
  TR835
Modal analysis
  Structural analysis: TA654.15
Mode-locked lasers
  Applied optics: TA1688
Model airplanes: TL770+
Model airships: TL775
Model analysis
  Structural engineering: TA643
Model engine
  Aircraft engines: TL704.6
Model gliders: TL774
Model helicopters: TL776
Model railways: TF197
Model rockets: TL844
Model space vehicles: TL844
Model testing
  Airplanes: TL671.8
  Airships: TL660.5
Modeling in clay
  Decorative crafts: TT916

Modelmaking
  Handicrafts: TT154+
Models
  Aeronautics: TL770+
  Airports: TL725.3.M63
  Airships: TL775
  Boilermaking: TJ295
  Bridges: TG307
  Cycles: TL438
  Flying machines: TL713.7+
  Handicrafts: TT154+
  Heavier-than-air craft: TL670.5
  Helicopters: TL776
  Locomotives: TJ630
  Motor vehicles: TL237+
  Motorcycles: TL438
  Ocean engineering: TC1680
  Paper airplanes: TL778
  Patents: T324
  Propellers: TL777
  Sloyd: TT188
  Steam engines: TJ480
  Tractors: TL233.8
Models for water testing
  Aeronautical research: TL567.M6
Models for wind tunnel testing
  Aeronautical research: TL567.M6
Modems
  Computer engineering: TK7887.8.M63
Moderators
  Nuclear reactors: TK9209
Modular coordination
  Architectural engineering: TH860
Modulators
  Electronics: TK7872.M6
Mohair
  Textile fiber: TS1548.M6
Moisture
  Grain: TS2149
  Packaging protection: TS198.8.M6
Moisture content
  Engineering materials: TA418.64
Molasses
  Cookery: TX819.M65
  Sugars and syrups: TP413
Molding
  Metal manufactures: TS243+
  Plastics: TP1150

Molding materials
  Metal manufactures: TS243.5
Molding sand
  Metal manufactures: TS243.5
Moldings (Exterior)
  Building construction: TH2482+
Moldings (Interior)
  Building construction: TH2553
Molecular electronics: TK7874.8
Molecular sieves
  Chemical technology: TP159.M6
Molten salt reactors
  Nuclear engineering: TK9203.M65
Molybdenum
  Chemical technology: TP245.M7
  Engineering and construction: TA480.M6
  Metallography: TN693.M64
  Metallurgy: TN799.M7
  Nuclear engineering: TK9185.2.M66
  Ore deposits and mining: TN490.M7
Molybdenum steel
  Metallurgy: TN757.M7
Moment distribution method: TA650+
Moments
  Aerodynamics: TL574.M6
Monazite
  Mining engineering: TN948.M7
Mond gas
  Gas industry: TP761.M7
Monitoring
  Biotechnology: TP248.25.M65
  Dynamoelectric machinery: TK2313
Monitoring receivers
  Radio apparatus: TK6564.M64
Monoclonal antibodies
  Biotechnology: TP248.65.M65
Monoplane characteristics: TL671.3
Monopulse radar: TK6592.M6
Monsters
  Photographic portraits: TR681.M65
Monte Carlo method
  Industrial engineering: T57.64
Montgolfiers: TL617
Montmorillonite
  Mining engineering: TN948.M72

Monuments
  Cement manufacture: TP885.M7
  Stonework: TS788
Moon
  Extraterrestrial radio
    communication: TK6571.5.M6
  Flight to: TL799.M6
Moon cars: TL480
Mooring berths
  Hydraulic engineering: TC373
Mooring masts
  Airports: TL731
Morals
  Household servants: TX333
Mordants
  Dyeing: TP927
Mordenite
  Mining engineering: TN948.Z4
Morphing
  Computer animation: TR897.75
Mortar
  Chemical technology: TP887
  Masonry materials: TA434+
Motels
  Energy conservation:
    TJ163.5.H67
Motherboards
  Computer engineering:
    TK7895.B33
Mothers
  Photographic portraits:
    TR681.M67
Mothproofing
  Textile industries: TS1517
Motion control devices
  Mechanical engineering: TJ214.5
Motion picture cameras
  Cinematography: TR880
Motion picture film
  Cinematography: TR886+
Motion picture films in
  storehouses
  Fire prevention and
    extinction: TH9445.T5
Motion picture machines
  Cinematography: TR878+
Motion picture theaters
  Electric power: TK4035.M6
  Fire prevention and
    extinction: TH9445.T4

Motion pictures
  Editing: TR899+
  Photography: TR845+
  Technical education: T65.5.M6
Motion pictures for television
  Cinematography: TR898
Motion study
  Industrial engineering: T60.7
  Machine shops: TJ1143
Motion time systems,
  Predetermined
  Industrial engineering: T60.5+
Motive power
  Canals: TC767+
  Dynamoelectric machinery:
    TK2000+
  Locomotives: TJ640+
Motor bicycles: TL443
Motor generators
  Dynamoelectric machinery:
    TK2695
Motor scooters: TL450+
Motor sledges: TL460
Motor vehicle driving: TL152.5+
Motor vehicle emissions
  Air pollutants: TD886.5
Motor vehicle fleets: TL165
Motor vehicle operation:
  TL151.5+
Motor vehicle scales
  Highway engineering: TE176.8
Motor vehicles: TL1+
  Human engineering in design:
    TL250
Motorboat cookery: TX840.M7
Motorboat racing
  Water pollution: TD428.M68
Motorcars
  Railway equipment: TF494+
Motorcycle riding: TL440.5
Motorcycles
  Technology: TL439+
Motorcyclists: TL440.2
  Photographic portraits:
    TR681.M69
Motormen's manuals
  Electric railways: TF965
Motors
  Aeronautics: TL701+
  Dynamoelectric machinery:
    TK2511+
  Gasoline automobiles: TL210+

Motors
  Mechanical engineering: TJ751+
  Motorcycles: TL445
  Types: TK2537
Motorsports
  Environmental effects:
    TD195.M67
Mountain climbing
  Airplanes: TL721.1
Mountain flying
  Airplanes: TL711.M68
Mountain photography: TR787
Mountain railways
  Technology: TF680+
Mountain roads
  Highway engineering: TE229.8
Mounting of prints
  Photographic processing: TR340
Movable bed models
  Hydraulic engineering: TC164.6
Movable boilers
  Hot water heating: TH7540
Movable bridges: TG420
Movable dams: TC549
Movable furnaces
  Hot water heating: TH7540
  Hydronic systems: TH7475
  Steam heating: TH7590
Moving loads
  Structural analysis: TA654.3
Moving of structures
  Building construction: TH153
Moving target indicator radar:
    TK6592.M67
Moving, Household: TX307
Mucilage
  Organic chemical industries:
    TP970
Mud fuel: TP360
Muds
  Well drilling: TN871.27
Muffin pans
  Cookery: TX657.M85
Muffins
  Cookery: TX770.M83
Mufflers
  Aircraft engines: TL702.M8
Mullet
  Cookery: TX748.M84
Mullite
  Mining engineering: TN948.M8

Multiengine flying
  Airplanes: TL711.T85
Multiphase current systems
  Electrical engineering: TK3158
Multiphase currents
  Electrical engineering: TK1168
Multiphase flow
  Applied fluid mechanics:
    TA357.5.M84
Multiplane characteristics:
    TL671.3
Multiple punches
  Machine shop: TJ1257
Multiplex telegraph system:
    TK5538
Multiplex telephone systems:
    TK6425
Multiplexers
  Electronics: TK7872.M8
Multistory frames
  Structural engineering:
    TA660.F73
Multitubular steam boilers
  Mechanical engineering: TJ311+
Municipal chemistry: TP149
Municipal engineering: TD159+
Municipal railways: TF701+
Municipal refuse
  Environmental technology:
    TD785+
Muscovite
  Mining engineering: TN948.M85
Museums
  Energy conservation:
    TJ163.5.M87
  Fire prevention and
    extinction: TH9445.M8
  Sanitary engineering:
    TH6057.M87
Mushrooms
  Cookery: TX804
  Food processing and
    manufacture: TP444.M8
  Food values: TX558.M9
  Preservation and storage:
    TX612.M8
Musicians
  Photographic portraits:
    TR681.M86
Mussels
  Cookery: TX754.M98

Must
  Beverages: TP560
Mustard
  Cookery: TX819.M87
Mustard oil
  Organic chemical industries:
    TP959.M8
Mutton
  Cookery: TX749.5.L35
Muzzle-loading firearms
  Manufactures: TS535.8
Muzzle-loading rifle:
    TS536.6.M8

N

Nacelles
  Airplanes: TL681.5
Nail care
  Professional operators: TT958.3
Nail craft
  Metalworking: TT213.6
Nails
  Metal manufactures: TS440+
Nails, Metal
  Engineering and construction:
    TA492.N2
Nanostructure materials
  Engineering materials:
    TA418.9.N35
Nanotechnology: T174.7
  Biotechnology: TP248.25.N35
Nanowires: TK7874.85
Naphtha
  Petroleum products: TP692.4.N3
Naphthazarin
  Textile dyes: TP918.N2
Narrow gauge railways: TF675
National Board of Fire
  Underwriters' rules
  Building construction: TH9176
National Research and Education
  Network
  Computer networks:
    TK5105.875.N37
Natto
  Food processing: TP438.S6
Natural carbons
  Metallurgy: TN845+
Natural draft
  Ventilation of buildings:
    TH7674+

Natural dyes: TP919+
  Textile decoration: TT854.3
Natural filtration
  Mechanical treatment of water
    purification: TD443
Natural flight
  Aeronautics: TL575
Natural foods
  Cookery: TX741
  Nutrition: TX369
Natural gas
  Air pollutants: TD885.5.N38
  Fuel: TP350
  Mining engineering: TN880+
Natural gas motor vehicles:
    TL228
Natural gas pipelines: TN880.5
Natural lighting
  Building construction: TH7791+
  Photography: TR590+
Natural paraffin
  Mineral oils and waxes: TP695
  Mining engineering: TN857
Natural sweeteners: TP426
Natural ventilation
  Ventilation of buildings:
    TH7674+
Nature cinematography
  Photography: TR893.4+
Nature photography: TR721+
Naval stations
  Fire prevention and
    extinction: TH9445.N3
Navigation computer
  Aeronautical instrument:
    TL589.2.N3
Navigation for air pilots:
    TL586+
Navigation lights
  Aircraft: TL691.N3
Navigation satellites: TL798.N3
Navigation systems
  Space vehicles: TL3250+
Navy yards
  Fire prevention and
    extinction: TH9445.N3
Near misses
  Airplane accidents: TL553.55
Neckties
  Men's tailoring: TT616
Needle dams: TC549
Needlepoint lace: TT805.N43

Needles industry
  Manufactures: TS2301.P5
Needlework (Kindergarten):
  TT708
Negative-resistance devices
  Electronics: TK7872.N4
Negatives
  Photographic processing: TR290+
Neodymium
  Chemical technology: TP245.N4
  Metallurgy: TN799.N47
Neon
  Chemical technology: TP245.N5
Neon lamps and tubes
  Electric lighting: TK4383
Neon tubes: TK7871.84.N4
Nepheline syenite
  Mining engineering: TN948.N37
Nephelite (Nepheline)
  Mining engineering: TN948.N4
Neptunium
  Metallurgy: TN799.N5
Nernst lamps
  Electric lighting: TK4359.N47
Net
  Balloons: TL625.N4
Net systems
  Fire prevention and
    extinction: TH9418
NetCruiser: TK5105.883.N43
NetObjects Fusion
  Web authoring software:
    TK5105.8885.N48
Nets
  Engineering mathematics:
    TA347.N46
Netscape: TK5105.883.N48
Netscape Communicator:
  TK5105.883.N49
Netscape Composer
  Web authoring software:
    TK5105.8885.N49
Netscape LiveConnect
  Web authoring software:
    TK5105.8885.N5
Netscape Navigator:
  TK5105.883.N48
Netscape SuiteSpot:
  TK5105.883.N493
Netting
  Textile arts: TT840.N48

Network analysis
  Industrial engineering: T57.85
Network systems theory
  Industrial engineering: T57.85
Neutralization
  Sewage disposal systems:
    TD747.9
Neutron optical devices: TA1773
Neutron sources
  Nuclear engineering: TK9182
New England style cookery:
  TX715.2.N48
New towns
  Environmental effects:
    TD195.N47
New York airbrakes: TF430
Newsprint: TS1160
Newsreel cinematography
  Photography: TR895
Nicaragua Canal: TC784
Nickel
  Chemical technology: TP245.N6
  Engineering materials: TA480.N6
  Environmental pollutants:
    TD196.N48
  Metallography: TN693.N5
  Metallurgy: TN799.N6
  Ore deposits and mining:
    TN490.N6
  Prospecting: TN271.N5
Nickel alloys
  Electronics: TK7871.15.N53
Nickel-cadmium batteries
  Electricity production:
    TK2945.N52
Nickel chromium alloys
  Metallurgy: TN757.N6
Nickel-hydrogen batteries
  Electricity production:
    TK2945.N53
Nickel plating
  Electroplating: TS690
Nickel steel
  Engineering materials: TA479.N5
  Metallurgy: TN757.N5
Nickel-titanium alloys
  Engineering materials:
    TA480.N63
Nicotine
  Tobacco manufacturing: TS2255
Night flying
  Airplanes: TL711.N5

Night views
  Photography: TR610
Niobium: TN490.N65
  Chemical technology: TP245.N7
  Engineering materials:
    TA480.N65
  Metallurgy: TN799.N7
Niter
  Inorganic chemicals: TP238
Nitrates
  Effect on food: TX572.N5
  Mining engineering: TN911
  Salts: TP237+
Nitration
  Chemical engineering: TP156.N5
Nitric acid
  Chemicals: TP217.N5
Nitrides
  Electronics: TK7871.15.N57
  Engineering materials: TA455.N5
Nitriding
  Steel metallurgy: TN752.C3
Nitrification
  Water treatment and
    conditioning: TD468
Nitrites
  Effect on food: TX572.N5
Nitrocellulose
  Chemical technology: TP248.N7
Nitrocellulose compounds
  Explosives: TP276
Nitrogen
  Chemical technology: TP245.N8
  Environmental pollutants:
    TD196.N55
  Fertilizers: TP963.4.N5
  Industrial electrochemistry:
    TP261.N7
  Metallurgy: TN757.N66
  Sewage treatment: TD758.5.N58
  Water pollutants: TD427.N5
Nitrogen compounds
  Chemical technology: TP248.N8
  Environmental pollutants:
    TD196.N55
  Explosives: TP290.N53
  Water pollutants: TD427.N5
Nitrogen oxides
  Air pollutants: TD885.5.N5
Nitrogen, Liquid, automobiles:
  TL229.L56

Nitrogylcerine compounds
  Explosives: TP285
Nobel: TP268.5.N7
Nodular iron
  Metallurgy: TN719.5
Noise
  Aerodynamics: TL574.N6
  Air conditioning: TH7687.5
  Aircraft propellers: TL706.N6
  Airplanes: TL671.65
  Airports: TL725.3.N6
  Electronic circuits: TK7867.5
  Environmental engineering:
    TD891+
  Motor vehicle dynamics: TL246
  Turbines: TJ267.5.N5
Noise generators
  Electronics: TK7872.N6
Noise in buildings
  Building construction: TH1725
Noise in machinery
  Mechanical engineering: TJ179
Noise measurement: TD894
Non-automatic electrolytic
  telegraphs: TK5515
Nonalcoholic beverages: TP620+
Noncarbonated fruit beverages:
  TP656+
Nonconvex programming
  Industrial engineering: T57.817
Nondestructive tests
  Testing of materials: TA417.2+
Nonferrous metal industries
  Electric power: TK4035.N6
  Environmental effects:
    TD195.N65
Nonferrous metals
  Assaying: TN580.N6
  Engineering and construction:
    TA479.3
  Manufactures: TS370+
  Metallurgy: TN758+
  Ore dressing and milling:
    TN538.N6
Nonlinear programming
  Industrial engineering: T57.8+
Nonmetallic bearings
  Machinery: TJ1072+
Nonmetallic materials
  Engineering materials:
    TA418.95+

Nonmetallic minerals
  Mining engineering: TN799.5+
  Prospecting: TN271.N63
Nonnutritive sweeteners
  Flavoring aids: TP422+
Nonpoint source pollution
  Water pollution: TD424.8
Nonrigid airships: TL656.2
Nonwoven fabrics
  Textile fiber: TS1828
Noodles
  Cookery: TX809.N65
Nori
  Food values: TX558.N6
Normal numbers
  Engineering mathematics:
    TA347.N6
Normandy cookery: TX719.2.N67
Northern style cookery
  Italian: TX723.2.N65
Notch effect
  Plastic properties and tests:
    TA418.17
Notions industry: TS2301.N5
Novell Netware networks:
  TK5105.8.N65
Novelties industry
  Manufactures: TS2301.N55
Nozzle forms
  Fire extinction: TH9323
Nozzles
  Aeronautical research: TL567.N6
  Chemical technology: TP159.N6
  Fire extinction: TH9380
  Hydrodynamics: TC173
  Jet engines: TL709.5.N68
  Rockets: TL784.N65
  Turbines: TJ267.5.N6
Nuclear counters
  Nuclear engineering: TK9180
Nuclear electric powerplants
  Space vehicles: TL1102.N8
Nuclear engineering: TK9001+
Nuclear engineering as a
  profession: TK9155.5
Nuclear facilities
  Air pollution: TD888.N8
  Environmental effects:
    TD195.N83
  Fire prevention and
    extinction: TH9445.N83
  Ventilation: TH7684.N83

Nuclear locomotives: TJ623
Nuclear power plants: TK1341+
  Airplanes: TL708+
  Fire prevention and
    extinction: TH9445.A85
  Water pollution: TD428.A86
Nuclear pressure vessels
  Nuclear reactors: TK9211.5
Nuclear propulsion
  Aeronautics: TL708+
Nuclear propulsion systems:
  TL783.5
Nuclear reactor
  instrumentation: TK9178+
Nuclear reactors
  Engineering: TK9202+
Nuclear reactors for
  propulsion: TK9230
Nuclear rockets: TL783.5
Nuclear safety
  Nuclear engineering: TK9152+
Nuclear saline water conversion
  plants: TD479.6
Nuclear weapons plants
  Environmental effects:
    TD195.N85
Nucleation
  Chemical engineering: TP156.N8
Nucleotides
  Chemical technology: TP248.N9
Nude
  Artistic photography: TR674+
Numerical control
  Machine tools: TJ1189
Numerical methods
  Engineering mathematics: TA335
Nursing homes
  Fire prevention: TH9445.A4
Nut oils
  Food values: TX560.N7
Nut products
  Food processing: TP439+
Nut runners and setters
  Machine shops: TJ1201.N8
Nutcrackers
  Cookery: TX657.N87
Nutrients
  Water pollutants: TD427.N87
Nutrition
  Home economics: TX341+
Nutrition policy: TX359

Nuts
  Cookery: TX814+
  Food processing: TP439+
  Food values: TX558.N8
  Nutrition: TX399
Nuts, Metal
  Engineering materials:
    TA492.B63
Nylon
  Chemical technology: TP1180.P55

O

Oakum
  Textile fiber: TS1747.O3
Oat bran
  Cookery: TX809.O22
  Food processing and
    manufacture: TP435.O37
Oat products
  Food processing and
    manufacture: TP435.O37
Oats
  Cookery: TX809.O23
  Food values: TX558.O3
Oblong stone blocks: TE265
Observers' handbooks
  Artificial satellites: TL796.8
Ocean engineering: TC1501+
Ocean flying
  Airplanes: TL711.O26
Ocean mining: TN291.5
  Environmental effects:
    TD195.O25
Ocean thermal energy
  conversion: TK1073
Ocean, Discharge into
  Sewage disposal: TD771.5
Oceans
  Sewage effluent discharge
    into: TD763+
Ocher
  Mining engineering: TN948.O2
Odontographs
  Mechanical movements: TJ186
Odor control
  Water purification: TD457
Odors
  Air pollutants: TD886
Off-road trucks: TL235.6+
Off-road vehicle driving:
  TL235.7

Off-road vehicles: TL235.6+
Office buildings
  Air conditioning: TH7688.O4
  Building operation and
    housekeeping: TX980
  Construction: TH4311+
  Electric lighting: TK4399.O35
  Energy conservation:
    TJ163.5.O35
  Fire prevention and
    extinction: TH9445.O4
  Heating and ventilation:
    TH7392.O35
  Plumbing: TH6515.O3
  Sanitary engineering: TH6057.O4
Office organization
  Telegraph enterprises: TK5285+
  Telephone enterprises: TK6185+
Office records
  Management of engineering
    works: TA190.5
Office systems
  Management of engineering
    works: TA190.5
Offices
  House remodeling: TH4816.3.O34
  Noise control: TD893.6.O34
Offshore oil industry
  Water pollution: TD428.O33
Offshore structures
  Air conditioning: TH7688.O44
  Fire prevention and
    extinction: TH9445.O43
  Ocean engineering: TC1665+
Ogee wings
  Airplanes: TL673.O4
Ohmmeters
  Electric meters: TK311
Oil
  Gas manufacture: TP751.7
  Hazardous substances and their
    disposal: TD1066.O55
  Insulating material: TK3441.O5
  Sewage treatment: TD758.5.O37
Oil analysis
  Petroleum refining: TP691
Oil burning installations
  Furnaces: TJ326
Oil companies outside of United
  States: TN879
Oil feeders
  Tribology: TJ1079

Oil filters
  Aircraft engines: TL702.O55
Oil fuels
  Central heating: TH7466.O6
Oil gas
  Petroleum products: TP692.4.O3
Oil gasification: TP759
Oil handling and storage:
  TP692.5
Oil heating of buildings:
  TH7402+
Oil hydraulic machinery: TJ843
Oil hydraulics: TJ843
Oil industries
  Waste control: TD899.O54
Oil inspection
  Petroleum refining: TP691
Oil mist lubrication
  Mechanical engineering:
    TJ1073.6
Oil processes
  Photography: TR443
Oil sands
  Petroleum geology: TN870.54
Oil sands extraction plants
  Air pollution: TD888.O35
  Water pollution: TD428.O35
Oil separators
  Steam powerplants: TJ444
Oil-shale industry
  Environmental effects: TD195.O4
Oil shales
  Mining engineering: TN858+
Oil-soluble preservatives
  Preservation of wood:
    TA424.6.O4
Oil standards
  Petroleum refining: TP691
Oil storage tanks
  Fire prevention and
    extinction: TH9445.O55
Oil stoves
  Convective heating: TH7449+
  Cookery: TX657.S8
Oil strainers
  Tribology: TJ1081
Oil system
  Gasoline automobiles: TL214.O5
Oil testing
  Petroleum refining: TP691
Oilcloth
  Floor covering: TS1779.O5

Oils
  Chemical technology: TP669+
  Food values: TX560.O3
  Hairdressing: TT969
Oils and fats, Edible
  Condiments: TX407.O34
Okra
  Cookery: TX803.O37
Olive butter
  Cookery: TX819.O4
Olive oil
  Chemical technology: TP683
  Cookery: TX819.O42
  Food values: TX560.O4
Olives
  Cookery: TX813.O4
  Food processing and
    manufacture: TP441.O4
  Food values: TX558.O5
Olympus (Artificial
  satellite): TK5104.2.O49
Omnirange system
  Aeronautical navigation
    equipment: TL696.O5
One-pipe systems
  House drainage: TH6602
  Low-pressure hot water
    heating: TH7525
  Steam heating: TH7567
Onions
  Cookery: TX803.O5
  Food processing and
    manufacture: TP444.O5
Opals
  Jewelry work: TS755.O73
  Mineral industries: TN997.O7
Open air views
  Photographic lighting: TR615
Open and enclosed arcs
  Electric lighting: TK4322
Open channels
  Hydrodynamics: TC175+
Open Document Architecture
  Computer network protocols:
    TK5105.577
Open dumps
  Municipal refuse: TD795+
Open fires
  Heating of buildings: TH7421+
Open hearth process
  Steel metallurgy: TN740+

Open Systems Interconnect
  Computer networks: TK5105.58
Open working
  Mining: TN291
Opening and closing system
  Aircraft engines: TL702.V3
Operation and management
  Electric railways: TF960+
  High speed ground
    transportation: TF1500+
Operation sequence analysis
  Manufacturing engineering:
    TS178.7
Operational amplifiers:
  TK7871.58.O6
Operations management: TS155+
Operations research
  Industrial engineering: T57.6+
Operations, Contractors':
  TA201+
Optic systems
  Telegraph: TK5515
Optical character recognition
  Optical data processing: TA1640
Optical coatings
  Optical instruments: TS517.2
Optical communications
  Electrical engineering:
    TK5103.59
Optical data processing:
  TA1630+
Optical data storage: TA1635
Optical devices, Neutron:
  TA1773
Optical equipment
  Aeronautics: TL697.O65
  Computer engineering: TK7895.O6
  Radar: TK6590.O67
  Space vehicles: TL1200
Optical fiber detectors: TA1815
Optical gyroscope
  Aeronautical instruments:
    TL589.2.O6
Optical instruments
  Manufactures: TS510+
Optical isomers
  Biotechnology: TP248.65.O65
Optical pattern recognition
  Optical data processing: TA1650
Optical properties
  Engineering materials: TA418.62
Optical radar: TK6592.O6

Optical surface preparation
  Optical instruments: TS517
Optical tests
  Engineering materials: TA418.62
Optics, Applied: TA1501+
Optics, Integrated
  Optical data processing: TA1660
Optimization, Structural
  Structural engineering: TA658.8
Optoelectronic devices
  Control engineering: TJ223.P5
  Electronics: TK8300+
Optoelectronics: TA1750+
Orange juice: TP562.5.O73
Orange oil
  Organic chemical industries:
    TP959.O7
Oranges
  Cookery: TX813.O6
  Food values: TX558.O7
Orbital mechanics: TL1050+
Orbital rendezvous
  Space vehicles: TL1095
Orbital transfer
  Space navigation: TL1075+
Orchids
  Nature photography: TR726.O73
Ordinary telegraph system:
  TK5523
Ore cars: TN342
  Railway equipment: TF479
Ore deposits
  Mining: TN400+
Ore dressing and milling:
  TN496+
Ore-dressing plants: TN504
  Dust removal: TH7697.O7
  Electric power: TK4035.O7
Ores
  Analysis: TN580.A+
  Sampling: TN560
Organic chemical industries:
  TP950+
Organic chemicals: TP247.A1+
Organic compounds
  Air pollutants: TD885.5.O74
  Biotechnology: TP248.65.O73
  Environmental pollutants:
    TD196.O73

Organic compounds
  Hazardous substances and their
    disposal: TD1066.O73
  Sewage treatment: TD758.5.O75
  Soil pollutants: TD879.O73
  Water pollutants: TD427.O7
Organic compounds, Chlorine
  Environmental pollutants:
    TD196.C5
Organic compounds, Halogen
  Environmental pollutants:
    TD196.H35
Organic moderated reactors
  Nuclear engineering: TK9203.O7
Organic wastes
  Waste disposal: TD804+
Organization
  Industrial research: T175.5
Organization of staff and force
  Railway operation: TF510+
Organohalogen compounds
  Waste disposal: TD812.5.O73
Organolead compounds
  Environmental pollutants:
    TD196.O75
Organometallic compounds
  Electronics: TK7871.15.O7
  Environmental pollutants:
    TD196.O76
Oriental rugs
  Textile industries: TS1778
Orienting mechanisms
  Assembling machines: TJ1317.5
Orifices
  Hydrodynamics: TC173
Ornamental bridges: TG430
Ornamental glass in buildings:
    TP863+
Ornamental glazing
  Decorative furnishings: TH8271+
Ornamental lathework: TT203
Ornamental stones
  Mining engineering: TN950+
Ornaments
  Hairwork: TT976
Ornithopters: TL717
Orthochromatic photography:
    TR453
Orthographic projection
  Mechanical drawing: T363

Oscillations
  Aerodynamics: TL574.S7
Oscillators
  Electronics: TK7872.O7
  Radar: TK6590.O7
  Radio: TK6565.O7
  Television: TK6655.O7
Oscillographs
  Electrical engineering: TK381
Oscilloscopes
  Electronic instruments:
    TK7878.7
Osmium
  Chemical technology: TP245.O7
Osmosis
  Chemical engineering: TP156.O7
Ostrich
  Cookery: TX750.5.O77
Outdoor cookery: TX823
Outdoor furniture
  Woodworking: TT197.5.O9
Outdoor photography: TR659.5
Outer space
  Mining: TN291.3+
Outfall sewers: TD711
Outhouses
  Building construction: TH4975
Outlet stores
  Consumer education: TX335+
Ovens
  Cookery: TX657.O57+
Over-the-horizon radar:
    TK6592.O94
Overcoats
  Men's tailoring: TT600
Overhang
  Airplanes: TL673.O8
Overhead lines
  Electric power: TK3231+
  Telegraph: TK5452+
  Telephone connections: TK6352
Overhead projectors
  Photography: TR508
Overhead systems
  Low-pressure hot water
    heating: TH7525
  Steam heating: TH7567
Overlays
  Highway maintenance: TE220.3
Overshot water wheels: TJ862
Overwater flying
  Airplanes: TL711.O26

Oxalic acid
  Chemical technology: TP248.O9
Oxidation
  Chemical engineering: TP156.O9
  Pollution control methods:
    TD192.45
  Sewage disposal: TD758
Oxidation ponds
  Sewage treatment: TD746.5
Oxidizing agents
  Chemical technology: TP159.O9
  Environmental pollutants:
    TD196.O95
Oxyacetylene welding: TS228+
Oxygen
  Chemical technology: TP245.O9
  Explosives: TP290.L5
  Fire prevention and
    extinction: TH9446.O95
  Industrial electrochemistry:
    TP261.O9
Oxygen cutting
  Welding: TS228.2
Oxygen equipment
  Airplanes: TL697.O8
Oxygen steelmaking: TN747
Oysters
  Cookery: TX754.O98
Ozokerite
  Mineral oils and waxes: TP695
  Mining engineering: TN857
Ozone
  Air pollutants: TD885.5.O85
  Chemical technology: TP245.O9
  Ventilation of buildings:
    TH7657
Ozone-depleting substances
  Air pollutants: TD887.O95
Ozone treatment
  Water purification: TD461
Ozotype
  Photography: TR433

P

Pacific Northwest style
  cookery: TX715.2.P32
Pacific submarine telegraph:
  TK5613
Package goods industry
  Energy conservation:
    TJ163.5.P33
  Environmental effects:
    TD195.P26
Packaging
  Food processing and
    manufacture: TP374+
  Manufactures: TS195+
Packaging waste
  Waste disposal: TD797.9+
Packed towers
  Chemical technology: TP159.P3
Packet switching: TK5105.3+
Packet transmission
  Radio: TK6562.P32
Packing
  Machinery: TJ246
  Plastics: TP1145
  Steam engines: TJ529
Packing for shipment: TS198.5+
Packinghouses
  Air conditioning: TH7688.P3
  Building construction: TH4534
  Equipment: TS1973
  Heating and ventilation:
    TH7392.P33
  Waste control: TD899.M4
PACSAT (Artificial satellite):
  TK5104.2.P33
Padlocks
  Locksmithing: TS531.5
Page turners industry:
  TS2301.P2
PageMill
  Web authoring software:
    TK5105.8885.A36
Pagodas
  Building construction: TH4224
Pail systems
  Sewage disposal: TD780
Paint analysis: TP936.5
Paint grinding machines:
  TP937.5

Paint industry
  Environmental effects:
    TD195.P35
  Waste control: TD899.P25
Paint machinery: TP937.5
Paint mixing machines: TP937.5
Paint removers
  Chemical technology: TP937.8
Paint shops
  Fire prevention and
    extinction: TH9445.P3
  Handicrafts: TT305.3
Paint testing: TP936.5
Painters' materials: TT324
Painting
  Buildings: TT320 +
  Decoys: TT199.75
  Handicrafts: TT300 +
  Metal finishing: TS698
  Metal finishing arts: TT382.4
  Motor vehicles: TL255.2
Painting, Industrial
  Handicrafts: TT300 +
Paintings
  Photography of art: TR658
Paintmixing
  Handicrafts: TT310
Paints
  Chemical technology: TP934 +
  Space vehicles: TL954.P35
Palapa project
  Artificial satellites:
    TK5104.2.P35
Palladium
  Chemical technology: TP245.P2
  Metallography: TN693.P3
  Metallurgy: TN799.P34
Pallets
  Packaging: TS198.6.P3
Palm frond weaving
  Decorative crafts: TT877.5
Palm oil
  Chemical technology: TP684.P3
Palm products industry:
  TS2301.P24
Palygorskite
  Mining engineering: TN948.P25
Panama affair: TC780
Panama Canal
  Construction and maintenance:
    TC774 +
  Hydraulic engineering: TC774 +

Panama Exposition: TC781 +
Pancakes
  Cookery: TX770.P34
Panel type electric radiant
  heating
  Building construction: TH7434.7
Paneling
  Wooden construction:
    TA666.5.P35
Panels
  Radio: TK6565.P3
  Reinforced concrete
    construction: TA683.5.P35
  Wooden construction:
    TA666.5.P35
Panoramic receivers
  Radio apparatus: TK6564.P35
Panoramic views
  Artistic photography: TR661
Pantograph
  Mechanical engineering: TJ181.9
Pantry plumbing
  Building construction: TH6507 +
Papaya
  Cookery: TX813.P3
Paper
  Insulating material: TK3441.P25
  Packaging materials: TS198.3.P3
Paper airplanes
  Aeronautical models: TL778
Paper-bag cookery: TX833
Paper boxes
  Manufactures: TS1200.A1 +
Paper characteristics
  Paper manufacture: TS1121
Paper coatings: TS1118.F5
Paper-cutting machines:
  TS1118.C8
Paper dolls
  Handicrafts: TT175 +
Paper finishing: TS1118.F5
Paper flowers
  Decorative crafts: TT892
Paper handling
  Papermills: TS1116.6
Paper industry
  Electric power: TK4035.P3
  Noise control: TD893.6.P35
  Waste control: TD899.P3
  Water pollution: TD428.P35
Paper manufacture: TS1080 +
  Chemistry: TS1120

Paper mills
  Air conditioning: TH7688.F27
  Air pollution: TD888.P8
  Building construction: TH4536
  Energy conservation:
    TJ163.5.P37
  Environmental effects:
    TD195.P37
  Paper manufacture: TS1116+
Paper properties
  Paper manufacture: TS1121
Paper recycling
  Paper manufacture: TS1120.5
Paper ribbon work
  Textile arts: TT850.5
Paper sizing: TS1118.S5
Paper toys
  Handicrafts: TT174.5.P3
Paper types
  Paper manufacture: TS1124+
Paper waste
  Waste disposal: TD805
Paperboard: TS1135+
  Housing material: TH4818.P3
  Packaging materials: TS198.3.P3
Paperboard, Corrugated: TS1138
Paperhanging
  Building decoration: TH8441
  Wall decoration: TH8423+
Papers
  Sensitive surfaces
    Photography: TR285
Papers, Special
  Paper manufacture: TS1124+
Paperwork
  Decorative crafts: TT870+
Papier mâché: TS1155
  Building construction: TH1550
Papier-mâché craft
  Decorative crafts: TT871
Papiers collés
  Crafts: TT910
Papyrus: TS1125
Parachutes: TL750+
Parachutes to carry airplanes:
  TL758
Paraffin
  Mineral oils and waxes: TP693
Paraffin, Natural
  Mining engineering: TN857
Paraffins
  Petroleum products: TP692.4.P3

Parakites: TL759.6.P3
Parallel circuit
  Electrical engineering:
    TK454.15.P37
Parallel driving
  Alternating-current machinery:
    TK2715
Parallel kinematic machines
  Manufactures: TS155.67
Parametric amplifiers:
  TK7871.24
Parametrons
  Computer engineering: TK7895.P3
Parasols
  Textile industries: TS1865
Parchment: TS1165
Park bridges: TG430
Park buildings
  Building construction: TH4711
Parking facilities
  Motor vehicles: TL175
Parking garages: TL175
Parking lots: TL175
Parks
  Sanitary engineering: TD931
Parlor cars
  Railway equipment: TF457
Parquetry
  Floors and flooring: TH2529.W6
Particle accelerators
  Nuclear engineering: TK9340
Particle board
  Wood products: TS875
Particle counting
  Water quality: TD368
Particle size determination
  Engineering materials: TA418.8
Particle technology
  Chemical engineering: TP156.P3
Particles
  Engineering materials:
    TA418.78+
  Water pollutants: TD427.P27
Particulate matter
  Air pollutants: TD884.5
Partitions
  Building design and
    construction: TH2541+
Parts catalogs
  Motor vehicles: TL159+
Party decorations
  Decorative crafts: TT900.P3

Passementerie
  Silk manufactures: TS1687
Passenger accommodations
  Airports: TL725.3.P3
Passenger cars
  Railway equipment: TF455+
Passenger conveyors: TJ1400
Passenger depots
  Railway structures: TF300+
Passenger planes: TL685.4+
Passenger tickets
  Railway operation: TF654
Passenger traffic
  Railway operation: TF653
Passenger trains: TF570+
Passivity-based control
  Mechanical engineering: TJ221
Passover
  Cookery: TX739.2.P37
Pasta
  Cookery: TX809.M17
  Food processing and
    manufacture: TP435.M3
Pasta products
  Cereals: TX394.5
Pasteboard: TS1135+
Pastes
  Organic chemical industries:
    TP970
Pastry
  Cookery: TX773
Patchwork
  Handicrafts: TT835
Patent leather
  Manufactures: TS970
Patent solicitors, Publications
  of: T339
Patents
  Aeronautical engineering: TL513
  Aeronautics: TL513
  Astronautics: TL788.35
  Biotechnology: TP248.175
  Building laws: TH257
  Chemicals: TP210
  Cycles: TL437
  Electrical engineering: TK257
  Electronics: TK7850.A1+
  Glass and glassmaking: TP858
  Iron and steel
    Metal manufactures: TS307
  Mechanical engineering: TJ758
  Metallurgy: TN708

Patents
  Motor vehicles: TL280
  Motorcycles: TL437
  Nuclear engineering: TK9152.5
  Ocean engineering: TC1660
  Pet food industry: TS2287
  Petroleum refining: TP690.5
  Plastics: TP1114
  Radio: TK6559
Patios
  Building construction: TH4970
Pattern recognition systems
  Electronics: TK7882.P3
Pattern recognition, Optical
  Optical data processing: TA1650
Patternmaking
  Dressmaking: TT520
  Men's tailoring: TT590
  Metal manufactures: TS240
Patterns
  Children's clothing: TT640
  Decorative needlework: TT753+
Pavements
  Airports: TL725.3.P35
Pavements and paved roads
  Highway engineering: TE250+
Pavilions
  Exhibitions: T396.5
PCMCIA cards
  Computer engineering:
    TK7895.P38
Peach palm
  Cookery: TX813.P38
Peaches
  Cookery: TX813.P4
  Food processing and
    manufacture: TP441.P4
  Food values: TX558.P3
Peanut butter: TP438.P4
  Cookery: TX814.5.P38
Peanut oil
  Chemical technology: TP684.P4
Peanuts: TP438.P4
  Cookery: TX803.P35
Pearls
  Jewelry work: TS755.P3+
Pears
  Cookery: TX813.P43

Peas
  Cookery: TX803.P4
  Food processing and
    manufacture: TP444.P4
  Food values: TX558.P35
Peat
  Air pollutants: TD887.P34
  Engineering materials: TA455.P4
  Fire prevention and
    extinction: TH9446.P38
  Fuel: TP340
  Mining: TN837+
  Prospecting: TN271.P27
Peat industry
  Electric power: TK4035.P33
Peat machinery: TN841
Peat mining
  Environmental effects:
    TD195.P38
Peat mull: TN842
Peat straw: TN842
Pecans
  Cookery: TX814.2.P4
  Food processing and
    manufacture: TP439.5.P42
Pectic substances
  Food constituent: TX553.P4
Pectin
  Chemical technology: TP248.P4
Pedal cars: TL483
Pedestrian areas
  Electric lighting: TK4399.P44
Pedestrian facilities
  Pavements: TE279.5+
Pegmatites
  Mining engineering: TN948.P38
  Prospecting: TN271.P3
Pelletizing
  Chemical engineering: TP156.P4
Pelton water wheels: TJ866
Pencils
  Stationery: TS1268
Penetrant inspections
  Testing of materials: TA417.55
Penetration mechanics: TA354.5
Pennsylvania-Dutch cookbooks:
  TX721
Pens
  Stationery: TS1262+
Penstocks
  Hydraulic powerplants: TJ849

Pentachlorophenol
  Industrial waste disposal:
    TD898.8.P45
Pentodes: TK7871.79.P4
Pentosan
  Chemical technology: TP248.P44
Pepper
  Cookery: TX819.P3
Peppermint
  In plumbing testing: TH6617
Peppermint oil
  Organic chemical industries:
    TP959.P4
Peppers
  Cookery: TX803.P46
Perceptrons
  Control engineering: TJ223.P4
Perchloric acid: TP217.P4
Perforating machinery
  Machine shops: TJ1250+
Performance
  Aircraft engines: TL701.6
  Aircraft propellers: TL706.P4
  Airplanes: TL671.4
  Airships: TL660.3
  Pavements and paved roads:
    TE251.5
Perfumes
  Organic chemical technology:
    TP983+
Perilla oil
  Chemical technology: TP684.P47
Perlite
  Engineering materials:
    TA455.P45
  Mining engineering: TN948.P4
Permanent makeup: TT959
Permanent way
  Railway construction: TF240+
Permits
  Building construction: TH11
Peroxides
  Chemical technology: TP248.P46
  Explosives: TP290.P5
Peroxyacetyl nitrate
  Environmental pollutants:
    TD196.P36
Perpetual motion
  Mechanical engineering: TJ181.3
Perry (Cider): TP564.5
Persimmons
  Cookery: TX813.P45

Personal communication service
  systems
  Wireless communication
    systems: TK5103.485
Personal propulsion units:
  TL717.5
Personal rapid transportation:
  TA1207
Personal robotics
  Mechanical engineering:
    TJ211.416
Personnel management
  Hotels, clubs, restaurants,
    etc.: TX911.3.P4
Personnel, Manufacturing:
  TS155.4+
Perspective projection
  Mechanical drawing: T369
PERT
  Production control: TS158.2
Pervaporation
  Biotechnology: TP248.25.P44
Pest control in buildings:
  TH9041
Pesticide residues
  Effect on food: TX571.P4
Pesticides
  Air pollutants: TD887.P45
  Chemical technology: TP248.P47
  Environmental pollutants:
    TD196.P38
  Hazardous substances and their
    disposal: TD1066.P47
  Soil pollutants: TD879.P37
  Water pollutants: TD427.P35
Pesticides industry
  Waste control: TD899.P37
Pestos
  Cookery: TX819.P45
Pests, Household: TX325
Pet food industry: TS2284+
Petrochemical industry
  Environmental effects:
    TD195.P39
Petroleum: TN860+
  Environmental pollutants:
    TD196.P4
  Fire prevention and
    extinction: TH9446.P4

Petroleum
  Fuel: TP355
  Prospecting: TN271.P4
  Soil pollutants: TD879.P4
  Water pollutants: TD427.P4
Petroleum chemicals industry
  Air pollution: TD888.P38
Petroleum engineering: TN860+
  Electric power: TK4035.P35
Petroleum gas
  Gas industry: TP761.P4
Petroleum geology: TN870.5+
Petroleum industry
  Environmental effects: TD195.P4
  Waste control: TD899.P4
Petroleum pipelines: TN879.5+
  Fire prevention and
    extinction: TH9445.P38
Petroleum products
  Chemical technology: TP690+
Petroleum refineries
  Air pollution: TD888.P4
  Energy conservation:
    TJ163.5.P47
  Fire prevention and
    extinction: TH9445.P4
  Noise control: TD893.6.P47
  Water pollution: TD428.P47
Petroleum refining
  Chemical technology: TP690+
Petroleum supplies
  Petroleum engineering: TN871.5
Petroleum waste
  Waste disposal: TD800
Pewter craft: TT266.3
Phantom circuits
  Telephone: TK6343
Pharmaceutical industry
  Water pollution: TD428.P54
Phase-locked loops
  Electronics: TK7872.P38
Phase meters
  Electrical engineering: TK381
Phase partition
  Biotechnology: TP248.25.P53
Phase shifters
  Electronics: TK7872.P39
Pheasant
  Cookery: TX750.5.P45
Phenol products
  Chemical technology: TP248.P5

Phenolic resins
  Plastics: TP1180.P39
Phenolite
  Plastics: TP1180.P4
Phenols
  Food constituents: TP453.P45
  Sewage treatment: TD758.5.P53
  Water pollutants: TD427.P53
Philosophy of machinery: TJ14
Phonograph industry: TS2301.P3
Phosphate coating
  Metal finishing: TS696
Phosphate industry
  Waste control: TD899.P45
Phosphate mines and mining
  Environmental effects:
    TD195.P46
Phosphates
  Environmental pollutants:
    TD196.P45
  Mining engineering: TN913+
  Ore dressing and milling:
    TN538.P43
  Prospecting: TN271.P45
  Water pollutants: TD427.P56
Phosphatic fertilizer industry
  Environmental effects:
    TD195.P47
Phosphatides
  Chemical technology: TP248.P55
Phosphogypsum
  Environmental pollutants:
    TD196.P46
Phosphoric acid: TP217.P5
Phosphoric acid industry
  Waste control: TD899.P46
Phosphors
  Electrical engineering:
    TK454.4.P5
  Electronics: TK7871.15.P4
Phosphorus
  Chemical technology: TP245.P5
  Food constituent: TX553.P45
  Industrial electrochemistry:
    TP261.P48
  Sewage treatment: TD758.5.P56
  Water pollutants: TD427.P56
Phosphorus compounds
  Water pollutants: TD427.P56
Photo CDs: TR502
Photo-oleographs
  Photographic processing: TR487

Photoaquatint
  Photography: TR445
Photoceramics
  Photographic processing: TR500
Photochemical telegraph
  system: TK5549
Photochronograph
  Cinematography: TR885
Photoconductive cells: TK8330+
Photocopying processes: TR824+
Photodiodes: TK8312
Photoelectric multipliers:
  TK8314
Photoelectronic devices
  Control engineering: TJ223.P5
  Electronics: TK8300+
Photoemissive tubes: TK8308+
Photoenamels
  Photographic processing: TR500
Photoengraving
  Photography: TR970
Photogalvanography
  Photography: TR990
Photoglyptie
  Photography: TR995
Photogrammetry
  Applied photography: TR693+
Photograms
  Artistic photography: TR688
Photographers
  Photographic portraits:
    TR681.P56
Photographers' reference
  handbooks: TR150
Photographic accessories and
  apparatus: TR570
Photographic amusements: TR148
Photographic chemicals: TR210+
Photographic chemistry: TR210+
  Photography: TR200+
Photographic criticism: TR187
Photographic equipment
  Collectors' manuals: TR6.5
Photographic image, Properties
  of: TR222
Photographic industry
  Waste control: TD899.P48
Photographic interpretation
  Photography: TR810
Photographic optics: TR220
Photographic patterns: TR682
Photographic physics: TR215+

Photographic processes: TR200+
Photographic processing: TR287+
Photographic reproduction: TR824+
Photographic triangulation: TA593.8+
Photographic waste, Recovery of: TR225
Photographs
Collectors' manuals: TR6.5
Photographs on metal, glass, cloth, etc.
Photographic processing: TR495
Photography: TR1+
Surveying: TA592+
Photography as a profession: TR154
Photography in criminology: TR822
Photography in education: TR816
Photography in engineering: TR702
Photography in law: TR822
Photography of airplanes: TR714
Photography of art: TR657+
Photography of colored objects
Photographic processes: TR453
Photography of handicraft: TR658.5
Photography of historic documents: TR825
Photography of manuscripts: TR825
Photography of railroads: TR715
Photography of the grotesque: TR686
Photography studios: TR550+
Photogravure
Photography: TR980
Photojournalism
Applied photography: TR820
Photolithography
Photography: TR940+
Photomechanical processes
Photography: TR925+
Photomontage
Photography: TR685
Photomultipliers: TK8314
Photon propulsion systems: TL783.57
Photon rockets: TL783.57
Photonics: TA1501+

Photoplasticity: TA418.15
Photopotentiometer: TK8360.P5
Photoresistors: TK8331
Phototelegraphy: TK6600
Phototransistors: TK8332
Phototubes: TK8308+
Photovoltaic cells: TK8322
Photovoltaic power generation
Solar energy: TK1087
Photovoltaic power systems
Solar energy: TK1087
Photoxylography
Photography: TR960
Photozincography
Photography: TR955
Phthalate esters
Environmental pollutants: TD196.P47
Phthalic acid
Chemical technology: TP248.P6
Phthalocyanins
Chemical technology: TP248.P62
Physical education facilities
Electric lighting: TK4399.P5
Physical metallurgy: TN689+
Physical properties
Engineering materials: TA418.5+
Physical requirements
Air pilots: TL555
Physical tests
Soils surveys: TE208+
Physics
Home economics: TX149
Phytoremediation
Pollution control methods: TD192.75
Pickles
Cookery: TX805
Pickling
Food preservation: TP371.44
Metal finishing: TS654
Picnic cooking: TX823
Picric acid
Chemical technology: TP248.P65
Picture telegraphy: TK6600
Picture transmission systems
Electrical engineering: TK5105.2
Picture tubes
Television: TK6655.P5
PID controllers
Control engineering: TJ223.P55

Piers
  Building design and
    construction: TH2140
  Fire prevention and
    extinction: TH9445.P5
  Harbor engineering: TC357
Pies
  Cookery: TX773
Piezoelectric devices
  Electronics: TK7872.P54
Pig iron
  Metallurgy: TN710+
Pigeons
  Food values: TX556.P6
Piggyback trailers
  Motor vehicles: TL297.6
Piggyback trains: TF582
Pigment processes
  Photography: TR440
Pigments
  Chemical technology: TP934+
  Mining engineering: TN948.P5
Pike
  Cookery: TX748.P54
Pile-driving: TA780+
Piles: TA780+
Pillaring
  Mining: TN289.8
Pillow blocks
  Machinery: TJ1065
Pillowcases
  Handicrafts: TT408
  Home furnishings: TX315
Pillows
  Handicrafts: TT410
Pilot balloons: TL630
Pilot ejection seats
  Airplanes: TL697.P5
Pilot lights
  Building gas supply: TH6887
Piloting
  Space vehicles: TL1090+
Pin proportioning
  Bridge design: TG301
Piña cloth
  Textile fiber: TS1544.P55
Pincushions
  Decorative crafts: TT899.3
Pine
  Woodpulp industry: TS1176.4.P5
Pine cone craft
  Decorative crafts: TT874.5

Pine needle crafts
  Decorative crafts: TT874
Pine oil
  Organic chemical industries:
    TP959.P5
Pineapple
  Food processing and
    manufacture: TP441.P54
Pineapples
  Cookery: TX813.P5
Pinfire
  Firearms: TS538.4
Pinhole photography: TR268
Pins
  Fastenings: TJ1328
Pins industry
  Manufactures: TS2301.P5
Pioneer project: TL789.8.U6P56
Pipe
  Cement manufacture: TP885.P5
  Chemical technology: TP159.P5
Pipe and fittings
  Steam powerplants: TJ415+
Pipe bending
  Building construction: TH6294
Pipe dampers
  Warm-air heating: TH7627
Pipe flanges
  Steam powerplants: TJ421
Pipe industry
  Noise control: TD893.6.P55
Pipefitting
  Building construction: TH6703+
  Building gas supply: TH6840
  Plumbing work: TH6293+
Pipefitting and plumbing
  Building construction: TH6101+
Pipefitting catalogs: TH6729
Pipeline radio: TK6570.P5
Pipelines
  Electric power: TK4035.P55
  Environmental effects: TD195.P5
  Hydraulic machinery: TJ930+
  Hydraulic powerplants: TJ849
  Structural engineering:
    TA660.P55
Pipes
  Freezing and thawing: TH6685
  Gas industry: TP757
  Hydrodynamics: TC174
  Metal manufactures: TS280+
  Railway structures: TF290

Pipes of cement, concrete, and clay: TA447
Pipes, Metal
  Engineering and construction: TA492.P6
Pipes, Plastic: TP1185.P5
  Engineering materials: TA448
Pipes, Tobacco
  Manufactures: TS2270
Piping
  Hot water heating: TH7543
  Hydronic systems: TH7478
  Steam heating: TH7593
  Warm-air heating: TH7625
Piping installation
  Building gas supply: TH6840
  Pipefitting: TH6703+
Pisé building construction: TH1421
Pistols
  Manufactures: TS537
Piston blowers
  Pneumatic machinery: TJ963
Piston pumps
  Hydraulic machinery: TJ915
Piston rings
  Steam engines: TJ533
Piston valve
  Steam engines: TJ546
Pistons
  Aircraft engines: TL702.P5
  Diesel engines: TJ798.5
  Gas engines: TJ774
  Gasoline automobiles: TL214.P57
  Internal combustion engines: TJ788
  Locomotives: TJ659
  Steam engines: TJ533
Pita bread
  Cookery: TX770.P56
Pitch
  Aerodynamics: TL574.M6
Pitch, Adjustable
  Aircraft propellers: TL707.P5
Pitch, Controllable
  Aircraft propellers: TL707.P5
Pivot bearings
  Machinery: TJ1067
Pizza
  Cookery: TX770.P58
Placer mining: TN421

Plain bearings
  Machinery: TJ1063
Plan reading
  Building construction: TH431
Plane table
  Surveying instruments: TA571
Planers
  Machine shops: TJ1206
Planes
  Machine shops: TJ1201.P55
Planetables
  Aeronautical research: TL567.P6
Planetary quarantine
  Space vehicles: TL943
Planimeter
  Surveying: TA614
Planing machines
  Machine shops: TJ1205+
Planing-mill products
  Manufactures: TS878
Planing mills
  Wood products: TS850
Plank roads
  Unpaved roads: TE245
Planning for machinery
  Manufacturing engineering: TS181+
Plans
  Photographic reproduction processes: TR920+
Plant biotechnology: TP248.27.P55
Plant design
  Manufacturing engineering: TS177
Plant engineering
  Production management: TS184+
Plant fibers
  Engineering materials: TA455.P49
Plant grounds
  Plant engineering: TS190+
Plant housekeeping
  Plant engineering: TS193
Plant layout
  Manufacturing engineering: TS178+
Plant lipids
  Biotechnology: TP248.65.P53
Plant maintenance
  Plant engineering: TS192

Plant performance monitoring
Plant engineering: TS194
Plant service facilities
Plant engineering: TS189+
Plant size
Manufacturing engineering:
TS177.3
Plant supervisors
Manufacturing personnel:
TS155.4
Plant utilities
Plant engineering: TS187
Planters
Agricultural machinery: TJ1483
Plants
Nature photography: TR724+
Plasma
Chemical engineering: TP156.P5
Plasma devices
Plasma engineering: TA2030
Plasma dynamics, Applied:
TA2001+
Plasma-enchanced chemical vapor
deposition
Metal finishing: TS695.15
Plasma engineering: TA2001+
Plasma jets
Chemical technology: TP159.P57
Metallurgical equipment: TN678
Plasma propulsion systems:
TL783.6
Plasma rockets: TL783.6
Plasma sheath effects
Astrionics: TL3028
Plaster
Decorative furnishings: TH8135+
Housing material: TH4818.P53
Plaster craft: TT295
Plaster products
Chemical technology: TP888
Plasterboard
Decorative furnishings: TH8139
Plastering
Building construction: TH8120+
Plastic analysis
Structural analysis: TA652
Plastic bearings
Mechanical engineering:
TJ1073.P6
Plastic construction
Structural engineering: TA668
Plastic craft: TT297+

Plastic design
Structural engineering: TA658.6
Plastic flooring: TH2529.P5
Plastic foam
Handicrafts: TT297+
Plastic furniture
Handicrafts: TT297.5
Plastic technology: TP1185.F8
Plastic lenses: TS517.5.P5
Plastic materials
Electronics: TK7871.15.P5
Plastic pipes: TP1185.P5
Engineering materials: TA448
Plumbing: TH6330
Plastic plants
Dust removal: TH7697.P5
Plastic properties and tests:
TA418.14+
Plastic roofing
Building construction: TH2447
Plastic scrap
Water pollutants: TD427.P62
Plastic tubes
Plumbing: TH6330
Plastic waste
Waste disposal: TD798
Plasticizers
Chemical technology: TP247.7
Plastics
Aeronautics: TL699.P6
Chemical technology: TP1101+
Effect on food: TX571.P63
Electrical engineering:
TK454.4.P55
Engineering materials:
TA455.P5+
Environmental pollutants:
TD196.P5
Fire prevention and
extinction: TH9446.P55
Fire-testing: TH9446.5.P45
Insulating material: TK3441.P55
Machine tools: TJ1194
Motor vehicle construction
materials: TL240.5.P42
Plumbing: TH6325+
Plastics (non-foil)
Packaging materials: TS198.3.P5
Plastics industry
Environmental effects:
TD195.P52
Waste control: TD899.P55

Plastics plants
  Chemical technology: TP1135
  Fire prevention and
    extinction: TH9445.P55
Plate-bonds
  Window and door openings:
    TH2261+
Plate girder bridges: TG360
Plate girders
  Structural engineering:
    TA660.P59
Plate glass
  Glassmaking: TP860
Plate towers
  Chemical technology: TP159.P6
Plates
  Sensitive surfaces
    Photography: TR281
  Structural engineering:
    TA660.P6
Plates, Folded
  Structural engineering:
    TA660.P63
Plates, Metal
  Engineering and construction:
    TA492.P7
Plates, Twisted
  Structural engineering:
    TA660.P65
Plating baths
  Electroplating: TS672
Platinum
  Assaying: TN580.P7
  Chemical technology: TP245.P7
  Electroplating: TS692.P55
  Manufactures: TS770
  Metallography: TN693.P55
  Metallurgy: TN799.P7
  Ore deposits and mining:
    TN490.P7
  Ore dressing and milling:
    TN538.P53
  Prospecting: TN271.P56
Platinum group
  Electroplating: TS692.P56
  Ore deposits and mining:
    TN490.P7
Platinum salts
  Photographic processes: TR420
Playground equipment
  Handicrafts: TT176

Playhouses, Children's
  Building construction: TH4967
Pleasures of the table
  Nutrition: TX631+
Plexiglas
  Plastics: TP1180.P5
Pliers
  Machine shops: TJ1201.T64
Plotting
  Railroad surveying: TF214
  Surveying: TA611
Plows
  Agricultural machinery: TJ1482
Plumbers' tools
  Building construction: TH6299
Plumbing and pipefitting
  Building construction: TH6101+
Plumbing fitting supplies
  Building construction: TH6249+
Plumbing fixtures supplies
  Building construction: TH6249+
Plumbing work
  Building construction: TH6291+
Plums
  Cookery: TX813.P55
  Food processing and
    manufacture: TP441.P55
Plush
  Silk manufactures: TS1680
Plutonium
  Metallurgy: TN799.P74
  Radioactive waste disposal:
    TD898.7.P48
  Water pollutants: TD427.P63
Plutonium as fuel: TK9365
Plywood
  Aeronautics: TL699.W7
  Wood products: TS870
Plywood working
  Woodworking: TT191
Pneumatic control systems
  Mechanical engineering: TJ219
Pneumatic equipment
  Aeronautics: TL697.P6
  Airports: TL725.3.P55
Pneumatic machinery
  Mechanical engineering: TJ950+
Pneumatic presses
  Lifting machinery: TJ1465
Pneumatic tools: TJ1005+
Pneumatic tubes and carriers:
  TJ1015

Pointing
  Masonry construction: TH5371
Pointing systems
  Space vehicles: TL3270
Points (English)
  Railway construction: TF266+
Polarized-light photography:
  TR757
Polders
  Hydraulic engineering: TC343+
Pole supports
  Electric power: TK3243
Poles
  Electric power: TK3242
  Reinforced concrete
    construction: TA683.5.P65
Police radio: TK6570.P6
Polishes
  Abrading machinery: TJ1296+
  Chemical technology: TP940
Polishing
  Optical instruments: TS517
Political aspects
  Hazardous substances and their
    disposal: TD1050.P64
Pollen
  Air pollutants: TD887.P65
  Food values: TX560.P6
Pollock
  Cookery: TX748.P64
Pollution
  Groundwater: TD426+
Pollution control devices
  Gasoline automobiles: TL214.P6
Pollution control methods
  Environmental pollution:
    TD191.5+
Pollution of streams: TD425
Pollution, Air
  Control: TD881+
Pollution, Environmental:
  TD172+
Pollution, Heat
  Water pollutants: TD427.H4
Pollution, Radioactive
  Environmental pollutants:
    TD196.R3
Pollution, Thermal
  Water pollutants: TD427.H4
Pollution, Water: TD419+
Polyacetylenes
  Plastics: TP1180.P53

Polyacrylamides
  Plastics: TP1180.P54
Polyamide textile fibers:
  TS1548.7.P57
Polyamides
  Plastics: TP1180.P55
Polybishloromethyloxetane
  Plastics: TP1180.P555
Polybutenes
  Plastics: TP1180.P56
Polycarbonates
  Plastics: TP1180.P57
Polychlorinated biphenyls
  Effect on food: TX572.P65
  Environmental pollutants:
    TD196.P65
  Hazardous substances and their
    disposal: TD1066.P64
  Industrial waste disposal:
    TD898.8.P64
  Sewage treatment: TD758.5.P64
  Soil pollutants: TD879.P64
  Water pollutants: TD427.P65
Polycyclic aromatic
  hydrocarbons
  Soil pollutants: TD879.P66
  Water pollutants: TD427.H93
Polycyclic systems
  Electrical engineering: TK3159
Polyelectrolytes
  Water pollutants: TD427.P67
Polyester textile fibers:
  TS1548.7.P58
Polyesters
  Plastics: TP1180.P6
Polyethylene
  Plastics: TP1180.P65
Polyethylene glycol
  Biotechnology: TP248.65.P58
  Plastics: TP1180.P653
Polyethylenimine
  Plastics: TP1180.P655
Polyhedra
  Structural engineering:
    TA660.P73
Polyimides
  Plastics: TP1180.P66
Polymer conductors
  Electric power: TK3311.P6
Polymerization
  Chemical engineering: TP156.P6

Polymers
  Biotechnology: TP248.65.P62
  Cementing substance: TA443.P58
  Chemical technology: TP1080+
  Electronics: TK7871.15.P6
  Engineering materials:
    TA455.P58
  Fire prevention and
    extinction: TH9446.P65
  Fire-testing: TH9446.5.P65
  Insulating material: TK3441.P58
  Manufacture: TP1080+
Polymethines
  Textile dyes: TP918.P65
Polymethylbenzenes
  Chemical technology: TP248.P67
Polyolefins
  Plastics: TP1180.P67
Polyphase alternating-current
  machinery: TK2731
Polyphase-current machinery
  Alternating-current machinery:
    TK2745
Polyphase current systems
  Electrical engineering: TK3155+
Polyphase currents
  Electrical engineering: TK1161+
Polyphase motors
  Alternating-current motors:
    TK2785
Polypropylene
  Plastics: TP1180.P68
Polypropylene textile fibers:
  TS1548.7.P6
Polysaccharides
  Biotechnology: TP248.65.P64
  Chemical technology: TP248.P68
  Food constituent: TX553.P65
  Food constituents: TP453.P64
  Gums and resins: TP979.5.P6
Polysulphides
  Plastics: TP1180.P685
Polytetrafluorethylene
  Plastics: TP1180.P7
Polythylene glycols
  Environmental pollutants:
    TD196.P67
Polyurethanes
  Plastics: TP1180.P8
  Textile fibers: TS1548.7.P63
Polyvinyl plastics: TP1180.V48

Ponds
  Water supply source: TD392
Pontoon bridges
  Bridge engineering: TG450
Poor
  Nutrition: TX361.P66
  Photographic portraits:
    TR681.P6
Popcorn
  Cookery: TX814.5.P66
Porcelain
  Ceramic technology: TP822
Porch roofs
  Building construction: TH2425
Pork
  Cookery: TX749.5.P67
  Food values: TX556.P8
Porosity and denseness
  Engineering materials: TA418.82
Porous materials
  Engineering materials:
    TA418.9.P6
Porridge
  Cookery: TX809.P67
Portable buildings
  Building construction: TH1098
Portable engines: TJ710
Portable radios: TK6564.P6
Porter
  Brewing and malting: TP578
Portland cement
  Cement manufacture: TP883
Portland cement concrete:
  TA439+
Portrait photography: TR575+
Portraits
  Artistic photography: TR680+
Positives
  Photographic processing: TR320+,
    TR540+
Post-tensioned prestressed
  concrete construction:
    TA683.94
Posters
  Industrial safety: T55.3.P67
Potash-bearing rocks and plants
  Mining engineering: TN919
Potassium
  Chemical technology: TP245.P8
  Ore dressing and milling:
    TN538.P6
  Prospecting: TN271.P6

Potassium salts
  Mining engineering: TN919
Potato chip industry
  Waste control: TD899.P6
Potato peeling machines
  Cookery: TX657.P6
Potato printing
  Decorative crafts: TT868
Potatoes
  Cookery: TX803.P8
  Food processing and
    manufacture: TP444.P6
  Food values: TX558.P8
  Nutrition: TX401.2.P67
Potential meters and
    measurements
  Electrical engineering: TK321
Potentiometer
  Electronics: TK7872.P6
Potpourris (Scented floral
    mixtures)
  Decorative crafts: TT899.4
Pottery
  Chemical technology: TP807+
  Chemistry of: TP810
Pottery craft
  Decorative crafts: TT919+
Pottery machinery: TP817
Potting compounds
  Aeronautics: TL699.P7
  Electronics: TK7871.15.P65
Poultry
  Cookery: TX750+
  Food values: TX556.P9
  Nutrition: TX375
Poultry houses
  Building construction: TH4930
Poultry industry
  Waste control: TD899.P65
Poultry processing
  Manufactures: TS1968
Powder magazines
  Explosives: TP295
Powder metallurgy
  Metal manufactures: TS245
  Metallurgy: TN695+
Powders
  Plastics: TP1183.P68
Power
  Mechanical engineering:
    TJ163.6+
Power amplifiers: TK7871.58.P6

Power and power transmission
  Machinery exclusive of prime
    movers: TJ1045+
Power electronics: TK7881.15
Power factor meters: TK351
Power hammers
  Machine shops: TJ1305+
Power meters and measurements
  Electrical engineering: TK351
Power plants
  Air pollution: TD888.P67
  Airports: TL725.3.P67
  Building construction: TH4581+
  Electric lighting: TK4399.P6
  Electrical engineering: TK1191+
  Energy conservation:
    TJ163.5.P68
  Noise control: TD893.6.P68
  Ventilation: TH7684.P7
  Water pollution: TD428.P67
Power plants utilizing heat
  energy: TK1221+
Power plants utilizing other
  power: TK1560
Power plants utilizing
  waterpower: TK1421+
Power plants utilizing wind:
  TK1541
Power plants, Atomic
  Water pollution: TD428.A86
Power plants, Coal-fired
  Water pollution: TD428.C58
Power plants, Hydraulic: TJ845+
Power plants, Nuclear: TK1341+
Power plants, Pumped storage:
  TK1083
Power plants, Solar: TK1545
Power production
  Telegraph: TK5371
  Telephone: TK6271+
Power production and
  distribution
  Electric railways: TF863
Power resources
  Mechanical engineering:
    TJ163.13+
Power resources development
  Environmental effects:
    TD195.E49
Power spectra
  Engineering mathematics: TA348

Power supply
  Computer engineering:
    TK7895.P68
  Electronic circuits: TK7868.P6
  High speed ground
    transportation: TF1480
Power tools
  Handicrafts: TT153.5
Power trains
  Motor vehicles: TL260+
Power transmission machinery
  Machinery exclusive of prime
    movers: TJ1051
Power transmission systems
  Electric railways: TF880+
PPP
  Computer network protocols:
    TK5105.582
Practical mining operations:
  TN275+
Praseodymium
  Chemical technology: TP245.P9
Precast concrete
  Housing material: TH4818.P7
  Roads: TE278.8
Precast concrete construction:
  TH1498
Precast concrete industry
  Noise control: TD893.6.P74
Precast construction
  Reinforced concrete
    construction: TA683.7
Precious metals
  Assaying: TN580.P74
  Manufactures: TS720+
  Metallography: TN693.P7
  Metallurgy: TN759+
  Ore deposits and mining: TN410+
Precious stones
  Jewelry manufacture: TS747+
  Machine tools: TJ1193
Precipitation
  Chemical engineering: TP156.P7
Precipitation, Chemical
  Sewage purification: TD751
Precise leveling
  Surveying: TA607
Precooked meat
  Food values: TX556.M43
Predetermined motion time
  systems
  Industrial engineering: T60.5+

Predictive control
  Mechanical engineering: TJ217.6
Prefabricated bridges: TG418
Prefabricated buildings
  Building construction: TH1098
Prefabricated construction:
  TH4819.P7
Preliminary processes
  Cotton manufactures: TS1577
  Spinning
    Textile industries: TS1480+
Preliminary surveying: TF213
Preparation of coal: TN816.A1+
Prepared cereals: TX395
Prepared foods
  Nutrition: TX389
Prepayment meters
  Electrical engineering: TK396
Preservation
  Motion picture film: TR886.3
Preservation of foods in the
  home: TX599+
Preservation of land from the
  sea: TC343+
Preservation of wood: TA422+
Preservation techniques
  Food processing: TP371.2+
Preservatives
  Wine and winemaking: TP548.5.P7
Press-tool work
  Metal manufactures: TS253
Pressed brick
  Chemical technology: TP831
Pressed-earth building
  construction: TH1421
Presses
  Lifting machinery: TJ1450+
Pressing
  Men's clothing: TT583
  Paper manufacture: TS1118.P74
Pressing machinery
  Mechanical engineering: TJ1425+
Pressure
  Aerodynamics: TL574.P7
Pressure airships: TL656+
Pressure cooker recipes
  Cookery: TX840.P7
Pressure distribution
  Aerodynamics: TL574.P7
Pressure gages
  Steam boilers: TJ370+

Pressure-impregnation
  Preservation of wood: TA424.4
Pressure instruments
  Aeronautical instruments:
    TL589.2.P7
Pressure packaging: TS198.P7
Pressure processes
  Chemical engineering: TP156.P75
Pressure regulators
  Furnaces: TJ357
Pressure suits
  Aeronautics: TL697.P7
Pressure tunneling
  Railway construction: TF232
Pressure vessels
  Metal manufactures: TS283
  Structural engineering:
    TA660.T34
Pressure welding: TS228.9
Pressurization
  Airplanes: TL681.P7
Pressurized water reactors
  Nuclear engineering: TK9203.P7
Prestressed concrete
  Roads: TE278.6
Prestressed concrete
  construction: TA683.9+
Prestressed construction
  Structural engineering: TA665
Pretreatment of saline waters
  Saline water conversion:
    TD479.8
Pretzels
  Cookery: TX770.P73
Prevention of accidents
  Aeronautics: TL553.5
Pricelists
  Children's clothing: TT645
  Men's clothing: TT620+
  Millinery: TT665
Prices
  Building construction: TH11
  Heating of buildings: TH7337
  Hotels, clubs, restaurants,
    etc.: TX911.3.P7
  Pipefittings: TH6723
Primary cells
  Electrical engineering: TK2921
Primates
  Nature photography: TR729.P74
Prime movers
  Machinery: TJ250+

Primitive construction: TH16
Primitive pumps
  Hydraulic machinery: TJ901
Principles of mechanism
  Mechanical engineering: TJ175
Printed circuits
  Electronic circuits: TK7868.P7
Printed circuits industry
  Air pollution: TD888.P73
  Waste control: TD899.P69
Printers' ink
  Chemical technology: TP949+
Printing
  Color photography: TR545
  Metal finishing: TS719
  Packaging: TS196.7
  Telegraph: TK5543
Printing industry
  Environmental effects: TD195.P7
  Waste control: TD899.P7
Printing machinery
  Electric driving: TK4059.P74
Printing of positives
  Photographic processing: TR330+
Printing plants
  Air conditioning: TH7688.P7
  Building construction: TH4536.5
  Noise control: TD893.6.P75
  Ventilation: TH7684.P75
Printing presses
  Electric driving: TK4059.P74
Printout equipment
  Computer engineering: TK7887.7
Prisoners
  Photographic portraits:
    TR681.P69
Prisons
  Heating and ventilation:
    TH7392.P8
Private aircraft
  Airports: TL725.3.P7
Private electric-light plants
  for country houses: TK4395
Private fire departments
  Fire prevention and
    extinction: TH9447
Private flying
  Airplanes: TL721.4
Private planes: TL685.1
Privies
  Building construction: TH4975
  Sewage disposal: TD775

Prizes
  Cookery: TX648
Probabilistic methods
  Engineering mathematics: TA340
Probability of safety
  Structural analysis: TA656.5
Probability theory
  Industrial engineering: T57.3+
Probes
  Electronic instruments:
    TK7878.6
Process control
  Production management: TS156.8
Process engineering
  Production management: TS176+
Process planning
  Manufacturing engineering:
    TS183.3+
Process recorders
  Electrical engineering: TK393
Processing methods
  Wood: TS936
Processing of exposed film
  Cinematography: TR886.2
Producer gas
  Gas industry: TP761.P9
Product design
  Product engineering: TS171+
Product engineering
  Production management: TS170+
Product safety
  Product engineering: TS175
Product testing
  Product engineering: TS175.5
Production capacity
  Industrial engineering: T58.7+
Production control
  Food processing and
    manufacture: TP372.7
  Production management: TS157+
  Sugar processing: TP380
Production lines
  Manufacturing engineering:
    TS178.4+
Production management: TS155+
Production of electric energy:
    TK1001+
  Diesel engine electric plants:
    TK1075
  Direct-current engineering:

Production of electric energy
    TK1111+
  Gas turbine power plants:
    TK1076
  Ocean thermal energy
    conversion: TK1073
  Production from atomic power:
    TK1078
  Production from gas: TK1061
  Production from geothermal
    energy: TK1055
  Production from steam (Coal):
    TK1051
  Production from waterpower:
    TK1081+
Production of electricity
  Chemical action: TK2901+
  Direct energy conversion
    devices: TK2896+
Production planning
  Production management: TS176+
Production standards
  Industrial engineering: T60.3+
  Machine shops: TJ1143
  Textile industries: TS1450.5
Production systems, Control of
  Production management: TS155.8+
Productivity
  Industrial engineering: T58.8
Profiles
  Railroad surveying: TF214
Profils d'ailes
  Aerodynamics: TL574.A4
Programmable controllers
  Control engineering: TJ223.P76
Programmed instruction
  Technical education: T65.5.P7
Programming
  Industrial engineering: T57.7+
  Mechanical engineering:
    TJ211.45
Project Apollo: TL789.8.U6A5
Project Gemini: TL789.8.U6G4
Project management
  Industrial engineering: T56.8
Project Mariner: TL789.8.U6M3
Project Pioneer: TL789.8.U6P56
Project Ranger: TL789.8.U6R3
Project SNAP
  Space vehicles: TL1102.N8
Project Surveyor: TL789.8.U6S9

Projection
  Cinematography: TR890
  Mechanical drawing: T362+
Projectors
  Photography: TR506+
Projects for boys
  Handicrafts: TT159+
Proline
  Chemical technology: TP248.P73
Promethium
  Chemical technology: TP245.P94
Propaganda balloons: TL633
Propane
  Gas industry: TP761.P94
Propellers
  Aeronautical engineering:
    TL705+
  Models: TL777
Properties of soils: TA710+
Propylene
  Chemical technology: TP248.P75
Prorating tables
  Freight: TF666
Prospecting: TN270+
  Use of airplanes: TL722.4
Prostitutes
  Photographic portraits:
    TR681.P73
Protection against corrosion
  Iron and steel: TA467
  Metals: TA462
Protection against sand
  Railway operation: TF541
Protection against snow
  Railway operation: TF542
Protection from fire
  Building construction: TH9111+
Protection from water
  Fire prevention and
    extinction: TH9431
Protection of structures
  Engineering: TA900
Protective clothing
  Fire prevention and
    extinction: TH9395+
  Industrial safety: T55.3.P75
Protective coatings
  Electrical engineering:
    TK454.4.P7
  Engineering materials: TA418.76

Proteins
  Biotechnology: TP248.65.P76
  Chemical technology: TP248.P77
  Food constituent: TX553.P7
  Food constituents: TP453.P7
Protoactinium
  Chemical technology: TP245.P95
Protozoan biotechnology:
  TP248.27.P75
Provençal cookery: TX719.2.P75
Proving grounds
  Environmental effects:
    TD195.P76
Proximity detectors
  Electronics: TK7882.P7
Prunes
  Cookery: TX813.P78
  Food processing and
    manufacture: TP441.P7
Psychiatric hospital patients
  Photographic portraits:
    TR681.P76
Psychological aspects
  Fatigue: T59.72
Psychological examination
  Drivers: TL152.35
Psychology
  Motor vehicle drivers: TL152.3+
  Photography: TR183
Public buildings
  Air conditioning: TH7688.P78
  Artificial lighting: TH7975.P82
  Building construction: TH4021+
  Building operation and
    housekeeping: TX985
  Electric lighting: TK4399.P8
  Fire prevention and
    extinction: TH9445.P8
  Heating and ventilation:
    TH7392.P9
  Sanitary engineering: TH6057.P8
  Ventilation: TH7684.P8
Public comfort stations
  Plumbing: TH6515.P9
Public land
  Surveying: TA622
Public relations
  Hotels, clubs, restaurants,
    etc.: TX911.3.P77
Public safety radio service:
  TK6570.P8

Public shelters
  Air conditioning: TH7688.P8
Puddings
  Cookery: TX773
Puddling and puddling furnaces
  Wrought iron: TN725
Pulleys
  Mechanical engineering: TJ1103
Pulp
  Analysis: TS1176.6.A5
Pulp consistency transmitters
  Paper manufacture: TS1118.P85
Pulp mills
  Air pollution: TD888.P8
  Building construction: TH4536
  Energy conservation:
    TJ163.5.P37
  Environmental effects:
    TD195.P37
Pulp, Bleaching of
  Woodpulp industry: TS1176.6.B6
Pulping processes
  Paper manufacture: TS1171+
Pulque
  Fermented beverage: TP588.P8
Pulse
  Electronic circuits: TK7868.P8
Pulse amplifiers: TK7871.58.P8
Pulse compression radar:
  TK6592.P85
Pulse generators
  Electronics: TK7872.P8
Pulse plating
  Electroplating: TS671
Pulsed power systems
  Electrical engineering: TK2986
Pulsed reactors
  Nuclear engineering: TK9203.P8
Pulsometers
  Hydraulic machinery: TJ921
Pultrusion
  Plastics: TP1175.P84
Pulverized coal
  Fuel: TP328
Pumice
  Mining engineering: TN948.P74
Pump placing
  Cement and concrete
    construction: TA682.45
Pumped storage power plants:
  TK1083

Pumping
  Chemical engineering: TP156.P8
Pumping by compressed air
  Hydraulic machinery: TJ925
Pumping machinery
  Chemical technology: TP159.P8
  Electric driving: TK4059.P85
  Hydraulic machinery: TJ899+
Pumping stations
  Sewers: TD725
  Water distribution systems:
    TD485+
Pumpkin
  Cookery: TX803.P93
Pumpkinseed oil
  Chemical technology: TP684.P85
Pumps
  Hydraulic machinery: TJ899+
  Water distribution systems:
    TD482
Punch work
  Metal manufactures: TS253
Punching machinery: TJ1255+
Punkas
  Ventilation of buildings:
    TH7683.P8
Punks
  Photographic portraits:
    TR681.P84
Puppets
  Handicrafts: TT174.7
Purchasing
  Airplanes: TL671.85
  Hotels, clubs, restaurants,
    etc.: TX911.3.P8
Pure-culture yeast
  Brewing and malting: TP581
Pure food shows
  Nutrition: TX346.A1+
Purification
  Chemical engineering: TP156.P83
  Gas industry: TP754
  Sewage disposal systems: TD745+
Purification, Water
  Environmental technology:
    TD429.5+
Purple
  Textile dyes: TP925.P9
Push technology
  Internet: TK5105.887
Pusher propellers: TL706.P8

Putty
  Chemical technology: TP941
Pyrdine
  Chemical technology: TP248.P8
Pyrite
  Mining engineering: TN948.P8
Pyrites
  Prospecting: TN271.P9
Pyrochlore
  Mining engineering: TN948.P82
Pyrography
  Woodworking: TT199.8
Pyrolysis
  Chemical engineering: TP156.P9
Pyrometallurgy: TN688.5
  Ferrous metals: TN706.5
Pyrophyllite
  Mining engineering: TN948.P85
Pyrotechnics: TP300+
  Rockets: TL784.P9
Pyrotechnics and explosives
  Chemical technology: TP267.5+

Q

Qanats
  Groundwater: TD404.7
QS-9000
  Motor vehicles: TL278.5
Quadraphonic sound systems
  Electronics: TK7881.8+
Quadratic programming
  Industrial engineering: T57.82
Quadruple expansion
  Steam engines: TJ505
Quadruplex telegraph system:
  TK5535
Quail
  Cookery: TX750.5.Q34
Qualities of water: TD370+
Quality assurance
  Production management: TS156.6
Quality control
  Building construction: TH438.2
  Engineering materials: TA403.6
  Food processing: TP372.5+
  Fur manufactures: TS1063
  Hotels, clubs, restaurants,
    etc.: TX911.3.Q34
  Machinery: TJ245.5
  Paper manufacture: TS1107
  Production management: TS156+

Quality standards
  Motor vehicles: TL278.5
Quantitative methods
  Industrial engineering: T57+
Quantities
  Engineering economy: TA183
  Heating of buildings: TH7335+
  Masonry construction: TH5330
  Plumbing: TH6234+
Quantities and costs
  Bridge engineering: TG313
  Building construction: TH434+
  Carpentry and joinery: TH5614+
  Commercial buildings: TH4315
  Houses: TH4815.8
Quantity meters and
  measurements
  Electrical engineering: TK341
Quantum dots: TK7874.88
Quarries
  Dangers and accidents: TN311+
  Dust removal: TH7697.Q37
  Environmental effects: TD195.Q3
  Mining: TN277
  Noise control: TD893.6.Q35
Quartz
  Electronics: TK7871.15.Q3
  Mining engineering: TN948.Q3
  Prospecting: TN271.Q4
Quays
  Harbor engineering: TC357
Quenching
  Steel metallurgy: TN752.Q4
Questions
  Building construction: TH166
Queuing theory
  Industrial engineering: T57.9
Quick and easy cookery: TX833.5
Quilting
  Handicrafts: TT835
Quilts
  Handicrafts: TT835

R

Rabbit
  Cookery: TX749.5.R32
Racetracks (Automobile)
  Construction: TE305
Racing automobiles: TL236
Racing motorcycles: TL442
Racing planes: TL685.6

Rack railroads: TF684
Racks and pinions
  Toothed gears: TJ190
Radar: TK6573+
  Aeronautical navigation
    equipment: TL696.R2
  Aircraft communication: TL693+
  Aircraft navigation equipment:
    TL695+
Radar air traffic control
  systems
  Aeronautical navigation
    equipment: TL696.R25
Radiant floor heating: TH7535.5
Radiant heaters
  Local heating: TH7434.5+
Radiation accidents: TK9152+
Radiation effects
  Engineering materials: TA418.6
Radiation environment
  procedures and equipment
  Nuclear engineering: TK9151.4+
Radiation safety
  Airports: TL725.3.R3
Radiation shielding
  Space vehicles: TL1490
Radiation tests
  Engineering materials: TA418.6
Radiative heating
  Heating of buildings: TH7421+
Radiator coils: TH7482+
Radiators
  Aircraft engines: TL702.R3
  Convective heating: TH7449+
  Gasoline automobiles: TL214.R3
  Hot water heating: TH7547
  Hydronic systems: TH7480+
  Steam heating: TH7597
Radio
  Aircraft communication: TL693+
  Aircraft navigation equipment:
    TL695+
  Amateurs' manuals: TK9956+
  Apparatus: TK6560+
  Electrical engineering: TK6540+
  Railway signaling: TF627+
  Space vehicles: TL3035
Radio and television towers:
    TK6565.R32
Radio compass
  Aeronautical navigation:
    TL696.C7

Radio control: TK6570.C6
Radio control systems
  Models and modelmaking: TT154.5
Radio data systems: TK6570.R27
Radio photographs: TK6600
Radio receiving apparatus:
    TK6563+
Radio stations: TK6557.5+
  Aircraft navigation: TL695.5
  Building construction: TH4655
  Directories: TK6555
Radioactive measurements
  Control engineering: TJ223.R3
Radioactive metals
  Air pollutants: TD887.R3
Radioactive minerals
  Ore deposits and mining:
    TN490.A3
  Prospecting: TN271.R33
Radioactive pollution
  Environmental pollutants:
    TD196.R3
  Soil pollutants: TD879.R34
Radioactive prospecting:
    TN269.7
Radioactive substances
  Fire prevention and
    extinction: TH9446.R3
  Nuclear engineering: TK9400+
  Transportation: TK9152.17
  Water pollutants: TD427.R3
Radioactive waste disposal
  Industrial wastes: TD897.85+
  Solid wastes: TD812+
Radioactive waste sites:
    TD898.15+
Radioactive waste treatment
  facilities: TD898.16
Radioactivity
  Effect on food: TX571.R3
Radiochemistry
  Nuclear engineering: TK9350
Radiographic examinations
  Testing of materials: TA417.25
Radiography
  Photography: TR750
Radioisotope components
  Aircraft: TL689
Radioisotope technology
  Aircraft: TL689
Radioisotopes
  Nuclear engineering: TK9400+

Radiotelegraph
  Electrical engineering: TK5700 +
  Stations: TK5771
  Systems and instruments:
    TK5811 +
Radiotelephone: TK6553
Radishes
  Cookery: TX803.R33
Radium
  Chemical technology: TP245.R2
  Ore deposits and mining:
    TN490.R3
Radomes
  Radar: TK6590.R3
Radon
  Air pollutants: TD885.5.R33
  Environmental pollutants:
    TD196.R33
Raffia
  Decorative crafts: TT875
  Textile fiber: TS1747.R2
Rafter gages
  Building construction: TH2397
Rafter tables
  Building construction: TH2398
Rafters
  Building construction: TH2393
Ragweed seed oil
  Chemical technology: TP684.R23
Rail bonds
  Electric railways: TF873
Rail fastenings
  Railway construction: TF261
Railroad buildings
  Heating and ventilation:
    TH7392.R3
Railroad car furnishings: TF440
Railroad cars
  Utilization and care: TF600 +
Railroad employees
  Training and education: TF518
Railroad engineering and
  operation: TF1 +
Railroad repair shops
  Electric power: TK4035.R3
  Ventilation: TH7684.R3
Railroad structures
  Heating and ventilation:
    TH7392.R3
Railroad surveying: TF210 +

Railroads
  Environmental effects:
    TD195.R33
  Noise control: TD893.6.R3
  Photography: TR715
  Radio: TK6570.R3
  Waste control: TD899.R26
Railroads, Model
  Photography: TR715
Rails
  Electric railways: TF872
  Railway construction: TF258 +
Railway bridges: TG445
Railway construction: TF200 +
Railway docks: TF315
Railway equipment and
  supplies: TF340 +
Railway ferries: TF320
Railway machinery and tools:
  TF350
Railway motors
  Electric railways: TF935
Railway operation and
  management: TF501 +
Railway patents: TF365
Railway shops: TF376
Railway structures and
  buildings: TF270 +
Rain loads
  Architectural engineering:
    TH893
Rainmaking
  Environmental effects:
    TD195.R34
Rainwater
  Water supply: TD418
Raisins
  Cookery: TX813.R34
Ramie
  Textile fiber: TS1544.R2, TS1747.R:
Ramjet engines
  Aeronautics: TL709.3.R3
Ramps
  Building design and
    construction: TH2259
Range
  Aeronautical navigation
    equipment: TL696.R3
Range water heaters
  Plumbing: TH6553 +
Ranger project: TL789.8.U6R3

Ranges
  Cookery: TX657.S3+
  Metal manufactures: TS425
Rape oil
  Adulteration: TX595.R37
  Chemical technology: TP684.R3
Rapid solidification processing
  Metal manufactures: TS247
Rapid transit question: TF710+
Rare earth metal alloys
  Metallography: TN693.R3
  Metallurgy: TN799.R37
Rare earth metals
  Engineering materials: TA480.R3
Rare earths
  Mining: TN490.A2
  Prospecting: TN271.A2
Rare gases
  Chemical technology: TP244.R3
Rare metals
  Mining: TN490.A2
  Prospecting: TN271.A2
Raspberries
  Cookery: TX813.R37
Rate of climb indicator
  Aeronautical instruments:
    TL589.2.R3
Rate tables
  Railroad freight: TF664
Rates
  Hotels, clubs, restaurants,
    etc.: TX911.3.R3
Rates, Water: TD360
Rattan furniture
  Woodworking: TT197.8
Rattan work
  Decorative crafts: TT876.5
Rayon
  Silk manufactures: TS1688.A1+
  Textile fiber: TS1544.R3
Razors
  Barbering: TT967
Reac computer: TK7889.R4
Reactor fuel reprocessing
  plants
  Air pollution: TD888.R4
  Environmental effects: TD195.R4
  Waste control: TD899.R3
Reactor fuels
  Nuclear engineering: TK9360+

Reading machines
  Computer engineering:
    TK7887.8.R4
Reading the clock: TS548
Reagents
  Metallurgical equipment:
    TN678.5
Real-time control
  Mechanical engineering: TJ217.7
Reamers
  Machine shops: TJ1270
  Machine tools: TJ1186
Reapers
  Agricultural machinery: TJ1485
Rebuilding
  Building construction: TH3401+
Receipts
  Home economics: TX151+
Receipts for barbers: TT977
Receivers, Telephone: TK6481
Receiving
  Aircraft communication
    equipment: TL694.R4
Receiving apparatus
  Radar: TK6588
  Television: TK6653
Recharge of groundwaters
  Disposal of sewage effluent:
    TD765
Recharge, Artificial
  Groundwater: TD404
Rechargeable batteries
  Electrical engineering: TK2941
Recipe books
  Cookery: TX765
Reciprocating engines of
  unusual form: TJ717
Reciprocating pumps
  Hydraulic machinery: TJ915
Reciprocating steam engines:
  TJ485+
Reclamation of bogs, swamps,
  lakes, etc.: TC975
Reclamation of land from the
  sea: TC343+
Reclamation of oil: TP687
Reclamation of wasteland:
  TC801+
Reconnaissance
  Railroad surveying: TF212
  Railway construction: TF200

Recording apparatus
  Radio: TK6565.R4
Recording meters
  Electrical engineering: TK393
Recording telephones: TK6500
Records
  Highway engineering: TE185
Recovery of wastes
  Precious metals: TS729
Recreation areas
  Electric lighting: TK4399.R4
  Sanitary engineering: TD931
Recreation buildings
  Building construction: TH4711
Recreation rooms
  Building design and
    construction: TH3000.R43
Recreational vehicle living:
  TX1110
Rectangular wings
  Airplanes: TL673.R4
Rectification
  Chemical engineering: TP156.R35
Rectifiers
  Electronics: TK7872.R35
  Radio: TK6565.R42
Recycle processes
  Chemical engineering: TP156.R38
Recycling
  Industrial and factory wastes:
    TD897.845
  Municipal refuse: TD794.5+
  Plastics: TP1175.R43
Redheads
  Photographic portraits:
    TR681.R44
Reduced gravity
  Testing of materials:
    TA417.7.R43
Reduced gravity environments
  Applied fluid mechanics:
    TA357.5.R44
Reducing valves
  Steam powerplants: TJ433
Reduction
  Chemical engineering: TP156.R4
  Photographic negatives: TR299
  Photographic processing: TR475
Reduction gears
  Mechanical movements: TJ202
Reductions
  Industrial photography: TR910

Reed
  Engineering materials: TA455.R4
Reentry communications
  Astrionics: TL3028
Refineries: TP690.3
  Building construction: TH4571
Refinery equipment: TP690.3
Refinery processes
  Wrought iron: TN725
Refining
  Paper manufacture: TS1118.R4
Refinishing
  Woodworking: TT199.4
Reflectors
  Lighting fixtures: TH7970.R4
Reflex cameras
  Photography: TR261
Refractories
  Architectural ceramics: TP838
Refractories industry
  Dust removal: TH7697.R4
  Waste control: TD899.R34
Refractory coating
  Metal finishing: TS695.9
Refractory materials: TA418.26
  Metallurgical furnaces: TN677.5
Refractory transition metal
  compounds
  Metallography: TN693.T7
Refrigerants
  Chemical technology: TP492.8+
Refrigeration
  Chemical technology: TP490+
Refrigeration and refrigerating
  machinery
  Electric power: TK4035.R4
Refrigerator cars
  Railway equipment: TF477
Refrigerator drainage
  Plumbing: TH6671.R3
Refrigerator service
  Freight: TF667
Refrigerators: TP496+
Refueling
  Airplanes: TL711.R4
Refugees
  Photographic portraits:
    TR681.R48
Refuse disposal
  Low temperature sanitary
    engineering: TD949
  Rural sanitary engineering:
    TD929+

Refuse drainage
  Low temperature sanitary
    engineering: TD949
Registers
  Hydrodynamics: TC177
  Ventilation of buildings:
    TH7683.R4
  Warm-air heating: TH7626
Regulation
  Explosives: TP297.A+
  Hydraulic engineering: TC530+
  Locomotive boilers: TJ642
Regulation and control of power
  Machinery exclusive of prime
    movers: TJ1055
Regulation devices
  Gas engines: TJ775
Regulators
  Building gas supply: TH6875
  Central heating: TH7466.5
  Dynamoelectric machinery:
    TK2851
  Hydraulic machinery: TJ857
  Sewer appurtenances: TD701
Reinforced concrete
  Fire-resistive building
    construction: TH1087
  Housing material: TH4818.R4
  Masonry materials: TA444+
  Pavements: TE278+
Reinforced concrete bridges:
    TG340
  Continuous girder bridges:
    TG414
Reinforced concrete
  construction
  Building construction: TH1501
  Structural engineering:
    TA682.92+
Reinforced materials
  Engineering materials:
    TA418.9.R4
Reinforced plastics: TP1177+
  Engineering materials:
    TA455.P55
Reinforcing bars
  Corrosion: TA445.5
  Reinforced concrete
    construction: TA683.42
Reinforcing materials
  Fire-resistive-building
    construction: TH1088

Relativistic effects in
    astrodynamics: TL1055
Relativistic rocket mechanics:
    TL1055
Relay (Artificial satellite):
    TK5104.2.R4
Relay control systems
  Mechanical engineering: TJ218.5
Relays
  Dynamoelectric machinery:
    TK2861
  Electronics: TK7872.R38
  Telegraph: TK5581+
Reliability
  Electronics: TK7870.23
  Industrial products
    Product engineering: TS173
  Petroleum pipelines: TN879.55
  Rockets: TL784.R4
Relief processes
  Photography: TR970
Relief wells
  Drainage: TC973
Religious institutions
  Energy conservation:
    TJ163.5.C57
Remanufacturing: TS183.8
Remington rifle: TS536.6.R44
Remodeling
  Building construction: TH3401+
  Houses: TH4816+
Remote handling
  Nuclear engineering: TK9151.6+
Remote sensing
  Environmental technology: TD158
  Petroleum geology: TN870.55
Remotely operated vehicles
  Ocean engineering: TC1662
Removal of dissolved minerals
  Water purification: TD466
Removal of sand
  Railway operation: TF541
Removal of snow and ice
  Railway operation: TF542
Removal of weeds
  Railway operation: TF546
Removal of wrecks
  Railway operation: TF544
Rendering apparatus
  Lard manufactures: TS1981
Renewable energy sources:
    TJ807+

Renewal theory
  Industrial engineering: T57.33
Renovating
  Hats: TS2193
Repair
  Airplanes: TL671.9
  Building construction: TH3401+
  Building gas supply: TH6860
  Buses: TL232.2
  Cycles: TL430
  Hotels, clubs, restaurants,
    etc.: TX928
  Houses: TH4817+
  Motor vehicle operation: TL152+
  Motorcycles: TL444
  Petroleum pipelines: TN879.58
  Plumbing: TH6681+
  Railway permanent way: TF530+
  Sewers: TD716+
  Tractors: TL233.2
  Trucks: TL230.2
Repair shops
  Airports: TL725.3.R4
  Railroads: TF376
Repairing
  Furniture: TT199
  Handicrafts: TT151
  Men's clothing: TT583
  Radio: TK6553
Repairing and adjusting
  Watches and clocks: TS547
Repeating firearms
  Manufactures: TS536
Replacement
  Equipment analysis: TS181.6
Reporting and forecasting
  Aeronautical meteorology:
    TL557.R4
Reprocessing
  Nuclear engineering: TK9360+
Reproduction paper: TS1167
Reptiles
  Nature photography: TR729.R47
Rescue work
  Fire extinction: TH9402+
  Mining engineering: TN297
Research
  Aeronautics: TL565+
  Technology: T175+
Research aircraft: TL567.R47
Research buildings
  Building construction: TH4652

Research equipment
  Aeronautics: TL566+
Research natural areas
  Environmental effects:
    TD195.R45
Research parks: T175.7
Reservations
  Hotels, clubs, restaurants,
    etc.: TX911.3.R47
Reservoir oil pressure
  Petroleum engineering: TN871.18
Reservoirs: TD395+
  Environmental effects:
    TD195.R47
  Hydrostatics: TC167
Reservoirs, Collecting
  Sewers: TD722
Reservoris
  Petroleum geology: TN870.57
Residual materials
  Engineering: TA709.5
Resin
  Cementing substance: TA443.R4
Resinography: TP979
Resistance boxes
  Electric meters: TK311
Resistance meters and
    measurements
  Electric meters: TK311
Resistors
  Electronics: TK7872.R4
  Radio: TK6565.R426
Resonance
  Electrical engineering: TK541
Resonators
  Radar: TK6590.R4
  Radio: TK6565.R43
Resource recovery facilities
  Air pollution: TD888.R48
  Environmental effects:
    TD195.R49
Respirators
  Industrial safety: T55.3.G3
Rest areas
  Roadside development: TE178.8
Restaurants: TX901+
  Building construction: TH4755
  Business mathematics:
    TX911.3.M33
  Electric power: TK4035.R46

Restaurants
  Fire prevention and
    extinction: TH9445.R44
  Food service: TX945+
  Passenger planes: TL685.5.R4
  Sanitary engineering: TH6057.R4
Restoration
  Airplanes: TL671.95
  Military airplanes: TL685.3
  Motor vehicle operation:
    TL152.2
  Motorcycles: TL444.2
  Photographs: TR465
  Tractors: TL233.25
Restoring
  Furniture: TT199
Restraints, Metal
  Locksmithing: TS531
Restyling
  Women's tailoring: TT550
Retaining rings
  Fastenings: TJ1327
Retaining walls
  Bridges: TG325
  Civil engineering: TA760+
  Earthwork: TA770
Retouching
  Photographic processing: TR310
Retractable landing gear
  Airplanes: TL683.R4
Reusable space vehicles
  (Astronautics): TL795.5+
Reveals
  Window and door openings:
    TH2261+
Reverse engineering: TA168.5
Reverse osmosis
  Chemical engineering: TP156.O7
Revolvers
  Manufactures: TS537
Rhenium
  Assaying: TN580.R48
  Engineering materials: TA480.R5
  Metallography: TN693.R45
  Metallurgy: TN799.R45
  Ore deposits and mining:
    TN490.R48
Rheology
  Chemical engineering: TP156.R45

Rheostats
  Dynamoelectric machinery:
    TK2851
Rhodium
  Electroplating: TS692.R5
  Metallurgy: TN799.R5
Rhodonite
  Mining engineering: TN948.R45
Rhubarb
  Cookery: TX803.R58
  Food values: TX558.R4
Ribbon work
  Textile arts: TT850.5
Ribbon work, Paper
  Textile arts: TT850.5
Ribs
  Airplanes: TL674
Rice
  Cookery: TX809.R5
  Food values: TX558.R5
  Milling: TS2159.R5
Rice beer
  Brewing and malting: TP579
Rice flour
  Cookery: TX809.R52
Rice oil
  Chemical technology: TP684.R5
Rice products
  Food processing and
    manufacture: TP435.R3
Rice vinegar: TP429.5
Rifles
  Manufactures: TS536.4+
Rigging
  Airplanes: TL671.5
  Airships: TL660.1
  Balloons: TL623
Right-of-way
  Railway operation: TF561
Rigid airships: TL657
Ring networks
  Computer networks: TK5105.72
Rip panel
  Balloons: TL625.R5
Risk assessment
  Environmental pollution:
    TD193.5
  Hazardous substances and their
    disposal: TD1050.R57

Risk assessment
  Nuclear engineering: TK9152.16
  Radioactive waste disposal:
    TD898.14.R57
Risk communication
  Technology: T10.68
Risk management
  Hotels, clubs, restaurants,
    etc.: TX911.3.R57
River crossings
  Sewers: TD705
River engineering: TC401+
River protective works: TC530+
Rivers
  Hydrodynamics: TC175+
  Water supply source: TD392
Riveting
  Iron and steel work: TA891
Riveting machines
  Machine shops: TJ1310
Rivets
  Fastenings: TJ1325
Rivets, Metal
  Engineering and construction:
    TA492.R6
Road binders for unpaved
  roads: TE221
Road construction
  Air pollution: TD888.R62
  Water pollution: TD428.R63
Road-marking materials: TE203
Road rollers
  Highway engineering: TE223+
Road surveys: TE209+
Roadbed
  Electric railways: TF865
  Railway construction: TF250
Roadmasters' manuroads: TF538
Roads
  Environmental effects:
    TD195.R63
  Highway engineering: TE1+
Roadside development: TE177+
Roadside litter control
  Highway maintenance: TE220.55
Roasting
  Cooking process: TX690
Robot dynamics: TJ211.4
Robot kinematics: TJ211.412
Robot motion: TJ211.4
Robot vision: TJ211.3

Robot wrists: TJ211.42
Robots
  Mechanical engineering:
    TJ210.2+
Robots, Industrial: TS191.8
Robust control
  Mechanical engineering: TJ217.2
Rock craft: TT293
Rock cuttings
  Railroad construction: TF220+
Rock drilling: TA743
Rock drills: TA745+
Rock excavation: TA740+
Rock mechanics: TA706+
  Petroleum geology: TN870.56
Rocket belts: TL717.5
Rocket propulsion: TL780+
Rocketry as a profession:
    TL782.8
Rockets
  Aeronautics: TL780+
Rockfills: TA709
Rocking chairs
  Wood manufactures: TS886.5.C45
Rocks
  Nature photography: TR732
Roll
  Aerodynamics: TL574.M6
Roller compacting
  Cement and concrete
    construction: TA682.455
Rolling contact
  Mechanical engineering: TJ183.5
Rolling mill machinery
  Electric driving: TK4059.R64
Rolling mills
  Building construction: TH4537
  Dust removal: TH7697.R6
  Electric power: TK4035.R6
  Energy conservation:
    TJ163.5.R64
  Manufactures: TS340
Rolling stock
  Railway equipment: TF371+
Rolls
  Ore dressing and milling: TN510
Roman cement
  Cement manufacture: TP884.R7
Roof details
  Building construction: TH2481+
Roof falls
  Mines: TN317

Roof framing
  Building construction: TH2391 +
Roof outlets
  House drainage: TH6666
Roof trusses
  Building construction: TH2392
Roofing
  Building construction: TH2430 +
Roofing industry
  Air pollution: TD888.R66
Roofs
  Building construction: TH2401 +
Roofs and roofing
  Building construction: TH2391 +
Roofs, Special: TH2421 +
Room service
  Hotels, clubs, restaurants,
    etc.: TX943 +
Rope systems
  Fire prevention and
    extinction: TH9414
Rope transmission
  Mechanical engineering: TJ1115
Ropework
  Textile arts: TT840.R66
Rose oil
  Organic chemical industries:
    TP959.R6
Roselle
  Cookery: TX814.5.R58
  Textile fiber: TS1747.R6
Roses
  Cookery: TX814.5.R6
  Nature photography: TR726.R66
Rosin oil
  Chemical technology: TP684.R7
Rotaries
  Dynamoelectric machinery:
    TK2796
Rotary blowers
  Pneumatic machinery: TJ966
Rotary combustion engines:
  TJ792
Rotary engines: TJ729
Rotary pumps
  Hydraulic machinery: TJ917
Rotor aircraft: TL714 +
Rotors
  Machinery: TJ1058
Roughing filtration
  Water purification: TD444

Roughing in
  House drainage: TH6615
Roundhouse management
  Trains: TF595
Roundhouses
  Railway structures: TF296
Routers
  Computer networks: TK5105.543
  Handicrafts: TT203.5
Routing
  Handicrafts: TT203.5
Routing tools
  Machine shops: TJ1208
Roving vehicles
  Astronautics: TL475 +
Rozhestvenskii (Aircraft
  manufacturer): TL686.R7
Rubber
  Aeronautics: TL699.R8
  Engineering materials: TA455.R8
  Fire prevention and
    extinction: TH9446.R8
  Wood preservative: TA424.6.R8
Rubber bands
  Manufactures: TS1920
Rubber bearings
  Mechanical engineering:
    TJ1073.R8
Rubber boots
  Manufactures: TS1910
Rubber industry: TS1870 +
  Electric power: TK4035.R82
  Energy conservation:
    TJ163.5.R82
  Waste control: TD899.R8
Rubber-seed oil
  Chemical technology: TP684.R83
Rubber shoes
  Manufactures: TS1910
Rubber stamp printing
  Decorative crafts: TT867
Rubber tires
  Manufactures: TS1912
Rubber to metal bonding
  Metal finishing: TS718
Rubbing craft
  Decorative crafts: TT912
Rubidium: TN490.R8
  Engineering materials: TA480.R8
Rubies
  Jewelry work: TS755.R82

Ruby lasers
  Applied optics: TA1705
Rudder
  Airplanes: TL677.R8
Ruger rifle: TS536.6.R84
Rugs
  Textile manufactures: TS1772+
Rugs, Hand-made
  Textile arts: TT850
Ruling-machinery
  Stationery: TS1260
Rum
  Distilled liquors: TP607.R9
Runners
  Nutrition: TX361.R86
Running gear
  Motor vehicles: TL260+
Runoff from roads
  Water pollution: TD428.R84
Runoff, Urban
  Sewage collection and disposal
    systems: TD657+
Runways
  Airports: TL725.3.R8
Rural sanitary engineering:
    TD920+
Rural telephones: TK6169
Rush work
  Decorative crafts: TT877
Russia leather: TS980.R8
Rustic works
  Woodworking: TT200
Rye
  Food values: TX558.R9

S

Saccharimetry
  Food processing and
    manufacture: TP382
Saccharin
  Sweeteners: TP424
Saddle roofs
  Building construction: TH2407
Saddlery hardware
  Manufactures: TS1035
Saddles
  Leather industries: TS1030+
Safes
  Metal manufactures: TS420
  Security in buildings: TH9734

Safety
  Dams: TC550
  Radio: TK6553
Safety appliances
  Furnaces: TJ350+
  Machine shops: TJ1177
Safety devices
  Aeronautics: TL697.S3
  Electric railways: TF947
  Elevators: TJ1377
  Highway engineering: TE228
Safety factors
  Motor vehicles: TL242
Safety helmets
  Industrial safety: T55.3.S23
Safety instrumentation
  Nuclear engineering: TK9183.S24
Safety lamps
  Mines: TN307
Safety manuals
  Authorship: T55.3.A87
Safety measures
  Airports: TL725.3.S34
  Airships: TL651
  Chemical technology: TP149
  Fire prevention and
    extinction: TH9182
  Food processing and
    manufacture: TP373.5
  Foundry work: TS238
  Gas in buildings: TH6830+
  Glass and glassmaking: TP858
  Hazardous substances and their
    disposal: TD1050.S24
  Hotels, clubs, restaurants,
    etc.: TX911.3.S24
  Hydraulic engineering: TC159
  Lighting
    Building construction: TH7720
  Management of engineering
    works: TA192
  Mechanical engineering: TJ166
  Metal finishing: TS653.5
  Metallurgical plants: TN676.A1+
  Mining engineering: TN295
  Petroleum pipelines: TN879.59
  Petroleum refining: TP690.6
  Plastics: TP1148
  Radioactive waste disposal:
    TD898.14.S34
  Railway operation: TF610

Safety measures
  School shops: TT170.4
  Steam boilers: TJ298
  Textile industries: TS1449
  Welding: TS227.8
Safety of consumer products
  Product engineering: TS175
Safety of exit
  Building construction: TH153
Safety probability
  Structural analysis: TA656.5
Safety standards
  Motor vehicles: TL242
Safety valves
  Furnaces: TJ352 +
Safety, Industrial: T55 +
Safflower
  Textile dyes: TP925.S23
Saffron
  Cookery: TX819.S24
Saggars
  Ceramic technology: TP815
Sago
  Cookery: TX814.5.S34
  Starch: TP416.S3
Saint Patrick's Day decorations
  Decorative crafts: TT900.S25
Saké
  Brewing and malting: TP579
Sal seed oil
  Chemical technology: TP684.S2
Salad dressing
  Cookery: TX819.S27
Salads
  Cookery: TX807
  Recipes: TX740
Saline springs
  Salt manufacture: TN907
Saline water conversion: TD478 +
Saline water pretreatment:
  TD479.8
Salmon
  Cookery: TX748.S24
Saloons: TX950 +
  Plumbing: TH6518.B2
Salsas
  Cookery: TX819.S29
Salt
  Mining engineering: TN900 +
  Preservation of wood:
    TA424.6.S3
  Soil stabilization: TE210.5.S3

Salt
  Street snow control: TD870
  Water pollutants: TD427.S24
  Wood composition: TS933.S2
Salt mines and mining
  Environmental effects:
    TD195.S26
Salt mining: TN900 +
Saltpeter: TP238
Salts: TP230 +
  Fire prevention and
    extinction: TH9446.S3
Salvage of material during
  fires
  Fire prevention and
    extinction: TH9431
Salvaging
  Building construction: TH449
Samarium
  Chemical technology: TP245.S2
Sample books
  Men's clothing: TT628
  Paper manufacturers: TS1220
Sampling
  Ores: TN560
  Pollution measurement: TD193 +
  Sewage analysis: TD735
Sampling theory
  Industrial engineering: T57.36
Sand
  Engineering materials: TA455.S3
  Mining engineering: TN939
Sand and gravel industry
  Dust removal: TH7697.S3
  Environmental effects: TD195.S3
Sand-blast process
  Ornamental glass: TP864
Sand bypassing
  Coast protective works: TC339.8
Sand casting
  Handicrafts: TT295
Sand crafts
  Decorative crafts: TT865
Sand filtration
  Mechanical treatment of water
    purification: TD445
Sand-lime brick
  Brickmaking: TP832.S2
Sand-lime products
  Cement manufacture: TP884.S3

Sand plants and bins
  Railway structures: TF292
Sandblast
  Pneumatic machinery: TJ1009
Sandstone
  Building stones: TN957
Sandwich construction elements,
  Metal
  Engineering and construction:
    TA492.S25
Sandwich elements
  Structural engineering:
    TA660.S3
Sandwiches
  Cookery: TX818
Sanitary crafts
  Environmental engineering of
    buildings: TH6071+
Sanitary engineering: TD1+
  Buildings: TH6014+
Sanitary landfills
  Municipal refuse: TD795.7
  Sewage disposal: TD771
Sanitation
  Food processing and
    manufacture: TP373.6
  Hotels, clubs, restaurants,
    etc.: TX911.3.S3
  Wine and winemaking:
    TP548.5.S35
Sapphires
  Mineral industries: TN997.S24
Saprolites
  Mining engineering: TN948.S24
Sapropel
  Mining engineering: TN851
Sardines
  Cookery: TX748.S26
Sashes
  Window and door: TH2272
Sassafras oil
  Organic chemical industries:
    TP959.S2
Satellite surveying: TA595.5
Satellite television
  Amateurs' manuals: TK9962
Sauces
  Cookery: TX819.A1+
Sauerkraut
  Food processing and
    manufacture: TP444.S27

Sausages
  Cookery: TX749.5.S28
  Meat-packing industries:
    TS1974.S3
Sautéing
  Cooking process: TX689.4
Saw filing
  Machine shops: TJ1235
Saw sets
  Machine shops: TJ1237
Saw sharpening
  Woodworking equipment: TS851
Sawing machinery
  Machine shops: TJ1230+
Sawmills
  Wood products: TS850
Saws
  Machine shops: TJ1233+
Scaffolding
  Building construction: TH5281
Scale
  Saline water conversion:
    TD479.8
Scales (Weighing instruments)
  Metal manufactures: TS410
Scaling ladder systems
  Fire prevention and
    extinction: TH9412
Scandium
  Chemical technology: TP245.S3
  Ore deposits and mining:
    TN490.S4
Scanning systems
  Electronics: TK7882.S3
Scenic byways
  Highway engineering: TE229.9
Scheduling
  Building construction: TH438.4
  Production control: TS157.5+
Schematic analysis
  Industrial engineering: T57.4
Schematic methods
  Engineering mathematics: TA337+
Scholars
  Photographic portraits:
    TR681.S36
School buildings
  Electric power: TK4025
  Fire prevention and
    extinction: TH9445.S3
  Heating and ventilation:
    TH7392.S35

School cafeterias
  Food service: TX945.2
School lunchrooms
  Food service: TX945.2
School photography: TR818
School shops
  Handicrafts: TT170+
Schools
  Brewing and malting: TP574
  Energy conservation: TJ163.5.U5
  Plumbing: TH6515.S4
Schools, Technical
  Industrial engineering: T61+
Schottky-barrier diodes
  Semiconductors: TK7871.89.S35
Schuetzen rifles: TS536.6.S3
Schungite
  Mining engineering: TN847
Scientific applications
  Photography: TR692+
Scientific cinematography
  Photography: TR893+
Scientific expeditions
  Photography: TR710
Scientific satellites: TL798.S3
Scissors
  Metal manufactures: TS381
Sconces
  Woodworking: TT197.5.L34
Scones
  Cookery: TX770.B55
Scooters
  Handicrafts: TT174.5.S35
Scramjet engines
  Aeronautics: TL709.3.S37
Scrap metal industry
  Environmental effects: TD195.S36
Scrap metals
  Manufactures: TS214
Scrapers
  Machine shops: TJ1201.S3
Scrapmetal craft
  Metalworking: TT214
Screen doors
  Building design: TH2278+
Screen process work
  Handicrafts: TT273
Screening
  Chemical engineering: TP156.S3
  Coal: TN816.A1+
  Mechanical water purification: TD439

Screening
  Ore dressing and milling: TN515
  Sewage purification: TD753
  Sewage treatment: TD748
Screening machinery: TJ1540
Screens
  Ore dressing and milling: TN515
  Window fittings: TH2276
Screw bevel gears
  Mechanical movements: TJ196
Screw-cutting machines
  Machine shops: TJ1222
Screw machines
  Machine shops: TJ1215+
Screw-piles
  Foundations: TA783
Screw press
  Lifting machinery: TJ1455
Screwdrivers
  Machine shops: TJ1201.S34
Screwjack
  Lifting machinery: TJ1433
Screws and screw threads
  Fastenings: TJ1338+
Screws, Metal
  Engineering and construction: TA492.S3
Scrolls and designs for
  carriage painters: TS2032
Scrubber process
  Chemical engineering: TP156.S32
Scrubbers
  Chemical technology: TP159.S34
Sculpture
  Photography of art: TR658.3
Scuttles
  Building construction: TH2491
Sea locks
  Harbor engineering: TC353
Sea water
  Effect on structures: TC200
  Salt manufacture: TN905
Seac computer: TK7889.S4
Seafood
  Cookery: TX747+
  Food values: TX556.5
Sealing
  Building construction: TH1719
  Chemical technology: TP988
  Machinery: TJ246

619

Sealing compounds
  Chemical technology: TP988
Seaplane flying: TL711.S43
Seaplanes: TL684+
Search and rescue
  Airplane accidents: TL553.8
Search engines
  Internet: TK5105.884+
Search radar: TK6592.S4
Search theory
  Industrial engineering: T57.97
Searchlights
  Aircraft: TL691.S4
  Electric lighting: TK4399.S4
Seashore photography: TR670+
Seasoning
  Lumber: TS837
  Meat-packing industries:
    TS1974.F5
Seats
  Motor vehicles: TL255.6
  Passenger planes: TL685.5.S4
  Space environment: TL1555
Seawalls
  Coast protective works: TC335
Secondary cells
  Electrical engineering: TK2941
Secondary recovery of oil
  Petroleum engineering: TN871.37
Secondary school courses
  Driver education: TL152.65
Section
  Airplanes: TL673.S4
Section-books
  Railway construction: TF260
Sectional radiators
  Hydronic systems: TH7487
Security
  Hotels, clubs, restaurants,
    etc.: TX911.3.S4
Security devices
  Security in buildings: TH9730+
Security in buildings
  Building construction: TH9701+
Security measures
  Airports: TL725.3.S44
  Electrical engineering:
    TK5102.85
Sediment
  Water pollutants: TD427.S33

Sediment analysis
  Geophysical surveying:
    TN269.885
Sediment transport
  Hydrodynamics: TC175.2
Sedimentation
  Chemical engineering: TP156.S4
  Mechanical of water
    purification: TD439
  Reservoirs: TD396
  Sewage treatment: TD749+
Sedimentation tanks and basins
  Mechanical water purification:
    TD439
Sedimentation with coagulation
  Sewage purification: TD751
Seed oils
  Food values: TX560.S4
Seed products
  Food processing: TP437+
Seeders
  Agricultural machinery: TJ1483
Seeding
  Pollution control methods:
    TD192.7
Seeds
  Cookery: TX814.5.S44
  Food processing: TP437+
Seismic prospecting: TN269.8+
Seismic reflection method
  Seismic prospecting: TN269.84
Seismic refraction method
  Seismic prospecting: TN269.85
Selection
  Equipment analysis: TS181.3
Selenium
  Chemical technology: TP245.S4
  Mining engineering: TN948.S4
  Water pollutants: TD427.S38
Self-purification of streams
  Disposal of sewage effluent:
    TD764
Semi-submersible offshore
  structures
  Ocean engineering: TC1702
Semiconductor lasers
  Applied optics: TA1700
Semiconductors
  Control engineering: TJ223.S45
  Electronics: TK7871.85+
Semikilled steel
  Metallurgy: TN757.S45

Semimetals
  Engineering materials:
    TA455.S35
Semirigid airships: TL656.4
Sending apparatus
  Radio: TK6561
Sensitive surfaces
  Photography: TR280+
Sensitometry
  Photography: TR280+
Sensory evaluation of food:
    TX546
Sensory qualities
  Water quality: TD375, TD380+
Separate sewerage system: TD664
Separation
  Biotechnology: TP248.25.S47
  Chemical engineering: TP156.S45
Separators (Machine)
  Chemical technology: TP159.S4
Septic tanks
  Sewage disposal: TD778
Series circuit
  Electrical engineering:
    TK454.15.S47
Serpentine
  Mining engineering: TN948.S45
Servants
  Household administration:
    TX331+
Service industries
  Electric power: TK4035.S4
  Fire prevention and
    extinction: TH9445.S4
Service life of materials:
    TA409.2
Service rules and regulations
  Railway operation: TF520+
Service stations
  Motor vehicles: TL153
  Waste control: TD899.S46
Serving, Table
  Dining-room service: TX881
Servomechanisms
  Mechanical engineering: TJ214
  Radar: TK6590.S4
Sesame
  Cookery: TX814.5.S47
Settings
  Boilermaking: TJ292

Settling
  Mechanical water purification:
    TD439
Settling tanks
  Sewage treatment: TD749+
Setup time
  Industrial engineering: T60.47
Sewage: TD730+
Sewage and wastes
  House drainage: TH6651+
Sewage collection and disposal
  systems: TD511+
Sewage disposal
  Low temperature sanitary
    engineering: TD949
  Rural sanitary engineering:
    TD929+
Sewage disposal plants: TD746
  Air pollution: TD888.S38
  Environmental effects:
    TD195.S47
  Noise control: TD893.6.S48
  Water pollution: TD428.S47
Sewage disposal systems: TD741+
Sewage drainage
  Low temperature sanitary
    engineering: TD949
Sewage effluent
  Disposal: TD759+
Sewage farming
  Disposal of effluent: TD760
Sewage irrigation: TD670, TD760
Sewage sludge: TD767.4+
  Disposal: TD772
  Treatment and disposal: TD767+
Sewage sludge ash
  Sewage disposal: TD770.3
Sewer appurtenances: TD695+
Sewer corrosion: TD691
Sewer explosions: TD690
Sewer gas: TD690
Sewer pipe
  Architectural ceramics: TP839
Sewerage: TD511+
  Water pollution: TD428.S47
Sewerage systems design: TD658
Sewers: TD673+
Sewing
  Textile arts: TT700+
Sewing (Kindergarten): TT708
Sewing by machine
  Textile arts: TT713

Sewing machines
  Mechanical engineering: TJ1501+
Sextant
  Aeronautical instruments:
    TL589.2.S4
Shades
  Dyeing: TP907
Shadows
  Lighting: TH7723
Shaft and journals
  Steam engines: TJ539
Shaft sinking
  Mining: TN283
Shafting
  Generators: TK2458.S5
  Machinery exclusive of prime
    movers: TJ1057
Shafting, Metal
  Engineering and construction:
    TA492.S5
Shale
  Engineering materials: TA455.S4
  Gas manufacture: TP751.7
  Mining engineering: TN948.S5
Shale oil
  Mineral oils and waxes: TP699
Shampoos: TP984
Shape
  Sewers: TD675+
Shape memory alloys
  Engineering and construction:
    TA487
Shapers
  Machine shops: TJ1208
Shaping machines
  Machine shops: TJ1300
Sharks
  Cookery: TX748.S5
Sharpening tools
  Machine shops: TJ1280+
Shaving
  Barbering: TT964
Shawls
  Knitting and crocheting: TT825
  Textile industries: TS1781
Shear
  Structural analysis: TA648.4
  Testing of materials:
    TA417.7.S5
Shear legs
  Hoisting machinery: TJ1361

Shears
  Machine shops: TJ1240
Shears, Hand
  Metal manufactures: TS381
Sheathing papers
  Building construction: TH1720
Sheer fabrics
  Textile fabrics: TS1770.S54
Sheet iron
  Metal manufactures: TS360
Sheet metal
  Building construction: TH1651+
Sheet metal walls
  Building design and
    construction: TH2247
Sheet metalwork
  Metal manufactures: TS250
Sheet-piling
  Foundations: TA785
Sheet steel
  Metal manufactures: TS360
Sheet systems
  Fire prevention and
    extinction: TH9418
Sheets
  Handicrafts: TT406
  Home furnishings: TX315
Shell roofs
  Building construction: TH2416+
Shellac
  Chemical technology: TP938
Shellcraft
  Decorative crafts: TT862
Shellfish
  Cookery: TX753+
  Nutrition: TX387
Shells
  Reinforced concrete
    construction: TA683.5.S4
  Structural engineering:
    TA660.S5
Shells (Sea shells)
  Engineering materials:
    TA455.S43
Shelving
  Building construction: TH2555
Shielding
  Aircraft communication
    equipment: TL694.I6
  Airplanes: TL673.T4
  Electronic circuits: TK7867.8
  Nuclear reactors: TK9210+

Shift registers
  Computer engineering:
    TK7895.S54
Shingle roofing
  Building construction: TH2441
Ship canals: TC770
Ship railways: TC771+
Shipment, Packing for: TS198.5+
Ships
  Air pollution: TD888.S54
  Seashore photography: TR670.5
  Water pollution: TD428.S55
Shipyards
  Electric power: TK4035.S5
Shirts
  Men's tailoring: TT612
Shisha mirror embroidery:
    TT778.S55
Shochu
  Distilled liquors: TP607.S5
Shock absorbers
  Airplanes: TL683.S4
  Machinery: TJ1060.2
  Motor vehicles: TL257.5
  Railroad cars: TF393
Shock tubes
  Aeronautical research: TL567.S4
Shock waves
  Aerodynamics: TL574.S4
Shoe making machinery
  Manufactures: TS1005
Shoemaking
  Leather industries: TS989+
Shoji screens
  Building construction: TH2544
Shone sewerage system: TD668
Shop kinks
  Machine shop practice: TJ1165
Shop management
  Hairdressing: TT965+
Shop mathematics
  Machine shop practice: TJ1165
Shop practice
  Locomotives: TJ683
Shop repairing
  Machine shop practice: TJ1165
Shopping
  Household administration:
    TX335+

Shopping centers
  Environmental effects:
    TD195.S52
  Fire prevention and
    extinction: TH9445.S8
Shopping guides
  Consumer education: TX335+
Shops
  Railway structures: TF298
Shoring
  Building construction: TH5281
Shortwave radios: TK6564.S5
Shortwave transmission
  Radio: TK6562.S5
Shotguns
  Manufactures: TS536.8
Shoulders
  Highway engineering: TE212.5
Show cards
  Painting: TT360.A1+
Show windows
  Electric lighting: TK4399.S5
Shower baths
  Plumbing: TH6492
Shrimp
  Cookery: TX754.S58
Shrines
  Fire prevention and
    extinction: TH9445.C5
Shunting
  Trains: TF592
Shunts
  Electric meters: TK311
  Generators: TK2487
Shutters
  Photography: TR272
  Window fittings: TH2276
Sicilian style cookery:
    TX723.2.S55
Siderite
  Ore deposits and mining:
    TN402.S5
Sidewalk lights
  Natural lighting: TH7799
Sidewalks
  Pedestrian facilities: TE280+
Siding
  Building design and
    construction: TH2238.5
Siemens process
  Steel metallurgy: TN740+

Sieves
  Metal manufactures: TS275
Sights
  Gunsmithing: TS535.2.S46
Sign lettering
  Painting: TT360.A1 +
Sign painting: TT360.A1 +
Signal generators
  Electronics: TK7872.S5
Signal lights
  Transportation engineering:
    TA1250
Signal processing
  Electrical engineering:
    TK5102.9
Signaling
  Aircraft: TL692
  High speed ground
    transportation: TF1510
  Railway operation: TF615 +
Signaling equipment
  Transportation engineering:
    TA1245 +
Signals
  Railway operation: TF610
Signboards
  Airports: TL725.3.S47
Signs
  Airports: TL725.3.S47
  Electric lighting: TK4399.S6
Silencers
  Gunsmithing: TS535.2.S5
Silica
  Mining engineering: TN948.S6
Silicates
  Engineering materials:
    TA455.S46
Silicides
  Electronics: TK7871.15.S54
Silicon
  Chemical technology: TP245.S5
  Electronics: TK7871.15.S55
Silicon alloys
  Engineering materials: TA479.S5
Silicon carbide
  Abrasive: TJ1298
Silicon industry
  Environmental effects:
    TD195.S54
Silicon nitride
  Electronics: TK7871.15.S558
  Insulating material: TK3441.S46

Silicon organic compounds
  Electronics: TK7871.15.S56
  Insulating material: TK3441.S47
Silicone rubber
  Manufactures: TS1927.S55
Silicones
  Chemical technology: TP248.S5
Siliconizing
  Metal finishing: TS695.5
Silk
  Dyeing: TP901
  Textile fiber: TS1546
Silk fabrics
  Textile dyeing: TP931.S6
Silk flowers
  Decorative crafts: TT890.7
Silk machinery
  Silk manufactures: TS1672
Silk ribbon embroidery:
  TT778.S64
Silk-screen printing
  Handicrafts: TT273
Sillimanite
  Mining engineering: TN948.S63
Sills
  Window and door openings:
    TH2261 +
Silos
  Building construction: TH4935
Siloxanes
  Insulating material: TK3441.S48
Silver
  Assaying: TN580.S5
  Chemical technology: TP245.S6
  Engineering materials: TA480.S5
  Environmental pollutants:
    TD196.S48
  Metallography: TN693.S5
  Ore deposits and mining: TN430 +
  Prospecting: TN271.S55
  Sewage disposal: TD758.5.S44
Silver and gold
  Metallurgy: TN760 +
  Ore deposits and mining: TN410 +
Silver and lead
  Metallurgy: TN770
Silver cleaning: TX324
Silver plating
  Electroplating: TS680
Silver salts
  Photographic processes: TR385 +

Silver work
  Manufactures: TS720+
Silvering
  Metal arts and crafts: TT382.8
  Metal finishing: TS715
Silversmithing
  Manufactures: TS730+
Silverware
  Manufactures: TS735
Simple Network Management
  Protocol (SNMP)
  Computer networks: TK5105.583
Simplex model
  Linear programming: T57.76+
Simplex telegraph system:
  TK5523
Simulation methods
  Hydraulic engineering: TC409
  Industrial engineering: T57.62+
  Mathematical models: TA343
  Structural engineering: TA643
Simultaneous telegraph and
  telephone: TK6525
Single cell lipids
  Biotechnology: TP248.65.S55
Single cell proteins
  Biotechnology: TP248.65.S56
Single heading
  Airplanes: TL711.S5
Single-phase current systems
  Electrical engineering: TK3151
Single-phase currents
  Electrical engineering: TK1145
Single-ply roofing
  Building construction: TH2452
Single-rail railways: TF694
Single shot rifle: TS536.6.S5
Single-sideband radio
  transmission: TK6562.S54
Sinks
  Kitchen plumbing: TH6511
Siphonage
  Plumbing: TH6631+
Sirens
  Electroacoustics: TK5990
Sisal
  Textile fiber: TS1747.S5
Size of airports: TL725.3.S5
Size of sewers: TD675+
Size reduction
  Chemical engineering: TP156.S5

Sizing
  Paper manufacture: TS1118.S5
  Textile industries: TS1488+
Skate industry
  Technology: TS2301.S5
Skateboards
  Handicrafts: TT174.5.S35
Skates (Fishes)
  Cookery: TX748.S58
Skewer cookery: TX834
Skidding
  Motor vehicles: TL295
Skids
  Airplanes: TL683.S5
Skillet cookery: TX840.S55
Skimming
  Sewage treatment: TD748
Skin care: TT958.5
Skins
  Leather industries: TS967
Skirts
  Women's tailoring: TT540
Skis
  Airplanes: TL683.S6
Skylights
  Building design and
    construction: TH2486+
Skynet Project
  Artificial satellites:
    TK5104.2.S5
Skyscrapers
  Fire prevention and
    extinction: TH9445.T18
  Security in buildings:
    TH9745.S59
Skywriting: TL722.5
Slab-on-ground construction:
  TH4819.S5
Slabs
  Cement and concrete
    construction: TA682.5.S5
  Reinforced concrete
    construction: TA683.5.S6
  Structural engineering:
    TA660.S6
Slacks
  Men's tailoring: TT605
  Women's tailoring: TT542
Slag
  Composition roofing: TH2451
  Engineering materials: TA455.S5
  Masonry materials: TA441
  Metallurgy: TN707

Slag cement
  Cement manufacture: TP884.S6
Slate: TN958
  Insulating material: TK3441.S5
Slate roofing
  Building construction: TH2445
Slaughterhouses
  Manufactures: TS1960+
  Ventilation: TH7684.S55
  Waste control: TD899.M4
Sleepers
  Railway construction: TF252+
Sleeping accommodations
  Passenger planes: TL685.5.S6
Sleeping cars
  Railway equipment: TF459
Sleeves
  Men's tailoring: TT603
Slide-rule calculations
  Carpentry and joinery: TH5613
Slide valve
  Steam engines: TJ545
Sliding and folding doors
  Building design: TH2278+
Sliding mode control
  Mechanical engineering: TJ220.5
Slime treatment
  Ore dressing and milling: TN525
Slip
  Aircraft propellers: TL706.S4
Slip stream
  Aeronautical engineering:
    TL706.S5
Slipcovers
  Handicrafts: TT395
Slope-deflection method: TA650+
Sloshing
  Applied fluid mechanics:
    TA357.5.S57
Slotted wings
  Airplanes: TL673.S6
Slotting machines
  Machine shops: TJ1210
Sloyd
  Woodworking: TT187+
Sludge digestion
  Sewage treatment: TD769+
Sludge gas
  Sewage treatment: TD769.4
Sluice gates
  Electric driving: TK4059.S55

Sluices
  Dams: TC553
  Hydraulic powerplants: TJ847
  Hydrostatics: TC169
  Technical hydraulics: TC175+
Small bridges
  Railway structures: TF282
Small gasoline engines
  Internal combustion engines:
    TJ790
Smart cards
  Computer engineering:
    TK7895.S62
Smart materials
  Engineering materials:
    TA418.9.S62
Smelt-water explosions
  Woodpulp industry: TS1176.6.S5
Smelting companies: TN400+
Smocking
  Textile arts: TT840.S66
Smocks
  Women's tailoring: TT546
Smog
  Air pollutants: TD884.3
Smoke
  Air pollutants: TD884
  In plumbing testing: TH6617
Smoke control systems
  Fire-resistive-building
    construction: TH1088.5
Smoke prevention
  Locomotives: TJ653
Smoked foods
  Cookery: TX835
Smokeless powder
  Explosives: TP273
Smokers, Facts for
  Tobacco industry: TS2249
Smokestacks, Powerplant
  Building construction: TH4591
Smoking
  Preservation of foods: TX609
Smoking and fires
  Fire prevention: TH9197
Smoking paraphernalia
  Manufactures: TS2280
Smoking, Enjoyment of
  Tobacco industry: TS2249
Smoking, Pipes for
  Manufactures: TS2270

Smoky chimneys
  Building construction: TH2284
SNA (Computer network
  systems): TK5105.8.S65
Snack foods: TP451.S57
Snails
  Cookery: TX754.S63
Snapshooters
  Photographic portraits:
    TR681.S6
(SNMP) Simple Network
  Management Protocol
  Computer networks: TK5105.583
Snow and ice control
  Roads and highways: TE220.5
  Streets: TD868+
  Use of salt and chemicals:
    TD870
Snow and ice loads
  Bridge design: TG304
Snow building construction:
  TH1431
Snow control
  Streets: TD868+
Snow guards
  Railway structures: TF277
Snow loads
  Architectural engineering:
    TH895
  Structural analysis: TA654.4
Snow mechanics
  Engineering: TA714
Snowmobiles: TL234.2
Soap
  Chemical technology: TP990+
Soaps: TP991
  Hairdressing: TT969
Soapstone
  Mining engineering: TN948.T2
Soaring: TL760+
  Aeronautics: TL576
Social aspects
  Biotechnology: TP248.23
  Radioactive waste disposal:
    TD898.14.S63
  Technology: T14.5
Social executives
  Hotels, clubs, restaurants,
    etc.: TX930
Sockets
  Electric lighting: TK4361+

Socks
  Knitting and crocheting: TT825
Sod
  Housing material: TH4818.S55
Soda deposits
  Mining engineering: TN899+
Soda fountains
  Beverage industry apparatus:
    TP635
  Plumbing: TH6518.S6
Soda process
  Woodpulp industry: TS1176.6.S6
Soda water: TP628+
Sodium
  Chemical technology: TP245.S7
  Food constituent: TX553.S65
Sodium graphite reactors
  Nuclear engineering: TK9203.S6
Sodium hydroxide
  Environmental pollutants:
    TD196.S52
Sodium salts
  Mining engineering: TN899+
Sodium sulphate
  Mining engineering: TN948.S7
Sodium sulphur batteries
  Electricity production:
    TK2945.S63
Soft home furnishings
  Handicrafts: TT387+
Soft sculpture
  Decorative crafts: TT925
Soft toys
  Handicrafts: TT174.3
Softness
  Water quality: TD372
Soil
  Engineering materials: TA455.S6
Soil bank failures
  Mines: TN318.5
Soil bioventing
  Soil remediation: TD878.6
Soil builder, Sewage disposal
  as: TD774+
Soil cement
  Housing material: TH4818.S6
  Soil stabilization: TE210.5.S6
Soil compaction
  Earthwork: TA749
  Highway engineering: TE210.4+
Soil dynamics: TA711+

Soil erosion prevention
  Building construction: TH383
Soil fixtures
  Plumbing: TH6497
Soil management
  Water pollution: TD428.S64
Soil mechanics: TA710 +
  Motor vehicle effects: TL243 +
Soil piping
  House drainage: TH6653
Soil pollution
  Environmental engineering:
    TD878 +
Soil profiles
  Highway engineering: TE208 +
Soil remediation
  Environmental engineering:
    TD878 +
Soil stabilization
  Earthwork: TA749
  Highway engineering: TE210.4 +
Soil stack systems
  House drainage: TH6651 +
Soil-structure interaction
  Soil mechanics: TA711.5
Soil surveys
  Highway engineering: TE208 +
Soil testing
  Soil mechanics: TA710.5
Soil vapor extraction
  Soil remediation: TD878.5
Soil working machines
  Agricultural machinery: TJ1482
Soils
  Airports: TL725.3.S6
  Properties: TA710 +
Solar air conditioning
  Ventilation of buildings:
    TH7687.9
Solar batteries
  Amateurs' manuals: TK9918
  Electrical engineering: TK2960
Solar cars: TL222
Solar cells
  Amateurs' manuals: TK9918
  Electrical engineering: TK2960
Solar collectors: TJ812
Solar cookery: TX835.5
Solar energy: TJ809 +
  Environmental effects:
    TD195.S64
  Production of electric energy:
    TK1056
  Production of electric power:

Solar engines: TJ812.5
Solar furnaces
  Building construction: TH7145
Solar gas turbines: TJ812.6
Solar heating
  Heating of buildings: TH7413 +
Solar houses
  Heating of buildings: TH7414
Solar materials: TJ812.7
Solar ponds: TJ812.8
Solar power plants: TK1545
Solar production of electric
  power: TK1085 +
Solar pumps
  Hydraulic machinery: TJ912
Solar sails: TL783.9
Solar saline water conversion
  plants: TD479.7
Solar vehicles: TL222
Solar water heaters
  Plumbing: TH6561.7
Solder
  Plumbing: TH6297
Soldering
  Handicrafts: TT267
  Plumbing: TH6297
  Tinsmithing: TS610
Sole leather: TS980.S6
Soliciting
  Electrical engineering: TK445
Solid fuel reactors
  Nuclear engineering: TK9203.S65
Solid lubricants
  Tribology: TJ1078
Solid propellant rockets:
  TL783.3
Solid state batteries
  Electrical engineering: TK2942
Solid-state fermentation
  Biotechnology: TP248.25.S64
Solid-state image
  intensifiers: TK8334
Solid-state lasers
  Applied optics: TA1705
Solid waste management,
  Integrated: TD794.2
  Local: TD788 +
Solid wastes
  Environmental technology:
    TD785 +

Solidification
  Chemical engineering: TP156.S55
  Hazardous substances: TD1063
  Radioactive waste disposal:
    TD898.18
Solions
  Control engineering: TJ223.S6
Soluble glass
  Glassmaking: TP869
Solution mining: TN278.5
Solvent wastes
  Waste disposal: TD898.8.S65
Solvents
  Chemical technology: TP247.5
  Effect on food: TX571.S65
  Environmental pollutants:
    TD196.S54
Solvents industry
  Air pollution: TD888.S6
SONET
  Synchronous transfer systems:
    TK5105.415
Sonic boom
  Aerodynamics: TL574.S55
Sonic coagulation
  Dust removal: TH7695.S6
Soot
  Environmental pollutants:
    TD196.S56
  Removal from chimneys: TH2285
Sorbents
  Chemical technology: TP159.S6
Sorbitol
  Chemical technology: TP248.S6
Sorghum
  Food values: TX558.S6
  Milling: TS2159.S65
  Sugars and syrups: TP405
Sorghum products
  Food processing and
    manufacture: TP435.S65
Sorting
  Ore dressing and milling: TN515
Sorting devices
  Mechanical engineering: TJ1555
Sound motion pictures
  Cinematography: TR897
Sound recording
  Electronics: TK7881.4+
Sound recording instruments
  industry: TS2301.S6

Sound reproduction
  Electronics: TK7881.4+
Sound systems
  Amateurs' manuals: TK9968
  Electronics: TK7881.4+
Sound transmitting systems
  Telephone: TK6401+
Sounders
  Telegraph: TK5581+
Sounding balloons
  Aeronautics: TL631
Sounding rockets: TL785.8.S6
Soundproof construction
  Building construction: TH1725
Soundproofing
  Airplanes: TL681.S6
Soups
  Cookery: TX757
  Food processing and
    manufacture: TP451.S67
Sour cream and milk
  Cookery: TX759.5.S68
Source reduction
  Waste minimization: TD793.95
Source separation
  Municipal refuse: TD794.8
Sourdough bread
  Cookery: TX770.S66
Southern Pacific Railroad:
  TJ603.3.S6
Southern style cookery
  American: TX715.2.S68
  Italian: TX723.2.S65
Southwestern style cookery:
  TX715.2.S69
Soy sauce
  Condiments: TX407.S69
  Cookery: TX819.S58
  Food processing: TP438.S6
  Nutrition: TX401.2.S69
Soybean
  Food values: TX558.S7
Soybean oil
  Chemical technology: TP684.S6
Soybean products
  Nutrition: TX401.2.S69
Soybeans
  Cookery: TX803.S6
  Nutrition: TX401.2.S69
Space-based radar: TL3285
Space cabin simulators: TL1572
Space colonies: TL795.7

Space communities: TL795.7
Space debris: TL1499
Space environment: TL1489+
Space environmental effects
  Engineering materials: TA418.59
Space flight computer
  simulation: TL1088
Space flight to Jupiter:
  TL799.J8
Space flight to Mars: TL799.M3
Space flight to the moon:
  TL799.M6
Space flight to the sun:
  TL799.S86
Space flight to Venus:
  TL799.V45
Space flight training: TL1085
Space frame structures
  Structural engineering:
  TA660.S63
Space mining: TN291.3+
Space navigation
  Astronautics: TL1065+
Space photography: TR713
Space probes (Astronautics):
  TL795.3
Space robotics: TL1097
Space safety: TL867
Space shuttles (Astronautics):
  TL795.5+
Space simulators
  Space environment: TL1495
Space spinoffs
  Astronautics: TL865
Space stations: TL797+
Space suits: TL1550
Space tools: TL1098
Space tracking
  Astronautics: TL4030
Space trajectories
  Space navigation: TL1075+
Space travel: TL787+
Space vehicles: TL795+
  Design and construction: TL875
  Operation: TL1090+
  Reliability: TL885
Space vehicles, Reuseable
  (Astronautics): TL795.5+
Space walk: TL1096
Spaceships: TL795+

Spaghetti
  Food processing and
  manufacture: TP435.M3
Spaghetti squash
  Cookery: TX803.S63
Spark ignition
  Miscellaneous motors and
  engines: TJ782+
Spark plugs
  Internal combustion engines:
  TJ787
Sparks and spark arresters
  Locomotives: TJ656
Spars
  Airplanes: TL674
Special effects
  Cinematography: TR858
  Photography: TR148
Special occasions
  Cookery: TX739+
Specifications
  Aircraft engines: TL701.7
  Aircraft propellers: TL706.S6
  Airplanes: TL671.1
  Airports: TL725.2
  Astronautics: TL869
  Bathrooms: TH6486
  Bridges: TG310
  Building construction: TH425
  Carpentry and joinery: TH5609
  Cement and concrete
  construction: TA682.25
  Concrete building
  construction: TH1465
  Dynamoelectric machinery:
  TK2321
  Electrical engineering: TK425
  Engineering economy: TA180+
  Engineering materials: TA404.5
  Environmental engineering of
  buildings: TH6051
  Foundry work: TS234
  Gas and electric lighting
  fixtures: TH7963
  Heating of buildings: TH7325
  Highway engineering: TE180
  Hot water heating: TH7513
  Hydraulic machinery: TJ902.5
  Incandescent lighting: TK4348
  Iron and steel: TA466

Specifications
  Knit goods: TT688
  Lighting: TH7715
  Machinery: TJ245
  Metals: TA461
  Optical instruments: TS515
  Packaging: TS195.6
  Pavements: TE252
  Photography in surveying:
    TA593.6
  Plumbing: TH6225
  Railroad engineering: TF195
  Railway equipment: TF363
  Reinforced concrete
    construction: TA683.24
  Steam engines: TJ474
  Steam heating: TH7563
  Telegraph: TK5281
  Telephone: TK6181
  Underground lines: TK3258
  Warm-air heating: TH7602
  Watches and clocks: TS544.5
  Water supply to buildings:
    TH6523
Spectrum analysis of food:
  TX547+
Speech processing systems
  Electronics: TK7882.S65
Speech recognition systems
  Computer engineering:
    TK7895.S65
Speed and revolution indicators
  Machinery exclusive of prime
    movers: TJ1054
Speedometers
  Locomotives: TJ669.S6
Spelt
  Cookery: TX809.S64
Spencer rifle: TS536.6.S64
Sphalerite
  Ore deposits and mining:
    TN482.S6
Spherical balloons: TL634
Spices
  Adulteration: TX587+
  Flavoring aids: TP420
  Nutrition: TX406+
Spiegel iron
  Metallurgy: TN757.S7

Spikes, Metal
  Engineering and construction:
    TA492.N2
Spillways
  Dams: TC555
  Environmental effects:
    TD195.S65
Spinach
  Food processing and
    manufacture: TP444.S65
Spindles
  Machine tools: TJ1187.4
Spinner
  Aircraft propellers: TL707.S6
Spinning
  Aerodynamics: TL574.S6
  Cotton manufactures: TS1577
  Flax industries: TS1727
  Silk manufactures: TS1667
  Textile industries: TS1480+
  Woolen manufactures: TS1627+
Spinning wheel
  Textile arts: TT847
  Textile industries: TS1484
Spirit leveling
  Surveying: TA607
Splicing
  Motion picture film: TR886.5
Splines
  Fastenings: TJ1329
SPM materials
  Engineering materials:
    TA418.9.S64
Sponge iron
  Metallurgy: TN727
Spool-knitting for children:
  TT829
Spoons
  Cookery: TX657.S28
Sport airplanes: TL685.1
Sport clothes: TT649
Sport utility vehicles: TL230+
Sporting goods industry
  Manufactures: TS2301.S7
Sporting surfaces
  Plastic: TP1185.S65
Sports cars: TL236
Sports cinematography
  Photography: TR895.6

Sports facilities
  Electric lighting: TK4399.S63
  Energy conservation:
    TJ163.5.S67
  Heating and ventilation:
    TH7392.S65
Sports photography: TR821
Spotting
  Commercial garment cleaning:
    TP932.6
Sprang
  Textile arts: TT840.S68
Spray painting
  Handicrafts: TT315
Spraying
  Chemical engineering: TP156.S6
Spraying with plastics:
    TP1175.S6
Sprays
  Plumbing: TH6492
Spread spectrum
  communications: TK5103.45
Springs
  Mechanical movements: TJ210
  Railroad cars: TF391
Springs and suspension
  Motor vehicles: TL257+
Sprinklers
  Water supply: TH6569.S7
Sprinkling carts
  Street cleaning: TD865
Sprouted bed processes
  Chemical engineering: TP156.S57
Sprouts
  Food values: TX558.S75
Spruce
  Aeronautics: TL699.S7
  Woodpulp industry: TS1176.4.S7
Spur gears
  Toothed gears: TJ189
Squares
  Machine shops: TJ1201.S68
Squash
  Cookery: TX803.S67
Squid
  Cookery: TX748.S68
Squirrel-cage motors
  Alternating-current motors:
    TK2785

Stability
  Aerodynamics: TL574.S7
  Electric power systems: TK1010
  Motor vehicle dynamics: TL245.8
  Rockets: TL784.S7
Stability of structures: TA656+
Stabilization
  Hazardous substances: TD1063
  Radioactive waste disposal:
    TD898.18
  Water treatment and
    conditioning: TD468
Stabilization ponds
  Sewage treatment: TD746.5
Stabilizers
  Airplanes: TL677.S8
  Airships: TL662.S7
Stabilizing devices
  Airplanes: TL697.S8
Stabilizing surfaces
  Airplanes: TL676+
Stadia surveying: TA588
Staff building construction:
    TH1550
Stage photography: TR817
Stagger
  Airplanes: TL673.S7
Staging
  Building construction: TH5281
  Rockets: TL784.S74
Stain fungi
  Deterioration of wood: TA423.4
Stained glazing
  Decorative furnishings: TH8271+
Stainless steel
  Engineering materials: TA479.S7
  Metallurgy: TN757.C5
Stair joinery
  Building construction: TH5671+
Stair railings
  Building construction: TH5675+
Stairbuilding
  Finish carpentry: TH5667+
Stall warning systems
  Aeronautical instruments:
    TL589.2.S7
Stalling
  Aerodynamics: TL574.S74
Stamping
  Decorative needlework
    Patterns: TT755

Stamps
  Ore dressing and milling: TN510
Standard clock systems
  Manufactures: TS544
Standard times of work
  Industrial engineering: T60.42
Standardization
  Industrial engineering: T59+
  Railway equipment: TF347
  Textile industries: TS1450
Standards
  Aircraft engines: TL701.7
  Aircraft propellers: TL706.S6
  Airplanes: TL671.1
  Cement and concrete
    construction: TA682.25
  Computer networks: TK5105.55+
  Dynamoelectric machinery:
    TK2311
  Engineering materials: TA404.5
  Food processing and
    manufacture: TP372.6
  Hydraulic machinery: TJ902.5
  Mechanical drawing: T357
  Optical instruments: TS515
  Packaging: TS195.6
  Photography in surveying:
    TA593.6
  Radio: TK6553
  Reinforced concrete
    construction: TA683.24
  Screws and screw threads:
    TJ1340
  Steam engines: TJ474
  Wells: TD407
  Wood: TA419.5
Standpipes
  Water distribution systems:
    TD489
Stannotype
  Photography: TR997
Star trackers
  Space vehicles: TL3255
Starch
  Chemical technology: TP248.S7
Starches: TP415+
  Food values: TX558.S8
Starching
  Laundry work: TT993
Starters
  Dynamoelectric machinery:
    TK2851

Starting devices
  Aircraft engines: TL702.S7
  Jet engines: TL709.5.S8
  Motor vehicles: TL272
Static electricity
  Aeronautical meteorology:
    TL557.S65
Static electricity and fires
  Fire prevention: TH9198.5
Static loading conditions
  Structural analysis: TA648+
Statics, Applied: TA351
Station management: TF652
Stationary boilers
  Hot water heating: TH7539
Stationary furnaces
  Hot water heating: TH7539
  Hydronic systems: TH7473
  Steam heating: TH7589
Stationery
  Paper manufacture: TS1228+
Stations
  Mining engineering: TN297
  Railway structures: TF300+
  Telephone: TK6211+
Statistical methods
  Engineering mathematics: TA340
  Hotels, clubs, restaurants,
    etc.: TX911.3.S73
  Industrial engineering: T57.35+
  Industrial safety: T55.3.S72
  Mining engineering: TN272.7
Statistically indeterminate
  structures: TA650+
Staves
  Manufactures: TS890
Steam accumulators
  Steam boilers: TJ393
Steam automobiles: TL200
Steam boiler explosions: TJ299+
Steam boilers: TJ281+
Steam coil tanks
  Hot water supply: TH6559
Steam condensation heating
  tanks
  Plumbing: TH6560
Steam engine accessories:
  TJ555+
Steam engineering: TJ268+
Steam engines
  Aircraft engines: TL704.4
  Mechanical engineering: TJ461+

INDEX

Steam engines,
  Non-reciprocating: TJ720+
Steam fire engines
  Fire extinction: TH9376
Steam fixtures of buildings:
    TH7561+
Steam gages
  Steam boilers: TJ370+
Steam hammers
  Machine shops: TJ1305+
Steam heating of buildings:
    TH7561+
Steam jacket
  Steam engines: TJ531
Steam-jacketed pans
  Chemical technology: TP159.S7
Steam-laundry work: TT990
Steam packing
  Steam powerplants: TJ435
Steam pipe covering
  Steam powerplants: TJ427
Steam power plants
  Air pollution: TD888.S7
  Mechanical engineering: TJ395+
  Waste control: TD899.S68
Steam pumps
  Hydraulic machinery: TJ906+
Steam separators
  Steam powerplants: TJ441
Steam shovels
  Railroad construction: TF225+
Steam syphons
  Hydraulic machinery: TJ921
Steam traps
  Steam powerplants: TJ438
Steam trucks: TJ705
Steam turbines: TJ735+
Steam valves
  Steam powerplants: TJ430+
Steam wagons: TJ705
Steam water heaters
  Hot water supply: TH6558+
Steaming
  Cooking process: TX691
Steaming apparatus
  Chemical technology: TP159.S73
Stearates
  Chemical technology: TP248.S76
Stearic acid
  Chemical technology: TP248.S8
Stearman (Aircraft
    manufacturer): TL686.S7

Steel
  Aeronautics: TL699.S8
  Electrical engineering:
    TK454.4.S7
  Heating: TS325
  Housing material: TH4818.S73
  Metal manufactures: TS300+
  Metallurgy: TN730+
  Structural engineering: TA684+
Steel alloys
  Aeronautics: TL699.S8
  Engineering materials: TA478+
  Metallurgy: TN756+
Steel and iron
  Engineering materials: TA464+
Steel beams
  Structural engineering:
    TA660.S66
Steel dams: TC549
Steel furniture
  Manufactures: TS408
Steel pens
  Stationery: TS1263
Steel piling
  Foundations: TA786
Steel pipe
  Sewers: TD686
Steel plants
  Metal manufactures: TS330
Steel roofing
  Building construction: TH2457
Steel square
  Carpentry and joinery: TH5619
Steel-wood I-beams
  Structural engineering:
    TA660.S67
Steel work
  Engineering: TA890+
Steelworking
  Metal manufactures: TS320
Steelworks
  Air pollution: TD888.S72
  Electric lighting: TK4399.I7
  Electric power: TK4035.S7
  Energy conservation:
    TJ163.5.S83
  Environmental effects: TD195.S7
  Waste control: TD899.S7
Steering apparatus
  Airships: TL662.S8
Steering gear
  Motor vehicles: TL259

Stencil cutting
  Handicrafts: TT270+
Stencil printing
  Textile decoration: TT852.6
Stencil work
  Handicrafts: TT270+
Stephanite: TN432.S7
Stepped gears
  Mechanical movements: TJ192
Stereo high fidelity systems
  Electronics: TK7881.8+
Stereophonic broadcasting
  Radio: TK6562.S7
Stereophotogrammetry: TA593.7
Stereophotography: TR780
Stereoscopic cameras
  Photography: TR259
Stereoscopic motion pictures:
  TR854
Stereotomy
  Masonry construction: TA672
Sterilization
  Canned foods: TP371.35
  Chemical engineering: TP156.S8
  Space vehicles: TL945
  Wine and winemaking: TP548.5.S7
Stevia
  Cookery: TX819.S75
Stewards' manuals
  Hotels, clubs, restaurants,
    etc.: TX921
Stewing
  Cooking process: TX693
Still life photography: TR656.5
Stir frying
  Cooking process: TX689.5
Stitches
  Decorative needlework: TT760
Stochastic processes
  Industrial engineering: T57.32+
Stochastic programming
  Industrial engineering: T57.79
Stock cars
  Motor vehicles: TL236.28
  Railway equipment: TF475
Stock photography: TR690.6
Stock preparation
  Paper manufacture: TS1118.S85
Stockkeeping
  Inventory control: TS163

Stockroom keeping
  Hotels, clubs, restaurants,
    etc.: TX911.3.S8
Stockrooms
  Machine shops: TJ1150
Stocks
  Cookery: TX819.S8
Stone
  Housing material: TH4818.S75
  Masonry construction: TA676
  Masonry materials: TA426+
  Pavements: TE257+
  Roadmaking material: TE200+
  Sidewalks: TE289
  Stairbuilding: TH5667+
Stone blocks
  Pavements: TE261+
Stone building construction:
  TH1201
Stone flooring: TH2529.S7
Stone roofing
  Building construction: TH2444+
Stone walls
  Building design and
    construction: TH2249
Stone, Coloring of
  Painting: TT370
Stonebreaking for roads: TE237
Stonecrushers for road
  material: TE239
Stonecutting
  Building construction: TH5401+
Stonemasonry
  Building construction: TH5401+
Stoneware
  Ceramic technology: TP820
Stonework
  Manufactures: TS780+
Stoping
  Mining: TN287
Stoppings
  Mining engineering: TN304
Storage
  Food: TP373.3
  Nuclear engineering: TK9152.165
Storage and handling
  Explosives: TP295
Storage batteries
  Electrical engineering: TK2941
  Locomotives: TJ669.S7
Storage buildings: TH4451+

Storage facilities
  Plant service facilities:
    TS189.6
Storage of coal: TN817
Storage of foods in the home:
  TX599+
Storage of hot water
  Plumbing: TH6562+
Storage of petroleum: TN871
Storage systems
  Cold water supply plumbing:
    TH6545
Storage tanks
  Cold water supply plumbing:
    TH6545
Storage tubes
  Electronics: TK7871.76
Store fixtures
  Wooden furniture: TS889
Storerooms
  Machine shops: TJ1150
  Plant service facilities:
    TS189.6
Stores, Retail
  Electric lighting: TK4399.S8
  Energy conservation:
    TJ163.5.S85
  Fire prevention and
    extinction: TH9445.S8
  Security in buildings:
    TH9745.S7
Storm sewer system: TD665
Stormproof construction
  Building construction: TH1096
Storms
  Aeronautical meteorology:
    TL557.S7
Stormwater infiltration:
  TD657.5
Stoves
  Cookery: TX657.S3+
  Metal manufactures: TS425
Stoves for commercial kitchens
  Building construction: TH7135
Stoves for heating
  Building construction: TH7435+
Straight-line mechanisms
  Mechanical engineering: TJ181.8
Straightening machines
  Machine shops: TJ1300
Strain gages
  Testing of materials: TA413.5

Strain hardening
  Plastic properties and tests:
    TA418.18
Strains
  Aircraft propellers: TL706.S7
  Airships: TL660.2
  Bridge engineering: TG260+
  Structural analysis: TA648.5
Stratified charge engines
  Internal combustion engines:
    TJ791
Straw
  Engineering materials: TA455.S8
  Floor covering: TS1779.M2
  Housing material: TH4818.S77
Straw plaiting
  Textile fiber: TS1747.S7
Straw work
  Decorative crafts: TT876
Strawberries
  Cookery: TX813.S9
Stray currents
  Electric railways: TF912
Streak cameras
  Photography: TR257.5
Stream channelization
  Hydraulic engineering: TC529
Stream gaging
  Hydrodynamics: TC175+
Stream motorcars
  Railway equipment: TF495
Stream pollution: TD425
Streambank planting
  River protective works: TC537
Streams
  Sewage effluent discharge
    into: TD763+
Streams, Discharge into
  Sewage disposal: TD771.5
Streams, Self-purification of
  Disposal of sewage effluent:
    TD764
Street cars
  Electric railways: TF920+
Street cleaning: TD813+
Street lighting: TP741
Street photography: TR659.8
Street railways: TF701+
Street rods: TL236.3
Street sprinkling
  Street cleaning: TD863+

Streets
  Highway engineering: TE279
  Lighting (nonelectric): TP741
  Use of salt and chemicals in
    ice control: TD870
Strela computer: TK7889.S7
Strength
  Boilermaking: TJ291
  Brick: TA433
  Cast iron: TA475
  Cement: TA435
  Concrete: TA440
  Iron and steel: TA465
  Metals: TA460
  Mortar: TA437
  Reinforced concrete: TA445
  Soils: TA710+
  Steel: TA473
  Stone: TA427
  Wood: TA420
  Wrought iron: TA470
Strength of materials: TA405+
Strengthening mechanisms
  Strength of materials: TA409.3
Stress analysis
  Strength of materials: TA407
Stress, Deformation of
  materials under: TA417.6
Stresses
  Aircraft propellers: TL706.S7
  Airships: TL660.2
  Bridge engineering: TG260+
  Structural analysis: TA648.3
Stresses, Thermal
  Engineering materials: TA418.58
  Structural engineering: TA654.8
String
  Decorative crafts: TT880
Strip adjustment
  Photographic triangulation:
    TA593.83
Strip mining: TN291
  Environmental effects:
    TD195.S75
Striped bass
  Cookery: TX748.S75
Stroboscopy: TA1820
Strontium: TN490.S8
  Chemical technology: TP245.S8

Structural analysis
  Air frames: TL671.6
  Bridges: TG260+
  Structural engineering: TA645+
Structural design: TA658+
Structural details
  Airplanes: TL674
Structural drawing
  Mechanical drawing: T355
Structural drawings
  Building design and
    construction: TH2031
Structural dynamics
  Bridge engineering: TG265
  Space vehicles: TL910
  Structural analysis: TA654+
Structural elements for
  landscape construction,
  Building of: TH4961+
Structural engineering: TA630+
Structural engineering of
  buildings
  Building construction: TH845+
Structural failure: TA656+
Structural iron and steel
  Manufactures: TS350
Structural optimization
  Structural engineering: TA658.8
Structural parts
  Airplanes: TL674
Structural protection
  Engineering: TA900
Structure-soil interaction
  Soil mechanics: TA711.5
Structures, Submerged
  Hydraulic engineering: TC201
Struts
  Airplanes: TL674
  Structural engineering:
    TA660.S7
Stucco
  Building construction: TH1461+
  Engineering materials:
    TA455.S84
  Masonry: TH5371
Studio lighting
  Photography: TR573
Studios
  Photography: TR550+
Stuffed foods
  Cookery: TX836

Stuffing box
  Steam engines: TJ529
Stump work embroidery:
    TT778.S75
Stun guns
  Electronics: TK7882.S78
Stunt driving: TL152.58
Stunt flying: TL711.S8
Styrene
  Effect on food: TX572.S79
  Plastics: TP1180.S7
Subdivisions
  Engineering: TH350
Subgrade soils
  Analysis: TE208+
Subgrade structure
  Highway engineering: TE211
Sublimation
  Chemical engineering: TP156.S9
Submachine guns
  Manufactures: TS536.9
Submarine blasting
  Hydraulic engineering: TC191+
Submarine building
  Hydraulic engineering: TC195+
Submarine drilling
  Hydraulic engineering: TC193
Submarine foundations
  Hydraulic engineering: TC197
Submarine telegraph
  Engineering: TK5601+
Submarine telephone cables:
    TK6370+
Submarine well drilling
  Petroleum engineering: TN871.3
Submersible pumps
  Hydraulic machinery: TJ927
Submillimeter waves
  Electronics: TK7877
Subsidences
  Mining: TN319
Substations
  Electric lighting: TK4237
  Electric power plants: TK1751
  Telephone: TK6241
Subsurface disposal
  Sewage effluent: TD761
Subterranean photography: TR788
Subways
  Engineering: TF845+
  Environmental effects: TD195.S9

Sucrose
  Chemical technology: TP375+
Suez Canal: TC791
Sugar
  Cookery: TX819.S94
  Food constituent: TX553.S8
  Food values: TX560.S9
Sugar byproducts: TP414.5
Sugar cane industry
  Environmental effects:
    TD195.S93
Sugar esters
  Chemical technology: TP248.S9
Sugar factories
  Air pollution: TD888.S77
  Electric power: TK4035.S9
Sugar industry
  Energy conservation:
    TJ163.5.S93
  Waste control: TD899.S8
Sugar-making machinery: TP381
Sugar products: TP414.3+
Sugarcane wax: TP679.S8
Sugars and syrups
  Chemical technology: TP375+
SuiteSpot (Netscape):
    TK5105.883.N493
Sulphate process
  Woodpulp industry: TS1176.6.S9
Sulphate waste liquor
  Woodpulp industry:
    TS1176.6.S915
Sulphates
  Air pollutants: TD887.S78
  Inorganic chemicals: TP240
Sulphide dyes
  Textile dyes: TP918.S8
Sulphides
  Ore deposits and mining:
    TN495.S9
  Ore dressing and milling:
    TN538.S84
  Prospecting: TN271.S88
  Water pollutants: TD427.S94
Sulphite liquor
  Woodpulp industry: TS1176.6.S92
Sulphite process
  Woodpulp industry: TS1176.6.S93
Sulphites
  Inorganic chemicals: TP240
Sulphonated oils: TP675

Sulphonitriding
  Metal finishing: TS695.7
Sulphur
  Air pollutants: TD887.S82
  Chemical technology: TP245.S9
  Engineering materials:
    TA455.S93
  Environmental pollutants:
    TD196.S95
  Mining engineering: TN890
  Prospecting: TN271.S9
  Water pollutants: TD427.S94
Sulphur cement
  Cement manufacture: TP884.S85
Sulphur compounds
  Petroleum products: TP692.4.S9
  Water pollutants: TD427.S94
Sulphur dioxide
  Air pollutants: TD885.5.S8
  Chemical technology: TP244.S83
Sulphur hexafluoride
  Insulating material: TK3441.S8
Sulphur-organic compounds
  Chemical technology: TP248.S93
Sulphur oxides
  Air pollutants: TD885.5.S85
Sulphuric acid: TP215
Sulphuric acid plants
  Air pollution: TD888.S8
Sulphurous acid
  Effect on food: TX572.S9
Summer homes
  Construction: TH4835
Summer pieces
  Building construction: TH7433
Sun
  Flights to: TL799.S86
Sunflower seed oil
  Chemical technology: TP684.S8
Sunspaces
  Building design and
    construction: TH3000.S85
Superchargers
  Aircraft engines: TL702.S8
  Gasoline automobiles: TL214.S8
  Miscellaneous motors and
    engines: TJ762.S95
Superconductors
  Electrical engineering:
    TK454.4.S93
  Electronics: TK7872.S8
  Metallography: TN693.S9

Superheated steam
  Locomotives: TJ693
  Steam engineering: TJ272
Superheaters
  Steam engineering: TJ272
Superheating reactors
  Nuclear engineering: TK9203.S86
Superintendence
  Bridge engineering: TG315
  Construction sites: TH438+
  Electrical enterprises: TK441+
  Heating of buildings: TH7338
  Plumbing: TH6238
Superphosphates
  Fertilizers: TP963.4.S9
Supersonic aerodynamics: TL571
Supersonic compressors
  Turbines: TJ267.5.C6
Supersonic nozzles
  Turbines: TJ267.5.N6
Superstructure
  Railway construction: TF240+
Supervisory control systems
  Mechanical engineering: TJ222
Suppers
  Cookery: TX738
Supplies
  Blacksmithing: TT224
  Color photography: TR515
  Electric railways: TF950+
  Heating of buildings: TH7345
  Machine shops: TJ1150
  Petroleum pipelines: TN879.54
  Photography: TR196+
  Pollution control methods:
    TD192
  Textile arts: TT845
  Woodworking: TT186
Support systems, Decision
  Industrial engineering: T58.62
Supporting surfaces
  Airplanes: TL672+
Supports
  Boilermaking: TJ293
  Pipelines: TJ930.5
SURAnet
  Computer networks:
    TK5105.875.S95
Surface
  Steam engines: TJ561

Surface active agents
  Organic chemical industries:
    TP994
Surface analysis
  Chemical engineering: TP156.S95
Surface effects
  Engineering materials: TA418.7+
Surface hardening
  Steel metallurgy: TN752.S8
Surface impoundments
  Hazardous waste treatment
    facilities: TD1054
Surface tests
  Engineering materials: TA418.7+
Surface transportation: TN341
Surround-sound systems
  Electronics: TK7881.83
Surveying: TA501+
  Railway construction: TF200
Surveying of cities
  City planning: TD167
Surveyor project: TL789.8.U6S9
Survival after airplane
  accidents: TL553.7
Survival and rescue narratives
  Aeronautics: TL553.9.A1+
Susidences
  Building construction: TH1094+
Suspended ceilings
  Building: TH2533.S88
Suspended railways: TF693
Suspension
  Motor vehicles: TL257+
Suspension bridges: TG400
Suspension roofs
  Building construction: TH2417
Swac computer: TK7889.S8
Swamps
  Reclamation: TC975
Sweaters
  Clothing manufacture: TT679+
  Knitting and crocheting: TT825
Sweepback
  Airplanes: TL673.S9
Sweet potatoes
  Cookery: TX803.S94
  Food processing and
    manufacture: TP444.S94
  Food values: TX558.S94
Sweeteners
  Flavoring aids: TP421+

Sweeteners, Artificial
  Effect on food: TX571.S9
Swimmers
  Photographic portraits:
    TR681.S88
Swimming pools
  Building construction: TH4763
Switchboards and accessories
  Dynamoelectric machinery:
    TK2821+
  Telegraph: TK5491
Switchboards and accessories
  for line connections:
    TK6391+
Switched capacitor circuits
  Electronic circuits: TK7868.S88
Switched multi-megabit data
  service
  Computer networks:
    TK5105.875.S97
Switches
  Dynamoelectric machinery:
    TK2831
  Railway construction: TF266+
Switchgear
  Radio: TK6565.S9
Switching
  Electronic circuits: TK7868.S9
Switching circuits
  Computer engineering: TK7888.4
Switching diodes
  Semiconductors: TK7871.89.S95
Switching of cars
  Trains: TF592
Switching systems
  Electrical engineering:
    TK5103.8
Syenite
  Mining engineering: TN948.S9
Symbols
  Industrial engineering: T55.52
  Technology: T8
Synchronizers
  Electrical engineering: TK381
Synchronous alternating-current
  machinery: TK2731
Synchronous digital hierarchy
  Synchronous transfer systems:
    TK5105.42
Synchronous motors
  Alternating-current motors:
    TK2787

Synchronous telegraph system: TK5535

Synchronous transfer systems
  Electrical engineering: TK5105.4+

Synthetic aperture radar: TK6592.S95

Synthetic dyes
  Textile decoration: TT854.5

Synthetic fibers
  Textile industries: TS1548.2+

Synthetic fuels industry
  Environmental effects: TD195.S95

Synthetic petroleum
  Fuel: TP355
  Mineral oils and waxes: TP698

Synthetic rubber
  Manufactures: TS1925

Synthetic textile fibers
  Dyeing: TP904
  Manufactures: TS1548.2+

Synthetic training devices
  Technical education: T65.5.S9

Syrups
  Carbonated beverages: TP636
  Cookery: TX819.S96

Systems analysis
  Industrial engineering: T57.6+

Systems engineering: TA168
  Astronautics: TL870+

Systems of electric lighting: TK4303+

Systems reliability: TA169+

T

Table
  Dining-room service: TX871+

Table arrangement
  Dining-room service: TX873

Table carving
  Dining-room service: TX885

Table covers
  Embroidery: TT775

Table decoration
  Dining-room service: TX879
  Hotels, clubs, restaurants, etc.: TX911.3.T32

Table furnishings
  Dining-room service: TX877

Table service
  Hotels, clubs, restaurants, etc.: TX925

Table serving
  Dining-room service: TX881

Table setting
  Hotels, clubs, restaurants, etc.: TX911.3.T32

Table-top photography: TR683.5

Table, Pleasures of
  Nutrition: TX631+

Tables
  Air navigation: TL587
  Chemical technology: TP151
  Home economics: TX151+
  Ore dressing and milling: TN520+
  Precious metals: TS729
  Wood manufactures: TS886.5.T3
  Woodworking: TT197.5.T3

Tabletop fountains
  Decorative crafts: TT899.74

Tablets
  Stonework: TS788

Tacan
  Aeronautical navigation equipment: TL696.T3

Tachometer
  Aeronautical instruments: TL589.7.T3

Taconite
  Ore deposits and mining: TN402.T3

TACV
  High speed ground transportation: TF1580

Tail skids
  Airplanes: TL683.S5

Taildragger flying
  Airplanes: TL711.T28

Tailings dam failures
  Mines: TN319.5

Tailless airplanes: TL684.6

Tailoring, Men's: TT570+

Tailplane
  Airplanes: TL677.S8

Takeoff
  Airplanes: TL711.T3

Talc
  Electrical engineering: TK454.4.T3
  Engineering materials: TA455.T3
  Mining engineering: TN948.T2

Tall buildings
  Fire prevention and
    extinction: TH9445.T18
  Heating and ventilation:
    TH7392.T34
  Plumbing: TH6515.T35
  Sanitary engineering:
    TH6057.T23
Tall oil
  Chemical technology: TP684.T3
Tallow
  Manufactures: TS1980+
Tangential water wheels: TJ866
Tank cars
  Railway equipment: TF481
Tank systems
  Hot water supply plumbing:
    TH6551
Tanks
  Aircraft engines: TL702.F8
  Plastic: TP1185.T3
  Structural engineering:
    TA660.T34
Tanneries
  Environmental effects:
    TD195.T35
  Fire prevention and
    extinction: TH9445.T2
  Waste control: TD899.T3
Tanning
  Manufactures: TS940+
Tanning materials
  Manufactures: TS985
Tannins
  Manufactures: TS985
Tantalum: TN490.T2
  Chemical technology: TP245.T2
  Engineering materials:
    TA480.T34
  Metallography: TN693.T34
  Metallurgy: TN799.T3
  Prospecting: TN271.T3
Taper
  Airplanes: TL673.T4
Tapes
  Packaging materials: TS198.3.A3
Tapestry
  Hand weaving: TT849
  Textile industries: TS1780
  Wall decoration: TH8481
Tapioca
  Starch: TP416.T3

Tapping of the line
  Electrical engineering: TK3101
Taps and dies
  Fastenings: TJ1335
Tar
  Composition roofing: TH2451
Tarred roads: TE244
Tartaric acid
  Chemical technology: TP248.T27
Tartrates
  Chemical technology: TP248.T3
Tassels
  Decorative crafts: TT899.5
Tatting
  Textile arts: TT840.T38
Taverns: TX950+
Taxicabs: TL232.5
TCP/IP
  Computer network protocols:
    TK5105.585
TDMA (Wireless communication
  systems): TK5103.486
Tea
  Adulteration: TX585
  Chemical technology: TP650
  Cookery: TX817.T3
  Nonalcoholic beverages: TP638+
  Nutrition: TX415
Tea making paraphernalia
  Cookery: TX657.T43
Teargas munitions
  Manufactures: TS538.5
Tearooms
  Food service: TX945+
Technetium
  Water pollutants: TD427.T42
Technical applications
  Photography: TR692+
Technical chemistry of plastics
  Analysis: TP1140
Technical education
  Industrial engineering: T61+
Technical hydraulics
  Hydraulic engineering: TC160+
Technical information
  Communication: T10.5+
Technical mensuration: T50
Technical processes
  Ceramic technology: TP814
  Plastics: TP1150+
Technical schools
  Industrial engineering: T61+

Technical writing: T11 +
Technological change: T173.2 +
Technological forecasting: T174
Technological innovations:
　T173.8
　Hazardous substances and their
　　disposal: TD1050.T43
Technology assessment: T174.5
Technology indicators: T174.2
Technology transfer: T174.3
　Astronautics: TL865
Tee stiffeners, Metal
　Engineering and construction:
　　TA492.T4
Tehuantepec Canal: TC785
Tehuantepec Ship Railway: TC786
Telecommunication
　Electrical engineering: TK5101 +
　Space vehicles: TL3025 +
Telecommunication as a
　profession: TK5102.6
Telecommunication lines:
　TK5103.15
Telegraph
　Aircraft communication: TL693 +
　Amateurs' manuals: TK9941 +
　Engineering: TK5107 +
Telegraph alphabets: TK5509
Telegraph apparatus, lines and
　material, Testing of: TK5385
Telegraph branch stations:
　TK5341
Telegraph circuits, Wiring of:
　TK5441 +
Telegraph codes
　Aircraft: TL694.C6
Telegraph enterprises,
　Management of: TK5283 +
Telegraph line: TK5301 +
Telegraph plants: TK5301 +
Telegraph stations: TK5301 +
Telegraph stations, Central:
　TK5321 +
Telegraph system
　Railway operation: TF627 +
Telegraph wires and cables:
　TK5481
Telegraphic equipment
　Railway operation: TF615 +
Telegraphing systems: TK5501 +
Telegraphones: TK6500

Telematics
　Computer networks: TK5105.6
Telemeter systems
　Electrical engineering: TK399
Telemetry
　Aircraft communication
　　equipment: TL694.T35
　Rockets: TL784.T5
Telephone: TK6001 +
　Amateurs' manuals: TK9951
Telephone companies
　Management: TK6183 +
Telephone connection systems:
　TK6394 +
Telephone lines
　Telephone connections: TK6351 +
Telephone plants: TK6201 +
Telephone receivers: TK6481
Telephone stations: TK6201 +
Telephone stations, Central:
　TK6211 +
Telephone system
　Railway operation: TF627 +
Telephone wiremen's manuals:
　TK6345
Telephone wires and cables:
　TK6381 +
Telephonographs: TK6500
Telephoto lenses
　Photography: TR271.T44
Telephotography: TR770
Telescopic sights
　Gunsmithing: TS535.2.T4
Teletext systems: TK6679.7
Teletype
　Aircraft communication
　　equipment: TL694.T4
Television: TK6630 +
　Aircraft communication: TL693 +
　Aircraft navigation equipment:
　　TL695 +
　Amateurs' manuals: TK9960 +
　Space vehicles: TL3040
　Technical education: T65.5.T4
Television as a profession:
　TK6644
Television camera operation
　Cinematography: TR882.5
Television cameras
　Cinematography: TR882 +
Television relay systems:
　TK6648 +

Television stations: TK6646
  Building construction: TH4656
Telford roads
  Unpaved roads: TE241
Tellurium: TN490.T5
  Chemical technology: TP245.T3
  Metallography: TN693.T4
Telpherage
  Conveying machinery: TJ1385+
Telstar (Artificial
  satellite): TK5104.2.T4
Tempeh
  Cookery: TX814.5.T45
  Food values: TX558.T39
Temperature
  Effects on viscous flow and
    yield strength: TA418.24+
Temperature-dependent
  properties and tests:
    TA418.24+
Temperature measurements
  Steel: TN731
Tempering
  Steel metallurgy: TN752.T4
Temporary storage of discarded
  materials
  Nuclear engineering: TK9152.165
Tenite
  Plastics: TP1180.T4
Tennis players
  Nutrition: TX361.T45
Tension
  Testing of materials:
    TA417.7.T4
Tension leg platforms
  Ocean engineering: TC1703
Tensionmeter
  Aeronautical instruments:
    TL589.2.T4
Tensor analysis
  Engineering mathematics:
    TA347.T4
Tent making
  Textile industries: TS1860
Tequila
  Distilled liquors: TP607.T46
Terbium
  Chemical technology: TP245.T4
Terephthalic acid
  Chemical technology: TP248.T46
Terminal management
  Trains: TF590+

Terminally ill
  Photographic portraits:
    TR681.T47
Terminals: TF300+
  Computer engineering:
    TK7887.8.T4
  Generators: TK2488
  Transportation engineering:
    TA1225
Termites
  Deterioration of wood: TA423.7
Terra-cotta
  Architectural ceramics: TP835
  Fire-resistive building
    construction: TH1077+
  Masonry materials: TA432+
Terrace houses
  Construction: TH4825
Terraces
  Building construction: TH4970
Test of vision
  Railway operation: TF620
Testing
  Aircraft engines: TL701.8
  Aircraft propellers: TL706.T4
  Airplanes: TL671.7
  Airships: TL660.4+
  Alternating-current machinery:
    TK2723
  Brick: TA433
  Building gas supply: TH6860
  Cast iron: TA475
  Cement: TA435
  Color photography: TR515
  Concrete: TA440
  Direct current machinery:
    TK2623
  Dynamoelectric machinery:
    TK2316
  Electric machinery and
    appliances: TK401
  Electric power distribution
    systems: TK3081
  Fuel: TP321+
  Heating of buildings: TH7341
  Iron and steel: TA465
  Leather industries: TS967
  Line insulators: TK3246
  Materials: TA410+
  Metals: TA460
  Military airplanes: TL685.3
  Mortar: TA437

Testing
  Motor vehicles: TL285
  Packaging: TS195.8
  Paper manufacture: TS1109
  Plumbing: TH6241
  Preservation of wood: TA424.2
  Prime movers: TJ253
  Radio: TK6553
  Railway equipment: TF361
  Railway operroadon: TF537
  Reinforced concrete: TA445
  Roadmaking materials: TE205
  Rocket manufacture: TL784.5.T4
  Sewage sludge: TD767.4+
  Space vehicles: TL920
  Steam boilers: TJ297
  Steel: TA473
  Stone: TA427
  Telephone apparatus: TK6285
  Telephone line and material:
    TK6285
  Textile industries: TS1449
  Tobacco industry: TS2249
  Watches and clocks: TS548
  Wine and winemaking: TP548.5.A5
  Wood: TA420
  Wood pulp: TS1176.6.T4
  Wrought iron: TA470
Testing laboratories
  Electrical engineering: TK411+
  Engineering: TA416+
Testing machines
  Testing of materials: TA413+
Testing methods
  Rock mechanics: TA706.5
Testing of soils
  Soil mechanics: TA710.5
Tests
  Air pilots: TL555
  Examination and analysis of
    food: TX551+
  Gas industry: TP754
  Steam engines: TJ475
Tethered satellites: TL798.T47
TETRA
  Wireless communication
    systems: TK5103.488
Textile arts and crafts: TT699+
Textile bleaching
  Chemical technology: TP890+
Textile chemistry: TS1474.5

Textile decoration
  Handicrafts: TT851+
Textile design
  Textile industries: TS1475
Textile dyeing
  Chemical technology: TP890+
  Textile decoration: TT853+
Textile fabrics
  Packaging materials: TS198.3.T5
  Textile industries: TS1760+
Textile factories
  Dust removal: TH7697.T4
  Electric power: TK4035.T4
  Fire prevention and
    extinction: TH9445.M5
  Heating and ventilation:
    TH7392.T47
  Ventilation: TH7684.T25
Textile fibers
  Textile industries: TS1540+
Textile finishing
  Textile arts: TT849.7
Textile industry
  Energy conservation:
    TJ163.5.T48
  Environmental effects:
    TD195.T48
  Manufactures: TS1300+
  Noise control: TD893.6.T4
  Waste control: TD899.T4
Textile machinery
  Electric driving: TK4059.T48
  Manufactures: TS1525
Textile mills
  Air conditioning: TH7688.F3
  Building construction: TH4521
Textile painting: TT851
Textile printing
  Chemical technology: TP890+
  Textile arts and crafts: TT852+
Textile roofing
  Building construction: TH2449
Textile setting: TS1511
Textile supplies
  Textile industries: TS1529+
Textured soy protein
  Cookery: TX814.5.T48
Textures
  Artistic photography: TR682

Thallium
  Chemical technology: TP245.T5
  Environmental pollutants:
    TD196.T45
Thanksgiving
  Cookery: TX739.2.T45
Thanksgiving decorations
  Decorative crafts: TT900.T5
Thatch roofing
  Building construction: TH2435
Thaw houses
  Explosives: TP295
Thawing of pipes
  Plumbing: TH6685
Theater photography: TR817
Theaters
  Electric lighting: TK4399.T6
  Electric sound control:
    TK7881.9
  Fire prevention and
    extinction: TH9445.T3+
  Heating and ventilation:
    TH7392.T5
  Sanitary engineering: TH6057.T3
  Ventilation: TH7684.T3
Theodolite
  Aeronautical instruments:
    TL589.2.T5
  Surveying instruments: TA575
Theory of structures
  Structural engineering: TA645+
Thermal analysis
  Food: TX544
Thermal batteries
  Electrical engineering: TK2953
Thermal conductivity
  Thermal properties: TA418.54
Thermal expansion
  Properties of materials:
    TA418.56+
Thermal pollution
  Water pollutants: TD427.H4
Thermal properties
  Electronic apparatus and
    materials: TK7870.25
  Walls: TH1715+
Thermal properties and tests
  Engineering materials:
    TA418.52+
Thermal stresses
  Engineering materials: TA418.58
  Structural engineering: TA654.8

Thermionic converters
  Electrical engineering: TK2955
Thermistors
  Electronics: TK7871.98
Thermodynamics
  Heat engines: TJ265
  Mechanical engineering: TJ756
  Refrigeration and icemaking:
    TP492.5
  Space vehicles: TL900
Thermoelectric cooling: TP492.9
Thermoelectric devices
  Space vehicles: TL1102.T4
Thermoelectricity
  Electrical engineering: TK2950+
Thermomechanical treatment
  Steel metallurgy: TN752.T54
Thermometers
  Aeronautical instruments:
    TL589.2.T53
  Control engineering: TJ223.T4
  Nuclear engineering: TK9183.T54
Thermoplastics
  Plastics: TP1180.T5
Thermosetting plastics
  Plastics: TP1180.T55
Thermostats
  Central heating: TH7466.5
  Range water heaters: TH6557
Thermosyphons: TJ263.2
Thick-walled elements
  Structural engineering:
    TA660.T48
Thin film devices
  Electronics: TK7872.T55
Thin film transistors:
  TK7871.96.T45
Thin films
  Engineering materials:
    TA418.9.T45
Thin layer chromatography
  Food analysis: TX548.2.T48
Thin-walled elements
  Structural engineering:
    TA660.T5
Thinners
  Paints: TP937.7
Third-rail railroads
  Electric railways: TF890

Thorium: TN490.T55
  Chemical technology: TP245.T6
  Metallography: TN693.T45
  Metallurgy: TN799.T4
  Prospecting: TN271.T4
Thread manufacture
  Cotton manufactures: TS1590
Thread numbers
  Textile industries: TS1450
Three-dimensional motion
  pictures: TR854
Three-moment theorem: TA650+
Three-phase current systems
  Electrical engineering: TK3156
Three-phase currents
  Electrical engineering: TK1165
Threshing machines
  Agricultural machinery: TJ1486
Thrift
  Foods and food supply: TX356
Thrust
  Aerodynamics: TL574.L5
  Aircraft propellers: TL706.T5
  Rockets: TL784.T4
Thrust reversers
  Jet engines: TL709.5.T5
Thulium
  Chemical technology: TP245.T7
Thyratrons
  Electronics: TK7871.83
Thyristors
  Electronics: TK7871.99.T5
Tidal power
  Hydraulic engineering: TC147
Tie-dyeing
  Textile decoration: TT853.5
Tie plates
  Railway construction: TF257
Ties
  Railway construction: TF252+
Tile
  Building construction: TH8541+
  Cement manufacture: TP885.P5
  Decorative furnishings: TH8521+
  Fire-resistive building
    construction: TH1077+
  Masonry materials: TA432+
Tile-concrete combination
  systems
  Fire-resistive-building
    construction: TH1089

Tile craft
  Decorative crafts: TT927
Tile industry
  Waste control: TD899.T55
Tile roofing
  Building construction: TH2448
Tilefish
  Cookery: TX748.T54
Tilelaying
  Decorative furnishings: TH8521+
Tiles
  Architectural ceramics: TP837
  Plastic: TP1185.T5
Tilt
  Photography in surveying:
    TA593.9.T54
Timber and concrete
  Masonry materials: TA442
Timbering
  Mine ground control: TN289
Timbers
  Aeronautics: TL699.W6
Time and motion study
  Industrial engineering: T60+
Time code
  Editing of motion pictures:
    TR899.5
Time dependent properties and
  tests: TA418.3+
Time-lapse photography
  Cinematography: TR857
Time measurement, Methods
  Industrial engineering: T60.52
Time measurements
  Electronics: TK7878.2
Time schedules
  Airports: TL725.3.T5
  Railway operation: TF565
Time stamps industry: TS2301.T5
Time study
  Industrial engineering: T60.4+
  Machine shops: TJ1143
Timekeeping
  Highway engineering: TE185
Timers
  Control engineering: TJ223.T5
Timing
  Electronic circuits: TK7868.T5
Timing belts
  Gasoline automobiles: TL214.T55
Timing chains
  Gasoline automobiles: TL214.T55

Tin
  Chemical technology: TP245.T8
  Effect on food: TX572.T6
  Engineering materials: TA480.T5
  Metallurgy: TN793
  Ore deposits and mining: TN470+
  Ore dressing and milling:
    TN538.T55
  Prospecting: TN271.T5
  Utilization of waste: TP996.T5
Tin can craft: TT266+
Tin industry
  Dust removal: TH7697.T5
Tin mines and mining
  Environmental effects:
    TD195.T56
Tin ores
  Assaying: TN580.T5
Tin roofing
  Building construction: TH2455
Tin shingling
  Building construction: TH2455
TINA (Computer network
  protocols): TK5105.586
Tinning
  Metal finishing: TS660
Tinplate
  Manufactures: TS590+
Tinsmithing: TS600+
Tinsmiths' supplies
  Manufactures: TS619
Tinting
  Mechanical drawing: T357
Tintype
  Photography: TR375
Tinware
  Manufactures: TS619
Tinwork
  Handicrafts: TT266+
Tipping
  Aircraft propellers: TL707.T5
Tips of wings
  Airplanes: TL673.T4
Tire houses
  Building construction:
    TH4818.T57
Tires
  Airplanes: TL683.T5
  Cycles: TL425
  Motor vehicles: TL270
Tissue paper: TS1168

Titanium: TN490.T6
  Aeronautics: TL699.T56
  Chemical technology: TP245.T85
  Electronics: TK7871.15.T56
  Electroplating: TS692.T5
  Engineering and construction:
    TA480.T54
  Manufactures: TS562
  Metallography: TN693.T5
  Metallurgy: TN799.T5
  Powder metallurgy: TN697.T5
  Prospecting: TN271.T55
Titanium steel
  Metallurgy: TN757.T5
Titling
  Motion picture film: TR886.9
TK toolkit
  Web authoring software:
    TK5105.8885.T54
TLV
  High speed ground
    transportation: TF1560+
TMN
  Electrical engineering:
    TK5105.45
TNT
  Explosives: TP290.T8
Toaster oven cookery: TX840.T63
Toasters
  Cookery: TX657.T58+
Tobacco industry
  Manufactures: TS2220+
Tocopherol
  Chemical technology: TP248.T55
Tofu
  Cookery: TX814.5.T63
  Food processing: TP438.S6
  Food values: TX558.T57
Toilet rooms
  Plumbing: TH6485+
Toilets
  Plumbing: TH6498
Tole painting: TT385
Tolerances
  Product engineering: TS172
Toluene
  Chemical technology: TP248.T6
  Petroleum products: TP692.4.T6
Tomato juice
  Cookery: TX814.5.T64
Tomato paste
  Cookery: TX814.5.T65

Tomatoes
  Adulteration: TX595.T6
  Cookery: TX803.T6
  Food processing and
    manufacture: TP444.T6
  Food values: TX558.T6
  Preservation and storage:
    TX612.T7
Tombstones
  Stonework: TS788
Ton-miles
  Railway operation: TF555
Tongs
  Machine shops: TJ1201.T64
Toning
  Photographic positives: TR335
Tool cars
  Railway equipment: TF485
Tool life
  Equipment analysis: TS181.4
Tool steel
  Metal manufactures: TS320
Toolboxes
  Woodworking: TT197.5.T65
Toolrooms
  Plant service facilities:
    TS189.3
Tools
  Building construction: TH915
  Carpentry: TH5618
  Engineering: TA213+
  Handrail joinery: TH5677
  Joinery: TH5618
  Stonecutting: TH5440
  Stonemasonry: TH5440
  Street cleaning: TD860
  Textile arts: TT845
  Woodworking: TT186
Toothed gears
  Mechanical engineering: TJ184+
Topographic drawing
  Surveying: TA616
Topographical surveying: TA590
TOPS: TK5105.8.T65
Torches: TP743
Torquemeters
  Machinery exclusive of prime
    movers: TJ1053.5
Torsion
  Testing of materials:
    TA417.7.T6

Tortillas
  Cookery: TX770.T65
Tote bags
  Clothing manufacture: TT667
Toupees
  Hairwork: TT975
Tourist trade
  Environmental effects:
    TD195.T68
Towels
  Textile industries: TS1781
Towers
  Building design and
    construction: TH2180
  Electric power: TK3242
  Structural engineering:
    TA660.T6
Towing
  Canals: TC767+
  Motor vehicles: TL153.7
Towing apparatus
  Aeronautical research: TL567.T6
Toy balloons: TL633
Toy industry
  Manufactures: TS2301.T7
Toy-knitting: TT829
Toys
  Handicrafts: TT174+
Trace elements
  Assaying: TN580.T73
  Environmental pollutants:
    TD196.T7
  Food constituent: TX553.T7
  Water pollutants: TD427.T7
Track
  Electric railways: TF870+
  Railway construction: TF240+
Track maintenance equipment
  Railway operation: TF538.5
Track tanks
  Railway structures: TF271
Tracked air cushion vehicle
  High speed ground
    transportation: TF1580
Tracked levitated vehicle
  High speed ground
    transportation: TF1560+
Tracking
  Hazardous substances and their
    disposal: TD1050.T73
Tracklaying machinery
  Railway construction: TF248

Tracklaying vehicles: TL234 +
Trackmasters' manuals: TF538
Traction
  Motor vehicles: TL295
Traction drives
  Mechanical engineering: TJ1095
Traction engines: TJ700
Traction tests
  Highway engineering: TE450
  Motor vehicles: TL295
Tractor driving: TL233.3
Tractor propellers: TL706.P8
Tractors: TL233 +
Trade publications
  Stationery: TS1238
Trade shows
  Technology: T391 +
Trademarks: T325
  Paper manufacture: TS1115
Traffic circles
  Highway engineering: TE176.5
Traffic control
  Airports: TL725.3.T7
Traffic control devices
  Highway engineering: TE228
Traffic operation
  Railway operation: TF650 +
Trafficability of soils:
  TE208.5
Trail bikes: TL441
Trailers
  Motor vehicles: TL297 +
Trails
  Highway engineering: TE304
Train dispatching
  Railroad operation: TF563
Train resistance
  Railway operation: TF552
Train rules
  Railway operation: TF559
Train running
  Railway operation: TF556
Train speed
  Railway operation: TF553 +
Train telegraph systems:
  TK5569.T7
Training
  Hotels, clubs, restaurants,
    etc.: TX911.3.T73
Training equipment
  Astronautics: TL1570 +

Trainload
  Railway operation: TF555
Trainmen's manuals
  Railway operation: TF557 +
Trains
  Railway operation: TF550 +
Transaxles: TL265
Transducers
  Control engineering: TJ223.T75
  Electronics: TK7872.T6
Transfer functions
  Engineering mathematics:
    TA347.T7
Transfer machines
  Machine tools: TJ1185.5
Transfer pictures industry:
  TS2301.T9
Transfer printing
  Textile decoration: TT852.7
Transfer tables
  Railway structures: TF276
Transfer work, Iron-on
  Textile decoration: TT852.7
Transfer, Technology: T174.3
Transformation of electricity
  Electrical engineering: TK3107
Transformers
  Amateurs' manuals: TK9915
  Electronics: TK7872.T7
  Radio: TK6565.T7
  Television: TK6655.T7
Transforming machinery
  Dynamoelectric machinery:
    TK2551
Transistor amplifiers
  Electronics: TK7871.2
Transistor radios: TK6564.T7
Transistors
  Semiconductors: TK7871.9 +
Transit and theodolite
  Surveying instruments: TA575
Transition metal compounds
  Metallography: TN693.T7
Transition spiral
  Railroad surveying: TF217
Translating
  Patents: T210.2
  Technical information: T11.5
Translating services
  Patents: T210.2
Transmission devices
  Motor vehicles: TL262 +

Transmission gears
  Mechanical engineering: TJ204
Transmission lines
  Electronics: TK7872.T74
  Radio: TK6565.T73
Transmission of electric power
  Electrical engineering: TK3001+
Transmit-receive tubes
  Radar: TK6590.T72
Transmitter-receiver units
  Radar: TK6587
Transmitters
  Radio: TK6561
  Telephone: TK6475+
Transmitting
  Aircraft communication
    equipment: TL694.T7
Transmitting apparatus
  Radar: TK6587
  Television: TK6651
Transmutation
  Radioactive waste disposal:
    TD898.178
Transoceanic flights: TL531
Transonic aerodynamics: TL571
Transpacific routes
  Air routes: TL726.15
Transparencies
  Photography: TR504+
Transport centers
  Transportation engineering:
    TA1225
Transport planes: TL685.7
Transport processes
  Chemical engineering: TP156.T7
Transportation
  Energy conservation: TJ163.5.T7
  Engineering materials: TA403.6
  Environmental effects: TD195.T7
  Food: TP373.2
  Noise control: TD893.6.T7
  Papermills: TS1116.6
  Radioactive substances:
    TK9152.17
Transportation engineering:
  TA1001+
Transportation industries
  Fire prevention and
    extinction: TH9445.T7
Transportation method
  Linear programming: T57.78

Transportation systems, Urban:
  TA1205+
Transportation, Air
  Environmental effects:
    TD195.A27
Transputers
  Computer engineering:
    TK7895.T73
Transvestites
  Photographic portraits:
    TR681.T7
Traps
  Petroleum geology: TN870.57
  Plumbing: TH6631+
Trashracks
  Dams: TC554
Travel cinematography: TR896.5
Travel photography: TR790
Traveling-wave tubes
  Electronics: TK7871.77
Travelling cranes
  Hoisting machinery: TJ1365
Traverses
  Surveying: TA585
Trays
  Wood products: TS913
Treadmills
  Renewable energy sources: TJ830
Tree houses
  Construction: TH4885
Tree planting
  Coast protective works: TC340
  River protective works: TC537
Trees
  Nature photography: TR726.T7
Trestle bridges: TG365+
Triangular wings
  Airplanes: TL673.T7
Triangulation for engineering
  works: TA583
Triangulation, Photographic:
  TA593.8+
Tributyltin
  Water pollutants: TD427.T73
Trichloroethylene
  Air pollutants: TD887.T75
  Chemical technology: TP248.T7
  Water pollutants: TD427.T75
Trick cinematography: TR858
Trick photography: TR148
Tricolor photography: TR520
Tricycles: TL410+

Trigger
  Electronic circuits: TK7868.T7
Trigonometric leveling
  Surveying: TA609
Trihalomethanes
  Water pollutants: TD427.T77
Trimming
  Women's tailoring: TT552
Trimming of prints
  Photographic processing: TR340
Trimmings
  Silk manufactures: TS1687
  Window and door openings:
    TH2261+
Trinitrotoluene
  Explosives: TP290.T8
Triplanes: TL684.5
Triple expansion
  Steam engines: TJ501+
Tripoli
  Mining engineering: TN948.T74
Triticale
  Food values: TX558.T7
Tritium
  Environmental pollutants:
    TD196.T74
Trochotrons: TK7871.79.T7
Troilite
  Ore dressing and milling:
    TN538.T74
Trolley (overhead wiring)
  Electric railways: TF885
Trona
  Mining engineering: TN948.T76
Tropical photography: TR795
Tropical woods
  Woodpulp industry: TS1176.4.T7
Tropospheric scatter
  communication systems:
    TK6570.T76
Trousers
  Men's tailoring: TT605
  Women's tailoring: TT542
Trout
  Cookery: TX748.T74
TRS-80 computer: TK7889.T77
Truck driver training: TL230.3
Truck driving: TL230.3
Truck-mounted campers: TL298
Truck-mounted coaches: TL298
Truck trailers
  Motor vehicles: TL297.6

Trucking
  Water pollution: TD428.T78
Trucks: TL230+
  Human engineering in design:
    TL250
Truffles
  Cookery: TX804.5
Trunked radio
  Wireless communication
    systems: TK5103.488
Trussed bridges: TG375+
Trusses
  Cement manufacture: TP885.T7
  Reinforced concrete
    construction: TA683.5.T7
  Structural engineering:
    TA660.T8
Try cocks
  Steam boilers: TJ363
Tube vehicle system
  High speed ground
    transportation: TF1620
Tubes
  Aeronautics: TL699.T8
  Manufactures: TS1920
  Metal manufactures: TS280+
Tubes, Metal
  Engineering and construction:
    TA492.T8
Tubs
  Plumbing: TH6493
Tubular bag systems
  Fire prevention and
    extinction: TH9416
Tubular bridges: TG390
Tubular radiators
  Hydronic systems: TH7488
Tuna
  Cookery: TX748.T84
Tunable lasers
  Applied optics: TA1706
Tuned amplifiers: TK7871.58.T8
Tuners
  Television: TK6655.T8
Tung oil
  Chemical technology: TP684.T8
Tungsten
  Chemical technology: TP245.T9
  Electronics: TK7871.15.T85
  Electroplating: TS692.T8
  Engineering and construction:

Tungsten
    TA480.T9
    Metallography: TN693.T94
    Metallurgy: TN799.T9
    Prospecting: TN271.T8
Tungsten lamps
    Electric lighting: TK4359.T9
Tungsten ores: TN490.T9
Tungsten steel
    Metallurgy: TN757.T9
Tunnel diodes
    Semiconductors: TK7871.87
Tunnel kilns: TP842.T8
Tunneling
    Engineering: TA800 +
    Mining: TN285
    Noise control: TD893.6.T86
Tunnels
    Engineering: TA800 +
    Fire prevention and
        extinction: TH9445.T8
    Railway construction: TF230 +
Turbine-propeller engines
    Aeronautics: TL709.3.T8
Turbines: TJ266 +
    Jet engines: TL709.5.T87
    Water wheels: TJ870 +
Turbochargers
    Gasoline automobiles: TL214.T87
Turbofan engines
    Aeronautics: TL709.3.T82
Turbojet engines
    Aeronautics: TL709.3.T83
Turbomachines: TJ266 +
    Electric driving: TK4059.T87
Turbulence
    Aerodynamics: TL574.T8
    Applied fluid mechanics:
        TA357.5.T87
Turkey
    Cookery: TX750.5.T87
Turn and bank indicator
    Aeronautical instruments:
        TL589.2.T8
Turning
    Handicrafts: TT201 +
Turning machines
    Machine shops: TJ1215 +
Turnouts
    Railroad surveying: TF216
    Railway construction: TF264

Turntables
    Railway structures: TF275
Turpentine
    Organic chemical industries:
        TP977 +
Turquoise
    Jewelry work: TS755.T8
Turtles
    Nutrition: TX388.T8
Tuscan style cookery:
    TX723.2.T86
TVS
    High speed ground
        transportation: TF1620
Twin-engine flying
    Airplanes: TL711.T85
Twine
    Textile fiber: TS1795
Twins
    Photographic portraits:
        TR681.T85
Twisted gears
    Mechanical movements: TJ192
Twisted plates
    Structural engineering:
        TA660.P65
Twisting and twisting machinery
    Textile industries: TS1487.5
Two-phase current systems
    Electrical engineering: TK3153
Two-phase currents
    Electrical engineering: TK1151
Two-phase flow
    Applied fluid mechanics:
        TA357.5.M84
Two-pipe systems
    House drainage: TH6604
    Low-pressure hot water
        heating: TH7525
    Steam heating: TH7567
Two-stroke cycle engines
    Gasoline automobiles: TL210.5
Two-stroke engines
    Internal combustion engines:
        TJ790
Two-way radio: TK6553
Typewriter art
    Decorative crafts: TT869
Tysonite
    Mining engineering: TN948.T9

U

U.S. Army world flight:
  TL721.U6
U.S. National Aeronautics and
  Space Administration:
  TL521.3+
Ultra large scale integrated
  circuits: TK7874.76
Ultrafax
  Facsimile transmission: TK6720
Ultrahigh frequency apparatus
  Television: TK6655.U6
Ultralight aircraft: TL685.15
Ultrasonic machining
  Machine tools: TJ1191
Ultrasonic testing
  Testing of materials: TA417.4
Ultrasonic transducers: TK5982
Ultrasonic welding: TS228.92
Ultrasonics
  Chemical engineering: TP156.A33
Ultrasound
  Food preservation: TP372.4
Ultraviolet ray treatment
  Sewage disposal: TD747.5
  Water purification: TD460
Ultraviolet technology
  Applied optics: TA1600
Umbrellas
  Textile industries: TS1865
Unauthorized users of water:
  TD497
Undercarriage
  Airplanes: TL682+
Underground conduits
  Electric railways: TF895
Underground construction: TA712
Underground factories
  Building construction: TH4518
Underground flow
  Hydrodynamics: TC176
Underground gasification of
  coal: TP759
Underground lines
  Electric power: TK3251+
  Telegraph: TK5465+
Underground railways
  Engineering: TF845+
Underground roads
  Mines: TN333

Underground shopping centers
  Fire prevention and
    extinction: TH9445.U5
Underground storage
  Gas industry: TP756.5
Underground telephone lines:
  TK6365
Underground utility lines
  City planning: TD168
Undershirts
  Clothing manufacture: TT675
Undershot water wheels: TJ864
Undertakers' supplies
  industry: TS2301.U5
Underwater cinematography:
  TR893.8
Underwater construction
  Cement and concrete
    construction: TA682.485
Underwater mining: TN291.5
Underwater photography: TR800
Underwater pipelines
  Ocean engineering: TC1800
Underwater television: TK6679.5
Underwear
  Clothing manufacture: TT669+
Unfermented apple juice: TP564
Unfermented grape juice
  Beverages: TP560
Unidentified flying objects:
  TL789+
Uniforms
  Fire prevention and
    extinction: TH9395+
  Men's clothing: TT625
Unit trains: TF583
Univac computer: TK7889.U6
Universal joints
  Machinery: TJ1059
Universities
  Energy conservation: TJ163.5.U5
  Plumbing: TH6515.S4
University buildings
  Heating and ventilation:
    TH7392.S35
Unloading and loading
  Materials handling: TS180.5
Unpaved roads
  Highway engineering: TE230+
Unsaturated fatty acids
  Food constituent: TX553.U5

Unsteady flow
  Aerodynamics: TL574.U5
  Applied fluid mechanics:
    TA357.5.U57
Upgrading
  Computer engineering: TK7887
Upholstering
  Handicrafts: TT198
Upholstery
  Fire-testing: TH9446.5.U63
  Motor vehicles: TL256
Upholstery leather: TS980.U6
Uppers
  Leather: TS980.U7
Ural computer
  Computer engineering: TK7889.U7
Uranium
  Chemical technology: TP245.U7
  Engineering materials: TA480.U7
  Metallography: TN693.U7
  Metallurgy: TN799.U7
  Ore deposits and mining:
    TN490.U7
  Ore dressing and milling:
    TN538.U7
  Prospecting: TN271.U7
Uranium as fuel: TK9363
Uranium industry
  Environmental effects: TD195.U7
  Waste control: TD899.U73
Uranium mines and mining
  Water pollution: TD428.U73
Uranium steel
  Metallurgy: TN757.U7
Urban runoff
  Sewage collection and disposal
    systems: TD657+
Urban transportation systems:
  TA1205+
Urea
  Chemical technology: TP248.U7
  Environmental pollutants:
    TD196.U73
  Fertilizers: TP963.4.U7
Urea-formaldehyde resins
  Plastics: TP1180.U7
Urethanes
  Effect on food: TX571.P63
Urinals
  Plumbing: TH6499

Usenet
  Computer networks:
    TK5105.875.U83
User's plant
  Electric power: TK3201+
Utensils
  Cookery: TX656+
Utility lines, Underground
  City planning: TD168

V

Vacation cinematography:
  TR896.5
Vaccines
  Biotechnology: TP248.65.V32
Vacuum lifters
  Hoisting machinery: TJ1360
Vacuum metallurgy
  Electrometallurgy: TN686.5.V3
Vacuum processes
  Cement and concrete
    construction: TA682.47
Vacuum pumps: TJ940.5
Vacuum system
  Dust removal: TH7695.V2
Vacuum technology
  Chemical engineering: TP156.V3
  Mechanical engineering: TJ940+
Vacuum-tube amplifiers
  Electronics: TK7871.2
Vacuum tubes
  Chemical technology: TP159.V3
  Electronics: TK7871.72+
  Radio: TK6565.V3
Valentine's Day
  Cookery: TX739.2.V34
Valentine's Day decorations
  Decorative crafts: TT900.V34
Valuation
  Engineering economy: TA178
  Hotels, clubs, restaurants,
    etc.: TX911.3.V34
Value analysis
  Cost control: TS168
Value engineering
  Cost control: TS168
Valve gears
  Locomotives: TJ665
  Steam engines: TJ547+

Valves
  Aircraft engines: TL702.V3
  Balloons: TL625.V3
  Chemical technology: TP159.V34
  Control engineering: TJ223.V3
  Gasoline automobiles: TL214.V3
  Hot water heating: TH7543
  Hydronic systems: TH7478
  Locomotives: TJ665
  Metal manufactures: TS277
  Plumbing explosion prevention:
    TH6566
  Steam heating: TH7593
  Water distribution systems:
    TD491
  Water supply plumbing: TH6528
Vanadium
  Chemical technology: TP245.V2
  Environmental pollutants:
    TD196.V35
  Metallography: TN693.V3
  Metallurgy: TN799.V3
  Ore deposits and mining:
    TN490.V2
Vanadium steel
  Engineering materials: TA479.V3
  Metallurgy: TN757.V3
Vanaspati
  Chemical technology: TP684.V36
Vanes
  Building construction: TH2495
Vanguard: TL796.5.U6V3
Vanilla
  Cookery: TX819.V35
Vanners
  Ore dressing and milling:
    TN520+
Vans: TL230+
Vapor lamps and systems
  Electric lighting: TK4381
Vapor-plating
  Metal finishing: TS695+
Varactors
  Semiconductors: TK7871.88
Variable air volume systems
  Air conditioning: TH7687.95
Variety meats
  Cookery: TX749.5.V37
Varistors
  Electronics: TK7871.99.V3
Varnish
  Insulating material: TK3441.V3

Varnishes
  Chemical technology: TP938
Varnishing
  Handicrafts: TT300+
  Wood finishing: TT340
Vat dyes
  Textile dyes: TP918.V37
Vaults
  Building design and
    construction: TH2160
  Security in buildings: TH9734
Vector analysis
  Engineering mathematics:
    TA347.V4
Vegetable fats
  Chemical technology: TP680+
Vegetable-fiber work
  Decorative crafts: TT873+
Vegetable fibers
  Textile industries: TS1541+
Vegetable foods
  Nutrition: TX391+
Vegetable juices
  Food values: TX558.V4
Vegetable oils
  Chemical technology: TP680+
  Fuel: TP359.V44
Vegetable products
  Food processing: TP443+
Vegetables
  Cookery: TX801+
  Food processing: TP443+
  Food values: TX557+
  Nutrition: TX401+
  Preservation and storage:
    TX612.V4
Vegetarian cookery: TX837+
Vegetarianism
  Nutrition: TX392+
Vegetation
  Roadside development: TE178
Vehicles
  Aerodynamics: TA359
  Fire prevention and
    extinction: TH9370+
  Handicrafts: TT174.5.V43
  Vibration: TA356
Vehicular tunnels
  Engineering: TA800+
Velocipedes: TL405
Velvets
  Silk manufactures: TS1675

Vending machines
  Mechanical engineering: TJ1560
Veneering
  Manufactures: TS870
Veneers
  Wall details: TH2251.5
  Wood products: TS870
Venison
  Food values: TX556.V4
Vent piping
  House drainage: TH6668
Vent stack
  House drainage: TH6666
Vent stack systems
  House drainage: TH6665+
Ventilating machines
  Mining engineering: TN303
Ventilation
  Buildings: TH7646.92+
  Prisons: TH7392.P8
  Railway equipment: TF445+
  Railway tunnels: TF235
  Sewers: TD692
  Transportation engineering:
    TA1280
  Tunneling: TA814
Ventilation of mines: TN301+
Ventilation radiators
  Hydronic systems: TH7490
Ventilators
  Artificial ventilation of
    buildings: TH7678+
  Building design and
    construction: TH2486+
  Ventilation of buildings:
    TH7683.V4
Venting for appliances
  Gas in buildings: TH6835
Vents
  Plumbing: TH6631+
Venturi scrubber
  Dust removal: TH7695.V45
Venus (Planet)
  Flight to: TL799.V45
Veranda roofs
  Building construction: TH2425
Vermiculite
  Engineering materials: TA455.V4
  Mining engineering: TN948.V4
Vertical drains: TC974.2

Vertical multitubular steam
  boilers
  Mechanical engineering: TJ312
Vertical seismic profiling:
  TN269.86
Vertical stabilizer
  Airplanes: TL677.F5
Vertically rising aircraft
  Aeronautical engineering: TL685
Very high speed integrated
  circuits
  Electronics: TK7874.7
Very large scale integrated
  circuits
  Electronics: TK7874.75
Vests
  Men's tailoring: TT615
Veterinary drug residues
  Effect on food: TX571.V48
Vibration
  Aerodynamics: TL574.V5
  Aircraft propellers: TL706.V4
  Bridge engineering: TG265
  Engineering: TA355
  Machinery: TJ177
  Motor vehicle dynamics: TL246
  Vehicles: TA356
Vibration methods
  Reinforced concrete
    construction: TA683.46
Vibration processes
  Cement and concrete
    construction: TA682.46
Vibrations
  Structural analysis: TA654+
Vibrators
  Chemical technology: TP159.V52
  Mechanical engineering: TJ208
Vibroseis
  Seismic prospecting: TN269.88
Vici kid
  Leather: TS980.V6
Victorium
  Chemical technology: TP245.V5
Vicuna
  Textile fiber: TS1548.V5
Video amplifiers: TK7871.58.V5
Video disc equipment
  Electronics: TK6685
Video discs
  Electronics: TK6685

Video game equipment
  Electronics: TK6681
Video games
  Amateurs' manuals: TK9971
Video recording
  Amateurs' manuals: TK9961
Video recording, Lighting for
  Cinematography: TR891
Video recordings
  Photography: TR845+
Video tape recorders
  Amateurs' manuals: TK9961
  Television: TK6655.V5
Video telephones: TK6505
View cameras
  Photography: TR258
Vigorit
  Explosives: TP290.V5
Vinegar
  Cookery: TX819.V5
  Flavoring aid: TP429+
VINES: TK5105.8.V56
Vinidur
  Plastics: TP1180.V42
Vinyl
  Plastics: TP1180.V48
  Textile fiber: TS1548.7.V5
Vinyl chloride
  Air pollutants: TD887.V55
Vinyl flooring: TH2529.P5
Viruses
  Water pollutants: TD427.V55
Viscoelasticity
  Plastic properties and tests:
    TA418.2
Viscous flow
  Applied fluid mechanics:
    TA357.5.V56
  Plastic properties and tests:
    TA418.2
  Temperature effects: TA418.24+
Vises
  Handtools: TJ1201.V5
Visibility
  Aeronautical meteorology:
    TL557.V5
Visitors, Foreign
  Photographic portraits:
    TR681.V58
Visual InterDev (Microsoft)
  Web authoring software:
    TK5105.8885.M55

Vitamins
  Biotechnology: TP248.65.V57
  Food constituent: TX553.V5
  Food constituents: TP453.V5
Vitrification
  Ceramic technology: TP815
  Radioactive waste disposal:
    TD898.179
Vocational guidance
  Carpentry and joinery: TH5608.8
  Hairdressing: TT958
  Hotels, clubs, restaurants,
    etc.: TX911.3.V62
  Pollution control personnel:
    TD177.8
  Textile industries: TS1463
  Watch and clock manufactures:
    TS545.9
  Welding: TS227.7
Vodka
  Distilled liquors: TP607.V6
Voice of the air
  Airplane advertising: TL722.5
Volcanic ash, tuff, etc.
  Water pollutants: TD427.V64
Voltage detectors
  Electrical engineering: TK321
Voltage dividers
  Electronics: TK7872.V53
Voltage-frequency converters
  Electronics: TK7872.V54
Voltage meters and measurements
  Electrical engineering: TK321
Voltage regulators
  Electronics: TK7872.V55
  Radar: TK6590.V6
  Radio: TK6565.V6
Voltage waveforms
  Electrical engineering: TK531
Voltameters
  Electrical engineering: TK331
Voltmeters
  Electrical engineering: TK321
  Electronics: TK7879+
Voltmeters, Vacuum tube
  Electronics: TK7879.2
Voltohmmeters: TK325
Vortex theory
  Aerodynamics: TL574.V6
Vortex tubes: TJ264.5

VSATs
  Artificial satellites:
    TK5104.2.V74
Vulcanizing
  Rubber industry: TS1891

W

Waffles
  Cookery: TX770.P34
Wagonmaking
  Manufactures: TS2001+
Wainscots
  Building construction: TH2547
Waiters, Manuals for
  Hotels, clubs, restaurants,
    etc.: TX925
Waiting line problems
  Industrial engineering: T57.9
Waitresses, Manuals for
  Hotels, clubs, restaurants,
    etc.: TX925
Wakes
  Aerodynamics: TL574.W3
Walkie-talkies
  Radio: TK6565.W25
Wall coils
  Radiators: TH7484
Wall decoration
  Building construction: TH8403+
Wall hangings
  Textile arts: TT850.2
Wall plugs
  Electric lighting: TK4361+
Wallboard
  Engineering materials: TA455.W3
Wallpaper
  Wall decoration: TH8423+
Walls
  Building construction: TH2201+
  Building details: TH2251+
  Reinforced concrete
    construction: TA683.5.W34
  Structural engineering:
    TA660.W3
Walls above surface
  Building design and
    construction: TH2231+
Walnuts
  Cookery: TX814.2.W3

Wankel engines
  Gasoline automobiles: TL210.7
  Internal combustion engines:
    TJ792
War
  Environmental effects:
    TD195.W29
War damage
  Airports: TL725.3.D35
War photography: TR820.6
War use of airships: TL664.2
Warehouses
  Air conditioning: TH7688.W3
  Building construction: TH4451
  Fire prevention and
    extinction: TH9445.W2
  Plant service facilities:
    TS189.6
Warm-air and steam heating
  systems: TH7635
Warm-air heating
  Building construction: TH7601+
Warm-air heating by
  convection: TH7633
Washin
  Airplanes: TL673.W3
Washing
  Photographic negatives: TR305
  Woodpulp industry: TS1176.6.W36
Washing of coal: TN816.A1+
Washington system
  Incandescent gas lighting:
    TH7955.W3
Washout
  Airplanes: TL673.W3
Washtubs
  Laundry plumbing: TH6505
Waste control
  Production management: TS169
Waste disposal sites
  Environmental effects:
    TD195.W295
Waste glass
  Glassmaking: TP859.7
Waste heat boilers: TJ319
Waste heat utilization
  Blast furnaces: TN718
  Municipal refuse: TD796.2
Waste minimization
  Hazardous substances and their
    disposal: TD1050.W36
  Industrial and factory wastes:
    TD897.847
  Municipal refuse: TD793.9+

Waste paint
  Waste disposal: TD800.5
Waste piping
  House drainage: TH6658+
Waste prevention
  Paper manufacture: TS1109
Waste stack systems
  House drainage: TH6655+
Waste tires
  Waste disposal: TD797.7
Waste treatment facilities:
  TD897.6
Waste treatment facilities,
  Radioactive: TD898.16
Waste utilization
  Chemical technology: TP995+
Waste, Plastic
  Waste disposal: TD798
Wastes, Hazardous
  Soil pollutants: TD879.H38
Wastes, Radioactive
  Waste disposal: TD812+
Wastes, Recovery of
  Precious metals: TS729
Wasteways
  Dams: TC555
  Hydraulic powerplants: TJ851
Watches
  Manufactures: TS540+
Watchmakers' lathes: TS546
Water
  Artistic photography: TR670+
  Brewing and malting: TP583
  Chemical industry: TP262+
  Food constituent: TX553.W3
Water analysis
  Geophysical surveying:
    TN269.885
Water at rest: TC165+
Water backs
  Range water heaters: TH6555
Water channels
  Aeronautical research: TL567.B4
Water chemistry
  Petroleum geology: TN870.515
Water closets
  Plumbing: TH6498
Water columns
  Railway structures: TF290
Water conservation: TD388+
Water conversion, Saline:
  TD478+

Water-cooled reactors
  Nuclear engineering: TK9203.W37
Water distribution systems
  Environmental technology:
    TD480.92+
Water gages
  Steam boilers: TJ360+
Water gas
  Gas industry: TP760
Water glass
  Glassmaking: TP869
Water glasses
  Steam boilers: TJ366
Water hammer
  Hydrodynamics: TC174
Water heaters
  Building construction: TH6551+
Water heating coils
  Range water heaters: TH6556
Water hyacinth craft
  Decorative crafts: TT877.8
Water in motion
  Hydraulic engineering: TC171+
Water mains
  Breaks in: TD495+
  Water distribution systems:
    TD491
Water meters and metering:
  TD499+
Water mills: TJ859
Water pipes
  Water distribution systems:
    TD491
Water pollution: TD419+
Water-pressure engines: TJ890
Water purification
  Environmental technology:
    TD429.5+
Water quality: TD370+
Water quality management
  Environmental technology:
    TD365+
Water quality monitoring:
  TD367+
Water rates: TD360
Water resistance: TC766
Water resources of a
  watershed: TC401+
Water reuse
  Environmental technology: TD429
Water softeners
  Steam boilers: TJ379

Water softening
  Chemical technology: TP263
  Water purification: TD466
Water-soluble polymers
  Plastics: TP1180.W37
Water-soluble preservatives
  Preservation of wood:
    TA424.6.W3
Water supply
  Communication of information:
    TD209 +
  Fire prevention and
    extinction: TH9311 +
  Low temperature sanitary
    engineering: TD947
  Papermills: TS1116.2
  Plumbing in buildings: TH6521 +
  Rural and farm sanitary
    engineering: TD927
  Space environment: TL1565
  Steam boilers: TJ377
Water-supply engineering:
    TC401 +
  Environmental effects: TD195.W3
Water-supply fixture catalogs:
    TH6529
Water supply, Domestic: TD201 +
Water supply, Industrial:
    TD201 +
Water tower systems
  Fire prevention and
    extinction: TH9332 +
Water towers
  Water distribution systems:
    TD489
Water treatment and
  conditioning
  Environmental technology:
    TD429.5 +
Water treatment plants
  Building construction: TH4538
  Environmental technology: TD434
  Noise control: TD893.6.W37
  Waste control: TD899.W3
Water tube boilers
  Mechanical engineering: TJ314 +
Water tunnels
  Hydrodynamics: TC171.5
Water waste prevention: TD495 +
Water wave loads
  Structural analysis: TA654.55

Water waves
  Hydrodynamics: TC172
Water wheels: TJ860 +
Water withdrawals
  Water distribution systems:
    TD493
Waterfront structures
  Fire prevention and
    extinction: TH9445.P5
Watermarks
  Paper manufacture: TS1115
Waterpower engineering: TC147
Waterpower power plants:
    TK1421 +
Waterproof construction
  Engineering: TA901
Waterproofing
  Protection of buildings: TH9031
  Textile industries: TS1520
Watershed management
  Hydraulic engineering: TC409
Waterways
  Inland navigation: TC601 +
Waterworks
  Energy conservation:
    TJ163.5.W36
  Water distribution systems:
    TD485 +
Watt-hour meters: TK351
Wattmeters: TK341
Waveguides
  Electronics: TK7871.6 +
  Radar: TK6590.W3
  Radio: TK6565.W3
Wax crafts
  Decorative crafts: TT866
Wax figures industry: TS2301.W3
Wax flowers
  Decorative crafts: TT894
Waxes
  Chemical technology: TP669 +
Weathering
  Protection of buildings from:
    TH9039
Weathering of coal: TN817
Weaving
  Cotton manufactures: TS1579
  Woolen manufactures: TS1629
Weaving, Hand
  Textile arts: TT848 +
Weaving, Industrial
  Manufactures: TS1490 +

Web authoring software
  Internet: TK5105.8883+
Web server software
  Internet: TK5105.8883+
Webcasting
  Internet: TK5105.887
WebTV (Trademark): TK5105.8887
Wedding photography: TR819
Wedges
  Handtools: TJ1201.W44
Weed-burners
  Railway operation: TF546
Weighing and measuring
  Chemical engineering: TP156.W4
Weighing systems
  Electronics: TK7882.W44
Weightlessness simulators:
  TL1575
Weirs
  Dams: TC555
  Hydrodynamics: TC175+
Welded joints, Metal
  Engineering materials: TA492.W4
Welding
  Airplanes: TL671.5
  Handicrafts: TT211
  Metalworking: TS227+
  Petroleum pipelines: TN879.6
  Plastics: TP1160
  Rocket manufacture: TL784.5.W4
Welding shops
  Dust removal: TH7697.W4
Well boring
  Water supply: TD412
Well digging
  Water supply: TD412
Well drilling
  Petroleum engineering: TN871.2+
Well logging
  Petroleum engineering: TN871.35
Well testing
  Petroleum engineering: TN871
Wellpoint system
  Drainage: TC974
Wells
  Pollution: TD426.8
  Steam boilers: TJ378
  Steam engines: TJ565
  Water supply: TD405+
Welsbach system
  Incandescent gas lighting:
  TH7955.W4

Western style cookery:
  TX715.2.W47
Westinghouse airbrakes: TF425
Wet cleaning
  Commercial garment cleaning:
  TP932.5
Wetting
  Chemical engineering: TP156.W45
Whale meat
  Cookery: TX748.W48
Whales
  Nutrition: TX388.W4
Whaling
  Use of airplanes: TL722.2
Wharves
  Harbor engineering: TC357
Wheat
  Cookery: TX809.W45
  Food values: TX558.W5
Wheat germ
  Cookery: TX809.W453
Wheat products
  Food processing and
    manufacture: TP435.W48
Wheatstone's bridge
  Electric meters: TK311
Wheel
  Mechanical engineering: TJ181.5
Wheels
  Airplanes: TL683.W5
  Cycles: TL422
  Electric railways: TF949.W5
  Locomotives: TJ669.W54
  Motor vehicles: TL270
  Railroad cars: TF383
Whirlwind computer: TK7889.W47
Whiskey
  Chemical technology: TP605
White chocolate
  Cookery: TX767.W48
White sauce
  Cookery: TX819.W5
White work embroidery:
  TT778.W55
Whitewashing
  Building decoration: TH8181
Whiting
  Mining engineering: TN948.C5
Whittling
  Woodworking: TT199.7+
Wicker furniture
  Woodworking: TT197.7

Wide-angle lenses
  Photography: TR271.W53
Wide-angle photography: TR687
Wide area networks
  Electrical engineering:
    TK5105.87+
Wide-screen processes
  Cinematography: TR855
Wigs
  Hairwork: TT975
Wild rice
  Cookery: TX809.W55
Wildlife
  Nature photography: TR729.W54
Wildlife cinematography:
  TR893.5
Willowware
  Manufactures: TS910
Winches
  Hoisting machinery: TJ1362
Winchester rifle: TS536.6.W55
Wind loads
  Structural analysis: TA654.5
Wind power: TJ820+
Wind power industry
  Environmental effects:
    TD195.W54
Wind pressure
  Architectural engineering:
    TH891
  Bridge design: TG303
Wind pumps
  Hydraulic machinery: TJ926
Wind resistant design
  Structural engineering:
    TA658.48
Wind tunnel models
  Aeronautical research: TL567.M6
Wind tunnels
  Aeronautical research: TL567.W5
Wind turbines: TJ828
Windchimes
  Decorative crafts: TT899.7
Winding
  Generators: TK2474+
Winding machines: TJ1535
  Electric driving: TK4059.W56
Windmills: TJ823+
Window fittings
  Building design and
    construction: TH2270+

Window guards
  Building design and
    construction: TH2273
  Burlgar proof construction:
    TH9725.W5
Window openings
  Building design and
    construction: TH2264
  Fittings: TH2261+
Window shade industry
  Manufactures: TS2301.W5
Windows
  Building design and
    construction: TH2275
  Motor vehicles: TL256.5
Winds
  Aeronautical meteorology:
    TL557.A5
Windshields
  Airplanes: TL681.W5
  Motor vehicles: TL256.5
Wine: TP544+
  Cookery: TX726
Wine lists
  Hotels, clubs, restaurants,
    etc.: TX911.3.M45
Wine service
  Hotels, clubs, restaurants,
    etc.: TX925
Winemaking: TP544+
Wineries
  Sanitary engineering:
    TH6057.W55
Wing load
  Aerodynamics: TL574.P7
Wing skids
  Airplanes: TL683.S5
Winged flight: TL717
Wire
  Aeronautics: TL699.W5
  Engineering and construction:
    TA492.W7
Wire broadcasting
  Radio: TK6562.W5
Wire craft
  Metalworking: TT214.3
Wire glass windows
  Fire-resistive building
    construction: TH1069
Wire-grass industry
  Wood technology: TS915

Wire netting
  Engineering and construction:
    TA492.W77
Wire rope
  Engineering materials: TA492.W8
  Textile fiber: TS1787
Wire rope transportation
  Conveying machinery: TJ1385 +
Wire screens
  Metal manufactures: TS273
Wireless communication systems
  Electrical engineering:
    TK5103.2 +
Wireless telegraph
  Amateurs' manuals: TK9946
  Electrical engineering: TK5700 +
Wireless telephone
  Amateurs' manuals: TK9956 +
Wiremaking
  Metal manufactures: TS270 +
Wiremen's manuals
  Telegraph: TK5445
Wires
  Airplanes: TL674
  Electric power: TK3301 +
  Standards and testing: TK3307
  Tables of properties and
    dimensions: TK3305
  Telegraph: TK5481
Wiretapping
  Telephone wires: TK6383
Wiring
  Aircraft: TL691.W5
  Electric lighting: TK4255
  Electrical engineering: TK3201 +
  Space vehicles: TL1102.W57
  Telephone circuits: TK6341 +
Woad
  Textile dyes: TP925.W8
Wok cookery: TX840.W65
Wolfram ores: TN490.T9
Wollastonite
  Mining engineering: TN948.W6
Women
  Hairdressing: TT972 +
  Nutrition: TX361.W55
  Photographic portraits:
    TR681.W6
Women in technology: T36
Women, Home arts for: TT697 +
Women's tailoring: TT500 +, TT519.5 +

Wood
  Aeronautics: TL699.W6
  Chemical processing: TS920 +
  Composition and chemistry:
    TS932 +
  Engineering materials: TA419 +
  Fire-resistive building
    construction: TH1073
  Fuel: TP324
  Housing material: TH4818.W6
  Packaging materials: TS198.3.W6
  Pavements: TE253
  Railway construction: TF254
  Sidewalks: TE285
  Stairbuilding: TH5667 +
  Trussed bridges: TG375
  Utilization of waste: TP996.W6
Wood adhesives: TS857
Wood alcohol
  Distilling: TP594
Wood bearings
  Mechanical engineering:
    TJ1073.W6
Wood building construction:
  TH1101
Wood chips
  Woodpulp industry: TS1176.6.W6
Wood distillation
  Chemical technology: TP997
Wood finishing
  Handicrafts: TT325 +
Wood fuels
  Central heating: TH7466.W66
Wood industry
  Air pollution: TD888.W6
  Waste control: TD899.W6
Wood products
  Manufactures: TS840 +
Wood staining
  Wood finishing: TT345
Wood-steel I-beams
  Structural engineering:
    TA660.S67
Wood stove heating
  Convective heating: TH7437 +
Wood stoves
  Convective heating: TH7438 +
  Cookery: TX657.S9
Wood technology
  Manufactures: TS800 +

Wood-using industries
  Energy conservation:
    TJ163.5.W66
  Environmental effects: TD195.W6
Wood waste
  Waste disposal: TD810
Woodburning
  Woodworking: TT199.8
Woodburytype
  Photography: TR995
Wooden ceilings
  Building: TH2533.W66
Wooden construction
  Structural engineering: TA666+
Wooden dams: TC545
Wooden flooring
  Building construction:
    TH2529.W6
Wooden stairbuilding
  Building construction: TH5670+
Wooden toys
  Handicrafts: TT174.5.W6
Wooden trestles
  Bridge engineering: TG365
Woodpulp industry
  Paper manufacture: TS1171+
  Waste control: TD899.W65
  Water pollution: TD428.W65
Woodpulp, Articles manufactured
  from: TS1177
Woodworking
  Handicrafts: TT180+
Woodworking industries
  Dust removal: TH7697.W6
  Fire prevention and
    extinction: TH9445.M6
  Noise control: TD893.6.W65
Woodworking, Industrial
  Manufactures: TS840+
Wool
  Dyeing: TP899
  Textile fiber: TS1547
Wool substitutes
  Woolen manufactures: TS1630
Woolen machinery
  Woolen manufactures: TS1633
Woolen manufactures: TS1600+
Worcestershire sauce
  Cookery: TX819.W65
Work clothes: TT649
Work design
  Industrial engineering: T60.8

Work diagrams
  Mechanical engineering: TJ173
Work measurement
  Industrial engineering: T60+
Work sampling
  Industrial engineering: T60.55
Work study
  Industrial engineering: T60+
Workbenches
  Woodworking: TT197.5.W6
Workers
  Nutrition: TX361.W6
Working class
  Photographic portraits:
    TR681.W65
Working drawings
  Mechanical drawing: T379
  Photographic reproduction
    processes: TR920+
Working environment
  Human engineering in industry:
    T59.77
Working women
  Nutrition: TX361.W7
Workmanship, Inspection of
  Management of engineering
    works: TA191
Workshop practice
  Handicrafts: TT153+
Workshop tools
  Handicrafts: TT153+
Workshops
  Artificial lighting: TH7975.F2
  Dust removal: TH7697.F2
  Electric lighting: TK4399.F2
  Handicrafts: TT152
World Wide Web
  Internet: TK5105.888
Worm gears
  Mechanical movements: TJ200
Worsted machinery
  Woolen manufactures: TS1633
Wrapping
  Packaging: TS198.W7
Wrapping machines: TJ1550
Wreaths
  Decorative crafts: TT899.75
Wrecking
  Building construction: TH447
Wrecking cars
  Railway equipment: TF490

Wrecking industry
  Waste control: TD899.W73
Wrenches
  Handtools: TJ1201.W8
Writing
  Telegraph: TK5545
Writing, Technical: T11+
Wrought iron: TA469+
  Metallurgy: TN720+
Wrought-iron work
  Handicrafts: TT240

X

X-15 program: TL789.8.U6X5
X-ray lasers
  Applied optics: TA1707
X-ray optics, Applied: TA1775
X-ray tubes: TK7871.79.X2
X.500
  Computer network protocols:
    TK5105.587
Xenium
  Chemical technology: TP245.X4
Xenobiotics
  Effect on food: TX571.X45
Xerography
  Electrostatic printing: TR1045
XY plotters
  Computer engineering:
    TK7887.8.X18
Xyloles
  Chemical technology: TP248.X9
Xylose
  Chemical technology: TP248.X95

Y

Y tracks
  Railway structures: TF274
Yard drainage
  Plumbing: TH6671.F6
Yard management
  Trains: TF590+
Yard waste
  Waste disposal: TD810.5
Yarn
  Textile industries: TS1449
Yashica cameras
  Photography: TR263.Y3
Yaw
  Aerodynamics: TL574.M6

Yeast
  Brewing and malting: TP580+
  Food values: TX560.Y4
  Leavening agents and baking
    aids: TP433
Yeast biotechnology:
  TP248.27.Y43
Yield strength
  Temperature effects: TA418.24+
Yield stress analysis
  Structural analysis: TA652
Yogurt
  Cookery: TX759.5.Y63
  Nutrition: TX380
Youth
  Nutrition: TX361.Y6
  Photographic portraits:
    TR681.Y6
Youth hostels: TX931
Ytterbium
  Chemical technology: TP245.Y8
Yttrium
  Chemical technology: TP245.Y9
  Engineering materials: TA480.Y8
Yurts
  Construction: TH4870

Z

Zebra mussel
  Water pollutants: TD427.Z43
Zener diodes
  Semiconductors: TK7871.89.Z46
Zeolites
  Mining engineering: TN948.Z4
Zeppelin: TL658.Z4
Zilog Model Z-80 computer:
  TK7889.Z54
Zinc
  Chemical technology: TP245.Z7
  Electroplating: TS692.Z5
  Engineering and construction:
    TA480.Z6
  Environmental pollutants:
    TD196.Z56
  Manufactures: TS640
  Metallurgy: TN796
  Ore deposits and mining: TN480+
  Powder metallurgy: TN697.Z54
  Prospecting: TN271.Z5

Zinc batteries
    Electricity production:
        TK2945.Z55
Zinc oxide
    Chemical technology: TP936 +
Zippers
    Women's tailoring: TT557
Zirconium: TN490.Z5
    Chemical technology: TP245.Z8
    Engineering materials:
        TA480.Z65
    Metallography: TN693.Z5
    Metallurgy: TN799.Z5
Zone melting
    Chemical engineering: TP156.Z6
    Electrometallurgy: TN686.5.Z6
Zoning
    Airports: TL725.3.Z6

NOTES